INTERNATIONAL MONETARY FUND

International
Financial Statistics

COUNTRY NOTES
2013

INTERNATIONAL FINANCIAL STATISTICS

Vol. LXVI, 2013
Prepared by the IMF Statistics Department
Louis Marc Ducharme, Director, Statistics Department

For information related to this publication, please:
> fax the Statistics Department at (202) 589-6460,
> or write Statistics Department
> > International Monetary Fund
> > Washington, D.C. 20431
> or e-mail your query to **StatisticsQuery@imf.org**

For copyright inquiries, please fax the Editorial Division at (202) 623-6579.
For purchases only, please contact Publication Services (see information below).

International Financial Statistics (IFS) is a standard source of statistics on all aspects of international and domestic finance. IFS publishes, for most countries of the world, current data on exchange rates, international liquidity, international banking, money and banking, interest rates, prices, production, international transactions (including balance of payments and international investment position), government finance, and national accounts. Information is presented in tables for specific countries and in tables for area and world aggregates. IFS is published monthly and annually.

Address orders to:
International Monetary Fund
Attention: Publication Services
P.O. Box 92780
Washington, D.C. 20090
U.S.A.
Telephone: (202) 623-7430
Telefax: (202) 623-7201
E-mail: publications@imf.org
Internet: http://www.imf.org

ISSN 0250-7463
ISBN 978-1-48434-309-8

POSTMASTER: Send address changes to International Financial Statistics, Publication Services, 700 19th St., N.W., Washington, D.C. 20431. Postage for periodicals paid at Washington, D.C. USPS 049-610

Contents

"Country" in this publication does not always refer to a territorial entity that is a state as understood by international law and practice; the term also covers the euro area and some nonsovereign territorial entities, for which statistical data are provided internationally on a separate basis.

Selection of statistical publications

International Financial Statistics (IFS)

Acknowledged as a standard source of statistics on all aspects of international and domestic finance, IFS publishes, for most countries of the world, current data on exchange rates, international liquidity, international banking, money and banking, interest rates, prices, production, international transactions (including balance of payments and international investment position), government finance, and national accounts. Information is presented in tables for specific countries and in tables for area and world aggregates. IFS is published monthly and annually. Price: Subscription price is US$847 a year (US$550 to university faculty and students) for twelve monthly issues and the yearbook. Single copy price is US$109 for a monthly issue and US$172 for a yearbook issue.

Balance of Payments Statistics Yearbook (BOPSY)

Issued in three parts, this annual publication contains balance of payments and international investment position data. Part 1 provides detailed tables on balance of payments statistics for approximately 177 countries and international investment position data for 123 countries. Part 2 presents tables of regional and world totals of major balance of payments components, net International Investment Position (IIP), plus Total Assets and Total Liabilities for the IIP. Part 3 contains descriptions of methodologies, compilation practices, and data sources used by reporting countries. Price: US$153.

Direction of Trade Statistics (DOTS)

Quarterly issues of this publication provide, for 160 countries, tables with current data (or estimates) on the value of imports from and exports to their most important trading partners. In addition, similar summary tables for the world, industrial countries, and developing countries are included. The yearbook provides, for the most recent seven years, detailed trade data by country for approximately 184 countries, the world, and major areas. Price: Subscription price is US$247 a year (US$212 to university faculty and students) for the quarterly issues and the yearbook. Price for a quarterly issue only is US$41 and the yearbook only is US$110.

Government Finance Statistics Yearbook (GFSY)

This annual publication provides detailed data on transactions in revenue, expense, net acquisition of assets and liabilities, other economic flows, and balances of assets and liabilities of general government and its subsectors. The data are compiled according to the framework of the 2001 Government Finance Statistics Manual, which provides for several summary measures of government fiscal performance. Price: US$102.

CD-ROM Subscriptions

International Financial Statistics (IFS), Balance of Payments Statistics (BOPS), Direction of Trade Statistics (DOTS), and Government Finance Statistics (GFS) are available on CD-ROM by annual subscription. The CD-ROMs incorporate a Windows-based browser facility, as well as a flat file of the database in scientific notation. Price of each subscription: US$690 a year for single-user PC license (US$414 for university faculty and students). Network and redistribution licenses are negotiated on a case-by-case basis. Please visit www.imfbookstore.org/onlineServicePricing.asp for information.

Subscription Packages

Combined Subscription Package

The combined subscription package includes all issues of IFS, DOTS, GFS, and BOPSY. Combined subscription price: US$1,349 a year (US$1,017 for university faculty and students). Expedited delivery available at additional cost; please inquire.

Combined Statistical Yearbook Subscription

This subscription comprises BOPSY, IFSY, GFSY, and DOTSY at a combined rate of US$537. Because of different publication dates of the three yearbooks, it may take up to one year to service an order. Expedited delivery available at additional cost; please inquire.

IFS, BOPS, DOTS, GFS on the Internet

The Statistics Department of the Fund is pleased to make available to subscribers the International Financial Statistics (IFS), Balance of Payments Statistics (BOPS), Direction of Trade Statistics (DOTS), and Government Finance Statistics (GFS) databases through the new, easy-to-use IMF eLibrary Data online service. New features include Data Reports, which provides quick access to predefined tables and charts aimed at satisfying many common data searches. From your data report, you can download to Excel, PDF, and Word. IMF eLibrary Data lets you create a basic custom-built data query in well under a minute, using the Query Builder tool and it offers greater flexibility to create larger and more complex queries. Once you have defined your query, you can structure the table the way you want it, and then convert your data into a chart or download it. A number of personalization options are available in the "My Data" section such as accessing your favorites and saved queries. Free registration for My Data can be obtained by clicking on the Sign In or Register link on the IMF eLibrary Data home page. Single user license price for each of the IFS, BOP, DOTS, GFS Online Service is $690, and $414 for academic users. Dependent on certain criteria, a range of scaled discounts is available. For full details of qualification for these discounts and online payment, please visit http://www.imfbookstore.org/statistical.asp or e-mail us directly at publications@imf.org.

Address orders to

Publication Services, International Monetary Fund, PO Box 92780, Washington, DC 20090, USA

Telephone: (202) 623-7430   Fax: (202) 623-7201   E-mail: publications@imf.org

Internet: http://www.imfbookstore.org

Note: Prices include the cost of delivery by surface mail. Expedited delivery is available for an additional charge.

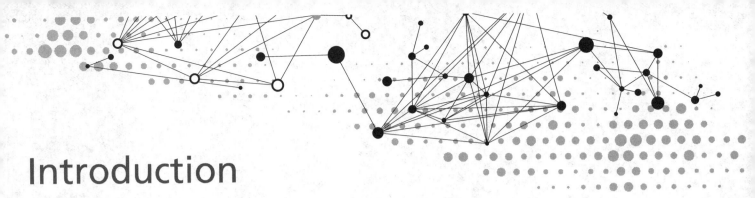

Introduction

The Fund's principal statistical publication, *International Financial Statistics (IFS)*, has been published monthly since January 1948. Beginning in 1961, the monthly was supplemented by a yearbook, and in 1991 and 2000, respectively, IFS was introduced on CD-ROM and the Internet. IFS contains country tables for most Fund members, as well as for Anguilla, Aruba, the Central African Economic and Monetary Community (CEMAC), Curaçao, the currency union of Curaçao and Sint Maarten, the Eastern Caribbean Currency Union (ECCU), the euro area , Montserrat, the former Netherlands Antilles, Sint Maarten, the West African Economic Monetary Union (WAEMU), West Bank and Gaza, and some nonsovereign territorial entities for which statistics are provided internationally on a separate basis. Also, selected series are drawn from the country tables and published in area and world tables.

International Financial Statistics, Country Notes presents, in two sections, brief information on the data published in IFS. The first section provides a description of the compilation techniques underlying selected area and world tables. The second identifies for each country the standard sources of the statistics and provides some explanatory material on each country's data, including any breaks in the series. Prior to the May 2003 issue of IFS, this information appeared within the individual world and country pages and often overflowed to the rear portion of the publication. As part of the redesign of IFS, the notes from the monthly and yearbook editions have been combined into this separate volume.

Although the topics addressed by the notes provided for each country may differ, they typically cover the following:

- Date of Fund Membership
- Standard Sources identified by the country (e.g., the Bank of Albania's *Monthly Statistical Report*)
- Exchange Rates
- International Liquidity
- Money and Banking
- Interest Rates
- Prices, Production and Labor
- International Transactions
- Government Finance
- National Accounts

Country Notes is designed to be a companion volume to each version of IFS: the monthly print edition, the yearbook, the CD-ROM, and the Internet. It will normally appear as an annual volume and will be shipped with the print edition of the *International Financial Statistics Yearbook* during August each year. Because one main volume of *Country Notes* will be produced each year, any supplementary notes will be provided on a cumulative basis at the rear of the monthly print edition of IFS until the next volume of *Country Notes* is published.

In addition, the complete set of updated country notes are accessible from the *IFS Online Service* Internet site at www.imfstatistics.org and appear on the CD-ROM edition of IFS. A print edition of the *Country Notes* volume may be ordered separately by subscribers of the CD-ROM.

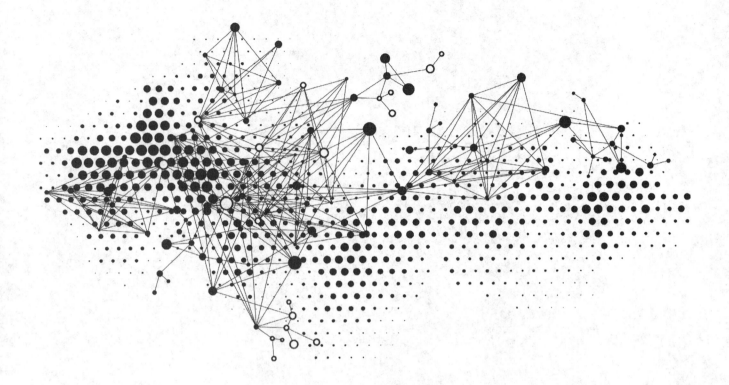

World Notes

Real Effective Exchange Rate Indices

Starting with the March 2010 IFS, the publication of the 65um, reu, and neu series are discontinued. They are being discontinued because their calculations were based on 17 advanced economies. In the old system, the historical data for the unit labor cost for manufacturing series were compiled from various ad-hoc exercises and the information of the sources is no longer available. The last exercise was completed in 2003 and subsequently the data extended forward using interpolated data from the most recent WEO database.

They are replaced by the **rel** and **nel** series.

The **rel** and **nel** series are the real and nominal effective exchange rates for the advanced economies based on a basket of 26 countries and euro area as a group. These 26 advanced economies include Austria, Belgium, Finland, France, Germany, Greece, Ireland, Italy, Luxembourg, Netherlands, Portugal, Spain, Australia, Canada, Denmark, Hong Kong SAR, Israel, Japan, Korea, New Zealand, Norway, Singapore, Sweden, Switzerland, United Kingdom, and United States.

The main source for the unit labor cost data is from the OECD Analytical Database (quarterly unit labor cost in manufacturing). However, for Australia, Hong Kong SAR, Singapore, and Israel, the unit labor cost data are provided by IMF staff (annual data interpolated into higher frequencies). The source for the United States' quarterly unit labor cost data, is from the Bureau of Labor Statistics.

Several of the measures of real effective exchange rates are subject to frequent and sometimes substantial revision. To an important extent, these revisions stem from the procedures used to estimate several of the indicators. Thus, the national data underlying the two labor cost series and the value-added deflator series are calculated by benchmarking the best available monthly or quarterly series on reasonably comprehensive and comparable, but periodically revised, annual data from the national accounts. While such benchmarking makes these series particularly susceptible to revision, it also permits the calculation of up-to-date quarterly series which, on an annual basis, are also reasonably comprehensive and comparable.

The total trade weights used to construct the nominal effective exchange rates and the associated real effective exchange rates for the five indices are designed to make them particularly relevant with respect to movements in costs and prices affecting exports and imports of manufactured goods. The weights, which are built up from aggregate trade flows for manufactured goods (SITC 5–8) averaged over the period 2004–2006, take into account the relative importance of a country's trading partners in its direct bilateral relations with them, in both the home and foreign markets; of the competitive relations with third countries in particular markets; and of the differences among countries in the importance of foreign trade to the manufacturing sector.

Estimates shown for the Euro Area for relative unit labor costs and relative normalized unit labor costs are generated using a subset of the trade weights described in the paragraph above, where the weights for the Euro Area relate to the trade of the Euro Area as a whole with its partners in the system. A synthetic euro has been constructed for the period before the introduction of the euro using trade weights drawn from the same weighting scheme, Euro Area member exchange rates, and the official lock-in rates, which were used to determine the initial value of the euro. This method (national currency series times lock-in rates times Euro Area member trade weights specific to this system) has also been used to estimate the Euro Area unit labor cost and normalized unit labor cost series denominated in euros.

The nature and scope of the various national indicators entering into the indices are briefly described below. While mention is made of specific deficiencies in some of the selected measures of costs and prices, the emphasis is on what they purport to measure. Because these measures of costs and prices contain a considerable amount of staff estimation, they are not published in *IFS*.

Unit labor costs are defined as compensation of employees per unit of real output (or value added) in the manufacturing sector. Account is taken of employer-paid social insurance premia and other employment taxes, as well as wages and salaries. For the most recent quarters, however, indices typically refer more narrowly to wages or wages and salaries per unit of total output of manufactured goods (rather than that of value added in the manufacturing sector).

Normalized unit labor costs in manufacturing are calculated by dividing an index of actual hourly compensation per worker by the normalized index of output per man-hour in local currency. The data printed are the product of this variable after weighting (to obtain the relative measure) and the nominal effective exchange rate (**neu**). The purpose of normalizing output per man-hour is to remove distortions arising from cyclical movements which occur largely because changes in hours worked do not correspond closely to changes in the effective inputs of labor. The Hodrick-Prescott filter, which smooths a time series by removing short-run fluctuations while retaining changes of larger amplitude, is the method used to normalize output per man-hour. The monthly series are estimated by extrapolating the quarterly local currency series for the period needed, interpolating these estimates from quarterly into monthly series and reweighting the interpolated monthly series to obtain the monthly relative series. **Where the monthly data are extrapolated, data for the corresponding quarters are not shown.** Monthly nominal effective exchange rates are computed using monthly exchange rates and the same weights as are used for quarterly nominal effective exchange rates, and real effective rates are calculated using the nominal effective rates and interpolated relative monthly normalized unit labor costs. The extrapolation and interpolation of the quarterly series is acceptable because the quarterly series have been smoothed and the trend of these series is retained in the extrapolation. The interpolated monthly trend series is used to adjust the more current nominal effective exchange rate. The annual series (for both relative, and relative normalized, unit labor costs) may not correspond with the average of the quarterly series because only the annual series include Switzerland.

An indicator of real effective exchange rates based on relative consumer prices is also shown *(line rec)* to afford comparison with a wider group of partner—or competitor—countries. The weighting scheme is based on disaggregated trade data for commodity, manufacturing, and tourism covering the three-year period 2004–06 and is derived according to the same methodology as that followed for other countries discussed in the Introduction (section 1). The consumer price index that is used as a cost indicator is that shown on the country pages *(line 64)*. However, it should be borne in mind that, especially for the industrial countries, consumer price indices are, in a number of respects, conceptually inferior to the other measures of domestic costs and prices discussed above for the purpose of compiling indices of real effective exchange rates, owing to the inclusion of various factors which may differ across countries, for example, net taxes on production.

Estimates shown for the Euro Area for relative consumer prices are generated using a subset of the trade weights described in the above, where the weights for the Euro Area relate to the trade of the Euro Area as a whole with its partners in the system. A synthetic euro has been constructed for the period before the introduction of the euro using trade weights drawn from the same weighting scheme, Euro Area member exchange rates, and the official lock-in rates, which were used to determine the initial value of the euro. The Euro Area consumer price series from January 1995 onward is the Harmonized Index of Consumer Prices, provided by the ECB, and prior to this period, it is the trade-weighted average of the individual member countries' consumer price indices. Trade weights used in the construction are specific to this system and are the same as those used in the construction of the synthetic euro.

As indicated in the Introduction, movements in these indices need to be interpreted with considerable caution. While every effort is made to use national data that are as internationally comparable as possible, the degree to which it is practicable to assure comparability is limited by the character of the available data. For this reason, the table provides a wide array of available indicators.

Industrial Production

The aggregate Industrial Production Index for the industrial countries as a group is calculated by the Statistics Department from industrial and manufacturing production indices that are published in the country pages. The index covers industrial activities in mining, quarrying, manufacturing, and electricity, gas, and water. The coverage of each country's production index is detailed in the footnotes of the country pages. No attempt has been made to standardize the coverage of industrial country series before aggregation.

Non-seasonally adjusted industrial production *(lines 66)* or manufacturing production *(lines 66ey)* indices are presented for 29 industrial countries. The aggregate index thus includes non-seasonally adjusted production data.

The aggregate index is calculated using a weighted geometric mean of country indices. The individual country production series are weighted by the 2005 value added in industry, as derived from individual countries' national accounts and expressed in U.S. dollars. Different weighting bases—1963, 1970, 1975, 1980, 1984–86, 1990, 1995, 2000, and 2005—have been used, and the index series are chain-linked by the technique of ratio splicing at the overlap years and are shifted to the reference base 2005=100. The weights used in the calculation are identical in concept for all countries and cover, where possible, mining, quarrying, manufacturing, and electricity, gas, and water.

Although industrial production data for some countries are not available for more recent periods, the aggregate index will be calculated for any period for which data for more than 60 percent of the area index aggregate have been reported.

Commodity Prices

Indices of market prices for primary commodities are prepared by the Commodities Unit, IMF Research Department. They are compiled as period averages in terms of U.S. dollars and expressed using a 2005=100 weights reference period in accordance with all indices published in *IFS*. The *All Non-Fuel Commodities* indices include 62 market price series (marked by an * in the Commodity Price table) which represent 45 primary commodities. They do not include fuel (petroleum, natural gas, and coal) and precious metals (gold and silver). The commodity price index for the *World* is calculated by weighting commodity price indices with the average export earnings of the commodities selected during the years 2002 through 2004 in 175 countries.

† For the periods prior to 1982 the *World* index and its components (food, beverages, agricultural raw materials, metals except fertilizers) were calculated by backward recursion of percent changes based on the previously used indices. (00176axd)

The World Bank Price Index for Primary Commodities for the Low- and Middle-Income Countries (LMICs) is compiled by the Commodity Policy and Analysis Unit of the World Bank's International Economics Department. The weights for the index are based on the average export earnings during the period 2002–04 of countries classified by the World Bank as being Low- and Middle-Income Countries, expressed in U. S. dollars, on a 2000=100 base.

The commodities covered and the weights used are as follows:

1. *Food Commodities*—16.7 percent: bananas—0.4 percent, cereals (maize, rice, and wheat)—3.6 percent, meat (beef, lamb, swine meat, and poultry)—3.7 percent, vegetable oils and protein meals (coconut oil, fishmeal, groundnuts, olive oil, palm oil, soybeans, soybean meal, soybean oil, and sunflower oil)—4.4 percent, seafood (fish and shrimp)—3.2 percent, oranges—0.5 percent, and sugar—0.9 percent. (00176exd)

2. *Beverages*—1.8 percent: cocoa beans—0.7 percent, coffee—0.9 percent, and tea—0.3 percent. (00176dwd)

3. *Agricultural Raw Materials*—7.7 percent: cotton—0.7 percent, hides—2.6 percent, rubber—0.5 percent, timber—3.4 percent, and wool (fine and coarse)—0.5 percent. (00176bxd)

4. *Metals*—10.7 percent: aluminum—3.9 percent, copper—2.8 percent, iron ore—1.3 percent, lead—0.2 percent, nickel—1.1 percent, tin—0.2 percent, uranium—0.5 percent, and zinc—0.6 percent. (00176ayd)

5. *Energy*—63.1 percent: coal—2.6 percent, natural gas—6.9 percent, and petroleum—53.6 percent. (00176end)

Aluminum: London Metal Exchange*, standard grade, spot price, minimum purity 99.5 percent, c.i.f. U.K. ports (*Wall Street Journal,* New York, and *Metals Week,* New York).[3] Prior to 1979, U.K. producer price, minimum purity 99 percent (*Metal Bulletin,* London). (15676drz)

Bananas: Latin America*: Central America and Ecuador, first class quality tropical pack, Chiquita, Dole and Del Monte, U.S. importer's price f.o.b. U.S. ports (Sopisco News, Guayaquil).[1] (24876u.z)

Barley: Canada*: Canadian No. 1 Western Barley, spot price (Winnipeg Commodity Exchange). (15676baz)

Beef: Australia/NZ (U.S. Ports)*: frozen boneless, 85 percent visible lean cow meat, U.S. import price, f.o.b. U.S. port of entry (*The Yellow Sheet,* The National Provisioner Daily Market and News Service, Chicago, Illinois).[3] Prior to December 1975, 90 percent visible. (19376kbz)

United States: Utility grade, all weights in New York, Chicago and San Francisco, mid-month. (11176k.z)

Argentina (frozen) unit value. (21374kaz)

Brazil (unit value). (22374m.z)

Butter: New Zealand (London). (19676flz)

New Zealand (unit value). (19674flz)

Coal: Australia*: Thermal coal. 12000 btu/pound, less than 1% sulfur, 14% ash, f.o.b. piers, Newcastle/Port Kembla (World Bank). (19376coz)

Australia (unit value). (19374vrz)

South Africa: Steam, f.o.b. Richards Bay, for period up to 2001, 11,500 btu/lb, less than 1% sulfur, 16% ash for 1990–2001; beginning 2002, 11,200 btu/lb. (19976coz)

Cocoa Beans: New York and London*: International Cocoa Organization daily price. Average of the daily prices of the nearest three active future trading months on the New York Cocoa Exchange at noon and the London Terminal market at closing time. c.i.f. U.S. and European ports (*The Financial Times,* London).[3] (65276r.zM44)

Brazil (unit value). (22374r.z)

Coconut Oil: Philippines/Indonesia (New York)*: Philippines. (56676aiz)

Coffee: Other milds*: Arithmetic average of El Salvador Central Standard, Guatemala prime washed, Mexico prime washed, prompt shipment, ex-dock, New York.[3] (38676ebz)

Brazil (New York): Unwashed arabica, Santos No. 4, ex-dock, New York.[3] (22376ebz).

Brazil (unit value). (22374e.z)

Uganda (New York)*: Robusta: New York cash price. Côte d'Ivoire Grade II, and Uganda Standard. Prompt shipment, ex-dock, New York. Prior to July 1982, arithmetic average of Angolan Ambriz and 2AA and Ugandan Native Standard (*Patton's Complete Coffee Coverage,* New York).[3] (79976ecz)

Copper: United Kingdom*: London Metal Exchange, grade A cathodes, spot price, c.i.f. European ports (*Wall Street Journal,* New York and *Metals Week,* New York).[3] Prior to July 1986, higher grade, wire bars or cathodes. (11276c.z)

Copra: Philippines: Phil/Indo, c.i.f. Northwest European ports (*Oil World,* Hamburg).[1] (56676agz)

Cotton: Liverpool Index*: Midd. 13/32 inches, Liverpool Index 'A', average of the cheapest five of fourteen styles; c.i.f. Liverpool (*Cotton Outlook,* Liverpool). From January 1968 to May 1981 strict middling, SM 11/16 inches; prior to 1968, Mexican SM 11/16 .[1] (11176f.zM40)

DAP (diammonium phosphate): US Gulf: Standard size, bulk spot, f.o.b. (11176arzM17)

Fish: Norway*: Fresh Norwegian Salmon, farm bred, export price (NorStat). (14276fiz)

Fish Meal: Peru Fish meal/pellets 65% protein, CIF (*DataStream*). Prior to 1964, FAO estimate, Peruvian. (29376z.z)

Iceland (unit value). (17674zaz)

Gasoline: Regular unleaded. Petroleum Product Assessments (Reuter's News Services). (11176rgz)

Gold: United Kingdom: 99.5 percent fine. London, afternoon fixing.[3] (11276krz)

Groundnuts: Any origin*: 40 to 50 count per ounce, in-shell, cif Argentina (DataStream) (69476bhz)

Groundnut Oil: Any Origin: c.i.f. Rotterdam (*Oil World,* Hamburg).[1]

Hides: United States*: Wholesale dealer's price, packer's heavy native steers, over 53 lbs. (formerly over 58 lbs.), Chicago, f.o.b.

shipping point (*Wall Street Journal,* New York).[3] Prior to November 1985, U.S. Bureau of Labor Statistics, Washington, D.C. (11176p.z)

Iron Ore: China: Iron Ore fines, 62 percent FE (iron) spot (CFR Tianjin port) (92476gaz)

Jute: Raw Bangladesh BWD, f.o.b. Chittagong/Chalna (World Bank, Washington, D.C. Beginning 1977, UNCTAD source.)[2] (51376x.z)

Lamb: New Zealand (London)*: PL, frozen, wholesale price at Smithfield Market, London (National Business Review, Auckland, New Zealand). (19676pfz)

Lead: United Kingdom*: London Metal Exchange, 99.97 percent pure, spot, c.i.f. European ports (*Wall Street Journal,* New York, and *Metals Week,* New York).[3] (11276v.z)

United States: Common grade domestic pigs in New York. (00176v.z)

Linseed Oil: Any origin, ex-tank Rotterdam (*Oil World,* Hamburg). (11176niz)

Maize: United States (U.S. Gulf Ports)*: U.S. No. 2 yellow, prompt shipment, f.o.b. Gulf of Mexico ports (USDA *Grain and Feed Market News,* Washington, D.C.).[3] (11176j.zM17)

Natural Gas: Russian Federation: Russian border price in Germany (World Gas Intelligence, New York). (92276ngz)

Indonesia: Indonesian Liquid Natural Gas in Japan (World Gas Intelligence, New York). (53676ngz)

United States: Natural Gas Spot Price, Henry Hub, Lousiana. (11176ngz)

Newsprint: Finland (unit value). (17274ulz)

Nickel: United Kingdom*: London Metal Exchange, melting grade, spot, c.i.f. North European ports (*Wall Street Journal,* New York, and *Metals Week,* New York). Prior to 1980, INCO price, c.i.f. Far East and American ports (*Metal Bulletin,* London).[3] (15676ptz)

Olive Oil: United Kingdom*: ex-tanker prices, crude extra virgin olive oil, 1%>ffa (free fatty acid) (DataStream). (11276liz)

Oranges: French import price*: miscellaneous oranges, (FRuiTROP and World Bank). (13276raz)

Palm Kernel Oil: Malaysia: c.i.f. Rotterdam (*World Oil,* Hamburg). (54876dfz)

Palm Oil: Crude Palm Oil Futures (first contract forward) 4–5 percent FFA (*Bursa Malaysian Derivatives Berhad*).[1] Prior to 1974, UNCTAD.[2] (54876dgz)

Malaysia (unit value). (54874dgz)

Pepper: Malaysia: Black, average U.S. wholesale price, bagged, carlots, f.o.b. New York. Average of daily quotations.(54876dlz)

Singapore: White Sarawak 100%, closing quotations (Market News Service, I.T.C., Geneva). (57676dlz)

Petroleum: Average Crude Price: U.K. Brent (light), Dubai (medium), and West Texas Intermediate, equally weighted. † Prior to 1983, Alaska North Slope (heavy) was used in the composition of this line instead of West Texas Intermediate. Annual data through 1994 for this earlier version are available in the 1995 *IFS* yearbook, with quarterly and monthly data available in the monthly issues through the January 1996 issue. (00176aaz)

Dubai: Medium, Fateh 32° API, spot, f.o.b. Dubai (*Petroleum Market Intelligence,* New York, *International Crude Oil and Product Prices,* Beirut, and *Bloomberg Business News*). † Prior to 1984, Middle East Light 34° API, spot (*Petroleum Intelligence Weekly,* New York). † Prior to 1974, Saudi Arabian Light 34° API, posted price, ex Ras Tanura (*Platt's Oil Price Handbook and Almanac,* New York). (46676aaz)

United Kingdom: Light, Brent Blend 38° API, spot, f.o.b. U.K. ports (*Petroleum Market Intelligence,* New York, *Platt's Oilgram Price Report,* New York, and *Bloomberg Business News*). † Prior to 1984,

North African Light 37/44° API (*Petroleum Intelligence Weekly,* New York). † Prior to 1974, Libyan Brega 40° API, posted price, ex Marsa El Brega (*Platt's Oil Price Handbook and Almanac,* New York). † Prior to 1961, Qatar Um Said 39° API posted price, f.o.b. (*Platt's Oil Price Handbook and Almanac,* New York). (11276aaz)

United States: West Texas Intermediate 40° API, spot, f.o.b. Midland Texas (New York Mercantile Exchange, New York). In 1983–84 (Platt's Oilgram Price Report, New York).[3] (11176aazM17)

Phosphate Rock: Morocco (Casablanca): 70 percent BPL, contract, f.a.s. Prior to 1981, 72 percent BPL, f.a.s.1 (68676awz)

Potash: Canada: Muriate of potash, f.o.b., Vancouver. Average of daily quotations. (15676qrz)

Plywood: Africa and South East Asia: Lauan, 3-ply, extra, 91 cm x 182 cm x 4 mm, wholesale price, spot, Tokyo. (56676wxz)

Pulp: Sweden (North Sea Ports): Softwood, sulphate bleached, air-dry weight, c.i.f. (14476slzz)

Rice: Thailand*: White milled 5 percent broken, nominal price quotes, f.o.b. Bangkok (USDA *Rice Market News,* Little Rock, Arkansas).[1] (57876n.zM81)

Thailand (unit value). (57874n.z)

Rubber: Malaysia*: No. 1 R.S.S., prompt shipment, f.o.b. Malaysian/Singapore ports (*The Financial Times,* London).[3] (548761.z)

Malaysia (unit value). (548741.z)

Thailand (unit value). (578741.z)

Shrimp: United States*: Mexican, west coast, white, No. 1 shell-on, headless, 26 to 30 count per pound, wholesale price at New York (World Bank). (11176blz)

Silver: United States: 99.9 percent grade refined, Handy and Harman, New York. Average of daily quotations. (11176y.z)

Sisal: East African, ungraded, c.i.f. European ports (UNCTAD).[2] (63976mlz)

Sorghum: United States: No. 2 yellow, prompt shipment, f.o.b. Gulf of Mexico ports (*USDA Grain and Feed Market News,* Washington, D.C.) (11176trz)

Soybeans: Soybean futures contract (first contract forward) No. 2 yellow and par*: (*Chicago Board of Trade*). (11176jfz)

Brazil (unit value). (22374s.z)

Soybean Meal: Soybean Meal Futures (first contract forward) Minimum 48 percent protein (*Chicago Board of Trade*). (11176jjz)

Soybean Oil: Crude Soybean Oil Futures (first contract forward) exchange approved grades (*Chicago Board of Trade*). Prior to April 1973, Dutch crude oil, ex-mill. (11176jiz)

Sugar: EU Import Price*: Unpacked sugar, c.i.f. European ports. Negotiated export price for sugar from ACP countries to EU under the Sugar Protocol (Lomé Convention). (EU office, Washington, D.C.).[3] (11276i.z)

Free Market*: CSCE contract No. 11, nearest future position (Coffee, Sugar and Cocoa Exchange, New York Board of Trade). (00176iaz)

U.S. Import Price*: CSCE contract No. 14, nearest future position (Coffee, Sugar and Cocoa Exchange, New York Board of Trade). (11176iazM02)

Brazil (unit value). (22374i.z)

Philippines (unit value): Centrifugal. (55674i.z)

Sunflower Oil: Sunflower Oil, crude, US export price from Gulf of Mexico (*DataStream*). (11276soz)

Superphosphate: United States (U.S. Gulf Ports): Triple-super-phosphate, bulk, spot, f.o.b. Gulf of Mexico Ports.[3] (11176asz)

Swine Meat: United States (Iowa)*: 51–52% (.8-.99 inches of back fat at measuring point) lean Hogs, USDA average base cost

price of back fat measured at the tenth rib (USDA). (11176smz)

Tea: Average Auction (London)*: Mombasa auction price for best PF1, Kenyan Tea. Replaces London auction price beginning July 1998.[3] (11276s.z)

Sri Lanka (unit value). (52474s.z)

Timber: Hardwood Logs*: Malaysia, meranti, Sarawak best quality, sale price charged by importers, Japan (World Bank, Washington, D.C.). From January 1988 to February 1993, average of Sabah and Sarawak in Tokyo weighted by their respective import volumes in Japan. From February 1993 to present, Sarawak only.[2] (54876vxz)

Hardwood Sawnwood*: Malaysian sawnwood, dark red meranti, select and better quality, standard density, c.i.f. U.K. Port (Tropical Timbers, Surrey, England).[2] (54876rmz)

Softwood Logs*: Average value of Douglas-fir, Western hemlock and other softwoods exported from Washington, Oregon, Northern California and Alaska (Pacific Northwest Research Station, USDA Forest Service, Portland, OR).[2] (11176vxz)

Softwood Sawnwood*: Average value of Douglas-fir, Western hemlock and other softwoods exported from Canada. (11176rmz)

Tin: Any Origin (London)*: London Metal Exchange, standard grade, spot, c.i.f. European ports (*Wall Street Journal,* New York). From December 1985 to June 1989, Malaysian Straits, minimum 99.85 percent purity, Kuala Lumpur Tin Market settlement price. Prior to November 1985, London Metal Exchange (*Wall Street Journal,* New York and *Metals Week,* New York).[3] (11276q.z)

Bolivia (unit value). (21874q.z)

Malaysia (unit value): Primary tin. (54874q.z)

Thailand (unit value): Tin metal. (57874q.z)

Tobacco: U.S. Import Unit Value of general unmanufactured tobacco. (USDA, Foreign Agricultural Service). (11176m.z)

Uranium: Restricted*: Metal Bulletin Nuexco Exchange Uranium (U308 restricted) price. (00176umz)

Urea: Ukraine: Bulk, spot, for 1985–91 (June) f.o.b. Eastern Europe; from f.o.b. Black Sea (primarily Yuzhnyy). (92676urz).

Wheat: Australia (unit value). (19374d.z)

United States*: No. 1, hard red winter, ordinary protein, prompt shipment, f.o.b. Gulf of Mexico ports (USDA *Grain and Feed Market News,* Washington, D.C.) (11176d.z)

Argentina (unit value). (21374d.z)

Wool: Australia-New Zealand 48's*: Coarse wool, 23 micron (AWEX, Australian Wool Exchange) Sydney, Australia. (11276hdz)

Australia-New Zealand 64's*: Fine wool, 19 micron (AWEX, Australian Wool Exchange) Sydney, Australia. (11276hez)

Australia (unit value): Greasy wool. (19374haz)

Zinc: United Kingdom*: London Metal Exchange, high grade, c.i.f. U.K. ports, 98 percent pure, spot (*Wall Street Journal,* New York, and *Metals Week,* New York).[3] Prior to January 1987, standard grade. (11276t.z)

Bolivia (unit value). (21874t.z)

---

[1] Average of weekly quotations.

[2] Monthly quotations.

[3] Average of daily quotations.

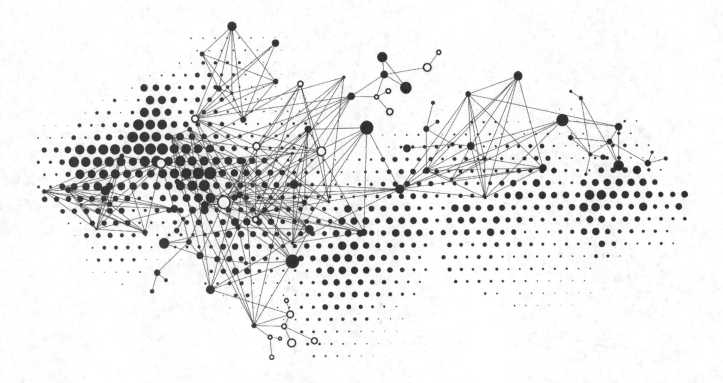

Country Notes

Afghanistan, I.R. of   512

Date of Fund Membership:
July 14, 1955

Standard Sources:
Da Afghanistan Bank
Central Statistics Office

Exchange Rates:

Official Rate: (End of Period and Period Average):
The official rate has been fixed at Afghani 2,000 per U.S. dollar since April 1996. It applies to transactions of the central government, official investment income, and transactions under bilateral payments agreements. Most other transactions are being conducted in the free market ("money bazaar") at a substantially depreciated exchange rate. † Between October 7, 2002 and January 2, 2003, the new Afghani was introduced. It replaced the previous Afghani at two distinct rates. Issues of the government of President Burhanuddin Rabbani were replaced at a rate of 1,000 to the new Afghani, while the issues of Abdul Rashid Dostum were replaced at a rate of 2,000 to the new Afghani. The new Afghani was valued at 43 Afghani to the U.S. dollar. Data refer to the midpoint rate calculated by the Da Afghanistan Bank as an average of the market midpoint rates of ten major money changers.

International Liquidity:
Data are compiled based on the Solar calendar, which ends on the 21st day of the Gregorian calendar month.

Central Bank:
Consists of the Da Afghanistan Bank (DAB) only.
Data are based on a standardized report form (SRF) for central banks, which accords with the concepts and definitions of the IMF's *Monetary and Financial Statistics Manual (MFSM)*, 2000. Data are compiled based on the Solar calendar, which ends on the 21st day of the Gregorian calendar month. Beginning in August 2007, data are derived from a new accounting system. Departures from the *MFSM* methodology are explained below.
Beginning in March 2007, gold is valued at a fixed price, which is equivalent to the market price of gold at the end of March 2007. For August and September 2007, assets do not equal liabilities due to the inconsistency in source data during the transition to a new accounting system for the DAB.
Other Items (Net) includes some positions with different sectors of the economy due to a lack of detailed information.
Positions of the central bank with other depository corporations are not fully consistent with those in the section for other depository corporations as data for private commercial banks are compiled based on the Gregorian calendar.

Other Depository Corporations:
Comprises commercial banks.
Data are based on a standardized report form (SRF) for other depository corporations, which accords with the concepts and definitions of the *Monetary and Financial Statistics Manual (MFSM)*. For other depository corporations in Afghanistan, departures from the *MFSM* methodology are explained below.

Private commercial banks report data based on the Gregorian calendar, while state-owned commercial banks report data based on the Solar calendar. This results in differences in the interbank positions for other depository corporations.
Positions of other depository corporations with the central bank are not fully consistent with those in the section for the central bank as data for private commercial banks are compiled based on the Gregorian calendar. Accrued interest on assets and liabilities is excluded from the data.
In September and October 2007, *Liabilities to Nonresidents* includes some other deposits in foreign currency with resident banks.

Depository Corporations:
See notes on central bank and other depository corporations.

Monetary Aggregates:

Broad Money:
Broad Money calculated from the liability data in the sections for the central bank and other depository corporations accords with the concepts and definitions of the *MFSM* and is consistent with M2 described below.

Money (National Definitions):
M1 comprises currency outside depository corporations and demand deposits of other financial corporations, public nonfinancial corporations, and private sector with the DAB and other depository corporations. Currency outside depository corporations is equal to the amount of currency notes and coins issued by the DAB *less* domestic currency note and coin holdings of the DAB and other depository corporations.
M2 comprises M1 and quasi-money. Quasi-money comprises other deposits of other financial corporations, public nonfinancial corporations, and private sector with the DAB and other depository corporations.

Interest Rates:

Money Market Rate:
Simple average of rates on deposits between financial corporations with maturity of one to 90 days in national currency.

Money Market Rate (Foreign Currency):
Simple average of rates on deposits between financial corporations with maturity of one to 90 days in foreign currency.

Savings Rate:
Simple average of rates offered by commercial banks on new savings deposits with maturity of one to 90 days in national currency. Savings deposits can be exchangeable on demand at par with little or no penalty.

Savings Rate (Foreign Currency):
Simple average of rates offered by commercial banks on new savings deposits with maturity of one to 90 days in foreign currency. Savings deposits can be exchangeable on demand at par with little or no penalty.

Deposit Rate (Foreign Currency):
Simple average of rates offered by commercial banks to on time deposits of nonbank customers with maturity of one to 90 days in foreign currency.

Lending Rate:
Simple average of rates charged by commercial banks on new loans to nonbank customers with maturity of 91 to 180 days in national currency.

Lending Rate (Foreign Currency):
Simple average of rates charged by commercial banks on new loans to nonbank customers with maturity of 91 to 180 days in foreign currency.

Prices:

Consumer Prices:
Source: Da Afghanistan Bank. Weights reference period: March 2011. Geographical coverage: National (Kabul, Herat, Kandahar, Jalalabad, Mazar-e-Sharif, and Khost, 10 provinces are now included). Number of items in basket: 290 important goods and services, typically consumed by urban middle and low-income households. Basis for calculation: Weights and commodity basket based on the Household Budget Survey conducted by the Central Statistics Office and the United Nations in 1987 with some modifications.

International Transactions:

Balance of Payments:
Data are compiled based on the Solar calendar, which ends on the 21st day of the Gregorian calendar month. Annual figures are presented according to fiscal year ending the first quarter following the reference year.

Albania   914

Date of Fund Membership:
October 15, 1991

Standard Sources:
Bank of Albania
Institute of Statistics

Exchange Rates:

Market Rate (End of Period and Period Average):
† Beginning in July 1992, a floating exchange rate system (independent float) was introduced. The exchange rate for the lek is the weighted average midpoint rate of six commercial banks and four foreign exchange bureaus that cover most of the foreign exchange transactions.

Central Bank:
Consists of the Bank of Albania only.
† Beginning in December 2002, data are based on a standardized report form (SRF) for central banks, which accords with the concepts and definitions of the IMF's *Monetary and Financial Statistics Manual (MFSM)* 2000. Departures from the *MFSM* methodology are explained below.
Long-term securities for investment and available for trading are valued at acquisition cost rather than at current market price or fair value.
For December 2001 through November 2002, data have less conformity with the *MFSM* methodology and therefore are not strictly comparable to data for later periods.

Other Depository Corporations:
Comprises commercial banks. † Beginning in December 2002, includes savings and loans associations.

† Beginning in December 2002, data are based on a standardized report form (SRF) for other depository corporations, which accords with the concepts and definitions of the *Monetary and Financial Statistics Manual (MFSM)*. For other depository corporations in Albania, departures from the *MFSM* methodology are explained below.
Long-term securities for investment and available for trading are valued at acquisition cost rather than at current market price or fair value.
Accrued interest of savings and loans associations, with the exception of loans, is included in *Other Items (Net)* rather than in the outstanding amounts of the financial assets and liabilities.
For December 2001 through November 2002, data have less conformity with the *MFSM* methodology and therefore are not strictly comparable to data for later periods.

Depository Corporations:
† See notes on central bank and other depository corporations.

Monetary Aggregates:

Broad Money:
Broad Money is calculated from the liability data in the sections for the central bank and other depository corporations.

Money (National Definitions):
M1 comprises currency outside depository corporations and demand deposits and sight deposits of residents other than central government in national currency.
M2 comprises M1 and term deposits of residents other than central government in national currency.
M3 comprises M2 and deposits of residents other than central government in foreign currency.

Interest Rates:

Central Bank Policy Rate (End of Period):
Main policy rate on weekly repurchase agreements.

Discount Rate (End of Period):
Basic rate at which the Bank of Albania lends to commercial banks.
Weighted average rate of accepted bids on three-month treasury bills during the last auction of the month.

Treasury Bill Rate:
Weighted average rate of accepted bids on three-month treasury bills during the last auction of the month.

Deposit Rate:
† Beginning in June 1993, guideline rate set by the Bank of Albania with the lower end of the band enforced as the minimum deposit rate. † Beginning in October 1995 weighted average rate on new 12-month deposits of the three commercial banks with the highest level of outstanding deposits.

Lending Rate:
† Beginning in June 1995, the Bank of Albania announced guideline rates to assist banks in setting their lending rates. Data refer to the guideline rate for loans of 12-month maturity. † Beginning in July 1995, the Bank of Albania ceased announcing the guideline rates and the banks are left on their own to determine their lending rates. Data refer to the maximum interest rate charged by a state-owned commercial bank on loans with 12-month maturity. † Beginning in October 1995, weighted average rate on new 12-month loans of the three commercial banks with the highest level of outstanding loans.

Prices:

Producer Prices:
Source: Institute of Statistics. Weight Reference Period: 1998; Sectoral Coverage: mining and quarrying, manufacturing, fishing, forestry, gas and electricity; Number of Items in the Basket: about 250 goods; Basis for Calculation: weights of goods and industries are based on the sales values for 1998.

Consumer Prices:
Source: Institute of Statistics. Weights Reference Period: 2007; Geographical Coverage: 11 cities; Number of Items in the Basket: 262 items; Basis for Calculation: weights are derived from the last Household Budget Survey by INSTAT.

Wages:
Source: Institute of Statistics. Average wages cover the public sector through The National Statistics Program implemented by INSTAT and data on wages by economic activities for all sectors based on data collected by the Structural Survey of Economic Enterprises. This survey is an annual one and covers the activities of Industry, Transport and Communication, Trade and some other sectors of Services.

International Transactions:

Source: Institute of Statistics.

Government Finance:

Annual data are as reported for the *Government Finance Statistics Yearbook (GFSY)* and cover general government. The fiscal year ends December 31.

National Accounts:

Source: Institute of Statistics. As indicated by the country, data are compiled according to the recommendations of the *1993 SNA*.

Algeria   612

Date of Fund Membership:
September 26, 1963

Standard Source:
Department of Statistics

Exchange Rates:
Official Rate: (End of Period and Period Average):
Central bank midpoint rate. The official rate is based on a fixed relationship between the dinar and a composite of currencies.

International Liquidity:
Gold (National Valuation) (line 1and) is equal to *Gold (Million Fine Troy Ounces) (line 1ad)*, valued at SDR 35 per fine troy ounce and converted into U.S. dollars at the dollar/SDR rate **sa** on the country page for the United States.

Central Bank:
Consists of the Bank of Algeria only, consolidating the accounts of headquarters and its 48 branches in the country.
Data are based on a standardized report form for central banks, which accords with the concepts and definitions of the IMF's *Monetary and Financial Statistics Manual (MFSM)*, 2000. Departures from the *MFSM* methodology are explained below.
Monetary gold is valued at a historic price of DA 4.93 per ounce.

Other Depository Corporations:
Comprises state-owned commercial banks (including the Caisse Nationale d'Épargne et de Prévoyance), private-sector-owned commercial banks, and a mutual bank (banking department of the Caisse Nationale de Mutualité Agricole). Data exclude the offshore bank established in Algeria.
Data are based on a standardized report form for other depository corporations, which accords with the concepts and definitions of the *Monetary and Financial Statistics Manual (MFSM)*. Departures from the *MFSM* methodology are explained below.
Accrual accounting and sectorization of counterpart transactors are not consistently applied by all reporting corporations.

Depository Corporations:
See notes on central bank and other depository corporations. In conformity with the MFSM, deposits from the public at the Centres des Chèques Postaux, which are units of the postal administration, and at the Treasury are not included in the depository corporations survey.

Other Financial Corporations:
Comprises finance companies ("établissements financiers" in accordance with the Algerian Law on Money and Credit). Data exclude insurance corporations and financial auxiliaries. There are no pension funds in Algeria.
Data are based on a standardized report form for other financial corporations, which accords with the concepts and definitions of the *Monetary and Financial Statistics Manual (MFSM)*. Departures from the *MFSM* methodology are explained below.
Accrual accounting and sectorization of counterpart transactors are not consistently applied by all reporting corporations.

Monetary Aggregates:
Broad Money:
Broad Money calculated from the liability data in the sections for the central bank and other depository corporations also includes some of the deposits of the public with the Centres des Chèques Postaux, which are units of the postal administration that is sectorized in Algeria as a public nonfinancial corporation (see line 59m.b), and with the Treasury, which is a unit of the central government (see line 59m.a). Broad money differs from M2 described below because broad money includes deposits of insurance corporations, finance companies, and households with the central bank and excludes blocked import deposits of nonfinancial corporations with commercial banks. Broad money excludes deposits of local governments with the Treasury. Beginning in January 2007, broad money is consistent with M2 described below.

Money (National Definitions):
M1 (means of payment) comprises banknotes and coins held by the public; demand deposits of nonfinancial corporations, households, other financial corporations, and local governments with other depository corporations; demand deposits of households and public nonfinancial quasi-corporations with the postal administration (Centres des Chèques Postaux); and demand deposits of households and social security funds with the Treasury.
M2 comprises M1; time, savings, and foreign currency deposits of nonfinancial corporations, households, other financial corporations, and social security funds with other depository corporations; and blocked import deposits of

nonfinancial corporations with commercial banks. † Beginning in January 2007 includes deposits of insurance corporations, finance companies, and households with the central bank and excludes blocked import deposits of nonfinancial corporations with commercial banks.

Interest Rates:

Discount Rate (End of Period):
Rate charged by the Bank of Algeria on loans to banks and finance companies through a call for tender system.

Money Market Rate:
Weighted average rate on transactions in the interbank market on the last working day of the period.

Treasury Bill Rate:
Weighted average rate at issuance for treasury bills with maturity of 26 weeks sold at the last auction of the period.

Deposit Rate:
Average rate offered by commercial banks on 12-month term deposits to nonfinancial corporations and households.

Lending Rate:
Average rate charged by commercial banks on short term rediscountable loans granted to nonfinancial corporations for general purpose.

Prices, Production, Labor:

Producer Prices:
Source: Department of Statistics. Weights Reference Period: 1989; Coverage: 157 public and private companies; Number of Items in Basket: 300.

Consumer Prices:
Source: Department of Statistics. Weights Reference Period: 2001; Geographic Coverage: Algiers; Number of Items in Basket: 261; Basis for Calculation: National Survey on Household Consumption conducted in 2000.

Industrial Production:
Source: Department of Statistics. Weights Reference Period: 1989.

Crude Petroleum Production:
Calculated from production quantities reported in the *Oil Market Intelligence.*

International Transactions:

Exports:
Annual data on the volume of petroleum exports are obtained by weighting volumes for crude and refined petroleum by their relative 1995 export values. Monthly data on volume of crude petroleum exports are based on production quantities shown in the *Petroleum Intelligence Weekly.*

Imports, c.i.f.:
Department of Statistics data.

Government Finance:

Annual data are as reported for the *Government Finance Statistics Yearbook (GFSY)* and cover budgetary central government. The fiscal year ends December 31.

National Accounts:

Source: Department of Statistics.

Angola   614

Date of Fund Membership:
September 19, 1989

Standard Sources:
National Bank of Angola
Instituto Nacional de Estatística

Exchange Rates:
On September 22, 1990, the new kwanza (NKZ) replaced the kwanza at par. Beginning in July 1995, a monetary reform took place, and the readjusted kwanza (KZR), equal to 1,000 new kwanzas, was introduced. On November 12, 1999, the kwanza, equal to 1,000,000 readjusted kwanzas, was introduced.

Market Rate (End of Period and Period Average):
Through June 1996, the market rate was determined by the National Bank of Angola (central bank) and applied to sales of foreign exchange to commercial banks on the basis of allocations that were administratively set at fixing sessions held from time to time. Beginning on July 1, 1996, the market rate was administratively fixed to the U.S. dollar. Beginning in June 1998, the market rate is determined weekly in accordance with a crawling peg scheme. On May 1999, a free market exchange rate system was introduced. The rate is determined as the weighted average of the rates quoted by banking institutions and exchange bureaus.

International Liquidity:
Foreign Exchange (line ld.d) is the U.S. dollar value of the central bank's deposits in foreign banks and holdings of foreign currency.

Monetary Authorities:
Comprises the National Bank of Angola (NBA) only. Data for 1995 and 1996 are partially estimated. Estimates are based on available balance sheet data of the NBA with adjustments to reconcile these data with information from foreign correspondent banks and operational data of the NBA. Counterpart entries to these adjustments are included in *Other Items (Net) (line 17r).* *Other Items (Net)* also reflect weaknesses in accounting data, which have been addressed beginning in the third quarter of 1997. † Beginning in December 1999, data are based on a new plan of accounts.

Banking Institutions:
Comprises the Banco Português do Atlântico, Banco Totta & Açores, Banco de Comércio e Indústria, Banco de Fomento e Exterior, Banco Africano de Investimentos, Banco de Poupança e Crédito, Banco Comercial Angolano, and Caixa de Crédito Agro Pecuário e Pescas, which was liquidated in May 2001. † See note on monetary authorities. Beginning in December 2001, includes Banco Sol. Beginning in January 2002, includes Banco Espírito Santo-Angola. Beginning in October 2003, includes Banco Regional do Keve.

Banking Survey:
† See note on monetary authorities.

Money (National Definitions):
Base Money comprises currency in circulation, banks' required and excess reserve deposits in national and foreign currency, and local government and private sector deposits in national currency with the BNA.

Reserve Money comprises base money, local government and private sector deposits in foreign currency with the BNA, and securities issued by the BNA held by commercial banks.

M1 comprises currency outside of depository corporations and transferable deposits in national and foreign currency of local governments, nonfinanicial public enterprises, and the private sector with depository corporations. Currency outside of depository corporations refers to the notes and coins issued by the BNA less the amount held by the BNA and commercial banks.

M2 comprises *M1* and time and other deposits in national and foreign currency of nonfinanical public enterprises and the private sector.

M3 comprises *M2* and BNA bonds, certificates of deposit, and repurchase agreements in national and foreign currency held with the depository corporations by nonfinancial public enterprises and the private sector.

Interest Rates:

Discount Rate (End of Period):
Rate charged by the National Bank of Angola on loans to commercial banks.

Deposit Rate:
Minimum rate set by the National Bank of Angola on commercial banks' time deposits in national currency with maturities of 91 to 180 days. † Beginning in May 1999, rate offered by commercial banks on 91- to 180-day time deposits in national currency. † Beginning in January 2000, average rate offered by commercial banks on time deposits of up to 90 days in national currency. † Beginning in December 2000, weighted average rate offered by commercial banks on time deposits of up to 90 days in national currency. The rate is weighted by deposit amounts.

Lending Rate:
Maximum rate set by the National Bank of Angola on commercial banks' loans in national currency with maturities of 180 days. † Beginning in May 1999, rate charged by commercial banks on 180-day loans in national currency. † Beginning in January 2000, average rate charged by commercial banks on loans of up to 180 days in national currency. † Beginning in December 2000, weighted average rate charged by commercial banks on loans of up to 180 days in national currency. The rate is weighted by loan amounts.

Prices:

Consumer Prices:
Source: Instituto Nacional de Estatística. Weights Reference Period: December 2010; Geographical Coverage: as of 2008–09 survey, coverage includes entire country; –Number of Items in Basket: 240; Basis for Calculation: weights are based on the results obtained from the Population Welfare Integrated Survey (IBEP), conducted from May 2008 to May 2009 on close to 1,300 randomly selected households.

International Transactions:

Source: National Bank of Angola. Trade data in U.S. dollars.

National Accounts:

Source: Instituto Nacional de Estatística. Data are prepared in accordance with the 1968 United Nations System of National Accounts.

Anguilla 312

Standard Sources:

Eastern Caribbean Central Bank
Central Statistical Office

Exchange Rates:

Official Rate: (End of Period and Period Average):
The official rate is pegged to the U.S. dollar.

Central Bank:

Data are based on a standardized report form (SRF) for central banks, which accords with the concepts and definitions of the IMF's *Monetary and Financial Statistics Manual (MFSM)*, 2000. Departures from the *MFSM* methodology are explained below.

Data refer to accounts in the balance sheet of the East Caribbean Central Bank (ECCB) attributable to Anguilla.

Financial derivatives are excluded from the data.

Claims on Nonresident comprises estimates of Anguilla's notional share of the ECCB's foreign assets.

Claims on Other Depository Corporations comprises the portion of the ECCB's claims on resident other depository corporations attributable to Anguilla.

Claims on Central Government and *Liabilities to Central Government* comprise the portion of the ECCB's claims on and liabilities to the central government attributable to Anguilla.

Financial assets with *other* financial corporations, state and local governments, public nonfinancial corporations, and private sector attributable to Anguilla are not included in the data in the absence of a country of these accounts in the balance sheet of the ECCB.

Currency in circulation comprises the portion of currency in circulation attributable to Anguilla less vault cash held by other depository corporations.

Some portion of other deposits to other depository corporations and interest accrued from these deposits are included in *Other Items (Net)*.

Share and other equity is not applicable to the member countries of the ECCU because the shares and other equity in the balance sheet of the ECCB exclusively belong to the ECCB.

Other Depository Corporations:

Comprises commercial banks. Data exclude credit unions, which accept deposits.

Data are based on a standardized report form (SRF) for other depository corporations, which accords with the concepts and definitions of the *Monetary and Financial Statistics Manual (MFSM)*. For resident other depository corporations in the member countries of the ECCU, departures from the *MFSM* methodology are explained below.

Financial derivatives and insurance technical reserves are excluded from the data.

Financial assets and liabilities for which economic sectorization is unavailable are allocated to the economic sector having the largest volume of transactions in the category.

Transferable Deposits Included in Broad Money includes all deposits of the private sector denominated in foreign currency.

Accounts receivable and payable are included in *Other Items (Net)* rather than in other depository corporations' claims or liabilities to the corresponding economic sectors.

Accrued interest on transactions with nonresidents is included in

Other Items (Net) rather than in the outstanding amount of foreign assets and liabilities.

Depository Corporations:

See notes on central bank and other depository corporations.

Monetary Aggregates:

Broad Money:

Broad Money is calculated from the liability data in the sections for the central bank and other depository corporations. Broad money differs from M2 described below as broad money includes the deposits of money holding sectors with the ECCB attributable to Anguilla and deposits of other financial corporations, state and local government, and public nonfinancial corporations in national and foreign currencies with commercial banks.

Money (National Definitions):

M1 comprises notes and coins held by the public and demand deposits in national currency of the private sector with commercial banks.

M2 comprises M1 plus time, savings, and foreign currency deposits of the private sector with commercial banks.

Interest Rates:

Discount Rate (End of Period):

Rate charged by the ECCB on loans of last resort to commercial banks.

Money Market Rate:

Fixed rate on loans between commercial banks. The rate includes the commission charged by the ECCB as agent. † Beginning in October 2001, weighted average rate on loans between commercial banks. The rate is weighted by loans amounts.

Savings Rate:

Maximum rate offered by commercial banks on savings deposits in national currency. † Beginning in June 2003, weighted average rate offered by commercial banks on savings deposits in national currency. The rate is weighted by deposit amounts.

Savings Rate (Foreign Currency):

Weighted average rate offered by commercial banks on savings deposits in foreign currency. The rate is weighted by deposit amounts.

Deposit Rate:

Maximum rate offered by commercial banks on three-month The rate is weighted by deposit amounts.

Deposit Rate (Foreign currency):

Weighted average rate offered by commercial banks on deposits in foreign currency. The rate is weighted by deposit amounts.

Lending Rate:

Maximum rate charged by commercial banks on prime loans. The rate is weighted by loan amounts.

Lending Rate (Foreign Currency):

Weighted average rate charged by commercial banks on loans in foreign currency. The rate is weighted by loan amounts.

Prices, Toursim, Labor:

Consumer Prices:
Source: Central Statistical Office.

International Transactions:

Exports and Imports:
Source: Central Statistical Office.

National Accounts:

Source: Eastern Caribbean Central Bank.

Antigua and Barbuda   311

Date of Fund Membership:

February 25, 1982

Standard Sources:

Eastern Caribbean Central Bank

Exchange Rates:

Official Rate: (End of Period and Period Average):
Rates are based on a fixed relationship to the U.S. dollar.

Central Bank:

Data are based on a standardized report form (SRF) for central banks, which accords with the concepts and definitions of the IMF's *Monetary and Financial Statistics Manual (MFSM)*, 2000. Departures from the *MFSM* methodology are explained below.

Data refer to accounts in the balance sheet of the East Caribbean Central Bank (ECCB) attributable to Antigua and Barbuda. Financial derivatives are excluded from the data.

Claims on Nonresident comprises estimates of Antigua and Barbuda's notional share of the ECCB's foreign assets.

Claims on Other Depository Corporations comprises the portion of the ECCB's claims on resident other depository corporations attributable to Antigua and Barbuda.

Claims on Central Government and *Liabilities to Central Government* comprise the portion of the ECCB's claims on and liabilities to the central government attributable to Antigua and Barbuda.

Financial assets with other financial corporations, state and local governments, public nonfinancial corporations, and private sector attributable to Antigua and Barbuda are not included in the data in the absence of a country of these accounts in the balance sheet of the ECCB.

Currency in circulation comprises the portion of currency in circulation attributable to Antigua and Barbuda less vault cash held by other depository corporations.

Some portion of other deposits to other depository corporations and interest accrued from these deposits are included in *Other Items (Net)*.

Share and other equity is not applicable to the member countries of the ECCU because the shares and other equity in the balance sheet of the ECCB exclusively belong to the ECCB.

Other Depository Corporations:

Comprises commercial banks. Data exclude finance companies, mortgage companies, and credit unions, which accept deposits.

Data are based on a standardized report form (SRF) for other depository corporations, which accords with the concepts and definitions of the *Monetary and Financial Statistics Manual (MFSM)*. For resident other depository corporations in the member countries of the ECCU, departures from the *MFSM* methodology are explained below.

Financial derivatives and insurance technical reserves are excluded from the data.

Financial assets and liabilities for which economic sectorization is unavailable are allocated to the economic sector having the largest volume of transactions in the category.

Transferable Deposits Included in Broad Money includes all deposits of the private sector denominated in foreign currency.

Accounts receivable and payable are included in *Other Items (Net)* rather than in other depository corporations' claims or liabilities to the corresponding economic sectors.

Accrued interest on transactions with nonresidents is included in *Other Items (Net)* rather than in the outstanding amount of foreign assets and liabilities.

Depository Corporations:

See notes on central bank and other depository corporations.

Monetary Aggregates:

Broad Money:

Broad Money is calculated from the liability data in the sections for the central bank and other depository corporations. Broad money differs from M2 described below as broad money includes the deposits of money holding sectors with the ECCB attributable to Antigua and Barbuda and deposits of other financial corporations, state and local government, and public nonfinancial corporations in national and foreign currencies with commercial banks.

Money (National Definitions):

M1 comprises notes and coins held by the public and demand deposits in national currency of the private sector with commercial banks.

M2 comprises M1 plus time, savings, and foreign currency deposits of the private sector with commercial banks.

Interest Rates:

Discount Rate (End of Period):

Rate charged by the ECCB on loans of last resort to commercial banks.

Money Market Rate:

Fixed rate on loans between commercial banks. The rate includes the commission charged by the ECCB as agent. † Beginning in October 2001, weighted average rate on loans between commercial banks. The rate is weighted by loans amounts.

Treasury Bill Rate:

Rate on three-month treasury bills.

Savings Rate:

Maximum rate offered by commercial banks on savings deposits in national currency. † Beginning in June 2003, weighted average rate offered by commercial banks on savings deposits in national currency. The rate is weighted by deposit amounts.

Savings Rate (Foreign Currency):

Weighted average rate offered by commercial banks on savings deposits in foreign currency. The rate is weighted by deposit amounts.

Deposit Rate:

Maximum rate offered by commercial banks on three-month time deposits. The rate is weighted by deposit amounts.

Lending Rate:

Maximum rate charged by commercial banks on prime loans. The rate is weighted by loan amounts.

Lending Rate (Foreign Currency):

Weighted average rate charged by commercial banks on loans in foreign currency. The rate is weighted by loan amounts.

International Transactions:

Data for exports and imports are from ECCB.

National Accounts:

Source: ECCB. As indicated by the country, data have been revised following the implementation of the *1993 SNA*.

Argentina   213

Date of Fund Membership:

September 20, 1956

Standard Sources:

Central Bank of the Republic
National Institute of Statistics and Census

Exchange Rates:

From January 1, 1970, the peso ley ($ ley) was established as the monetary unit replacing the peso moneda nacional at the exchange rate of one peso ley for 100 peso moneda nacional (m$n). On June 1, 1983, the peso argentino ($a), equal to 10,000 peso ley was introduced. On June 14, 1985, the austral (A), equal to 1,000 peso argentino was introduced. On January 1, 1992 the peso, equal to 10,000 australes, was introduced. The *Official Rate (End of Period* and *Period Average)* was pegged to the U.S. dollar through 2001. By the end of 2001, and amidst a partial freeze on bank deposits and the introduction of exchange and capital controls, Argentina abandoned the Convertibility System and devalued the peso through Law 25.561: "Public Emergency and Reform of the Exchange Regime." By means of this law a new exchange regime was established, based on an Official Exchange Market with a fixed rate of 1.40 pesos per U.S. dollar for trade and financial transactions, and a Free Exchange Market for all other transactions. A unified floating exchange rate regime was introduced on February 11, 2002, with the exchange rate determined by market conditions.

International Liquidity:

As of April 1, 1991, international reserve assets back the monetary liabilities of the Central Bank of the Republic of Argentina. *Gold (National Valuation) (line 1and)* is the U.S. dollar value of official holdings of gold as reported in the country's standard sources. *Foreign Exchange (line 1d.d):* The decline in foreign exchange holdings of the Central Bank in August 1995 was partly due to a decrease in reserve requirements at the Central Bank that could be met by a corresponding increase in the banks' deposits abroad in certain foreign banks. *Line 3..d* mainly comprises payments agreements balances and export bills held by the Central Bank of Argentina.

Argentina's national definition of international reserves includes the central bank's holdings of gold, SDR holdings, reserve position in the Fund, foreign exchange, net assets of the ALADI agreement (multilateral payment system), and domestic government securities payable in foreign exchange.

Monetary Authorities:

Comprises the Central Bank of the Republic of Argentina (CBRA) only. Accounts classified as central government include also positions with nonfinancial public enterprises.

The definition of foreign assets of the monetary authorities in

IFS differs from the definition of foreign assets in the *Bulletin* in that the latter excludes the foreign exchange received by the CBRA under swaps from domestic financial entities' current account balances in foreign currencies. † Beginning in January 1990, data may not be comparable with data for earlier periods because of a change in the valuation system and adjustments to the accounts of the CBRA. † Beginning in January 1994, data are based on more detailed sectorization of the accounts.

Deposit Money Banks:

Comprises national, provincial, and municipal banks, Caja Nacional de Ahorro y Seguro (savings bank), and private commercial banks including branches of foreign banks. Holdings of public securities and accrued income on loans, which are classified as *Claims on Central Government (line 22a),* include also positions with state and local governments and nonfinancial public enterprises. *Claims on Official Entities (line 22bx)* comprise mainly claims on nonfinancial public enterprises. Positions in financial derivatives are included in unclassified assets and liabilities which are shown in other items net. † Beginning in January 1990, data are based on an improved reporting system. † See note on monetary authorities.

Monetary Survey:

Money (line 34) excludes deposits of other banking institutions. † See notes on monetary authorities and deposit money banks.

Other Banking Institutions:

Comprises investment finance companies, credit cooperatives, and savings and loan associations for housing. † See notes on monetary authorities and deposit money banks.

Banking Survey:

† See notes on monetary authorities and deposit money banks.

Money (National Definitions):

Base Money comprises currency in circulation, reserve deposits, and correspondent accounts of banking institutions in national currency with the CBRA. Currency in circulation refers to notes and coins issued by the CBRA less the amount held by the CBRA. *M1* comprises currency in circulation outside the banking system and transferable deposits in national and foreign currency. Currency in circulation outside the banking system refers to notes and coins issued by the CBRA less the amount held by banking institutions, including the CBRA. Transferable deposits refer to current account deposits of state and local governments, public nonfinancial corporations, private sector, and residents abroad with banking institutions.
M2 comprises M1 and savings deposits in national and foreign currency of state and local governments, public nonfinancial corporations, private sector, and residents abroad with banking institutions.
M3 comprises M2, fixed deposits, and other deposits in national and foreign currency of state and local governments, public nonfinancial corporations, private sector, and residents abroad with banking institutions.
M3 Total comprises M3 and transferable, savings, time, and other deposits of nonresidents (in national and foreign currency).

Interest Rates:

Money Market Rate:
Average rate on loans denominated in national currency of up to 15 days between domestic financial institutions. The rate is weighted by daily loan amounts.

Money Market Rate (Foreign Currency):
Average rate on loans denominated in U.S. dollars of up to 15 days between domestic financial institutions. The rate is weighted by daily loan amounts.

Savings Rate:
Weighted average rate offered by financial institutions in Buenos Aires and surrounding areas on savings deposits in national currency. The rate is weighted by deposit amounts.

Savings Rate (Foreign Currency):
Weighted average rate offered by financial institutions in Buenos Aires and surrounding areas on savings deposits in U.S. dollars. The rate is weighted by deposit amounts.

Deposit Rate:
Weighted average rate offered by financial institutions in Buenos Aires and surrounding areas on 30- to 59-day time deposits in national currency. The rate is weighted by deposit amounts.

Deposit Rate (Foreign Currency):
Weighted average rate offered by financial institutions in Buenos Aires and surrounding areas on 30- to 59-day time deposits in U.S. dollars. The rate is weighted by deposit amounts.

Lending Rate:
Arithmetic average rate at which a selected group of banks is willing to lend to most creditworthy business customers on 30-day loans denominated in national currency. † Beginning in January 2009, weighted average rate charged by domestic financial institutions in Buenos Aires and surrounding areas on loans to private nonfinancial corporations in national currency. The loans are in the form of current account advances of one- to seven-days and of ten million pesos or more. The rate is weighted by loan amounts.

Lending Rate (Foreign Currency):
Arithmetic average rate at which a selected group of banks is willing to lend to most creditworthy business customers on 30-day loans denominated in U.S. dollars. † Beginning in January 1994, weighted average rate charged by domestic financial institutions on loans to the private nonfinancial sector in U.S. dollars. The loans are in the form of bills of up to 89 days. The rate is weighted by loan amounts.

Prices and Production:

Share Prices:
Composite stock price index (MERVAL) of the Buenos Aires Stock Exchange, base June 30, 1986. The index covers shares based on their trading volume and is weighted by market capitalization. The component companies and their weights are updated on a quarterly basis according to their participation in the market during the last six months.

Producer Prices:
Source: National Institute of Statistics and Census. Weights Reference Period: 1993; Coverage: agriculture, fisheries, minerals,

manufacturers, and electric energy; Number of Items in Basket: 2800 prices are monitored every month; Basis for Calculation: weights are based on the gross production value for the primary sector, the results of the National Economic Census of 1994 for the manufacturing sector, and the foreign trade data for exports and imports.

Consumer Prices:
Source: National Institute of Statistics and Census. Weights Reference Period: 2004–2005; Geographical Coverage: Greater Buenos Aires; Number of Items in Basket: 440; Basis for Calculation: weights are derived from the National Household Expenditure Survey, 2004–2005. The data for Argentina are officially reported data. The IMF has, however, issued a declaration of censure and called on Argentina to adopt remedial measures to address the quality of the official CPI-GBA data. Alternative data sources have shown considerably higher inflation rates than the official data since 2007. In this context, the Fund is also using alternative estimates of CPI inflation for the surveillance of macroeconomic developments in Argentina.

Wages: Monthly Earnings (Manufacturing):
Source: National Institute of Statistics and Census. Index, weights reference period: 2001. Data cover wages, including overtime pay and holiday pay, of production workers in manufacturing firms employing 10 or more people.

Manufacturing Production, Seasonally Adjusted:
Source: National Institute of Statistics and Census. Weights reference period: 1993. Calculated by main economic activities in accordance with ISIC Rev. 3. Data are based on surveys of 83 leading enterprises, supplemented by information from trade associations and administrative information on 100 products.

Crude Petroleum Production:
Index based on data (in thousands of cubic meters) directly supplied by the Central Bank.

International Transactions:

Value of Exports and Imports:
Trade data are from the National Institute of Statistics and Census, with the exception of imports f.o.b. which are supplied by the Central Bank.
Trade indices are from the National Institute of Statistics and Census. Weights reference period: 1993. Aggregate volume data are Laspeyres, and unit value indices are Paasche indices.

Government Finance:

Monthly, quarterly, and annual data cover the consolidated central government and are derived from *Public Sector Accounts—Public Sector on a Cash Basis—Savings, Investment, and Financing,* a monthly publication of the Ministry of Economy, Public Works, and Services. Revenue and expenditure data are adjusted to exclude taxes collected by the central government and shared with provincial governments, and expenditure data include transfers to nonfinancial public enterprises. The fiscal year ends December 31.

National Accounts:

Source: National Institute of Statistics and Census. As indicated by the country, concepts and definitions are broadly in accordance with the recommendations of the *System of National Ac-*

counts 1993 (1993 SNA); Coverage: the entire economy; Gross Domestic Product (GDP) is compiled by the production, expenditure and income approaches. Line 93i (changes in inventories) includes a statistical discrepancy. Adjustments to account for services to households, informal activities in trade and transport services, and some illegal activities are made by using employment data and information on income per employee from the household surveys. GDP volume measures are calculated based on the prices and weights for 1993 and are presented at annual levels. The data are not seasonally adjusted. The data for Argentina are officially reported data. the IMF has, however, issued a declaration of censure and called on Argentina to adopt remedial measures to address the quality of the official GDP data. Alternative data sources have shown significantly lower real growth than the official data since 2008. In this context, the Fund is also using alternative estimates of GDP growth for the surveillance of macroeconomic developments in Argentina. Quarterly data are adjusted at annual rates.

Armenia   911

Date of Fund Membership:
May 28, 1992

Standard Sources:
Central Bank of Armenia
National Statistical Service

Exchange Rates:
The ruble was the legal tender in Armenia until November 21, 1993. The dram, equal to 200 rubles, was introduced on November 22, 1993.

Official Rate: (End of Period and Period Average):
The official rate is determined by the Central Bank of Armenia (CBA) and is set on a daily basis as a weighted average of the previous day's interbank and foreign exchange auction rates.

International Liquidity:
Prior to January 1996, *Foreign Exchange (line 1d.d)* includes convertible and nonconvertible currencies.

Central Bank:
Consists of the Central Bank of Armenia (CBA) only.
Data are based on a standardized report form (SRF) for central banks, which accords with the concepts and definitions of the IMF's *Monetary and Financial Statistics Manual (MFSM),* 2000.
Claims on Central Government and *Liabilities to Central Government* include positions with local governments because they are not financially independent from central government. For central bank, departures from the *MFSM* methodology are explained below. Securities other than shares issued are valued at face value rather than at market price or fair value.

Other Depository Corporations:
Comprises commercial banks and credit organizations. Prior to May 2008, comprises commercial banks only. *Claims on Central Government* and *Liabilities to Central Government* include positions

with local governments because they are not financially independent from central government.

Data are based on a standardized report form (SRF) for other depository corporations, which accords with the concepts and definitions of the *Monetary and Financial Statistics Manual (MFSM)*. For other depository corporations in the Republic of Armenia, departures from the MFSM methodology are explained below.

Securities other than shares issued are recorded at face value rather than at the market price or fair value.

Depository Corporations:

See notes on central bank and other depository corporations.

Other Financial Corporations:

Comprises insurance companies and investment companies.

Data are based on a standardized report form (SRF) for other financial corporations, which accords with the concepts and definitions of the *Monetary and Financial Statistics Manual (MFSM)*. For other financial corporations in the Republic of Armenia, departures from the *MFSM* methodology are explained below.

Financial assets and liabilities for which financial instrument breakdown is unavailable are allocated to the financial instrument having the largest volume of transactions in the category.

Financial assets and liabilities for which economic sectorization is unavailable are allocated to the economic sector having the largest volume of transactions in the category.

Claims on Depository Corporations includes some claims on other financial corporations.

Claims on Private Sector includes claims on public nonfinancial corporations.

Loans includes some liabilities to other financial corporations.

Financial Corporations:

See notes on central bank, other depository corporations, and other financial corporations.

Monetary Aggregates:

Broad Money:

Broad Money calculated from the liability data in the sections for the central bank and other depository corporations accords with the concepts and definitions of the *MFSM* and is consistent with M2X described below.

Money (National Definitions):

Reserve Money comprises notes and coins issued by the CBA, required reserve and other deposits of other depository corporations with the CBA, and deposits of the private sector in national and foreign currency with the CBA.

M1 comprises currency in circulation and transferable deposits. Currency in circulation refers to notes and coins issued by the CBA less the amount held by other depository corporations. Transferable deposits refer to current account deposits in national currency of other financial corporations, public nonfinancial corporations, and private sector with the CBA and other depository corporations.

M2 is designated as national currency broad money and comprises M1 and term deposits in national currency of other financial corporations, public nonfinancial corporations, and private sector with the CBA and other depository corporations.

M2X is designated as broad money and comprises M2 and foreign currency deposits of other financial corporations, public nonfinancial corporations, and private sector with the CBA and other depository corporations.

Interest Rates:

Central Bank Policy Rate (End of Period):

Repo rate at which the CBA conducts repurchase agreements with resident banks. Beginning in January 2006, the rate is used as operational target under CBA's adopted inflation targeting strategy.

Discount Rate (End of Period):

Corresponds to the credit auction rate, which is the basic rate at which the CBA lends to commercial banks.

Refinancing Rate (End of Period):

Basic rate at which the CBA lends to the central government.

Money Market Rate:

Loan-amount-weighted average rate of interbank loans and deposits.

Treasury Bill Rate:

Weighted average yield on 91-day treasury bills. † Beginning in May 1996, weighted average yield on three- to six-month (including 182-day) treasury bills. † Beginning in March 2001, weighted average yield on nine- to twelve-month treasury bills.

Deposit Rate:

Weighted average rate offered by commercial banks on new deposits in domestic currency with maturities of 15 days to less than a year. The rate is weighted by deposit amounts.

Lending Rate:

Weighted average rate charged by commercial banks on new loans in domestic currency with maturities of 15 days to less than a year. The rate is weighted by loan amounts.

Government Bond Yield:

Weighted average yield on medium-term coupon bonds with partial repayment sold in the primary market. Several types of bonds with maturities ranging between one to five years are included.

Prices, Production, Labor:

Source: Ministry of Statistics of Republic of Armenia.

Producer Prices:

Source: Ministry of Statistics of Republic of Armenia. Weights Reference Period: 2008; Sectoral coverage: Mining and quarrying manufacturing electricity, gas, steam and air conditioning supply, water supply; sewerage, waste management and remediation activities; Number of Items: Prices are monitored for 417 products at 413 base industrial enterprises. Basis for Calculation: Sources of weights are data on total volume of industrial production value derived as a result of entire branch-wise statistical surveys.

Consumer Prices:

Source: Ministry of Statistics of Republic of Armenia. Weights Reference Period: 2010; Geographical Coverage: Yerevan and eleven large population centers in the Republic; Number of Items in Basket: 470; Basis for Calculation: the weights for goods and services that are used to aggregate indices are calculated on the basis of 2010 data from surveys covering about 6,816 households.

Industrial Production:
Source: Ministry of Statistics of Republic of Armenia. The index is derived from a monthly survey covering approximately 1,200 large and medium-sized industrial organizations, and another 1000 micro- and small-sized organizations quarterly; it measures production volumes of the mining and quarrying industry, manufacturing industry, electricity, gas, steam and air conditioning supply, water supply; waste management and remediation activities. Basis for Calculation: survey of industrial organizations.

Wages:
Source: Ministry of Statistics of Republic of Armenia. Average monthly nominal wages, including benefits in kind per worker, are compiled on the basis of monthly reports provided by 9,000 economic entities. All branches and occupations are covered, excluding military personnel. Calculation of average wages/earnings and labor compensation of employees correspond to the principles of *1993 SNA*.

International Transactions:

Source: Ministry of Statistics of Republic of Armenia. *Exports* and *Imports* are based on customs records that include coverage of citizens' (shuttle) trade.

Government Finance:

Cash data cover the operations of the consolidated central government. The fiscal year ends December 31.

National Accounts:

Source: Ministry of Statistics of Republic of Armenia. *Gross Domestic Product, Production Approach (line 99b)* is compiled from the production approach using data on gross output and intermediate consumption from production surveys. Because official GDP is calculated using the production approach, the statistical discrepancy (*line 99bs*) represents the difference between GDP from the production approach (*line 99b*) and the sum of the expenditure components shown. Concepts, definitions, and methodology are in accordance with the *1993 SNA*, as indicated by the country. Estimates include hidden activities but exclude illegal activities.

Aruba   314

Standard Sources:

Centrale Bank van Aruba
Central Bureau of Statistics

Exchange Rates:

Official Rate: (End of Period and Period Average):
The official rate is pegged to the U.S. dollar.

International Liquidity:

Gold (National Valuation) (line 1and) is obtained by converting the value in national currency terms, as reported in the country's standard source, using the prevailing exchange rate, as given in *line ae.* Title to the gold held in various forms by the Central Bank of the Netherlands Antilles as of December 31, 1985 was formally transferred to the Gold Fund of the Netherlands Antilles and Aruba by means of a deed of transfer dated December 19,

1986. The Gold Fund then distributed gold to the Bank van de Nederlandse Antillen and the Centrale Bank van Aruba based on the Mutual Regulation. During 1998, the distribution of gold was finalized. *Lines 7a.d* and *7b.d* are derived from the accounts of the commercial banks and exclude the nonresident assets and liabilities of offshore banks operating in Aruba.

Monetary Authorities:

Comprises the Central Bank of Aruba (CBA), which was established on January 1, 1986, when Aruba obtained a separate status within the Kingdom of the Netherlands. Prior to that date, Aruba formed part of the Netherlands Antilles. *Central Government Deposits (line 16d)* includes development funds received from the Netherlands Government and held temporarily pending expenditures on current development projects in Aruba.

Deposit Money Banks:

Data refer to the four commercial banks licensed to carry out operations with residents and nonresidents. The two offshore banks established in Aruba transact exclusively with nonresidents and are themselves classified as such in national sources. *Claims on Private Sector (line 22d)* includes claims on nonfinancial public enterprises.

Money (National Definitions):

Narrow Money comprises currency in circulation and demand deposits of the private sector in national and foreign currency at the CBA and commercial banks. Currency in circulation refers to notes and coins issued by the CBA less the amount held by commercial banks.
Quasi-Money comprises time and savings deposits of the private sector in national and foreign currency at the CBA and commercial banks.
Broad Money comprises narrow money, quasi-money, and treasury bills held by the private sector.

Interest Rates:

Discount Rate:
The rate at which the central bank makes collateralized loans to commercial banks. Data are end-of-period.

Money Market Rate:
Rate paid on seven-day interbank advances.

Deposit Rate:
Beginning in September 1998, data refer to the weighted-average rate on new deposits. Prior to September 1998, data are end-of period and refer to deposit money banks' offered rates on six-month deposits above Af. 10,000.

Lending Rate:
Beginning in September 1998, data refer to the weighted average rate on new loans. Prior to September 1998, data are end-of-period and refer to deposit money banks' current account lending rate.

Prices and Tourism:

Consumer Prices:
Source: Central Bureau of Statistics. Weights Reference Period: December 2006; Basis for Calculation: weights are based on the Income and Expenditure Survey held during the period April-May 2006, which consisted of 796 households.

International Transactions:

Source: Central Bureau of Statistics. Data through December 1999 exclude imports into and exports from the Free Zone. Mineral fuels trade is also excluded.

National Accounts:

Source: Central Bureau of Statistics. As indicated by the country, the National Accounts of Aruba follows the guidelines, concepts, definitions, classifications, and accounting rules of *1993 SNA*.

Australia 193

Date of Fund Membership:

August 5, 1947

Standard Sources:

Reserve Bank of Australia
Commonwealth Cash Flow Statements
Department of the Treasury/Australian Office of Financial Management
Department of Finance
Australian Bureau of Statistics

Exchange Rates:

Market Rate (End of Period and Period Average):
Central bank midpoint rate.

International Liquidity:

Gold (National Valuation) (line 1and) is obtained by converting the value in national currency terms, as reported in the country's standard sources, using the prevailing exchange rate, as given in *line* **ae**. This line follows national valuation procedures which revalue gold monthly on the basis of the average U.S. dollar price of gold prevailing in the London market during the month.

Central Bank:

Consists of the Reserve Bank of Australia (RBA) only.
† Beginning in January 2007, data are based on a standardized report form (SRF) for central banks which accords with the concepts and definitions of the IMF's *Monetary and Financial Statistics Manual (MFSM), 2000*. Departures from the *MFSM* methodology are explained, below.
Financial assets and liabilities for which the financial instrument breakdown is unavailable are allocated to the financial instrument having the largest volume of transactions in the category.
Financial assets and liabilities for which economic sectorization is unavailable are allocated to the economic sector having the largest volume of transactions in the category.
Accounts receivable and payable are included in *Other Items (Net)* rather than in central bank's claims on or liabilities to the corresponding economic sectors.
For January 2007 through February 2010, data are for the last Wednesday of every month. Beginning in March 2010, data are for the last day of every month.
For December 2001 through December 2006, data in the SRF format are compiled from pre-SRF data which are not fully based

on the *MFSM* methodology. Departures from the *MFSM* methodology, in addition to departures from January 2007 listed above, are explained below.
Data are for the last Wednesday of every month.
Some positions with resident sectors are included in *Other Items (Net)* rather than as claims on or liabilities to the corresponding economic sectors.
Current year result and retained earnings are included in *Other Items (Net)* rather than in *Shares and Other Equity*.

Other Depository Corporations:

Comprise authorized deposit-taking institutions, namely banks, credit unions, and building societies. Data exclude registered financial corporations, cash management trusts, and specialist credit card institutions. Data are collected by the Australian Prudential Regulatory Authority (APRA).
† Beginning in January 2007, data are based on a standardized report form (SRF) for other depository corporations which accords with the concepts and definitions of the IMF's Monetary *and Financial Statistics Manual (MFSM), 2000*. For other depository corporations in Australia, departures from *MFSM* methodology are explained below.
Financial assets and liabilities for which financial instrument breakdown is unavailable are allocated to the financial instrument having the largest volume of transactions in the category.
Financial assets and liabilities for which economic sectorization is unavailable are allocated to the economic sector having the largest volume of transactions in the category.
Data on public sector securities are reported net of short positions which may result in negative values of *Claims on Central Government* and *Claims on State and Local Governments*.
Currency includes holdings of foreign currency.
Trade credit and advances are included in *Other Items (Net)* rather than as claims on or liabilities to the corresponding economic sectors.
Transferable deposit assets and liabilities with other depository corporations in foreign currency are included as other deposits.
Some other deposits of other depository corporations are included as transferable deposits and settlement accounts.
Holdings of securities other than shares and shares and other equity issued by other nonfinancial corporations in foreign currency are included as shares and other equity.
Holdings of shares and other equity issued by other nonfinancial corporations in national currency may be underestimated slightly as holdings of securities other than shares and shares and other equity issued by other nonfinancial corporations in foreign currency are subtracted from holdings of shares and other equity issued by other nonfinancial corporations in national currency.
Financial derivatives are classified as with other financial corporations, except those with the central bank.
Settlement account assets with other financial corporations are included as other deposits.
Settlement account liabilities in foreign currency are included as with other financial corporations.
Asset and liability settlement account balances between other depository corporations may not be consistent due to timing differences.
The holder of securities issued by other depository corporations

is unavailable. Promissory notes, commercial paper, and certificates of deposit issued by other depository corporations are included as securities other than shares included in broad money held by other nonfinancial corporations. Bill acceptances and other short-term securities issued by other depository corporations are included as securities other than shares excluded from broad money held by other nonfinancial corporations. Loan capital and hybrid securities issued by other depository corporations are included as securities other than shares excluded from broad money held by other financial corporations. Long-term securities issued by other depository corporations are included as securities other than shares excluded from broad money held by other resident sectors. Securities other than shares issued by other depository corporations in foreign currency are included as held by other nonfinancial corporations.

Holdings of own bankers acceptances are included as claims.

Securities sold under agreements to repurchase are included in *Other Items (Net)* rather than as liabilities to the corresponding economic sectors.

Securities other than shares and shares and other equity held for investment are valued at amortized cost, in accordance with Australian accounting standards in AASB 139 www.aasb.gov.au/admin/file/content105/c9/AASB139_07–04_ COMPoct10_01–11.pdf, rather than at current market price or fair value.

Securities other than shares issued are generally valued at amortized cost, in accordance with Australian accounting standards in AASB 139, rather than at current market price or fair value.

† For March 2002 through December 2006, data in the SRF format are compiled from pre-SRF data which are not fully based on the *MFSM* methodology and are, therefore, not strictly comparable to data for later periods. Departures from the *MFSM* methodology, in addition to departures from January 2007 listed above, are explained below.

Some positions with resident sectors are included in *Other Items (Net)* rather than as claims on or liabilities to the corresponding economic sectors.

Claims on Other Financial Corporations and *Financial Derivatives* include positions in financial derivatives with other depository corporations.

Securities Other than Shares Included in Broad Money and *Securities Other than Shares Excluded from Broad Money* include securities held by other depository corporations.

Securities other than shares and shares and other equity held for investment purposes are valued at acquisition cost, in accordance with Australian accounting standards in AASB 139, rather than at current market price or fair value.

† For December 2001 through February 2002, data in the SRF format are compiled from pre-SRF data which are not fully based on the *MFSM* methodology and are, therefore, not strictly comparable to data for later periods.

Depository Corporations:

† See notes on central bank and other depository corporations.

Other Financial Corporations:

Comprises money market corporations and finance companies. Data exclude life insurance corporations, other insurance corporations, pension funds, securitization vehicles, other financial institutions, central borrowing authorities, and financial auxiliaries. Data are collected by the APRA.

Data are based on a standardized report form (SRF) for other financial corporations which accords with the concepts and definitions of the IMF's Monetary *and Financial Statistics Manual (MFSM), 2000.*). For other financial corporations in Australia, departures from the *MFSM* methodology are explained below.

Financial assets and liabilities for which economic sectorization is unavailable are allocated to the economic sector having the largest volume of transactions in the category.

Financial assets and liabilities for which financial instrument breakdown is unavailable are allocated to the financial instrument having the largest volume of transactions in the category.

Claims on Depository Corporations includes holdings of foreign currency.

Other deposits with other depository corporations are included as transferable deposits.

Other Items (Net) includes discrepancies which result from data inaccuracies.

Securities Other than Shares held by other nonfinancial corporations includes all short-term securities other than shares issued by other financial corporations to resident sectors.

Securities Other than Shares held by other resident sectors includes all long-term securities other than shares issued by other financial corporations to resident sectors.

Financial derivatives are classified as with other financial corporations, except those with the central bank.

Settlement accounts between other financial corporations are included as other deposits.

Securities other than shares and shares and other equity held for investment are valued at amortized cost, in accordance with Australian accounting standards in AASB 139 www.aasb.gov.au/admin/file/content105/c9/AASB139_07–04_ COMPoct10_01–11.pdf, rather than at current market price or fair value.

Securities other than shares issued are generally valued at amortized cost, in accordance with Australian accounting standards in AASB 139, rather than at current market price or fair value.

Monetary Aggregates:

Broad Money:

Broad Money (line *59m*) calculated from the liability data in the sections for the central bank and other depository corporations accords with the concepts and definitions of the *MFSM*. Broad money includes currency issued by the central government. Broad money (line 59m) differs from broad money (line 59mea) as line 59mea includes deposits of the private sector with registered financial corporations and cash management trusts; certificates of deposit and commercial paper issued by registered financial corporations held by the private sector; and bills drawn by the nonfinancial intermediary private sector and accepted by other depository corporations and other financial corporations, net of bank holdings of those acceptances.

Money (National Definitions):

Money Base comprises currency in circulation, deposits of banks with the central bank, and other liabilities issued by the central bank to the private sector and other financial corporations.

Currency comprises notes and coins outside the central bank and banks.

M1 comprises currency and current account deposits of public nonfinancial corporations, and private sector with the central bank and banks.

M3 comprises M1; other deposits (including certificates of deposit) of other financial corporations, public nonfinancial corporations, and private sector with banks in national currency; and deposits of other financial corporations, public nonfinancial corporations, and private sector with the rest of other depository corporations in national currency.

Broad Money comprises M3; deposits of public nonfinancial corporations and private sector with other financial corporations; and commercial paper, promissory notes, and bill acceptances issued by all financial intermediaries held by the private sector.

Interest Rates:

Central Bank Policy Rate (End of Period):
Rediscount rate offered by the RBA to holders of treasury notes. Rates shown are average for period.† Beginning in August 1990, Target cash rate set by the RBA at each Board meeting. The RBA targets the weighted average of the interest rates at which banks have borrowed and lent exchange settlement funds on the interbank overnight market. The 11am call rate is used prior to July 1998.

Money Market Rate:
Weighted average short-term rate of outstanding loans. † Beginning in January 1995, rate paid on unsecured overnight loans of cash as calculated by the Australian Financial Markets Association and published on Reuters page at 11 a.m. † Beginning in January 1999, weighted average rate of the interest rates at which banks have borrowed and lent exchange settlement funds during the day. The rate is weighted by loan amounts.

Treasury Bill Rate:
Weighted average yield on thirteen-week treasury notes allotted at last tender of month. †Beginning in January 1995, estimated closing yield in the secondary market on thirteen-week treasury notes. No treasury notes were issued between May 2002 and March 2009.

Savings Rate:
Rate on bonus savings accounts which are deposit accounts of at least $10,000 Australian dollars that pay a higher rate of interest if at least one deposit and no withdrawals are made each month. Rate is an average of the five largest banks' rates assuming these requirements are met. Prior to April 2003, the average is for three of the five largest banks and, between April 2003 and April 2005, the average is for four of the five largest banks.

Deposit Rate:
Investment rate offered by savings banks. † Beginning in December 1981, average rate offered by major banks on three-month fixed deposits of 10,000 Australian dollars.† Beginning in February 2002, average rate on $10 000 term deposits across all terms offered by the five largest banks, including their advertised 'specials' and regular rates.

Lending Rate:
Maximum rate charged by banks on overdrafts of less than 100,000 Australian dollars. † Beginning in January 1977, rate charged by banks on loans to large businesses. † Beginning in January 2007, rate charged by banks on standard housing loans.

Government Bond Yield:
Short-Term: Yield on two-year Treasury bonds. † Beginning in June 1981, assessed secondary market yield on two-year non-rebate bonds. † Beginning in June 1992, assessed secondary market yield on three-year non-rebate bonds. Yield is calculated before brokerage and on the last business day of the month. *Long-Term:* Yield on 15-year Treasury bonds † Beginning in July 1969, assessed secondary market yield on ten-year non-rebate bonds. Yield is calculated before brokerage and on the last business day of the month.

Prices, Production, Labor:

Share Prices (End of Month):
Share price index covering shares quoted in the Australian Stock Exchange (ASX) refers to the All Ordinaries Index, base December 31, 1979. † Beginning in December 1979, share price index refers to the S&P/ASX 200, base December 31, 1979.

Prices: Manufacturing Output:
Australian Bureau of Statistics index of articles produced by manufacturing industry, weights reference period: 1998–99 The index includes prices of articles produced by domestic manufacturers for sale or transfer to other domestic sectors or for export or for use as capital equipment.

Consumer Prices:
Source: Australian Bureau of Statistics. Weights Reference Period: 2009–10; Geographical Coverage: Eight capital cities; Number of Items in Basket: Goods and services actually acquired by the reference population in the weighting base period; Basis for Calculation: Weights are based on Household Expenditure Survey and are updated at approximately five-yearly intervals.

Wages:
Average weekly earnings, ordinary time (excludes overtime) for full-time adult employees for the pay period ending on or before the middle of the quarter.

Industrial Production, Seasonally Adjusted:
Source: Australian Bureau of Statistics. Weights Reference Period: 2008–2009; Sectoral Coverage: mining, manufacturing and electricity, gas and water industrial sectors; Basis for Calculation: from 1985–86 the elemental volume indexes are aggregated together to form annually reweighted chain Laspeyres indexes which are referenced to the current price values of the latest but one complete financial year.

Manufacturing Employment, Seasonally Adjusted:
Australian Bureau of Statistics data for the middle month of the quarter on civilians employed in manufacturing establishments. For coverage see the explanatory notes to "The Labor Force, Australia," published by the Australian Bureau of Statistics.

International Transactions:

All trade value and volume data are from the Australian Bureau of Statistics. Beginning July 1985, non-merchandise trade is excluded from total trade value. Non-merchandise trade includes such items as coin being legal tender and goods for temporary exhibition.

Exports:
Data refer to total exports, f.o.b.

Imports, c.i.f.:

Prior to June 1976, data are based on imports, f.o.b., adjusted by the f.o.b./c.i.f. factor supplied by the Australian Bureau of Statistics. Since July 1976, the Australian Bureau of Statistics has supplied imports, c.i.f. data. † Beginning October 1985, import statistics exclude posted articles with a value of less than $1,000 inclusive (previously $250) and will not be strictly comparable with data for previous periods.

Volume of Exports:

Laspeyres index of exports of merchandise annually chained. Volume indices for individual commodities are based on data in physical quantities.

Volume of Imports:

Laspeyres index of imports of merchandise annually chained.

Export Prices:

Australian Bureau of Statistics Laspeyres export prices index (including re-exports), weights reference period: annually reweighted and chained.

Wheat:

Australian Bureau of Statistics Australian Wheat Board price.

Coal/Greasy Wool (Unit Value):

Data are calculated by *IFS* from reported value and volume data.

Import Prices:

Reserve Bank of Australia Laspeyres import price index, f.o.b., weights reference period: annually reweighted and chained.

Balance of Payments:

The Australian Bureau of Statistics (ABS) has compiled data on a *BPM6* basis since Q32009 and also re-published previous periods on a *BPM6* basis.

Government Finance:

Prior to May 2003, monthly cash data are derived from Commonwealth Cash Flow Statements and Department of the Treasury/Australian Office of Financial Management. Commonwealth Cash Flow Statements are used for revenue, expenditure, and financing, whereas Department of the Treasury/Australian Office of Financial Management is used for debt. Monthly data cover the operations of the budgetary central government (Commonwealth Public Account) and include the budget appropriations to central government agencies with individual budgets. Excluded are own revenues of central government agencies with individual budgets and the expenditures from those revenues. Total debt, *line 63* for budgetary central government includes government securities on issue. From July 1995, debt data include Income Equalization Deposits and exclude Treasury Bond holdings by the Loan Consolidation and Investment Reserve Trust Fund.

† Owing to changes associated with the introduction of accrual accounting cash data provided from September quarter 1999 are not comparable with earlier data. From 1999 onward, data for the month of June are derived as a residual.

From July 2003, quarterly accrual data are reported by the Australian Bureau of Statistics.

From Jan 2011, monthly cash data are reported by the Department of Finance, and cover the operations of the consolidated central government (the Commonwealth Public Account and central government entities operating outside the Commonwealth Public Account).

† Starting in July 2008, defense weapons platforms are capitalized and included in net acquisition or nonfinancial assets. Through June 2008, these outlays are treated as expense.

National Accounts:

† Data have been revised from mid-quarter 1959 onwards following the implementation of improved compilation methods and the *2008 SNA*. *Lines 99a.c* and *99b.c* include a statistical discrepancy. GDP chain-linked volume measures are calculated based on the prices and weights of the previous year, using Laspeyres formula in general. Quarterly data are no longer adjusted at annual rates.

Austria   122

Data are denominated in schillings prior to January 1999 and in euros from January 1999 onward. An irrevocably fixed factor for converting schillings to euros was established at 13.7603 schillings per euro. Beginning in January 1999, with the implementation of Stage Three of the European Economic and Monetary Union (EMU), a euro area-wide definition of residency was introduced: All positions with residents of other euro area (EA) countries, including the European Central Bank (ECB), are classified as domestic positions, and foreign assets and foreign liabilities include only positions with non-euro area residents. In 2002, the schilling was retired from circulation and replaced by euro banknotes and coins. Descriptions of the changes in the methodology and presentation of Austria's accounts following the introduction of the euro are shown in the introduction to *IFS* and the notes on the euro area page.

Date of Fund Membership:

August 27, 1948

Standard Sources:

National Bank
Statistical Office
Eurostat

Exchange Rates:

Official Rate: (End of Period and Period Average):

Prior to January 1999, the official rate referred to the midpoint rate in the Vienna market. In January 1999, the schilling became a participating currency within the Eurosystem, and the euro market rate became applicable to all transactions. In 2002, the schilling was retired from circulation and replaced by euro banknotes and coins. For additional information, refer to the section on Exchange Rates in the introduction to *IFS* and the footnotes on the euro area page.

International Liquidity:

Beginning in January 1999, *Total Reserves minus Gold (line 1l.d)* is defined in accordance with the Eurosystem's statistical definition of international reserves. The international reserves of Austria per the Eurosystem statistical definition at the start of the monetary union (January 1, 1999) in billions of U.S. dollars were as follows: *Total Reserves minus Gold,* $17,257; *Foreign Exchange,* $15,676; *SDR holdings,* $149; *Reserve Position in the Fund,* $1,433; *Other Reserve Assets,* $0; *Gold,* $3,972; *Gold (million fine troy ounces),*

13.820 ounces. *Foreign Exchange (line 1d.d)*: Between January 1995 and December 1998, gold and foreign exchange holdings excluded deposits at the European Monetary Institute (EMI), and the holdings of European currency units (ECUs) issued against these deposits were included in *line 1d.d*. *Gold (Eurosystem Valuation) (line 1and)*: Prior to January 1999, the value of gold was obtained by converting the value in national currency, as reported in the country's standard sources, using the schilling/dollar conversion rates utilized for balance sheet purposes. These conversion rates differed from the prevailing exchange rates reported in *IFS*. Beginning in December 1979, gold in national sources was valued at 60,000 schillings per kilogram. From January 1999 onward, gold is valued at market prices at the end of each month. Memorandum data are provided on *Non-Euro Claims on Euro Area Residents* and *Euro Claims on Non-Euro Area Residents,* which represent positions as of the last Friday in each month. For additional information, refer to the section on International Liquidity in the introduction to *IFS* and the footnotes on the euro area page.

Central Bank:

Consists of the National Bank of Austria, which beginning in January 1999 is part of the Eurosystem, only. For a description of the accounts, refer to the section on *Central Bank - Euro Area* in the introduction to *IFS*.

Other Depository Corporations:

Comprises all resident units classified as other monetary financial institutions (other MFIs), in accordance with *1995 ESA* standards, including money market funds. Monthly statistical reports are not required for several hundred small MFIs, but data are estimated to represent the entire MFI sector. For a description of the accounts, refer to the section on *Other Depository Corporations - Euro Area* in the introduction to *IFS*.

Depository Corporations (National Residency):

For a description of the methodology and accounts, refer to the section on *Depository Corporations (National Residency) - Euro Area* in the introduction to *IFS*.

Depository Corporations (Euro Area-wide Residency):

For a description of the methodology and accounts, refer to the section on *Depository Corporations (Euro Area-wide Residency)* in the introduction to *IFS*.

Interest Rates:

Discount Rate (End of Period):
Prior to January 1999, rate at which the National Bank of Austria discounted eligible paper. The National Bank of Austria also lent against government and other eligible securities at the lombard rate, which was usually above the discount rate. Beginning in January 1999, central bank policy rates are discontinued. See Eurosystem policy rate series on the euro area page.

Money Market Rate:
Rate on one-day interbank loans among banks in Vienna. Monthly data are unweighted averages of daily mean rates.

Deposit Rate:
Rate on deposits up to one year at monetary financial institutions. † Prior to December 1997, data refer to rates on savings deposits without agreed maturity (due at call).

Deposit Rate (lines 60lhs, 60lhn, 60lcs, and 60lcn):
See notes in the introduction to *IFS* and *Euro-area Interest Rates*.

Lending Rate:
Rate on loans to enterprises up to one year.

Lending Rate (lines 60phs, 60pns, 60phm, 60phn, 60pcs, and 60pcn):
See notes in the introduction to *IFS* and *Euro-area Interest Rates*.

Government Bond Yield:
Data refer to all government bonds issued and not yet redeemed and are weighted with the share of each bond in the total value of government bonds in circulation. The data include bonds benefiting from tax privileges under the tax reduction scheme. For additional information, refer to the section on interest rates in the introduction to *IFS* and the footnotes on the euro area page. †Beginning January 1985, refers to secondary market yields of government bonds with a 10-year maturity. This rate is used to measure long-term interest rates for assessing convergence among the European Union member states.

Prices, Production, Labor:

Share Prices (End of Month):
Index refers to average quotations of 41 shares on the Vienna Stock Exchange, base March 1, 1938. † Beginning in December 1967, share price index, base December 31, 1967. Prior to January 1986, data refer to end-of-period quotations; thereafter, to monthly averages of daily quotations. † Beginning in January 1993, data refer to a capitalization-weighted index of the most heavily traded stocks on the Vienna Stock Exchange, base January 2, 1991. The equities use free float adjusted shares in the index calculation.

Wholesale Prices:
Source: Statistical Office. Weights Reference Period: 2008; Sectoral Coverage: all wholesale industries excluded importers; Number of Items in Basket: 385 items; Basis for Calculation: weights are based on the results of the structural business statistics of 2008 for wholesale trade.

Consumer Prices:
Source: Statistical Office. Weights Reference Period: 2009/2010; Geographical Coverage: entire country; Number of Items in Basket: 791; Basis for Calculation: weights are derived from a household budget survey (HBS), which is carried out every five years.

Wages: Monthly Earnings (line 65):
Data are from the Statistical Office, covering manufacturing and mining and excluding sawmills.

Wages (line 65a):
Source: Statistical Office, covering all employed persons within the Austrian Economy. Index based on agreed minimum wages for employees over 18 years of age.

Industrial Production:
Source: Statistical Office. Weights Reference Period: 2005; Sectoral Coverage: starting in 1996, mining and quarrying, manufacturing, electricity, gas and steam, and construction; Basis for Calculation: weights are based on gross value added to factor costs derived from structural statistics and applied to quantity relatives or, in some cases, to deflated value relatives.

Employment:
Data are from the Austrian social security office, based on social security statistics covering total employment at the end of each month.

International Transactions:

Value data on total *Exports* and *Imports* are from the Statistical Office.

Government Finance:

Prior to 1999, annual cash data on federal government are as reported for the *Government Finance Statistics Yearbook (GFSY)* and cover consolidated central government operations, including social security and extrabudgetary operations. However, data on central government outstanding debt relate to the budgetary central government only. Quarterly data differ from the National Bank in which budgetary and extrabudgetary accounts are reported separately, whereas they are consolidated in *IFS*. From 1999, accrual data on general government are derived from Eurostat. The fiscal year ends December 31.

National Accounts:

Source: National Bank. As indicated by the country, data are compiled according to the recommendations of the *ESA 95*. Beginning in 1999, euro data are sourced from the Eurostat database. Eurostat introduced chain-linked GDP volume measures to annual data with the release of the third quarter 2005 on November 30, 2005. Chain linked GDP volume measures are expressed in the prices of the previous year and re-referenced to 2005.

Azerbaijan, Rep. of   912

Date of Fund Membership:

September 18, 1992

Standard Sources:

National Bank of Azerbaijan
State Committee on Statistics

Exchange Rates:

The manat, which was first introduced on August 15, 1992 and circulated alongside the Russian ruble at a fixed rate of 10 rubles per manat, became the sole legal tender in Azerbaijan on January 1, 1994. On January 1, 2006, the new manat, equivalent to 5,000 of the old manat was introduced.

Official Rate: (End of Period and Period Average):
Multiple exchange rates were in existence from 1992 through February 1995. The official exchange rate was pegged to the ruble at the rate of 10 rubles per manat until end-November 1993, when the National Bank of Azerbaijan (NBA) fixed the exchange rate for the manat against the U.S. dollar at a rate of US$1=118 manats. The fixed exchange rate against the U.S. dollar was maintained until March 25, 1994, when the NBA reverted to a ruble peg for the manat at a rate of 10 rubles per manat. On March 25, 1994, with the re-pegging of the manat to the ruble, the official exchange rate moved from 118 manats to 174 manats per U.S. dollar. On May 24, 1994, the NBA began quoting the official manats per U.S. dollar exchange rate on the basis of a weighted average of exchange rates quoted by commercial banks. Starting in March 1995, the exchange rate was unified and the official exchange rate is determined by the NBA at the rate established by the Baku Interbank Currency Exchange

(BICEX), the Organized Interbank Foreign Exchange Market (OIFEM), the Common Interbank Foreign Exchange Market (CIFEM), and the commercial banks.

International Liquidity:

Data for *Foreign Exchange (line .1d.d)* comprise the NBA's convertible currency cash and other liquid claims on nonresidents denominated in convertible currencies and in post–1993 Russian rubles.

Central Bank:

Consists of the National Bank of Azerbaijan (NBA) only.
Data are based on a standardized report form (SRF) for central banks, which accords with the concepts and definitions of the IMF's *Monetary and Financial Statistics Manual (MFSM)*, 2000.

Other Depository Corporations:

Comprises commercial banks.
Data are based on a standardized report form (SRF) for other depository corporations, which accords with the concepts and definitions of the *Monetary and Financial Statistics Manual (MFSM)*.

Depository Corporations:

See notes on central bank and other depository corporations.

Monetary Aggregates:

Broad Money:
Broad Money calculated from the liability data in the sections for the central bank and other depository corporations accords with the concepts and definitions of the *MFSM* and is consistent with M3 described below.

Money (National Definitions):
Reserve Money comprises notes and coins issued by the NBA, deposits of other depository corporations with the NBA, and deposits of other financial corporations, public nonfinancial corporations, and private sector with the NBA.
M1 comprises currency outside depository corporations and transferable deposits. Currency outside depository corporations refers to notes and coins issued by the NBA less the amount held by other depository corporations.
Transferable deposits refer to current account deposits in national currency of other financial corporations, public nonfinancial corporations, and private sector with the NBA and other depository corporations.
M2 comprises M1; savings and time deposits in national currency of other financial corporations, public nonfinancial corporations, and private sector with the NBA and other depository corporations; and securities other than shares in national currency issued by other depository corporations held by other financial corporations, public nonfinancial corporations, and private sector.
M3 comprises M2; foreign currency deposits of other financial corporations, public nonfinancial corporations, and private sector with the NBA and other depository corporations; and securities other than shares in foreign currency issued by other depository corporations held by other financial corporations, public nonfinancial corporations, and private sector.

Interest Rates:

Central Bank Policy Rate (End of Period):
Basic six-month rate at which the NBA lends to commercial banks.

Treasury Bill Rate:

Weighted average rate on three-month treasury bills sold at auction.

Deposit Rate:

Weighted average rate offered by commercial banks on 12-month deposits in national currency. The rate is weighted by deposit amounts.

Deposit Rate (Foreign Currency):

Weighted average rate offered by commercial banks on 12-month deposits in foreign currency. The rate is weighted by deposit amounts.

Lending Rate:

Weighted average rate charged by commercial banks on 12-month loans in national currency. The rate is weighted by loan amounts.

Lending Rate (Foreign Currency):

Weighted average rate charged by commercial banks on 12-month loans in foreign currency. The rate is weighted by loan amounts.

Prices:

Consumer Prices:

Source: State Committee on Statistics. Weights Reference Period: the weights are updated anually and were last updated in 2011. Number of Items: Prices are collected for 565 products. Basis for calculation: Percent changes derived from annually chained Laspeyres index which includes 268 items, uses weight from the Household Budget Survey representative for all socio-economic groups and geographic areas.

International Transactions:

Source: State Committee on Statistics. Data exclude military goods, precious metals, and goods procured in foreign ports.

Government Finance:

Through 1999, annual data are as reported for the *Government Finance Statistics Yearbook* and cover the consolidated central government. The fiscal year ends December 31.

National Accounts:

Source: State Committee on Statistics.

Bahamas, The   313

Date of Fund Membership:
August 21, 1973

Standard Sources:
Central Bank
Department of Statistics

Exchange Rates:

The official exchange rate is pegged to the U.S. dollar and applies to most transactions. An investment currency rate, which is also pegged to the U.S. dollar, applies to certain capital transactions between residents and nonresidents and to direct investments outside The Bahamas.

Principal Rate relates to the official rate.

Secondary Rate relates to the investment currency rate.

International Liquidity:

† Prior to January 1977, data for *line 1d.d* include small foreign exchange holdings by the government, which were transferred to the Central Bank of The Bahamas as of this date. *Lines 7a.d* and *7b.d* relate to the foreign accounts of commercial banks. There are numerous other financial institutions in The Bahamas, primarily branches of foreign banks, that engage exclusively in foreign operations. Their assets and liabilities with the monetary system are regarded as part of the foreign sector in sections 10, 20, and 30. Hence, *lines 7a.d* and *7b.d* include accounts of commercial banks with offshore banks. Data are not available on the accounts of all such Bahamian-based intermediaries.

Monetary Authorities:

Comprises the Central Bank of The Bahamas only.

Deposit Money Banks:

Comprises commercial banks and the authorized dealers that are permitted to undertake domestic business and are licensed to deal in gold and all foreign currencies.

Other Banking Institutions:

Comprises licensed banks and trust companies that are permitted to undertake domestic business, other than commercial banks (reported in section 20). These data exclude the accounts of numerous financial intermediaries transacting primarily, and in most cases exclusively, with nonresidents for which complete data are not available (see note in the international liquidity section).

Money (National Definitions):

Base Money comprises currency in circulation, banker's correspondent and other accounts with the Central Bank of The Bahamas (CBB), and transferable deposits of nonbank depository corporations CBB in national currency. Currency in circulation refers to notes and coins issued by the CBB.

M1 comprises currency in circulation and transferable deposits. Currency in circulation refers to notes and coins issued by the CBB less the amount held by banking institutions. Transferable deposits refer to current account deposits in national currency of nonbank financial institutions, public nonfinancial corporations, private sector, and the national insurance fund with the CBB and banking institutions.

M2 comprises M1 and fixed and savings deposits in national currency of nonbank financial institutions, public nonfinancial corporations, and private sector with banking institutions.

M3 comprises M2 and foreign currency deposits of nonbank financial institutions, public nonfinancial corporations, and private sector with banking institutions.

Interest Rates:

All interest rate data are from the Central Bank.

Central Bank Policy Rate (End of Period):

Rate at which the Central Bank of The Bahamas makes loans and advances to the commercial banks.

Treasury Bill Rate:

Average discount rate for three-month bills denominated in Bahamian dollars.

Savings Rate:

Average of rates quoted by commercial banks for savings deposits.

Deposit Rate:

Average of rates quoted by commercial banks for three-month time deposits.

Lending Rate:

Prime rate, which is the rate that commercial banks charge their most creditworthy business customers on short-term loans.

Prices:

Consumer Prices:

Source: Department of Statistics. Weights Reference Period: February 2010; Basis for Calculation: Weights were derived from the 2006 Household Budgetary Survey.

Tourist Arrivals:

Source: Central Bank.

International Transactions:

All trade data are from the Central Bank. Trade data since 1988 are those compiled by the Central Bank of the Bahamas and published in the Central Bank, *Quarterly Statistical Digest, Quarterly Economic Review*. These data differ significantly from *DOTS* which are compiled by the Department of Statistics and published in Department of Statistics, *Quarterly Statistical Summary, Statistical Abstract 1978*. Beginning in 1990, trade statistics exclude certain oil and chemical products.

Government Finance:

Data are derived from the Central Bank. Data originate from monthly Treasury Statistical Summary Printouts and annual Treasury Accounts. † Data beginning in 1988 cover the budgetary central government and no longer cover operations of the National Insurance Board, which is a social security fund. The discrepancies between the annual data and the sum of the monthly and quarterly data result from the annual data revisions, which could not be allocated by months and quarters. † From 1993 onward, fiscal years begin on July 1, rather than on January 1. † Prior to July 2004, to the extent possible, existing subannual *IFS* data were converted to the main aggregates that are presented in the *GFSM 2001* Statement of Sources and Uses of Cash (see the Introduction of the monthly *IFS* publication for details). The fiscal year ends June 30.

National Accounts:

Source: Department of Statistics. As indicated by the country, beginning in 1989, data have been revised following the implementation of improved compilation methods and the *1993 SNA. Gross Saving (line 99s)* is derived from the gross national disposable income account. A statistical discrepancy exists with gross savings derived from gross capital formation.

Bahrain, Kingdom of   419

Date of Fund Membership:

September 7, 1972

Standard Sources:

Central Bank of Bahrain
Ministry of Finance and National Economy (MOFNE)
Central Statistics Organization

Exchange Rates:

Official Rate: (End of Period and Period Average):

Central bank midpoint rate. The official rate shows limited flexibility against the U.S. dollar. Since 1980 the Bahraini Dinar has been fixed to the SDR at a rate of BD 0.47619 per SDR. As of December 25, 2001 the Bahraini Dinar was formally pegged to the U.S. Dollar at a rate of $2.659 per BD.

International Liquidity:

Gold (National Valuation) (line 1and) is obtained by converting the value in national currency terms, as reported in the country's standard sources, using the prevailing exchange rate, as given in *line* **ag** or *line* **wg**.

Offshore banking units (OBUs), which began operations in 1976, deal freely with nonresidents but are permitted to undertake only limited domestic operations, essentially with the monetary system and the government. OBUs are treated as residents of Bahrain. † Prior to 1991, data for *lines 7a.d* and *7b.d* include positions with offshore banking units, which were classified as nonresident institutions. Data are as given in the Central Bank of Bahrain.

Monetary Authorities:

Consolidates the Central Bank of Bahrain (CBB), which effective September 7, 2006 is the successor to the Bahrain Monetary Agency (BMA), with monetary functions undertaken by the MOFNE. The contra-entry to MOFNE IMF accounts and government foreign assets is included in *line 16d*. † See note on deposit money banks.

Deposit Money Banks:

Beginning in February 2008, comprises Retail banks which succeeded to the operations of the former Full commercial banks (FCBs) and some of the former Offshore banking units (OBUs) under the provisions of *Regulation No. (1) of 2007 Pertaining to the Central Bank of Bahrain Regulated Services* (issued on December 27, 2007). Prior to February 2008, comprises Full commercial banks (FCBs).

† Beginning in 1991, data are compiled from a new set of statistical returns, under which Offshore banking units (OBUs) and Investment banks (IBs), previously classified as nonresidents, are classified as resident financial corporations. Beginning in 1991, FCBs' claims on and liabilities to nonresidents therefore exclude positions with OBUs and IBs (previously treated as nonresident positions), and FCBs claims on and liabilities to resident banks include positions with OBUs and IBs.*Reserves (line 20)* includes vault cash and balances held with the Central Bank of Bahrain.

Monetary Survey:

† See note on deposit money banks.

Other Banking Institutions:

Beginning in February 2008, comprises Wholesale banks which succeeded to the operations of some of the former Offshore banking units (OBUs) and Investment banks (IBs) under the provisions of *Regulation No. (1) of 2007 Pertaining to the Central Bank of Bahrain Regulated Services* (issued on December 27, 2007). Prior to February 2008, comprises OBUs and IBs.

Money (National Definitions):

M1 comprises currency outside banks and demand deposits in national and foreign currency of resident non-bank non-government sectors with the Central Bank of Bahrain and Retail banks (prior to February 2008, with Full commercial banks).

M2 comprises M1 plus time and savings deposits in national and foreign currency and certificates of deposit in national and foreign currency of resident non-bank non-government sectors with the Central Bank of Bahrain and Retail banks (prior to February 2008, with Full commercial banks).

M3 comprises M2 plus central government and social insurance system deposits in national and foreign currency with the Central Bank of Bahrain and Retail banks (prior to February 2008, with Full commercial banks).

Interest Rates:

Central Bank Policy Rate (End of Period):
Rate offered on the CBB's one-week deposit facility.

Central Bank Repo Rate (End of Period):
Rate charged by the CBB on overnight repurchase agreements using government securities as collateral.

Money Market Rate:
Rate offered on three-month interbank deposits.

Treasury Bill Rate:
Average rate (discount basis) per annum on allotted treasury bills with 91 days to maturity. Monthly averages are simple averages of weekly averages. For periods during which no auctions of treasury bills were held, no data are published.

Savings Rate:
Weighted average rate offered on savings deposits in national currency.

Deposit Rate:
Weighted average of interest rates on time deposits with maturities of at least three months and under six months. † Beginning in June 1998, rate offered on three- to twelve-month time deposits between BD10,000–50,000. Through June 2009, data refer to rates offered during the last month of each quarter.

Lending Rate:
Maximum recommended rate on consumer loans with maturities of at least twelve months and under fifteen months. † Beginning in September 1988, weighted average of interest rates on consumer loans with maturities of at least twelve months and under fifteen months. † Beginning in June 2009, weighted average rate on all personal loans extended in the last month of the quarter. The interest-rate survey is conducted quarterly with deposit money banks.

Prices, Production, Labor:

Share Prices (End of Month):
Data refer to the Bahrain All Share Index, base July 1, 2004. Bahrain All Share Index is a capitalization-weighted index of all Bahraini public share-holding companies listed on the Bahrain Stock Exchange (BSE). It is a benchmark index consisting of all the local-publicly listed companies on the BSE.

Consumer Prices:
Source: Central Bank of Bahrain. Weights Reference Period: 2005–2006; Geographical Coverage: whole national territory; Number of Items in Bakset: 1371; Basis for Calculation: Laspeyres type index that uses the annual base year expenditure weights from the Household Expenditure Survey of the Sultanate conducted in 2005/2006.

Petroleum Production:
Source: Ministry of Oil and Industry data.

International Transactions:

Exports and Imports, c.i.f.:
All data are from the Central Bank of Bahrain. If uncurrent, total value data are obtained as the sum of petroleum and other trade (excluding gold). The latter series are supplied by the Central Bank of Bahrain and are not published.

Government Finance:

Annual data are as reported for the *Government Finance Statistics Yearbook (GFSY)* and cover budgetary central government. The fiscal year ends December 31.

National Accounts:

Source: Ministry of Finance and National Economy.

Bangladesh   513

Date of Fund Membership:
August 17, 1972

Standard Sources:
Bangladesh Bank
Bangladesh Bureau of Statistics

Exchange Rates:

Official Rate: (End of Period and Period Average):
As of January 1, 1992, the official exchange rate and the secondary exchange market rate were unified.

International Liquidity:

Gold (National Valuation) (line 1 and) is obtained by converting the value in national currency terms, as reported in the country's standard sources, using the prevailing exchange rate, as given in line **ae** or **we.** Data on gold in national sources revalue gold monthly at 75 percent of the average London market prices for the preceding month.

Central Bank:

Consists of the Bangladesh Bank (BB) only.
Data are based on a standardized report form (SRF) for central banks, which accords with the concepts and definitions of the IMF's *Monetary and Financial Statistics Manual (MFSM)*, 2000. Departures from the *MFSM* methodology are listed below:
Accrued interest is included in *Other Items (Net)* rather than in the outstanding amounts of financial assets and liabilities.

Other Depository Corporations:

Comprises commercial banks, National Savings Scheme, and nonbank depository corporations (Grameen Bank, private finance and leasing companies, land mortgage cooperative banks, cooperative banks, and cooperative societies).
Data are based on a standardized report form (SRF) for other depository corporations, which accords with the concepts and definitions of the *Monetary and Financial Statistics Manual (MFSM)*. Departures from the *MFSM* methodology are listed below:
Accrued interest is included in Other items (net) rather than in the outstanding amounts of financial assets and liabilities.

Depository Corporations:

See notes on central bank and other depository corporations.

Monetary Aggregates:

Broad Money:
Broad Money calculated from the liability data in the sections for the central bank and other depository corporations accords with the concepts and definitions of the *MFSM* and is consistent with M3 described below. Broad money includes currency issued by the central government.

Money (National Definitions):
Reserve Money comprises currency in circulation, transferable deposits in national and foreign currency of other depository corporations with the BB, and other deposits in national currency of other financial corporations with the BB. Currency in circulation refers to notes and coins issued by the BB and the Treasury less note and coin holdings of the BB.
M1 comprises currency outside commercial banks, transferable deposits, and other deposits. Currency outside commercial banks refers to the amount of currency in circulation *less* the note and coin holdings of commercial banks. Transferable deposits refer to the current account deposits in national currency of other financial corporations, state and local governments, public nonfinancial corporations, and the private sector with commercial banks. Other deposits refer to time and savings deposits in national currency of other financial corporations with the BB.
M2 comprises M1 and quasi-money. Quasi-money comprises time, savings, and foreign-currency deposits of other financial corporations, state and local governments, public nonfinancial corporations, and private sector with commercial banks.
M3 comprises M2 and transferable and other deposits in national and foreign currency with the National Savings Scheme and nonbank depository corporations.

Interest Rates:

Reverse Repurchase Agreement Rate (End of Period):
Rate on one-two day reverse repurchase agreements between the BB and commercial banks.

Repurchase Agreement Rate (End of Period):
Rate on one-two day repurchase agreements between the BB and the commercial banks.

Discount Rate (End of Period):
Discount rate offered by the BB on loans to commercial banks.

Deposit Rate:
Average rate offered by commercial banks on three- to six-month fixed or term deposits.

Lending Rate:
Maximum rate charged by commercial banks on loans and advances for agricultural production, including forestry and fisheries.

Prices, Production, Labor:

Share Prices (End of Month):
Composite stock price index of the Dhaka Stock Exchange Limited, base November 24, 2001.

Consumer Prices:
Source: Bangladesh Bank. Weights Reference Period: 1995–96; Geographical Coverage: national index; Number of Items in Basket: covers items relating to eight commodity groups; Basis for

Calculation: weights are determined based on the Household Expenditure Survey of 1995–96.

Industrial Production:
Bangladesh Bureau of Statistcis quantum index of industrial production, all industries, weights reference period 1988–89. The index covers manufacturing, mining, and electricity.

International Transactions:

Trade data are from Bangladesh Bank. Value of *Exports* refers to total exports receipts which include cash, barter, and special trade. *Imports, c & f* data include cost and freight, but exclude insurance.

International Investment Position:
The data on Other Investment, General Government are compiled on a fiscal year ending June 30.

Government Finance:

Annual data are as reported for the *Government Finance Statistics Yearbook (GFSY)* and cover budgetary central government. The fiscal year ends June 30.

National Accounts:

Source: Bangladesh Bank. As indicated by the country, data from 1990 onwards are according to the *1993 SNA*.

Barbados   316

Date of Fund Membership:
December 29, 1970

Standard Sources:
Central Bank of Barbados
Statistical Service

Exchange Rates:

Official Rate: (End of Period and Period Average):
The official rate is pegged to the U.S. dollar.

International Liquidity:

† Beginning in 1972, *line 1dbd* includes sinking funds held against domestic government debt.

Central Bank:

Consists of the Central Bank of Barbados (CBB) only.
† Beginning in September 2006, data are based on a standardized report form (SRF) for central banks, which accords with the concepts and definitions of the IMF's *Monetary and Financial Statistics Manual (MFSM), 2000*. Departures from the *MFSM* methodology are explained below.
Financial derivatives are excluded from the data.
Accrued interest is included in *Other Items (Net)* rather than in the outstanding amounts of the financial assets or liabilities.
Held-to-maturity securities are valued at acquisition cost rather than at current market price or fair value. Holdings of equity shares are valued at acquisition cost rather than at current market price or fair value.
For December 2001 through August 2006, data in the SRF format are compiled from pre-SRF data not based on the *MFSM* methodology.
Departures from the *MFSM* methodology are explained below.

Financial derivatives are excluded from the data.

Financial assets and liabilities for which economic sectorization is unavailable are allocated to the economic sector having the largest volume of transactions in the category.

Some deposits of other financial corporations, public nonfinancial corporations, other nonfinancial corporations, and other resident sectors are included in *Other Items (Net)* rather than in *Transferable Deposits Included in Broad Money* and *Other Deposits Included in Broad Money*.

Accrued interest is included in *Other Items (Net)* rather than in the outstanding amounts of the financial assets or liabilities.

Other Depository Corporations:

Comprises commercial banks, most of the credit unions, trusts and mortgage finance companies, finance companies, and merchant banks. Data exclude the Barbados Development Bank and the rest of the credit unions.

† Beginning in September 2006, data are based on a standardized report form (SRF) for other depository corporations, which accords with the concepts and definitions of the IMF's *Monetary and Financial Statistics Manual (MFSM)*. For other depository corporations in Barbados, departures from the *MFSM* methodology are explained below.

Data for the credit unions are only available on a quarterly basis. Data for intervening months and current months after the last quarter have been estimated by carrying forward the data from the last quarter.

Financial assets and liabilities not disaggregated by economic sector are allocated to the economic sector having the largest volume of transactions in that category.

Positions with nonresidents are not clearly identifiable in the data and could be included as claims on or liabilities to residents.

Claims on Other Financial Corporations, Transferable Deposits Included in Broad Money, and *Other Deposits Included in Broad Money* include some positions with other depository corporations.

Financial assets and liabilities for which financial instrument breakdown is unavailable are allocated to the financial instrument having the largest volume of transactions in the category.

Currency held by credit unions is included in *Other Items (Net)*.

Transferable deposits of other resident sectors with credit unions are included in *Other Deposits Included in Broad Money* rather than in *Transferable Deposits Included in Broad Money*.

Accrued interest is included in *Other Items (Net)* rather than in the outstanding amounts of the financial assets or liabilities.

For December 2001 through August 2006, data in the SRF format are compiled from pre-SRF data not based on the *MFSM* methodology.

Departures from the *MFSM* methodology are explained below.

Data for the credit unions are only available on a quarterly basis. Data for intervening months and current months after the last quarter have been estimated by carrying forward the data from the last quarter.

Financial assets and liabilities not disaggregated by economic sector are allocated to the economic sector having the largest volume of transactions in that category.

Positions with nonresidents are not clearly identifiable in the data and could be included as claims on or liabilities to residents.

Claims on Other Financial Corporations, Transferable Deposits Included in Broad Money, and *Other Deposits Included in Broad Money* include some positions with other depository corporations.

Financial assets and liabilities for which financial instrument breakdown is unavailable are allocated to the financial instrument having the largest volume of transactions in the category.

Currency held by credit unions is included in *Other Items (Net)*.

Transferable deposits of other resident sectors with credit unions are included in *Other Deposits Included in Broad Money* rather than in *Transferable Deposits Included in Broad Money*.

Held-to-maturity securities are valued at acquisition cost rather than at current market price or fair value. Holdings of equity shares are valued at acquisition cost rather than at current market price or fair value.

Depository Corporations:

† See notes on central bank and other depository corporations.

Monetary Aggregates:

Broad Money:

Broad Money calculated from the liability data in the sections for the central bank and other depository corporations accords with the concepts and definitions of the *MFSM*. Broad money differs from Total Monetary Liabilities described below as Total Monetary Liabilities exclude the deposits of money holding sectors with credit unions, trusts and mortgage finance companies, finance companies, and merchant banks.

Money (National Definitions):

Money comprises currency held by the public; demand deposits of other financial corporations, public nonfinancial corporations, and private sector (other nonfinancial corporations and other resident sectors); and demand deposits of nonresidents in foreign currency with the CBB and commercial banks.

Quasi-money comprises time and savings deposits of other financial corporations, public nonfinancial corporations, and private sector (other nonfinancial corporations and other resident sectors) and time and savings deposits of nonresidents in foreign currency with commercial banks.

Total Monetary Liabilities comprise money and quasi-money excluding deposits of nonresidents in foreign currency.

Interest Rates:

Discount Rate (End of Period):
CBB's general rediscount rate.

Treasury Bill Rate:
Average tender rate for three-month treasury bills.

Savings Rate:
Rate offered by commercial banks on savings deposits.

Deposit Rate:
Weighted average rate offered by commercial banks on time and savings deposits. The rate is weighted by deposit amounts.

Lending Rate:
Prime lending rate charged by commercial banks. Data represent the maximum of the range of rates quoted by commercial banks.

Prices and Production:

Consumer Prices:
Source: Central Bank of Barbados. Base Period: July 2001; Geographical Coverage: Whole national territory; Number of Items in Basket: 340; Basis for Calculation: Weights are derived from the household budget survey of 1998–1999.

Industrial Production:
Source: Central Bank of Barbados. Index covers mining and quarrying, electricity and gas, manufacturing industries, base 1994, as compiled by the Statistical Service.

International Transactions:

Exports and Imports:
All trade data are from the Central Bank of Barbados. Total exports include domestic exports and re-exports.

International Investment Position:
Starting 2010, IIP data include position data covering offshore institutions as well as real estate position data that are consistent with Barbados data submitted for publication in the Coordinated Direct Investment Survey (CDIS) and the Coordinated Portfolio Investment Survey (CPIS). However, offshore institutions are, in general, treated as nonresidents for balance of payments purposes.

Government Finance:

Data are derived from the Central Bank of Barbados and cover budgetary central government. The statistical discrepancy results from net errors and omissions in the recording of financing transactions. The fiscal year ends March 31.

National Accounts:

Central Bank data as reported by the national authorities. Data for *line 96f* include increases or decreases in stocks.

Belarus   913

Date of Fund Membership:
July 10, 1993

Standard Sources:
National Bank of the Republic of Belarus
Ministry of Finance of the Republic of Belarus
National Statistical Committee of the Republic of Belarus

Exchange Rates:

Official Rate: (End of Period and Period Average):
The official rate is the rate used by the National Bank of the Republic of Belarus (NBRB) and, since December 1993, has been determined in auctions organized by the Interbank Currency Exchange.
On August 20, 1994, the rubel (Rbl) replaced the Belarusian ruble (Br) as the unit of account at the rate of ten Belarusian rubles per rubel. On January 1, 2000, the national currency was redenominated. The new rubel is equal to 1,000 old rubels.

International Liquidity:

Data for *Total Reserves minus Gold (line 11.d)* comprise the country's holdings of SDRs, reserve position in the Fund, and convertible foreign exchange.

Central Bank:

Consists of the National Bank of the Republic of Belarus (NBRB) only. † Beginning in December 2004, data are based on a standardized report form (SRF) for central banks, which accords with the concepts and definitions of the IMF's *Monetary and Financial Statistics Manual (MFSM)*, 2000.
For December 2001 through November 2004, data in the SRF format are compiled from pre-SRF data not based on the *MFSM* methodology. Departures from the MFSM methodology are explained below.
Prior to March 2003 , monetary gold is valued at acquisition cost rather than at current market price or fair value.

Other Depository Corporations:

Comprises banks, including banks in liquidation.
† Beginning in December 2004, data are based on a standardized report form (SRF) for other depository corporations, which accords with the concepts and definitions of the *Monetary and Financial Statistics Manual (MFSM)*.
For December 2001 through November 2004, data in the SRF format are compiled from pre-SRF data not based on the *MFSM* methodology.

Depository Corporations:

† See notes on central bank and other depository corporations.

Other Financial Corporations:

Comprises insurance organizations. Beginning in January 2012, includes the Development Bank of the Republic of Belarus and Agency of Deposit Compensation. Data exclude leasing companies.
Data are based on a standardized report form (SRF) for other financial corporations, which accords with the concepts and definitions of the *Monetary and Financial Statistics Manual (MFSM)*.

Financial Corporations:

See notes on central bank, other depository corporations, and other financial corporations.

Monetary Aggregates:

Broad Money:
Broad Money calculated from the liability data in the sections for the central bank and other depository corporations accords with the concepts and definitions of the *MFSM* and is consistent with M3 described below.

Money (National Definitions):
Base Money comprises currency in circulation, required reserves deposits of banks in the NBRB, banks' correspondent and other accounts at the NBRB, and transferable and time deposits of public nonfinancial corporations, and private sector with the NBRB. Currency in circulation refers to notes and coins issued by the NBRB less the amount held in cash offices of the NBRB.
M1 comprises currency in circulation and transferable deposits. Currency in circulation refers to notes and coins issued by the NBRB less the amount held in cash offices of the NBRB and banks. Transferable deposits refer to the current account deposits and other demand accounts including accrued interest in national currency of other financial corporations, public nonfinancial corporations, and private sector with the NBRB and banks.
M2 comprises M1 and time deposits. Time deposits include time and savings deposits, deposits in escrow, and accrued interest in national currency of other financial corporations, public nonfinancial corporations, and private sector with the NBRB and banks.
M2* comprises M2 and securities other than shares issued by

banks in national currency held by other financial corporations, public nonfinancial corporations, and private sector.

M3 comprises M2* plus transferable and time deposits in foreign currency and deposits in precious metals of other financial corporations, public nonfinancial corporations, and private sector with the NBRB and banks and securities other than shares issued by banks in foreign currency held by other financial corporations, public nonfinancial corporations, and private sector.

Interest Rates:

Central Bank Policy Rate (End of Period):
Announced rate at which the NBRB lends to banks.

Discount Rate (End of Period):
Actual average rate at which the NBRB lends to banks. Includes concessionary rates charged on directed loans. The practice of directed lending to banks at concessionary rates was discontinued.

Deposit Rate:
Weighted average rate offered by banks on deposits in national currency. Rate is weighted by deposit amounts.

Lending Rate:
Weighted average rate charged by banks on loans in national currency. Rate is weighted by loan amounts.

Prices and Labor:

Producer Prices:
Source: National Statistical Committee of the Republic of Belarus. Weights Reference Period: December of the previous year; Sectoral Coverage: mining and quarrying, manufacturing production and distribution of electricity, gas and water; Number of Items in the Basket: more than 700 commodity groups; Basis for Calculation: weights are based on the data of industrial statistical survey of the value of shipped products.

Consumer Prices:
Source: National Statistical Committee of the Republic of Belarus. Weights Reference Period: 2010; Geographical Coverage: 31 urban areas that comprise more than 50 percent of the total population; Number of Items in the Basket: 442; Basis for Calculation: based on data on families' expenditures for purchases of goods and services obtained from the Annual Household.

Wages:
Source: National Statistical Committee of the Republic of Belarus. The nominal gross wage index reflects changes in the nominal wages of an employee during the reference period relative to the base period.

International Transactions:

Source: National Statistical Committee of the Republic of Belarus. Data consist from merchandise trade data compiled by the State Customs Committee (SCC) of the Republic of Belarus on the basis of customs declarations and export/import of goods not recorded by the SCC.

Government Finance:

Monthly data are derived from the Ministry of Finance of the Republic of Belarus and cover the central budget sector excluding social security. Annual data are as reported for the *Government Finance Statistics Yearbook (GFSY)* and cover consolidated central government. † Prior to 2003, to the extent possible, existing subannual *IFS* data were converted to the main aggregates that are presented in the *GFSM 2001* Statement of Sources and Uses of Cash (see the Introduction of the monthly *IFS* publication for details). The fiscal year ends December 31.

National Accounts:

Source: National Statistical Committee of the Republic of Belarus. As indicated by the country, data are compiled according to the recommendations of the *1993 SNA*. The base year for constant price estimates is changed every five years and GDP volume 2009 is computed, making it possible to link the series and obtain a longer-term series in uniform prices. On January 1, 2000, the denomination of the Belarusian rubel took place (1000 times decrease in the face value of money unit).

Belgium   124

Data refer to Belgium except where noted. Data are denominated in Belgian francs prior to January 1999 and in euros from January 1999 onward. An irrevocably fixed factor for converting Belgian francs to euros was established at 40.3399 Belgian francs per euro. Beginning in January 1999, with the implementation of Stage Three of the European Economic and Monetary Union (EMU), a euro area-wide definition of residency was introduced: All positions with residents of other euro area (EA) countries, including the European Central Bank (ECB), are classified as domestic positions, and foreign assets and foreign liabilities include only positions with non-euro area residents. In 2002, the franc was retired from circulation and replaced by euro banknotes and coins. Descriptions of the changes in the methodology and presentation of Belgium's accounts following the introduction of the euro are shown in the introduction to *IFS* and in the notes on the euro area page.

Date of Fund Membership:
December 27, 1945

Standard Sources:
National Bank
National Institute of Statistics
Eurostat

Exchange Rates:

Market Rate (End of Period and Period Average):
Prior to March 5, 1990, there was a dual exchange rate system, in which the primary rate, maintained within the cooperative exchange arrangement under the European Monetary System (EMS), was applicable to most current transactions, and the secondary, or free market rate, was applicable to most capital transactions. Between March 5, 1990 and December 31, 1998, the market rate maintained within the EMS was applicable to all transactions. Prior to January 1999, the market rate was the midpoint rate in the official market in Brussels. In January 1999, the Belgian franc became a participating currency within the Eurosystem, and the euro market rate became applicable to all transactions. In 2002, the franc was retired from circulation and

replaced by euro banknotes and coins. For additional information, refer to the section on Exchange Rates in the introduction to *IFS* and on the euro area page.

International Liquidity:

Beginning in January 1999, *Total Reserves minus Gold (line 1l.d)* is defined in accordance with the Eurosystem's statistical definition of international reserves. The international reserves of Belgium per the Eurosystem statistical definition at the start of the monetary union (January 1, 1999) in billions of U.S. dollars were as follows: *Total Reserves minus Gold*, $12,670; *Foreign Exchange*, $10,166; *SDR holdings*, $609; *Reserve Position in the Fund*, $1,895; *Other Reserve Assets*, $0; *Gold*, $2,738; *Gold (million fine troy ounces)*, 9.525 ounces. From December 1998 through May 1999, holdings of monetary gold include an amount of gold on loan to Luxembourg. *Foreign Exchange (line 1d.d)*: Beginning in March 1979, gold and foreign exchange holdings excluded deposits at the European Monetary Cooperation Fund (EMCF), and the holdings of European currency units (ECUs) issued against these deposits were included in *line ld.d. Gold (Eurosystem Valuation) (line 1and)*: Prior to January 1990, only 20 percent of official gold was valued at market prices. From January 1990 onward, all official gold has been valued at market prices. Memorandum data are provided on *Non-Euro Claims on Euro Area Residents* and *Euro Claims on Non-Euro Area Residents,* which represent positions as of the last Friday in each month. For additional information, refer to the section on International Liquidity in the introduction to *IFS* and on the euro area page.

Central Bank:

Consists of the National Bank of Belgium, which beginning in January 1999 is part of the Eurosystem, only. *Currency Issued* includes coins issued by the Treasury. For a description of the accounts, refer to the section on *Central Bank - Euro Area* in the introduction to *IFS*.

Other Depository Corporations:

Comprises all resident units classified as other monetary financial institutions (other MFIs), in accordance with *1995 ESA* standards, including money market funds. For a description of the accounts, refer to the section on *Other Depository Corporations - Euro Area* in the introduction to *IFS*.

Depository Corporations (National Residency):

For a description of the methodology and accounts, refer to the section on *Depository Corporations (National Residency) - Euro Area* in the introduction to *IFS*.

Depository Corporations (Euro Area-wide Residency):

For a description of the methodology and accounts, refer to the section on *Depository Corporations (Euro Area-wide Residency)* in the introduction to *IFS*.

Interest Rates:

Discount Rate (End of Period):
Before January 1999, official rate applied by the National Bank of Belgium to rediscounts of commercial paper and bank acceptances presented by financial intermediaries. The discount rate was abolished on December 15, 1998. From January 1999 onward, see Eurosystem policy rate series on the euro area page.

Money Market Rate:
† Before 1991, the call money rate. From 1991 until January 1999, the averages of borrowing and lending rates for three-month interbank transactions. From January 1999 onward, the three-month EURIBOR rate, which is an interbank deposit bid rate. See euro area page.

Deposit Rate:
† Before 1993, the indicative rates published by banks; thereafter, the rate on three-month time deposits, weighted by volume of deposits in a monthly survey of banks.

Deposit Rate (lines 60lhs, 60lhn, 60lcs, and 60lcn):
See notes in the introduction to *IFS* and *Euro-area Interest Rates*.

Lending Rate:
Published rate for liquidity credit from the four major banks; banks can charge a higher or lower rate to certain customers.

Lending Rate (lines 60phs, 60pns, 60phm, 60phn, 60pcs, and 60pcn):
See notes in the introduction to *IFS* and *Euro-area Interest Rates*.

Government Bond Yield:
Yield on ten-year government bonds. † Beginning September 1963, refers to yield on government bonds of more than five years. † Beginning January 1980, refers to secondary market yields of government bonds with a ten-year maturity. This rate is used to measure long-term interest rates for assessing convergence among the European Union member states.

Prices, Production, Labor:

Share Prices:
Industrial share price index, base 1963. † Beginning in 1951, data refer to 10th-of-month quotations for all industrial shares on the Brussels and Antwerp exchanges, base 1970. † Beginning in January 1992, data refer to the BEL 20 Index, base January 1, 1991. The BEL 20 Index is a modified capitalization-weighted index of the 20 most capitalized and liquid Belgian stocks that are traded on the Brussels Stock Exchange. The equities use free float shares in the index calculation.

Producer Prices:
Source: National Institute of Statistics. Weights Reference Period: weights are updated annually; Sectoral Coverage: total industry, excluding construction; Basis for Calculation: weights are based on value of sales of product categories in the latest available year (from monthly Prodcom survey) and are revised annually.

Industrial Production Prices:
Data are sourced from the OECD database; Weights Reference Period: weights are updated every 5 years; Sectoral Coverage: mining and quarrying, manufacturing, electricity, gas and water supply, construction.

Consumer Prices:
Source: National Institute of Statistics. Weights Reference Period: January-December 2004; Geographical Coverage: whole national territory; Number of Items in Basket: 535; Basis for Calculation: the Household Budget Survey was organized by the National Statistical Institute, covering the period January-December 2004.

Wages:
Source: National Institute of Statistics. Weights reference period: Q3 1980. The index covers male members over 21 years old in industry.

Industrial Production:

Data are sourced from the OECD database, weights reference period: annually re-weighted and chained. The indices exclude construction.

International Transactions:

Source: National Bank. BLEU trade data refer to the Belgium-Luxembourg Economic Union and exclude transactions between the two countries. Beginning in 1997, trade data are for Belgium only, which includes trade between Belgium and Luxembourg. (For 1997, certain goods transiting from non-EU members to EU members through the Belgium-Luxembourg Economic Union are recorded as imports and exports of the BLEU.) BLEU trade data and Belgium trade data are not comparable, owing to differences in compilation methods. The Laspeyres volume and Paasche unit value indices of trade, weights reference period: 1993, are from the *Monthly Bulletin of Foreign Trade*. The annual, but not the quarterly or monthly, indices of *Volume of Exports* are adjusted for changes in coverage.

Import Prices:

† National Bank Index, weights reference period: 1980 refers to the import component of the Industrial products group of the general wholesale price index of Belgium (country code 124).

Government Finance:

Data on general government are derived from Eurostat. Monthly cash data are provided by the Ministry of Finance. Transactions and debt data cover budgetary operations of the central government Treasury but exclude operations of social security funds and other central government agencies with individual budgets. Lending minus repayments receipts are included in revenue, and payments are included in expenditure. † Beginning in 1999, monthly, quarterly, and annual data cover only budgetary operations and are not comparable to data from previous years. † Beginning in 1970, annual data on central government are as reported for the *Government Finance Statistics Yearbook (GFSY)* and cover consolidated central government. † From 1996 onwards, annual data are compiled on the basis of European Standard Accounting rules and are not comparable with data for previous years. The fiscal year ends December 31.

National Accounts:

Source: National Bank. As indicated by the country, from 1985 onwards data have been revised following the implementation of the *ESA 95*. Beginning in 1999, euro data are sourced from the Eurostat database. Eurostat introduced chain-linked GDP volume measures to both annual and quarterly data. Chain-linked GDP volume measures are expressed in the prices of the previous year and re-referenced to 2010.

Belize   339

Date of Fund Membership:

March 16, 1982

Standard Sources:

Central Bank of Belize
Central Statistical Office

Exchange Rates:

Official Rate: (End of Period and Period Average):
Rates are based on a fixed relationship to the U.S. dollar.

Central Bank:

Consists of the Central Bank of Belize (CBB) only.
† Beginning in January 2006, data are based on a standardized report form (SRF) for central banks, which accords with the concepts and definitions of the IMF's *Monetary and Financial Statistics Manual (MFSM)*, 2000.
For December 2001 through December 2005, data in the SRF format are compiled from pre-SRF data not based on the *MFSM* methodology. Departures from the *MFSM* methodology are explained below.
Financial assets and liabilities not disaggregated by economic sector are allocated to the economic sector having the largest volume of transactions in the category.
Some financial assets with the other financial corporations and private sector are included in *Other Items (Net)*.
Small amounts of liabilities to the central government are included in *Other Items (Net)*.
Share and other equity comprises funds contributed by owners and retained earnings only.
Small amounts of accounts receivable and payable with some economic sectors are included in *Other Items (Net)* rather than in claims on and liabilities to the corresponding sectors.
Accrued interest is included in *Other Items (Net)* rather than in the outstanding amounts of the financial assets and liabilities.

Other Depository Corporations:

Comprises commercial banks. Data exclude credit unions, which accept deposits.
† Beginning in January 2006, data are based on a standardized report form (SRF) for other depository corporations, which accords with the concepts and definitions of the *Monetary and Financial Statistics Manual (MFSM)*.
For December 2001 through December 2005, data in the SRF format are compiled from pre-SRF data not based on the *MFSM* methodology. Departures from the *MFSM* methodology are explained below.
Financial assets and liabilities not disaggregated by economic sector are allocated to the economic sector having the largest volume of transactions in the category.
Claims on Nonresidents and *Liabilities to Nonresidents* include some consolidation adjustments between the head office and branches abroad and small amounts of claims on and liabilities to resident economic sectors in foreign currency.
Shares and Other Equity excludes current year result.
Accounts receivable and payable with some economic sectors are included in *Other Items (Net)* rather than in claims on and liabilities to the corresponding sectors.
Accrued interest is included in *Other Items (Net)* rather than in the outstanding amounts of the financial assets and liabilities.

Depository Corporations:

See notes on central bank and other depository corporations.

Monetary Aggregates:

Broad Money:

Broad Money is calculated from the liability data in the sections for the central bank and other depository corporations. Broad money for December 2001 through December 2005 differs from M2 described below as the data used to calculate broad money does not have sufficient disaggregation of deposits by currency and economic sector.

Money (National Definitions):

M1 comprises currency in circulation outside the banking system and transferable deposits. Transferable deposits comprise demand and checkable savings deposits of other financial corporations, local governments, nonfinancial public corporations, and the private sector in national and foreign currency and demand deposits of nonresidents in national currency with commercial banks.

M2 comprises M1, time and savings deposits of other financial corporations, local governments, nonfinancial public corporations, and the private sector in national and foreign currency, time deposits of nonresidents in national and foreign currency, and savings deposits of nonresidents in national currency with commercial banks. Beginning in January 2006, M2 comprises M1, time and savings deposits of other financial corporations, local governments, nonfinancial public corporations, and the private sector in national and foreign currency and time and savings deposits of nonresidents in national currency with commercial banks.

Interest Rates:

Discount Rate (End of Period):

Rate at which the CBB makes advance to commercial banks against government securities.

Treasury Bill Rate:

Discount rate on treasury bills.

Savings Rate:

Rate offered by commercial banks on savings deposits.

Deposit Rate:

Weighted average rate offered by commercial banks on deposits. Rate is weighted by deposit amounts.

Lending Rate:

Weighted average rate charged by commercial banks on loans. Rate is weighted by loan mounts.

Prices:

Consumer Prices:

Source: Central Bank of Belize, Weights Reference Period: 1990; Geographical Coverage: National index; Number of Items in the Basket: More than 277 items. Data are compiled on a monthly basis starting February 2011; Basis for Calculation: Index was derived from a national household expenditure survey conducted from June 1990 through May 1991.

International Transactions:

Central Statistical Office data.

Government Finance:

Annual data cover budgetary accounts only. The fiscal year ends March 31.

National Accounts:

Line 99b includes a statistical discrepancy.

Benin   638

Date of Fund Membership:

July 10, 1963

Standard Sources:

Banque Centrale des Etats de l'Afrique de l'Ouest (Central Bank of West African States)

Institut National de la Statistique et de l'Analyse Economique Benin is a member of the West African Economic and Monetary Union, together with Burkina Faso, Côte d'Ivoire, Guinea-Bissau, Mali, Niger, Senegal, and Togo. The Union, which was established in 1962, has a common central bank, the Central Bank of West African States (BCEAO), with headquarters in Dakar, and national branches in the member states. Mali and Guinea-Bissau joined the Union on June 1, 1984 and May 2, 1997, respectively. Direction Générale des Statistiques

Exchange Rates:

Official Rate: (End of Period and Period Average):

Prior to January 1999, the official rate was pegged to the French franc. On January 12, 1994, the CFA franc was devalued to CFAF 100 per French franc from CFAF 50 at which it had been fixed since 1948. From January 1, 1999, the CFAF is pegged to the euro at a rate of CFA franc 655.957 per euro.

International Liquidity:

Gold is revalued on a quarterly basis at the rate communicated by the BCEAO, which corresponds to the lowest average fixing in the London market.

Monetary Authorities:

Comprises the national branch of the BCEAO only. The amount of currency outside banks is estimated by subtracting from the amount of CFA franc notes issued by Benin the estimated amounts of Benin's currency in the cash held by the banks of all member countries of the Union.

Deposit Money Banks:

Comprises commercial banks and the Development Bank, and includes certain banking operations of the Treasury and the Post Office. The Treasury accepts customs duty bills (reported separately in *line 22d.i*). Through its many branches, the Postal Checking System acts as the main depository for the private sector in the interior of Benin. *Claims on the Private Sector (line 22d)* include doubtful and litigious debts. † Beginning in 1979, *Central Government Deposits (line 26d)* include the deposits of the public establishments of an administrative or social nature (EPAS) and exclude those of the savings bank; *Demand and Time Deposits (lines 24 and 25)* include deposits of the savings bank and exclude deposits of EPAS; and *Claims on Private Sector (line 22d)* exclude claims on other financial institutions.

Monetary Survey:

The data reported agree with Banque Centrale des Etats de l'Afrique de l'Ouest aggregates, as given in the table on the position of the monetary institutions. Valuation differences exist as a result of the *IFS* calculations of reserve position in the Fund and the SDR holdings, both components of *line 11,* based on Fund record. † Beginning in 1979, *Claims on Other Financial Institutions (line 32f)* includes claims of deposit money banks on other financial institutions; see deposit money bank notes for explanation of other break symbols.

Other Banking Institutions:

Liquid Liabilities (line 55l): † See notes on deposit money banks and monetary survey.

Interest Rates:

Discount Rate (End of Period):
Basic discount rate offered by the BCEAO.

Repurchase Agreement Rate (End of Period):
Rate on repurchase agreements between the BCEAO and the banks.

Money Market Rate:
Rate paid on overnight interbank advances.

Deposit Rate:
Rate offered by banks on time deposits of CFAF 500,000–2,000,000 for under six months.

Prices:

Consumer Prices:
Source: Institut National de la Statistique et de l'Analyse Economique. Weights Reference Period: 2008; Geographical Coverage: largest metropolitan area of Benin (Cotonou, Calayi and Agblagandan); Number of Items in Basket: 626; Basis for Calculation: The weights come from a household expenditure survey in 2008 in the country's largest metropolitan area.

International Transactions:

All trade data are from Banque the Centrale des Etats de l'Afrique de l'Ouest . Ships' stores, bunkers, and imports of gold are included. Data on trade crossing land frontiers may be understated.

Government Finance:

Annual data are as reported for the *Government Finance Statistics Yearbook (GFSY)* and cover budgetary central government. The fiscal year ends December 31.

National Accounts:

Source: Institut National de la Statistique et de l'Analyse Economique. Data are prepared in accordance with the 1993 United Nations System of National Accounts.

Bhutan   514

Date of Fund Membership:

September 28, 1981

Standard Sources:

Royal Monetary Authority of Bhutan
National Statistics Bureau

Exchange Rates:

Official Rate: (End of Period and Period Average):
Official midpoint rate. Since Bhutan's currency was introduced in 1974, the ngultrum has been pegged at par to the Indian rupee, which also circulates freely within Bhutan.

International Liquidity:

Foreign Exchange (line 1d.d) consists of all foreign assets of the Royal Monetary Authority of Bhutan and the convertible currency and Indian rupee-denominated foreign assets of other depository corporations.

Central Bank:

Consists of the Royal Monetary Authority of Bhutan (RMA), which was established in 1983, only.

Data are based on a standardized report form for central bank, which accords with the concepts and definitions of the IMF's *Monetary and Financial Statistics Manual (MFSM)*, 2000. Departures from the *MFSM* methodology are explained below. Securities other than shares and shares and other equity are recorded at acquisition cost rather than at market price or fair value.

Accrued interest is included in *Other Items (Net)* rather than in the outstanding amounts of the financial assets and liabilities.

Other Depository Corporations:

Comprises commercial banks.

Data are based on a standardized report form for other depository corporations, which accords with the concepts and definitions of the *Monetary and Financial Statistics Manual (MFSM)*. Departures from the *MFSM* methodology are explained below. Securities other than shares and shares and other equity are recorded at acquisition cost rather than at market price or fair value.

Accrued interest is included in *Other Items (Net)* rather than in the outstanding amounts of the financial assets and liabilities.

Depository Corporations:

See notes on central bank and other depository corporations.

Monetary Aggregates:

Broad Money:
Broad Money calculated from the liability data in the sections for the central bank and other depository corporations accords with the concepts and definitions of the *MFSM* and is consistent with M2 described below.

Money (National Definitions):
M1 comprises currency outside banks and demand deposits. *Currency outside banks* is equal to the amount of currency notes and coins issued by the RMA *less* currency note and coin holdings of the RMA and commercial banks. Demand deposits consist of current accounts and savings deposits. Savings deposits are interest-bearing deposits that can be withdrawn on demand without penalty.
M2 comprises M1 and quasi-money. *Quasi-money* comprises time and foreign-currency deposits that other financial corpora-

tions, public nonfinancial corporations, and private sector hold at the RMA and commercial banks.

Interest Rates:

Bank Rate (End of Period):
Rate determined by the Monetary Operation Committee of the RMA on the RMA bills of 91-day maturity that are sold to the commercial banks.

Deposit Rate:
Minimum rate offered by commercial banks on three- to six-month deposits.

Lending Rate:
Maximum rate charged on loans for general trade by the financial corporations operating in Bhutan.

Prices, Production, and Tourism:

Consumer Prices:
National Statistics Bureau index for all Bhutan, weights reference period: 2003. The indices prior to Q3 2003 represent half-yearly averages. The quarterly index and the half-yearly index cannot be directly compared because of a different periodicity and a considerable break in continuity (the expenditure basket has been completely changed).

Electricity Production:
The large increase in 1986–87 is due to the beginning of production of the Chukha hydroelectric facility. From July 1988 onwards, the data refer to Chukha production only.

Tourist Arrivals:
The data refer to tourists on package tours paid for in convertible currencies. Tourists from India are not included.

International Transactions:

All value data for merchandise trade are customs data, as adjusted by the Department of Trade and Industry to include, inter alia, exports of electricity and imports of aircraft.

Balance of Payments:
The Royal Monetary Authority (RMA) of Bhutan compiles Bhutan's balance of payments and international investment position statistics on the basis of the IMF's *Balance of Payments Manual*. Data sources include reports published by government departments and data collected through balance of payments survey forms and questionnaires sent out to financial institutions, government corporations, private companies, and other private sector sources. Surveys are augmented by other reports received from various government sources. Notably, the Department of Revenue and Customs and the Department of Public Accounts under the Ministry of Finance provide the Bhutan trade statistics and external public debt data, respectively. The RMA reports annual fiscal year (end-June) balance of payments statistics.

International Investment Position:
Annual IIP data are available beginning with the 2007 reference year. The sources of information are similar to those used for the balance of payments.

Government Finance:

Annual data are as reported for the *Government Finance Statistics Yearbook (GFSY)* and cover budgetary central government. † Through 1986, fiscal year begins April 1; from 1988 onward, fis-

cal year ends June 30. Data for 1988 fiscal year cover 15 months. † From 1989 onward, data on grants include grants received in kind. Also, data on expenditure include the value of grants in kind.

National Accounts:
Source: National Statistics Bureau.

Bolivia   218

Date of Fund Membership:
December 27, 1945

Standard Source:
Central Bank of Bolivia
National Statistics Institute

Exchange Rates:
On January 1, 1987 the boliviano, equal to 1,000,000 pesos, was introduced.
Market Rate (End of Period and *Period Average)* is determined through auction held by the Central Bank of Bolivia.

International Liquidity:
Gold (National Valuation) (line 1and) is the U.S. dollar value of official holdings of gold as reported in the country's standard sources.

Central Bank:
Consists of the Central Bank of Bolivia (CBB) only.
Data are based on a standardized report form (SRF) for central banks, which accords with the concepts and definitions of the IMF's *Monetary and Financial Statistics Manual (MFSM)*, 2000. Departures from the *MFSM* methodology are explained below.
Liabilities to Other Depository Corporations includes securities issued by the CBB held by other financial corporations.

Other Depository Corporations:
Comprises commercial banks, credit unions, savings and loans associations, and private finance funds.
Data are based on a standardized report form (SRF) for other depository corporations, which accords with the concepts and definitions of the *Monetary and Financial Statistics Manual (MFSM)*. Departures from the *MFSM* methodology are explained below.
Prior to December 2005, *Claims on Central Government* includes holdings of CBB securities by commercial banks.
Claims on Private Sector includes loans to other sectors.
Other Items (Net) includes some repurchase agreements with the central bank.
Deposits Included in Broad Money includes deposits of investment funds with other depository corporations and some deposits of foreign embassies and diplomatic missions.
For December 2001 through May 2004, data also contain misclassifications of financial instruments and economic sectors.

Depository Corporations:
See notes on central bank and other depository corporations.

Other Financial Corporations:
Comprises insurance corporations, pension funds, and the state-owned Banco de Desarrollo Productivo (former Nacional

Financiera Boliviana - NAFIBO). Data exclude the Fund for the Development of the Financial System (FONDESIF), leasing companies, and financial auxiliaries.

Data are based on a standardized report form (SRF) for other financial corporations, which accords with the concepts and definitions of the *Monetary and Financial Statistics Manual* (*MFSM*).

Financial Corporations:

See notes on central bank, other depository corporations, and other financial corporations.

Monetary Aggregates:

Broad Money calculated from the liability data in the sections for the central bank and other depository corporations accords with the concepts and definitions of the *MFSM*. Broad money includes treasury bills held by the nonfinancial private sector. Broad money differs from M4' described below as M4' excludes the deposits of state and local governments, and public nonfinancial corporations with the CBB and other depository corporations.

Money (National Definitions):

Base money comprises notes and coins in circulation and deposits of other depository corporations with the CBB.

M1 comprises notes and coins in circulation outside the banking system and current account and sight deposits in national currency of the private sector with other depository corporations.

M1' comprises M1 and current account and sight deposits in foreign currency and national currency with value maintenance of the private sector with other depository corporations.

M2 comprises M1 and savings deposits in national currency of the private sector with other depository corporations.

M2' comprises M1' and savings deposits in national currency, foreign currency, and national currency with value maintenance of the private sector with other depository corporations.

M3 comprises M2 and time deposits and other deposits in national currency of the private sector with other depository corporations.

M3' comprises M2' and time deposits and other deposits in national currency, foreign currency, and national currency with value maintenance of the private sector with other depository corporations.

M4 comprises M3 and treasury bills in national currency held by the nonfinancial private sector.

M4' comprises M3' and treasury bills in national currency, foreign currency, and national currency with value maintenance held by the nonfinancial private sector.

Interest Rates:

Discount Rate (End of Period):

Rate charged by the CBB on loans in national currency to financial corporations collateralized by public (Treasury or CBB) securities.

Discount Rate (Foreign Currency) (End of Period):

Rate charged by the CBB on loans in foreign currency to financial corporations collateralized by public (Treasury or CBB) securities.

Money Market Rate:

Weighted average rate on loans between financial corporations in national currency. The rate is weighted by daily loan amounts and the maturity of the loan.

Money Market Rate (Foreign Currency):

Weighted average rate on loans between financial corporations in foreign currency. The rate is weighted by daily loan amounts and the maturity of the loan.

Treasury Bill Rate:

Rate on 91-day treasury bills denominated in national currency auctioned by the CBB.

Treasury Bill Rate (Foreign Currency):

Rate on 91-day treasury bills denominated in foreign currency auctioned by the CBB.

Savings Rate:

Average rate offered by commercial banks on savings deposits in national currency.

Savings Rate (Foreign Currency):

Average rate offered by commercial banks on savings deposits in foreign currency.

Deposit Rate:

Average rate, including surcharges and commissions, offered by commercial banks on time deposits in national currency. † Beginning in January 1987, weighted average rate, including surcharge and commissions, paid by commercial banks on time deposits in national currency.

Deposit Rate (Foreign Currency):

Weighted average rate, including surcharge and commissions, paid by commercial banks on time deposits in foreign currency.

Lending Rate:

Average rate, including surcharge and commissions, charged by commercial banks on loans in national currency. † Beginning in January 1987, weighted average rate, including surcharge and commissions, charged by commercial banks on loans in national currency.

Lending Rate (Foreign Currency):

Weighted average rate, including surcharge and commissions, charged by commercial banks on loans in foreign currency.

Prices and Production:

Consumer Prices:

Source: Central Bank of Bolivia. Weights Reference Period: 2007; Geographical Coverage: the capital cities of the whole country (including El Alto); Number of Items in the Basket: 364 items; Basis for Calculation: the weights are derived from the household survey conducted in 2003–2004.

Crude Petroleum Production:

Central Bank of Bolivia data (in thousand cubic meters).

International Transactions:

Value of Exports and Imports:

All data are from Central Bank of Bolivia. Exports of *Tin* refer to tin concentrates and tin metallic. Total export values are adjusted downward for smelting of minerals abroad. Commodity export values include smelting costs.

Volume of Exports:

IFS average of tin, natural gas, zinc, antimony, silver, and wolfram with a 1995 value of exports as weights. *Export Volume* indices for individual commodities are based on Central Bank of Bolivia data in physical quantities.

Unit Value of Exports:

IFS average of tin, natural gas, zinc, antimony, silver, and wolfram with a 1995 value of exports as weights. *Export Unit Value* indices for individual commodities are calculated for *IFS* from reported value and volume data.

Government Finance:

Monthly, quarterly, and annual data are as reported by Central Bank of Bolivia and are derived from data provided by the Fiscal Programming Unit of the National Secretariat of Finance. Data cover the consolidated general government comprising the budgetary central government, decentralized agencies including the social security institutions, and regional and local governments. Revenue data include grants and repayments of loans extended by the government. Expenditure data include lending by the government. The fiscal year ends December 31.

National Accounts:

Source: Central Bank of Bolivia. As indicated by the country, data are compiled according to the recommendations of the *1968 SNA* and the *1993 SNA*.

Bosnia & Herzegovina   963

Date of Fund Membership:

December 20, 1995

Standard Sources:

Central Bank of Bosnia and Herzegovina
Agency for Statistics of Bosnia and Herzegovina

Exchange Rates:

Official Rate: (End of Period and Period Average):
The official rate is pegged to the euro. Prior to January 1999, the official rate was pegged to the deutsche mark at a 1:1 rate.

Central Bank:

Comprises the Central Bank of Bosnia and Herzegovina (CBBH) only.
† Beginning in January 2006, data are based on a standardized report form for central banks, which accords with the concepts and definitions of the IMF's *Monetary and Financial Statistics Manual (MFSM)*.
For December 2001 through December 2005, data have less conformity with the *MFSM* methodology and therefore are not strictly comparable to data for later periods.

Other Depository Corporations:

Comprises commercial banks.
† Beginning in January 2006, data are based on a standardized report form for other depository corporations, which accords with the concepts and definitions of the IMF's *Monetary and Financial Statistics Manual (MFSM)*. For other depository corporations in Bosnia and Herzegovina, departures from the *MFSM* methodology are explained below.
For January 2006 through November 2010, loans to the economic sectors exclude nonperforming loans of all banks. Beginning in December 2010, loans to the economic sectors exclude nonperforming loans of banks in the Federation of Bosnia and Herzegovina.
For December 2001 through December 2005, data have less conformity with the *MFSM* methodology and therefore are not strictly comparable to data for later periods.

Depository Corporations:

† See notes on central bank and other depository corporations.

Monetary Aggregates:

Broad Money:
Broad Money calculated from the liability data on the sections for the central bank and other depository corporations accords with the concepts and definitions of the *MFSM* and is consistent with M2 described below.

Money (National Definitions):
M0 comprises currency in circulation, commercial banks' deposits with the CBBH in national and foreign currency, and demand deposits of other financial corporations, cantonal and municipal governments, public nonfinancial corporations, and private sector with the CBBH in national currency. Currency in circulation refers to notes and coins issued by the CBBH.
M1 comprises currency outside depository corporations and demand deposits of other financial corporations, cantonal and municipal governments, public nonfinancial corporations, and private sector with depository corporations in national currency.
M2 comprises M1 and quasi-money. Quasi-money comprises demand deposits in foreign currency and time and savings deposits in national and foreign currency of other financial corporations, cantonal and municipal governments, public nonfinancial corporations, and private sector with depository corporations.

Interest Rates:

Deposit Rate:
Average of end-of-period minimum and maximum rates offered by commercial banks on time and savings deposits of households. † Beginning in January 2002, weighted average rate offered by commercial banks on time and savings deposits of households in national currency. The rate is weighted by the amount of new deposits accepted during the reference period.

Lending Rate:
Average of end-of-period minimum and maximum rates charged by commercial banks on short-term loans to private nonfinancial enterprises. † Beginning in January 2002, weighted average rate charged by commercial banks on short-term loans to private nonfinancial enterprises and cooperatives. The rate is weighted by the amount of new loans extended during the reference period.

Prices:

Share Prices (End of Period):
Bosnian Investment Fund Index (BIFX), base July 2004. The index covers shares traded on the Sarajevo Stock Exchange.
Investment Funds Index of Republika Srpska (FIRS), base July 2004. The index covers shares traded on the Banja Luka Stock Exchange.

Consumer Prices:
Source: Agency for Statistics of Bosnia and Herzegovina. Weights Reference Period: weights are updated every year according to changes in prices in a previous year; Geographical Coverage: 12 large cities; Number of Items in the Basket: 599 items; Basis for Calculation: the weights are derived from the Household Budget Survey 2007, updated every year according to changes in prices in a previous year.

International Transactions:

Exports and imports data are sourced from the *Annual Report* of the Central Bank of Bosnia and Herzegovina. Data are compiled by the Customs Administration of the Federation of Bosnia and Herzegovina and the Customs Administration of Republika Srpska.

International Investment Position:

The main data sources used by the Central Bank of Bosnia and Herzegovina (CBBH) for compiling the IIP are three sets of statistics compiled within the CBBH: foreign investment statistics, monetary and financial statistics, and external debt statistics.

Data for direct investment in banks are derived from a survey on direct investment conducted by the CBBH. The survey covers the equity investments both in BH and abroad.

The survey on direct investments provides separate data on portfolio investments. However, only portfolio investments in commercial banks are classified in this IIP category. Assets of monetary authorities configured as debt securities are included in reserve assets.

Data on stocks of foreign loans and deposits of nonresidents held at residential commercial banks are obtained from the CBBH's monetary and financial statistics.

Reserve assets are gross foreign reserves of the CBBH, which consist of balance sheet positions of short-term foreign assets of the CBBH (gold, SDR holdings, foreign exchange in the CBBH vault, short-term foreign exchange deposits with nonresident banks, and other) and investment in long-term foreign securities. Data are derived from monetary and financial statistics.

Government Finance:

Data are derived from Central Bank of Bosnia and Herzegovina and cover the operations of the consolidated budgetary central government institutions (BiH common institutions, the two entities' governments, 10 cantonal governments, and Brcko District Government) along with all Social Security Funds (two entity level pension funds, health funds, and unemployment funds; one entity child protection fund, 10 cantonal health funds and 10 cantonal unemployment funds). The fiscal year ends December 31.

National Accounts:

Source: Agency for Statistics of Bosnia and Herzegovina. As indicated by the country, data are compiled in accordance with the methodology of the *1995 ESA* and the *1993 SNA*.

Botswana   616

Date of Fund Membership:

July 24, 1968

Standard Sources:

Bank of Botswana
Department of Customs and Excise
Central Statistics Office

Exchange Rates:

Official Rate: (End of Period and Period Average):
The official rate is pegged to a basket of currencies.

Central Bank:

Consists of the Bank of Botswana (BOB) only.
Data are based on a standardized report form (SRF) for central banks, which accords with the concepts and definitions of the IMF's *Monetary and Financial Statistics Manual (MFSM)*, 2000.

Other Depository Corporations:

Comprises commercial banks, African Banking Corporation, Botswana Building Society, and Botswana Savings Bank. Data are based on a standardized report form (SRF) for other depository corporations, which accords with the concepts and definitions of the *Monetary and Financial Statistics Manual (MFSM)*. For other depository corporations in Botswana, departures from the *MFSM* methodology are explained below.

Holdings of securities other than shares and shares and other equity not disaggregated by economic sector are allocated to *Claims on Central Government*.

Depository Corporations:

See notes on central bank and other depository corporations.

Monetary Aggregates:

Broad Money:
Broad Money from the liability data in the sections for the central bank and other depository corporations accords with the concepts and definitions of the *MFSM* and is consistent with *M3* described below.

Money (National Definitions):
M1 comprises notes and coins in circulation outside the depository corporations and transferable deposits in national and foreign currency of other financial institutions, local government, public nonfinancial corporations, and private sector with depository corporations.

M2 comprises M1 and other deposits in national and foreign currency of other financial institutions, local government, public nonfinancial corporations, and private sector with the depository corporations.

M3 comprises *M2* and certificates issued by the BOB held by other financial institutions, local government, public nonfinancial corporations, and private sector.

Interest Rates:

Discount Rate (End of Period):
The BOB's lending rate.

Savings Rate:
Rate offered by commercial banks on savings deposits.

Deposit Rate:
Rate offered by commercial banks on 88-day-notice fixed deposits. Quarterly and annual data are averages of end-of-period monthly data.

Deposit Rate (Foreign Currency):
Rate offered by commercial banks on 88-day-notice fixed deposits in US dollars. Quarterly and annual data are averages of end-of-period monthly data.

Lending Rate:
Commercial banks' prime lending rate. Quarterly and annual data are averages of end-of-period monthly data.

Government Bond Yield:
Yield on 12-year government bonds.

Prices, Production, Labor:

Share Prices (End of Month):
Index is based on a domestic company index as determined by the Botswana Stock Exchange, base June 19, 1989.

Consumer Prices:

Source: Central Statistics Office. Weights Reference Period: September 2006; Geographical Coverage: cities and towns throughout the country; Number of Items in Basket: 384; Basis for Calculation: weights are determined based on the Household Income and Expenditure Survey (HIES) of 2002–03.

International Transactions:

All value data on trade are derived from Department of Customs and Excise. *Imports, c.i.f.* and *Imports, f.o.b.* include duty and are therefore not comparable to corresponding balance of payments data.

Government Finance:

† Beginning in 1986, data are reported from the records of the Ministry of Finance and Development Planning and are reported by Bank of Botswana. The data cover the operations of budgetary central government. † Beginning in 2000, annual data are derived from monthly and quarterly data. Annual data between 1986–1999 were reported separately from monthly and quarterly data. Prior to 1986 data are as reported from the *Government Finance Statistics Yearbook (GFSY)* and cover budgetary central government. The fiscal year ends March 31.

National Accounts:

Source: Central Statistics Office. Data are prepared in accordance with the 1968 United Nations System of National Accounts.

Brazil   223

Date of Fund Membership:

January 14, 1946

Standard Sources:

Central Bank of Brazil
Ministry of Industry, Commerce and Tourism, Secretariat of Foreign Commerce (SECEX)
Brazilian Institute of Statistics and Geography (IBGE)

Exchange Rates:

Beginning on November 1, 1942, a cruziero (Cr$) was worth a thousand réis. On February 13, 1967 the new cruzeiro (NCr$) was instituted as a transitory monetary unit equivalent to 1,000 cruzeiros. Effective May 15, 1970 the cruziero (Cr$) was re-established at par with the new cruzeiro. On February 28, 1986, the cruzado (Cz$), equal to 1,000 cruzeiros, was introduced. On January15, 1989 the new cruzado (NCz$), equal to 1,000 old cruzados, was introduced. On March 16, 1990 the cruzeiro (Cr$) replaced the new cruzado at an exchange rate of one new cruzado for one cruzeiro. On August 1, 1993 the cruzeiro real (Cr$), equal to 1,000 cruzeiros, was introduced. On July 1, 1994 the real (R$), equal to 2,750 cruzeiros reais, was introduced.

Principal Rate (End of Period and Period Average):
From March 1990 through September 1994, the official rate floated independently with respect to the U.S. dollar. From October 1994 through January 17, 1999, the official rate was determined by a managed float. Since January 18, 1999, the official rate floats independently with respect to the U.S. dollar.

International Liquidity:

Foreign Exchange (line 1d.d) includes domestic government securities payable in foreign currency. *Gold (National Valuation) (line 1and)* is valued on the basis of the daily average closing quotations in London during the preceding two months. *Other Liquid Foreign Assets (line 1e.d)* comprises the value of liquid export bills. The Brazilian definition of liquid international reserves comprises the sum of *Total Reserves minus Gold (line 1l.d)*, *Gold (National Valuation) (line 1and)*, and *Other Liquid Foreign Assets (line 1e.d)*. † Prior to January 1986, data for *Total Reserves minus Gold (line 1l.d)* and *Foreign Exchange (line 1d.d)* include foreign exchange held by the Central Bank of Brazil (CBB) and Bank of Brazil. Beginning in 1986, data include the foreign exchange held by the CBB only. Beginning January 1999 data reflect inclusion of gold deposits in lines *1and* and *.1ad*.

Central Bank:

Consists of the Central Bank of Brazil (CBB) only.
† Beginning in July 2007, data are based on a standardized report form (SRF) for central banks, which accords with the concepts and definitions of the IMF's *Monetary and Financial Statistics Manual (MFSM)*, 2000. Departures from the *MFSM* methodology are explained below.
Securities lending backed by securities is treated as a transaction and included in *Other Items (Net)* rather than recorded off-balance sheet. Loans to financial corporations in liquidation are valued at market price rather than at nominal value.
For December 2001 through June 2007, data in the SRF format are compiled from pre-SRF data which are not fully based on the *MFSM* methodology. Departures from the *MFSM* methodology are explained below.
Financial assets and liabilities for which economic sectorization is unavailable are allocated to the economic sector having the largest volume of transactions in the category.
Foreign Assets are partly calculated using balance of payments data rather than entirely calculated from the balance sheet of the BCB.
Shares and Other Equity includes some provisions for losses.
Accounts receivable and payable are included in *Other Items (Net)* rather than in the CBB's claims on or liabilities to the corresponding economic sectors.
Securities lending backed by securities is treated as a transaction and included in *Other Items (Net)* rather than recorded off-balance sheet.
Some securities other than shares issued by the central government are valued at acquisition cost rather than at current market price or fair value.
Loans to financial corporations in liquidation are valued at market price rather than at nominal value.

Other Depository Corporations:

Comprises commercial banks, Bank of Brazil; multiple banks; Federal Savings Bank; investment banks; National Bank for Economic and Social Development (BNDES); development banks; finance and investment companies; housing credit companies, mortgage companies; money market financial investment funds; and savings, loans, and credit cooperatives.
† Beginning in December 2004, data are based on a standardized report form (SRF) for other depository corporations, which accords with the concepts and definitions of the *Monetary and*

Financial Statistics Manual (*MFSM*). For other depository corporations in Brazil, departures from the *MFSM* methodology are explained below.

Some data for other depository corporations were not directly distinguished from data for other financial corporations, in which case separation is derived by using counterparty records with residual amounts allocated to the private sector.

For December 2001 through November 2004, coverage of other depository corporations excludes credit cooperatives. Data in the SRF format are compiled from pre-SRF data which are not fully based on the *MFSM* methodology. Departures from the *MFSM* methodology are explained below.

Financial assets and liabilities for which economic sectorization is unavailable are allocated to the economic sector having the largest volume of transactions in the category.

Though some data for other depository corporations were not directly distinguished from data for other financial corporations, separation of the data was based on the characteristics of the financial asset or liability.

Loans to other financial corporations are included in *Other Items (Net)*. *Loans* include some loans from other depository corporations.

Claims on Other Financial Corporations includes debentures issued by other nonfinancial corporations.

Other Deposits Included in Broad Money includes some deposits of other depository corporations.

Deposits Excluded from Broad Money includes other deposits of other financial corporations and nonresidents.

Shares and Other Equity includes provisions for loan losses.

Some financial derivatives and accounts receivable and payable are included in *Other Items (Net)* rather than in the other depository corporations' claims on or liabilities to the corresponding economic sectors.

Depository Corporations:

† See notes on central bank and other depository corporations.

Other Financial Corporations:

Comprises leasing companies, stock brokerage houses, distributor companies, and fostering agencies. † Beginning in December 2006, includes closed pension funds, non-money market financial investment funds, microfinance societies, and exchange banks. Data exclude insurance corporations, open pension funds, capitalization funds, and exchange houses.

Data are based on a standardized report form (SRF) for other financial corporations, which accords with the concepts and definitions of the *Monetary and Financial Statistics Manual* (*MFSM*). For other financial corporations in Brazil, departures from the *MFSM* methodology are explained below.

Data for the closed pension funds are available only on a quarterly basis. Data for the intervening months and the two months after the latest quarter are estimated by carrying forward the data for the last month of the previous quarter.

Some data for other depository corporations were not directly distinguished from data for other financial corporations, in which case separation is derived by using counterparty records with residual amounts allocated to the private sector.

For December 2001 through November 2006, data in the SRF format are compiled from pre-SRF data which are not fully based on the *MFSM* methodology. For other financial corporations in the Brazil, departures from the *MFSM* methodology are explained below.

Financial assets and liabilities for which financial instrument breakdown is unavailable are allocated to the financial instrument having the largest volume of transactions in the category.

Though some data for other financial corporations were not directly distinguished from data for other depository corporations, separation of the data was based on the characteristics of the financial asset or liability. *Claims on Depository Corporations* includes some deposits with other financial corporations and shares and other equity issued by other financial corporations and private sector.

Shares and Other Equity includes provisions for loan losses.

Some financial derivatives and accounts receivable and payable are included in *Other Items (Net)* rather than in the other financial corporations' claims on or liabilities to the corresponding economic sectors.

Monetary Aggregates:

Broad Money:

Broad Money calculated from the liability data in the sections for the central bank and other depository corporations differs from M4 described below as M4 includes deposits of the central government and transferable deposits of nonresidents with depository corporations; the net position of the repurchase agreements conducted with money holding sectors using only central government securities; and federal, state, and municipal liquid securities held by the public.

Money (National Definitions):

Base Money (B) comprises notes and coins issued and non-interest bearing required and excess reserves on sight deposits with financial corporations. Sight deposits include demand deposits, advance notice deposits, third party float, collection of taxes, cashier's checks, and realized guarantees.

B1 comprises B and interest-bearing required reserves on sight deposits with financial corporations.

BA comprises B1, required cash reserves on savings and time deposits and federal securities valued by their yield curve outside the CBB, except the *Letras do Banco Central-Série Especial* (LBC-E) used for the swap of state securities.

B2 comprises BA and state and local securities outside the CBB, at face value, and LBC-E.

M1 comprises currency held by the public, and demand deposits. Demand deposits include deposits of the private sector; of the federal, state, and municipal governments; of the federal, state, and municipal enterprises; and of the financial institutions that are not subject to reserve requirements. M1 also includes domestic currency deposits of nonresidents, travelers' checks issued and not cashed, certified checks with a fixed payment date, payroll checks, and customers' credit balances on loan and financing accounts.

M2 comprises M1 plus interest-bearing deposits, savings deposits, and securities issued by depository corporations.

M3 comprises M2 plus shares in financial investment funds and the net position of the securities used in the repurchase agreements transactions with money holding sectors.

M4 comprises M3 plus federal, state, and municipal liquid securities held by the public.

Interest Rates:

Central Bank Policy Rate (End of Period):
Target rate for overnight interbank loans collateralized by government bonds, registered with and traded on the Sistema Especial de Liquidacao e Custodia (SELIC). The actual SELIC rate is used to determine the discount rate charged by the CBB.

Discount Rate (End of Period):
Bank rate (TBAN) charged by the CBB on noncollateralized loans to financial institutions. † Beginning in March 2000, TBAN was abolished, and the CBB established new rules for lending to financial institutions, taking into account the maturity of the operation and the collateral used by the borrowing institutions. The CBB decided to use the SELIC rate (see note on money market rate) plus two points as the discount rate. In April 2002, the CBB introduced a new payments system and changed the method for calculating the discount rate based on repurchase agreements using government securities. Beginning in April 2002, corresponds to SELIC plus one point. Beginning in July 2002, corresponds to SELIC plus six points.

Money Market Rate:
Average rate on loans between commercial banks. † Beginning in January 1980, the SELIC overnight rate is a weighted average rate on loans between financial institutions involving firm sales of or repurchase agreements based on federal securities in the SELIC. The rate is weighted by loan amounts.

Treasury Bill Rate:
Effective yield on *Letras do Tesouro Nacional* (LTN) of 31 days or longer, calculated from the discount. The yield is that of the last issue of the month, is calculated on a daily basis, and applies only to business days.

Treasury Bill Rate (Foreign Currency):
Effective yield on *Notas do Tesouro Nacional-Emissão D* (NTN-Series D) of three months or longer issued with exchange rate guarantee. The yield includes the purchase discount or premium and the coupon rate of six percent per year, compounded twice a year for notes for longer than six months and paid at maturity for shorter terms. The yield is that of the last issue of the month and does not include the exchange rate change.

Savings Rate:
Rate paid by the Brazilian savings and loan system (SBPE) on 30-day savings deposits.

Deposit Rate:
Average rate offered by banks on 60-day time deposits. † Beginning in January 1989, average rate offered by banks on certificates of deposit of 30 days or longer.

Lending Rate:
Weighted average of the rates charged by banks on loans with fixed interest rates and with own funds to individuals and corporations. The rate is weighted by loan amounts.

Prices, Production, Labor:

Share Prices (Period Average and End of Month):
Average and end of month indices of daily share prices in the São Paulo Securities Exchange (BOVESPA), weights reference period: January 2, 1968.

Wholesale Prices:
Source: Brazilian Institute of Statistics and Geography. Weights Reference Period: August 1994; Coverage: the index is structured to measure the rate of change of prices of a sample of merchandise at the wholesale level in business to business transactions in the following productive areas of the country: Alagoas, Amazonas, Bahia, Ceara, Espírito Santo, Goiás, Maranhão, Mato Grosso do Sul, Minas Gerais, Pará, Paraíba, Panará, Pernambuco, Piauí, Rio de Janeiro, Rio Grande do Norte, Rio Grande do Sul, Rondônia, Santa Catarina, Sergipe, São Paulo e Tocantis; Number of Items in Basket: 462 commodities/products; Basis for Calculation: weights are revised monthly due to relative changes in the components of the index.

Consumer Prices:
Source: Brazilian Institute of Statistics and Geography. Weights Reference Period: July 2002-July 2003; Geographical Coverage: whole national territory; Number of Items in Basket: 512; Basis for Calculation: weights are derived from Consumer Expenditure Survey performed between July 2002 and July 2003.

Industrial Production, Seasonally Adjusted:
Source: Brazilian Institute of Statistics and Geography. Weights Reference Period: 2004; Sectoral Coverage: mining sector and processing industry; Basis for Calculation: the weighting system is fixed and follows the structure of the "Industrial Value Added of 1998/2000" based on the relative importance of each product in the Value Added of General Industry.

Labor Force, Employment, Unemployment, Unemployment Rate:
† For data from 2003 onwards, the methodology has been changed with the introduction of a new monthly survey (monthly and annual data are not consistent). In 2001 it underwent a methodology review aimed at increasing the level of detail of labor characteristics and forms of classes of workers in the productive market, updating its thematic coverage and adapting it to recent international patterns recommended by the International Labour Organization - ILO. The main methodological changes introduced in this revision refer to the implementation of conceptual changes in the topic labor and to a greater coverage of the research, in order to obtain a better understanding of the employed population and the population searching for work.

International Transactions:

All trade value and volume data are from Ministry of Industry, Commerce and Tourism, Secretariat of Foreign Commerce.

Volume of Exports and Imports:
Data on total volume are based on quantities in metric tons.*Unit Value of Exports* and *Imports* indices are calculated from value and volume indices.
Export Volume indices for coffee are based on Central Bank of Brazil data in metric tons. *Export Unit Value* indices for coffee are calculated for *IFS* from reported value and volume data. The coffee wholesale price index is the Brazil (New York) index shown in the commodity prices world table.

Government Finance:

Operations Statement data are from the Central Bank and Ministry of Finance. The Central Bank of Brazil revised the data series for financial data (flows and stocks), correcting some classification and consolidation problems. † In the Balance Sheet, beginning December 2006 onwards, the Central/General Government Gross Debt excludes the Central Government securities that are under the Central Bank's outright ownership. The financial asset "currency and deposits" was corrected by the same amount. (For additional information on this methodological break, please consult the note published by the Central Bank of Brazil in www.bcb.gov.br/ftp/notaecon/ni200802pfi.zip.)

National Accounts:

Data are from Central Bank of Brazil. *Line 93i* data are included in *line 96f* when they are not separately shown. † As indicated by the country, data have been revised following the implementation of the *1993 SNA*. Annual GDP volume data are at 2000 prices: while we await the publication of quarterly data at 2000 prices, quarterly GDP volume, quarterly GDP volume index and deflator are being published at 1995 prices and are not compatible with the annual series.

Brunei Darussalam   516

Date of Fund Membership:

October 10, 1995

Standard Sources:

Brunei Currency and Monetary Board
Ministry of Finance
Department of Economic Planning and Development

Exchange Rates:

Official Rate: (End of Period and Period Average):
Refers to Singapore's midpoint interbank rate at noon. The Brunei dollar is legal tender in Brunei Darussalam and the Singapore dollar is a customary tender. Under the Currency Interchangeability Agreement of 1967, Brunei Darussalam and Singapore accept each other's currency at par without charge.

International Liquidity:

Foreign Exchange (line 1d.d) comprises the Brunei Currency and Monetary Board's foreign currency holdings, liquid correspondent accounts with nonresidents banks, and holdings of foreign securities and shares.

Central Bank:

Consists of the Brunei Currency and Monetary Board (BCMB) only.
† Beginning in January 2010, data are based on a standardized report form (SRF) for central banks, which accords with the concepts and definitions of the IMF's *Monetary and Financial Statistics Manual (MFSM)*, 2000.
For December 2001 through December 2009, data in the SRF format are compiled from pre-SRF data which are not fully based on the *MFSM* methodology. Departures from the *MFSM* methodology are explained below.
Financial assets and liabilities for which financial instrument breakdown is unavailable are allocated to the financial instrument having the largest volume of transactions in the category.
Claims on Nonresidents and *Liabilities to Nonresidents* include small positions with resident sectors.
Some accounts payable are included in *Other Items (Net)* rather than in the BCMB's liabilities to the corresponding economic sectors.

Accrued interest not disaggregated by financial instrument is allocated to the financial instrument having the largest volume of transactions in the category.

Other Depository Corporations:

Comprises commercial banks, finance companies, and a trust fund. Data exclude an offshore banking institution.
† Beginning in January 2010, data are based on a standardized report form (SRF) for other depository corporations, which accords with the concepts and definitions of the *Monetary and Financial Statistics Manual (MFSM)*. For other depository corporations in Brunei Darussalam, departures from the *MFSM* methodology are explained below.
Financial derivatives are excluded from the data.
Held-to-maturity securities are valued at acquisition cost rather than at current market price or fair value.
For December 2001 through December 2009, data in the SRF format are compiled from pre-SRF data which are not based on the *MFSM* methodology. Departures from the *MFSM* methodology are explained below.
Financial assets and liabilities for which economic sectorization is unavailable are allocated to the economic sector having the largest volume of transactions in the category.
Financial assets and liabilities for which financial instrument breakdown is unavailable are allocated to the financial instrument having the largest volume of transactions in the category.
Other Items (Net) includes claims on other financial corporations.
Some accounts receivable and payable are included in *Other Items (Net)* rather than in the other depository corporations' claims on or liabilities to the corresponding economic sectors.
Accrued interest is included in *Other Items (Net)* rather than in the outstanding amounts of the financial assets and liabilities.
Securities other than shares and shares and other equity are valued at acquisition cost rather than at current market price or fair value.

Depository Corporations:

† See notes on central bank and other depository corporations.

Other Financial Corporations:

Comprises insurance companies. Data exclude pension funds, securities companies, asset management companies, mutual funds, offshore financial institutions, money remittance companies, and money changing companies.
† Beginning in June 2011, data are based on a standardized report form (SRF) for other financial corporations, which accords with the concepts and definitions of the *Monetary and Financial Statistics Manual (MFSM)*. For other financial corporations in Brunei Darussalam, departures from the *MFSM* methodology are explained below.
Claims on Private Sector includes some trade credit/advances to other depository corporations, other financial corporations, public nonfinancial corporations, and nonresidents.
Some trade credit/advances of nonresidents are included in *Other Items (Net)* rather than in *Liabilities to Nonresidents*.
Held-to-maturity securities other than shares and shares and other equity are valued at acquisition cost rather than at current market price or fair value.

For December 2007 through May 2011, data in the SRF format are compiled from pre-SRF data which are not fully based on the *MFSM* methodology. Departures from the *MFSM* methodology are explained below.

Financial assets and liabilities for which economic sectorization is unavailable are allocated to the economic sector having the largest volume of transactions in the category. *Claims on Nonresidents* and *Claims on Depository Corporations* include positions with other financial corporations. *Claims on Nonresidents* includes holdings of securities issued by other depository corporations.

Financial assets and liabilities for which financial instrument breakdown is unavailable are allocated to the financial instrument having the largest volume of transactions in the category. Some transferable deposits with nonresidents are included in *Claims on Depository Corporations* rather than in *Claims on Nonresidents*.

Some accounts receivable and payable are included in *Other Items (Net)* rather than in the other financial corporations' claims on or liabilities to the corresponding economic sectors.

Accrued interest is included in *Other Items (Net)* rather than in the outstanding amounts of the financial assets and liabilities. Securities other than shares and shares and other equity are valued at acquisition cost rather than at current market price or fair value.

Monetary Aggregates:

Broad Money (line 59m) calculated from the liability data in the sections for the central bank and other depository corporations accords with the concepts and definitions of the *MFSM* and is consistent with broad money (*line 59mea*) described below.

Money (National Definitions):
M0 comprises currency in circulation.

Money comprises currency outside depository corporations and demand and call deposits of other financial corporations, public nonfinancial corporations, and private sector with commercial banks and trust fund. † Beginning in January 2010, comprises currency outside depository corporations and demand deposits of other financial corporations, public nonfinancial corporations, and private sector with commercial banks and trust fund.

Quasi Money comprises fixed deposits of other financial corporations, public nonfinancial corporations, and private sector with other depository corporations and securities other than shares issued by other depository corporations held by the private sector in national currency. † Beginning in January 2010, comprises call and fixed deposits of other financial corporations, public nonfinancial corporations, and private sector with other depository corporations.

Broad Money comprises money and quasi money.

Interest Rates:

Deposit Rate:
Average rate offered by commercial banks on three-month time deposits in national currency.

Lending Rate:
Minimum rate, fixed by the Brunei Association of Banks, charged by commercial banks on loans to preferred customers in national currency. † Beginning on May 16, 2005, the minimum rate is market determined.

Prices:

Consumer Prices:
Source: Department of Economic Planning and Development. Base Year: 2005; Geographical Coverage: all income groups and all districts of the country; Number of Items in Basket: 557 items, of which 247 food items, 310 non-food items; Basis for Weights Calculation: the basket of goods and services and the weights are derived from the Household Expenditure Survey (HES) 2005. The CPI calculation uses the chained index method, whereby the ratio of the average prices of the current month and the previous month is multiplied with the index value of the previous month.

International Transactions:

Source: Department of Economic Planning and Development. Based on customs data.

Balance of Payments:
Income excludes receipts by government.

National Accounts:

Source: Department of Economic Planning and Development. Series based on the recommendations of the *1993 SNA* and based to the year 2000.

Bulgaria   918

Date of Fund Membership:
September 25, 1990

Standard Sources:
Bulgarian National Bank
National Statistical Institute
Eurostat

Exchange Rates:

On July 5, 1999 the lev was re-denominated: the post-July 5, 1999 lev is equal to 1,000 of the pre-July 5, 1999 leva. All data are expressed in terms of the post-July 5, 1999 lev.

Official Rate: (End of Period and Period Average):
Beginning July 1, 1997, the official rate is pegged to the deutsche mark at one Bulgarian lev (LEV) per 1 deutsche mark. When the euro became the legal tender in the Federal Republic of Germany, the official exchange rate of the lev to the euro was determined by the conversion rate of the deutsche mark to the euro. The established exchange rate, published by the Bulgarian National Bank in the State Gazette, is LEV 1 per euro 0.5113 (euro 1 per LEV 1.95583). Prior to July 1997, data refer to market rate, calculated as the volume weighted average of the previous day's interbank rates.

International Liquidity:

Gold (National Valuation) (line 1and) is the U.S. dollar value of official holdings of gold which, beginning in February 2005, are valued at market prices. †For the period July 1997 to January 2005, gold was valued at either 500 Bulgarian leva per fine troy ounce or at the end-of-period London gold market price, whichever is lower. † Prior to July 1997, gold was valued at US$300 per fine troy ounce.

Central Bank:

Consists of the Bulgarian National Bank only.

Data are based on a new accounting system and compiled in accordance with the European Central Bank's framework for monetary statistics using the national residency approach.

Other Depository Corporations:

Beginning in February 2007, comprises credit institutions (licensed commercial banks) and monetary market funds, which represent all resident units classified as other monetary financial institutions (other MFIs) in accordance with *1995 ESA* standards. Prior to February 2007, comprises only licensed commercial banks (non-operating banks were excluded).

Data are based on a new accounting system and are compiled in accordance with the European Central Bank's framework for monetary statistics using the national residency approach.

Depository Corporations:

See notes on central bank and other depository corporations.

Monetary Aggregates:

Broad Money:

Broad Money calculated from the liability data in the sections for the central bank and other depository corporations.

Money (National Definitions):

M1 comprises currency outside MFIs and overnight deposits of non-central government non-MFI resident sectors with resident MFIs.

M2 is equal to M1 plus deposits with agreed maturity up to two years and deposits redeemable at notice with terms up to three months of non-central government non-MFI resident sectors with resident MFIs.

M3 is equal to M2 plus marketable instruments (which comprise repurchase agreements contracted by MFIs with non-government non-MFI resident sectors, shares/units of money market funds, and debt securities issued by resident MFIs with maturity of up to two years).

Interest Rates:

Central Bank Policy Rate (End of Period):

Data refer to Basic Interest Rate (BIR). BIR is the official reference rate announced by the Bulgarian National Bank (BNB) and published in the State Gazette. † Since February 1, 2005, BIR is equal to the arithmetic average of the LEONIA reference rates for the business days of the previous calendar month (the LEONIA (Lev OverNight Index Average) reference rate is a weighted average of rates on all overnight unsecured lending transactions in the interbank market in Bulgaria by a representative panel of banks). The BIR is in effect from the first to the last day of the calendar month to which it refers. † During period July 1, 1997 (the date of establishment of the currency board) to January 31, 2005, BIR was set equal to the annual yield on the three-month government securities based on the outcome of the primary auction. This rate was in effect from the day of the auction and was recalculated based on the results of the subsequent auction. † Prior to January 1997, BIR was one of BNB's main policy instruments and was determined by its Board of Directors based on the annual yield on short-term (7 to 28-day) government securities.

Money Market Rate:

Beginning in December 2004, the LEONIA reference rate. † Prior to December 2004 weighted average rate on deposits transacted in the interbank market.

Treasury Bill Rate:

Beginning in January 2006, weighted average yield to maturity on treasury bonds with terms over one year traded in secondary market. † Prior to January 2006, weighted average yield on newly issued government bonds with terms over one year sold at primary auctions.

Deposit Rate:

Beginning in February 2000, weighted average rate offered by credit institutions on new one-month deposits in leva to the household sector. † Prior to February 2000, weighted average rate offered by credit institutions on time deposits in leva to the non-financial corporations and the household sectors.

Lending Rate:

Weighted average rate charged by credit institutions on new loans (including overdrafts) in leva to the non-financial corporations and household sectors with terms up to one year.

Government Bond Yield:

Beginning in January 2006, weighted average yield to maturity on treasury bonds with terms over one year traded in secondary market. † Prior to January 2006, weighted average yield on newly issued government bonds with terms over one year sold at primary auctions.

Prices and Production:

Share Prices (End of Month):

Data refer to the SOFIX index, base October 20, 2000. The SOFIX is a correlation of the sum of market capitalization of the companies within the SOFIX index portfolio on the current day and the sum of the market capitalization of the same on the previous day. The issues should have been traded on the regulated markets for three months at least and the market capitalization of each issue should not be less than BGN 2 million.

Producer Prices:

Source: National Statistical Institute. Weights Reference Period: weights are updated every five years; Sectoral Coverage: mining, manufacturing industries, the production and distribution of electricity, steam, natural gas and air conditioning supply; Number of Items in the Basket: the sampling method compilation involves a three-stage sampling process: first of PROD-COM groups, second of reporting units, and then of specific products (transactions); Basis for Calculation: weights are based on the mandatory Annual Structural Business Statistics (SBS) survey.

Consumer Prices:

Source: National Statistical Institute. Weights Reference Period: 2011; Geographical Coverage: entire country; Number of Items in Basket: 664; Basis for Calculation: the commodity basket is reweighted each year based on the annual Household Budget Survey (HBS) data.

International Transactions:

Source: Bulgarian National Bank. Based on customs data.

Government Finance:

Cash data cover operations of consolidated central government, comprising budgetary, extrabudgetary, and social security funds. † Beginning in 1994, quarterly and annual data are reported by the Bulgarian National Bank and are taken from Eurostat and unpublished reports on the operations of the consolidated central government. Beginning in 1996, annual and quarterly data are obtained by aggregating monthly data. Beginning in January 2006, central government data is reported in the *GFSM 2001* Statement of Sources and Uses of Cash as compiled by the Ministry of Finance. Monthly central government debt data are compiled according to the national methodology, at face value, and are the same as those disseminated on the SDDS national summary data page. Beginning 1999, preliminary accrual data on general government are presented in the *GFSM 2001* Operations Statement and Balance Sheet as compiled by Eurostat. The fiscal year ends December 31. Beginning in January 2002, general government data are presented in the *GFSM 2001* Statement of Sources and Uses of Cash. The fiscal year ends December 31.

National Accounts:

Source: National Statistical Institute. As indicated by the country, data are compiled according to the recommendations of the *1995 ESA* and the *1993 SNA*. Chain linked GDP volume measures are expressed in 2005 prices.

Burkina Faso   748

Date of Fund Membership:
May 2, 1963

Standard Source:
Banque Centrale des Etats de l'Afrique de l'Ouest (Central Bank of West African States
Institut National de la Statistique et de la Démographie
Burkina Faso is a member of the West African Economic and Monetary Union, together with Benin, Côte d'Ivoire, Guinea-Bissau, Mali, Niger, Senegal, and Togo. The Union, which was established in 1962, has a common central bank, the Central Bank of West African States (BCEAO), with headquarters in Dakar, and national branches in the member states. Mali and Guinea-Bissau joined the Union on June 1, 1984 and May 2, 1997, respectively.

Exchange Rates:

Official Rate: (End of Period and Period Average):
Prior to January 1999, the official rate was pegged to the French franc. On January 12, 1994, the CFA franc was devalued to CFAF 100 per French franc from CFAF 50 at which it had been fixed since 1948. From January 1, 1999, the CFAF is pegged to the euro at a rate of CFA franc 655.957 per euro.

International Liquidity:

Gold is revalued on a quarterly basis at the rate communicated by the BCEAO, which corresponds to the lowest average fixing in the London market.

Monetary Authorities:

Comprises the national branch of the BCEAO only. The amount of currency outside banks is estimated by subtracting from the amount of CFA franc notes issued by Burkina Faso the estimated amounts of Burkina Faso's currency in the cash held by the banks of all member countries of the Union.

Deposit Money Banks:

Comprises commercial banks and specialized development banks, and includes certain banking operations of the Treasury and the Post Office. The Treasury accepts customs duty bills (reported separately in *line 22d.i*). Through its many branches, the Postal Checking System acts as the main depository for the private sector in the interior of Burkina Faso. *Claims on the Private Sector (line 22d)* include doubtful and litigious debts. † Beginning in 1979, *Central Government Deposits (line 26d)* include the deposits of the public establishments of an administrative or social nature (EPAS) and exclude those of the savings bank; *Demand and Time Deposits (lines 24 and 25)* include deposits of the savings bank and exclude deposits of EPAS; and *Claims on Private Sector (line 22d)* exclude claims on other financial institutions.

Monetary Survey:

The data reported agree with Banque Centrale des Etats de l'Afrique de l'Ouest (Central Bank of West African States), aggregates, as given in the table on the position of the monetary institutions. Valuation differences exist as a result of the *IFS* calculations of reserve position in the Fund and the SDR holdings, both components of *line 11*, based on Fund record. † Beginning in 1979, *Claims on Other Financial Institutions (line 32f)* includes claims of deposit money banks on other financial institutions; see deposit money bank notes for explanation of other break symbols.

Other Banking Institutions:

Liquid Liabilities (line 55l): † See notes on deposit money banks and monetary survey.

Interest Rates:

Discount Rate (End of Period):
Basic discount rate offered by the BCEAO.

Repurchase Agreement Rate (End of Period):
Rate on repurchase agreements between the BCEAO and the banks.

Money Market Rate:
Rate paid on overnight interbank advances.

Deposit Rate:
Rate offered by banks on time deposits of CFAF 500,000–2,000,000 for under six months.

Prices and Labor:

Consumer Prices:
Source: Banque Centrale des Etats de l'Afrique de l'Ouest. Weights Reference Period: 2008; Geographical Coverage: City of Ouagadougou; Number of Items in Basket: 722; Basis for Calculation: The weights are derived from a household expenditure survey conducted in the city of Ouagadougou in 2008.

International Transactions:

Trade data for goods are from the Institut National de la Statistique et de la démographie. Trade data for services are from the BCEAO.

Government Finance:

Data are derived from information provided by Banque Centrale des Etats de l'Afrique de l'Ouest (Central Bank of West African States), and cover budgetary central government and capital expenditure financed by foreign grants. The fiscal year ends December 31.

National Accounts:

Source: Institut National de la Statistique et de la Démographie. Data are prepared in accordance with the 1968 United Nations System of National Accounts.

Burundi   618

Date of Fund Membership:

September 28, 1963

Standard Source:

Central Bank
Institut de Statisques et d'Etudes Economiques

Exchange Rates:

Official Rate: (End of Period and Period Average):
The official rate is pegged to an undisclosed basket of currencies and is adjusted from time to time.

International Liquidity:

Gold (National Valuation) (line 1and) is obtained by converting the value in national currency terms, as reported in the country's standard sources, using the prevailing exchange rate, as given in *line* **ae** or **we.** This line follows national valuation procedures which revalue gold semiannually beginning December 1977 at the average price of the opening and closing quotations on the London market of the last day of each period.

Central Bank:

Consists of the Banque de la République du Burundi (BRB) only, consolidating the accounts of headquarters and its two branches in the country.
Data are based on a standardized report form for central banks, which accords with the concepts and definitions of the IMF's *Monetary and Financial Statistics Manual (MFSM),* 2000. Departures from the *MFSM* methodology are explained below.
Claims on Other Depository Corporations includes the net position of the claims of the BRB with banks in liquidation.
Claims on Central Government excludes accrued interest before maturity on credits to the central government.

Other Depository Corporations:

Comprises commercial banks. Data exclude microfinance institutions allowed to collect deposits from the public.
Data are based on a standardized report form for other deposi-

tory corporations, which accords with the concepts and definitions of the *Monetary and Financial Statistics Manual (MFSM).* For other depository corporations in Burundi, departures from the *MFSM* methodology are explained below.
Accrual accounting and sectorization of counterpart transactors are not consistently applied by all reporting corporations.

Depository Corporations:

Consolidation of central bank and other depository corporations.

Other Financial Corporations:

Comprises finance companies ("établissements financiers" in accordance with Burundi's banking law). Data exclude insurance corporations, exchange bureaus, microfinance institutions allowed to grant credits, pension funds, and solidarity funds. In April 2002 and in May 2003, a finance company became a commercial bank.
Data are based on a standardized report form for other financial corporations, which accords with the concepts and definitions of the *Monetary and Financial Statistics Manual (MFSM).* For other financial corporations in Burundi, departures from the *MFSM* are explained below.
Accrual accounting and sectorization of counterpart transactors are not consistently applied by all reporting corporations.

Monetary Aggregates:

Broad Money:
Broad Money calculated from the liability data in the sections for the central bank and other depository corporations accords with the concepts and definitions of the *MFSM.* Broad money includes demand and term deposits of nonfinancial corporations and households with the postal administration (Comptes de Chèques Postaux). Broad money is consistent with M3 described below.

Money (National Definitions):
M1 *(means of payment)* comprises banknotes and coins held by the public; demand deposits in national currency of nonfinancial corporations, households, other financial corporations, and local government with depository corporations; and demand deposits of nonfinancial corporations and households with the postal administration (Comptes de Chèques Postaux).
M2 *(money stock in national currency)* comprises M1 and time and savings deposits in national currency of nonfinancial corporations, households, and other financial corporations with other depository corporations.
M3 *(money stock in national and foreign currency)* comprises M2 and foreign currency deposits of nonfinancial corporations, households, and other financial corporations with other depository corporations.

Interest Rates:

Discount Rate (End of Period):
The discount rate is applicable for the refinancing of short-term commercial claims held by commercial banks.

Treasury Bill Rate:
Rate on one-month treasury bills.

Lending Rate:
Rate offered by commercial banks on short-term cash advances (two years or less).

Prices:

Consumer Prices:
Source: Institut de Statisques et d'Etudes Economiques. Weights Reference Period: January 1991; Geographical Coverage: Bujumbura, Gitega, Muyinga, Ngozi, Ruyigi, Rugombo and Rumonge; Basis for Calculation: household consumption expenditure survey conducted in 1991.

International Transactions:

All trade data are from Institut de Statisques et d'Etudes Economiques. *Value of Exports* and *Imports* are based on customs data.

Government Finance:

Data are derived from the Central Bank and cover central government operations. They comprise receipts and outlays from the ordinary and extraordinary budget as well as Treasury receipts and outlays from extrabudgetary accounts. Data on government operations do not cover operations of the National Social Security Institute or of other central government agencies with own budgets. † Beginning in 1992, data are presented in a new format and are not directly comparable with data for earlier periods. Debt data cover outstanding debt of the nonfinancial public sector comprising direct government debt, onlent government debt, and debt guaranteed by the government. The fiscal year ends December 31.

National Accounts:

Source: Institut de Statisques et d'Etudes Economiques.

Cambodia   522

Date of Fund Membership:

December 31, 1969

Standard Source:

National Bank of Cambodia
National Institute of Statistics

Exchange Rates:

Official Rate: (End of Period and Period Average):
Official buying rate of the National Bank of Cambodia (NBC).

International Liquidity:

† Prior to 1994, *Foreign Exchange (line 1d.d)* excludes portion of official reserves that was held by the Foreign Trade Bank. Beginning in 1994, official foreign reserves were centralized at the National Bank of Cambodia.

Central Bank:

Consists of the National Bank of Cambodia (NBC) only. Beginning in July 2004, covers the accounts of the NBC's head office and provincial branches. Prior to July 2004, the NBC's provincial branches were classified as other depository corporations.
† Beginning in December 2004, data are based on a standardized report form (SRF) for central banks, which accords with the concepts and definitions of the IMF's *Monetary and Financial Statistics Manual (MFSM)*. 2000.

For December 2001 through November 2004, data have less conformity with the *MFSM* methodology and therefore are not strictly comparable to data for later periods.

Other Depository Corporations:

Comprises commercial banks, a rural development bank, branches of foreign banks, and NBC's provincial branches. Beginning in July 2004, excludes the NBC's provincial branches, which were reclassified as part of the central bank. Data exclude the microfinance institutions which accept deposits.
† Beginning in December 2004, data are based on a standardized report form (SRF) for other depository corporations, which accords with the concepts and definitions of the IMF's *Monetary and Financial Statistics Manual (MFSM)*.
For December 2001 through November 2004, data have less conformity with the *MFSM* methodology and therefore are not strictly comparable to data for later periods.

Depository Corporations:

† See notes on central bank and other depository corporations.

Monetary Aggregates:

Broad Money:
Broad Money calculated from the liability data in the sections for the central bank and other depository corporations accords with the concepts and definitions of the *MFSM* and is consistent with M2 described below.

Money (National Definitions):
M1 comprises currency outside banks and demand deposits of other financial corporations, public nonfinancial corporations, and private sector with the NBC and other depository corporations. *Currency outside banks* is equal to the amount of domestic currency notes issued by the NBC *less* domestic currency note holdings of the NBC and other depository corporations.
M2 comprises M1 and quasi-money. *Quasi-money* comprises time, savings, and foreign-currency deposits of other financial corporations, public nonfinancial corporations, and private sector with the NBC and other depository corporations.

Interest Rates:

Deposit Rate:
Simple average of rates on domestic-currency savings deposits reported by the ten banks with the largest deposit holdings up to December 2006. Since January 2007, NBC started compiling portfolio-weighted interest rates using data from all banks.

Lending Rate:
Simple average of rates on foreign currency loans to private enterprises reported by ten banks with the largest deposit holdings up to December 2006. Since January 2007, NBC started compiling portfolio-weighted interest rates using data from all banks.

Prices and Labor:

Consumer Prices:
Source: National Institute of Statistics. Weight Reference Period: October-December 2006; Geographical Coverage: Phnom Penh and five provincial cities; Number of Items in Basket: 225 (227 for Phnom Penh); Basis for Calculation: weights are based on the 2004 Cambodian socio-economic survey.

International Transactions:

All trade data are from the National Bank of Cambodia.

Government Finance:

Monthly accrual data are provided by the Ministry of Finance. The data cover the operations of central government. Preliminary monthly GFS data are compiled from the table of financial operations (TOFE). Adjustment lines in the monthly TOFE can result in the appearance of negative amounts in expenses in the monthly GFS table. Annual data appearing in *IFS* are obtained by aggregating monthly data. The negative amounts are rectified in the annual data published in the *GFS Yearbook*. The fiscal year ends December 31.

National Accounts:

Source: National Institute of Statistics.

Cameroon   622

Date of Fund Membership:

July 10, 1963

Standard Sources:

Banque des Etats d'Afrique Centrale (BEAC) (Bank of the Central African States)

Institut National de la Statistique (National Institute of Statistics)

Exchange Rates:

Official Rate: (End of Period and Period Average):

Prior to January 1999, the official rate was pegged to the French franc. On January 12, 1994, the CFA franc was devalued to CFAF 100 per French franc from CFAF 50 at which it had been fixed since 1948. From January 1, 1999, the CFAF is pegged to the euro at a rate of CFA franc 655.957 per euro.

International Liquidity:

Gold (National Valuation) (line 1and) is obtained by converting the value in national currency, as reported in the country's standard sources, using the prevailing exchange rate, as given in *line* **ae**. Prior to January 1999, the national currency/dollar conversion rates utilized for balance sheet purposes are used. These conversion rates differ from the prevailing exchange rates reported in *IFS*. This line follows the national valuation procedure which corresponds to that of the Bank of France (*cf* the international liquidity note on the *IFS* page for France).

Central Bank:

Consists of the national office of the Banque des Etats de l'Afrique Centrale (BEAC), consolidating the accounts of all its branches located in Yaoundé, Douala, Bafoussam, Garoua, Limbe, and Nkongsamba.

Data are based on a standardized report form for central banks, which accords with the concepts and definitions of the IMF's *Monetary and Financial Statistics Manual (MFSM)*, 2000. Departures from the *MFSM* methodology are explained below.

Held-to-maturity securities are valued at amortized cost rather than at current market price or fair value.

Other Depository Corporations:

Comprises commercial banks. Data exclude credit unions and microfinance institutions which accept deposits.

Data are based on a standardized report form for other depository corporations, which accords with the concepts and definitions of the *Monetary and Financial Statistics Manual (MFSM)*. For other depository corporations in Cameroon, departures from the *MFSM* methodology are explained below.

Financial assets and liabilities for which currency breakdown is unavailable are allocated to assets and liabilities denominated in national currency.

Held-to-maturity securities are valued at acquisition cost rather than at current market price or fair value.

Depository Corporations:

See notes on central bank and other depository corporations.

Monetary Aggregates:

Broad Money:

Broad Money calculated from the liability data in the sections for the central bank and other depository corporations accords with the concepts and definitions of the *MFSM*. Broad money differs from M2 described below as M2 excludes holdings of currency by the central government.

Money (National Definitions):

M1 comprises currency in circulation and transferable deposits. Transferable deposits refer to current account deposits of other financial corporations, public nonfinancial corporations, and private sector with depository corporations in national currency.

M2 comprises M1 and quasi-money. Quasi-money refers to fixed and saving deposits of other financial corporations, public nonfinancial corporations, and private sector with depository corporations in national currency.

Interest Rates:

Discount Rate (End of Period):

Basic rediscount rate offered by the BEAC. † Beginning in July 1994, rate charged by the BEAC on refinancing operations to financial institutions.

Deposit Rate:

Minimum rate offered by other depository corporations on savings accounts.

Lending Rate:

Maximum rate charged by financial institutions on loans.

Prices and Production:

Industrial Production:

Source: National Institute of Statistics. Laspeyres-type index. The industrial production index (IPI) covers the manufacturing industry as well as the production and distribution of water, electricity, gas, and oil refining. It measures changes in the volume of production of a basket of 242 goods representative of the 18 manufacturing branches covered. Data are collected through on-site visits to 170 enterprises in Cameroon. The IPI product weights in the index are based on the gross value added calculated on the basis of the 1995/96 Annual Survey of Industry (EAI).

Consumer Prices:

Source: National Institute of Statistics. Weights reference period: 1993; Geographical Coverage: weighted average of the price indices of five major towns, Yaoundé, Douala, Bafoussam, Bamenda, and Garoua; Number of Items in Basket: 266; Basis for Calculation: Cameroonian Household Survey of 1996, conducted on 1,733 households.

International Transactions:

All trade data are from Bank of the Central African States. Data on total exports may not include all crude oil exports.

Government Finance:

Annual data are as reported for the *Government Finance Statistics Yearbook (GFSY)* and cover budgetary central government. Annual data refer to a fiscal year different from calendar year. The fiscal year ends June 30.

National Accounts:

Line 99b includes a statistical discrepancy. The framework of the national accounts for data corresponding to the new weights reference period 1989/90 is patterned on the *1993 SNA*.

Canada   156

Date of Fund Membership:

December 27, 1945

Standard Sources:

Bank of Canada
Statistics Canada

Exchange Rates:

Market Rate (End of Period and Period Average):
The exchange rate floats independently. Midpoint rate quoted by the Bank of Canada at noon in the Montreal-Toronto interbank exchange market.

International Liquidity:

Lines 7a.d and *7b.d* comprise Canadian dollar and foreign currency accounts of nonresidents booked in Canada.

Central Bank:

Consists of the Bank of Canada (BOC) only.
Data are based on a standardized report form (SRF) for central banks, which accords with the concepts and definitions of the IMF's *Monetary and Financial Statistics Manual (MFSM)*, 2000. Data in the SRF format are compiled from pre-SRF data which are not fully based on *MFSM* methodology. Departures from the *MFSM* methodology are explained below.
Financial assets and liabilities for which economic sectorization is unavailable are allocated to the economic sector assumed to have the largest volume of transactions in the category.
Claims on and liabilities to nonresidents are determined based on the currency of the transaction rather than residency of the institutional unit.
Currency in circulation includes a small amount of notes issued by the government of Canada and banks before the BOC became the sole issuer of currency in Canada and assumed the liability for these notes.
Shares and Other Equity comprises funds contributed by owners and statutory reserves only.
Accounts receivable and payable are included in *Other Items (Net)* rather than in the BOC's claims on or liabilities to the corresponding sectors.
Accrued interest is included in *Other items (Net)* rather than in the outstanding amounts of the financial assets and liabilities.
Securities other than shares are valued at acquisition cost amortized for premium or discount rather than at current market price of fair value.

Other Depository Corporations:

Comprises chartered banks, trust and mortgage loan companies, local credit unions, life insurance company annuities, government owned savings institutions, money market mutual funds, and non-money market mutual funds. Data exclude caisses populaires, which have small amounts of short-term liabilities.
Data are based on a standardized report form (SRF) for other depository corporations, which accords with the concepts and definitions of the *Monetary and Financial Statistics Manual (MFSM)*. Data in the SRF format are compiled from data contained in balance sheet of other depository corporations and are not fully based on the *MFSM* methodology. For other depository corporations in Canada, departures from the *MFSM* methodology are explained below.
Data for trust and mortgage loan companies and local credit unions are available only on a quarterly basis. Data for the intervening months are estimated by interpolation. Data for the two months after the latest quarter are estimated by extrapolation.
Data include only the deposits with life insurance company annuities and government owned savings institutions and shares issued by money market mutual funds and non-money market mutual funds. The corresponding assets to the deposits and shares are included in *Other Items (Net)* rather than allocated to the corresponding economic sectors.
Financial assets and liabilities for which economic sectorization is unavailable are allocated to the economic sector assumed to have the largest volume of transactions in the category.
Claims on Nonresidents and *Liabilities to Nonresidents* include some accounts in foreign currency with resident economic sectors.
Claims on Private Sector includes financial assets with public nonfinancial corporations.
Accounts receivable and payable are included in *Other Items (Net)* rather than in the other depository corporations' claims on or liabilities to the corresponding economic sectors.
Accrued interest is included in *Other items (Net)* rather than in the outstanding amounts of the financial assets and liabilities.
Securities other than shares are valued at acquisition cost rather than at market price or fair value.
Valuation accounts are included in *Other Items (Net)* rather than in *Shares and Other Equity*.
Loans are reported net of provisions.

Depository Corporations:

See notes on central bank and other depository corporations.

Other Financial Corporations:

Comprises nondepository credit intermediaries, insurance companies, segregated funds, and investment funds. Nondepository credit intermediaries are establishments, both public (government sponsored enterprises) and private, that primarily engage in extending credit or lending funds raised by credit- market borrowing and by borrowing from financial corporations other than themselves.

Data are based on a standardized report form (SRF) for other financial corporations, which accords with the concepts and definitions of the *Monetary and Financial Statistics Manual (MFSM)*. Data in the SRF format are compiled from data contained in the balance sheets of other financial corporations and are not fully based on the *MFSM* methodology. For other financial corporations in Canada, departures from the *MFSM* methodology are explained below.

Data for other financial corporations are available only on a quarterly basis. Data for the intervening months are estimated by interpolation.

Financial derivatives are excluded from the data.

Financial assets and liabilities for which economic sectorization is unavailable are allocated to the economic sector assumed to have the largest volume of transaction in the category.

Claims on Nonresidents and *Liabilities to Nonresidents* include some accounts in foreign currency with resident economic sectors.

Claims on Depository Corporations includes some holdings of cash. Financial assets and liabilities with public nonfinancial corporations are included in *Other Items (Net*.

Retained earnings, current year result, general and special reserves, and valuation adjustment are included in *Other Items (Net)* rather than in *Shares and Other Equity*.

Accrued interest is included in *Other items (Net)* rather than in the outstanding amounts of the financial assets and liabilities.

Some securities other than shares are valued at acquisition cost rather than at market price or fair value.

Loans are reported net of provisions.

Financial Corporations:

See notes on central bank, other depository corporations, and other financial corporations.

Monetary Aggregates:

Broad Money:

Broad Money calculated from the liability data in the sections for the central bank and other depository corporations differs from *M2++* described below because broad money includes foreign currency deposits, non-personal term deposits held at chartered banks, and does not include continuity adjustments. In addition, broad money may be overstated due to the estimates to allocate deposits to money holding sectors described in the note on the other depository corporations.

Money (National Definitions):

The gross monetary aggregates include float. The float denotes funds in transition between the time a check is deposited or a payment is sent and the time the payment is settled. Continuity adjustments are made to reconstruct past data and make them consistent with how the current data are structured. Changes in the financial industry can result in new data that are inconsistent with the former presentation causing significant discontinuities in the series and making the data useless for econometric work. The Bank of Canada adjusts its monetary aggregates each time one of the following events takes place: the acquisition of a trust company by a bank, the acquisition of an entity in a sector that was not previously included in the monetary aggregates (i.e., an investment dealer), the formation of a bank from a trust company or companies, and the acquisition of a bank by a trust company. Monetary aggregates are also adjusted to exclude interbank deposits. Continuity adjustments have been made to eliminate discontinuities resulting from the 1980 Bank Act revision and the introduction of a new reporting system for the banks.

M1+ Gross comprises currency outside banks, personal and non-personal chequable deposits held at chartered banks, all chequable deposits at trust and mortgage loan companies, credit unions and caisses populaires (excluding deposits of these institutions) and continuity adjustments.

M1++ Gross comprises M1+ Gross, non-chequable notice deposits held at chartered banks, all non-chequable deposits at trust and mortgage loan companies, credit unions and caisses populaires less interbank non-chequable notice deposits and continuity adjustments.

M2 Gross comprises currency outside banks, personal deposits and non-personal demand and notice deposits held at chartered banks and continuity adjustments.

M2+ Gross comprises M2 Gross, deposits of non-banks (trust and mortgage loan companies, government savings institutions, deposits and shares at credit unions and caisses populaires, life insurance company individual annuities and money market mutual funds) and continuity adjustments.

M2++Gross comprises M2+Gross, Canada Savings Bonds and other retail instruments, cumulative net contributions to mutual funds other than Canadian dollar money market mutual funds (which are already included in M2+ Gross) and continuity adjustments.

M3 Gross comprises M2 Gross, non-personal term and foreign currency deposits of residents with chartered banks, and continuity adjustments.

Interest Rates:

Central Bank Policy Rate (End of Period):

Refers to the overnight money market (financing) rate, which is a measure or estimate of the collateralized overnight rate compiled at the end of the day by the Bank of Canada through a survey of major participants in the overnight market. It comprises the weighted-average funding cost of major money market dealers, including (SPRAs) with the Bank of Canada and trades that are conducted directly between dealers.

Borrowing Facility Rate (End of Period):

Rate at which the BOC is prepared to respond to requests of chartered banks for temporary advances and enter into purchase and resale agreements with money market dealers. Rate is se at ¼ of 1 percent above the latest average rate on three-month treasury bills established at the preceding weekly tender.

Money Market Rate:

Rate refers to the overnight money market financing rate. Monthly figures are the average for the seven days ending the last Wednesday of the month.

Corporate Paper Rate:
Rate of 90-day prime corporate paper. Quarterly and annual data are averages of data for the last Wednesday in each month.

Treasury Bill Rate:
Weighted average of the yields on successful bids for three-month bills. Monthly data related to the tender rates of the last Wednesday of the month.

Savings Rate:
Rate offered by chartered banks on non-checkable savings deposits in national currency.

Deposit Rate:
Rate offered by chartered banks on 90-day deposits in national currency.

Lending Rate:
Rate that chartered banks charge on large business loans to their most creditworthy customers; when there are differences among banks, the most typical rate is taken. Monthly figures are for the last Wednesday of the month.

Government Bond Yield:
Average yield to maturity. Medium-term series refers to issues with original maturity of 3–5 years. Long-term series refers to issues with original maturity of 10 years and over.

Prices, Production, Labor:

Share Prices (Period Average and End of Month):
Data refer to closing quotations on the Toronto Stock Exchange for a composite of 300 shares, base 1975.

Prices: Industry Selling:
Source: Statistics Canada. Data on aggregate industry selling prices (gross weighted), weights reference period 1997, covering about 90 percent of the value of manufacturing output in 1997.

Industrial Product Price Index:
Source: Statistics Canada. Weights Reference Period: 2002; Sectoral Coverage: manufacturing sectors; Number of Items in Basket: 944 Principal Commodity Aggregates (PCGAs); Basis for Calculation: weights are derived from shipment values reported for the 2002 Annual Survey of Manufactures (ASM) and edited to conform to the industry classification (i.e. NAICS). The weights are generally revised every five years.

Consumer Prices:
Source: Statistics Canada. Weights Reference Period: 2002; Geographical Coverage: All provinces of Canada, and the territorial cities of Whitehorse, Yellowknife, and Iqaluit; Number of Items in Basket: 177 item categories; Basis for Calculation: Weights are derived from 2009 Survey of Household Spending and are generally revised every four years. The index is re-based approximately every ten years.

Industrial Production, Seasonally Adjusted:
Statistics Canada. Weights Reference Period: 1997; Sectoral Coverage: entire economy of Canada; Basis for Calculation: GDP in constant 1997 prices based on the production approach for all industries using the 1997 North American Industrial Classification.

Gold Production:
Data are from *Statistics Canada* and are expressed in kilograms.

Wages: Hourly Earnings:
Source: Statistics Canada. Data in dollars per hour, covering manufacturing firms employing 20 or more persons. Data refer to the last pay period of the month including overtime, vacation pay, cost of living, allowances, etc.

Manufacturing Employment:
Source: Statistics Canada. Data covering manufacturing firms employing 20 or more persons. Data relate to the last pay period of the month.

International Transactions:

Exports:
Statistics Canada data on merchandise exports multiplied by a factor for inland freight adjustment, derived from the *Balance of Payments Statistics Yearbook*. Beginning January 1990, the inland freight adjustment is not made to these data, because the valuation basis for exports was revised to include these expenses.

Imports, f.o.b.:
Statistics Canada data on merchandise imports.
The general trade indices are Statistics Canada data. The *Unit Value* indices are constant weighted and are calculated as a Laspeyres index, weights reference period 1997. The *Volume* indices are Statistics Canada Laspeyres indices, seasonally adjusted, weights reference period: 1997.

Government Finance:

Quarterly general government data are provided by Statistics Canada and are derived from the national accounts. The data are prepared on a calendar year basis and therefore differ from the Canadian fiscal year, which begins on April 1.

National Accounts:

Data are derived from Statistics Canada. *Lines 99a.c* and *99b.c* include a statistical discrepancy. As indicated by the country, from 1995 onwards data have been revised following the implementation of the *1993 SNA*. GDP chain linked volume measures are calculated based on prices and weights of the previous year, using Laspeyres formula in general. Quarterly data are seasonally adjusted at annual rates.

Cape Verde   624

Date of Fund Membership:
November 20, 1978

Standard Source:
Bank of Cape Verde
Ministry of Finance
Instituto Nacional de Estatística

Exchange Rates:

Official Rate: (End of Period and Period Average):
On March 30, 1998, the Cape Verde escudo began to be pegged to the Portuguese escudo. Beginning January 1, 1999, the official rate is pegged to the euro at a rate of CVEsc 110.27 per euro.

International Liquidity:

Data on foreign exchange *(line 1d.d)* are derived from data denominated in national currency from components of monetary authorities' foreign assets *(line 11)*, using the end-of-period market rate *(line **ae**)* for conversion to U.S. dollars.

Central Bank:

Consists of the Bank of Cape Verde (BCV) only.

Data are based on a standardized report form (SRF) for central banks, which accords with the concepts and definitions of the IMF's *Monetary and Financial Statistics Manual (MFSM)*, 2000. Departures from the *MFSM* methodology are explained below.

Financial assets and liabilities for which economic sectorization is unavailable are allocated to the economic sector having the largest volume of transactions in the category.

Securities other than shares are valued at acquisition cost adjusted for any amortization of premium or accretion of discounts rather than at market price. Shares and other equity are valued at acquisition cost rather than at market price. Any expected loss arising from a change in the fair value of securities other than shares and equity instruments are recognized directly in equity.

Other Depository Corporations:

Comprises commercial banks.

Data are based on a standardized report form (SRF) for other depository corporations, which accords with the concepts and definitions of the *Monetary and Financial Statistics Manual (MFSM)*. For other depository corporations in Cape Verde, departures from the *MFSM* methodology are explained below.

Financial assets and liabilities for which economic sectorization is unavailable are allocated to the economic sector having the largest volume of transactions in the category.

Where data for other depository corporations were not directly distinguished from data for other financial corporations, separation of the data was based on the characteristics of the financial asset or liability.

Depository Corporations:

See notes on central bank and other depository corporations.

Monetary Aggregates:

Broad Money:

Broad Money calculated from the liability data in the sections for the central bank and other depository corporations and differs from the M2 described below because of the money holder/issuer classification used in M2.

Money (National Definitions):

Base Money comprises notes and coins in circulation outside the BCV, deposits of other depository corporations with the BCV in national and foreign currency, and central bank securities held by other depository corporations.

M1 comprises notes and coins in circulation outside depository corporations and demand deposits of other financial corporations, public nonfinancial corporations, and other resident sectors in national currency with depository corporations.

M2 comprises M1and demand deposits in foreign currency; time, saving, and restricted deposits in national and foreign currency; and payment orders of other financial corporations, public nonfinancial corporations, and other resident sectors with depository corporations.

Interest Rates:

Rediscount Rate (End of Period):

Rate at which the BCV lends to commercial banks in national currency.

Treasury Bill Rate:

Average yield on 182-day treasury bills denominated in national currency.

Deposit Rate:

Maximum rate offered by commercial banks on 90-day time deposits. † Beginning in January 1995, maximum rate offered by commercial banks on 61- to 90-day time deposits. † Beginning in May 2006, weighted average rate offered by commercial banks on 31- to 90-day deposits in national currency.

Lending Rate:

Maximum rate charged by commercial banks on 90-day loans. † Beginning in May 2006, weighted average rate offered by commercial banks on 90- to 181-day loans in national currency.

Prices:

Consumer Prices:

Source: Instituto Nacional de Estatística. Weights Reference Period: 2002; Geographical Coverage: regions of Santiago, São Vicente, and Santo Antão; Basis for Calculation: Household Expenditure and Income Survey (*IDRF*), conducted between October 2001 and October 2002.

International Transactions:

Source: Bank of Cape Verde.

Government Finance:

Source: Ministry of Finance. Quarterly data are derived from the accounting system of the Ministry of Finance. Data for budgetary central government also cover extrabudgetary central government units and entities.

National Accounts:

Source: Instituto Nacional de Estatística. Data are prepared in accordance with the 1968 United Nations System of National Accounts.

CEMAC   758

The treaty establishing the Central African Economic and Monetary Community (Communauté économique et Monétaire de l'Afrique Centrale (CEMAC)) was signed in March 1994 and entered into force on August 1999, after its ratification by the six member states: Cameroon, the Central African Republic, Chad, the Republic of Congo, Equatorial Guinea, and Gabon. The treaty was built on the achievements of the monetary cooperation arrangement in effect under the common central bank since 1959 and on those of the Customs and Economic Union of Central Africa (Union Douanière et économique de l'Afrique Centrale (UDEAC)) established in 1966.

The main objective of the treaty is to provide macroeconomic stability and credibility required to sustain the fixed exchange rate for the common currency. To achieve this objective, the member countries share a common regional central bank established in 1972, the Bank of Central African States (Banque des états de l'Afrique Centrale (BEAC)), which has issued the common currency, the CFA franc (CFA stands for "Coopération Financière en Afrique Centrale"), since 1972. Equatorial Guinea, which is not a founding member, joined the BEAC in 1985. Prior to 1972, the countries shared the Central Bank of Equatorial African States and of Cameroon (Banque Centrale des états de l'Afrique équatoriale et du Cameroun (BCEAEC)), which issued the common currency, the CFA franc (CFA stood for "Communauté Financière Africaine). The CEMAC Treaty integrates the Central African Monetary Union (Union Monétaire en Afrique Centrale (UMAC)) Covenant and the Central African Economic Union (Union Économique en Afrique Centrale (UEAC)) Covenant. The BEAC and the regional banking commission (Commission Bancaire en Afrique Centrale (COBAC)), a banking supervision agency established in 1990, are the UMAC's principal bodies.

Compared to the data published in the individual *IFS* pages for the CEMAC member countries, the consolidated data published for the CEMAC as a whole embody two major methodological differences: (1) where relevant, a CEMAC-wide residency criterion is applied instead of a national residency criterion; (2) BEAC headquarters' transactions are included in the data presented in the sections "International Liquidity" and "Monetary Authorities." BEAC headquarters' transactions are not allocated to the member countries' national data.

Date of Fund Membership:

Cameroon, the Central African Republic, Chad, the Republic of Congo, and Gabon on July 10, 1963; Equatorial Guinea on December 22, 1969.

Standard Source:

Banque des Etats d'Afrique Centrale (BEAC) (Bank of the Central African States)

Exchange Rates:

Official Rate: (End of Period and Period Average):
Prior to January 1999, the official rate was pegged to the French franc. On January 12, 1994, the CFA franc (CFAF) was devalued to CFAF 100 per French franc from CFAF 50 at which it had been fixed since 1948. From January 1, 1999 onward, the CFAF is pegged to the euro at the rate of CFAF 655.957 per euro.

Fund Position:

Data are the aggregation of positions of CEMAC countries. *SDR holdings (line 1b.d)* includes SDR holdings by BEAC headquarters.

International Liquidity:

Data include holdings by BEAC headquarters and BEAC member country national directorates. *Gold (National Valuation) (line 1and)* is obtained by converting the value in national currency, as reported by the BEAC, using the prevailing exchange rate, as given in *line* **ae**. Prior to January 1999, the national currency/dollar conversion rates utilized for balance sheet purposes were used. These conversion rates differ from the prevailing exchange rate reported in *IFS*. The national valuation procedure for gold corresponds to that of the Bank of France (see note on International Liquidity on the *IFS* page for France).

Monetary Authorities:

Data, compiled from the BEAC balance sheet, cover headquarters and national directorates.

Deposit Money Banks:

This section consolidates national data by application of a CEMAC-wide residency criterion. For more details on national data, see country notes.

Interest Rates:

Discount Rate (End of Period):
Basic rediscount rate offered by the BEAC. † Beginning July 1994, rate charged by the BEAC to financial institutions on refinancing operations.

Deposit Rate:
Minimum rate offered by deposit money banks on savings accounts.

Lending Rate:
Maximum rate charged by deposit money banks on all loans, excluding charges and fees.

Central African Rep.   626

Date of Fund Membership:
July 10, 1963

Standard Sources:

Banque des Etats d'Afrique Centrale (BEAC) (Bank of the Central African States)
Direction Générale de la Statistique, des Etudes Economiques et Sociales (Division of Statistics and Economic Studies, DSEES) Ministry for Economy, Finance, Planification, and International Cooperation

Exchange Rates:

Official Rate: (End of Period and Period Average):
Prior to January 1999, the official rate was pegged to the French franc. On January 12, 1994, the CFA franc was devalued to CFAF 100 per French franc from CFAF 50 at which it had been fixed since 1948. From January 1, 1999, the CFAF is pegged to the euro at a rate of CFA franc 655.957 per euro.

International Liquidity:

Gold (National Valuation) (line 1and) is obtained by converting the value in national currency, as reported in the country's standard sources, using the prevailing exchange rate, as given in *line* **ae**. Prior to January 1999, the national currency/dollar conversion rates utilized for balance sheet purposes are used. These conversion rates differ from the prevailing exchange rates reported in *IFS*. This line follows the national valuation procedure which corresponds to that of the Bank of France (*cf* the international liquidity note on the *IFS* page for France).

Central Bank:

Consists of the national office of the Banque des Etats de l'Afrique Centrale (BEAC), consolidating the accounts of all its branches located in Bangui and Berberati.

Data are based on a standardized report form for central banks, which accords with the concepts and definitions of the IMF's *Monetary and Financial Statistics Manual (MFSM)*, 2000. Departures from the *MFSM* methodology are explained below.

Held-to-maturity securities are valued at amortized cost rather than at current market price or fair value.

Other Depository Corporations:

Comprises commercial banks. Data exclude credit unions and microfinance institutions which accept deposits.

Data are based on a standardized report form for other depository corporations, which accords with the concepts and definitions of the *Monetary and Financial Statistics Manual (MFSM)*. For other depository corporations in Central African Republic, departures from the *MFSM* methodology are explained below.

Financial assets and liabilities for which currency breakdown is unavailable are allocated to assets and liabilities denominated in national currency.

Held-to-maturity securities are valued at acquisition cost rather than at current market price or fair value.

Depository Corporations:

See notes on central bank and other depository corporations.

Monetary Aggregates:

Broad Money:

Broad Money calculated from the liability data in the sections for the central bank and other depository corporations accords with the concepts and definitions of the *MFSM*. Broad money differs from M2 described below as M2 excludes holdings of currency by the central government.

Money (National Definitions):

M1 comprises currency in circulation and transferable deposits. Transferable deposits refer to current account deposits of other financial corporations, public nonfinancial corporations, and private sector with depository corporations in national currency.

M2 comprises M1 and quasi-money. Quasi-money refers to fixed and saving deposits of other financial corporations, public nonfinancial corporations, and private sector with depository corporations in national currency.

Interest Rates:

Discount Rate (End of Period):

Basic rediscount rate offered by the BEAC. † Beginning in July 1994, rate charged by the BEAC on refinancing operations to financial institutions.

Deposit Rate:

Minimum rate offered by other depository corporations on savings accounts.

Lending Rate:

Maximum rate charged by financial institutions on loans.

Prices and Labor:

All data on prices are from Centre National de la Statistique et des Études Économiques (National Center for Statistics and Economic Studies).

Wholesale Prices:

Data refer to the wholesale price index in Bangui, weights reference period: 1981. The weights are derived from import and production data for 1982. The index includes 63 items and covers foodstuffs, fuel, electricity, and industrial materials and products.

Consumer Prices:

Weights Reference Period: 1975/1976; Geographical coverage; all African households in the capital city of Bangui; Number of items in basket: 160 items; Basis for calculation: the weight factors/index are derived from the 1975 Budget Consumption Survey conducted among 5,000 households throughout the country.

International Transactions:

Source: Division of Statistics and Economic Studies.

National Accounts:

Source: Division of Statistics and Economic Studies. As indicated by the country, the national accounts are compiled primarily with reference to the *1993 SNA*.

Chad   628

Date of Fund Membership:

July 10, 1963

Standard Source:

Banque des Etats d'Afrique Centrale (BEAC) (Bank of the Central African States)

Institut National de la Statistique, des Études Économiques et Demographiques (National Institute of Statistical Studies Economic and Demographics)

Exchange Rates:

Official Rate: (End of Period and Period Average):

Prior to January 1999, the official rate was pegged to the French franc. On January 12, 1994, the CFA franc was devalued to CFAF 100 per French franc from CFAF 50 at which it had been fixed since 1948. From January 1, 1999, the CFAF is pegged to the euro at a rate of CFA franc 655.957 per euro.

International Liquidity:

Gold (National Valuation) (line 1and) is obtained by converting the value in national currency, as reported in the country's standard sources, using the prevailing exchange rate, as given in *line* **ae**. Prior to January 1999, the national currency/dollar conversion rates utilized for balance sheet purposes are used. These conversion rates differ from the prevailing exchange rates reported in *IFS*. This line follows the national valuation procedure which corresponds to that of the Bank of France (*cf* the international liquidity note on the *IFS* page for France).

Central Bank:

Consists of the national office of the Banque des Etats de l'Afrique Centrale (BEAC), consolidating the accounts of all its branches located in N'Djaména, Moundou, and Sarh.

Data are based on a standardized report form for central banks, which accords with the concepts and definitions of the IMF's *Monetary and Financial Statistics Manual (MFSM)*, 2000. Departures from the *MFSM* methodology are explained below.

Held-to-maturity securities are valued at amortized cost rather than at current market price or fair value.

Other Depository Corporations:

Comprises commercial banks. Data exclude credit unions and microfinance institutions which accept deposits.

Data are based on a standardized report form for other depository corporations, which accords with the concepts and definitions of the *Monetary and Financial Statistics Manual (MFSM)*. For other depository corporations in Chad, departures from the *MFSM* methodology are explained below.

Financial assets and liabilities for which currency breakdown is unavailable are allocated to assets and liabilities denominated in national currency.

Held-to-maturity securities are valued at acquisition cost rather than at current market price or fair value.

Depository Corporations:

See notes on central bank and other depository corporations.

Monetary Aggregates:

Broad Money:

Broad Money calculated from the liability data in the sections for the central bank and other depository corporations accords with the concepts and definitions of the *MFSM*. Broad money differs from M2 described below as M2 excludes holdings of currency by the central government.

Money (National Definitions):

M1 comprises currency in circulation and transferable deposits. Transferable deposits refer to current account deposits of other financial corporations, public nonfinancial corporations, and private sector with depository corporations in national currency.

M2 comprises M1 and quasi-money. Quasi-money refers to fixed and saving deposits of other financial corporations, public nonfinancial corporations, and private sector with depository corporations in national currency.

Interest Rates:

Discount Rate (End of Period):

Basic rediscount rate offered by the BEAC. † Beginning in July 1994, rate charged by the BEAC on refinancing operations to financial institutions.

Deposit Rate:

Minimum rate offered by other depository corporations on savings accounts.

Lending Rate:

Maximum rate charged by financial institutions on loans.

Prices and Labor:

Consumer Prices:

Source: National Institute of Statistical Studies Economic and Demographics. Weights reference period: 2003–2004. Geographical Coverage: N'Djamena, Moundou, Sarh, and Abéché. Number of items in basket: 332; Basis for Calculation: Survey on Consumption and Informal Sector in Chad, conducted in 2003–2004, covering 1024 national households in N'Djamena, Laspeyres index.

International Transactions:

Beginning with 1982, trade data are obtained from the *Balance of Payments Statistics*.

Government Finance:

† Prior to 1986, data cover budgetary central government only. Beginning in 1986, data are as reported for *the Government Finance Statistics Yearbook* by the Bank of the Central African States and cover budgetary central government and the Autonomous Amortization Fund accounts. † Beginning in 1991, data are as reported by the Banque des Etats de l'Afrique Centrale. The fiscal year ends December 31.

National Accounts:

Data are from the National Institute of Statistical Studies Economic and Demographics. Data are prepared in accordance with the *SNA93*.

Chile   228

Date of Fund Membership:

December 31, 1945

Standard Source:

Central Bank of Chile
National Institute of Statistics

Exchange Rates:

Market Rate (End of Period and Period Average):

Weighted average of the midpoint rates between the buying and selling rates of U.S. dollars by banks and foreign exchange houses that are part of the official exchange market. Since 1985, the exchange regime was based on a system of floating bands. In January 1997, the exchange rate band was broadened to 12.5 percent on either side of the reference rate (basket of currencies of the country's three major trading partners readjusted for domestic inflation discounted by relevant external inflation). In June 1998, the fluctuation margin was reduced from 25 percent to 5.5 percent. In September 1998, the margins of the band were broadened to 7 percent and a band broadening factor 0.013575 percent was introduced. In December 1998, it was broadened to 16 percent and the daily broadening factor retained. On September 2, 1999, the fluctuation band was indefinitely suspended and the peso was allowed to float freely.

International Liquidity:

Gold (National Valuation) (line 1and) is the U.S. dollar value of official holdings of gold as reported in the country's standard sources. Gold is valued at market prices in the London Metal Exchange.

Central Bank:

Consists of the Central Bank of Chile (CBCh) only.

Data are based on a standardized report form (SRF) for central banks, which accords with the concepts and definitions of the IMF's *Monetary and Financial Statistics Manual (MFSM)*, 2000.

† Beginning in January 2009, the adoption of international financial reporting standards prompted a reclassification of financial instruments.

Other Depository Corporations:

Comprises commercial banks and the government-owned Banco Estado. Data exclude savings and credit cooperatives, which have short-term deposits.

Data are based on a standardized report form (SRF) for other depository corporations, which accords with the concepts and definitions of the *Monetary and Financial Statistics Manual* (*MFSM*). † Beginning in January 2008, the adoption of international financial reporting standards prompted a reclassification of financial instruments.

Depository Corporations:

† See notes on central bank and other depository corporations.

Other Financial Corporations:

Comprises pension funds. Beginning in March 2008, includes insurance companies. Data exclude investment funds, mutual funds, general funds, housing funds, foreign capital investment funds, factoring societies, leasing companies, and financial auxiliaries.

Data are based on a standardized report form (SRF) for other financial corporations, which accords with the concepts and definitions of the *Monetary and Financial Statistics Manual* (*MFSM*). Departures from the *MFSM* methodology are explained below. Data for insurance companies are only available on a quarterly basis. Data for the intervening and current months have been estimated by carrying forward the data from the last quarter.

Financial assets and liabilities for which economic sectorization is unavailable are allocated to the economic sector having the largest volume of transactions in the category.

Claims on Private Sector includes holding of securities issued by public nonfinancial corporations. Prepaid premiums and reserves against outstanding claims of the central government are included in *Insurance Technical Reserves* rather than as *Liabilities to the Central Government*.

Monetary Aggregates:

Broad Money:
Broad Money calculated from the liability data in the sections for the central bank and other depository corporations accords with the concepts and definitions of the *MFSM*. Broad money differs from M3 described below as M3 includes treasury bills and securities issued by nonfinancial corporations held by the private sector.

Money (National Definitions):
Base money comprises notes and coins in circulation and deposits of other depository corporations at the CBCh.

M1 comprises notes and coins in circulation outside the banking system, checks issued by the CBCh, demand deposits of the private sector in national currency (net of checks to be cleared), other sight deposits of the private sector in national currency, and savings deposits of the private sector in national currency with a maturity of less than 30 days.

M2 comprises M1, time deposits of the private sector in national currency, savings deposits of the private sector in national currency with a maturity longer than 30 days, mutual funds' shares of the private sector with a maturity of less than one year, plus credit unions' deposit liabilities, less investment of mutual funds and credit unions in instruments included in M2.

M3 comprises M2, foreign currency deposits of the private sector, central bank bills held by the private sector in other depository corporations, treasury promissory notes held by the private sector in other depository corporations, letters of credit held by the private sector in other depository corporations, mutual

funds' shares of the private sector with a maturity longer than one year, plus voluntary savings quotas of pension funds, less investment of mutual funds and pension funds in instruments included in M3.

Interest Rates:

Central Bank Policy Rate (End of Period):
Refers to the Monetary Policy Rate (MPR) which is the target interest rate for the interbank money market.

Discount Rate (End of Period):
Rediscount rate charged by the CBCh on liquidity loans to banks.

Money Market Rate:
Weighted average overnight rate on loans between other depository corporations in national currency.

Savings Rate:
Weighted average rate paid by other depository corporations on savings deposits with unconditional withdrawal in national currency.

Deposit Rate:
Weighted average rate paid by banks on 30- to 89-day deposits in national currency. The rate is converted to percent per annum by compounding monthly rates of interest.

Deposit Rate (Foreign currency):
Weighted average rate paid by other depository corporations on 30- to 89-day deposits in foreign currency. The rate is converted to percent per annum by compounding monthly rates of interest.

Lending Rate:
Weighted average rate charged by banks on 30- to 89-day loans in national currency. † Beginning in January 1985, weighted average rate charged by other depository corporations on 30- to 89-day loans in national currency. The rate is converted to percent per annum by compounding monthly rates of interest.

Lending Rate (Foreign Currency):
Weighted average rate charged by other depository corporations on 30- to 89-day loans in foreign currency. The rate is converted to percent per annum by compounding monthly rates of interest.

Prices, Production, Labor:

Share Prices:
Selective Price Index (IPSA), base January 2, 2003, is a market capitalization weighted index representing the performance of the 40 companies with the highest average annual trading volume in the Santiago Stock Exchange. The index constituents are revised on a quarterly basis.

General Share Prices (End of Month):
General Index of Share Prices (IGPA), base December 30, 1980, is a market capitalization weighted index representing the performance of eligible companies listed on the Santiago Stock Exchange.

Industrial Share Prices:
Index of industrial share prices, base December 1974. † Beginning in January 1978, index of industrial share prices, base December 29, 1978. † Beginning in June 1980, index of industrial share prices, base December 30, 1980, refers to the average of daily quotations. † Beginning in January 2001, industrial share price index, base December 2007.

Wholesale Prices:

Source: Central Bank of Chile. Data are disseminated on the "Indice de Precios al por Mayor" (wholesale price index), a Laspeyres index (weights reference period November 2007), covering the agriculture and livestock, mining, fishing, and manufacturing production sectors. The weights used for the index were established on the basis of the internal absorption or destination side of the 1986 input output matrix.

Producer Prices:

Source: National Institute of statistics; Weights Reference Period: 2001; Sectoral coverage: Mining, manufacturing, electricity, gas and water. Number of items in basket: 8238 for all the sectors: Basis for calculation: Laspeyres, weights are derived from different sectoral studies.

Consumer Prices:

Source: National Institute of Statistics. Weights Reference Period: December 1998; Geographical Coverage: The Great Santiago Area; Number of Items in Basket: 482; Basis for Calculation: The relevant weights were established on the basis of a survey of family budgets carried out in Greater Santiago from August 1996 to July 1997. † Beginning January 2009, CPI is updated in accordance with international standards and calculated at national level. It will be updated at least every five years in line with international recommendations. National Institute of Statistics. Weights Reference Period: January 2009; Geographical Coverage: includes all regional capitals and their conurbations.

Wages:

Hourly earnings, weights reference period July 2009.

Employment:

Data are derived from the results of the new National Employment Survey, based on the Population and Households Census of 2009.

Industrial Production:

Source: National Institute of statistics; Weights Reference Period: 2009; Sectoral coverage: Mining, manufacturing, electricity, gas and water; Basis for calculation: Laspeyres, weights for the different sector are obtained from the aggregated values issued from the 2008 National accounts compilation made by the Central Bank of Chile.

Data are sourced from the OECD database.

Manufacturing Production:

Source: National Institute of Statistics. Weights Reference Period: 2000; Sectoral Coverage: entire manufacturing industry; Basis for Calculation: the sample is based on the importance of products and establishments, as determined by gross production value and value added.

Mining Production:

Source: National Institute of Statistics. Weight Reference Period: 2009. The index is based on surveys of Chile's mining establishments, excluding limestone.

International Transactions:

Source: Central Bank of Chile. Value data on trade, which are derived from customs returns, have been updated with central bank exchange record data for current periods. Value data on *Exports* and *Imports, c.i.f.* are from the Central Bank of Chile.

Import Prices:

Source: Central Bank of Chile. Index on wholesale import prices, weights reference period June 1992, compiled by INE.

Government Finance:

Monthly provisional data are provided by the Ministry of Finance as reported in the *GFSM 2001* analytical framework and cover the operations of the budgetary central government. Annual data are as reported for the *Government Finance Statistics Yearbook (GFSY)* and represent final data for the budgetary central government. The fiscal year ends December 31.

National Accounts:

Source: Central Bank of Chile. As indicated by the country, the national accounts are compiled according to the recommendations of the *1993 SNA*.

China, P.R.: Mainland   924

The data refer to the People's Republic of China, excluding the Hong Kong Special Administrative Region (HKSAR) and the Macao Special Administrative Region (MSAR). Data on transactions and assets and liabilities vis-à-vis HKSAR and MSAR are treated as international transactions and external positions respectively.

Date of Fund Membership:

December 27, 1945

Standard Sources:

Ministry of Finance
National Bureau of Statistics
Ministry of Finance
People's Bank of China

Exchange Rates:

† Beginning January 1, 1994, the People's Bank of China quotes the midpoint rate against the U.S. dollar based on the previous day's prevailing rate in the interbank foreign exchange market. Banks which are licensed to conduct foreign exchange business will quote their transaction rates within the floating margins set by the People's Bank of China. Prior to this date, the official exchange rate of renminbi was adjusted according to movements in the value of a basket of internationally traded currencies.

International Liquidity:

Foreign Exchange (line 1d.d): † Beginning in 1984, data include foreign government securities. † Prior to 1992, *Foreign Exchange* includes foreign exchange holdings of the Bank of China. Starting in that year, *line 1d.d* comprises foreign exchange holdings of the People's Bank of China only.

Banking Institutions: Liabilities (line 7b.d) includes specialized banks' borrowings from overseas affiliates, deposits of foreign banks, bonds issued abroad, and loans from foreign governments.

Monetary Authorities:

Comprises the accounts of the People's Bank of China (PBC). † Data classification from 1993 onwards has been revised. *Claims on Central Government (line 12a)* and *Central Government Deposits (line 16d)* relate to the units of the central government included in the budget. † Prior to 1997, *Central Government Deposits (line 16d)* also includes some deposits of provincial and local government units. † For the period 1993 to 1996, data on foreign assets are net figures. † Beginning in January 2002, *Claims on Other Banking Institutions (line 12f)* exclude nonbank financial institutions. *Reserve Money (line 14)* does not include deposits of the non-central government units.

Banking Institutions:

The data cover the Bank of China, the Agriculture Bank of China, the People's Construction Bank of China, the Industrial and Commercial Bank of China, and the Rural Credit Cooperatives. † Beginning in January 2002, other sectors *(line 22d: Claims on Other Sectors)* exclude nonbank financial institutions. Beginning in January 2004, Postal Savings Bureaus (PSBs) are classified as other depository corporations due to changes in regulations governing PSBs' financial activities. PSBs are not subject to reserve requirements but to a required amount of deposits at the People's Bank of China.

Banking Survey:

Consolidates the accounts of the People's Bank of China and the Banking Institutions. † Data prior to 1985 exclude rural credit cooperatives and the People's Construction Bank of China. *Money (line 34)* does not include deposits of the non-central government units. † See notes on monetary authorities and banking institutions.

Money (National Definitions):

M0 comprises currency issued by the PBC less the amount held by banking institutions.
M1 comprises currency in circulation plus demand deposits in national currency of resident non-bank non-government sectors with the PBC and banking institutions. Currency in circulation refers to notes and coins by the PBC less the amount held by banking institutions.
M2 comprises M1 plus time and savings deposits in national currency of resident non-bank financial corporations and non-bank non-government sectors with the PBC and banking institutions.

Interest Rates:

Discount Rate (End of Period):
Rate charged by the People's Bank of China on 20-day loans to financial institutions.

Deposit Rate (End of Period):
Interest rates on institutional and individual deposits of one-year maturity.

Lending Rate (End of Period):
† Prior to 1989, rate on working capital loans to state industrial enterprises. Thereafter, rate on working capital loans of one-year maturity.

Prices, Production, Labor:

Share Prices:
Data refer to the composite index of share prices for Shanghai Stock Exchange, which is calculated as Paasche weighted average of daily closing prices, base December 19, 1990.

Producer Prices:
Source: National Bureau of Statistics. The series provides changes from the corresponding period of the previous year and is the ex-factory prices of industrial products.

Consumer Prices:
Source: National Bureau of Statistics. The series provides changes from the corresponding period of the previous year and covers urban and rural residents.

Industrial Production:
Source: National Bureau of Statistics. The series provides changes from the corresponding period of the previous year and is the growth rate of the value added of industry.

International Transactions:

Sources C and S. Trade data are based on customs records. Prior to 1980, the data are provided by the Ministry of Foreign Trade and exclude exports of complete plants in the form of foreign aid. Beginning 1980, data are provided by the National Bureau of Statistics and are more comprehensive.

Government Finance:

Prior to 1990, data are from the State Statistical Bureau and represent a consolidation of the central government, provinces, counties, and municipal governments. Revenue includes repayments of loans extended and foreign borrowing, and Expenditure include lending. Beginning in 1990, annual data are from the Ministry of Finance. The data cover the budgetary central government. The deficit/surplus does not equal financing due to unavailability of complete financing data on a monthly basis. The fiscal year ends December 31.

National Accounts:

Source: National Bureau of Statistics. Constant price estimates are based on index numbers and use data with several base years chained together.

China, P.R.:Hong Kong   532

The data refer to the Hong Kong Special Administrative Region (HKSAR). Data on transactions and assets and liabilities vis-à-vis The Mainland of China are treated as international transactions and external positions respectively.

Standard Sources:

Hong Kong Monetary Authority
Census and Statistics Department, Hong Kong

Exchange Rates:

Market Rate (End of Period and Period Average):
The closing midpoint (average of selling and buying rates) telegraphic transfer rates provided by the Hang Seng Bank Limited.

International Liquidity:

Foreign Exchange (line 1d.d): † Beginning in July 1997, the data include foreign exchange reserves of the HKSAR Government's Land Fund. † Beginning in November 1998, assets of the Land Fund are placed with the Exchange Fund. † Beginning in January

2013, foreign currency deposits held in banks located in Hong Kong SAR are excluded.

Monetary Authorities:

Comprises the Hong Kong Monetary Authority. † Beginning in January 1999, *Reserve Money (line 14)* also includes Exchange Fund bills and notes. *Currency Outside Banks (line 14a):* Currency issuance corresponds to the amount of noninterest-bearing certificates of indebtedness (CI) that the Hong Kong Monetary Authority issues to three commercial banks as backing for the Hong Kong banknotes that these commercial banks issue. The CIs are issued at a rate of HK$7.8 per U.S. dollar under the exchange rate system established in October 1983 whereby the Hong Kong dollar was officially linked to the U.S. dollar. In the accounts of the banking institutions, banknote liabilities are exactly offset by the CI holdings of the three banks that issue the banknotes. Beginning in November 1998, assets of the HKSAR Government's Land Fund are placed with the Exchange Fund. The Land Fund's foreign exchange assets are included in *Foreign Assets (line 11)*, and its other assets are included in *Other Items (Net) (line 17r)*. The contra-entry to the Land Fund's total assets is included in *Government Deposits (line 16d)*.

Banking Institutions:

Comprises all authorized banking institutions, covering licensed banks, restricted licence banks, and deposit-taking companies. *Foreign Assets (line 21)* and *Foreign Liabilities (line 26c):* Data are based on information collected in a separate monthly survey of banking institutions. Because these data are not fully reconcilable with banking institutions' balance sheet accounts in respect of what may be inferred as foreign assets and liabilities, corresponding adjustments are made to the data in order to derive estimates of domestic assets and liabilities within the balance sheet framework.

Money (National Definitions):

Base Money comprises currency in circulation, clearing accounts of banking institutions in the Hong Kong Monetary Authority (HKMA) in national currency and foreign currency, and exchange funds issued by the HKMA. Currency in circulation refers to certificates of indebtedness and notes and coins issued by the HKMA.

M1 comprises currency in circulation and demand deposits in national currency and foreign currency of other financial corporations, public nonfinancial corporations, and private sector with licensed banks. Currency in circulation refers to certificates of indebtedness and notes and coins issued by the HKMA less the amount held by licensed banks.

M2 comprises M1 plus time and savings deposits in national currency and foreign currency of other financial corporations, public nonfinancial corporations, and private sector with licensed banks and negotiable certificates of deposit issued by licensed banks in national currency and foreign currency held by other financial corporations, public nonfinancial corporations, and private sector.

M3 comprises M2 plus deposits in national and foreign currency with restricted license banks and deposit taking companies and negotiable certificates of deposit issued by restricted license banks and deposit taking companies in national currency and foreign currency held by other financial corporations, public nonfinancial corporations, and private sector.

Interest Rates:

Discount Rate (End of Period):
Exchange Fund's overnight liquidity adjustment facility offer rate.

Money Market Rate (End of Period):
Midpoint (average of offer and bid rates) overnight closing rates in the interbank money market quoted by the Standard Chartered Bank.

Treasury Bill Rate (End of Period):
Annualized yields on Exchange Fund bills of 91-day maturity.

Deposit Rate:
Rate on average one-month time deposits of ten major banks. Prior to January 1995, data refer to the maximum rates paid by licensed banks under the interest rate rules of the Hong Kong Association of Banks.

Lending Rate (End of Period):
Rate quoted by the Hongkong and Shanghai Banking Corporation Limited.

Prices, Production, Labor:

Share Prices:
Data refer to daily values of closing Hang Seng indices, base July 31, 1964. The constituent stocks of the Hang Seng index are 33 stocks representative of the market. The aggregate market value of these stocks accounts for 75 percent of the total market capitalization on the Stock Exchange of Hong Kong Limited.

Producer Prices:
Source: Census and Statistics Department. Weights reference period: annually re-weighted and chained; Laspeyres index which measures the changes in producer prices of manufactured goods. The index covers the more important products identified from the Annual Survey of Industrial Production, and the data are obtained from the Quarterly Survey of Industrial Production. The survey sample covers about 1700 establishments.

Consumer Prices:
Source: Census and Statistics Department. Weights reference period: 2004–2005; Geographical Coverage: The whole HKSAR territory; Number of Items in Basket: 984; Basis for Calculation: The weights are derived from the expenditure patterns of households collected from the Household Expenditure Survey, and the indices are re-based and the weights revised every five years.

Wages: Average Earnings (Manufacturing):
Census and Statistics Department index, weights reference period: first quarter 1999. Payroll per person. Payroll covers wages and salaries, bonuses and gratuities, commissions, and cash payments in other forms paid directly to employees for normal work time and overtime.

Wage Rates (Manufacturing):
Census and Statistics Department index, weights reference period: September 1992. Data are based on the Labor Earnings Survey and refer to nominal wage indices for September of each year. Data cover a similar range of remuneration as the payroll per person index but only for normal work time.

Manufacturing Production:
Source: Census and Statistics Department. Weights reference period: weights are annually re-weighted; Sectoral Coverage: all

manufacturing industries; Basis for Calculation: sales data are used as weights for aggregating production indices at product level into indices at industry level.

International Transactions:

All trade data are from the Census and Statistics Department. Trade statistics refer to movements of merchandise between the HKSAR and its trading partners, by land, air, ocean, and to a limited extent, post. Imports are c.i.f. values, whereas exports are f.o.b. values. Value index, unit value index, and quantum index. Weights reference period: 2010.

National Accounts:

As indicated by the authorities, concepts and definitions are in accordance with the *1993 SNA*.

Data have been revised due to the release of the new data series of chain volume measures of GDP and components in October 2007. In calculating the chained (2005) dollar series, the current price value in the reference year of 2005 is extrapolated backwards and forwards using the corresponding chain volume index. Because the extrapolation process is carried out for the GDP and its components independently, the extrapolated values of the components do not, in general, aggregate exactly to the extrapolated value of GDP.

China, P.R.:Macao   546

The data refer to the Macao Special Administrative Region (MSAR). Data on transactions and assets and liabilities vis-à-vis the Mainland of China are treated as international transactions and external positions, respectively.

Standard Sources:

Monetary Authority of Macao
Statistics and Census Service of Macao
Revenue Bureau of Macao

Exchange Rates:

Market Rate (End of Period and Period Average):
The midpoint rate of the average buying and selling rates quoted by Reuters and fixed at 9:00 a.m. each day.

International Liquidity:

Foreign Exchange (line 1d.d) includes the claims on banks abroad, financial investments abroad, and other foreign exchange reserves of the Monetary Authority of Macao (AMCM) but does not include the foreign assets of the Reserve Fund, which are considered not to be readily available for use by the AMCM for balance of payments purposes. According to the Fiscal Reserves Act that came into effect on January 1, 2012, the fiscal reserves and foreign exchange reserves are managed under separate accounts. Due to the official transfer of the relevant assets in February 2012, Macao SAR's foreign exchange reserves fell significantly at end-February.

Central Bank:

Consists of the Monetary Authority of Macao only.
Data are based on a standardized report form (SRF) for central banks, which accords with the concepts and definitions of the

IMF's *Monetary and Financial Statistics Manual (MFSM)*, 2000. Departures from the *MFSM* methodology are explained below. Accrued interest is included in *Other Items (Net)* rather than in the outstanding amounts of the financial assets and liabilities. Provisions for losses are included in *Shares and Other Equity* rather than in *Other Items (Net)*.
Held-to-maturity securities are valued at acquisition cost rather than at market price or fair value.

Other Depository Corporations:

Comprises all authorized banking institutions and the postal savings bank.

Data are based on a standardized report form (SRF) for other depository corporations, which accords with the concepts and definitions of the *Monetary and Financial Statistics Manual (MFSM)*. Departures from the *MFSM* methodology are explained below. Accrued interest is included in *Other Items (Net)* rather than in the outstanding amounts of the financial assets and liabilities. Provisions for losses are included in *Shares and Other Equity* rather than in *Other Items (Net)*.
Held-to-maturity securities are valued at acquisition cost rather than at market price or fair value.

Depository Corporations:

See notes on central bank and other depository corporations.

Monetary Aggregates:

Broad Money:
Broad Money calculated from the liability data in the sections for the central bank and other depository corporations accords with the concepts and definitions of the *MFSM* and is consistent with M2 described below.

Money (National Definitions):
M1 comprises currency in circulation outside depository corporations and transferable deposits of resident non-central government sectors with depository corporations.
M2 comprises M1 and savings, notice, time, and certificates of deposits of non-central government sectors with depository corporations.

Interest Rates:

Interbank Rate (End of Period):
One-month MAIBOR, the Macao Interbank Offered Rates.

Deposit Rate:
Weighted average rate quoted by three major banks on three-month deposits; the weights are the shares of each bank in the volume of deposits.

Lending Rate:
Weighted average rate quoted by three major banks on loans; the weights are the shares of each bank in the volume of loans.

Prices and Labor:

Consumer Prices:
Source: Statistics and Census Service of Macao. Weights Reference Period: April 2008-March 2009; Geographical Coverage: whole national territory; Number of Items in Basket: 661; Basis for Calculation: weights are derived from the 2002–2003 Household Budget Survey.

International Transactions:

All trade data are from the Statistics and Census Service of Macao. The trade statistics are based on information given by the importers and exporters in the trade licenses and declarations.

Government Finance:

Annual data are as reported for the *Government Finance Statistics Yearbook (GFSY)* and cover Macao SAR consolidated general government. † Beginning in 2003, quarterly data are as reported in the *GFSM 2001* analytical framework and cover consolidated general government. The fiscal year ends December 31.

National Accounts:

Source: Statistics and Census Service of Macao.

Colombia   233

Date of Fund Membership:

December 27, 1945

Standard Sources:

Bank of the Republic
National Department of Statistics

Exchange Rates:

The exchange rate was operated as a managed float within an intervention band. On September 25, 1999 the crawling band was abandoned and the peso was allowed to float independently.

International Liquidity:

Monetary Authorities: Other Assets (line 3..d) comprises contributions to nonmonetary international organizations and net bilateral payments agreements assets.
Data for *lines .3..d, .4..d, .7a.d, .7b.d,* and *.7f.d* are converted from pesos to U.S. dollars at a booking rate different from exchange rate **ae**.

Central Bank:

Consists of the Bank of the Republic (BR) only.
Data are based on a standardized report form (SRF) for central banks, which accords with the concepts and definitions of the IMF's *Monetary and Financial Statistics Manual (MFSM)*, 2000. Departures from the *MFSM* methodology are explained below.
For December 2001 through November 2004, some financial assets and liabilities for which economic sectorization is unavailable are allocated to the economic sector having the largest volume of transactions in the category and accrued interest on various financial instruments is included in *Other Items (Net)* rather than in the outstanding amounts of the financial assets and liabilities.

Other Depository Corporations:

Comprises commercial banks, financial corporations, commercial financing companies, Central Mortgage Bank, a specialized cooperative (COOPCENTRAL), savings and loan associations, financial cooperatives, and special financial institutions (BANCOLDEX, FEN, and FINDETER). Beginning in March 2002, the savings and loan associations became commercial banks. Data exclude mutual funds and capitalization societies, which issue short-term liabilities.

Data are based on a standardized report form (SRF) for other depository corporations, which accords with the concepts and definitions of the *Monetary and Financial Statistics Manual (MFSM)*. Departures from the *MFSM* methodology are explained below. For December 2001 through November 2004, some financial assets and liabilities for which economic sectorization is unavailable are allocated to the economic sector having the largest volume of transactions in the category and accrued interest on various financial instruments is included in *Other Items (Net)* rather than in the outstanding amounts of the financial assets and liabilities.

Depository Corporations:

See notes on central bank and other depository corporations.

Other Financial Corporations:

Comprises mutual funds (institutions for collective investment), general and life insurance corporations, capitalization societies, insurance cooperatives, pension funds, severance funds, trusts, and society management of pension and severance funds. Beginning in November 2002, includes specialized financial institutions (Caja de Vivienda Militar, Fondo de Garantías de Entidades Cooperativas—FOGACOOP, Fondo Financiero de Proyectos de Desarrollo—FONADE, Fondo Nacional de Garantías, Fondo Nacional de Instituciones Financieras—FOGAFIN, Fondo Nacional del Ahorro—FNA, and Instituto Colombiano de Crédito y Estudios Técnicos en el Exterior—ICETEX). Beginning in January 2004, includes pension liabilities. Data exclude other institutions for collective investment management and special purpose entities specialized in the securitization of assets.
Data are based on a standardized report form (SRF) for other financial corporations, which accords with the concepts and definitions of the Monetary and Financial Statistics Manual (MFSM). For other financial corporations in Colombia, departures from the MFSM methodology are explained below.
For December 2001 to December 2009, data for general and life insurance corporations, capitalization societies, and insurance cooperatives are only available on a quarterly basis.

Financial Corporations:

See notes on central bank, other depository corporations, and other financial corporations.

Monetary Aggregates:

Broad Money:
Broad Money calculated from the liability data in the sections for the central bank and other depository corporations accords with the concepts and definitions of the *MFSM*. Broad money differs from M3 as described below as M3 includes central government and decentralized agencies deposits.

Money (National Definitions):
Reserve money comprises notes and coins issued and deposits of other depository corporations, special financial institutions, and BR employees with the BR.
M1 comprises notes and coins in circulation outside the banking system and demand deposits of the central, state, and municipal governments, decentralized agencies, public nonfinancial corporations, and private sector with depository corporations.
M2 comprises M1 and savings deposits and certificates of time

deposits of the central, state, and municipal governments, decentralized agencies, public nonfinancial corporations, and private sector with other depository corporations.

M3 comprises M2, fiduciary and other sight deposits of the central, state, and municipal governments, decentralized agencies, public nonfinancial corporations, and private sector with other depository corporations, mortgage certificates issued by the Central Mortgage Bank held by the public, and bonds in circulation issued by other depository corporations held by the public. Other sight deposits include guaranteed and tax deposits; cashier's, certified, and traveler's checks; and canceled accounts.

Interest Rates:

Central Bank Policy Rate (End of Period):
Intervention rate determined by the BR to either increase or decrease liquidity in the economy.

Discount Rate (End of Period):
Rate charged by the BR on loans to commercial banks. † Beginning in September 1986, corresponds to DTF (see note for deposit rate) plus two points. Beginning in October 1990, corresponds to DTF plus eight points. Beginning in June 1992, corresponds to DTF plus seven points. Beginning in December 1999, corresponds to DTF plus five points. Beginning in September 2001, corresponds to the Lombard rate plus one point. The Lombard rate is the maximum rate charged by the BR to provide liquidity to financial corporations.

Money Market Rate:
Weighted average rate on loans between financial corporations.

Deposit Rate:
Fixed-term deposits (FTD): Weighted average rate paid by other depository corporations on 90-day certificates of deposit.

Lending Rate:
Weighted average rate charged by other depository corporations on loans. † Beginning in May 1999, weighted average rate charged by other depository corporations on commercial, ordinary, short-term (tesorería), and long-term preferential loans. The rate is weighted by loan amounts and, owing to the revolving nature of the short-term preferential loans, their weight was established as one fifth of the daily disbursement.

Prices, Production, Labor:

Share Prices (End of Month):
Index of prices on the Bogotá Stock Exchange, base, March 15, 1976. † Beginning in January 1991, index of prices on the Bogotá Stock Exchange, base January 2, 1991. † Beginning in July 2001, general share price index on the Colombia Stock Exchange, base July 3, 2001.

Producer Prices:
Bank of the Republic index, fixed-weight Laspeyres index (June 1999=100). The PPI covers 76 percent of domestically produced goods and 24 percent of imports. The index is based on the prices of 730 goods traded in the wholesale market, and classified by origin; 460 goods are locally produced and 270 are imported. The PPI is calculated on the basis of 6,900 quotes for the various articles it comprises. Prices are obtained every month from a survey of a sample of 2,200 reporting entities. It covers 18 cities in which the Banco de la República has branches. Basic information for calculating the weights was obtained from the national accounts reported by Departamento Administrativo Nacional de Estadísticas

(DANE) for 1994, and from the Annual Manufacturing Survey and the Foreign Trade Yearbooks. The Index weights are fixed, and at the beginning of 1999 have been revised on the basis of the 1994 national accounts compiled by DANE.

Consumer Prices:
National Department of Statistics index, weights reference period December 2008. The index covers prices of a basket of 181 items (so-called basic expenditure) purchased by individual households located in the urban areas, which include the country's 24 largest cities, namely, Bogotá, Medellín, Cali, Barranquilla, Bucaramanga, Manizales, Pasto, Pereira, Cartagena, Neiva, Montería, Cúcuta, and Villavicencio, Riohacha, Quibdo, Tunja, Armenia, Popayan, Florencia, Sincelejo, Ibague, and San Andres (the data exclude the population of rural areas). The weights were last revised in 2008, with data from the 2006–2007 Income and Expenditure Survey.

Manufacturing Production:
Source: National Department of Statistics. Weights Reference Period: 1990; Sectoral Coverage: the manufacturing sector; Basis for Calculation: the index measures output and sales values and is presented in nominal and real terms.

Crude Petroleum Production:
Bank of the Republic data (in thousands of barrels). Data for January 1996 onwards are based on production quantities as reported in the Oil Market Intelligence.

Employment:
Prior to 2001, the National Household Survey covered the seven principal cities of the country. From 2001 onward, the survey includes the 13 main cities.

International Transactions:

Total Exports and Imports in U.S. dollars are from the National Department of Statistics. Current data on Exports and Imports f. o. b. are transmitted by the Bank of the Republic and are based on preliminary registration figures of the Colombian External Trade Institute (INCOMEX). Coffee exports in U.S. dollars are from Bank of the Republic (table 5.2.2), as compiled by the National Federation of Colombian Coffeegrowers.

Volume of Exports for Coffee are based on Bank of the Republic (table 5.2.2) data in physical quantities.

Export and Import Prices:
Data refer to Bank of the Republic indices of wholesale/producer prices of export goods and of import goods, respectively. The coffee export price index refers to the Bank of the Republic New York price quotation, as reported by the National Federation of Colombian Coffeegrowers.

Government Finance:

Data are derived from Bank of the Republic. Data cover budgetary central government and exclude the transactions of the decentralized agencies and the social security institutes. Revenue data include the repayments of loans granted to entities that do not form part of the nonfinancial public sector, and financing data include privatization receipts. The fiscal year ends December 31.

National Accounts:

Beginning in 1970, data are compiled by the National Department of Statistics (DANE). As indicated by the country, beginning in 1994, data are compiled according to the 1993 SNA.

Comoros   632

Date of Fund Membership:

September 21, 1976

Standard Source:

Banque Centrale des Comores

Exchange Rates:

Official Rate: (End of Period and Period Average):

Prior to January 1999, the official rate was pegged to the French franc. On January 12, 1994, the Comorian franc was devalued to CF 75 per French franc from CF 50 at which it had been fixed since 1948. From January 1, 1999, the CFAF is pegged to the euro at a rate of CFA franc 491.9677 per euro.

International Liquidity:

Data expressed in U.S. dollars on *Foreign Exchange (line 1d.d)* and *Gold (line 1and)* are derived from data denominated in national currency from components of the central bank's *Foreign Assets (line 11),* using the end-of-period market rate (*line* **ae**).

Central Bank:

Consists of the Banque centrale des Comores (BCC) only, consolidating the accounts of headquarters located in Grande Comore and its two branches located in Anjouan and Moheli.

Data are based on a standardized report form for central banks, which accords with the concepts and definitions of the IMF's *Monetary and Financial Statistics Manual (MFSM)*, 2000.

Other Depository Corporations:

Comprises commercial banks, savings and credit cooperatives (Union des mutuelles d'épargne et de crédit des Comores beginning in December 2005 and Union régionale des caisses Sanduk d'Anjouan beginning in December 2006), and banking activities of the Société nationale des postes et des services financiers including the Caisse nationale d'épargne (a national saving bank) and Comptes de chèques postaux (the post office checking accounts department). Beginning in March 2011, includes the Banque de développement des Comores.

Data are based on a standardized report form for other depository corporations, which accords with the concepts and definitions of the *Monetary and Financial Statistics Manual (MFSM)*. Departures from the *MFSM* methodology are explained below.

Accrual accounting and sectorization of counterpart transactors are not consistently applied by all reporting corporations.

Depository Corporations:

See notes on central bank and other depository corporations.

Other Financial Corporations:

Comprises the Banque de développement des Comores, the national development bank. Beginning in March 2011, the Banque de Développement des Comores was reclassified as an other depository corporation.

Data exclude insurance corporations and financial auxiliaries. There are no pension funds in Comoros.

Data are based on a standardized report form for other financial corporations, which accords with the concepts and definitions of the *Monetary and Financial Statistics Manual (MFSM)*.

Monetary Aggregates:

Broad Money:

Broad Money calculated from the liability data in the sections for the central bank and other depository corporations accords with the concepts and definitions of the *MFSM* and is consistent with M2 described below.

Money (National Definitions):

M1 comprises banknotes and coins held by the public, and demand deposits of nonfinancial corporations, households (including diaspora), other financial corporations, and local governments with depository corporations.

M2 comprises M1 and time, savings, and foreign currency deposits of nonfinancial corporations, households (including diaspora), other financial corporations, and local governments with depository corporations.

Interest Rates:

Discount Rate (End of Period):

Rediscount rate charged by the BCC and set at the Euro Overnight Index Average + 1.5 percent.

Deposit Rate:

Rate offered by commercial banks on saving passbooks.

Lending Rate:

Commercial bank lending rates are regulated by the BCC in the form of a minimum and a maximum rate. Data provided is a simple average of the minimum and maximum rates.

International Transactions:

All trade data are from Banque Centrale des Comores. Based on customs records.

Government Finance:

Annual data are as reported for the *Government Finance Statistics Yearbook (GFSY)* and cover the central government. The fiscal year ends December 31.

Congo, Dem. Rep. of   636

Date of Fund Membership:

September 28, 1963

Standard Sources:

Central Bank of Congo
Institut National des Statistiques

Exchange Rates:

On July 1, 1998 the Congo franc, equal to 100,000 new zaïres, was introduced. On October 22, 1993 the new zaïre, equal to three million old zaïres, was introduced.

Official Rate: (End of Period and Period Average):

The market rate is freely determined in the interbank foreign exchange market. Beginning in December 2003, data refer to the official exchange rate as set by the Central Bank of Congo.

International Liquidity:

Line 1and is equal to *line 1ad,* converted into U.S. dollars at the dollar price of gold used by national sources, as reported to *IFS*.

Monetary Authorities:

Comprises the Central Bank of Congo and the monetary authority functions of the Treasury. Prepayments for exchange are required to be made at commercial banks for the full c.i.f. value of imports when the banks open letters of credit abroad on behalf of importers. Import deposits are required to be made at commercial banks for 40 percent of the c.i.f. value of goods when applications for import licenses are presented. Both forms of import prepayments absorb liquidity. Prepayments for exchange at the Central Bank of Congo include outstanding external payment arrears.

Deposit Money Banks:

Aggregates commercial banks.

Monetary Survey:

In the monetary survey (see Introduction for the standard method of calculation), *line 34* includes *Post Office Checking Deposits (line 24..i)* with the contra-entry in *line 32an.*

Interest Rates:

Discount Rate (End of Period):
Rate charged by the Central Bank of Congo when providing liquidity over-the-counter through short-term loans (one week maximum) at a pre-specified interest rate to commercial banks against eligible assets. This rate is determined by the Central Bank of Congo as the annualized inflation rate plus ten percent at minimum. This rate reflects the stance of the monetary policy of the Central Bank of Congo and, thus, should be considered as the leading rate.

Standing Facility (End of Period):
Rate charged by the Central Bank of Congo when providing liquidity over-the-counter through very short-term loans (24 hours maximum) to commercial banks against eligible assets. This rate is determined by the Central Bank of Congo as the leading rate (see above) plus a few percentage points.

Interbank Rate (Minimum):
Minimum rate observed during the period on transactions between commercial banks.

Interbank Rate (Maximum):
Maximum rate observed during the period on transactions between commercial banks.

Deposit Rate (End of Period):
Simple average of rates offered by commercial banks on time deposits of all maturities in national currency.

Deposit Rate (Foreign Currency) (End of Period):
Simple average of rates offered by commercial banks on time deposits of all maturities in foreign currency.

Lending Rate (End of Period):
Simple average of rates charged by commercial banks on loans of all maturities in national currency.

Lending Rate (Foreign Currency) (End of Period):
Simple average of rates charged by commercial banks on loans of all maturities in foreign currency.

Prices:

All data are from Institut National des Statistiques.

Consumer Prices:
Weights reference period: August 1995; Geographical coverage: Kinshasa; Number of items in basket: 214; Basis for calculation: 1995 household budget survey.

International Transactions:

Trade data are on a payments basis. As of January 1984, all trade data are reported in SDRs and converted into U.S. dollars by *IFS* using the average exchange rate.

Government Finance:

Annual data are as reported for the *Government Finance Statistics Yearbook (GFSY)* and cover budgetary central government. The fiscal year ends December 31.

National Accounts:

Source: Institut National des Statistiques. Data are prepared in accordance with the *SNA93.*

Congo, Republic of   634

Date of Fund Membership:
July 10, 1963

Standard Source:

Banque des Etats d'Afrique Centrale (BEAC) (Bank of the Central African States)
Centre National de la Statistique et des Études Économiques (National Center for Statistics and Economic Studies)

Exchange Rates:

Official Rate: (End of Period and Period Average):
Prior to January 1999, the official rate was pegged to the French franc. On January 12, 1994, the CFA franc was devalued to CFAF 100 per French franc from CFAF 50 at which it had been fixed since 1948. From January 1, 1999, the CFAF is pegged to the euro at a rate of CFA franc 655.957 per euro.

International Liquidity:

Gold (National Valuation) (line 1and) is obtained by converting the value in national currency, as reported in the country's standard sources, using the prevailing exchange rate, as given in *line* **ae**. Prior to January 1999, the national currency/dollar conversion rates utilized for balance sheet purposes are used. These conversion rates differ from the prevailing exchange rates reported in *IFS*. This line follows the national valuation procedure which corresponds to that of the Bank of France (*cf* the international liquidity note on the *IFS* page for France).

Central Bank:

Consists of the national office of the Banque des Etats de l'Afrique Centrale (BEAC), consolidating the accounts of all its branches located in Brazzaville, Pointe-Noire, and Ouesso.
Data are based on a standardized report form for central banks, which accords with the concepts and definitions of the IMF's *Monetary and Financial Statistics Manual (MFSM)*, 2000. Departures from the *MFSM* methodology are explained below.

Held-to-maturity securities are valued at amortized cost rather than at current market price or fair value.

Other Depository Corporations:

Comprises commercial banks. Data exclude credit unions and microfinance institutions which accept deposits.

Data are based on a standardized report form for other depository corporations, which accords with the concepts and definitions of the *Monetary and Financial Statistics Manual (MFSM)*. For other depository corporations in Congo, departures from the *MFSM* methodology are explained below.

Financial assets and liabilities for which currency breakdown is unavailable are allocated to assets and liabilities denominated in national currency.

Held-to-maturity securities are valued at acquisition cost rather than at current market price or fair value.

Depository Corporations:

See notes on central bank and other depository corporations.

Monetary Aggregates:

Broad Money:

Broad Money calculated from the liability data in the sections for the central bank and other depository corporations accords with the concepts and definitions of the *MFSM*. Broad money differs from M2 described below as M2 excludes holdings of currency by the central government.

Money (National Definitions):

M1 comprises currency in circulation and transferable deposits. Transferable deposits refer to current account deposits of other financial corporations, public nonfinancial corporations, and private sector with depository corporations in national currency. *M2* comprises M1 and quasi-money. Quasi-money refers to fixed and saving deposits of other financial corporations, public nonfinancial corporations, and private sector with depository corporations in national currency.

Interest Rates:

Discount Rate (End of Period):

Basic rediscount rate offered by the BEAC. † Beginning in July 1994, rate charged by the BEAC on refinancing operations to financial institutions.

Deposit Rate:

Minimum rate offered by other depository corporations on savings accounts.

Lending Rate:

Maximum rate charged by financial institutions on loans.

Prices and Production:

All data on prices are from Centre National de la Statistique et des Études Économiques (National Center for Statistics and Economic Studies).

Consumer Prices:

Weights reference period: 1997 for Brazzaville, 1989 for Pointe-Noire. Geographical coverage: Brazzaville and Pointe-Noire. Number of items in basket: 232 per city. Basis for Calculation: budget/consumption survey in 1997 for Brazzaville, and in 1989 for Pointe-Noire using Laspeyres type index.

Crude Petroleum Production:

Data refer to the volume of production in thousand metric tons.

International Transactions:

All trade data are from Banque des Etats d'Afrique Centrale (BEAC) (Bank of the Central African States)

Value of Exports and Imports:

Bunkers and ship's stores are included. Data exclude imports from other countries of the Union douanière et économique de l'Afrique centrale (UDEAC) (Central African Customs Union). *Imports* are adjusted to include diamond imports as derived from diamond exports minus 10 percent for diamond handling. *Imports, f.o.b.* are calculated from *Imports, c.i.f.* by applying a freight and insurance factor estimated for *IFS*.

Government Finance:

Annual data are as reported for the *Government Finance Statistics Yearbook* and cover the consolidated central government. The fiscal year ends December 31.

National Accounts:

Source: National Center for Statistics and Economic Studies. Data are prepared in accordance with the framework of SNA 1968.

Costa Rica   238

Date of Fund Membership:

January 8, 1946

Standard Source:

Central Bank of Costa Rica

Exchange Rates:

Market Rate (End of Period and Period Average):

A system of managed floating is in effect.

International Liquidity:

Gold (National Valuation) (line 1and) is obtained by converting the value in national currency terms, as reported in the country's standard sources, using the prevailing exchange rate, as given in line **de,** line **ae,** or line **we.** This line follows national valuation procedures, which revalue gold monthly at the price of gold in London on the last day of each month.

Central Bank:

Consists of the Central Bank of Costa Rica (CBCR) only.

Data are based on a standardized report form (SRF) for central banks, which accords with the concepts and definitions of the IMF's *Monetary and Financial Statistics Manual (MFSM)*, 2000. Departures from the *MFSM* methodology are explained below.

Securities issued are allocated to holding sectors using information that does not provide full sectorization.

Financial instruments that cannot be valued at market prices are valued at acquisition cost.

Accrued interest not disaggregated by economic sector is allocated to the economic sector by estimation (weights according to principal outstanding).

Other Depository Corporations:

Comprises commercial banks, finance companies, savings and loan associations, credit and savings cooperatives, and Mutual de Vivienda.

Data exclude money market investment funds and offshore banks, which accept deposits from residents in Costa Rica.

Data are based on a standardized report form (SRF) for other depository corporations, which accords with the concepts and definitions of the *Monetary and Financial Statistics Manual (MFSM)*. For other depository corporations in Costa Rica, departures from the *MFSM* methodology are explained below.

Financial assets and liabilities for which economic sectorization is unavailable are allocated to the economic sector having the largest volume of transactions in the category.

Transferable Deposits Included in Broad Money, Other Deposits Included in Broad Money, and *Securities Other than Shares Included in Broad Money* include positions with nonresidents.

Financial assets that cannot be valued at market prices are valued at acquisition cost. Liabilities are valued at historical or issue prices.

Depository Corporations:

See notes on central bank and other depository corporations.

Monetary Aggregates:

Broad Money:

Broad Money calculated from the liability data in the sections for the central bank and other depository corporations accords with the concepts and definitions of the *MFSM*. Broad money differs from M3 described below as M3 excludes accrued interest on deposits, and securities issued by the CBCR held by money holding sectors.

Money (National Definitions):

Base Money comprises currency in circulation and reserve deposits and correspondent accounts of commercial banks in national currency with the CBCR. Currency in circulation refers to notes and coins issued by the CBCR.

M1 comprises currency in circulation and transferable deposits. Currency in circulation refers to notes and coins issued by the CBCR less the amount held by commercial banks. Transferable deposits refer to current account deposits in national currency of other financial corporations, state and local governments, public nonfinancial corporations, and private sector with commercial banks.

M2 comprises M1 and quasi-money in national currency. Quasi-money refers to fixed, savings, and overdue deposits; certificates of deposit; certified checks; and deposits in litigation of other financial corporations, state and local governments, public nonfinancial corporations, and private sector with commercial banks and securities other than shares issued by commercial banks held by other financial corporations, state and local governments, public nonfinancial corporations, and private sector.

M3 comprises M2 and quasi-money in foreign currency. Quasi-money refers to demand, fixed, savings, and overdue deposits; certificates of deposit; certified checks; and deposits in litigation of state and local governments, public nonfinancial corporations, and private sector with the CBCR and commercial banks and securities other than shares issued by commercial banks held by other financial corporations, state and local governments, public nonfinancial corporations, and private sector.

Interest Rates:

Central Bank Policy Rate (End of Period):

Monetary Policy Rate on 30-day investments. Beginning on March 15, 2006, rate on overnight deposits in the CBCR's financial services website. Beginning on May 29, 2008, rate charged by the CBCR on one-day loans in the Interbank Money Market. Beginning in August 2009, rate charged by the CBCR on one-day loans in the Integrated Liquidity Market. Beginning June 3, 2011, target rate used by the CBCR as a reference for one-day operations within a band in the Integrated Liquidity Market.

Discount Rate (End of Period):

Rediscount rate offered by the CBCR to commercial banks and other financial intermediaries.

Deposit Rate:

Rate offered by state-owned commercial banks on one-month time deposits. Data refer to a simple arithmetic average of the rates reported by each of the three state-owned commercial banks.

Lending Rate:

Rate charged by state-owned commercial banks on loans to the agricultural sector. Data refer to a simple arithmetic average of the rates reported by each of the three state-owned commercial banks.

Prices:

Producer Prices:

Source: Central Bank. Modified Laspeyres index, reference period December 1999=100. Weights were derived from a 1997 industrial survey. Index covers manufacturing industry with production for domestic market.

Consumer Prices:

Source: Central Bank. Weights Reference Period: April 2004-April 2005; Geographical Coverage: The first four sub-regions of the central region of Costa Rica; Number of Items in Basket: 292; Basis for Calculation: The weights were derived from the 2004/2005 ENIG that was conducted during the period April 2004 through April 2005. This survey covered households from all socio-economic groups in both the urban and rural sectors of the entire country.

International Transactions:

Exports and Imports:

Central Bank data, compiled by the Directorate General of Statistics and Census in U.S. dollars.

Government Finance:

Monthly, quarterly, and annual data are as reported by the Central Bank and are derived from the cash flow of the Directorate of the National Treasury in the Ministry of Finance. Data cover operations of the central administration (budgetary accounts and special Treasury accounts). The central administration does not receive grants in cash and does not engage in lending minus repayments operations. Data do not cover operations of the Costa Rican Social Security Fund or of any other central government units with individual budgets. Domestic and foreign debt data have the same coverage as the cash flow data of the Directorate of the National Treasury and are derived from the *Balance de la Hacienda Pública* of the Directorate of National Accounting in the Ministry of Finance. † From 1987 onwards, monthly and quarterly data were revised to have the same presentation as the Treasury cash flow. † Beginning in 2003, annual data are as reported for the *Government Finance Statistics Yearbook (GFSY)* and cover budgetary central government. † Beginning in January 2006, data are as reported in the *GFSM 2001* analytical framework and cover budgetary central government. The fiscal year ends December 31.

National Accounts:

Source: Central Bank. Beginning in 1991, data are compiled according to the *1993 SNA*, as indicated by the country.

Côte d'Ivoire   662

Date of Fund Membership:

March 11, 1963

Standard Source:

Banque Centrale des Etats de l'Afrique de l'Ouest (Central Bank of West African States)
Institut National de la Statistique
Côte d'Ivoire is a member of the West African Economic and Monetary Union, together with Benin, Burkina Faso, Guinea-Bissau, Mali, Niger, Senegal, and Togo. The Union, which was established in 1962, has a common central bank, the Central Bank of West African States (BCEAO), with headquarters in Dakar, and national branches in the member states. Mali and Guinea-Bissau joined the Union on June 1, 1984 and May 2, 1997, respectively.

Exchange Rates:

Official Rate: (End of Period and Period Average):
Prior to January 1999, the official rate was pegged to the French franc. On January 12, 1994, the CFA franc was devalued to CFAF 100 per French franc from CFAF 50 at which it had been fixed since 1948. From January 1, 1999, the CFAF is pegged to the euro at a rate of CFA franc 655.957 per euro.

International Liquidity:

Gold is revalued on a quarterly basis at the rate communicated by the BCEAO, which corresponds to the lowest average fixing in the London market.

Monetary Authorities:

Comprises the national branch of the BCEAO only. The amount of currency outside banks is estimated by subtracting from the amount of CFA franc notes issued by Côte d'Ivoire the estimated amounts of Côte d'Ivoire's currency in the cash held by the banks of all member countries of the Union.

Deposit Money Banks:

Comprises commercial banks and specialized development banks, and includes certain banking operations of the Treasury and the Post Office. The Treasury accepts customs duty bills (reported separately in *line 22d.i*). Through its many branches, the Postal Checking System acts as the main depository for the private sector in the interior of Côte d'Ivoire. *Claims on the Private Sector (line 22d)* include doubtful and litigious debts. † Beginning in 1979, *Central Government Deposits (line 26d)* include the deposits of the public establishments of an administrative or social

nature (EPAS) and exclude those of the savings bank; *Demand and Time Deposits (lines 24 and 25)* include deposits of the savings bank and exclude deposits of EPAS; and *Claims on Private Sector (line 22d)* exclude claims on other financial institutions.

Monetary Survey:

The data reported agree with Central Bank of West African States aggregates, as given in the table on the position of the monetary institutions. Valuation differences exist as a result of the *IFS* calculations of reserve position in the Fund and the SDR holdings, both components of *line 11*, based on Fund record. † Beginning in 1979, *Claims on Other Financial Institutions (line 32f)* includes claims of deposit money banks on other financial institutions; see deposit money bank notes for explanation of other break symbols.

Other Banking Institutions:

Liquid Liabilities (line 55l): † See notes on deposit money banks and monetary survey.

Interest Rates:

Discount Rate (End of Period):
Basic discount rate offered by the BCEAO.

Repurchase Agreement Rate (End of Period):
Rate on repurchase agreements between the BCEAO and the banks.

Money Market Rate:
Rate paid on overnight interbank advances.

Deposit Rate:
Rate offered by banks on time deposits of CFAF 500,000–2,000,000 for under six months.

Prices, Production, Labor:

Consumer Prices:
Source: Institut National de la Statistique. Weights Reference Period: 2008; Geographical Coverage: Abidjan metropolitan area; Number of Items in Basket: 684; Basis for Calculation: The weights come from a household budget survey conducted in Abidjan in 2008.

Industrial Production:
Source: Institut National de la Statistique. Laspeyres type index, weights reference 1984/Q4–1985/Q3. The index covers mining, manufacturing, and energy; sectors are weighted by their share of total value added at factor cost of 1985.

International Transactions:

All data are from the Central Bank of West African States.

Government Finance:

Annual data are as reported for the *Government Finance Statistics Yearbook* and cover the budgetary central government. The fiscal year ends December 31.

National Accounts:

Source: Institut National de la Statistique. Data are prepared in accordance with the 1993 United Nations System of National Accounts.

Croatia   960

Date of Fund Membership:
December 14, 1992

Standard Sources:
Croatian National Bank
Statistics Office of the Republic of Croatia

Exchange Rates:

Market Rate (End of Period and Period Average):
The midpoint rate announced by the Croatian National Bank based on the results of the interbank foreign exchange auctions. From December 23, 1991 to May 30, 1994, the Croatian dinar was the official currency of Croatia. On May 30, 1994 the kuna, equal to 1000 dinars, was introduced.

Central Bank:
Consists of the Croatian National Bank (CNB) only.
Claims on Central Government comprises claims on central government budgetary units and central government funds and includes claims arising from the assumption by the government of certain liabilities of the central bank of the Former Socialist Federal Republic of Yugoslavia to the CNB. *Central Government Deposits* comprises deposits of the central government budgetary units and central government funds. Data are based on a standardized report form (SRF) for central banks, which accords with the concepts and definitions of the IMF's *Monetary and Financial Statistics Manual (MFSM)*, 2000. Departures from the *MFSM* methodology are explained below.
For December 2001 through November 2010, liabilities to the Croatian Bank for Reconstruction and Development are included in *Liabilities to Central Government* rather than in *Liabilities to Other Sectors* and *Deposits Excluded from Broad Money.*
For December 2001 through December 2003, accrued interest is included in *Other Items (Net)* rather than in the outstanding amounts of financial assets and liabilities.
Securities other than shares issued are at face value rather than at market price or fair value.

Other Depository Corporations:
Comprises banks licensed by the CNB in accordance with the *Banking Act.* Beginning in December 2010, includes housing and savings banks.
Claims on Central Government comprises claims on central government budgetary units and central government funds and includes claims arising from the assumption by the government of certain liabilities of the central bank of the Former Socialist Federal Republic of Yugoslavia to Croatian banks. *Central Government Deposits* comprises deposits of the central government budgetary units and central government funds. Data are based on a standardized report form (SRF) for other depository corporations, which accords with the concepts and definitions of the IMF's *Monetary and Financial Statistics Manual (MFSM)*. Departures from the *MFSM* methodology are explained below.
For December 2001 through November 2010, claims on and liabilities to the Croatian Bank for Reconstruction and Development are included in *Claims on Central Government* rather than in

Claims on Other Financial Corporations and *Other Deposits Included in Broad Money* and *Deposits Excluded from Broad Money*, respectively. For December 2001 through November 2010, claims on and liabilities to the Croatian Motorways Authority are included in *Claims on Central Government* and *Liabilities to Central Government*, rather than in *Claims on Public Nonfinancial Corporations,Transferable Deposits Included in Broad Money, Other Deposits Included in Broad Money,* and *Deposits Excluded from Broad Money*, respectively. For December 2001 through December 2003, accrued interest is included in *Other Items (Net)* rather than in the outstanding amounts of financial assets and liabilities.
For December 2001 through April 2004, positions on financial derivatives are included in *Other Items (Net)* rather than attributed to claims on and liabilities to the counterparty sector.
Securities other than shares issued are at face value rather than at market price or fair value.

Depository Corporations:
See notes on central bank and other depository corporations.

Monetary Aggregates:

Broad Money:
Broad Money calculated from the liability data in the sections for the central bank and other depository corporations accords with the concepts and definitions of the *MFSM*. Beginning in January 2004, Broad Money differs from M4 described below as *M4* excludes accrued interest.

Money (National Definitions):
Reserve Money comprises currency in circulation and deposits of licensed banks, housing savings banks, savings and loan cooperatives, investment funds, and other resident non-central government sectors with the CNB. Currency in circulation refers to currency and coins issued by CNB.
M1 comprises currency outside licensed banks, and transferable deposits in national currency of housing savings banks, investment funds, savings and loan cooperatives, and other resident non-central government sectors with the CNB and licensed banks.
M4 (broad money) comprises M1, savings, time, and foreign currency deposits of housing savings banks, investment funds, savings and loan cooperatives, and other resident non-central government sectors, and bonds and money market instruments in national and foreign currency issued by licensed banks and held by other resident non-central government sectors.

Interest Rates:

Discount Rate (End of Period):
Basic rate at which the CNB lends to commercial banks.

Money Market Rate:
Short-term rate determined on the Zagreb Money Market.

Savings Rate (Foreign Currency):
Weighted average rate offered by commercial banks on foreign currency savings deposits of nonfinancial corporations, public sector, other financial corporations, nonprofit institutions, and nonresidents. The rate is weighted by the total end-of-month deposit amount. Beginning in January 2002, weighted average rate offered by commercial and savings banks on foreign currency savings deposits of nonfinancial corporations and households.

Deposit Rate:
Average rate offered by commercial banks on deposits weighted by volume of new deposits received during the last reporting month.

Deposit Rate (Indexed to Foreign Currency):
Weighted average rate offered by commercial banks on Kuna deposits indexed to foreign currency of nonfinancial corporations, public sector, other financial corporations, nonprofit institutions, and nonresidents. The rate is weighted by amount of new deposits received during the month. Beginning in January 2002, weighted average rate offered by commercial and savings banks on Kuna deposits indexed to foreign currency of nonfinancial corporations and households.

Deposit Rate (Foreign Currency):
Weighted average rate offered by commercial banks on foreign currency deposits of nonfinancial corporations, public sector, other financial corporations, nonprofit institutions, and nonresidents. The rate is weighted by amount of new deposits received during the month. Beginning in January 2002, weighted average rate offered by commercial and savings banks on foreign currency deposits of nonfinancial corporations and households.

Lending Rate:
Average rate charged by commercial banks on credits weighted by volume of new credits granted during the last reporting month. † Beginning in January 2002, rates on interbank loans and loans to the central government which carry lower interest rates, are excluded. Thus, the average rate has increased reflecting mainly rates on overdrafts to households and enterprises.

Lending Rate (Indexed to Foreign Currency):
Average rate charged by commercial banks on credits in Kuna indexed to foreign currency weighted by volume of new credits granted to nonfinancial corporations, public sector, other financial corporations, nonprofit institutions, and nonresidents during the last reporting month. Beginning in January 2002, average rate charged by commercial and savings banks on credits in Kuna indexed to foreign currency weighted by volume of new credits granted to nonfinancial corporations and households during the last reporting month.

Lending Rate in Euros:
Average rate charged by commercial banks on credits to nonfinancial corporations, public sector, other financial corporations, nonprofit institutions, and nonresidents in German marks weighted by volume of new credits granted during the last reporting month. Beginning in January 2002, average rate charged by commercial and savings banks on credits in Euros weighted by volume of new credits granted to nonfinancial corporations and households during the last reporting month.

Prices, Production, Labor:

Share Prices:
CROBEX share price index of Zagreb Stock Exchange, base July 1, 1997.

Wholesale Prices:
Source: Statistics Office of the Republic of Croatia. Weights Reference Period: 2009; Sectoral Coverage: mining and quarrying, manufacturing, electricity, gas and steam, air conditioning, and water supply; Number of Items in Basket: 1,344 products; Basis for Calculation: weights are annually price-updated to December of previous year.

Consumer Prices:
Source: Statistics Office of the Republic of Croatia. Weights Reference Period: 2005; Geographical Coverage: whole territory of the Republic of Croatia; Number of Items in Basket: 765; Basis for Calculation: weights are based on the Household Budget Survey, conducted on a regular basis since 1998.

Industrial Production:
Statistics Office of the Republic of Croatia. Weights Reference Period: 2005; Sectoral Coverage: mining and quarrying, manufacturing and energy supply; Basis for Calculation: weights are calculated as the value added relating to data sources.

Wages and Employment:
Source: Statistics Office of the Republic of Croatia. Data are based on a regular monthly sample of 70 percent of all employees, including the self-employed. Annual data represent averages of the monthly data. Prior to 1996, data did not include private farmers and employed persons at the Ministry of Internal Affairs and Ministry of Defense. Since 1996, these areas and estimates of employees in small businesses (up to 10 employed persons) have been included.

International Transactions:

Statistics Office of the Republic of Croatia data on *Exports and Imports, c.i.f.* are provisional customs statistics pending improvements in the management of customs declarations. Beginning in 1992, the data include foreign trade with countries of the Former Socialist Federal Republic of Yugoslavia.

Government Finance:

Monthly and quarterly data are as reported by the Ministry of Finance and cover budgetary central government. Annual data are obtained by aggregating of quarterly data. † Prior to January 2004, to the extent possible, existing subannual IFS data were converted to the main aggregates that are presented in the *GFSM 2001* Statement of Sources and Uses of Cash (see the Introduction of the monthly *IFS* publication for details). Beginning in January 2004, monthly data are as reported in the *GFSM 2001* analytical framework and cover budgetary central government. The fiscal year ends December 31.

National Accounts:

As indicated by the country, data are in accordance with the *ESA 95.* Beginning in 1995, data are sourced from the Eurostat database. Eurostat introduced chain-linked GDP volume measures to both annual and quarterly data. Chain linked GDP volume measures are expressed in the prices of the previous year and re-referenced to 2005.

Curaçao   354

Following the dissolution of the Netherlands Antilles on October 10, 2010, Curaçao became an autonomous country within the Kingdom of the Netherlands.

Standard Sources:

Central Bank of Curaçao and Sint Maarten
Bureau of Statistics

Exchange Rates:

Official Rate: (End of Period and Period Average):
Central bank midpoint rate. The official rate is pegged to the U.S. dollar.

Prices:

Consumer Prices:
Source: Bureau of Statistics. Weights Reference Period: October 2006; Geographical Coverage: Curaçao.

Curaçao & St Maarten   355

Following the dissolution of the Netherlands Antilles on October 10, 2010, the currency union of Curaçao and Sint Maarten was formed.

Standard Sources:

Central Bank of Curaçao and Sint Maarten
Bureau of Statistics

Exchange Rates:

Official Rate: (End of Period and Period Average):
Central bank midpoint rate. The official rate is pegged to the U.S. dollar.

International Liquidity:

According to national practice, *Gold (National Valuation) (line 1and)* is determined using the average of the lowest market values of the last three years minus a spread of 30%.

Cyprus   423

Data are denominated in Cyprus pounds prior to January 2008 and in euros from January 2008 onward. An irrevocably fixed factor for converting pounds to euros was established at 0.585274 Cyprus pounds per euro. With Cyprus's entry into Stage Three of the European Economic and Monetary Union (EMU) in January 2008, a euro area-wide definition of residency was introduced: all positions with residents of other euro area (EA) countries, including the European Central Bank (ECB), are classified as domestic positions, and foreign assets and foreign liabilities include only positions with non-EA residents. In 2008, the pound was retired from circulation and replaced by euro banknotes and coins. Descriptions of the methodology and presentation of Cyprus's accounts following the introduction of the euro are discussed under *European Economic and Monetary Union* in the Introduction to *IFS* and in the notes on the euro area page.

Date of Fund Membership:

December 21, 1961

Standard Sources:

Central Bank
Statistics and Research Department

Exchange Rates:

Market Rate (End of Period and Period Average):
In January 2008, the Cyprus pound became a participating currency within the Eurosystem, and the euro market rate became applicable to all transactions. In 2008, the pound was retired from circulation and replaced by euro banknotes and coins. For additional information, refer to the section on Exchange Rates in the *Introduction to IFS* and the notes on the euro area page. Prior to January 2008, midpoint of the official U.S. dollar/pound exchange rate, which was adjusted daily by the Central Bank of Cyprus.

International Liquidity:

Beginning in January 2008, *Total Reserves minus Gold (line 1l.d)* and *Foreign Exchange (line.1d.d)* are defined in accordance with the Eurosystem's statistical definition of international reserves. *Gold (Eurosystem Valuation) (line 1and)* is revalued monthly at market prices. Memorandum data are provided on *Non-Euro Claims on Euro Area Residents*. Prior to January 2008, *line 1d.d* includes Treasury foreign exchange, and gold is obtained by converting the value in national currency terms, as reported in the country's standard sources, using the prevailing exchange rate, as given in *line* **dg** or *line* **ag**. For additional information, refer to the section on International Liquidity in the introduction to *IFS* and the notes on the euro area page.

Central Bank:

Consists of the Central Bank of Cyprus (CBC) only, which beginning in January 2008 is part of the Eurosystem (for a description of accounts refer to the section on *Central Bank - Euro Area* in the introduction to *IFS*). Beginning in January 2008, *Currency Issued* comprises euro banknotes and coins and unretired pounds. Beginning in January 2008, data are compiled in accordance with the European Central Bank's framework for monetary statistics. For a description of accounts, refer to the section on *Central Bank - Euro Area* in the introduction to *IFS*.

Prior to January 2008, data do not fully conform with the European Central Bank's framework for monetary statistics and are not strictly comparable to data for later periods.

Other Depository Corporations:

Comprises commercial banks, Cooperative Central Bank which channel the excess liquidity of village cooperative societies to other societies, specialized credit institutions; cooperative credit institutions, and international banking units. Beginning in January 2008, comprises all resident units classified as other monetary financial institutions (other MFIs), in accordance with *1995 ESA* standards, including money market funds. Beginning in January 2008, data are compiled in accordance with the European Central Bank's framework for monetary statistics. For a description of accounts, refer to the section on *Other Depository Corporations - Euro Area* in the introduction to *IFS*.

Prior to January 2008, data do not fully conform with the European Central Bank's framework for monetary statistics and are not strictly comparable to data for later periods.

Depository Corporations (National Residency):

See notes on central bank and other depository corporations. For a description of the methodology and accounts, refer to the section on *Depository Corporations (Based on National Residency) - Euro Area* in the introduction to *IFS*.

Depository Corporations (Euro Area-wide Residency):

See notes on central bank and other depository corporations. For a description of the methodology and accounts, refer to the section on *Depository Corporations (Based on Euro Area-wide Residency) - Euro Area* in the introduction to *IFS*.

Money (National Definitions):

Beginning in January 2008, national monetary aggregates series were discontinued. The euro area aggregates are presented on the euro area page.

M1 comprises currency in circulation and transferable deposits. Currency in circulation refers to notes and coins issued by the CBC less the amount held by other depository corporations. Transferable deposits refer to the demand and sight deposits in national and foreign currency of other financial corporations, state and local governments, public nonfinancial corporations, and private sector with the CBC and other depository corporations.

M2 comprises M1, time and savings deposits in national and foreign currency of other financial corporations, state and local governments, public nonfinancial corporations, and private sector with other depository corporations, and sinking funds of public nonfinancial corporations with the CBC.

Interest Rates:

Discount Rate (End of Period):
Rate charged by the CBC for the discount of treasury bills. † Beginning in January 1996, marginal lending rate charged by the CBC for its overnight facility with collateral. In January 2008, the central bank rate was discontinued. See Eurosystem policy rate series on the euro area page.

Money Market Rate:
Average rate for overnight deposits in the interbank market. Beginning in January 2008, data refer to EURIBOR1M rate.

Treasury Bill Rate:
Weighted average rate on 13-week treasury bills sold at auctions during the month.

Deposit Rate (line 60l):
Deposit rate ceiling set by the CBC for time (fixed or notice) deposits of one year in the amount of over CYP 5,000. † For the period of March 1997 to December 2000, deposit rate ceiling set by the CBC for all types of time (fixed or notice) deposits. † Beginning in January 2001, average of the representative nominal interest rates on one-year fixed deposits as reported by the three largest banks.

Deposit Rate (lines 60lhs, 60lhn, 60lcs, and 60lcn):
See notes in the introduction to *IFS* and *Euro-area Interest Rates*.

Lending Rate (line 60p):
Lending rate ceiling set by the CBC. † For the period of January-November 2001, simple average of minimum nominal interest rates on loans to enterprises as reported by the three largest banks. † Beginning in December 2001, simple average of the representative nominal interest rates on loans to enterprises as reported by the three largest banks.

Lending Rate (lines 60phs, 60pns, 60phm, 60phn, 60pcs, and 60pcn):
See notes in the introduction to *IFS* and *Euro-area Interest Rates*.

Government Bond Yield:
Primary market weighted average yield on ten-year development stocks sold at auctions during the month. This rate is used to measure long-term interest rates for assessing convergence among the European Union member states.

Prices, Production, Labor:

Wholesale Prices:
Source: Statistics and Research Department. Weights reference period: 2005; Sectoral Coverage: mining and quarrying, manufacturing, electricity, water supply and materials recovery; Number of Items in Basket: 1100 prices; Basis for Calculation: annual industry survey on sales of industrial products and services.

Consumer Prices:
Source: Statistics and Research Department. Weights Reference Period: 2010; Geographical Coverage: entire country; Number of items in basket: 850; Basis for Calculation: the weights used in the index are based on the Family Budget Survey conducted by the Statistical Service of Cyprus every 5 years.

Industrial Production:
Source: Statistics and Research Department. Weights Reference Period: 2005.

Mining Production:
Source: Statistics and Research Department. Weights Reference Period: 2005.

International Transactions:

Exports and Imports, c.i.f.:
Source: Statistics and Research Department. Data methodology is defined by European Union regulations and relevant methodology for Intra and Extra EU trade.

Government Finance:

Monthly, quarterly, and annual data are derived from the Statistics and Research Department and cover consolidated central government. The fiscal year ends December 31.

National Accounts:

Beginning in 1999, data are sourced from the Eurostat database. Chain linked GDP volume measures are expressed in the prices of the previous year and re-referenced to 2005.

Czech Republic   935

Date of Fund Membership:
January 1, 1993

Standard Sources:
Czech National Bank
Czech Statistical Office
Eurostat

Exchange Rates:

Official Rate: (End of Period and Period Average):
Czech National Bank midpoint rate.

International Liquidity:

Gold (National Valuation) (line 1and) is valued at the price of 60.61 koruny per gram.

Central Bank:

Consists of the Czech National Bank only.

† Beginning in January 2002, data are compiled in accordance with the European Central Bank's framework for monetary statistics using the national residency approach.

For December 2001, data do not fully conform with the European Central Bank's framework for monetary statistics and are not strictly comparable to data for later periods. *Monetary Base* includes positions that are subsequently shown as *Other Liabilities to Other Depository Corporations*.

Other Depository Corporations:

Comprises financial institutions with bank licenses, namely the commercial banks, savings banks, and building societies. Beginning in January 2004, comprises all resident units classified as other monetary financial institutions (other MFIs) in accordance with *1995 ESA* standards, including the money market funds.

† Beginning in January 2002, data are compiled in accordance with the European Central Bank's framework for monetary statistics using the national residency approach.

For December 2001, data do not fully conform with the European Central Bank's framework for monetary statistics and are not strictly comparable to data for later periods. *Claims on General Government* and *Liabilities to Central Government* include positions with local governments and the National Property Fund. *Reserve Deposits and Securities* includes positions that are subsequently shown separately as *Claims on Central Bank: Other Claims*.

Depository Corporations:

See notes on central bank and other depository corporations.

Monetary Aggregates:

Broad Money:

Broad Money calculated from the liability data in the sections for the central bank and other depository corporations.

Money (National Definitions):

M1 comprises currency outside depository corporations and overnight deposits of resident non-MFI, noncentral government sectors with MFIs.

M2 comprises M1, deposits with agreed maturity up to two years, and deposits redeemable at notice up to three months of resident non-MFI, noncentral government sectors with MFIs .

M3 comprises M2, repurchase agreements contracted with other (non-MFI, noncentral government) resident sectors, money market fund shares/units, and debt securities issued by commercial banks with maturity up to two years.

Interest Rates:

Repurchase Agreement Rate:

Rate on a 14-day repurchase agreement between the Czech National Bank and the commercial banks.

Money Market Rate:

Rate on the three-month interbank deposits.

Treasury Bill Rate:

Average rate weighted by volume, on the three-month Treasury bills sold at auctions.

Deposit Rate:

Beginning in January 2001, average rate, weighted by stocks, offered by commercial banks on the outstanding koruny-denomi-nated deposits of non-financial sectors. † Prior to January 2001, average rate offered by commercial banks on all deposits weighted by stocks.

Lending Rate:

Beginning in January 2001, average rate, weighted by stocks, charged by commercial banks on the outstanding koruny-denominated credits to non-financial sectors. † Prior to January 2001, average rate charged by commercial banks on all outstanding credits weighted by stocks.

Government Bond Yield:

Secondary market yield of government bonds with a ten-year maturity. This rate is used to measure long-term interest rates for assessing convergence among the European Union member states.

Prices, Production, Labor:

Share Prices:

Data refer to the PX–50 index. The PX–50 index is a market capitalization weighted value ratio index of 50 stocks traded on the Prague Stock Exchange, base April 5, 1994. Beginning March 20, 2006 data refer to the PX Index, the official index of the Prague Stock Exchange, which replaced the PX50 and PX-D indices. The PX index took over the historical values of the PX–50. The PX index is a market capitalization weighed value ratio index of major stocks traded on the Prague Stock Exchange. The PX index is a price index and dividend yields are not considered in the calculation.

Producer Prices:

Source: Czech Statistical Office. Weights reference period: 2010; Sectorial Coverage: mining, quarrying, manufacturing, electricity, and water supply; Number of Item in Basket: 4,600 items; Basis for Calculation: weights are calculated from the structure of sales of the industrial enterprises on the domestic market.

Consumer Prices:

Source: Czech Statistical Office. Weights Reference Period: 2010; Geographical Coverage: entire country; Number of Items in Basket: 700; Basis for Calculation: the weights are based on 2010 Household Budget Survey (HBS).

Wages:

Source: Czech Statistical Office. Data refer to average monthly wages in Koruny, including agricultural cooperatives.

Industrial Production:

Source: Czech Statistical Office. Weights Reference Period: 2005; Sectoral Coverage: mining and quarrying, manufacturing and electricity, gas and water supply sectors; Basis for Calculation: weights are calculated as the shares of value added created in the whole industry based on a 2005 survey.

Industrial Employment:

Data on average number of workers employed in enterprises of 25 or more employees, reported in thousands. † Beginning 1995, the data cover enterprises of 100 or more employees. Starting in 1997, data cover enterprises of 20 or more employees. Since January 2007(Eurostat methodology) besides employees, the indicator of industrial employment has covered persons working out of employment, too, i.e. persons working base on contract of services and other employed but not just employees. It is an amount adapted to full time. It also induces figures of average monthly wages and productivity of labor. A year-on-year comparability is guaranteed.

International Transactions:

Source: Czech Statistical Office. Data are based on two systems of data collection: Intrastat measures the movement of goods within the EU Member States and Extrastat measures trade with other than EU Member States.

Government Finance:

Budgetary central government data are as supplied by the Ministry of Finance. Preliminary data on general government are compiled by Eurostat. The fiscal year ends December 31.

National Accounts:

Source: Czech Statistical Office. Concepts and definitions are in accordance with the *ESA 95*, as indicated by the country. Eurostat introduced chain-linked GDP volume measures to both annual and quarterly data with the release of the third quarter 2005 on November 30, 2005. Chain linked GDP volume measures are expressed in the prices of the previous year and re-referenced to 2005.

Denmark   128

Date of Fund Membership:

March 30, 1946

Standard Sources:

National Bank of Denmark
Statistical Office

Exchange Rates:

Market Rate (End of Period and Period Average):
Midpoint rate in the Copenhagen market fixed at 11:50 a.m. by the Danmarks National Bank each business day in a meeting attended by authorized foreign exchange dealers.

International Liquidity:

Gold (National Valuation) (line 1and) is valued according to the gold fixing price in London on the last banking day of each month. † prior to June 2005, *Gold (National Valuation)* was obtained by converting the value in national currency terms, as reported in the country's standard sources, using the prevailing exchange rate, as given in *line* **ae** or **we**. Prior to 2005, valuation of gold holdings took place only at the end of each calendar year.
Foreign Exchange (line 1d.d) is based on market value. † Prior to June 2005, these data were adjusted to market value only at year end.
Monetary Authorities: Other Liabilities (line 4..d) is based on market value. † Prior to June 2005, these data were adjusted to market value only at year end.

Central Bank:

Consists of the Danmarks Nationalbank.
Data are compiled in accordance with the European Central Bank's framework for monetary statistics using the national residency approach.
Claims on Nonresidents includes euros issued against the deposit with the European Central Banks (ECB) of U.S. dollars and gold.

Other Depository Corporations:

Comprises other monetary financial institutions in accordance with *1995 ESA* standards, including the money market funds.

Data are compiled in accordance with the European Central Bank's framework for monetary statistics using the national residency approach.

Depository Corporations:

See notes on central bank and other depository corporations.

Monetary Aggregates:

Broad Money:
Broad Money calculated from the liability data in the sections for the central bank and other depository corporations.

Money (National Definitions):
M1 comprises currency outside banks and demand deposits of resident non-MFI, noncentral government sectors with MFIs.
M2 comprises M1, time deposits with original maturity less than two years, and deposits at notice with original maturity less than three months of resident non-MFI, noncentral government sectors with MFIs.
M3 comprises M2, repurchase agreements, money-market securities and shares, and bonds with an original maturity less than two years issued by MFIs held by other (non-MFI, non-government) resident sectors..

Interest Rates:

Central Bank Policy Rate (End of Period):
Rate signals the overall level of Danmarks Nationalbank's interest rates. Changes in the discount rate normally lead the banks to carry out an equivalent general adjustment of the interest rates for deposits from and lending to customers.

Money Market Rate:
Average overnight interbank rate. † Beginning in January 1982, weighted average of three-month interbank rates. † Beginning in January 1993, average of offered interbank rates. † Beginning in January 2007, average of bidded interbank rates. † Beginning in January 2011, rate for uncollateralized money-market lending calculated as a turnover-weighted average of the rates of 12 reporters.

Deposit Rate:
Calculated from interest accrued on krone-denominated deposit accounts (excluding deposits under capital pension schemes) divided by average deposit balance in the quarter. † Prior to 2002, other depository corporations' deposit rates were based on information collected by the Danish Financial Supervisory Authority. Since then, Denmark's Nationalbank has been responsible for collecting these data and a number of methodological changes were introduced. These include a reduction in the number of reporters from 98 to 23 other depository corporations, and a refocusing of the data on other depository corporations' domestic deposit taking operations. † Prior to second quarter of 1993, calculated from interest accrued on both krone- and foreign currency-denominated deposit accounts (including deposits under capital pension schemes) divided by average deposit balance in the quarter. † Prior to 1990, weighted average of rates on time deposits for one to less than twelve months.

Lending Rate:
Calculated from interest accrued on krone-denominated loan accounts divided by average loan balance in the quarter. † Prior to 2002, other depository corporations' lending rates were based on information collected by the Danish Financial Supervisory

Authority. Since then, Denmark's Nationalbank has been responsible for collecting these data and a number of methodological changes were introduced. These include a reduction in the number of reporters from 98 to 23 other depository corporations, and a refocusing of the data on other depository corporations' domestic lending operations. † Prior to second quarter of 1993, calculated from interest accrued on both krone- and foreign currency-denominated loan accounts divided by average loan balance (including nonperforming loans from 1991) in the quarter. † Prior to 1990, weighted average rates on overdrafts.

Government Bond Yield:
Yield on five-year government bonds. † Beginning June 1983, refers to secondary market yields of government bonds with a ten-year maturity. This rate is used to measure long-term interest rates for assessing convergence among the European Union member states.

Mortgage Bond Yield:
Yield on 20-year mortgage credit bonds.

Prices, Production, Labor:

Share Prices (Period Average and End of Month):
Market capitalization weighted index of all stocks traded on the Copenhagen Stock Exchange, base December 31, 1995.

Industrial and Shipping Share Prices (End of Month):
Data are represented by a Laspeyres-type index, base 1935. The index covers a sample of shares on the Copenhagen exchange, refers to end-of-month quotations and covers a sample of shares on the Copenhagen exchange. † Beginning in January 1957, share price index, base 1958. † Beginning in January 1964, share price index, base 1960. † Beginning in January 1965, share price index, base 1971. † Beginning in January 1970, share price index, base January 1, 1983.

Prices, Home and Import Goods:
Source: Statistical Office. Weights reference period: 2005; Sectoral Coveragel: the sum of the import and production values for the home market excluding VAT and excise duties; Number of Items in Basket: about 800 enterprises; Basis for calculation: weights are based on the supply and use tables from national accounts.

Consumer Prices:
Source: Statistical Office. Weights Reference Period: weights are updated every four to five years; Geographical Coverage: whole country; Number of Items in Basket: 25,000 prices; Basis for Calculation: weights are based on a Household Budget Survey combined with the weights of the consumer groups in the national accounts.

Wages: Hourly Earnings:
Source: Statistical Office. Data are in kroner and represent mainly male workers in manufacturing industries, excluding agriculture and fishing, employing 10 or more persons. † Prior to 1988, enterprises employing six or more persons were sampled. Annual data are calculated independently and are not an average of quarterly data.

Unemployment:
Source: Statistical Office. The statistics on the registered number of unemployed persons are, to the greatest possible extent, compiled in accordance with the guidelines set forth by the ILO. Ac-

cording to these guidelines a person has to meet 3 requirements to be defined as unemployed: 1) out of work, 2) available for work and 3) actively in search of work. The data cover include those between the ages of 16–66.

Industrial Production:
Data are sourced from the OECD database, weights reference period: 2005. The sample is stratified by activity (approximately 50). Enterprises employing at least 200 persons in industry activities are surveyed. A sample is drawn for units employing between 20 and 199 persons. 1200 enterprises are surveyed, which represents a universe of 3000 enterprises with at least 20 persons employed. The sample covers about 85 percent of the turnover in this universe.

Agricultural Production:
The series is from the Statistical Office, weights reference period: 1985.

International Transactions:

Value of Exports and Imports:
Source: Statistical Office. Trade data before 1988 does not include ships etc.
Trade data are all published in the *Monthly Bulletin of External Trade*.

Trade indices:
Source: Statistical Office. Fisher indices, weights reference period: 1995.

Import Prices:
Statistical Office, weights reference period: 1995. The series is a component of the *Home and Import Goods* producer price index.

Government Finance:

From 1990 to 1999, annual data are as reported for the *Government Finance Statistics Yearbook (GFSY)* and cover consolidated central government. From 1999, accrual data on general government are derived from source V. The fiscal year ends December 31.

National Accounts:

Source: Statistical Office. † Beginning in 1988, data have been revised significantly following the implementation of the *1993 SNA*, as indicated by the country. Beginning in 1999, euro data are sourced from the Eurostat database. Eurostat introduced chain-linked GDP volume measures to both annual and quarterly data with the release of the third quarter 2005 on November 30, 2005. Chain-linked GDP volume measures are expressed in the prices of the previous year and re-referenced to 2005.

Djibouti 611

Date of Fund Membership:
December 29, 1978

Standard Source:
Le Ministere de l'Economie et des Finances Charge de l'Industrie et de la Planification (The Ministry of Economy and Finance Charge of Industry and Planning

Exchange Rates:

Official Rate: (End of Period and Period Average):
The official rate is pegged to the U.S. dollar. Cross rates are based on a fixed relationship to the U.S. dollar.

International Liquidity:

Data expressed in U.S. dollars for *Foreign Exchange (line 1d.d)* are derived from data denominated in national currency for components of the monetary authorities' *Foreign Assets (line 11),* using the end-of-period market rate *(line* **ae**).

Monetary Authorities:

Data cover the National Bank's accounts and certain accounts of the Treasury related to its monetary authority functions.

Deposit Money Banks:

Data cover the Banque Indo-Suez Mer-Rouge, Banque pour le Commerce et l'Industrie, and Commercial Bank of Ethiopia. Prior to 1998, coverage also includes Banque de Credit et du Commerce, Commercial and Savings Bank of Somalia, and Banque de Djibouti et du Moyen Orient which were operating at that time.

Other Banking Institutions:

Data cover the Caisse de Developpement de Djibouti.

Interest Rates:

Deposit Rate:
Simple average of minimum and maximum rates offered by commercial banks on time deposits of at least 1,000,000 Djibouti Francs with maturity of one month and more.

Lending Rate:
Simple average of minimum and maximum rates charged by commercial banks on overdrafts of under 10,000,000 Djibouti Francs.

Prices:

Source: The Ministry of Economy and Finance Charge of Industry and Planning. Weights Reference Period: March-April 1999. Geographic Coverage: The city of Djibouti. Number of Items in Basket: 223 Basis for Calculation: Djibouti Survey on Household Consumption conducted in 1999 and the Household Survey conducted in 1986.

International Transactions:

All trade data are from The Ministry of Economy and Finance Charge of Industry and Planning. Trade indices: Data are compiled on weights reference period: 1990.

Dominica   321

Date of Fund Membership:
December 12, 1978

Standard Sources:
Eastern Caribbean Central Bank
Ministry of Finance, Trade and Industry, Statistical Division

Exchange Rates:

Official Rate: (End of Period and Period Average):
The official rate is pegged to the U.S. dollar. Rates are based on a fixed relationship to the U.S. dollar.

Central Bank:

Data are based on a standardized report form (SRF) for central banks, which accords with the concepts and definitions of the IMF's *Monetary and Financial Statistics Manual (MFSM)*, 2000. Departures from the *MFSM* methodology are explained below.
Data refer to accounts in the balance sheet of the East Caribbean Central Bank (ECCB) attributable to Dominica.
Financial derivatives are excluded from the data.
Claims on Nonresident comprises estimates of Dominica's notional share of the ECCB's foreign assets.
Claims on Other Depository Corporations comprises the portion of the ECCB's claims on resident other depository corporations attributable to Dominica.
Claims on Central Government and *Liabilities to Central Government* comprise the portion of the ECCB's claims on and liabilities to the central government attributable to Dominica.
Financial assets with other financial corporations, state and local governments, public nonfinancial corporations, and private sector attributable to Dominica are not included in the data in the absence of a country of these accounts in the balance sheet of the ECCB.
Currency in circulation comprises the portion of currency in circulation attributable to Dominica less vault cash held by other depository corporations.
Some portion of other deposits to other depository corporations and interest accrued from these deposits are included in *Other Items (Net)*.
Share and other equity is not applicable to the member countries of the ECCU because the shares and other equity in the balance sheet of the ECCB exclusively belong to the ECCB.

Other Depository Corporations:

Comprises commercial banks. Data exclude mortgage companies, building societies, and credit unions, which accept deposits.
Data are based on a standardized report form (SRF) for other depository corporations, which accords with the concepts and definitions of the *Monetary and Financial Statistics Manual (MFSM)*.
For resident other depository corporations in the member countries of the ECCU, departures from the *MFSM* methodology are explained below.
Financial derivatives and insurance technical reserves are excluded from the data.
Financial assets and liabilities for which economic sectorization is unavailable are allocated to the economic sector having the largest volume of transactions in the category.
Transferable Deposits Included in Broad Money includes all deposits of the private sector denominated in foreign currency.
Accounts receivable and payable are included in *Other Items (Net)* rather than in other depository corporations' claims or liabilities to the corresponding economic sectors.
Accrued interest on transactions with nonresidents is included in *Other Items (Net)* rather than in the outstanding amount of foreign assets and liabilities.

Depository Corporations:

See notes on central bank and other depository corporations.

Monetary Aggregates:

Broad Money:

Broad Money is calculated from the liability data in the sections for the central bank and other depository corporations. Broad money differs from M2 described below as broad money includes the deposits of money holding sectors with the ECCB attributable to Dominica and deposits of other financial corporations, state and local government, and public nonfinancial corporations in national and foreign currencies with commercial banks.

Money (National Definitions):

M1 comprises notes and coins held by the public and demand deposits in national currency of the private sector with commercial banks.

M2 comprises M1 plus time, savings, and foreign currency deposits of the private sector with commercial banks.

Interest Rates:

Discount Rate (End of Period):

Rate charged by the ECCB on loans of last resort to commercial banks.

Money Market Rate:

Fixed rate on loans between commercial banks. The rate includes the commission charged by the ECCB as agent. † Beginning in October 2001, weighted average rate on loans between commercial banks. The rate is weighted by loans amounts.

Treasury Bill Rate:

Rate on three-month treasury bills.

Savings Rate:

Maximum rate offered by commercial banks on savings deposits in national currency. † Beginning in June 2003, weighted average rate offered by commercial banks on savings deposits in national currency. The rate is weighted by deposit amounts.

Savings Rate (Foreign Currency):

Weighted average rate offered by commercial banks on savings deposits in foreign currency. The rate is weighted by deposit amounts.

Deposit Rate:

Maximum rate offered by commercial banks on three-month time deposits. The rate is weighted by deposit amounts.

Deposit Rate (Foreign currency):

Weighted average rate offered by commercial banks on deposits in foreign currency. The rate is weighted by deposit amounts.

Lending Rate:

Maximum rate charged by commercial banks on prime loans. The rate is weighted by loan amounts.

Lending Rate (Foreign Currency):

Weighted average rate charged by commercial banks on loans in foreign currency. The rate is weighted by loan amounts.

Prices:

Consumer Prices:

Source: Ministry of Finance, Trade and Industry, Statistical Division. Weights Reference Period: January 2001; Geographical

Coverage: whole national territory; Number of Items in Basket: 394; Basis for Calculation: weights are derived from the 1997–1998 Household Expenditure Survey.

International Transactions:

All trade data are from the Ministry of Finance, Trade and Industry, Statistical Division.

National Accounts:

Source: Eastern Caribbean Central Bank. As indicated by the country, data have been revised following the implementation of the *1993 SNA.*

Dominican Republic 243

Date of Fund Membership:

December 28, 1945

Standard Source:

Central Bank of the Dominican Republic

Exchange Rates:

Until September 4, 2000, the exchange rate system was based on an independent float of the peso. On September 5, 2000, the exchange rate was devalued 2 percent under a managed floating regime; since then, and through November 19, 2001, the central bank was setting once a week, the official exchange rate equal to the previous week's average of the commercial bank rate. Effective November 20, 2001, the buying exchange rate is the weighted average buying rate on the private market on the business day immediately prior to the operation date. Effective March 13, 2002, the selling exchange rate is the weighted average selling rate on the private foreign exchange market on the business day immediately preceding the operation. The above-mentioned private market includes commercial banks and foreign exchange dealers.

International Liquidity:

Gold (National Valuation) (line 1and) is obtained by converting the value in national currency terms, as reported in the country's standard sources, using the prevailing exchange rate, as given in *line* **ae** or **we**. This line follows national valuation procedures which revalued gold monthly beginning June 1978 through January 1981 on the basis of the average minimum gold price in the Zurich and London markets during the month, and thereafter on the basis of the daily average price in the London market.

Central Bank:

Consists of the Central Bank of the Dominican Republic (CBDR) only.

Data are based on a standardized report form (SRF) for central banks, which accords with the concepts and definitions of the IMF's *Monetary and Financial Statistics Manual (MFSM)*, 2000. Departures from the *MFSM* methodology are explained below.

Securities other than shares issued are allocated to holding sectors using information that does not provide full sectorization.

Financial instruments that cannot be valued at market prices are valued at acquisition cost.

Other Depository Corporations:

Comprises multiple banks, development and credit banks, savings and loan associations, finance companies, loan houses, savings and credit corporations, and savings and credit associations. Beginning in January 2009, includes savings and credit cooperatives. Data exclude offshore banks, which accept deposits from residents, and money market investment funds.

Data are based on a standardized report form (SRF) for other depository corporations, which accords with the concepts and definitions of the *Monetary and Financial Statistics Manual (MFSM)*. For other depository corporations in the Dominican Republic, departures from the *MFSM* methodology are explained below.

Financial assets and liabilities for which financial instrument breakdown is unavailable are allocated to the financial instrument having the largest volume of transactions in the category. Financial assets and liabilities for which economic sectorization is unavailable are allocated to the economic sector having the largest volume of transactions in the category.

Before June 2006, *Claims on Private Sector* includes loans to public nonfinancial corporations.

Financial assets and liabilities that cannot be valued at market prices are valued at acquisition cost.

Depository Corporations:

See notes on central bank and other depository corporations.

Other Financial Corporations:

Comprises insurance corporations and pension funds. Data exclude non money market investment funds, securities dealers, foreign exchange houses, and warehouses.

Data are based on a standardized report form (SRF) for other financial corporations, which accords with the concepts and definitions of the *Monetary and Financial Statistics Manual (MFSM)*. For other financial corporations in the Dominican Republic, departures from the *MFSM* methodology are explained below.

Financial assets and liabilities for which financial instrument breakdown is unavailable are allocated to the financial instrument having the largest volume of transactions in the category.

Financial assets and liabilities for which economic sectorization is unavailable are allocated to the economic sector having the largest volume of transactions in the category.

Claims on Nonresidents include some positions with domestic sectors.

Claims on Central Government includes holdings of securities issued by public nonfinancial corporations.

Some accrued interest is included in *Claims on Other Depository Corporations* rather than in the underlying financial instrument and sector.

Financial assets and liabilities that cannot be valued at market prices are valued at acquisition cost.

Financial Corporations:

See notes on central bank, other depository corporations, and other financial corporations.

Monetary Aggregates:

Broad Money:
Broad Money calculated from the liability data in the sections for the central bank and other depository corporations accords with the concepts and definitions of the *MFSM* and is consistent with M3 described below.

Money (National Definitions):
Beginning in December 2001, the CBDR adopted the harmonized definition as the official definition of monetary aggregates. The harmonized definitions follow the methodology established by the Central American Monetary Council.

Narrow Monetary Base comprises currency in circulation, legal reserve deposits and clearing balances of multiple banks and development and credit banks with the CBDR in national currency, and securities issued by the CBDR held by multiple banks and, development and credit banks to satisfy legal reserve requirements in national currency. Currency in circulation refers to notes and coins issued by the CBDR.

Broad Monetary Base comprises narrow monetary base, legal reserve deposits and clearing balances of multiple banks and development and credit banks with the CBDR in foreign currency, other nonrestricted deposits of multiple banks and development and credit banks with the CBRD in national and foreign currency, and short-term securities issued by the CBRD held by multiple banks and development and credit banks in national and foreign currency.

M1 comprises currency held by the public, transferable deposits of other financial corporations, state and local government, public nonfinancial corporations, and private sector with other depository corporations in national currency, and cashiers and certified checks held by other financial corporations, state and local government, public nonfinancial corporations, and private sector in national currency.

M2 comprises M1, other deposits of other financial corporations, state and local government, public nonfinancial corporations, and private sector with other depository corporations, short-term securities issued by the BCRD held by the private sector in national currency, and short-term securities issued by other depository corporations held by other financial corporations, state and local government, public nonfinancial corporations, and private sector in national currency.

M3 comprises M2 and deposits of other financial corporations, state and local government, public nonfinancial corporations, and private sector with other depository corporations in foreign currency.

Interest Rates:

Central Bank Policy Rate (End of Period):
Refers to the Monetary Policy Rate (MPR) which is the reference rate for overnight liquidity operations as established by the Monetary Board of the CBDR.

Money Market Rate:
Simple average of rates at which multiple banks borrow funds in the interbank market.

Savings Rate:
Average rate offered by multiple banks on savings deposits in national currency.

Savings Rate (Foreign Currency):
Average rate offered by multiple banks on savings deposits in U.S. dollars.

Deposit Rate:

Average rate offered by multiple banks on time deposits. Beginning in January 1996, weighted average rate offered by commercial banks on time deposits in national currency. The rate is weighted by deposit amounts.

Deposit Rate (Foreign Currency):

Average rate offered by multiple banks on time deposits in U.S. dollars.

Lending Rate:

Average rate charged by multiple banks on non-preferential loans. Beginning in January 1996, weighted average rate charged by commercial banks on non-preferential loans in national currency. The rate is weighted by loan amounts.

Lending Rate (Foreign Currency):

Average rate charged by multiple banks on non-preferential loans in U.S. dollars.

Prices:

Consumer Prices:

Source: Central Bank of the Dominican Republic. National consumer price index, weights reference period: December 2010; Geographical Coverage: Four regions that were identified in the Household Budget Survey estimated 2007 (Ozama, North, East and South); Number of Items in Basket:305; Basis for Calculation: weights are derived from the 2007 Household Budget Survey. Prior to 1978, data refer only to consumer prices in Santo Domingo.

International Transactions:

Exports and Imports, f.o.b.:

All trade data are from the Central Bank of the Dominican Republic. Export and import values exclude trade in the processing zone.

Volume of Exports:

IFS average of sugar, ferronickel, coffee, and cocoa beans with a 1995 value of exports as weights.

Unit Value of Exports:

IFS average of sugar, ferronickel, coffee, and cocoa beans with a 1995 value of exports as weights.

Government Finance:

Monthly, quarterly, and annual data are derived from tables prepared by the Central Bank of the Dominican Republic and cover budgetary central government. Data do not cover operations of the social security funds or of other central government agencies with own budgets. Data differ from national presentations in that some transactions are reclassified according to Government Finance Statistics methodology. The fiscal year ends December 31.

National Accounts:

Data are from the Central Bank of the Dominican Republic. As indicated by the country, data are compiled according to the recommendations of the *1993 SNA*.

ECCU   309

The Eastern Caribbean Currency Union (ECCU) was formed when the Eastern Caribbean Central Bank (ECCB) was created.

The governments participating in the East Caribbean Currency Authority (ECCA) signed the Eastern Caribbean Central Bank Agreement Act 1983 on July 5, 1983 to establish the ECCB. In accordance with the Agreement, the ECCB was formally established on October 1, 1983, on which date the ECCA was deemed to have ceased to exist. Effective from this date, all the assets and liabilities of the ECCA, together with all its rights and obligations that are not inconsistent with the provisions of this Agreement, were transferred to the ECCB.

The ECCB is the monetary authority for the governments of Anguilla, Antigua and Barbuda, Dominica, Grenada, Montserrat, St. Kitts and Nevis, St. Lucia, and St. Vincent and the Grenadines. The ECCB is governed by two acts: the Eastern Caribbean Central Bank Agreement of 1983 which establishes and defines the powers and operations of the ECCB and the Uniform Banking Act of 1993 which defines the operations of financial institutions within the ECCU area including their relations with the ECCB. The Monetary Council, the governing body of the ECCB, comprises the Finance Minister of each of the eight members. The core purposes of the ECCB are to regulate the availability of money and credit, promote and maintain monetary stability, promote credit and exchange conditions and a sound financial structure conducive to the balanced growth and development of the territories of the participating governments, and actively promote the economic development of the territories of the participating governments.

The ECCB issues and manages a common currency for the area, the Eastern Caribbean dollar, with a fixed exchange rate pegged at EC$2.70 to US$1.00 since July 1976. The ECCB has the sole right to issue notes and coins for its member countries. The ECCB serves as a banker to its participating governments as well as to the commercial banks operating in the area. Governments maintain accounts with the ECCB through which transactions are conducted. Commercial banks maintain accounts with the ECCB to satisfy legal reserve requirements, to facilitate interbank transactions, and as a means of holding excess funds. The ECCB may grant advances to commercial banks to meet short-term liquidity needs.

The consolidated data published for the ECCU has one major methodological difference compared to the data published in *IFS* for the individual countries. The ECCU-wide residency criterion is applied instead of the national residency criterion.

Date of Fund Membership:

Antigua and Barbuda (February 25, 1982), Dominica (December 12, 1978), Grenada (August 27, 1975), Saint Kitts and Nevis (August 15, 1984), Saint Lucia (November 15, 1979), and Saint Vincent and the Grenadines (December 28, 1979). Anguilla and Montserrat are not members of the IMF.

Standard Sources:

Eastern Caribbean Central Bank

Exchange Rates:

Official Rate: (End of Period and Period Average):
The official rate is pegged to the U.S. dollar.

Central Bank:

Consists of the Eastern Caribbean Central Bank (ECCB) only. The ECCB is the monetary authority for the eight governments of the member countries of the ECCU and its headquarters is in St. Kitts. The ECCB is governed by two acts: the Eastern Caribbean Central Bank Agreement of 1983 which establishes and defines the powers and operations of the ECCB and the Uniform Banking Act of 1993 which defines the operations of financial institutions within the ECCU territories including their relations with the ECCB. The Monetary Council, the governing body of the ECCB, comprises the Finance Minister of each of the eight members. The core purposes of the ECCB are to regulate the availability of money and credit, promote and maintain monetary stability, promote credit and exchange conditions and a sound financial structure conducive to the balanced growth and development of the territories of the participating governments, and actively promote the economic development of the territories of the participating governments. The ECCB issues and manages a common currency for the area, the Eastern Caribbean dollar. The ECCB has the sole right to issue notes and coins for its member countries. The ECCB serves as a banker to its participating governments as well as to the commercial banks operating in the area. Governments maintain accounts with the ECCB through which transactions are conducted. Commercial banks maintain accounts with the ECCB to satisfy legal reserve requirements, to facilitate interbank transactions, and as a means of holding excess funds.

Data are based on a standardized report form (SRF) for central banks, which accords with the concepts and definitions of the IMF's *Monetary and Financial Statistics Manual (MFSM)*, 2000. The ECCU-wide residency criterion is applied to the ECCB's claims on and liabilities to resident economic sectors and nonresidents. Resident economic sectors include those having center of economic interest within the ECCU area. Departures from the *MFSM* methodology are explained below.

Financial assets and liabilities for which economic sectorization is unavailable are allocated to the economic sector having the largest volume of transactions in the category.

Claims on Public Nonfinancial Corporations includes some accounts with other financial corporations.

Financial derivatives are recorded on a net basis.

Other Depository Corporations:

Comprises commercial banks. Data exclude finance companies, mortgage companies, building societies, and credit unions, which accept deposits.

Data are based on a standardized report form (SRF) for other depository corporations, which accords with the concepts and definitions of the *Monetary and Financial Statistics Manual (MFSM)*. This section consolidates national data of the member countries of the ECCU by application of an ECCU-wide residency criterion for the distinction between resident economic sectors and nonresidents. Claims on and liabilities to nonresidents comprise other depository corporations accounts with nonresidents that do not have center of economic interest within the ECCU area. For resident other depository corporations in the member countries of the ECCU, departures from the *MFSM* methodology are explained below.

Financial derivatives and insurance technical reserves are not included in the data.

Financial assets and liabilities for which economic sectorization is unavailable are allocated to the economic sector having the largest volume of transactions in the category.

Financial derivatives and *Insurance Technical Reserves* are not included in the data.

Transferable Deposits Included in Broad Money includes all deposits of the private sector denominated in foreign currency.

Accounts receivable and payable are included in *Other Items (Net)* rather than in other depository corporations' claims or liabilities to the corresponding economic sectors.

Accrued interest on transactions with nonresidents is included in *Other Items (Net)* rather than in the outstanding amount of foreign assets and liabilities.

Depository Corporations:

See notes on central bank and other depository corporations..

Monetary Aggregates:

Broad Money:

Broad Money is calculated from the liability data in the sections for the central bank and other depository corporations. Broad money differs from M2 described below as broad money includes deposits of money holding sectors with the ECCB and deposits of other financial corporations, state and local government, and public nonfinancial corporations in national and foreign currency with commercial banks.

Money (National Definitions):

M1 comprises notes and coins held by the public and demand deposits in national currency of the private sector with commercial banks.

M2 comprises M1 plus time, savings, and foreign currency deposits of the private sector with commercial banks.

Interest Rates:

Discount Rate (End of Period):

Rate charged by the ECCB on loans of last resort to commercial banks.

Money Market Rate:

Fixed rate on loans between commercial banks. The rate includes the commission charged by the ECCB as agent. † Beginning in October 2001, weighted average rate on loans between commercial banks. The rate is weighted by loans amounts.

Savings Rate:

Maximum rate offered by commercial banks on savings deposits in national currency. † Beginning in June 2003, weighted average rate offered by commercial banks on savings deposits in national currency. The rate is weighted by deposit amounts.

Savings Rate (Foreign Currency):

Weighted average rate offered by commercial banks on savings deposits in foreign currency. The rate is weighted by deposit amounts.

Deposit Rate:

Maximum rate offered by commercial banks on three-month The rate is weighted by deposit amounts.

Deposit Rate (Foreign currency):

Weighted average rate offered by commercial banks on deposits in foreign currency. The rate is weighted by deposit amounts.

Lending Rate:

Maximum rate charged by commercial banks on prime loans. The rate is weighted by loan amounts.

Lending Rate (Foreign Currency):

Weighted average rate charged by commercial banks on loans in foreign currency. The rate is weighted by loan amounts.

National Accounts:

Source: Eastern Caribbean Central Bank.

Ecuador   248

Date of Fund Membership:

December 28, 1945

Standard Source:

Central Bank of Ecuador

Exchange Rates:

Market Rate (End of Period):

Through December 1999, the principal rate refers to the market-determined rate. On January 7, 2000, the Ecuadorian government passed a decree dollarizing the economy. On March 13, 2000, the Ecuadorian congress approved a new exchange system, whereby the U.S. dollar is adopted as the main legal tender in Ecuador for all purposes, including means of payment, store of value, and unit of account. On March 20, the Central Bank of Ecuador started to exchange the existing local currency (sucres) for U.S. dollars at the fixed exchange rate of 25,000 sucres per U.S. dollar. Beginning on April 30, 2000, all transactions are denominated in U.S. dollars. The exchange of sucres for U.S. dollars officially ended on June 8, 2001. A limited issue of domestic coins of small value remains in circulation to facilitate small transactions. These coins are fully backed by U.S. dollars.

International Liquidity:

Gold (National Valuation) (line 1and) is obtained by converting the value in national currency terms, as reported in the country's standard sources, using the prevailing exchange rate, as given in *line* **ae** or **we.**

Central Bank:

Comprises the Central Bank of Ecuador (CBE) only.

Data are based on a standardized report form (SRF) for central banks, which accords with the concepts and definitions of the IMF's *Monetary and Financial Statistics Manual (MFSM)*, 2000. Departures from the *MFSM* methodology are explained below.

Claims on Central Government and *Liabilities to Central Government* include small positions with other financial corporations and public nonfinancial corporations.

Other Depository Corporations:

Comprises private banks (both open and in the process of liquidation), private finance companies, National Development Bank, Housing Bank of Ecuador, savings and loans associations, and financial cooperatives. Beginning in March 2002, includes credit card companies. Beginning in July 2002, excludes Filabanco (private bank) due to the lack of reporting. Beginning in January 2004, excludes the Housing Bank of Ecuador. Beginning in February 2004, includes offshore banks. Data exclude investment funds, which issue short-term liabilities to money holding sectors.

† Beginning in July 2002, data are based on a standardized report form (SRF) for other depository corporations, which accords with the concepts and definitions of the *Monetary and Financial Statistics Manual (MFSM)*. For other depository corporations in Ecuador, departures from the *MFSM* methodology are explained below.

Claims on Central Government and *Liabilities to Central Government* include small positions with other financial corporations and public nonfinancial corporations.

For December 2001 through June 2002, data have less conformity with the *MFSM* methodology and therefore are not strictly comparable to data for later periods.

Depository Corporations:

† See notes on central bank and other depository corporations.

Other Financial Corporations:

Comprises the National Finance Corporation and credit card companies only. Beginning in March 2002, excludes credit card companies. Beginning in January 2004, includes the Housing Bank of Ecuador. Data exclude insurance corporations and the Mortgage Securitization Corporation.

† Beginning in July 2002, data are based on a standardized report form (SRF) for other financial corporations, which accords with the concepts and definitions of the *Monetary and Financial Statistics Manual (MFSM)*. For other financial corporations in Ecuador, departures from the *MFSM* methodology are explained below.

Claims on Central Government and *Liabilities to Central Government* include small positions with other financial corporations and public nonfinancial corporations.

For December 2001 through June 2002, data have less conformity with the *MFSM* methodology and therefore are not strictly comparable to data for later periods.

Interest Rates:

Discount Rate (End of Period):

Legal rate charged by the CBE to discount eligible commercial paper offered by commercial banks in national currency. † Beginning in March 2000, legal rate charged by the CBE to discount eligible commercial paper offered by commercial banks in U.S. dollars. Nominal interest rates published from March 2000 to July 2007 were recalculated and expressed as annual effective rates. † Beginning in August 2007, annual effective legal rate charged by the CBE to discount eligible commercial paper offered by all other depository corporations.

Savings Rate:

Weighted average rate offered by private banks on savings deposits in national currency. † Beginning in January 1999, weighted average rate offered by private banks on savings deposits in U.S. dollars. Nominal interest rates published from January 1999 to July 2007 were recalculated and expressed as annual effective rates. † Beginning in January 2008, weighted average of the annual effective rates offered by all other depository corporations on savings deposits in U.S. dollars.

Deposit Rate:

Weighted average rate offered by private banks on 30- to 83-day time deposits in national currency. † Beginning in January 1999, weighted average rate offered by private banks on 30- to 83-day time deposits in U.S. dollars. Nominal interest rates published from January 1999 to July 2007 were recalculated and expressed as annual effective rates. † Beginning in September 2007, weighted average of the annual effective rates offered by all other depository corporations on 30- to 60-day time deposits in U.S. dollars.

Lending Rate:
Weighted average rate charged by private banks on 92- to 172-day loans in national currency. † Beginning in January 1999, weighted average rate charged by private banks on 92- to 172-day loans in U.S. dollars. Nominal interest rates published from January 1999 to July 2007 were recalculated and expressed as annual effective rates. † Beginning in September 2007, weighted average of the annual effective rates charged by all other depository corporations on 121- to 180-day loans in U.S. dollars.

Prices and Production:

Producer Prices:
Source: Central Bank of Ecuador. Weight Reference Period: 1995; Coverage: main production centers; Number of Items in the Basket: covers a total of 1,419 items (368 agricultural and livestock goods, 72 fishing goods, and 979 mining and manufacturing goods) and approximately the same number of establishments; Basis for Calculation: measured for agricultural and livestock goods are in farm and ex-factory for the manufacturing and mining goods and port for the fishing goods.

Consumer Prices:
Source: Central Bank of Ecuador. Weights Reference Period: 2004; Geographical Coverage: covering eight cities with a population of more than 20,000; Number of Items in the Basket: 299 items; Basis for Calculation: Survey of Incomes and Expenses of Urban Homes, conducted during the period from February 2003 to January 2004.

Crude Petroleum Production:
Central Bank of Ecuador data in thousands of barrels.

International Transactions:

Source: Central Bank of Ecuado.

Government Finance:

† Beginning in 1973, annual data are identical to data reported in the *Government Finance Statistics Yeabook* and cover budgetary central government. † Beginning in 1986, annual data are derived from monthly data. Monthly, quarterly, and annual data are derived from the Central Bank of Ecuador and cover budgetary central government. The fiscal year ends December 31.

National Accounts:

Data are from the Central Bank of Ecuador. Prior to the first quarter of 1999 and annual of 1993, data in national currency has been converted using the average exchange rate (*line* **rf**). For subsequent periods, the data are reported in U.S. dollars. As indicated by the country, data are compiled according to the recommendations of the *1993 SNA*.

Egypt   469

Date of Fund Membership:
December 27, 1945

Standard Sources:
Central Bank of Egypt
Central Agency for Public Mobilization and Statistics

Exchange Rates:

Market Rate (End of Period and Period Average):
† Beginning in October 1991, data refer to the rate quoted by the Central Bank of Egypt based on Egypt's foreign exchange market conditions.

Beginning in October 1991, a unified exchange rate replaced the multiple exchange rate system. Since then, the Egyptian Pound is traded freely in a single exchange market with the authorities intervening to maintain the rate in a tight band against U.S. dollars. Egypt's exchange rate regimes prior to October 1991 are as follows: Until May 11, 1987, the *central bank pool,* which continues to exist, handled (1) on the receipts side, exports of petroleum, cotton, and rice; Suez Canal dues and Sumed pipeline royalties; and (2) on the payments side, imports of certain essential foodstuffs (including wheat, wheat flour, edible oils, tea, and sugar); insecticide and fertilizers; and specified public sector capital transactions. It covered all public sector external debt service payments except for service payments on suppliers' credits related to public sector capital goods imports. The *commercial bank pool,* which was formally closed in March 1988, received proceeds of workers' remittances, tourism, and exports not going through the central bank pool, while providing foreign exchange for public sector payments not covered by the central bank pool. In addition, transactions involving residents' holdings of foreign exchange deposits in free accounts with domestic banks were effected outside the banking system, and there also existed an unofficial market in Port Said (a free trade zone) and illegal street markets. The outside-banks markets shared common sources of supply with the commercial bank pool (workers' remittances and tourism) and satisfied demand by the private sector for exchange for both visible and invisible transactions.

A *new bank foreign exchange market* (the new bank market), in which all authorized commercial banks and two travel agencies were permitted to operate, began operations on May 11, 1987. In opening the market, the authorities set the initial exchange rate to reflect the rates in the outside-banks markets; subsequently, the daily rate for the market has been determined de jure by a committee of representatives from eight participating banks on the basis of market supply, demand, and other factors as evolved by the committee. On the supply side, the new bank markets' resources are drawn mainly from workers' remittances, tourist expenditures, the purchase of foreign bank notes, and specified public and private sector export earnings. On the uses side, the new market is permitted to provide foreign exchange for specified public sector visible and invisible transactions, private sector imports, and certain private sector invisible payments primarily related to imports. Authorized banks are permitted to sell for private sector debt servicing up to 10 percent of their foreign exchange receipts, provided that the debtors' own foreign exchange accounts have been drawn down.

Over 1987/88–1988/89, transactions through the central bank pool accounted for approximately two thirds and one fourth of merchandise exports and imports, respectively, and 40 percent of invisible transactions. Although the buying rate in the central bank pool was changed on August 15, 1989 from LE 0.7=US$1 to

LE 1.1=US$1, the Central Bank established three subaccounts to shield most transactions in the pool from the rate change, and most transactions continue to be carried out effectively at the rate of LE 0.7 = US$1.

Principal Rate relates to the central bank fixed official rate through December 1978, the unified exchange rate from January 1979 through July 1981, and the central bank pool rate thereafter.

Secondary Rate relates to the parallel market exchange rate through December 1978, the official incentive buying rate established by the authorities that applies to exchange transactions by authorized banks from August 1981 through December 1984, the premium rate quoted at authorized banks from January 1985 through June 1986, the authorized commercial bank (flexible) rate from July 1986 through March 1988, and the new bank free market rate thereafter. The banks free market rate was established in May 1987 and gradually absorbed most transactions from the authorized banks rate until the latter was abolished in March 1988.

Tertiary Rate relates to transactions effected outside banks and can only be considered as indicative of the exchange rates at which such transactions take place.

Since February 27, 1991, foreign exchange transactions were carried out through two markets, the primary market and the free market. Effective October 8, 1991, the primary market was eliminated, and all foreign exchange transactions are effected through the free market.

International Liquidity:

Gold (National Valuation) (line 1and) is the U.S. dollar value of official holdings of gold, which is valued at the daily average of gold fixing in London during the preceding three months, less a discount of 25 percent or at 75 percent of its final fixing on the last working day in June, whichever is less.

Central Bank:

Consists of the Central Bank of Egypt (CBE) only.

† Beginning in January 2004, data are based on a standardized report form (SRF) for central banks, which accords with the concepts and definitions of the IMF's *Monetary and Financial Statistics Manual (MFSM)*. Departures from the *MFSM* methodology are explained below.

Monetary gold is valued annually at 75 percent of the average end-of-period London market prices of the latest three months instead of end-of-period market price.

Held-to-maturity securities are valued at acquisition cost or fair value, whichever is lower, rather than at end-period market price or fair value.

For December 2001 through December 2003, data have less conformity with the *MFSM* methodology and therefore are not strictly comparable to data for later periods.

Other Depository Corporations:

Comprises commercial banks, business and investment banks (except the Arab International Bank), and specialized banks.

† Beginning in January 2004, data are based on a SRF for other depository corporations, which accords with the concepts and definitions of the IMF's *Monetary and Financial Statistics Manual (MFSM)*. Departures from the *MFSM* methodology are explained below.

Held-to-maturity securities are valued at acquisition cost or fair value, whichever is lower, rather than at current market price or fair value.

For December 2001 through December 2003, data have less conformity with the *MFSM* methodology and therefore are not strictly comparable to data for later periods.

Depository Corporations:

See notes on central bank and other depository corporations.

Monetary Aggregates:

Broad Money:

Broad Money calculated from the liability data in the sections for the central bank and other depository corporations accords with the concepts and definitions of the *MFSM*. Broad money differs from M2 as M2 excludes currency issued by the central government.

Money (National Definitions):

M1 (*Money Supply*) comprises currency outside the banking system and demand deposits of resident nonbank nongovernment sectors in national currency.

M2 (*Domestic Liquidity*) comprises M1 and quasi-money. Quasi-money consists of time and savings deposits of resident nonbank nongovernment sectors in national currency and demand, time, and savings deposits of resident nonbank nongovernment sectors in foreign currency.

Interest Rates:

Discount Rate (End of Period):

The rate at which the CBE discounts eligible commercial paper to commercial banks.

Treasury Bill Rate:

Weighted average based on the last auction of the month.

Deposit Rate:

Upper margin offered on fixed term deposits of less than one year.

Lending Rate:

Upper margin on commercial bank loans to the general public; the rates on agricultural and export credits are generally lower.

Industrial Share Price (End of Period):

Weighted average based on daily closing quotations, covering the whole industrial sector. Base 1992.

Prices and Labor:

Industrial Share Prices (End of Month):

Industrial goods and services and automobiles share price index on the Cairo and Alexandria Stock Exchange, base 1992.

Producer Prices:

Central Bank of Egypt index, weights reference period: 2004–2005, covering 786 commodities whose prices are received by domestic producers of goods and services in Egypt.

Consumer Prices:

Central Bank of Egypt index, weights reference period: January 2010; Geographical Coverage: whole country; Number of Items in Basket: 826; Basis for Calculation: weights are used derived from the household income and expenditure survey (HIES) 2008–2009.

International Transactions:

Exports and Imports, c.i.f.:

Central Agency for Public Mobilization and Statistics data. Exports cover domestic exports. Import data refer to goods cleared through customs and differ from balance of payments data, which are based on exchange control statistics, i.e., on actual payments for imports. The large differences are due to differences in both coverage and valuation, especially with regard to goods released from customs under the temporary admissions system. Both sets of statistics also substantially underestimate the value of petroleum imports. Data on Suez Canal dues are received directly from the Central Bank of Egypt.

Government Finance:

From fiscal year 2005/2006, quarterly cash data on the budgetary central government are derived from data published in the Central Bank of Egypt's *Monthly Statistical Bulletin*. Annual data are as reported for the *Government Finance Statistics Yearbook (GFSY)* and cover budgetary central government. The fiscal year ends June 30.

National Accounts:

Source: Central Bank of Egypt. † Compilation procedures were revised in 1970. Data for 1970 to 1979 relate to calendar year. Beginning in 1980, data relate to a fiscal year ending June 30. *Line 99b* includes a statistical discrepancy.

El Salvador 253

Date of Fund Membership:

March 14, 1946

Standard Sources:

Central Reserve Bank of El Salvador

Exchange Rates:

Market Rate (End of Period):

On June 1, 1990 the exchange system was unified. The exchange rate is determined by commercial banks and exchange houses authorized to operate in the foreign exchange market. Since January 1993, the central bank has intervened in the market to maintain the value of the colón at C 8.755 per U.S. dollar. Beginning in January 2001, because of the introduction of the 'Integration Law-*La Ley de Integración Monetaria,*' that makes the U.S. dollar legal tender, the exchange rate has been fixed to colón 8.75 per U.S. dollar.

International Liquidity:

Line 1and is equal to *line 1ad,* converted into U.S. dollars at the dollar price of gold used by national sources, as reported to *IFS.* † Beginning in November 2010, *line 1and* is estimated according to the gold price in the international market.

Central Bank:

Consists of the Central Reserve Bank of El Salvador (CRBES) only. Data are based on a standardized report form (SRF) for central banks, which accords with the concepts and definitions of the IMF's *Monetary and Financial Statistics Manual (MFSM)*, 2000.

Other Depository Corporations:

Comprises commercial banks, cooperative banks, savings and loans societies, and the two credit cooperatives supervised by the Superintendence of the Financial System. Data exclude the rest savings and credit cooperatives.

Data are based on a standardized report form (SRF) for other de-

pository corporations, which accords with the concepts and definitions of the *Monetary and Financial Statistics Manual (MFSM)*. For other depository corporations in El Salvador, departures from the *MFSM* methodology are explained below.

Loans are not fully sectorized owing to problems of misreporting and quality of the information received.

Data on deposits and repurchase agreements do not distinguish between resident and nonresident units.

Claims on Nonresidents includes deposits in resident other depository corporations.

Claims on Private Sector includes loans to other depository corporations, other financial corporations, and public nonfinancial corporations.

Transferable Deposits Included in Broad Money and *Other Deposits Included in Broad Money* include also deposits of nonresidents.

Held-to-maturity securities are valued at acquisition cost rather than at current market price or fair value.

Holdings of equity shares not traded in active markets are valued at acquisition cost rather than at market price or fair value.

Depository Corporations:

See notes on central bank and other depository corporations.

Other Financial Corporations:

Comprises insurance corporations, pension funds, and the Development Bank of El Salvador. Data exclude the Fondo Social para la Vivienda, Fondo Nacional de Vivienda Popular, Fondo de Saneamiento y Fortalecimiento Financiero, leasing companies, exchange houses, and stock brokers.

Data are based on a standardized report form (SRF) for other financial corporations, which accords with the concepts and definitions of the *Monetary and Financial Statistics Manual (MFSM)*. Departures from the *MFSM* methodology are explained below.

Accrued interest on securities issued by domestic sectors is included in *Claims on Central Government* rather than on claims on other domestic sectors.

Held-to-maturity securities are valued at acquisition cost rather than at current market price or fair value.

Holdings of equity shares not traded in active markets are valued at acquisition cost rather than at market price or fair value.

Financial Corporations:

See notes on central bank, other depository corporations, and other financial corporations.

Monetary Aggregates:

Broad Money:

Broad Money (line 59m) calculated from the liability data in the sections for the central bank and other depository corporations accords with the concepts and definitions of the *MFSM* and is consistent with broad money (line 59mea) described below.

Money (National Definitions):

Beginning in December 2001, the CRBES adopted the harmonized definition as the official definition of monetary aggregates. The harmonized definitions follow the methodology established by the Central American Monetary Council. *Base money* comprises national notes and coins in circulation, deposits of other depository corporations with the CRBES, deposits of other financial corporations and public nonfinancial corporations with the CRBES, and securities issued by the CRBES held by other depository corporations and other resident sectors.

M1 comprises national notes and coins in circulation outside the depository corporations and demand deposits of the private sector with other depository corporations.

M2 comprises M1 and savings and time deposits of the private sector with other depository corporations.

M3 comprises M2 and securities other than shares issued by other depository corporations held by other financial corporations.

Broad money comprises M3; demand and time deposits of other financial corporations and public nonfinancial corporations with the CRBES; demand, savings, and time deposits of other financial corporations, state and local governments, and public nonfinancial corporations with other depository corporations; and securities issued by the CRBES held by other financial corporations and private sector.

Interest Rates:

Money Market Rate:
Average of rates on 1- to 7-day loans between commercial banks.

Deposit Rate:
Rate offered by commercial banks, cooperative banks, and savings and loans societies on 180-day time deposits in national currency.

Deposit Rate (Foreign currency):
Rate offered by commercial banks, cooperative banks, and savings and loans societies on 180-day time deposits in foreign currency.

Lending Rate:
Rate charged by commercial banks, cooperative banks, and savings and loans societies on loans of one year or less in national currency.

Lending Rate (Foreign Currency):
Rate charged by commercial banks, cooperative banks, and savings and loans societies on loans of one year or less in foreign currency.

Prices:

Consumer Prices:
Source: Central Reserve Bank of El Salvador. Weights Reference Period: August 2005- September 2006; Geographical Coverage: Six departments of the country (Sonsonate, Santa Ana, La Libertad, San Salvador, La Paz y San Miguel); Number of Items in Basket: 238; Basis for Calculation: The weights are derived from the ENIGH, which covers the period from August to September 2006.

Wholesale Prices:
Central Reserve Bank of El Salvador index. Weights reference period: January 1978. The index covers 176 articles and relates to goods both produced and consumed in the country, as well as exports and imports. Coffee is included.

Producer Prices:
Central Reserve Bank of El Salvador index. Weights reference period: 1993. Its geographic coverage includes the San Salvador, La libertad and Santa Ana metropolitan areas. The index covers 140 producer goods. The index weights are based on the 1993 Economic Censuses developed by the General Bureau for Statistics and Censuses.

International Transactions:

Trade values are Central Reserve Bank of El Salvador data, as compiled by the General Directorate of Statistics and Census.

Government Finance:

† Beginning in January 1994, monthly, quarterly, and annual data are derived from the *Quarterly Review* of the Central Reserve Bank of El Salvador and cover budgetary central government. Until 1993, the data covered the central government's budgetary operations recorded in the General Account of the Treasury, the Development Loan Fund, and the IDB Revolving Loan Fund. Debt data cover central government and official entities. The fiscal year ends December 31.

National Accounts:

Source: Central Reserve Bank of El Salvador. Prior to 1978, *lines 99a* and *99b* include a statistical discrepancy. As indicated by the country, the national accounts are compiled according to the recommendation of the *1968 SNA*.

Equatorial Guinea   642

Date of Fund Membership:
December 22, 1969

Standard Source:
Banque des Etats d'Afrique Centrale (BEAC) (Bank of the Central African States)

Exchange Rates:

Official Rate: (End of Period and Period Average):
Prior to January 1999, the official rate was pegged to the French franc. On January 12, 1994, the CFA franc was devalued to CFAF 100 per French franc from CFAF 50 at which it had been fixed since 1948. From January 1, 1999, the CFAF is pegged to the euro at a rate of CFA franc 655.957 per euro.

Central Bank:

Consists of the national office of the Banque des Etats de l'Afrique Centrale (BEAC), consolidating the accounts of all its branches located in Malabo and Bata.

Data are based on a standardized report form for central banks, which accords with the concepts and definitions of the IMF's *Monetary and Financial Statistics Manual (MFSM)*, 2000. Departures from the *MFSM* methodology are explained below.

Held-to-maturity securities are valued at amortized cost rather than at current market price or fair value.

Other Depository Corporations:

Comprises commercial banks. Data exclude credit unions and microfinance institutions which accept deposits.

Data are based on a standardized report form for other depository corporations, which accords with the concepts and definitions of the *Monetary and Financial Statistics Manual (MFSM)*. For other depository corporations in Equatorial Guinea, departures from the *MFSM* methodology are explained below.

Financial assets and liabilities for which currency breakdown is unavailable are allocated to assets and liabilities denominated in national currency.

Held-to-maturity securities are valued at acquisition cost rather than at current market price or fair value.

Depository Corporations:

See notes on central bank and other depository corporations.

Monetary Aggregates:

Broad Money:

Broad Money calculated from the liability data in the sections for the central bank and other depository corporations accords with the concepts and definitions of the *MFSM*. Broad money differs from M2 described below as M2 excludes holdings of currency by the central government.

Money (National Definitions):

M1 comprises currency in circulation and transferable deposits. Transferable deposits refer to current account deposits of other financial corporations, public nonfinancial corporations, and private sector with depository corporations in national currency.

M2 comprises M1 and quasi-money. Quasi-money refers to fixed and saving deposits of other financial corporations, public nonfinancial corporations, and private sector with depository corporations in national currency.

Prices and Production:

Consumer Prices:

Source: Dirección Général de Estadística y Cuentas Nacionales.

Interest Rates:

Discount Rate (End of Period):

Basic rediscount rate offered by the BEAC. † Beginning in July 1994, rate charged by the BEAC on refinancing operations to financial institutions.

Deposit Rate:

Minimum rate offered by other depository corporations on savings accounts.

Lending Rate:

Maximum rate charged by financial institutions on loans.

National Accounts:

Source: Dirección Général de Estadística y Cuentas Nacionales.

Eritrea   643

Date of Fund Membership:

July 6, 1994

Standard Source:

Bank of Eritrea

Exchange Rates:

Official Rate: (End of Period and Period Average):

Central bank midpoint rate. Until October 1997, the Ethiopian birr was the legal tender. In November 1997, the Eritrean nakfa was introduced, at par with the birr.

International Liquidity:

Gold (National Valuation) (line 1and) is obtained by converting for current periods the value in national currency as recorded by the Bank of Eritrea, using the prevailing exchange rate, as given in *line ae*. The Bank of Eritrea adjusts the value of its gold holdings once a year at end-December, to bring it close to a valuation based on the London exchange quotation, using the official exchange rate. Thereafter, the valuation in nakfa remains constant during the year, except for changes in stock.

Central Bank:

Consists of the Bank of Eritrea only.

Data are based on a standardized report form (SRF) for central banks, which accords with the concepts and definitions of the IMF's *Monetary and Financial Statistics Manual (MFSM)*, 2000. Departures from the *MFSM* methodology are explained below.

Financial assets and liabilities not disaggregated by economic sector are allocated to the economic sector having the largest volume of transactions in that category.

Some accrued interest is included in *Other Items (Net)* rather than in the outstanding amounts of the financial assets and liabilities.

Foreign assets excludes a claim on the National Bank of Ethiopia, consisting of demonetized Ethiopian birr notes, and foreign liabilities excludes some account balances due to the National Bank of Ethiopia.

Other Depository Corporations:

Comprises commercial banks.

Data are based on a standardized report form (SRF) for other depository corporations, which accords with the concepts and definitions of the *Monetary and Financial Statistics Manual (MFSM)*. For other depository corporations in Eritrea, departures from the *MFSM* methodology are explained below.

Financial assets and liabilities not disaggregated by economic sector are allocated to the economic sector having the largest volume of transactions in that category.

Some accrued interest is included in *Other Items (Net)* rather than in the outstanding amounts of the financial assets or liabilities.

Depository Corporations:

See notes on central bank and other depository corporations.

Monetary Aggregates:

Broad Money:

Broad Money calculated from the liability data in the sections for the central bank and other depository corporations accords with the concepts and definitions of the *MFSM* and is consistent with M3 described below.

Money (National Definitions):

Reserve Money comprises currency in circulation, deposits of depository corporations in national and foreign currency with the Bank of Eritrea, and deposits of local governments, public financial corporations, and the private sector in national currency with the Bank of Eritrea.

M1 comprises currency in circulation outside depository corporations and demand deposits in national currency, other than those of the central government, with the Bank of Eritrea and other depository corporations.

M2 comprises M1 and savings and fixed deposits in national currency, other than those of the central government, with depository corporations.

M3 comprises M2 and foreign currency deposits, other than those of the central government, with depository corporations.

Estonia   939

Data are denominated in Estonian krooni prior to January 2011 and in euros from January 2011 onward. An irrevocably fixed factor for converting krooni to euros was established at 15.6466 Estonian krooni per euro. With Estonia's entry into Stage Three of the European Economic and Monetary Union (EMU) in January 2011, a euro area-wide definition of residency was introduced: all positions with residents of other euro area (EA) countries, including the European Central Bank (ECB), are classified as domestic positions, and foreign assets and foreign liabilities include only positions with non-EA residents. In 2011, the Estonian kroon is being retired from circulation and replaced by euro banknotes and coins. Descriptions of the methodology and presentation of Estonia's accounts following the introduction of the euro are discussed under *European Economic and Monetary Union* in the introduction to *IFS* and in the notes on the euro area page.

Date of Fund Membership:
May 26, 1992

Standard Sources:
Bank of Estonia
Statistical Office of Estonia

Exchange Rates:

Official Rate: (End of Period and Period Average):
The kroon was introduced in June 1992 and was pegged to the Deutsche mark. Effective January 1, 1999, the official rate was pegged to the euro. In January 2011, the euro, which has a market determined exchange rate, was adopted.

Market Rate (End of Period and Period Average):
Beginning in January 2011, Estonia adopted the euro and the euro market rate became applicable to all transactions. In 2011, the kroon was retired from circulation and replaced by euro banknotes and coins. For additional information, refer to the section on Exchange Rates in the introduction to *IFS* and the notes on the euro area page.

International Liquidity:
Beginning in January 2011, *Total Reserves minus Gold (line 1l.d)* and *Foreign Exchange (line.1d.d)* are defined in accordance with the Eurosystem's statistical definition of international reserves. *Gold (Eurosystem Valuation) (line 1and)* is revalued monthly at market prices. Memorandum data are provided on *Non-Euro Claims on Euro Area Residents and Euro Claims on Non-Euro Area Residents*. For additional information, refer to the section on International Liquidity in the introduction to *IFS* and the notes on the euro area page.

Central Bank:
Consists of the Bank of Estonia (Eesti Pank) only, which beginning in January 2011 became part of the Eurosystem (for a de-

scription of its accounts refer to the section *Central Bank - Euro Area* in the introduction to *IFS*).

† Beginning in January 2004, data are compiled in accordance with the European Central Bank's framework for monetary statistics using the national residency approach.

For December 2001 through December 2003, data do not fully conform with the European Central Bank's framework for monetary statistics and are not strictly comparable to data for later periods.

Other Depository Corporations:
Comprises banks and savings and lending associations. Beginning in January 2004, comprises all resident units classified as other monetary financial institutions (other MFIs) in accordance with *1995 ESA* standards. Beginning in January 2008, comprises credit institutions, savings and loan associations, and a money market fund.

† Beginning in January 2004, data are compiled in accordance with the European Central Bank's framework for monetary statistics using the national residency approach.

For December 2001 through December 2003, data do not fully conform with the European Central Bank's framework for monetary statistics and are not strictly comparable to data for later periods.

Depository Corporations (National Residency):
Beginning in January 2011, see section on *Depository Corporations (Based on National Residency)* in the introduction to *IFS*.

Depository Corporations (Euro Area-wide Residency):
Beginning in January 2011, see section on *Depository Corporations (based on Euro Area-wide Residency)* in the introduction to *IFS*.
For periods prior to January 2011, see notes on central bank and other depository corporations.

Monetary Aggregates:
Beginning in January 2011, national monetary aggregate series were discontinued. The euro area aggregates are presented on the euro area page. For periods prior to January 2011, monetary aggregates included:

Broad Money:
Broad Money is calculated from the liability data in the sections for the central bank and other depository corporations. Broad money differs from M2 described below because separate data on the issuance by MFIs of *money market funds/shares* and *debt securities* with maturity up to two years to the money holding sectors were not available under the ECB reporting framework.

Money (National Definitions):
M0 comprises currency in circulation and money on accounts held with the Bank of Estonia. The item money on accounts held with the Bank of Estonia comprises the deposits of banks and domestic financial and nonfinancial corporations.

M1 comprises currency outside MFIs, demand deposits in national and foreign currency of resident non-MFIs other than central government with MFIs (exclusive of deposits of the Deposit Guarantee Fund with the Bank of Estonia), and demand deposits of other MFIs (savings and loans associations, money market funds, and credit institutions) with commercial banks. Beginning in December 2000, excludes demand deposits of other MFIs (savings and loans associations, money market funds, and credit institutions) with commercial banks.

M2 comprises M1; time, savings, and other deposits (excluding repurchase agreements) in national and foreign currency of resident non-MFIs other than central government with MFIs; and time, savings, and other deposits (including repurchase agreements) of other MFIs (savings and loans associations, money market funds, and credit institutions) with commercial banks. Beginning in December 2000, excludes time, savings, and other deposits (including repurchase agreements) of other MFIs (savings and loans associations, money market funds, and credit institutions) with commercial banks.

Interest Rates:

Beginning in January 2011, euro area policy rates became applicable, and national policy rates were discontinued. See *Interest Rates* in the notes for the euro area page. For periods prior to January 2011:

Money Market Rate:
Weighted average rate on overnight loans between banks in national currency. The rate is weighted by daily loan amounts. † Beginning in January 2000, three-month Tallinn Interbank Offered Rate (TALIBOR).

Deposit Rate:
Weighted average rate offered by banks on time and savings deposits in national currency to individuals and other financial corporations. The rate is weighted by deposit amounts.

Deposit Rate (lines 60lhs, 60lhn, 60lcs, and 60lcn):
See notes in the introduction to *IFS* and *Euro-area Interest Rates.*

Lending Rate:
Weighted average rate charged by banks on short-term loans in national currency to individuals and other financial corporations. The rate is weighted by loan amounts.

Lending Rate (lines 60phm, 60pcs, and 60pcn):
See notes in the introduction to *IFS* and *Euro-area Interest Rates.*

Government Bond Yield:
Data refer to new loans in national currency to nonfinancial corporations and households with maturities over five years. A large part of the underlying claims is linked to variable interest rates and is subject to different credit risk than government bonds. Due to the fact that Estonia has very limited government debt and that there are no suitable long-term government bonds available in financial markets, the European Central Bank uses this rate for assessing convergence among the European Union member states.

Prices and Labor:

Share Prices:
Tallinn Stock Exchange (TALSE) index, base June 3, 1996. The index covers common shares traded in the TALSE and is weighted by market capitalization. The monthly index is calculated from the average of the daily closing quotations.

Producer Prices:
Source: Statistical Office of Estonia. Weights Reference Period: 2010; Sectoral Coverage: mining and quarrying, manufacturing, and energy supply industries; Number of Items in Basket: about 1000 prices; Basis for Calculation: the weights are derived from the sales data obtained from the annual survey "PRODCOM" conducted by Statistical Office of Estonia (SOE).

Consumer Prices:
Source: Statistical Office of Estonia. Weights Reference Period: 2011; Geographical Coverage: Whole territory of Estonia; Number of Items in Basket: 600 items; Basis for Calculation: derived from the quarterly Household Budget Survey, national accounts estimates, administrative data, business statistics data, as well as information received from some enterprises.

Monthly Earnings:
Source: Statistical Office of Estonia. The published average gross wages and salaries have been converted into full-time units (part-time employees converted into full-time units) that allow comparing different average wages regardless of the length of working time. The average gross wages include payments for actual worked time and remuneration for time not worked. The average gross wages and salaries exclude payments to employees with contract of agreement. Since 1999, sick benefits to employees from social security funds are not included in the average gross wages as, according to changes made in the law, the employer no longer calculates and pays out sick benefits.

International Transactions:

Exports and *Imports, c.i.f.*: Statistical Office of Estonia. Beginning in January 2000, the Special Trade System replaced the General Trade System as the coverage basis for data compilation.

Government Finance:

Annual data are as reported for the *Government Finance Statistics Yearbook (GFSY)* and cover budgetary central government. The fiscal year ends December 31.

National Accounts:

Source: Statistical Office of Estonia. As indicated by the country, concepts and definitions are in accordance with the *ESA 95*. Beginning in 1999, data are sourced from the Eurostat database. Eurostat introduced chain-linked GDP volume measures to both annual and quarterly data with the release of the third quarter 2005 on November 30, 2005. Chain linked GDP volume measures are expressed in the prices of the previous year and re-referenced to 2005.

Ethiopia   644

Date of Fund Membership:
December 27, 1945

Standard Source:
National Bank
Central Statistical Agency of Ethiopia

Exchange Rates:

Official Rate: (End of Period and Period Average):
Until May 1993, the birr was pegged to the U.S. dollar. During May 1993–July 25, 1995, the exchange rate system in Ethiopia consisted of two exchange rates: the official and auction exchange rates. On July 25, 1995, these exchange rates were unified, with the official exchange rate set as the marginal rate resulting from auctions. Effective October 25, 2001, the exchange rate is determined by the interbank foreign exchange market.

International Liquidity:

Gold (National Valuation) (line 1and) is obtained by converting the value in national currency terms, as reported in the country's standard sources, using the prevailing exchange rate, as given in *line* **ae** or **we.**

Monetary Authorities:

Comprises the National Bank of Ethiopia (NBE) only.

Deposit Money Banks:

Comprises the Commercial Bank of Ethiopia, Construction and Business Bank Awash International Bank S.C., Dashen Bank S.C., Bank of Abyssinia S.C., Wegagen Bank S.C., United Bank S.C., and Nib International Bank S.C. † Prior to December 1979, loans and advances of the commercial banks were included in *Claims on Private Sector (line 22d)*. Beginning in December 1979, these loans and advances are separated into *line 22d* and *Claims on Other Financial Institutions (line 22f)*. † Beginning in September 1983, data are based on an improved sectorization and classification of the accounts and exclude the Djibouti branch of the Commercial Bank of Ethiopia.

Monetary Survey:

See note on deposit money banks.

Other Banking Institutions:

Comprises the Development Bank of Ethiopia only.

Banking Survey:

See note on deposit money banks.

Money (National Definitions):

Base Money comprises notes and coins issued, deposits of commercial banks and Development Bank of Ethiopia, statutory deposits of insurance companies, and deposits of regional governments with the National Bank of Ethiopia (NBE).
M1 comprises currency in circulation outside the banking system and demand deposits. Demand deposits include statutory deposits of insurance companies and deposits of regional governments with the NBE; and demand deposits of the private sector, regional governments, nonfinancial public enterprises, nonfinancial cooperatives, and nonbank financial agencies and nontransferable nonresident deposits in national currency with commercial banks.
M2 comprises M1 plus fixed and savings deposits of the private sector, regional governments, nonfinancial public enterprises, nonfinancial cooperatives, and nonbank financial agencies with commercial banks in national and foreign currency.

Interest Rates:

Discount Rate:
Rate charged by the NBE on loans to commercial banks.
Treasury Bill Rate:
Average rate of yields on 28-, 91-, and 182-day treasury bills issued at face value. † Beginning in July 2003, weighted average yield on 91-day treasury bills.
Savings Rate:
Minimum rate offered by commercial banks on savings deposits.

Deposit Rate:
Weighted average rate offered by commercial banks on time deposits of less than one year. The rate is weighted by deposit amounts.
Lending Rate:
Rate charged by the Commercial Bank of Ethiopia on loans for exports. † Beginning in July 2003, minimum rate charged by commercial banks on loans to various sectors of the economy.
Government Bond Yield:
Rate paid by the NBE on its holdings of government bonds. † Beginning in November 2003, simple average yield on government bonds.

Prices and Labor:

Producer Prices:
Source: Central Statistical Agency of Ethiopia. Weights Reference Period: December 2006; Sectoral Coverage: selling prices received by farmers for their output in 463 representative Farmers Associations identified as enumeration areas across the country; Number of Items in Basket: about 99; Basis for Calculation: 2005/06 agricultural sample survey.

Consumer Prices:
Source: Central Statistical Agency of Ethiopia. Weights Reference Period: December 2006; Geographical Coverage: Whole national territory; Number of Items in Basket: varies between regions, from 103 to 193; Basis for Calculation: The weights are derived from the results of the Household Income, Consumption and Expenditure Survey (HICES) conducted in 2004/2005.

International Transactions:

Value of Exports and *Imports* are customs data. Data on imports are unadjusted for the undervaluation of crude petroleum imports.

Government Finance:

Data are as reported in the *Government Finance Statistics Yearbook* and cover budgetary central government. The fiscal year ends July 7.

National Accounts:

Source: Central Statistical Agency of Ethiopia. Data are prepared in accordance with the 1993 United Nations System of National Accounts. † Beginning 1992, data excludes Eritrea. † Beginning 1992, *line 96f* includes a statistical discrepancy.

Euro Area   163

The original participating members of Stage Three of the EMU are Austria, Belgium, Finland, France, Germany, Ireland, Italy, Luxembourg, Netherlands, Portugal, and Spain. Greece joined in January 2001, Slovenia in January 2007, Cyprus and Malta in January 2008, Slovak Republic in January 2008, and Estonia in January 2011. The euro area is an official descriptor for the monetary union and is defined by its actual membership as of a specified date. Thus, the accession of Greece, Slovenia, Cyprus, Malta, the Slovak Republic, and Estonia created breaks in series.
The European Economic Community, established in 1958,

formed the basis for European integration and creation of the EMU through a three-stage process. On July 1, 1990, the European Community entered Stage One of monetary union, which led to freedom of capital movements, increased cooperation among central banks, free usability of the European currency unit (ECU), and improvement of economic convergence among member states of the European Union (EU). The Maastricht Treaty, signed in February 1992, provided the legal basis for Stage Two, which began with the establishment of the European Monetary Institute (EMI). During Stage Two, the member states achieved greater economic convergence, enhanced coordination of monetary policies, and prohibited monetary financing of governments by central banks. The European Central Bank (ECB), successor to the EMI, was established on June 1, 1998, as part of Stage Two. Stage Three began on January 1, 1999 when the euro—the euro area currency unit—was introduced, the conversion rates for national currencies were irrevocably fixed, the new exchange rate mechanism (ERM II) became effective for two of the four EU countries that did not join the initial EMU, and the Eurosystem (the ECB and the national central banks of the countries that adopted the euro) began conducting a single monetary policy for the euro area. In 2002, euro banknotes issued by the Eurosystem and euro coins issued by the national authorities replaced the national currencies of the euro area countries. A description of the methodology and presentation of accounts for the euro area is presented in the introduction to *IFS*. † Following the participation of Greece in the Eurosystem, a break occurs in all series beginning with January 2001. Similar breaks in series resulted from accession into the Eurosystem of Slovenia in January 2007, Cyprus and Malta in January 2008, the Slovak Republic in January 2009, and of Estonia in January 2011.

Standard Sources:

European Central Bank
Eurostat

Exchange Rates:

Market Rate (End of Period and Period Average):
The euro was created on January 1, 1999 as the legal currency of the euro area countries, with an initial value established by setting one euro equal to one European currency unit (ECU), which was the accounting unit of the European Union. During 1999–2001, national denominations coexisted with the euro as physical circulating currencies and for denomination of financial instruments and transactions. The national currencies have irrevocable fixed conversion factors against the euro, based on the configuration of exchange rates when the euro was created. The irrevocably fixed, six significant digit conversion factors of national currencies per euro are as follows: Austrian schilling 13.7603, Belgian franc 40.3399, Cyprus pound 0.585274, Estonian krooni 15,6466, Finnish markka 5.94573, French franc 6.55957, German mark 1.95583, Greek drachmas 340.750, Irish pound .787564, Italian lira 1,936.27, Luxembourg franc 40.3399, Maltese lira 0.4293, Netherlands guilder 2.20371, Portuguese escudo 200.482, Slovak koruna 30.1260, Slovenian tolar 239.640, and Spanish peseta 166.386. In 2002, euro banknotes issued by the Eurosystem and euro coins issued by national authorities re-

placed the national currencies of the euro area countries. Only euro exchange rates are presented. For further information see the section on Exchange Rates in the introduction to *IFS*.

International Liquidity:

Total Reserves Minus Gold (Eurosystem Definition) (line 1l.d): Beginning in January 1999, the statistical definition of the international reserves for the Eurosystem (the ECB and euro area national central banks) is based on the Eurosystem's statistical definition of international reserves, adopted by the ECB's Statistics Committee in December 1998. Reserves are defined on a euro area-wide residency basis to include only positions with non-euro area residents. Claims denominated in euros are excluded from reserves. The international reserves of the euro area per the Eurosystem statistical definition at the start of the monetary union (January 1, 1999) in billions of U.S. dollars were as follows: *Total Reserves minus Gold*, $269,140; *Foreign Exchange*, $235,103; *SDR holdings*, $6,982; *Reserve Position in the Fund*, $26,238; *Other Reserve Assets*, $820; *Gold*, $116,094; *Gold (million fine troy ounces)*, 403.778 ounces. *Gold (Eurosystem Valuation) (line 1and)* from January 1999 onward is revalued at market rates and prices at the end of each month. Memorandum data are provided on *Non-Euro Claims on Euro Area Residents* and *Euro Claims on Non-Euro Area Residents*, which represent positions as of the last Friday in each month. For additional information, see the section on International Liquidity in the introduction to *IFS*.

Central Bank: (Eurosystem):

Covers the aggregated accounts of the Eurosystem. Includes coin issue of governments, with the contra-entries recorded in *Other Items (Net)*. The classifications of economic sectors and financial instruments used in the accounts are based on the Eurosystem's regulatory standards for monetary statistics. *Claims on* and *Liabilities to the Euro Area Depository Corporations* include claims on, and liabilities to, the ECB, national central banks, and other depository corporations (other MFIs) in the euro area. In contrast, Eurosystem members' Intra-Eurosystem claims/liabilities related to banknote issue are recorded as part of *Other Items (Net)*, where they effectively net to zero, and not as part of *Claims on* and *Liabilities to the Euro Area Depository Corporations*. *Bonds and Money Market Instruments* include subordinated debt in the form of securities, other bonds, and money market paper. For additional information and description of the accounts, see the section on *Monetary Statistics for Euro Area* in the introduction to *IFS*.

Other Depository Corporations: (Other Monetary Financial Institutions):

Comprises the aggregated accounts of all units in the euro area classified as other monetary financial institutions (other MFIs), defined in accordance with 1995 *ESA* standards. *Claims on* and *Liabilities to the Euro Area Depository Corporations* include claims on and liabilities to the ECB, national central banks, and other depository corporations (other MFIs) in the euro area. *Money Market Fund Shares* includes shares/units issued by money market funds. *Bonds and Money Market Instruments* includes subordinated debt in the form of securities, other bonds, and money market paper. For additional information and description of the accounts, see the section on *Monetary Statistics for Euro Area* in the introduction to *IFS*.

Depository Corporations (Euro Area-wide Residency):

Consolidated accounts of the depository corporations of the euro area, comprising the Eurosystem and other depository corporations (other MFIs). Euro area residency is based on the membership in the Eurosystem as any specific date. Euro area membership increased in January 2001 when Greece joined, in January 2007 when Slovenia joined, in January 2008 when Cyprus and Malta joined, in January 2009 when the Slovak Republic joined, and in January 2011 when Estonia joined. For additional information and description of the accounts, see the section on *Monetary Statistics for Euro Area* in the introduction to *IFS*.

Money (Eurosystem Definition):

Euro area monetary aggregates comprise monetary liabilities of MFIs (the Eurosystem and other depository corporations) and central government monetary liabilities to non-MFI euro area residents. Monetary liabilities of governments consist primarily of postal system savings accounts and Treasury Department deposit facilities in some euro area countries. Beginning in 2002, includes euro banknotes and coins and unretired national currency banknotes and coins.

M1 comprises currency in circulation and overnight deposits.

M1 Growth Rate. The M1 growth rates are calculated by the European Central Bank on the basis of adjusted flows rather than a simple comparison of end-of-period levels. The flows for the current period are calculated by adjusting the difference between the stock at the end of the period and the stock at the end of the previous period for effects that do not arise from transactions, such as reclassifications, foreign exchange revaluations, and other revaluations. Flows data used to compile the M1 Growth Rate are adjusted to eliminate the net effect on stocks caused by the changing composition of the euro area membership. Annual percentage changes for monthly data refer to end-of-month, whereas quarterly and annual data refer to the annual percentage change in the period average. Further details on methodology are available on the European Central Bank website.

M2 comprises M1 plus deposits with agreed maturity up to two years and deposits redeemable at notice up to three months.

M3 comprises *M2* plus repurchase agreements, money market fund shares and money market paper, and debt securities up to two years.

M3 Growth Rate . The M3 growth rates are calculated by the ECB on the basis of adjusted flows rather than a simple comparison of end-of-period levels. The flows for the current period are calculated by adjusting the difference between the stock at the end of the period and the stock at the end of the previous period for effects that do not arise from transactions, such as reclassifications, foreign exchange revaluations, and other revaluations. Flows data used to compile the M1 Growth Rate are adjusted to eliminate the net effect on stocks caused by the changing composition of the euro area membership. Annual percentage changes for monthly data refer to end-of-month, whereas quarterly and annual data refer to the annual percentage change in the period average. Further details on methodology are available on the European Central Bank website.

Nonmonetary Liabilities of MFIs comprises the other liabilities of MFIs-deposits with agreed maturity over two years, deposits re-

deemable at notice over three months, debt securities over two years, and capital and reserves.

Interest Rates:

Central Bank Policy Rate (End of Period):
Refers to the Eurosystem Main Refinancing Operations Rate, which is rate for the main open-market operations in the form of regular liquidity-providing reverse transactions with a frequency and maturity of one week. Reverse transactions refer to repurchase agreements or collateralized loans. The weekly main refinancing operations are carried out through a fixed-rate tender procedure with full allotment at the interest rate on the main refinancing operations. † Beginning in June 2000, the main refinancing operations are carried out as variable rate tenders, where the minimum bid rate refers to the minimum interest rate at which counterparties may place their bids. † Beginning in October 2008, the main refinancing operations are again carried out through a fixed-rate tender procedure with full allotment at the interest rate on the main refinancing operations.

Eurosystem Marginal Lending Facility Rate:
Rate at a Eurosystem standing facility at which eligible counterparties can obtain overnight credit against eligible assets. The terms and conditions of the facility are identical throughout the euro area.

Eurosystem Refinancing Rate:
Rate for the Eurosystem's main open-market refinancing operations in the form of regular liquidity-providing reverse transactions with a weekly frequency and two-week maturity.

Eurosystem Deposit Facility Rate:
Rate at a Eurosystem standing facility at which eligible counterparties can make overnight deposits with national central banks.

Interbank Rate (Overnight) and Eurepo Rate (3-month):
Average monthly rate on the 3-month Eurepo. The Eurepo rate is an average of the daily rates offered by a representative panel of prime banks, excluding the highest and lowest 15 percent of all the quotes collected.

Deposit Rate:
Weighted average euro area retail bank deposit rate for deposits with an agreed maturity up to one year, using instrument specific weights drawn from monthly MFI balance sheet statistics.

Deposit Rate (lines 60lhs, 60lhn, 60lcs, 60lcn, and 60lcr):
See notes in the introduction to *IFS* and *Euro-area Interest Rates*.

Lending Rate (lines 60phs, 60pns, 60phm, 60phn, 60pcs, and 60pcn):
See notes in the introduction to *IFS* and *Euro-area Interest Rates*.

Government Bond Yield:
Euro area yield for 10-year government bonds calculated on the basis of harmonized national government bond yields weighted by GDP. For additional information, refer to the introduction to *IFS*.

Prices, Production, Labor:

Producer Prices:
Eurostat index, weights reference period: 2005, an aggregation for the euro area of the industrial price indices of the 11 member countries, using 2005 industry sales weights excluding construction.

Harmonized CPI:

Eurostat index, the Harmonized Index of Consumer Prices (HICP), referring to a basket consisting of commodity groups common to all member states of the European Union with expenditure weights annually updated, excluding the imputed consumption cost of owner-occupied housing and certain other items.

Wages/Labor Costs:

Eurostat index. Average labor costs in the whole economy. Data for 1997 and earlier can be obtained from Eurostat.

Industrial Production:

Eurostat index, weights reference period: 2005, seasonally adjusted. An aggregation for the euro area of the industrial production indices of the 11 member countries, using 2005 industry value-added weights excluding construction.

Employment, Unemployment and Unemployment Rate:

Source: Eurostat. Seasonally adjusted compiled following the recommendations of the International Labor Office.

International Transactions:

Merchandise Exports and Imports:

Eurostat. Excludes intra-euro area trade. Refers to customs sources for trade with nonmember countries of the European Union and survey sources for trade with those EU countries that are not members of the EMU. Data for 1997 and earlier can be obtained from Eurostat.

Volume and Unit Value data:

Eurostat, weights reference period: 2000.

Balance of Payments:

Statistics for the euro area are compiled by the European Central Bank (ECB). Statistics are compiled by aggregating gross cross-border transactions of euro area residents vis-à-vis non-euro area residents as reported by the participating countries. The BOP data represents the moving concept of the Euro Area. There is a break sign to reflect a new country's membership in the union. Transactions between residents of the participating member states are not included. The methodological concepts follow international standards i.e., the IMF's *Balance of Payments Manual*; in addition, further harmonization proposals in special fields have been developed and agreed within the European System of Central Banks (ESCB), in consultation with the European Commission (Eurostat).

Government Finance:

Data are derived from Eurostat. For a description of the definitions, refer to section 8 in the introduction. The fiscal year ends December 31.

National Accounts:

Source: Eurostat. As indicated by Eurostat, series are based on the *ESA 95. Line 99b.r* is based on Eurostat data at 1995 prices. Data for 1997 and earlier can be obtained from Eurostat. Eurostat introduced chain-linked GDP volume measures to both annual and quarterly data with the release of the third quarter 2005 on November 30, 2005. Chain linked GDP volume measures are expressed in the prices of the previous year and re-referenced to 2000.

Fiji 819

Date of Fund Membership:

May 28, 1971

Standard Sources:

Reserve Bank of Fiji
Fiji Bureau of Statistics

Exchange Rates:

Official Rate: (End of Period and Period Average):
Central bank midpoint rate. The official rate has a fixed relationship with a weighted basket of currencies.

International Liquidity:

Line 1d.d includes treasury foreign exchange holdings.
Gold (National Valuation) (line 1and) is obtained by converting the value in national currency terms, as reported in the country's standard sources, using the prevailing exchange rate, as given in *line* **ae** or **we.**

Central Bank:

Consists of the Reserve Bank of Fiji (RBF) only.

† Beginning in January 2004, data are based on a standardized report form (SRF) for central banks, which accords with the concepts and definitions of the IMF's *Monetary and Financial Statistics Manual (MFSM)*, 2000. Departures from the *MFSM* methodology are explained below.

Some accrued interest is included in *Other Items (Net)* rather than in the outstanding amounts of the financial assets and liabilities. Held-to-maturity securities are valued at acquisition cost rather than at current market price or fair value.

For December 2001 through December 2003, data in the SRF format are compiled from pre-SRF data not based on the *MFSM* methodology. Departures from the *MFSM* methodology are explained below.

Financial assets and liabilities for which financial instrument breakdown is unavailable are allocated to the financial instrument having the largest volume of transactions in the category.

Financial assets and liabilities for which economic sectorization is unavailable are allocated to the economic sector having the largest volume of transactions in the category.

Accrued interest and trade credit are included in *Other Items (Net)* rather than in the outstanding amounts of the financial assets and liabilities.

Held-to-maturity securities are valued at acquisition cost rather than at current market price or fair value.

Other Depository Corporations:

Comprises commercial banks and credit institutions. Beginning in June 2002, includes the Fiji Development Bank and Housing Authority. Data exclude credit unions and microfinance institutions.

† Beginning in January 2009, data are based on a standardized report form (SRF) for other depository corporations, which accords with the concepts and definitions of the *Monetary and Financial Statistics Manual (MFSM)*. For other depository corporations in Fiji, departures from the *MFSM* methodology are explained below.

Holdings of national currency by credit institutions are included in *Other Items (Net)* rather than in *Currency*.

Financial assets and liabilities for which financial instrument breakdown is unavailable are allocated to the financial instrument having the largest volume of transactions in the category.

Financial assets and liabilities for which economic sectorization is unavailable are allocated to the economic sector having the largest volume of transactions in the category.

Though data for other depository corporations were not directly distinguished from data for other financial corporations, separation of the data was based on the characteristics of the financial asset or liability. *Claims on Other Financial Corporations, Transferable Deposits Included in Broad Money,* and *Other Deposits Included in Broad Money* include some positions with the Fiji Development Bank and Housing Authority.

Some accrued interest is included in *Other Items (Net)* rather than in the outstanding amounts of the financial assets and liabilities.

Securities other than shares and shares and other equity are valued at acquisition cost rather than at current market price or fair value.

For December 2001 through December 2008, data in the SRF format are compiled from pre-SRF data not based on the *MFSM* methodology. Departures from the *MFSM* methodology are explained below.

Holdings of national currency by credit institutions are included in *Other Items (Net)* rather than in *Currency*.

Financial assets and liabilities for which financial instrument breakdown is unavailable are allocated to the financial instrument having the largest volume of transactions in the category.

Financial assets and liabilities for which economic sectorization is unavailable are allocated to the economic sector having the largest volume of transactions in the category.

Though data for other depository corporations were not directly distinguished from data for other financial corporations, separation of the data was based on the characteristics of the financial asset or liability. *Claims on Other Financial Corporations, Transferable Deposits Included in Broad Money,* and *Other Deposits Included in Broad Money* include some positions with the Fiji Development Bank and Housing Authority.

Securities Other than Shares Included in Broad Money includes some securities held by other depository corporations.

For June 2002 through June 2006, some savings deposits of the private sector with the Fiji Development Bank are included in *Other Items (Net)* rather than in *Other Deposits Included in Broad Money*.

Accrued interest and trade credit are included in *Other Items (Net)* rather than in the outstanding amounts of the financial assets and liabilities.

Securities other than shares and shares and other equity are valued at acquisition cost rather than at current market price or fair value.

Depository Corporations:

† See notes on central bank and other depository corporations.

Other Financial Corporations:

Comprises insurance companies, Fiji National Provident Fund, Asset Management Bank, and insurance brokers, Beginning in March 2009, includes unit trusts. Data exclude finance companies, private money lenders, pawn shops, restricted foreign exchange dealers, and money changers.

Data are based on a standardized report form (SRF) for other financial corporations, which accords with the concepts and definitions of the *Monetary and Financial Statistics Manual (MFSM)*. Data in the SRF format are compiled from pre-SRF data not based on the *MFSM* methodology. For other financial corporations in Fiji, departures from the *MFSM* methodology are explained below.

Financial assets and liabilities for which financial instrument breakdown is unavailable are allocated to the financial instrument having the largest volume of transactions in the category.

Financial assets and liabilities for which economic sectorization is unavailable are allocated to the economic sector having the largest volume of transactions in the category.

Though data for other depository corporations were not directly distinguished from data for other financial corporations, separation of the data was based on the characteristics of the financial asset or liability. *Other Items (Net)* includes some positions with credit institutions, Fiji Development Bank, and Housing Authority.

Claims on Public Nonfinancial Corporations includes some holdings of securities issued by other depository corporations.

Claims on Private Sector includes some holdings of securities issued by public nonfinancial corporations and other depository corporations and trade credit of public nonfinancial corporations.

For December 2001 through December 2010, positions with nonresidents are included as assets and liabilities with resident sectors.

Accrued interest is included in *Other Items (Net)* rather than in the outstanding amounts of the financial assets and liabilities.

Securities other than shares and shares and other equity are valued at acquisition cost rather than at current market price or fair value.

Financial Corporations:

† See notes on central bank and other depository corporations.

Monetary Aggregates:

Broad Money:

Broad Money (line 59m) calculated from the liability data in the sections for the central bank and other depository corporations accords with the concepts and definitions of the *MFSM* and is consistent with broad money (*line 59mea*) described below.

Money (National Definitions):

Monetary Base comprises currency in circulation, statutory reserve deposits, and excess reserves of commercial banks.

M1 comprises currency in circulation outside commercial banks, demand deposits, and local bills payable. Demand deposits include transferable deposits of local governments, public nonfinancial corporations, and private sector less checks in the process of clearance in national currency with commercial banks. † Beginning in December 2001, comprises currency in circulation outside commercial banks and transferable deposits of other financial corporations, local governments, public nonfinancial corporations, and private sector in national currency with commercial banks.

Quasi Money comprises transferable deposits of other financial corporations, local governments, public nonfinancial corporations, and private sector with depository corporations in foreign currency and other deposits of other financial corporations, local governments, public nonfinancial corporations and private sector with other depository corporations in national and foreign currency.

M2 comprises M1 and quasi money. † See note to M1.

M3 comprises M2 and securities other than shares issued by other depository corporations held by other financial corporations, public nonfinancial corporations and private sector.

Interest Rates:

Central Bank Policy Rate (End of Period):
Policy indicator rate (PIR) determined by the RBF indicating the monetary policy stance. † Beginning in May 2010, overnight policy rate (OPR) indicating the monetary policy stance taken by the RBF. The RBF influences liquidity conditions to move the overnight interbank rate toward the OPR. A change in the OPR signals a change in the monetary policy stance of the RBF and is expected to transmit changes in other interest rates in the market. The OPR is reviewed regularly and changed depending on the policy stance of the RBF.

Discount Rate (End of Period):
Minimum rate charged by the RBF on short-term loans to commercial banks and public nonfinancial enterprises.

Money Market Rate:
Weighted average rate of interbank overnight loans.

Treasury Bill Rate:
Weighted average rate on 91-day treasury bills.

Savings Rate:
Weighted average rate offered by commercial banks on savings deposits. The rate is weighted by deposit amounts.

Deposit Rate:
Rate offered by deposit money banks on one- to three-month time deposits of less than F$250,000; these rates are regulated by the RBF.† Beginning in October 1992, weighted average rate offered by commercial banks on time deposits. The rate is weighted by deposit amounts.

Lending Rate:
Maximum rate charged by commercial banks on loans and advances. † Beginning in October 1992, weighted average rate charged by commercial banks on loans and advances. The rate is weighted by loan amounts.

Government Bond Yield:
Weighted average yield on five-year government bonds.

Prices, Production, Labor:

Share Prices: (Period Average and End of Month):
Kontiki South Pacific Stock Exchange Index (KSPX), base January 4, 2000. The index covers common stocks and is weighted by market capitalization.

Consumer Prices:
Source: Bureau of Statistics. Weights Reference Period: 2005; Geographical Coverage: covers price changes of goods and services consumed by all households in the seven urban areas of the Fiji islands (Suva, Lami, Nausori, Lautoka, Nadi, Ba, and Labasa); Number of Items in the Basket: 331 elementary groups of goods or services; Basis for Calculation: urban households extracted from the Household Income and Expenditure Survey of 2002–2003.

Wage Rates:
Source: Bureau of Statistics. Covers all employees. The data are derived from annual employment survey.

Industrial Production:
Source: Bureau of Statistics. Weight Reference Period: 1995; Coverage: covers the production of mining and quarrying, manufacturing, and electricity and water industries.

Tourist Arrivals:
Source: Bureau of Statistics. Index calculated from total number of visitor arrivals by sea and air. Data exclude residents and persons in transit.

Industrial Employment:
Data are derived from annual sample surveys of nonagricultural establishments.

International Transactions:

Reserve Bank of Fiji. Export data include re-exports.

Government Finance:

Data are provided by the Ministry of Finance. External debt data are from the Commonwealth Secretariat Debt Recording Management System, and domestic debt data are from the Reserve Bank of Fiji. The fiscal year ends December 31.

National Accounts:

Source: Bureau of Statistics. As indicated by the country, data are compiled according to the recommendations of the *1968 SNA*. *Line 99b* includes a statistical discrepancy.

Finland   172

Data are denominated in markkaa prior to January 1999 and in euros from January 1999 onward. The markka's irrevocable fixed conversion factor to the euro is 5.94573 markkaa per euro. Beginning in January 1999, with the implementation of Stage Three of the European Economic and Monetary Union (EMU), an alternative euro area-wide definition of residency was introduced: All positions with residents of other euro area (EA) countries, including the European Central Bank (ECB), are classified as domestic positions, and foreign assets and foreign liabilities include only positions with non-euro area residents. In 2002, the markka was retired from circulation and replaced by euro banknotes and coins. Descriptions of the changes in the methodology and presentation of Finland's accounts following the introduction of the euro are shown in the introduction to *IFS* and in the footnotes on the euro area page.

Date of Fund Membership:
January 14, 1958

Standard Sources:
Bank of Finland
Ministry of Finance
Statistics Finland
Eurostat

Exchange Rates:

Official Rate: (End of Period and Period Average):
Prior to January 1999, the market rate referred to the markka's central bank midpoint rate. In January 1999, the markka became a participating currency within the Eurosystem, and the euro market rate became applicable to all transactions. In 2002, the markka was retired from circulation and replaced by euro banknotes and coins. For additional information, refer to the section on Exchange Rates in the introduction to *IFS* and the footnotes on the euro area page.

International Liquidity:

Beginning in January 1999, *Total Reserves minus Gold (line 1l.d)* is defined in accordance with the Eurosystem's statistical definition of international reserves. The international reserves of Finland per the Eurosystem statistical definition at the start of the monetary union (January 1, 1999) in billions of U.S. dollars were as follows: *Total Reserves minus Gold,* $9,196; *Foreign Exchange,* $8,025; *SDR holdings,* $344; *Reserve Position in the Fund,* $826; *Other Reserve Assets,* $0; *Gold,* $575; *Gold (million fine troy ounces),* 2.002 ounces. *Foreign Exchange (line 1d.d)*: Beginning in January 1995, gold and foreign exchange holdings excluded deposits at the European Monetary Institute (EMI), and the holdings of European currency units (ECUs) issued against these deposits are included in *line 1d.d. Gold (Eurosystem Valuation) (line 1and)* is obtained by converting the value in national currency terms as reported in the country's standard sources, using the prevailing exchange rate, as given in *line de, line ae,* or *line we.* In December 1979 gold was revalued at the average daily quotations in London during November 1979 less a discount of 25 percent. From January 1999 onward, gold is revalued at market prices at the end of each month. Memorandum data are provided on *Non-Euro Claims on Euro Area Residents* and *Euro Claims on Non-Euro Area Residents,* which represent positions as of the last Friday in each month. For additional information, refer to the section on International Liquidity in the introduction to *IFS* and on the euro area page.

Central Bank:

Consists of the Bank of Finland, which beginning in January 1999 is part of the Eurosystem, only. For a description of the accounts, refer to the section on *Central Bank - Euro Area* in the introduction to *IFS*.

Other Depository Corporations:

Comprises all resident units classified as other monetary financial institutions (other MFIs), in accordance with *1995 ESA* standards, including money market funds. For a description of the accounts, refer to the section on *Other Depository Corporations - Euro Area* in the introduction to *IFS*.

Depository Corporations (National Residency):

For a description of the accounts and the methodology, refer to the section on *Depository Corporations (National Residency) - Euro Area* in the introduction to *IFS*.

Depository Corporations (Euro Area-wide Residency):

For a description of the accounts and the methodology, refer to the section on *Depository Corporations (Euro Area-wide Residency)* in the introduction to *IFS*.

Interest Rates:

Discount Rate (End of Period):
Prior to January 1999, the discount rate provided the basis for determining the interest rates charged by commercial banks. Over time, it had minor significance and was used mostly as a reference rate for loans and deposits. Beginning in January 1999, central bank policy rates are discontinued. See Eurosystem policy rate series on the euro area page.

Money Market Rate:
Three-month Helibor rate and, beginning in January 1999, the three-month EURIBOR rate. Monthly data are the average of daily rates for the month.

Deposit Rate:
Stock-weighted average of deposit rates of total deposits with credit institutions at end-of-month.

Deposit Rate (lines 60lhs, 60lhn, 60lcs, and 60lcn):
See notes in the introduction to *IFS* and *Euro-area Interest Rates.*

Lending Rate:
Mean value of the end-of-month lending rates weighted by market value of stocks.

Lending Rate (lines 60phs, 60pns, 60phm, 60phn, 60pcs, and 60pcn):
See notes in the introduction to *IFS* and *Euro-area Interest Rates.*

Government Bond Yield:
Data are period averages of secondary market quotations for a fixed rate serial bond with an average remaining maturity of 10 years. For additional information, refer to the section on interest rates in the introduction to *IFS* and on the euro area page. This rate is used to measure long-term interest rates for assessing convergence among the European Union member states.

Prices, Production, Labor:

Share Prices:
Industrial share price index, base 1948. † Beginning in January 1957, industrial share price index, base 1970. † Beginning in January 1967, industrial share price index, base 1975. † Beginning in January 1987, OMX Helsinki all share price index, base December 28, 1990. Index refers to the average of daily buying quotations.

Prices: Domestic Supply:
Source: Statistics Finland. Basic price index of domestic supply, Weights Reference Period: 2005; Sectoral Coverage: domestic and imported goods; Number of Items in Basket: 850 headings and 4,300 prices; Basis for Calculation: weights are derived from national accounts, Board of Customs foreign trade statistics and Statistics on industrial production.

Producer Manufacturing:
Source: Statistics Finland. Weights Reference Period: 2010; Sectoral Coverage: mining and quarrying, manufacturing and electricity, gas and water supply; Number of Items in Basket: about 2690 items; Basis for Calculation: weights are from national accounts, Board of Customs foreign trade statistics and Statistics on industrial production.

Consumer Prices:
Source: Statistics Finland. Weights Reference Period: calendar year 2010; Geographical Coverage: the whole country; Number of Items in Basket: 51,000 price observations; Basis for Calcula-

tion: weights are derived from the National Accounts 2009 updated to 2010 consumption level, covering all households and population groups.

Wages: Hourly Earnings:
Source: Statistics Finland. Weights reference period: 2005; Index includes wages of working-age population 15–69; Sectoral Coverage: All industries except fishing.

Industrial Production:
Source: Statistics Finland. Weights Reference Period: 2005; Sectoral Coverage: industrial sector; Basis for Calculation: the variable weight chain index in which the weights are changed yearly both within the industry and between industries is used.

Industrial Employment:
Index constructed from Statistics Finland data on employment in mining, manufacturing, electricity, gas, and water.

International Transactions:

Export and Import Prices:
Bank of Finland, weights reference period 2000.

Government Finance:

From 1999 onward annual, quarterly, and monthly cash data on central government are as reported by the Bank of Finland. Debt data on central government do not include the outstanding debt of the social security funds and selected extrabudgetary funds. Data on general government are derived from Eurostat. The fiscal year ends December 31.

National Accounts:

Source: Statistics Finland. *Line 93i* includes a statistical discrepancy. As indicated by the country, from 1988 onwards data have been revised following the implementation of the *ESA 95.* Beginning in 1999, euro data are sourced from the Eurostat database. Eurostat introduced chain-linked GDP volume measures to both annual and quarterly data with the release of the third quarter 2005 on November 30, 2005. Chain linked GDP volume measures are expressed in the prices of the previous year and re-referenced to 2005.

France   132

Data are denominated in French francs prior to January 1999 and in euros from January 1999 onward. An irrevocably fixed factor for converting French francs to euros was established at 6.55957 French francs per euro. Beginning in January 1999, with the implementation of Stage Three of the European Economic and Monetary Union (EMU), a euro area-wide definition of residency was introduced: All positions with residents of other euro area (EA) countries, including the European Central Bank (ECB), are classified as domestic positions, and foreign assets and foreign liabilities include only positions with non-euro area residents. In 2002, the franc was retired from circulation and replaced by euro banknotes and coins. Descriptions of the changes in the methodology and presentation of France's accounts following the introduction of the euro are shown in the introduction to *IFS* and in the footnotes on the euro area page.

Date of Fund Membership:
December 27, 1945

Standard Sources:

Bank of France
National Council of Credit
OECD
Ministry of Economics, Finance and Budget
National Institute of Statistics and Economic Research (INSEE)
Eurostat

Exchange Rates:

Market Rate (End of Period and Period Average):
In January 1999, the French franc became a participating currency within the Eurosystem, and the euro market rate became applicable to all transactions. In 2002, the franc was retired from circulation and replaced by euro banknotes and coins. For additional information, refer to the section on exchange rates in the introduction to *IFS* and on the euro area page.

International Liquidity:

Beginning in January 1999, *Total Reserves minus Gold (line 1l.d)* is defined in accordance with the Eurosystem's statistical definition of international reserves. The international reserves of France per the Eurosystem statistical definition at the start of the monetary union (January 1, 1999) in billions of U.S. dollars were as follows: *Total Reserves minus Gold,* $39,422; *Foreign Exchange,* $33,862; *SDR holdings,* $1,107; *Reserve Position in the Fund,* $4,453; *Other Reserve Assets,* $0; *Gold,* $29,425; *Gold (million fine troy ounces),* 102.370 ounces. *Foreign Exchange (line 1d.d):* Between March 1979 and December 1998, gold and foreign exchange holdings excluded deposits at the European Monetary Cooperation Fund (EMCF), and the holdings of European currency units (ECUs) issued against these deposits were included in *line 1.d.d. Gold (Eurosystem Valuation) (line 1and):* For January–May 1975, gold was valued at the average dollar price quoted on the London market on January 7 and converted into French francs at the dollar rate in Paris. During June 1975 to December 1998, the gold was the average over the three preceding months of the dollar price of gold in London converted to French francs at the franc/dollar rate in Paris. From January 1999 onward, gold is valued at market prices at the end of each month. Memorandum data are provided on *Non-Euro Claims on Euro Area Residents* and *Euro Claims on Non-Euro Area Residents,* which represent positions as of the last Friday in each month. For additional information, refer to the section on International Liquidity in the introduction to *IFS* and on the euro area page.

Central Bank:

Consists of the Bank of France, which beginning in January 1999 is part of the Eurosystem, only. *Currency Issued* includes coins issued by the Treasury. For a description of the accounts, refer to the section on *Central Bank - Euro Area* in the introduction to *IFS.*

Other Depository Corporations:

Comprises all resident units classified as other monetary financial institutions (other MFIs), as defined by the 1995 *ESA* standards. Accounts of the Caisse Nationale des Télécommunications and the Caisse Nationale des Autoroutes–affiliates of the

Institutions financières spécialisées et assimilées-and private sector deposits with the Postal System and Treasury are not included, but the money market funds are included. For a description of the accounts, refer to the section on *Other Depository Corporations - Euro Area* in the introduction to *IFS*.

Depository Corporations (National Residency):

For a description of the accounts and the methodology, refer to the section on *Depository Corporations (National Residency) - Euro Area* in the introduction to *IFS*.

Depository Corporations (Euro Area-wide Residency):

For a description of the accounts and the methodology, refer to the section on *Depository Corporations (Euro Area-wide Residency)* in the introduction to *IFS*.

Interest Rates:

Rate on Repurchase Agreements:
Prior to January 1999, data refer to the interest rate for official repurchase agreements with the Bank of France. The rate typically served as the lower bound for short-term market rates. In January 1999, central bank policy rates were discontinued. Refer to Eurosystem policy rate series on the euro area page.

Money Market Rate:
Prior to January 1999, data refer to the monthly average of rates for overnight loans against private bills, based on opening quotations. From January 1999 onward, data refer to the three-month EURIBOR rate, which is an interbank deposit bid rate. See euro area page.

Treasury Bill Rate:
End-of-month bid rate on new issues of 12-month treasury bills. † Beginning June 1989, refers to the monthly average yield on three-month treasury bills.

Deposit Rate:
Rate on tax-exempt "A" passbook deposits at savings bank.

Deposit Rate (lines 60lhs, 60lhn, 60lcs, 60lcn, and 60lcr):
See notes in the introduction to *IFS* and *Euro-area Interest Rates*.

Lending Rate:
Rate on short-term bank loans.

Lending Rate (lines 60phs, 60pns, 60phm, 60phn, 60pcs, and 60pcn):
See notes in the introduction to *IFS* and *Euro-area Interest Rates*.

Government Bond Yield:
Average yield to maturity on public sector bonds with original maturities of more than five years. Monthly yields are based on weighted averages of weekly data. For additional information, refer to the introduction to *IFS* and the notes on the euro area page. † Beginning January 1980, refers to secondary market yields of government bonds with a ten-year maturity. This rate is used to measure long-term interest rates for assessing convergence among the European Union member states.

Prices, Production, Labor:

Share Prices (Period Average and End of Month):
Industrial share price index, base 1949. † Beginning in December 1958, industrial share price index, base December 31, 1958. † Beginning in December 1960, industrial share price index, base December 30, 1960. † Beginning in December 1961, industrial share price index, base December 29, 1961. † Beginning in December 1972, industrial share price index, base December 29, 1972. † Beginning in January 1981, industrial share price index, base December 31, 1981. † Beginning in December 1983, industrial share price index, base December 28, 1984. † Beginning in December 1984, industrial share price index, base December 31, 1985. † Beginning in December 1985, share price index, base December 31, 1986. Index calculated from the sample of 180 shares on the Paris exchange. † Beginning in December 1987, share price index, base December 31, 1987. The index covers the common shares of the 40 enterprises having the largest capitalization.

Producer Prices:
Source: National Institute of Statistics and Economic Research. Beginning in 1999, in addition to the Prices of intermediate industrial goods (*line 63a*, weights reference period: 2005) and the imported raw materials index (*line 63b*, weights reference period: 2000), France publishes a Producer Price Index covering all sectors of the industry. The PPI, Weights Reference Period: 2005; Sectoral Coverage: all sectors of the industry; Number of Items in Baskey: about 29,000 prices; Basis for Calculation: weights are updated continuously, as per visits by field officers, which visit approximately one-fifth of the overall sample each year, ensuring a complete review of all weights and products every five years.

Consumer Prices:
Source: National Institute of Statistics and Economic Research. Weights Reference Period: year t–2; Geographical Coverage: all cities of mainland France and of the overseas departments (Guadeloupe, Martinique, French Guiana, Réunion) with a population greater than 2,000; Number of Items in Basket: 305; Basis for Calculation: weights for these groupings are derived from national accounts final consumption data of the antepenultimate year.

Labor Costs:
Source: National Institute of Statistics and Economic Research. Include wages and other labor costs established by law or contracts. The index covers manufacturing of mechanical and electrical machinery and equipment.

Industrial Production:
Source: National Institute of Statistics and Economic Research. Weights Reference Period: 2005; Sectoral Coverage: manufacturing, mining, construction and energy; Basis for Calculation: the weighting system is renewed every five years. Data are sourced from the OECD database.

Industrial Employment:
Source: National Institute of Statistics and Economic Research index. The series covers all salaried personnel in manufacturing and mining.

International Transactions:

Exports and *Imports, f.o.b.*: National Institute of Statistics and Economic Research data. *Imports c.i.f.*: Data are from the *Statistics of Foreign Trade* of Customs. Beginning in 1997, reported exports and imports data include trade of French Guiana, Guadeloupe, Martinique, and Reunion. The f.o.b./c.i.f. factor is established at the beginning of each year by the Customs director of forecasting.
Volume data: National Institute of Statistics and Economic Research, weights reference period: 1995 fixed weight indices.

Unit Value data: National Institute of Statistics and Economic Research, weights reference period: 1995, current weights indices. The indices exclude electricity, military and railway equipment, electronics, analyzing and controlling instruments, shipbuilding and aeronautics, and machine tools. From January 1994 onwards, the methodology was changed to broaden the geographical coverage and improve the validation procedures and the representativeness of the products selected. From January 2005 onward, the indices take into account the enlargement of the European Union. Both Volume Indices and Unit Value Indices have been discontinued in 2009.

Price Data: National Institute of Statistics and Economic Research, the indices track the changes in transaction prices of imported industrial goods and services and the ones sold abroad.

Government Finance:

Monthly and quarterly cash data are derived from National Institute of Statistics and Economic Research and cover Treasury accounts only. Monthly, quarterly, and annual debt data on central government are derived from Bank of France. Data on general government are derived from Eurostat. The fiscal year ends December 31.

National Accounts:

Source: National Institute of Statistics and Economic Research (INSEE). As indicated by the country, from 1997 onwards data have been revised following the implementation of the ESA 95. Beginning in 1999, euro data are sourced from the Eurostat database. Eurostat introduced chain-linked GDP volume measures to annual data with the release of the third quarter 2005 on November 30, 2005. Chain linked GDP volume measures are expressed in the prices of the previous year and re-referenced to 2005.

Gabon   646

Date of Fund Membership:
September 30, 1963

Standard Source:
Banque des Etats d'Afrique Centrale (BEAC) (Bank of the Central African States)
Direction Générale des Statistiques

Exchange Rates:

Official Rate: (End of Period and Period Average):
Prior to January 1999, the official rate was pegged to the French franc. On January 12, 1994, the CFA franc was devalued to CFAF 100 per French franc from CFAF 50 at which it had been fixed since 1948. From January 1, 1999, the CFAF is pegged to the euro at a rate of CFA franc 655.957 per euro.

International Liquidity:

Gold (National Valuation) (line 1and) is obtained by converting the value in national currency, as reported in the country's standard sources, using the prevailing exchange rate, as given in line **ae**. Prior to January 1999, the national currency/dollar conversion rates utilized for balance sheet purposes are used. These conver-

sion rates differ from the prevailing exchange rates reported in IFS. This line follows the national valuation procedure which corresponds to that of the Bank of France (cf the international liquidity note on the IFS page for France).

Central Bank:

Consists of the national office of the Banque des Etats de l'Afrique Centrale (BEAC), consolidating the accounts of all its branches located in Libreville, Port-Gentil, Franceville, and Oyem.

Data are based on a standardized report form for central banks, which accords with the concepts and definitions of the IMF's Monetary and Financial Statistics Manual (MFSM), 2000. Departures from the MFSM methodology are explained below.

Held-to-maturity securities are valued at amortized cost rather than at current market price or fair value.

Other Depository Corporations:

Comprises commercial banks. Data exclude credit unions and microfinance institutions which accept deposits.

Data are based on a standardized report form for other depository corporations, which accords with the concepts and definitions of the Monetary and Financial Statistics Manual (MFSM). For other depository corporations in Gabon, departures from the MFSM methodology are explained below.

Financial assets and liabilities for which currency breakdown is unavailable are allocated to assets and liabilities denominated in national currency.

Held-to-maturity securities are valued at acquisition cost rather than at current market price or fair value.

Depository Corporations:

See notes on central bank and other depository corporations.

Monetary Aggregates:

Broad Money:
Broad Money calculated from the liability data in the sections for the central bank and other depository corporations accords with the concepts and definitions of the MFSM. Broad money differs from M2 described below as M2 excludes holdings of currency by the central government.

Money (National Definitions):
M1 comprises currency in circulation and transferable deposits. Transferable deposits refer to current account deposits of other financial corporations, public nonfinancial corporations, and private sector with depository corporations in national currency.
M2 comprises M1 and quasi-money. Quasi-money refers to fixed and saving deposits of other financial corporations, public nonfinancial corporations, and private sector with depository corporations in national currency.

Interest Rates:

Discount Rate (End of Period):
Basic rediscount rate offered by the BEAC. † Beginning in July 1994, rate charged by the BEAC on refinancing operations to financial institutions.

Deposit Rate:
Minimum rate offered by other depository corporations on savings accounts.

Lending Rate:
Maximum rate charged by financial institutions on loans.

Prices and Production:

All data on prices are from Bank of the Central African States.

Consumer Prices:
Source: Direction Générale des Statistiques. Weights reference period: 2003; Laspeyres index; Coverage: cities of Libreville and Owendo; Number of Items in Basket: 394; Basis for Calculation: household expenditure survey conducted in Libreville in 2003.

Crude Petroleum Production:
Calculated from production quantities reported in the *Oil Market Intelligence.*

International Transactions:

All trade data are from Bank of the Central African States.

Value of Exports and Imports:
Data exclude transactions to and from other countries of the Union douanière et économique de l'Afrique centrale (UDEAC) (Central African Customs Union). If uncurrent, export data are derived by adding the value of oil exports and the value of other exports. Current monthly entries on other exports are estimated by carrying forward latest available entries. *Imports, c.i.f., from DOTS:* Data are based on reported data and estimates from *Direction of Trade Statistics (DOTS).*

National Accounts:

All trade data are from Bank of the Central African States. As indicated by the country, data are compiled according to the *1968 SNA.*

Gambia, The   648

Date of Fund Membership:
September 21, 1967

Standard Sources:
Central Bank of The Gambia
Gambia Bureau of Statistics

Exchange Rates:

Market Rate (End of Period and Period Average):
Cross rates are based on a fixed relationship to the pound sterling. † Beginning in July 1986, a floating rate system was introduced. The rate is determined by demand and supply factors.

International Liquidity:

Data for *line 1d.d* include small foreign exchange holdings by the government.

Central Bank:

Consists of the Central Bank of The Gambia (CBG) only.
† Beginning in December 2002, data are based on a standardized report from (SRF) for central banks, which accords with the concepts and definitions of the IMF's *Monetary and Financial Statistics Manual (MFSM).* Departures from the MFSM methodology are explained below:
Accrued interest is included in Other Items (Net) rather than in

the outstanding amounts of the underlying financial assets and liabilities.
For December 2001 through December 2002, data in the SRF format are compiled from pre-SRF data not based on the *MFSM* methodology. Departures from the *MFSM* methodology are explained below.
Deposits of nonresidents are included in *Other Items (Net)* rather than in *Liabilities to Nonresidents.*
Transferable deposits of other financial corporations and private sector with the CBG are included in *Other Items (Net)* rather than in *Reserve Money.*
Accrued interest is included in *Other Items (Net)* rather than in the outstanding amounts of the financial assets and liabilities.

Other Depository Corporations:

Comprises commercial banks and an Islamic bank. Data exclude credit institutions, microfinances, and Post Office Savings banks, which issue short-term liabilities.
† Beginning in December 2002, data are based on a standardized report form (SRF) for other depository corporations, which accords with the concepts and definitions of the *Monetary and Financial Statistics Manual (MFSM).* For other depository corporations in The Gambia, departures from the *MFSM* methodology are explained below:
Financial assets and liabilities for which economic sectorization in unavailable are allocated to the economic sector having the largest volume of transactions in the category.
Financial assets and liabilities not disaggregated by national and foreign currencies are allocated to the currency that is predominantly used in transactions in the category.
For December 2001 through December 2002, data in the SRF format are compiled from pre-SRF data not based on the *MFSM* methodology. Departures from the *MFSM* methodology are explained below.
Financial Assets and liabilities for which economic sectorization is unavailable are allocated to the economic sector having the largest volume of transactions in the category.
Financial assets and liabilities not disaggregated by national and foreign currencies are allocated to the currency that is predominantly used in transactions in the category.
Deposits of nonresidents are included in *Transferable* and/or *Other Deposits Included in Broad Money* rather than in *Liabilities to Nonresidents.*
Holdings of treasury bills issued by the central government based on Sharia Principles (SUKUK) are included in *Claims on Private Sector* rather than *Claims on Central Government.*
Accrued interest is included in *Other Items (Net)* rather than in the outstanding amounts of the financial assets and liabilities.

Depository Corporations:

† See notes on central bank and other depository corporations.

Monetary Aggregates:

Broad Money:
Broad Money calculated from the liability data in the sections for the central bank and other depository corporations accords with the concepts and definitions of the *MFSM.* Broad money differs from M2 as M2 excludes transferable deposits of other financial corporations and private sector with the CBG and includes de-

posits of nonresidents with the other depository corporations.

Money (National Definitions):

M0 (Reserve Money) comprises currency in circulation and deposits of other depository corporations with the CBG for reserve requirement. Currency in circulation refers to notes and coins issued by the CBG.

M1 (Narrow Money) comprises currency outside depository corporations, transferable deposits of public nonfinancial corporations with the CBG in national currency, and transferable deposits of public nonfinancial corporations, private sector, and nonresidents with other depository corporations in national currency. Currency outside depository corporations refers to currency in circulation less the notes and coins held by other depository corporations.

Quasi Money comprises savings and time deposits of public nonfinancial corporations, private sector, and nonresidents with other depository corporations in national and foreign currency.

M2 (Broad Money) comprises narrow money and quasi money.

Interest Rates:

Central Bank Policy Rate (End of Period):

Rate at which the CBG rediscounts treasury bills. This rate is determined by the Monetary Policy Committee on a quarterly basis.

Discount Rate (End of Period):

Rate at which the CBG discounts commercial paper for banks. The rate was discontinued in June 2004.

Treasury Bill Rate:

End-of-period yield on 12-month treasury bills sold in the primary market.

Savings Rate:

Minimum rate offered by commercial banks on savings deposits in national currency.

Deposit Rate:

Minimum rate offered by commercial banks on three-month time deposits in national currency.

Lending Rate:

Maximum rate charged by commercial banks on industrial loans in national currency.

Prices:

Consumer Prices:

Source: Gambia Bureau of Statistics. Weights Reference Period: August 2004; Geographical Coverage: National; Number of Items in the Basket: 293 items; Basis for Calculation: Integrated Household Survey conducted in 2003/2004 by the Gambia Bureau of Statistics (GBOS).

International Transactions:

Export data include re-exports.

Government Finance:

Annual data are as reported in the *Government Finance Statistics Yearbook (GFSY)* and cover budgetary central government. The fiscal year ends June 30.

National Accounts:

Source: Gambia Bureau of Statistics. As indicated by the country, concepts and definitions are broadly in accordance with the *1993 SNA*.

Georgia 915

Date of Fund Membership:
May 5, 1992

Standard Sources:
National Bank of Georgia
Ministry of Finance
National Statistics Office of Georgia

Exchange Rates:
The lari was introduced and made the sole legal tender in October 1995.

Official Rate: (End of Period and Period Average):
Beginning in April 1993, the official rate has been set by the NBG on the basis of the rate determined by the periodic auctions conducted by the Tbilisi Interbank Currency Exchange (TICEX). This exchange was established by the NBG and a group of commercial banks. Beginning in August 1996, rate set by the NBG on the basis of the average weighted rate in the interbank market.

International Liquidity:
Gold (National Valuation) (line 1and) is equal to *Gold (Million Fine Troy Ounces) (line 1ad)* valued at the London fixing rate, discounted by ten percent, for the end of period. *Foreign Exchange (line 1d.d)* comprises the NBG's cash holdings, liquid correspondent accounts with nonresident banks, and foreign government securities.

Central Bank:
Consists of the National Bank of Georgia (NBG) only.

Data are based on a standardized report form (SRF) for central banks, which accords with the concepts and definitions of the IMF's *Monetary and Financial Statistics Manual (MFSM)*, 2000.

Other Depository Corporations:
Comprises domestic commercial banks and branches of foreign banks. Data exclude credit unions.

Data are based on a standardized report form (SRF) for other depository corporations, which accords with the concepts and definitions of the *Monetary and Financial Statistics Manual (MFSM)*.

Depository Corporations:
See notes on central bank and other depository corporations.

Monetary Aggregates:

Broad Money:

Broad Money calculated from the liability data in the sections for the central bank and other depository corporations accords with the concepts and definitions of the *MFSM* and is consistent with M3 described below.

Money (National Definitions):

Reserve Money comprises currency in circulation, required reserves of other depository corporations with the NBG, and correspondent and other accounts of other depository corporations with the NBG (excluding banks with licenses withdrawn).

M2 comprises currency outside other depository corporations and deposits of other financial corporations, public nonfinancial corporations, and private sector with the NBG and other depository corporations in national currency.

M3 comprises M2 and deposits of other financial corporations, public nonfinancial corporations, and private sector with other depository corporations in foreign currency.

Interest Rates:

Central Bank Policy Rate (End of Period):
NBG's refinancing rate on one-week loans to commercial banks.

Money Market Rate:
Weighted average rate on loans determined in the interbank credit auction market in national currency. The rate is weighted by loan amounts. † Beginning in February 2008, weighted average rate on short-term interbank loans in national currency. The rate is weighted by loan amounts.

Money Market Rate (Foreign Currency):
Weighted average rate on loans determined in the interbank credit auction market in foreign currency. The rate is weighted by loan amounts. † Beginning in August 2008, rate on short-term interbank loans in foreign currency. The rate is weighted by loan amounts.

Treasury Bill Rate:
Weighted average rate on treasury bills. The rate is weighted by issuance amounts.

Deposit Rate:
Weighted average rate offered by commercial banks on deposits of other financial corporations, public nonfinancial corporations, nonresidents, and private sector in national currency. The rate is weighted by deposit amounts. Beginning in December 2002, excludes deposits of nonresidents.

Deposit Rate (Foreign Currency):
Weighted average rate offered by commercial banks on deposits of other financial corporations, public nonfinancial corporations, nonresidents, and private sector in foreign currency. The rate is weighted by deposit amounts. Beginning in December 2002, excludes deposits of nonresidents.

Lending Rate:
Weighted average rate charged by commercial banks on loans to other financial corporations, public nonfinancial corporations, nonresidents, and private sector in national currency. The rate is weighted by loan amounts. Beginning in January 2003, excludes loans to nonresidents.

Lending Rate (Foreign Currency):
Weighted average rate charged by commercial banks on loans to other financial corporations, public nonfinancial corporations, nonresidents, and private sector in foreign currency. The rate is weighted by loan amounts. Beginning in January 2003, excludes loans to nonresidents.

Prices:

Producer Prices:
Source: National Statistics Office of Georgia. Weights Reference Period: 2011; Coverage: Mining and quarrying; Manufacturing (except production of nuclear fuel and manufacture of aircraft); Electricity, gas and water supply; export goods are also included; Number of Items in the Basket: 400 price quotations reported by 200 enterprises; Basis for Calculation: the weights are revised annually based on production values for the previous year.

Consumer Prices:
Source: National Statistics Office of Georgia. Weights Reference Period: 2011; Geographical Coverage: five largest cities, which represent the major regions of Georgia; Number of Items in the Basket: 288 items; Basis for Calculation: the weights are revised every two years on the basis of a household budget survey of approximately 3,500 households.

International Transactions:

Source: National Statistics Office of Georgia.
Exports and *Imports (c.i.f.)* are compiled from the monthly customs statistics. Adjustments to the customs data are made to account for humanitarian aid (since 1998 data on humanitarian aid are included in the customs data) and the exports and imports of electricity and gas. Informal trade is excluded from the data coverage.

Government Finance:

† Prior to 2006, annual data are as reported for the *Government Finance Statistics Yearbook (GFSY)* and cover general government. Data are as reported by the Ministry of Finance. Beginning in January 2006, monthly data are as reported in the *GFSM 2001* analytical framework and cover the general government. The fiscal year ends December 31.

National Accounts:

Source: National Statistics Office of Georgia.
Data are as reported by the State Department for Statistics of Georgia. The GDP volume series are based on the production approach and the expenditure approach are included in series 99bs.

Germany   134

With the coming into effect on July 1, 1990 of the treaty on German Economic, Monetary, and Social Union (GEMSU) between the former Federal Republic of Germany (FRG) and the former German Democratic Republic (GDR), the deutsche mark became the sole currency of the GEMSU area, and customs borders between the two states were abolished. On October 3, 1990, the former GDR became part of the FRG under international law. The membership of the FRG in the Fund, under the designation Germany, remains unchanged. The presentation of exchange rates and Fund accounts shown for Germany in *IFS* is unaffected by the unification of the former FRG and the former GDR.

Data on international liquidity, money and banking, and international transactions cover the former FRG and the former GDR beginning with end-June (second quarter) 1990 for stock data and July 1990 for flow data. Data on prices, production, labor market, and national accounts cover the former FRG and the former GDR from 1991 onward. Data on industrial employment and wages refer only to the former FRG.

Data are denominated in deutsche marks prior to January 1999 and in euros from January 1999 onward. An irrevocably fixed factor for converting deutsche marks to euros was established at 1.95583 deutsche marks per euro. In 2002, the deutsche mark was retired from circulation and replaced by euro banknotes and coins. Beginning in January 1999, with the implementation of Stage Three of the European Economic and Monetary Union

(EMU), a euro area-wide definition of residency was introduced: All positions with residents of other euro area (EA) countries, including the European Central Bank (ECB), are classified as domestic positions, and foreign assets and foreign liabilities include only positions with non-euro area residents. Descriptions of the changes in the methodology and presentation of Germany's accounts following the introduction of the euro are shown in the introduction to *IFS* and in the notes on the euro area page.

Date of Fund Membership:
August 14, 1952

Standard Sources:
Deutsche Bundesbank
Federal Statistical Office
Eurostat

Exchange Rates:

Market Rate (End of Period and Period Average):
Prior to January 1999, the market rate was the midpoint rate determined during official sessions of the Frankfurt foreign exchange market. In January 1999, the deutsche mark became a participating currency within the Eurosystem, and the euro market rate became applicable to all transactions. In 2002, the deutsche mark was retired from circulation and replaced by euro banknotes and coins. For additional information, refer to the section on Exchange Rates in the introduction to *IFS* and the notes on the euro area page.

International Liquidity:
Beginning in January 1999, *Total Reserves minus Gold (line 1l.d)* is defined in accordance with the Eurosystem's statistical definition of international reserves. The international reserves of Germany per the Eurosystem statistical definition at the start of the monetary union (January 1, 1999) in billions of U.S. dollars were as follows: *Total Reserves minus Gold,* $75,408; *Foreign Exchange,* $65,536; *SDRs,* $2,609; *Reserve Position in the Fund,* $7,263; *Other Reserve Assets,* $0; *Gold,* $34,200; *Gold (million fine troy ounces),* 118.925 ounces. *Foreign Exchange (line 1d.d)*: Between March 1979 and December 1998, gold and foreign exchange holdings excluded deposits at the European Monetary Cooperation Fund (EMCF), and the holdings of European currency units (ECUs) issued against these deposits were included in *line 1d.d. Gold (Eurosystem Valuation) (line 1and)*: Prior to January 1999, gold was valued using the prevailing exchange rate given in *line* **ae** to convert the value in national currency terms, as reported in the country's standard sources. From January 1999 onward, gold is revalued at market prices at the end of each month. Memorandum data are provided on *Non-Euro Claims on Euro Area Residents* and *Euro Claims on Non-Euro Area Residents,* which represent positions as of the last Friday in each month. For additional information, refer to the section on International Liquidity in the introduction to *IFS* and the notes on the euro area page.

Central Bank:
Consists of the Deutsche Bundesbank, which beginning in January 1999 is part of the Eurosystem, only. *Currency Issued* includes coins issued by the Treasury. For a description of the accounts, refer to the section on *Central Bank - Euro Area* in the introduction to *IFS*.

Other Depository Corporations:
Comprises all resident units classified as other monetary financial institutions (other MFIs), in accordance with *1995 ESA* standards, including money market funds. For a description of the accounts, refer to the section on *Other Depository Corporations - Euro Area* in the introduction to *IFS*.

Depository Corporations (National Residency):
For a description of the accounts and the methodology, refer to the section on *Depository Corporations (National Residency) - Euro Area* in the introduction to *IFS*.

Depository Corporations (Euro Area-wide Residency):
For a description of the accounts and the methodology, refer to the section on *Depository Corporations (Euro Area-wide Residency)* in the introduction to *IFS*.

Interest Rates:

Discount Rate (End of Period):
Prior to January 1999, the central bank policy rate which was discontinued as of January 1999. See Eurosystem policy rate series on the euro area page.

Money Market Rate:
Period averages of ten daily average quotations for overnight credit.

Treasury Bill Rate:
Rate on 12-month Federal debt register claims.

Deposit Rate:
Rate on three-month deposits in denominations of less than five hundred thousand euro.

Deposit Rate (lines 60lhs, 60lhn, 60lcs, and 60lcn):
See notes in the introduction to *IFS* and *Euro-area Interest Rates*.

Lending Rate:
Rate on current-account credit in denominations of less than five hundred thousand euro.

Lending Rate (lines 60phs, 60pns, 60phm, 60phn, 60pcs, and 60pcn):
See notes in the introduction to *IFS* and *Euro-area Interest Rates*.

Government Bond Yield: Long-Term (line 61):
Bonds issued by the Federal government, the railways, the postal system, the Länder governments, municipalities, specific purpose public associations, and other public associations established under special legislation. Average yields on all bonds with remaining maturity of more than three years, weighted by amount of individual bonds in circulation.

For additional information, refer to the section on interest rates in the introduction to *IFS* and the notes on the euro area page. † Beginning January 1980, refers to yields on listed federal securities which can be delivered on the German Financial Futures and Options Exchange (DTB) with a remaining maturity of nine- to- ten years. This rate is used to measure long-term interest rates for assessing convergence among the European Union member states.

Prices, Production, Labor:

Share Prices (End of Month):
Share price index, base December 30, 1987, refers to the CDAX share price index (previously called all-share price index FWBX)

of the Deutsche Börse A.G. It shows average price movements of all ordinary and preference shares officially listed on the Frankfurt stock exchange of companies with headquarters in Germany.

Producer Prices:

Source: Federal Statistical Office. Weights Reference Period: 2005; Sectoral Coverage: mining, manufacturing, power and water supply (excludes goods for export); Number of Items in Basket: approximately 8,400 prices; Basis for Calculation: the monthly survey of mining and manufacturing units.

Consumer Prices:

Source: Federal Statistical Office. Weights Reference Period: 2005; Geographical Coverage: all regions of the Federal Republic of Germany; Number of Items in Basket: 700; Basis for Calculation: the weights are based on surveys of household expenditures on goods and services, and are revised every five years.

Industrial Production:

Data are sourced from the OECD database, weights reference period: 2005. The indices exclude construction.

International Transactions:

Trade indices are from the Federal Statistical Office, weights reference period: 2005.

Government Finance:

Transactions and debt data cover the budgetary federal government but exclude operations of the Federal Equalization Office and social insurance institutions. † Data cover government operations within the territory of the united Germany. † Data for social security funds and the European Recovery Program are on a cash basis only beginning in 1974 and 1975, respectively. † Beginning in 1990, central government extrabudgetary operations include operations of the German Unity Fund. † From 1992 onward, annual data refer to government operations within the territory of unified Germany; through 1991 annual data cover government operations within the territory of the former Federal Republic of Germany. † From 1995 onward, the debts of the Treuhandanstalt, classified as a nonfinancial corporation, have been assumed by the Redemption Fund for the Inherited Liabilities, a central government body. Preliminary data on general government are compiled by Eurostat. The fiscal year ends December 31.

National Accounts:

Source: Eurostat. From 1991 onwards, concepts and definitions are in accordance with the *ESA 95*, as indicated by the country, and GDP *(line 99b.c)* is calculated as the sum of the components. Beginning in 1999, euro data are sourced from the Eurostat database. Eurostat introduced chain-linked GDP volume measures to both annual and quarterly data with the release of the third quarter 2005 on November 30, 2005. Chain-linked GDP volume measures are expressed in the prices of the previous year and re-referenced to 2005.

Population:

† Beginning in 1991, data cover unified Germany.

Ghana   652

Date of Fund Membership:
September 20, 1957

Standard Sources:
Bank of Ghana
Ghana Statistical Service (GSS)

Exchange Rates:

In July 2007 the Ghanaian cedi (GHC) was redenominated. The new Ghana cedi (GHS) is equal to 10,000 old Ghanaian cedis (1 GHS = 10,000 GHC). The old currency remained in circulation alongside the new until December 2007.

Market Rate (End of Period and Period Average):

The exchange rate of the cedi is determined in the interbank foreign exchange market. In October 1999, the Bank of Ghana adopted a new procedure to calculate the market exchange rate from actual commercial bank transactions instead of from indicative rates.

International Liquidity:

Data for *line 1d.d* include government holdings. *Line 1and* is equal to *line 1ad,* converted into U.S. dollars at the dollar price of gold used by national sources, as reported to *IFS.*

Central Bank:

Consists of the Bank of Ghana only.

† Beginning in December 2006, data are based on a standardized report form (SRF) for central banks, which accords with the concepts and definitions of the IMF's *Monetary and Financial Statistics Manual (MFSM),* 2000. Departures from the *MFSM* methodology are explained below.

Financial derivatives are excluded from the data.

Accrued interest is included in *Other Items (Net)* rather than in the outstanding amounts of the financial assets or liabilities.

Held-to-maturity securities are valued at acquisition cost rather than at current market price or fair value. Holdings of equity shares are valued at acquisition cost rather than at current market price or fair value.

From December 2001 through November 2006, data in the SRF format are compiled from pre-SRF data not based on the *MFSM* methodology. Departures from the *MFSM* methodology are explained below.

Financial derivatives are excluded from the data.

Claims on Central Government and *Liabilities to Central Government* include claims on or liabilities to nonfinancial public corporations, respectively, because the central government subsector is not clearly distinguishable in the source data.

Financial assets and liabilities for which economic sectorization is unavailable are allocated to the economic sector having the largest volume of transactions in the category.

Some deposits of other financial corporations, public nonfinancial corporations, other nonfinancial corporations, and other resident sectors are included in *Other Items (Net)* rather than in *Transferable Deposits Included in Broad Money* and *Other Deposits Included in Broad Money.*

Accrued interest is included in *Other Items (Net)* rather than in the outstanding amounts of the financial assets or liabilities.

Held-to-maturity securities are valued at acquisition cost rather than at current market price or fair value. Holdings of equity shares are valued at acquisition cost rather than at current market price or fair value.

Other Depository Corporations:

Comprises commercial banks. Data exclude rural banks, savings and loans companies, finance houses, credit unions, and money-market mutual funds, which issue short-term liabilities.

† Beginning in December 2006, data are based on standardized report form (SRF) for other depository corporations, which accords with the concepts and definitions of the IMF's *Monetary and Financial Statistics Manual (MFSM)*. For other depository corporations in Ghana, departures from the *MFSM* methodology are explained below.

Some accrued interest is included in *Other Items (Net)* rather than in the outstanding amounts of the financial assets or liabilities. From December 2001 through November 2006, data in the SRF format are compiled from pre-SRF data not based on the *MFSM* methodology. Departures from the *MFSM* methodology are explained below.

Claims on Central Government and *Liabilities to central government* include claims on or liabilities to nonfinancial public corporations and social security, respectively, because the central government subsector is not clearly distinguishable in the source data.

Financial assets and liabilities not disaggregated by economic sector are allocated to the economic sector having the largest volume of transactions in that category.

Positions with nonresidents are not clearly identifiable in the data and could be included as claims on or liabilities to residents.

Claims on Other Financial Corporations, Transferable Deposits Included in Broad Money, and *Other Deposits Included in Broad Money* include some positions with other depository corporations.

Accrued interest is included in *Other Items (Net)* rather than in the outstanding amounts of the financial assets or liabilities.

Held-to-maturity securities are valued at acquisition cost rather than at current market price or fair value. Holdings of equity shares are valued at acquisition cost rather than at current market price or fair value.

Depository Corporations:

† See notes on central bank and other depository corporations.

Monetary Aggregates:

Broad Money:

Broad Money calculated from the liability data in the sections for the central bank and other depository corporations accords with the concepts and definitions of the *MFSM* and is consistent with M2+ described below.

Money (National Definitions):

M1 comprises currency in circulation outside depository corporations and demand deposits of other financial corporations, nonfinancial corporations, and other resident sectors in national currency with depository corporations.

M2 comprises M1, time and savings deposits, and certificates of deposits of other financial corporations, nonfinancial corporations, and other resident sectors in national currency with the other depository corporations.

M2+ comprises M2 and foreign currency deposits of other financial corporations, nonfinancial corporations, and other resident sectors with other depository corporations.

Interest Rates:

Discount Rate (End of Period):

Rate at which the Bank of Ghana makes advances against treasury bills. A rate of one percent higher is used in discounts of direct credit to business. There are no quantitative limits on credit to banks at the discount rate. The volume of these operations is relatively small.

Money Market Rate:

Weighted average rate on interbank loans. The rate is weighted by loan amounts.

Treasury Bill Rate:

Rate of discount on 91-day treasury bills.

Savings Rate:

Rate offered by commercial banks on savings deposits.

Deposit Rate:

Rate on offered by commercial banks on three-month time deposits.

Government Bond Yield:

Yield on three-year government bonds.

Prices and Labor:

Producer Prices:

Source: Ghana Statistical Service. Weights Reference Period: September 2006; Sectoral Coverage: 209 establishments from every industry in the mining, manufacturing, and utilities sectors of the economy; Number of Items in Basket: 950.

Consumer Prices:

Source: Ghana Statistical Service. Weights Reference Period: 1998/1999; Geographical Coverage: National; Number of Items in the Basket: 242 items; Basis for Calculation; the weights of the Laspeyres index are based on the Ghana Living Standard Household Budget Survey (GLSS4) which was conducted September 1998 to August 1999.

International Transactions:

All trade data are from Ghana Statistical Service.

Value of Exports and Imports:

Imports of military goods, purchase and sale of ships and aircraft, and purchase of fish from foreign fishing vessels are excluded.

Government Finance:

† Beginning in 2001, annual data are as reported for the *Government Finance Statistics Yearbook (GFSY)* and cover budgetary central government. The fiscal year ends December 31.

National Accounts:

All trade data are from Ghana Statistical Service. As indicated by the country, data are compiled according to the recommendations of the *1968 SNA*. As of the beginning of 2011, the GSS has reintroduced the use of the expenditure approach for GDP data.

Greece 174

Data are denominated in drachmas prior to January 2001 and in euros from January 2001, onward. An irrevocably fixed factor for converting drachmas to euros was established at 340.750 drachmas per euro. With Greece's entry into Stage Three of the European Economic and Monetary Union (EMU) in January 2001, a euro area-wide definition of residency is introduced. All positions with residents of other euro area (EA) countries, including the European Central Bank (ECB), are classified as domestic positions, and foreign assets and foreign liabilities include only positions with non-euro residents. In 2002, the drachma was retired from circulation and replaced by euro banknotes and coins. Descriptions of the changes in the methodology and presentation of Greece's accounts following the introduction of the euro are shown in the introduction to *IFS* and in the notes on the euro area page.

Date of Fund Membership:
December 27, 1945

Standard Sources:
Bank of Greece
National Statistical Service
Eurostat

Exchange Rates:

Market Rate (End of Period and Period Average):
Prior to January 2001, the market rate was the central bank midpoint rate. In January 2001, the drachma became a participating currency within the Eurosystem, and the euro market rate became applicable to all transactions. In 2002, the drachma was retired from circulation and replaced by euro banknotes and coins. For additional information, refer to the section on Exchange Rates in the introduction to *IFS* and the notes on the euro area page.

International Liquidity:

Beginning in January 2001, *Total Reserves minus Gold (line 11.d)* is defined in accordance with the Eurosystem's statistical definition of international reserves and is revalued at market prices at the end of each quarter. † For the period January 1986 to December 2000, data on *Gold (line 1ad)* and *Foreign Exchange (line 1d.d)* exclude the deposits made with the European Monetary Institute (EMI) of gold and gross U.S. dollar holdings: the holdings of European currency units (ECUs) issued by the EMI against these deposits are included in *1d.d.* †Prior to December 1975, data on import documentary credits are excluded from *line 1d.d* at the time of account opening. After this date, such credits are excluded at the time of payment. *Gold (Eurosystem Valuation) (line 1and)* : Prior to December 1985, gold was valued at SDR 35 per fine troy ounce and converted into U.S. dollars at the dollar/SDR rate **sa** on the country page for the United States. † For the period December 1985 to December 2000, gold is revalued each December at 65 percent of the average buying market price of gold during that month. From January 2001 onward, gold is revalued at market prices at the end of each month. Memorandum data are provided on *Non-Euro Claims on Euro Area Residents* and *Euro Claims on Non-Euro Area Residents*, which represent positions as of the last Friday in each month. For additional information, refer to the section on International Liquidity in the introduction to *IFS* and the notes on the euro area page.

Central Bank:
Consists of the Bank of Greece, which beginning in January 2001 is part of the Eurosystem, only. *Currency Issued* includes coins issued by the Treasury. For a description of the accounts, refer to the section on *Central Bank - Euro Area* in the introduction to *IFS*.

Other Depository Corporations:
Comprises all resident units classified as other monetary financial institutions (other MFIs), in accordance with *1995 ESA* standards, including money market funds. Monthly statistical reports are not required for several hundred small MFIs, but data are estimated to represent the entire MFI sector. For a description of the accounts, refer to the section on *Other Depository Corporations - Euro Area* in the introduction to *IFS*.

Depository Corporations (National Residency):
For a description of the methodology and accounts, refer to the section on *Depository Corporations (National Residency) - Euro Area* in the introduction to *IFS*.

Depository Corporations (Euro Area-wide Residency):
For a description of the methodology and accounts, refer to the section on *Depository Corporations (Euro Area-wide Residency)* in the introduction to *IFS*.

Interest Rates:

Discount Rate (End of Period):
Refers to the discount rate offered by the Bank of Greece prior to April 1998 and, thereafter, refers to the interest rate applied to deposits of 14-days maturity placed with the Bank of Greece; the Bank of Greece has made regular interventions in the domestic money market by conducting activities (every Wednesday) for accepting deposits with 14-days maturity. Accordingly, the interest rate applied to these deposits provides an indication of the liquidity conditions as well as the monetary stance. In January 2001, the central bank rates were discontinued. See Eurosystem policy rate on the euro area page.

Treasury Bill Rate:
Beginning in January 2000, data refer to the monthly average yield on 12-month treasury bills. Prior to that date, data refer to the end-month rate on new issues of 12-month treasury bills.

Deposit Rate:
Before December 1987, refers to the maximum rate offered by commercial banks on three to six month drachma deposits by individuals and enterprises. Beginning in 1988, data refer to deposits with a maturity of 12 months.

Deposit Rate (lines 60lhs, 60lhn, 60lcs, 60lcn, and 60lcr):
See notes in the introduction to *IFS* and *Euro-area Interest Rates*.

Lending Rate:
Prior to January 1999, refers to short-term loans to enterprises and households and, thereafter, refers to short-term loans to enterprises only. Beginning in June 1987, this rate was liberalized and includes commissions. Before June 1987, maximum rate charged by commercial banks for short-term working capital loans to industry.

Lending Rate (lines 60phs, 60pns, 60phm, 60phn, 60pcs, and 60pcn):
See notes in the introduction to *IFS* and *Euro-area Interest Rates*.

Government Bond Yield (Line 61):
Refers to the average daily secondary market yield on 10-year fixed-rate government bonds. This rate is used to measure

long-term interest rates for assessing convergence among the European Union member states.

Prices, Production, Labor:

Share Prices (End of Month):
The Athens Stock Exchange General Index is a capitalization-weighted index, base December 31, 1980.

Producer Prices:
Source: National Statistical Service. Weights Reference Period: 2005; Sectoral coverage: mining and quarrying, manufacturing, electricity and water supply; Number of Items in Basket: 398 products for the domestic market and 172 products for the non-domestic market; Basis for Calculation: based on sales to the domestic and non-domestic market in the year 2000. The index is rebased and the weights are revised every five years (PPI replaced WPI that has been compiled from 1962–2004).

Consumer Prices:
Source: National Statistical Service. Weights Reference Period: 2008; Geographical Coverage: the entire country; Number of Items in Basket: 800; Basis for Calculation: the weights are calculated on the basis of the results of the 2008 Household Budget Survey.

Wages: Monthly Earnings:
Source: National Statistical Service. Base Year: 1999Q1=100; Basis for Calculation: gross average monthly earnings in Euros obtained from the quarterly Labor Force Survey of 30,000 households. The index is broken down by primary, secondary, and tertiary sector of economic activity.

Industrial Production:
Source: National Statistical Service. Weights Reference Period: 2005; Sectoral Coverage: mining, electricity, gas and manufacturing ; Basis for Calculation: weighting is done according to the value added at factor cost of the weights reference period. Data are sourced from the OECD database.

International Transactions:

Exports and Imports, c.i.f.:
Beginning in 2002, euro trade data are sourced from the National Statistical Service of Greece (NSSG).

Government Finance:

Quarterly data (1999 to present) on general government are derived from Eurostat. A "Report on Greek government deficit and debt statistics" is available on the Eurostat website at epp.eurostat.ec.europa.eu/portal/page/portal/product_details/publication?p_product_code=COM_2010_report_greek.
Monthly, quarterly and annual cash data reported through 1998 are derived from Bank of Greece and cover budgetary central government. Data in the budgetary central government series differ from the corresponding national presentation in that *Revenue* is adjusted to include foreign transfers. *Expenditure* in Bank of Greece is also adjusted to exclude amortization. However, expenditures include refunds of taxes and restitutions of revenue to third parties. The fiscal year ends December 31.

National Accounts:

Source: Bank of Greece. Beginning in 1988, a statistical discrepancy is included in *line 93i* but, prior to 1988, is in *lines 99a* and *99b*. As indicated by the country, beginning in 1995, concepts and definitions are in accordance with the *1995 ESA*. Beginning

in 2001, national accounts data are sourced from the Eurostat database. Eurostat introduced chain-linked GDP volume measures to both annual and quarterly data with the release of the third quarter 2005 on November 30, 2005. Chain linked GDP volume measures are expressed in the prices of the previous year and re-referenced to 2005.

Grenada   328

Date of Fund Membership:
August 27, 1975

Standard Sources:
Eastern Caribbean Central Bank

Exchange Rates:

Official Rate: (End of Period and Period Average):
Rates are based on a fixed relationship to the U.S. dollar.

Central Bank:

Data are based on a standardized report form (SRF) for central banks, which accords with the concepts and definitions of the IMF's *Monetary and Financial Statistics Manual (MFSM)*, 2000. Departures from the *MFSM* methodology are explained below. Data refer to accounts in the balance sheet of the East Caribbean Central Bank (ECCB) attributable to Grenada.
Financial derivatives are excluded from the data.
Claims on Nonresident comprises estimates of Grenada's notional share of the ECCB's foreign assets.
Claims on Other Depository Corporations comprises the portion of the ECCB's claims on resident other depository corporations attributable to Grenada.
Claims on Central Government and *Liabilities to Central Government* comprise the portion of the ECCB's claims on and liabilities to the central government attributable to Grenada.
Financial assets with other financial corporations, state and local governments, public nonfinancial corporations, and private sector attributable to Grenada are not included in the data in the absence of a country of these accounts in the balance sheet of the ECCB.
Currency in circulation comprises the portion of currency in circulation attributable to Grenada less vault cash held by other depository corporations.
Some portion of other deposits to other depository corporations and interest accrued from these deposits are included in *Other Items (Net)*.
Share and other equity is not applicable to the member countries of the ECCU because the shares and other equity in the balance sheet of the ECCB exclusively belong to the ECCB.

Other Depository Corporations:

Comprises commercial banks. Data exclude finance companies, building societies, and credit unions, which accept deposits.
Data are based on a standardized report form (SRF) for other depository corporations, which accords with the concepts and definitions of the *Monetary and Financial Statistics Manual (MFSM)*. For resident other depository corporations in the member countries of the ECCU, departures from the *MFSM* methodology are explained below.

Financial derivatives and insurance technical reserves are excluded from the data.

Financial assets and liabilities for which economic sectorization is unavailable are allocated to the economic sector having the largest volume of transactions in the category.

Transferable Deposits Included in Broad Money includes all deposits of the private sector denominated in foreign currency.

Accounts receivable and payable are included in *Other Items (Net)* rather than in other depository corporations' claims or liabilities to the corresponding economic sectors.

Accrued interest on transactions with nonresidents is included in *Other Items (Net)* rather than in the outstanding amount of foreign assets and liabilities.

Depository Corporations:

See notes on central bank and other depository corporations.

Monetary Aggregates:

Broad Money:

Broad Money is calculated from the liability data in the sections for the central bank and other depository corporations. Broad money differs from M2 described below as broad money includes the deposits of money holding sectors with the ECCB attributable to Grenada and deposits of other financial corporations, state and local government, and public nonfinancial corporations in national and foreign currencies with commercial banks.

Money (National Definitions):

M1 comprises notes and coins held by the public and demand deposits in national currency of the private sector with commercial banks.

M2 comprises M1 plus time, savings, and foreign currency deposits of the private sector with commercial banks.

Interest Rates:

Discount Rate (End of Period):

Rate charged by the ECCB on loans of last resort to commercial banks.

Money Market Rate:

Fixed rate on loans between commercial banks. The rate includes the commission charged by the ECCB as agent. † Beginning in October 2001, weighted average rate on loans between commercial banks. The rate is weighted by loans amounts.

Treasury Bill Rate:

Rate on three-month treasury bills.

Savings Rate:

Maximum rate offered by commercial banks on savings deposits in national currency. † Beginning in June 2003, weighted average rate offered by commercial banks on savings deposits in national currency. The rate is weighted by deposit amounts.

Savings Rate (Foreign Currency):

Weighted average rate offered by commercial banks on savings deposits in foreign currency. The rate is weighted by deposit amounts.

Deposit Rate:

Maximum rate offered by commercial banks on three-month time deposits. The rate is weighted by deposit amounts.

Deposit Rate (Foreign currency):

Weighted average rate offered by commercial banks on deposits in foreign currency. The rate is weighted by deposit amounts.

Lending Rate:

Maximum rate charged by commercial banks on prime loans. The rate is weighted by loan amounts.

Lending Rate (Foreign Currency):

Weighted average rate charged by commercial banks on loans in foreign currency. The rate is weighted by loan amounts.

Prices:

Consumer Prices:

Source: Eastern Caribbean Central Bank. Weights reference period: January 2010; Geographical Coverage: Total of 193 Outlet spread out over all six parishes including Carriacou; Number of Items in Basket: 197 products with approximately 1102 varieties; Basis for Calculation: The average price method used in the new CPI Computation is based on the Geometric average and not arithmetic average as applied in computing the average price in the old, since is less affected by extreme values (that is items with large price variance).

International Transactions:

All trade value data are reported directly to *IFS* by the Ministry of Trade, Trade and Industry. *Exports* include re-exports.

Government Finance:

Annual data are as reported for the *Government Finance Statistics Yearbook (GFSY)* and cover budgetary central government. The fiscal year ends December 31.

National Accounts:

Data are as reported by national authorities. As indicated by the country, the national accounts are compiled according to the recommendations of the *1993 SNA*.

Guatemala   258

Date of Fund Membership:

December 28, 1945

Standard Sources:

Bank of Guatemala

Exchange Rates:

Market Rate (End of Period and Period Average):

Central bank midpoint rate. Effective June 1, 1990, the principal rate refers to the average of the buying and selling rates, set on a weekly basis, for official receipts and payments, imports of petroleum, and coffee exports. In addition, there is a market exchange rate determined by commercial banks and exchange houses. Prior to that date, a system of independent floating was in effect. A multiple exchange rate system, introduced on November 16, 1984, was modified on June 4, 1986 and was abolished in 1991.

International Liquidity:

Line 1and is equal to *line 1ad,* converted into U.S. dollars at the U.S. official gold rate of US$ 42.222 per fine troy ounce. Beginning in August 2008, Line *1and* is valued, according to national practice, in U.S. dollars.

Central Bank:

Comprises the Bank of Guatemala (BoG) only.

Data are based on a standardized report form (SRF) for central banks, which accords with the concepts and definitions of the IMF's *Monetary and Financial Statistics Manual* (*MFSM*), 2000.

Other Depository Corporations:

Comprises private commercial banks, the government-owned Crédito Hipotecario Nacional, and finance companies. Beginning in December 2003, includes offshore banks that accept deposits from residents. Beginning in December 2005, includes savings and loans associations.

Data are based on a standardized report form (SRF) for other depository corporations, which accords with the concepts and definitions of the *Monetary and Financial Statistics Manual* (*MFSM*). Departures from the *MFSM* methodology are explained below.

The classification of financial instruments is hampered by a chart of accounts that does not allow a proper sectorization of financial assets and liabilities, nor a distinction between resident and nonresident units.

Claims on Private Sector includes loans to public nonfinancial corporations.

Holdings of domestic securities are valued at acquisition cost rather than at current market price or fair value.

Depository Corporations:

See notes on central bank and other depository corporations.

Other Financial Corporations:

Comprises insurance companies. Beginning in November 2006, includes warehouses and exchange houses. Data exclude credit card companies, securities dealers. other financial intermediaries, and other financial auxiliaries.

Data are based on a standardized report form (SRF) for other financial corporations, which accords with the concepts and definitions of the *Monetary and Financial Statistics Manual* (*MFSM*). For other financial corporations in Guatemala, departures from the *MFSM* methodology are explained below.

Financial assets and liabilities for which economic sectorization is unavailable are allocated to the economic sector having the largest volume of transactions in the category.

Claims on Private Sector includes settlement accounts with all resident sectors.

Accrued interest is included in *Other Items (Net)* rather than as claims on and liabilities to the corresponding economic sectors.

Held-to-maturity securities are valued at amortized cost rather than at current market price or fair value.

Financial Corporations:

See notes on central bank, other depository corporations, and other financial corporations.

Monetary Aggregates:

Broad Money:

Broad Money calculated from the liability data in the sections for the central bank and other depository corporations accords with the concepts and definitions of the *MFSM* and is consistent with M3 described below.

Money (National Definitions):

Base Money comprises notes and coins issued; legal reserve requirements, excess deposits, and obligatory investments of commercial banks; and deposits of finance companies, offshore banks, and savings and loans associations with the BoG.

M1 comprises currency in circulation outside depository corporations and transferable deposits of other financial corporations, state and local governments, public nonfinancial corporations, and private sector in national currency with other depository corporations.

M2 comprises M1 and time and savings deposits in national currency and deposits in foreign currency of other financial corporations, state and local governments, public nonfinancial corporations, and private sector with the BoG and other depository corporations.

M3 comprises M2 and securities other than shares issued by the BoG and other depository corporations in national and foreign currency held by other financial corporations, state and local governments, public nonfinancial corporations, and private sector.

Interest Rates:

Central Bank Policy Rate (End of Period):

Leading monetary policy rate determined by the Monetary Board of the BoG.

Discount Rate (End of Period):

Rate charged by the BoG on eligible paper presented by commercial banks.

Money Market Rate:

Weighted average rate on loans between commercial banks. The rate is weighted by loan amounts.

Savings Rate:

Weighted average rate offered by commercial banks on savings deposits. The rate is weighted by deposit amounts.

Deposit Rate:

Maximum rate offered by commercial banks on time and savings deposits. † Beginning in January 1997, weighted average rate offered by commercial banks on time and savings deposits. The rate is weighted by deposit amounts.

Lending Rate:

Maximum rate charged by commercial banks on loans. † Beginning in January 1997, weighted average rate charged by commercial banks on loans. The rate is weighted by loan amounts.

Prices:

Consumer Prices:

Source: Bank of Guatemala. Weights Reference Period: December 2010. Geographical Coverage: Urban area of 15 cities (most departmental) with the largest number of inhabitants of the country and have the highest economic dynamics; Number of Items in Basket: 279; Basis for Calculation: Weights are based on the household income and expenditure survey conducted by the National Survey of Family Income and Expenditure (ENIGFAM) between July 2009 to June 2010.

International Transactions:

All trade data are from Bank of Guatemala.

Government Finance:

Monthly, quarterly, and annual data are derived from Bank of Guatemala. Data cover the operations of the budgetary central government but exclude receipt and use of own resources by budgetary units. Data do not cover the operations of the Guatemalan Social Security Institute or of other decentralized agencies with individual budgets. Expenditure and lending minus repayments data are adjusted to a cash basis by including the changes in floating debt. Data on foreign financing differ from those published in Bank of Guatemala in that bonds held by nonresidents are included in foreign financing, while in Bank of Guatemala, they are included in domestic financing. † Prior to 1994, revenue data included grants, and expenditure data included lending minus repayments, without adjustment to a cash basis. The fiscal year ends December 31.

National Accounts:

Data are from Bank of Guatemala. As indicated by the country, data are compiled according to the recommendations of the *1953 SNA*.

Guinea 656

Date of Fund Membership:
September 28, 1963

Standard Source:
Central Bank of the Republic of Guinea

Exchange Rates:
The official exchange rate of the Guinean franc was set and quoted weekly against the U.S. dollar until end-October 1994; beginning November 1, 1994, the exchange rate of the Guinean franc is determined in the interbank market for foreign exchange.

International Liquidity:
Data expressed in U.S. dollars on *Foreign Exchange (line 1d.d)* and *Gold (line 1and)* are derived from data denominated in national currency from components of the monetary authorities' *Foreign Assets (line 11),* using the end-of-period market rate (*line* **ae**).

Monetary Authorities:
Comprises the Central Bank of the Republic of Guinea and the operations of the government with the Fund. Beginning in December 1996, *Claims on Other Banking Institutions (line 12f)* excludes the Caisse Nationale de Sécurité Sociale (CNSS), which is included under *Claims on Central Government (line 12a).*

Deposit Money Banks:
Comprises commercial banks.

Interest Rates:
Refinancing Rate (End of Period):
Central bank lending rate for preferential refinancing.

Savings Rate:
Minimum rate on passbook savings deposits.

Deposit Rate:
Minimum rate on term deposits of at least three months.

Lending Rate:
Ceiling rate on medium- and long-term bank loans.

Prices and Production:
Consumer Prices:
Source: National Statistics Office (DNS). The consumer price index refers to Conakry and the surrounding area only. The consumer price index is published as a whole in a breakdown

of seven consumption functions. It also contains 23 consumption groups. The food function is itself subdivided into 11 product groups.

Government Finance:
Data are as reported in the *Government Finance Statistics Yearbook* and cover budgetary central government The fiscal year ends December 31.

National Accounts:
Source: National Statistics Office (DNS). The methodology is *SNA68*, although a plan is in place to introduce the changes in accordance with the new system of national accounts (*SNA93*).

Guinea-Bissau 654

Date of Fund Membership:
March 24, 1977

Standard Source:
Banque Centrale des États de l'Afrique de l'Ouest
Instituto Nacional de Estatística

Exchange Rates:
Official Rate: (End of Period and Period Average):
Beginning in end-December 1993, the official exchange rate was adjusted daily to keep the spread between the buying rate in the official and free markets at 2 percent. The free market exchange rate is determined by supply and demand conditions. As of May 2, 1997, Guinea-Bissau adopted as the national currency the CFA franc following its membership in the West African Monetary Union and the BCEAO. The currency conversion between the Guinean peso and the CFA franc was set at the rate of PG 65 per CFA franc, on the basis of the December 31, 1996 market rates. Prior to January 1999, the official rate was pegged to the French franc at the rate of CFAF 100 per French franc. Beginning January 1, 1999, the CFAF is pegged to the euro at a rate of CFA franc 655.957 per euro.

International Liquidity:
Gold is revalued on a quarterly basis at the rate communicated by the BCEAO, which corresponds to the lowest average fixing in the London market.

Monetary Authorities:
Comprises the national branch of the BCEAO only. The amount of currency outside banks is estimated by subtracting, from the amount of CFA franc notes issued by Guinea-Bissau, the estimated amounts of Guinea-Bissau's currency in the cash held by the banks of all member countries of the Union. Beginning in 1997, data reflect Guinea-Bissau's entry into the West African Monetary Union and the compilation of the data on the Central Bank of West African States' (BCEAO's) basis.

Deposit Money Banks:
Comprises commercial banks and development banks and includes certain banking operations of the Treasury and the Post Office. The Treasury accepts customs duty bills (reported separately in *line 22d.i*). Through its many branches, the Postal Checking Sys-

tem acts as the main depository for the private sector in the interior of Guinea-Bissau. † See note on monetary authorities.

Monetary Survey:

The data reported agree with Banque Centrale des États de l'Afrique de l'Ouest aggregates, as given in the table on the position of the monetary institutions. Valuation differences exist as a result of the *IFS* calculations of reserve position in the Fund and the SDR holdings, both components of *line 11,* based on Fund record. † See note on monetary authorities.

Interest Rates:

Discount Rate (End of Period):
Basic discount rate offered by the BCEAO.

Repurchase Agreement Rate (End of Period):
Rate on repurchase agreements between the BCEAO and the banks.

Money Market Rate:
Rate paid on overnight interbank advances.

Deposit Rate:
Rate offered by banks on time deposits of CFAF 500,000–2,000,000 for under six months.

Lending Rate:
Average lending rate charged by banks.

Prices:

Consumer Prices:
Source: Instituto Nacional de Estatística. Weights Reference Period: 2008; Geographical Coverage: Bissau metropolitan area; Number of Items in Basket: 655; Basis for Calculation: The weights are derived from a survey of household expenditure conducted between March 2008–February 2009 on a sample of 1008 households.

International Transactions:

All trade data are from Banque Centrale des États de l'Afrique de l'Ouest.

Balance of Payments:
The figures shown are derived from reports, in terms of U.S. dollars, sent to the IMF by the Central Bank of Guinea-Bissau.

Government Finance:

† Prior to 1987, data are as reported in the *Government Finance Statistics Yearbook (GFSY)* and cover budgetary central government. Beginning in 1987, data are derived from Ministry of Finance sources and cover budgetary central government. The fiscal year ends December 31.

National Accounts:

Source: Instituto Nacional de Estatística. Data are prepared in accordance with the 1968 United Nations System of National Accounts.

Guyana   336

Date of Fund Membership:
September 26, 1966

Standard Sources:
Bank of Guyana
The Statistical Bureau, Ministry of Economic Development

Exchange Rates:

Market Rate (End of Period and Period Average):
Central bank midpoint rate. From 1984 through February 1991, the Guyana dollar was pegged to a basket of currencies.

Central Bank:

Consists of the Bank of Guyana (BOG) only.

Data are based on a standardized report form (SRF) for central banks, which accords with the concepts and definitions of the IMF's *Monetary and Financial Statistics Manual (MFSM),* 2000. Departures from the *MFSM* methodology are explained below.

Financial assets and liabilities for which economic sectorization is unavailable are allocated to the economic sector having the largest volume of transactions in the category.

Some securities other than shares are valued at acquisition cost rather than at current market price or fair value.

Accrued interest is included in *Other Items (Net)* rather than in the outstanding amounts of the financial assets and liabilities.

Loans are reported net of provisions.

Other Depository Corporations:

Comprises commercial banks, new building societies, and trust companies.

Data are based on a standardized report form (SRF) for other depository corporations, which accords with the concepts and definitions of the *Monetary and Financial Statistics Manual (MFSM).* For other depository corporations in Guyana, departures from the *MFSM* methodology are explained below.

Financial assets and liabilities for which economic sectorization is unavailable are allocated to the economic sector having the largest volume of transactions in the category.

Claims on Nonresidents and *Liabilities to Nonresidents* include some accounts in foreign currency with resident economic sectors.

Claims on Other Financial Corporations and *Claims on Private Sector* include some portion of financial assets with nonresidents.

For December 2001 through November 2002, accrued interest is included in *Other items (Net)* rather than in the outstanding amounts of the financial assets and liabilities.

Account receivables and payables are included in *Other Items (Net)* rather than in claims on and liabilities to the corresponding economic sectors.

Securities other than shares are valued at acquisition cost rather than at current market price or fair value.

Valuation adjustments are included in *Other Items (Net)* rather than in *Shares and Other Equity* for of the new building societies and trust companies.

Depository Corporations:

See notes on central bank and other depository corporations.

Other Financial Corporations:

Comprises finance companies, life insurance companies, nonlife insurance companies, and pension funds. Beginning in September 2005, the data include asset management companies.

Data are based on a standardized report form (SRF) for other financial corporations, which accords with the concepts and definitions of the *Monetary and Financial Statistics Manual* (*MFSM*). For other financial corporations in Guyana, departures from the *MFSM* methodology are explained below.

Data for life insurance companies, nonlife insurance companies, and pension funds are available only on a quarterly basis. Even though monthly data are available for the finance companies, data for other financial corporations are shown only on a quarterly basis to maintain consistency in the institutional coverage.

Financial assets and liabilities for which economic sectorization is unavailable are allocated to the economic sector having the largest volume of transactions in the category.

Claims on Nonresidents and *Liabilities to Nonresidents* include some accounts in foreign currency with resident economic sectors.

Claims on Other Financial Corporations and *Claims on Private Sector* include some portion of financial assets with nonresidents.

Accrued interest is included in *Other items (Net)* rather than in the outstanding amounts of the financial assets and liabilities.

Account receivables and payables are included in *Other Items (Net)* rather than in claims on and liabilities to the corresponding economic sectors.

Securities other than shares are valued at acquisition cost rather than at current market price or fair value.

Valuation adjustments are included in *Other Items (Net)* rather than in *Shares and Other Equity*.

Financial Corporations:

See notes on central bank, other depository corporations, and other financial corporations.

Monetary Aggregates:

Broad Money:

Broad Money calculated from the liability data in the sections for the central bank and other depository corporations differs from *M2* described below as broad money includes the deposits of other financial corporations, state and local governments, public nonfinancial corporations, and private sector with commercial banks, new building societies and trust companies.

Money (National Definitions):

Base Money comprises currency issued by the BOG.

Reserve Money comprises currency issued and deposits of the commercial banks with the BOG including the External Payment Deposit Scheme. The external payment deposits were local currency deposits made by commercial banks on behalf of importers when restrictions were imposed on foreign exchange transactions. By depositing money in external payment deposits with commercial banks, resident importers could expect to receive foreign currency with which to make their payments. Although this scheme was discontinued after 1990, those depositors that disagreed to take losses arising from the discontinuation still keep the questioned amount in the account pending final settlement.

M1 comprises currency in circulation, demand deposits in national currency of the private sector with commercial banks, and checks outstanding.

M2 comprises M1 and time and savings deposits in national currency of the private sector with commercial banks.

Interest Rates:

Central Bank Policy Rate (End of Period):

Rate charged by the Bank of Guyana on short-term loans to commercial banks.

Treasury Bill Rate:

Average tender rate for three-month treasury bills.

Savings Rate:

Rate offered by commercial banks on small savings deposits in national currency.

Deposit Rate:

Rate offered by commercial banks on three-month time deposits.

Lending Rate:

Prime rate charged by commercial banks on loans to preferred customers.

Prices:

Consumer Prices:

Source: The Statistical Bureau, Ministry of Economic Development. Weights Reference Period: 2005/2006; Geographical Coverage: Georgetown only; Number of Items in Basket: 217; Basis for Calculation: weights were derived from the Household Budget Survey (HBS) conducted in 2005/2006.

International Transactions:

Exports and Imports:

All trade value data are from Bank of Guyana as compiled by the Statistical Bureau. *Exports* include re-exports.

Volume of Exports:

IFS average of sugar, bauxite, and rice with a 1995 value of exports as weights.

Government Finance:

† Beginning in 1970, data are as reported by the Central Bank of Guyana and cover budgetary central government. † Beginning in 1986, foreign debt includes central government, public guaranteed debt, and Bank of Guyana debt. The fiscal year ends December 31.

National Accounts:

Source: The Statistical Bureau, Ministry of Economic Development.

Haiti 263

Date of Fund Membership:

September 8, 1953

Standard Source:

Bank of the Republic of Haiti

Exchange Rates:

Market Rate (End of Period):

Central bank average rate weighted by the volume of transactions in the banking and informal markets. Since April 1995, the Bank of the Republic of Haiti (BRH) has operated a dollar clearinghouse. Commercial banks quote buying and selling rates for certain other currencies based on the buying and selling rates of the dollar in exchange markets abroad. The market is dominated by commercial banks, with the money changers and other informal market agents following this market.

Central Bank:

Consists of the Bank of the Republic of Haiti (BRH) only.

† Beginning in October 2006, data are based on a standardized report form (SRF) for central banks, which accords with the concepts and definitions of the IMF's *Monetary and Financial Statistics Manual (MFSM), 2000*. Departures from the *MFSM* methodology are explained below.

Accrued interest on a small portion of financial instruments is included in Other Items (Net) rather than in the outstanding amounts of the financial assets and liabilities.

Insurance technical reserves are included in *Other Items (Net)*.

For December 2001 through September 2006, data in the SRF format are compiled from pre-SRF data not fully based on the *MFSM* methodology.

Other Depository Corporations:

Comprises commercial banks. Data exclude cooperatives for savings and credit, which accept deposits.

† Beginning in October 2006, data are based on a standardized report form (SRF) for other depository corporations, which accords with the concepts and definitions of the *Monetary and Financial Statistics Manual (MFSM)*. For other depository corporations in Haiti, departures from the *MFSM* methodology are explained below. Accrued interest on a small portion of financial instruments is included in *Other Items (Net)* rather than in the outstanding amounts of the financial assets and liabilities.

Insurance technical reserves are included in *Other Items (Net)*.

The residency criterion is not applied uniformly by all other depository corporations. Consequently certain financial instruments are included in *Foreign Assets* or *Foreign Liabilities* rather than as claims on/liabilities to the corresponding domestic sector.

For December 2001 through September 2006, data in the SRF format are compiled from pre-SRF data not fully based on the *MFSM* methodology.

Depository Corporations:

† See notes on central bank and other depository corporations.

Monetary Aggregates:

Broad Money:

Broad Money calculated from the liability data in the sections for the central bank and other depository corporations accords with the concepts and definitions of the MFSM and is consistent with M3 described below.

Money (National Definitions):

Monetary Base comprises currency in circulation; banker's correspondent and other accounts at the BRH; commercial banks' investment in BRH securities; and transferable and time deposits in national and foreign currency of state and local governments, public nonfinancial corporations, private sector, and other financial corporations with the BRH. Currency in circulation refers to notes and coins issued by the BRH less

currency in the vaults of the BRH.

M1 comprises currency in circulation and transferable deposits. Currency in circulation refers to notes and coins issued by the BRH less the amount held by commercial banks. Transferable deposits refer to the current account deposits in national currency of the private sector with commercial banks.

M2 comprises M1, savings and time deposits, and securities other than shares issued by commercial banks in national currency held by the private sector. Time deposits refer to both conventional time deposits and bonds and debentures in national currency of the private sector with commercial banks.

M3 comprises M2, and transferable, savings, and time deposits in foreign currency of the private sector with commercial banks.

Interest Rates:

Central Bank Bill Rate:

Rate on the last monthly issue of 91-day central bank bonds auctioned by the BRH.

Savings Rate:

Minimum rate offered by commercial banks on savings deposits in national currency.

Savings Rate (Foreign Currency):

Minimum rate offered by commercial banks on savings deposits in foreign currency.

Deposit Rate:

Minimum rate offered by commercial banks on time deposits in national currency.

Deposit Rate (Foreign Currency):

Minimum rate offered by commercial banks on time deposits in foreign currency.

Lending Rate:

Maximum rate charged by commercial banks on loans in national currency.

Lending Rate (Foreign Currency):

Maximum rate charged by commercial banks on loans in foreign currency.

Prices:

Consumer Prices:

Bank of the Republic of Haiti. Weights Reference Period August 2004. Geographical Coverage: 36 towns and rural communities and 9 sectors of the metropolitan region of Port-au-Prince; Number of Items in the Basket: 140 items commonly used by the population, and broken into 278 varities; Basis for Calculation: Weights are based on the results of the 2000 household consumption budget survey and updated in the light of price trends between 2000 and August 2004; in particular, it takes into account the elimination of the subsidy for prices of petroleum products.

International Transactions:

All trade data are supplied directly by the national authorities; they are compiled by the General Customs Office.

Government Finance:

Monthly and annual data are as reported by the Bank of the Republic of Haiti and cover consolidated central government.

Annual data refer to a fiscal year different from calendar year. The fiscal year ends September 30.

National Accounts:

Line 99b includes a statistical discrepancy. *Line 96f* includes government consumption expenditures.

Honduras 268

Date of Fund Membership:
December 27, 1945

Standard Source:
Central Bank of Honduras

Exchange Rates:

Market Rate (End of Period and Period Average):
Since July 1994, the exchange rate has been determined through daily auctions by the Central Bank. From February 13, 1992 through June 30, 1992, the principal rate referred to the interbank rate which was the average exchange rate in the exchange house market in the preceding week. In addition, there was a market exchange rate determined by the foreign exchange houses. Prior to that period, the exchange rates had been unified. Effective July 1, 1992, the interbank exchange rate was eliminated, and all foreign exchange transactions are effected through the free market.

International Liquidity:

Gold (National Valuation) (line 1and) is obtained by converting the value in national currency terms, as reported in the country's standard sources, using the prevailing exchange rate, as given in *line* **ae** or **we**.

Central Bank:

Consists of the Central Bank of Honduras (CBH) only.
Data are based on a standardized report form (SRF) for central banks, which accords with the concepts and definitions of the IMF's *Monetary and Financial Statistics Manual (MFSM)*, 2000. Departures from the *MFSM* methodology are explained below.
Financial assets that cannot be valued at market prices are valued at acquisition cost.

Other Depository Corporations:

Comprises commercial banks, development banks, savings and loan associations, credit and saving cooperatives, and finance companies.
Data are based on a standardized report form (SRF) for other depository corporations, which accords with the concepts and definitions of the *Monetary and Financial Statistics Manual (MFSM)*. For other depository corporations in Honduras, departures from the *MFSM* methodology are explained below.
For December 2001 through December 2004, *Other Items (Net)* includes holdings of securities issued by nonresidents; *Claims on Central Government* and *Claims on Other Financial Corporations* include holdings of securities issued by other nonfinancial corporations; *Claims on Private Sector* includes loans to other financial

corporations and nonresidents; and financial assets and liabilities for which economic sectorization is unavailable are allocated to the economic sector having the largest volume of transactions in the category.
Financial assets and liabilities that cannot be valued at market prices are valued at acquisition cost.

Depository Corporations:
See notes on central bank and other depository corporations.

Other Financial Corporations:
Comprises Banhprovi, formerly Fondo Nacional de la Producción y Vivienda. Beginning in January 2003, includes insurance companies. Beginning in July 2012, includes private financial development organizations. Data exclude pension funds and financial auxiliaries.
Data are based on a standardized report form (SRF) for other financial corporations, which accords with the concepts and definitions of the *Monetary and Financial Statistics Manual (MFSM)*. For other financial corporations in Honduras, departures from the *MFSM* methodology are explained below.
Financial assets and liabilities that cannot be valued at market prices are valued at acquisition cost.
Financial assets and liabilities for which economic sectorization is unavailable are allocated to the economic sector having the largest volume of transactions in the category.

Monetary Aggregates:

Broad Money:
Broad Money calculated from the liability data in the sections for the central bank and other depository corporations accords with the concepts and definitions of the *MFSM* and is consistent with M3 described below.

Money (National Definitions):
Base Money comprises notes and coins issued, deposits of other depository corporations with the CBH in national currency, and securities issued by the CBH used to constitute compulsory investments in addition to the required reserves.
M1 comprises currency outside the depository corporations and demand deposits in national currency of the private sector with the CBH, commercial banks, and development banks. Beginning in December 2001, M1 includes demand deposits of the private sector in national currency with credit and saving cooperatives. Beginning in January 2005, M1 reflects a more accurate sectorization of money holding sectors.
M2 comprises *M1*; time, savings, and other deposits in national currency of the private sector with commercial banks, development banks, savings and loans associations, and finance companies; other deposits, including deposits for foreign currency purchase in auctions, in national currency of the private sector with the CBH; and securities issued by the CBH held by the private sector. Beginning in December 2001, M2 includes time, savings, and other deposits in national currency of the private sector with credit and saving cooperatives. Beginning in January 2005, M2 reflects a more accurate sectorization of money holding sectors.
M3 comprises *M2* and time, savings, and other deposits in foreign currency of the private sector with commercial banks, development banks, savings and loans associations, and finance compa-

nies. Beginning in December 2001, M3 includes time, savings, and other deposits in foreign currency of the private sector with credit and saving cooperatives. Beginning in January 2005, M3 reflects a more accurate sectorization of money holding sectors.

Interest Rates:

Central Bank Policy Rate (End of Period):
The maximum rate to purchase government securities in weekly auctions exclusively for the institutions of the financial system and in accordance with the guidelines of the Board of Directors of the CBH. The auctions last seven or fourteen days.

Discount Rate (End of Period):
Rate charged by the CBH on loans to commercial banks.

Savings Rate:
Average rate offered by commercial banks on savings deposits in national currency.

Savings Rate (Foreign Currency):
Average rate offered by commercial banks on savings deposits in foreign currency.

Deposit Rate:
Weighted average rate offered by commercial banks on time deposits in national currency. The rate is weighted by deposit amounts for all maturities.

Deposit Rate (Foreign Currency):
Weighted average rate offered by commercial banks on time deposits in foreign currency. The rate is weighted by deposit amounts for all maturities.

Lending Rate:
Weighted average rate charged by commercial banks on loans in national currency. The rate is weighted by loan amounts for all maturities.

Lending Rate (Foreign Currency):
Weighted average rate charged by commercial banks on loans in foreign currency. The rate is weighted by loan amounts for all maturities.

Government Bond Yield:
Weighted average yield on government bonds. Yields are calculated as volume-weighted yields on government bonds of different maturities traded through weekly public auctions.

Prices:

Consumer Prices:
Source: Central Bank Laspeyres index. Weights Reference Period; 1998–1999. Geographical Coverage: Whole national territory; Number of Items in Basket: 282; Basis for Calculation: Weights are derived from a Household Expenditure Survey conducted in 1998–1999 on 3746 urban and rural households.

International Transactions:

All trade data are from the Central Bank.

Volume of Exports:
IFS average of bananas, coffee, frozen beef, sugar, and wood with a 1995 value of exports as weights.

Export Prices:
IFS average of bananas, coffee, frozen beef, sugar, and wood with a 1995 value of exports as weights.

Government Finance:

Data are derived from the Central Bank and cover budgetary central government. The fiscal year ends December 31.

National Accounts:

Source: Central Bank. As indicated by the country, the national accounts are compiled according to the recommendation of the *1953 SNA*.

Hungary   944

Date of Fund Membership:

May 6, 1982

Standard Sources:

National Bank of Hungary
Central Statistical Office
Eurostat

Exchange Rates:

Official Rate: (End of Period and Period Average):
National Bank of Hungary midpoint rate. Beginning October 1991, data refer to a unified exchange rate.

International Liquidity:

Foreign Exchange (line 1d.d) comprises holdings of convertible currencies plus swapped gold.

Central Bank:

Consists of the National Bank of Hungary (NBH) only.
† Beginning in January 2003, data are compiled in accordance with the European Central Bank's framework for monetary statistics using the national residency approach.
For December 2001 to December 2002, data do not fully conform with the European Central Bank's framework for monetary statistics and are not strictly comparable to data for later periods.
Claims on General Government includes debt of the central budget, owing to valuation differences previously included in *Other Items (Net)*.
Other Liabilities to Other Depository Corporations includes foreign currency deposits, repurchase agreement deposits, syndicated loans, and noncallable deposits in national currency of other monetary financial institutions (other MFIs) with the NBH.

Other Depository Corporations:

Comprises all resident units classified as other MFIs in accordance with the *1995 ESA* standards, including money market funds.
† Beginning in January 2003, data are compiled in accordance with the European Central Bank's framework for monetary statistics using the national residency approach.
For December 2001 to December 2002, data do not fully conform with the European Central Bank's framework for monetary statistics and are not strictly comparable to data for later periods.
Other Claims on Central Bank includes foreign currency deposits, repurchase agreement deposits, syndicated loans, and noncallable national currency deposits of other MFIs with the NBH.

Transferable Deposits Included in Broad Money includes sight deposits in national currency of households, previously included in *Other Deposits included in Broad Money*.

Depository Corporations:

† See notes on central bank and other depository corporations.

Monetary Aggregates:

Broad Money:

Broad Money is calculated from the liability data in the sections for the central bank and other depository corporations. Broad money differs from M3 described below because separate data on the issuance by MFIs of *money market funds/shares* and *debt securities with maturity up to two years* to the money holding sectors are not currently available under the ECB reporting framework.

Money (National Definitions):

Monetary Base comprises currency in circulation and current account balances and overnight deposits of other MFIs with the NBH.

M1 comprises currency outside MFIs and sight deposits in national currency of resident non-MFIs other than central government with MFIs. Beginning in January 1993, M1 comprises currency outside MFIs and overnight deposits of resident non-MFIs other than central government with MFIs.

M2 comprises M1, time and savings deposits in national currency, and all foreign currency deposits of resident non-MFIs other than central government with MFIs. Beginning in January 1993, M2 comprises M1 and deposits with agreed maturity up to two years of resident non-MFIs other than central government with MFIs.

M3 comprises M2 and securities issued by other MFIs (e.g., bonds, CDs, and other debt securities, as defined by the Securities Act). Beginning in January 1993, M3 comprises M2, money market fund shares/units, repurchase agreements, and debt securities with original maturity of up to two years issued by MFIs to residents other than MFIs and central government.

M4 comprises M3, government securities (bonds and treasury bills), and domestic NBH bills held by resident non-MFIs.

Interest Rates:

Discount Rate (End of Period):

Basic rate at which NBH offers loans with maturity of more than one year to other MFIs. As of July 13, 2001, the base rate and rate on two-week deposit facilities at the NBH are identical.

Treasury Bill Rate:

Weighted average yield on 90-day Treasury bills sold at auctions.

Deposit Rate:

Simple arithmetic rate offered by banks on deposits with maturity of over one month and up to one year. † Beginning in January 1990, weighted average rate offered by banks on deposits with maturity of over one month and up to one year. † Beginning in January 1995, average rate offered by other MFIs on deposits with maturity of up to one year to nonfinancial corporations, weighted by volume of new deposits received during the last reporting month.

Lending Rate:

Average rate charged by other MFIs on loans with maturity of less than one year to nonfinancial corporations, weighted by volume of new credit extended during the last reporting month.

Government Bond Yield:

Average daily secondary market yield on ten-year fixed-rate government bonds. This rate is used to measure long-term interest rates for assessing convergence among the European Union member states.

Prices, Production, Labor:

Share Prices:

Refers to the Budapest Stock Exchange Index (BUX), base January 2, 1991. The BUX is a capitalization-weighted index adjusted for free float that tracks the daily price performance of large, actively traded shares accounting for the majority of domestic market capitalization on the BUX.

Producer Prices:

Source: Central Statistical Office. Weights reference period: 2 years prior to current year; Sectoral Coverage: mining and quarrying, manufacturing, electricity, gas, steam, air conditioning, and water supply, sewerage, waste management, and remediation activities; Number of Items in Basket: about 1200 enterprises; Basis for Calculation: weights are based on annual industry survey on production of industrial products and services.

Consumer Prices:

Source: Central Statistical Office. Weights reference period: 2 years prior to the current year; Geographical Coverage: entire country; Number of Items in Basket: approximately 1000 items; Basis for Calculation: weights are based on the data of the National Accounts completed with the data of Household Budget Survey (HBS) and other additional sources. The weights refer to the household expenditure sructure of the t–2 year.

Industrial Production:

Source: Central Statistical Office. Weights Reference Period: weights are updated every year; Sectoral Coverage: mining and quarrying, manufacturing, electricity, gas, steam, and water supply sectors; Basis for Calculation: weights are derived from Industry surveys and are updated every year.

Wages:

Source: Central Statistical Office. Base Year: 1995; Net monthly earning: based on persons employed full-time and include the basic wages and salaries, supplements, wages in kind, bonuses, premiums, 13th month salary, and payments for time not worked; Basis for Calculation: data are derived from surveys based on a full enumeration for economic units employing more than 50 persons and all public organizations, and a sample drawn from economic units with 5–50 employees.

International Transactions:

Exports and Imports:

Source: Central Statistical Office. Prior to January 1996, exports and imports data exclude customs free zones. Prior to January 1997, volume of exports and imports exclude customs free zones. *Exports* and *Imports* c.i.f. exclude repairs on goods and operating leasing. Imports f.o.b. only exclude repairs on goods and operating leasing from 1997 onwards. Data on exports and imports include re-exports until June 1989; from July 1989 onward the data exclude re-exports.

Unit values:

Source: Central Statistical Office, weights reference period: 1995. The series comprise chainlinked versions of indices compiled on a cumulative basis with the corresponding periods of the preceding year as the base.

Government Finance:
Cash data are as reported by the Ministry of Finance and cover the budgetary central government. Data on general government are derived from source V. The fiscal year ends December 31.

National Accounts:
Source: Central Statistical Office. As indicated by the country, data are compiled in accordance with the methodology of the *1995 ESA* and the *1993 SNA*. Chain linked GDP volume is expressed according to 2005 prices.

Iceland 176

Date of Fund Membership:
December 27, 1945

Standard Sources:
Central Bank of Iceland
Statistics Iceland

Exchange Rates:
Official Rate: (End of Period and Period Average):
Central bank midpoint rate. The official rate is determined on the basis of a trade-weighted basket of currencies. Effective March 28, 2001, rates are market determined.

International Liquidity:
Gold (National Valuation) (line 1and) is obtained by converting the value in national currency, as reported in the country's standard sources, using the national currency/dollar conversion rates utilized for balance sheet purposes. These conversion rates differ from the prevailing exchange rates reported in *IFS*. † Beginning in December 1999, gold valuation is based on market prices.

Central Bank:
Consists of the Central Bank of Iceland (CBI) only.
Data are based on a standardized report form (SRF) for central banks, which accords with the concepts and definitions of the IMF's *Monetary and Financial Statistics Manual (MFSM)*, 2000. For the period October 2008-November 2009, *Claims on Other Depository Corporations* include claims on former commercial and savings banks that were subject to liquidation; in December 2009, these claims were transferred to a special financial holding company established by the CBI. Beginning in December 2009, *Claims on Other Financial Corporations* include claims on a special financial holding company established by the CBI to which it transferred its claims on former commercial and savings banks that were subject to liquidation. Departures from the *MFSM* methodology are explained below.
Securities issued by the CBI are recorded at the sale price rather than at current market price or fair value.
In the data for December 2010, the notional amounts of financial derivative contracts are included in *Claims on Other Depository Corporations* and Other *Liabilities to Other Depository Corporations* rather than the fair value of the financial derivative.

Other Depository Corporations:
Comprises commercial and savings banks and branches of Icelandic banks abroad. Beginning in October 2008, comprise commercial and savings banks resident in Iceland.
† Beginning in July 2007, data are based on a standardized report form (SRF) for other depository corporations, which accords with the concepts and definitions of the IMF's *Monetary and Financial Statistics Manual (MFSM)*. Data on public sector securities are reported net of short positions, which may result in negative values of *Claims on Central Government*. For other depository corporations in Iceland, departures from the *MFSM* methodology are explained below.
For July 2007 through September 2008, data cover commercial and savings banks and branches of Icelandic banks abroad. For July 2007 through September 2008, *Claims on Nonresidents* includes claims of branches of Icelandic banks abroad on nonresidents and *Liabilities to Nonresidents* includes liabilities of branches of Icelandic banks abroad to nonresidents.
Financial assets and liabilities for which economic sectorization is unavailable are allocated to the economic sector having the largest volume of transactions in the category. *Claims on Public Nonfinancial Corporations* includes some claims on private nonfinancial corporations and *Claims on Other Nonfinancial Corporations* may include some claims on public nonfinancial corporations.
For July through December 2007, claims on the holding companies engaged in financial intermediation are included in *Claims on Private Sector* rather than in *Claims on Other Financial Corporations*. Beginning in January 2008, claims on holding companies which do not engage in financial intermediation are included in *Claims on Other Financial Corporations* rather than in *Claims on Private Sector*.
For December 2001 through June 2007, data have less conformity with the *MFSM* methodology and therefore are not strictly comparable to data for later periods. Data cover commercial and savings banks and branches of Icelandic banks abroad. † Beginning in January 2002, data reflect changes in the coverage of other depository corporations and in the classification and sectorization of financial instruments. Departures from the *MFSM* methodology are explained below.
Claims on Nonresidents includes claims of branches of Icelandic banks abroad on nonresidents and *Liabilities to Nonresidents* includes liabilities of branches of Icelandic banks abroad to nonresidents.
Some claims on and liabilities to nonresidents are not separately identified in reported data and are consequently included in claims on and liabilities to the resident sectors.
Claims on the holding companies engaged in financial intermediation are included in *Claims on Private Sector* rather than in *Claims on Other Financial Corporations*.

Depository Corporations:
† See notes to central bank and other depository corporations.

Monetary Aggregates:
Broad Money:
Broad Money calculated from the liability data in the sections for the central bank and other depository corporations accords with the concepts and definitions of the *MFSM* and differs from M3 described below as M3 includes small amounts of central government deposits with commercial and savings banks.

Money (National Definitions):
Base Money comprises currency in circulation and deposits, certificates of deposit, and other claims of other depository corporations on the CBI. Currency in circulation refers to notes and coins issued by the CBI.

M1 comprises notes and coins in circulation, including those held by other depository corporations, and current account deposits in national and foreign currency of resident non-bank non-central government sectors with other depository corporations.

M2 comprises M1 and sight deposits in national and foreign currency of resident non-bank non-central government sectors with other depository corporations.

M3 comprises M2, central government deposits with commercial and savings banks; indexed, supplementary pension, holiday pay, money market rate, and other time deposits in national and foreign currency of resident non-bank non-central government sectors with other depository corporations and savings departments of cooperatives.

M4 comprises M3 and domestic bond issues of other depository corporations held by resident non-bank non-central government sectors.

Interest Rates:

Discount Rate (End of Period):
Rate on overdrafts of other depository corporations. † Beginning in June 1994, central bank rate on loans against the 15-day notes issued by the borrowing institutions. † Beginning in March 1998, central bank's discount rate on overnight loans.

Money Market Rate:
End-of-month yield on the interbank overnight market.

Treasury Bill Rate:
Yield set by the government in the primary market. † Beginning in November 1992, annualized secondary market yield on 90-day treasury bills.

Deposit Rate:
Rate offered by other depository corporations on three-month deposits. † Beginning in January 2003 onward, rate offered by other depository corporations on money market accounts.

Housing Bond Rate:
Annualized secondary market real yield on indexed housing bonds of 25-year maturity.

Lending Rate:
Weighted average interest rate on general purpose loans.

Government Bond Yield:
Annualized secondary market real yield on indexed 10-year government bonds.

Prices, Production, Labor:

Share Prices:
Free float adjusted market capitalization weighted index of the 15 largest and most traded Icelandic companies of the OMX Stock Exchange, base December 31, 1997. † Beginning in January 2009, the index covers the six most traded Icelandic companies of the OMX Stock Exchange, base December 31, 2008. The index is rebalanced twice a year, on December 10 and June 10.

Consumer Prices:
Source: Statistics Iceland. Weights Reference Period: 12 months, March-March; Geographical Coverage: entire country; Number of Items in Basket: approximately 3,500 items; Basis for Calculation: the weights are based on the Household Expenditure Surveys (HES), continuous since year 2000.

Wages:
Source: Statistics Iceland. Weights reference period: December 1988. Wage index is calculated and published according to law no. 89/1989. The wage index is based on average for fixed hour earnings each month, calculated and published in the month following calculation. Basis for Calculation: The overall weighting for the three main groups are fixed as follows: General labor market (private market) 60 percent; public sector 34 percent and the banking sector 6 percent.

Total Fish Catch:
Source: Statistics Iceland.

International Transactions:

Exports and Imports, c.i.f.:
Source: Statistics Iceland. No estimates are made for under reported or missing trade such as smuggling activity or shuttle trade.

Volume of Exports and Imports:
Source: Statistics Iceland indices of volume of exports and imports, weights reference period 2000. The indices are chain indices computed with preceding year weights.

Unit Value of Exports:
Source: Statistics Iceland chain index with current year weights of unit values of all merchandise exports, weights reference period 2000.

Unit Value of Imports:
Source: Statistics Iceland chain unit value index with current year weights of general merchandise imports, base 2000. The volume indices and both unit value indices are interdependent and have been discontinued in 2007.

Government Finance:

From 1998 onward, monthly cash flow data are derived from Financial Management Authority and cover the operations of the budgetary central government. The quarterly accrual data are compiled and reported by Statistics Iceland and cover the general government. Beginning in January 2004, monthly and quarterly data are reported in the GFSM 2001 analytic framework. The central government's debt assumption of 192.2 billion Kronur in 2008q4 is excluded from the quarterly accrual data. The fiscal year ends December 31.

National Accounts:

Source: Statistics Iceland. As indicated by the country, the Icelandic National Accounts follow the structure, concepts, definitions and classifications of the System of National Accounts *1993 SNA* and *ESA 95*, implemented in 2000. Historical series have been revised back to 1990 according to the new system. Chain linked GDP volume measures are expressed in the prices of the previous year and re-referenced to 2005.

India   534

Date of Fund Membership:

December 27, 1945

Standard Sources:

Reserve Bank of India
Ministry of Statistics and Programme Implementation

Exchange Rates:

Market Rate (End of Period and Period Average):
Effective March 1, 1993, the exchange rate of the rupee is market-determined.

International Liquidity:

Gold (National Valuation) (line 1and) is obtained by converting the value in national currency terms, as reported in the country's standard sources, using the prevailing exchange rate, as given in *line* **ae**. Beginning September 2010, Gold is valued according to national practice, in U.S. dollars.

Monetary Authorities:

Consolidates the Reserve Bank of India (RBI) and monetary authority functions undertaken by the central government. The contra-entry to Treasury IMF accounts, SDR holdings, and currency issues is included in *line 12a. Foreign Liabilities* are mainly *Use of Fund Credit: Gen. Dept.* (see *line 2e.s*).

Deposit Money Banks:

Comprises commercial and cooperative banks. † Since 1978, a new classification of *Demand and Time Deposits* has reduced *lines 24* and *34* and increased *lines 25* and *35*. Latest monthly data are preliminary.

Money (National Definitions):

M0 or reserve money comprises currency in circulation, bankers' deposits with the RBI, and other deposits with the RBI. Currency in circulation includes the notes and coins in circulation. Notes of denomination two rupee notes and above are a monetary liability of the RBI; one rupee notes and all coins are a monetary liability of the central government. Bankers' deposits with the RBI comprise required reserves as well as excess reserves maintained by banks with the RBI. Other deposits with the RBI comprise deposits of quasi government, select domestic financial institutions, primary dealers, foreign central banks and governments, and international agencies. Reserve money is compiled with a weekly frequency each Friday, based on the weekly statement on assets and liabilities of the RBI.

M1 or narrow money comprises currency outside the banking system, demand deposits of other financial corporations, state and local government, public nonfinancial corporations and the private sector with the banking system, and other deposits of quasi government, select domestic financial institutions, primary dealers, foreign central banks and governments, and international agencies with the RBI. Currency outside the banking system comprises currency notes and coins in circulation less currency notes and coins held by deposit money banks. Demand deposits comprises all liabilities which are payable on demand and primarily include current deposits and the transferable liabilities portion of savings deposits.

M3 or broad money comprises M1 and time deposits of other financial corporations, state and local government, public nonfinancial corporations and the private sector with the banking system. Time deposits comprise deposit liabilities, which are payable otherwise than on demand, including fixed deposits and the time liabilities' portion of savings deposits.

Interest Rates:

Discount Rate (End of Period):
Standard rate at which the Reserve Bank makes advances to scheduled banks against commercial paper and government securities.

Money Market Rate:
Rate offered in Bombay interbank market. Quarterly and annual data are weighted averages of weekly series.

Lending Rate:
Rate charged on advances from the Reserve Bank of India to the commercial banks. This benchmark prime lending rate (BPLR) regulates all interest rates charged by the commercial banks on various categories of loans. † Beginning in July 2010, refers to the base lending rate charged by India's five largest commercial banks.

Government Bond Yield:
† Beginning in 1971, this rate is the average yield on government 5½ percent bonds maturing in the years 1999 and 2000.

Prices, Production, Labor:

Share Prices:
Share price index, base 1938, † Beginning in 1952, share price index, base 1949–50. † Beginning in July 1957, share price index, base 1952–53. † Beginning in April 1964, share price index, base 1961–62. † Beginning in April 1973, index of security prices of ordinary shares in all industries, average of weeks ending Saturday, base 1970–71. † Beginning in April 1979, monthly average of daily closing figures for the Bombay Stock Exchange Sensitive Index (SENSEX), base 1978–79.

Wholesale Prices:
Data refer to Laspeyres index numbers of wholesale prices, base 2004–05 covering 98 primary articles, 318 manufactured products and 19 fuel and power items.

Consumer Prices:
Source: Reserve Bank of India. Weights Reference Period: 2001; Geographical Coverage: 78 industrial cities/towns; Number of Items in Basket: 260; Basis for Calculation: Weights are based on Household Expenditure Survey and are updated at approximately 10-yearly intervals.

Industrial Production:
Source: Reserve Bank of India. Weights Reference Period: 2004–05; Sectoral Coverage: mining, manufacturing, and electricity; Basis for Calculation: the weights for the three sectors (mining, manufacturing, and electricity) are based on gross value added in the base year.

Employment:
Data refer to public sector and establishments of non-agricultural private sector with 10 or more persons employed.

International Transactions:

Value of Exports and Imports:
Source: Reserve Bank of India. Data include indirect transit trade of Nepal, Tibet, Sikkim, and Bhutan and exclude military goods, fissionable materials, bunkers, ships, and aircraft. The general system of recording trade transactions is used.

Unit Value of Exports and Imports:
Data refer to Reserve Bank of India Paasche indices, base 1978–79.

Government Finance:

Annual data are as reported for the *Government Finance Statistics Yearbook (GFSY)* and cover budgetary central government. Annual data refer to a fiscal year different from calendar year. The fiscal year ends March 31.

National Accounts:

Lines 99a and *99b* include a statistical discrepancy. As indicated by the country, from 1987 onwards data have been revised following the implementation of the *1993 SNA*.

Indonesia   536

Date of Fund Membership:

April 15, 1954
Withdrew from membership: August 17, 1965
Readmitted to membership: February 21, 1967

Standard Sources:

Bank Indonesia
Ministry of Finance
Statistics Indonesia

Exchange Rates:

Market Rate (End of Period and Period Average):
Central bank midpoint rate.

International Liquidity:

IFS line land follows national valuation procedures, which revalue gold quarterly at 80 percent of the London market quotation on the fifteenth day of the last month of every quarter. *Line land* is equal to *line lad* converted into U.S. dollars at the dollar price of gold used by national sources as reported to *IFS*.

Central Bank:

Consists of the Bank Indonesia (BI) only.
† Beginning in June 2004, data are based on a standardized report form (SRF) for central banks, which accords with the concepts and definitions of the IMF's *Monetary and Financial Statistics Manual (MFSM)*, 2000.
For December 2001 through May 2004, data in the SRF format are compiled from pre-SRF data not based on the *MFSM* methodology. Departures from the *MFSM* methodology are explained below.
All deposits of other depository corporations are included in *Liabilities to Other Depository Corporations* in the absence of data separating the deposits included in and excluded from the monetary base.
All certificates issued by the BI are included in *Other Liabilities to Other Depository Corporations* in the absence of data on an individual economic sector's holdings, recognizing that other depository corporations are the principal holders of BI certificates.
Accrued interest is included in *Other Items (Net)* rather than in the outstanding amounts of the financial assets and liabilities.

Other Depository Corporations:

Comprises commercial banks, which are grouped into state banks, regional government banks, private domestic banks and foreign and joint venture banks. † Beginning in June 2004, the data include rural banks. Coverage excludes mutual funds (*Reksa Dana*), which issue short-term liabilities.
† Beginning in June 2004, data are based on a standardized report form (SRF) for other depository corporations, which accords with the concepts and definitions of the *Monetary and Financial Statistics Manual (MFSM)*. For other depository corporations in Indonesia, departures from the *MFSM* methodology are explained below.
Restricted other deposits are included in *Other Deposits Included in Broad Money* rather than in *Deposits Excluded from Broad Money*. The classification of securities included in broad money is based on original maturity rather than on remaining maturity. Short-term certificates of deposit are included in *Securities Other than Shares Excluded from Broad Money* rather than in *Securities Included in Broad Money*. Acceptances not eligible for rediscounting are included in *Securities Other than Shares Included in Broad Money* and *Securities Excluded from Broad Money* rather than in *Loans*.
† Beginning in January 2010, data are based on a new reporting system which provides improved classification and sectorization of the accounts.
For December 2001 through May 2004, data in the SRF format are compiled from pre-SRF data not based on the *MFSM* methodology. Departures from the *MFSM* methodology are explained below.
Financial derivatives are included in *Other Items (Net)*.
Financial assets and liabilities not disaggregated by economic sector are allocated to the economic sector having the largest volume of transactions in the category.
Claims on Central Government includes holdings of rupiah denominated shares and other equity issued by other financial corporations, public nonfinancial corporations, and nonresidents.
Holdings of securities issued by other financial corporations are not identified.
Securities Other than Shares Included in Broad Money are not distinguished from *Securities Other than Shares Excluded from Broad Money*.
Loans to nonresidents are included in *Other Items (Net)*.
Accrued interest is included in *Other Items (Net)* rather than in the outstanding amounts of the financial assets and liabilities.

Depository Corporations:

† See notes on central bank and other depository corporations.

Other Financial Corporations:

Comprises finance companies. Data exclude insurance companies, pension funds, pawnshops, and other financial auxiliaries.
Data are based on a standardized report form (SRF) for other financial corporations, which accords with the concepts and definitions of the *Monetary and Financial Statistics Manual (MFSM)*. For other financial corporations in Indonesia, departures from the *MFSM* methodology are explained below.
Financial assets and liabilities for which financial instrument breakdown is unavailable are allocated to the financial instrument having the largest volume of transactions in the category.
Financial assets and liabilities for which economic sectorization is unavailable are allocated to the economic sector having the largest volume of transactions in the category.
Financial derivatives are included in *Other Items (Net)*.
Accrued interest is included in *Other Items (Net)* rather than in the outstanding amounts of the financial assets and liabilities.

Monetary Aggregates:

Broad Money:

Broad Money calculated from the liability data in the sections for the central bank and other depository corporations accords with the concepts and definitions of the *MFSM* and is consistent with M2 described below.

Money (National Definitions):

Base Money comprises currency in circulation, transferable deposits in national and foreign currencies that other depository corporations, and other deposits in national currency that other depository corporations, other financial corporations, state and local governments, and the private sector (other nonfinancial corporations and other resident sectors), hold in the BI. *Currency in circulation* is Rupiah currency notes and coins issued by the BI *less* note and coin holdings of BI.

M1 comprises currency outside depository corporations and transferable deposits. *Currency outside depository corporations* is the amount of currency in circulation *less* the Rupiah currency note and coin holdings of other depository corporations. *Transferable deposits* are current account deposits in national currency that other financial corporations, state and local governments, and the private sector hold in the BI and other depository corporations.

M2 comprises M1, quasi-money, and securities issued by other depository corporations held by other financial corporations, state and local governments, public nonfinancial corporations, and the private sector. *Quasi-money* comprises time, savings, and foreign-currency deposits that other financial corporations, state and local governments, public nonfinancial corporations, and the private sector hold in the BI and other depository corporations.

Interest Rates:

Central Bank Policy Rate (End of Period):

Refers to the Bank Indonesia rate, which is the policy rate reflecting the monetary policy stance adopted by Bank Indonesia and announced to the public.

Discount Rate (End of Period):

Rate on one-month Bank Indonesia Certificates (SBIs).

Money Market Rate:

Rate on one-day loans between commercial banks.

Deposit Rate:

Average rate offered by commercial banks on six-month time deposits. † Beginning in January 1990, weighted average rate offered by commercial banks on three-month time deposits in national currency. Rate is weighted by deposit amounts.

Deposit Rate (Foreign currency):

Weighted average rate offered by commercial banks on three-month time deposits in foreign currency. Rate is weighted by deposit amounts.

Lending Rate:

Weighted average rate charged by commercial banks on loans to the private sector for working capital in national currency. Rate is weighted by loan amounts.

Lending Rate (Foreign Currency):

Weighted average rate charged by commercial banks on loans to the private sector for working capital in foreign currency. Rate is weighted by loan amounts.

Prices, Production, Labor:

Share Prices (End of Month):

Stock price index of the Jakarta Stock Exchange, base August 10, 1982.

Wholesale Prices:

Source: Statistics Indonesia. Data are disseminated on the General Wholesale Price Index (2005=100), a Laspeyres index covering the agricultural, mining and quarrying, industry, import and export sectors. The weights used in the index are based on marketed surplus, including taxes, in the 2005 weights reference period.

Consumer Prices:

Source: Statistics Indonesia. Weights Reference Period: 2007; Geographical Coverage: 66 major urban areas throughout Indonesia; Number of Items in Basket: Between 287 and 441; Basis for Calculation: The weights used in the index are based on the 2007 Cost of Living Survey (CLS).

Industrial Production:

Manufacturing production index measuring changes in real production of large and medium non-oil manufacturing establishments.

Manufacturing Production:

Source: Statistics Indonesia. Weights Reference Period: 2010; Sectoral Coverage: non-oil manufacturing establishments; Basis for Calculation: the production index computation methodology is done using the Discrete Divisia procedure.

International Transactions:

Exports and Imports, c.i.f.:

Data are based on customs statistics.

Trade indices: Bank Indonesia indices computed according to the Fisher ideal formula with weights reference period 1990.

Government Finance:

† Beginning in 1990, annual data are as reported for the *Government Finance Statistics Yearbook (GFSY)* and cover consolidated central government. Also beginning in 2000, quarterly data are derived from the Ministry of Finance. Development expenditure are classified as *net acquisition of nonfinancial assets*. These data may include some current expenses. Sales of nonfinancial assets are included in *revenue*. The fiscal year ends December 31.

National Accounts:

Source: Bank Indonesia. Data compiled in accordance with the *1993 SNA*.

Iran, I.R. of   429

Data refer to the Islamic Republic of Iran. Revised annual data in financial sections 10, 20, 30, and 40 relating to Iranian years ending March 20 appeared in the January through March 1972 issues. Beginning with the April 1972 issue, these data refer to December 20.

Date of Fund Membership:

December 29, 1945

Standard Sources:

Central Bank Markazi Jomhouri Islami Iran

Exchange Rates:

Official Rate: (End of Period and Period Average):
The exchange rate system is based on a dual official exchange rate structure; the floating rate and the export rate. The floating rate applies mainly to the imports of essential goods, and the export rate applies to all other transactions. Beginning in March 1993, the exchange rate refers to the official floating rate. Prior to that date, the exchange rate referred to the basic official exchange rate of the Iranian rial, which was pegged to the SDR. † Beginning from March 2002, a unified exchange rate, determined at the inter-bank foreign exchange market, has replaced the dual foreign exchange rate system.

Market Rate:
Data refer to end-of-month average rate determined at the Tehran Stock Exchange.

Weighted Average:
Calculated as a weighted average of the exchange rates that prevailed during the month, where the weights are based on the authorities' estimates of the shares of transactions conducted at various exchange rates.

International Liquidity:

Gold holdings are for months ending the 20th, while *SDR* holdings and the *Reserve Position in the Fund* are as of the end of the month. *Monetary Authorities: Other Assets (line 3..d)* comprise foreign currency subscriptions to other international agencies and net payment agreement balances.

Gold (National Valuation) (line 1and) is equal to *Gold (Million Fine Troy Ounces) (line 1ad),* valued at SDR 35 per fine troy ounce and converted into U.S. dollars at the dollar/SDR rate **sa** on the country page for the United States.

Monetary Authorities:

Comprises Bank Markazi Jomhouri Islami Iran only.

Deposit Money Banks:

Comprises commercial banks.

Other Banking Institutions:

Comprises the Agricultural Bank, the Housing Bank, and the Industrial and Mining Bank.

Interest Rates:

Deposit Rate (End of Period):
Data refer to weighted average provisional rate of profits from non-public sectors' deposits with state-owned banks. The rate is weighted by the outstanding amount of the aforementioned deposits at the end of the reference period.

Lending Rate (End of Period):
Data refer to weighted average rate of expected returns on lending facilities extended by state-owned banks to public and non-public sectors. The rate is weighted by the outstanding amount of lending facilities extended to various economic sectors at the end of the reference period.

Prices and Production:

Share Prices:
Data cover all companies listed in Tehran Stock Exchange and are produced as a Laspeyres-type index based on average daily prices, base 1990–1991.

Wholesale Prices:
General index for Iran, includes exports, imports, and home goods, weights reference period: 1997–98.

Wholesale Prices, Home Goods:
Index for domestically produced and consumed goods, with weights reference period: 1997–98.

Consumer Prices:
Source: Central Bank Markazi Jomhouri Islami Iran. Weights Reference Period: 2004; Number of Items: 359; Basis for calculation: The CPI is compiled using the standard Laspeyres formula and the weights from the 1383 (2004) Household Expenditure Survey conducted by the CBI are used.

Crude Petroleum Production:
Source: Central Bank Markazi Jomhouri Islami Iran data, updated for current periods using production quantities as reported in the *Oil Market Intelligence.*

International Transactions:

Source: Central Bank Markazi Jomhouri Islami Iran.

Exports:
Data include oil and gas. The volume index for petroleum is obtained by weighting volume indexes for crude petroleum and refined petroleum by their relative values of exports in 1980. Since April 1979, bunker oil has been included in the refined petroleum exports series. Beginning October 1980, data on the value and volume of oil exports and on the value of total exports are rough estimates based on information published in various petroleum industry journals.

Government Finance:

Data are compiled and reported by Central Bank Markazi Jomhouri Islami Iran, using unpublished Ministry of Finance data. Data cover the budgetary central government and exclude the operations of the special purpose funds, the Social Insurance Organization, the pension funds, and the procurement and distribution centers. The fiscal year ends March 20.

National Accounts:

Data are as reported by national authorities. *Lines 99a* and *99b* include a statistical discrepancy.

Iraq   433

Date of Fund Membership:
December 27, 1945

Standard Source:
Central Bank of Iraq

Exchange Rates:

On October 15, 2003, the new national currency known as the "new Iraqi dinar" replaced the existing "old dinar" and the currency used in the North of Iraq, the"swiss dinar." The conversion rates for the new Iraqi dinar were as follows: one "old dinar" for one new Iraqi dinar and one unit of the "swiss" dinar for 150 new Iraqi dinars.

Market Rate (End of Period and Period Average):
Prior to 2003, a fixed exchange rate (US dollar per Iraqi dinar) was used. † Beginning in October 2003, a managed exchange

rate system was introduced. The exchange rate for the Iraqi dinar against the US dollar is determined daily in Central Bank of Iraq auctions.

International Liquidity:

Gold (National Valuation) (line 1and):
Prior to December 1994, gold was valued at acquisition cost. † Beginning in December 2004, gold is valued according to the price of the last business day of the reference month (in US Dollars) on the London market and converted to Iraqi Dinar according to the list issued by the CBI on the last business day of the reference month on exchange rates of Iraqi Dinar against foreign currencies.

Central Bank:

Consists of the Central Bank of Iraq (CBI) only.
Data are based on a standardized report form for central banks, which accords with the concepts and definitions of the IMF's *Monetary and Financial Statistics Manual (MFSM)*. Departures from the *MFSM* methodology are explained below.
Financial derivatives are excluded from the data.
Prior to July 2005, assets and liabilities denominated in foreign currency are converted to national currency using period-average exchange rates.
Tradable securities and shares are valued at acquisition cost rather than at current market price or fair value.
Accrued interest on instruments other than treasury bills is included in *Other Items (Net)* rather than in the outstanding amounts of the financial assets or liabilities.
Loans are net of provisions for loan losses.

Other Depository Corporations:

Comprises commercial banks, including state- and privately-owned banks, and specialized banks. Data from the Kurdistan branches of Rafidain Bank, Rasheed Bank, Industrial Bank, and Agricultural and Cooperative Bank have been unavailable since 1991 and are not included. Only data from the Kurdistan branch of the Trade Bank of Iraq (in Erbil) are included.
Data are based on a standardized report form for other depository corporations, which accords with the concepts and definitions of the *Monetary and Financial Statistics Manual* (*MFSM*). For other depository corporations in Iraq, departures from the *MFSM* methodology are explained below.
Financial derivatives are excluded from the data.
Claims on Central Government includes holdings of the CBI bills.
Other Deposits Included in Broad Money excludes guaranteed deposits of the private sector.
Prior to July 2006, assets and liabilities denominated in foreign currency are converted to national currency using period-average exchange rates.
Tradable securities and shares are valued at acquisition cost, rather than at current market price or fair value.
Accrued interest on instruments other than treasury bills are included in *Other Items (Net),* rather than in the outstanding amounts of the financial assets and liabilities. Loans are net of provisions for loan losses.

Depository Corporations:

See notes on central bank and other depository corporations.

Monetary Aggregates:

Broad Money:
Broad Money calculated from the liability data in the sections for the central bank and other depository corporations accords with the concepts and definitions of the *MFSM*. Broad money includes post office savings deposits of money holding sectors. Broad money differs from M2 described below as M2 excludes deposits of public nonfinancial corporations in national and foreign currency with the central bank and cash items in the process of collection with other depository corporations and includes guarantee deposits of the private sector.

Money (National Definitions):
M0 comprises currency in circulation and reserves of other depository corporations. Currency in circulation refers to notes and coins issued by the CBI less the amount held by other depository corporations. Reserves comprise national currency holdings in the vaults of commercial banks, current accounts, and overnight deposits in national currency of other depository corporations with the CBI. Beginning in July 1, 2007, overnight deposits in national currency were replaced with seven day deposits, and thus no longer included in M0.
M1 comprises currency in circulation and demand deposits of residents (public nonfinancial corporations and private sector) other than central government, with other depository corporations in national and foreign currency, less cash items in process of collection. Currency in circulation refers to notes and coins issued by the CBI less the amount held by other depository corporations.
M2 comprises M1 and savings, term, and guaranteed deposits of residents (public nonfinancial corporations and private sector) other than central government, in national and foreign currency with depository corporations and post office savings deposits.

Interest Rates:

Central Bank Policy Rate (End of Period):
CBI's main policy rate. Beginning in August 2004, the CBI sets the benchmark policy rate as the basis from which the rates of its standing facilities are calculated. Currently, the rates for the primary and secondary credit facilities are set at the policy rate plus two and three percentage points, respectively.

Treasury Bill Rate:
Rate on 91-day treasury bills. Data are simple monthly averages of auctions held during the month.

Savings Rate:
Simple average of rates offered by commercial banks on savings deposits in national currency. Rates are set by commercial banks on a monthly basis.

Savings Rate (Foreign Currency):
Simple average of rates offered by commercial banks on savings deposits in foreign currency. Rates are set by commercial banks on a monthly basis.

Deposit Rate:
Simple average of rates offered by commercial banks on one-year time deposits in national currency. Rates are set by commercial banks on a monthly basis.

Deposit Rate (Foreign Currency):
Simple average of rates offered by commercial banks on one-year time deposits in foreign currency. Rates are set by commercial banks on a monthly basis.

Lending Rate:

Simple average of rates charged by commercial banks on medium-term (more than one-year) loans in national currency. Rates are set by commercial banks on a monthly basis.

Lending Rate (Foreign Currency):

Simple average of rates charged by commercial banks on medium-term (more than one-year) loans in foreign currency. Rates are set by commercial banks on a monthly basis.

Prices and Production:

Consumer Prices:

Source: Central Bank. Reference Period 2007. Geographic Coverage: All urban areas in the 18 Governorates of Iraq. Number of Items in Basket: 416. Basis for Calculation: Iraqi Household Social and Economic Survey (IHSES) of 2007 which cover the whole country including the three governorates of Kurdistan.

Crude Petroleum Production:

Calculated from production quantities reported in the *Oil Market Intelligence.*

International Transactions:

Imports, c.i.f., from DOTS:

Data are based on reported data and estimates from *Direction of Trade Statistics (DOTS).*

Balance of Payments:

The Central Bank of Iraq (CBI) is responsible for compiling Iraq's balance of payments statistics. The Balance of Payments Statistics Division (BOPSD) of the Statistics and Research Department (SARD) at the CBI has set the methodology for estimating the various components of the Balance of Payments (BOP) consistent with the methodology of the International Monetary Fund's (IMF) *Balance of Payments Manual.* The CBI obtains primary data from various sources, including internal sources, the Central Organization for Statistics and Information Technology (COSIT), the Ministry of Finance (MOF), other ministries and governmental agencies, commercial banks, and enterprises. The CBI prepares the data on an annual and quarterly basis in U.S. dollars and publishes the data in its *Quarterly Statistical Bulletin* and in its *Annual Bulletin.* Data are also available at the internet address www.cbi.iq.

Transactions carried out in other currencies are converted to U.S. dollars using the valid exchange rate at the time the transaction took place. Given the difficulty of obtaining accurate and timely information, estimates for certain components and items might not be comprehensive and will be subject to revisions as more data become available and new estimate models are developed.

International Investment Position:

Annual IIP data are available beginning with the 2006 reference year. The sources of information on Iraq's IIP are similar to those used for the balance of payments. The IIP does not fully cover the asset and liability positions of *other sectors* due to the unavailability of source data.

Ireland   178

Data are denominated in pounds prior to January 1999 and in euros from January 1999 onward. The pound's irrevocable fixed conversion factor to the euro is 0.787564 pounds per euro. In 2002, the pound was retired from circulation and replaced by euro banknotes and coins. Beginning in January 1999, with the implementation of Stage Three of the European Economic and Monetary Union (EMU), an alternative euro area-wide definition of residency was introduced: All positions with residents of other euro area (EA) countries, including the European Central Bank (ECB), are classified as domestic positions, and foreign assets and foreign liabilities include only positions with non-euro area residents. Descriptions of the changes in the methodology and presentation of Ireland's accounts following the introduction of the euro are shown in the introduction to *IFS* and in the footnotes on the euro area page.

Date of Fund Membership:

August 8, 1957

Standard Sources:

Central Bank of Ireland
Central Statistics Office
Eurostat

Exchange Rates:

Prior to January 1999, the market rate related to the midpoint rate quoted at 2:30 p.m. in the Dublin Market. In January 1999, the pound became a participating currency within the Eurosystem, and the euro market rate became applicable to all transactions. In 2002, the pound was retired from circulation and replaced by euro banknotes and coins. For additional information, refer to the section on Exchange Rates in the introduction to *IFS* and the footnotes on the euro area page.

International Liquidity:

Beginning in January 1999, *Total Reserves minus Gold (line 1l.d)* is defined in accordance with the Eurosystem's statistical definition of international reserves. The international reserves of Ireland per the Eurosystem statistical definition at the start of the monetary union (January 1, 1999) in billions of U.S. dollars were as follows: *Total Reserves minus Gold,* $7,295; *Foreign Exchange,* $6,677; *SDRs,* $193; *Reserve Position in the Fund,* $426; *Other Reserve Assets,* $0; *Gold,* $130; *Gold (million fine troy ounces),* .451 ounces. *Foreign Exchange (line 1d.d):* Beginning in March 1979, gold and foreign exchange holdings exclude deposits at the European Monetary Cooperation Fund (EMCF), and the holdings of European currency units (ECUs) issued against these deposits are included in *line 1d.d. Gold (Eurosystem Valuation) (line 1and):* During 1994–98, gold was revalued at the midmarket closing price at the valuation date. From January 1999 onward, gold is valued at market prices at the end of each month. Memorandum data are provided on *Non-Euro Claims on Euro Area Residents* and *Euro Claims on Non-Euro Area Residents,* which represent positions as of the last Friday in each month. For additional information, refer to the section on International Liquidity in the introduction to *IFS* and on the euro area page.

Central Bank:

Consists of the Central Bank of Ireland, which is part of the Eurosystem beginning in January 1999, only. For a description of the accounts, refer the section on *Central Bank - Euro Area* in the introduction to *IFS.* Data refer to the Central Bank and Financial Services Authority of Ireland through September 2010.

Other Depository Corporations:

Comprises all resident units classified as other monetary financial institutions (other MFIs), in accordance with *1995 ESA* standards, including money market funds. For a description of the accounts, refer to the section on *Other Depository Corporations - Euro Area* in the introduction to *IFS*.

Depository Corporations (National Residency):

For a description of the accounts and the methodology, refer to the section on *Depository Corporations (National Residency) - Euro Area* in the introduction to *IFS*.

Depository Corporations (Euro Area-wide Residency):

For a description of the methodology and accounts, refer to the section on *Depository Corporations (Euro Area-wide Residency)* in the introduction to *IFS*.

Interest Rates:

Discount Rate (End of Period):
Short-term facility rate charged by the Bank of Ireland on funds, up to a specified quota, lent to banks experiencing day-to-day liquidity shortages. Beginning in January 1999, central bank policy rates are discontinued. See Eurosystem policy rate series on the Euro Area page.

Money Market Rate:
Rate on one-month fixed interbank deposits (data refer to closing rates).

Treasury Bill Rate:
Yield on 90-day exchequer notes.

Deposit Rate:
Rate offered by licensed banks on demand deposits in the range of six to thirty thousand euro.

Deposit Rate (lines 60lhs and 60lcs):
See notes in the introduction to *IFS* and *Euro-area Interest Rates*.

Lending Rate:
Lower point of range of rates charged on short-term loans to large commercial customers by the associated banks. Prior to 1991, data refer to the rate charged to AAA customers in the primary, manufacturing, and service sectors.

Lending Rate (lines 60phs, 60pns, 60phm, 60phn, 60pcs, and 60pcn):
See notes in the introduction to *IFS* and *Euro-area Interest Rates*.

Government Bond Yield (Line 61):
Representative yield on government securities with 15-year maturities. For additional information, refer to the section on interest rates in the introduction to *IFS* and the notes on the euro area page. † Beginning August 1988, refers to secondary market yields of government bonds with a ten-year maturity. This rate is used to measure long-term interest rates for assessing convergence among the European Union member states.

Prices, Production, Labor:

Share Prices (End of Month):
Share price index, base 1953. † Beginning in March 1972, share price index, base January 1963. † Beginning in January 1986, share price index, base 1975. † Beginning in January 1989, Irish Stock Exchange's equity index of all Official List and USM equities, excluding UK-registered companies, base January 4, 1988.

Wholesale Prices: Manufacturing Industry Output:
Source: Central Statistics Office. Weights Reference Period: weights are updated every 5 years; Sectoral Coverage: the index refers to a family of indices that measure the average change over time in the selling prices received by domestic producers of goods and services; Number of Items in Basket: approximately 7,000 price quotations; Basis for Calculation: weights are based on 2005 Census of Industrial Production, 1998 Building & Construction survey, 2005 National Income and Expenditure Accounts.

Consumer Prices:
Source: Central Statistics Office. Weights Reference Period: weights are updated every five years; Geographical Coverage: whole national territory; Number of Items in Basket: 632; Basis for Calculation: weights are derived from the 2009–2010 Household Budget Survey (HBS).

Wages: Weekly Earnings:
Source: Central Statistics Office. Average weekly earnings by all industrial workers in manufacturing. The new Hours and Employment Costs Survey (EHECS) has been collecting data for all sectors since Q1 2008 and from that time other earnings surveys were discontinued.

Industrial Production:
Source: Central Statistics Office. Weights Reference Period: weights are updated every 5 years; Sectoral Coverage: mining and quarrying, manufacturing, electricity, gas and water supply sectors; Basis for Calculation: weights are sourced from Census of Industrial Production (CIP) for the production industries.

Industrial Employment:
Central Statistics Office data, unadjusted; for data from 2004 onwards, the index covers all industries; numbers are derived from the *Quarterly National Household Survey* (QNHS).

International Transactions:

All value data on trade are from the Central Statistics Office.

Volume of Exports:
Source: Central Statistics Office. Annual indices of volume are Fisher ideal indices derived from an annual unit value index. Monthly indices are derived from monthly value and unit value indices, base: 1990.

Volume of Imports:
Central Statistics Office data derived similarly to volume of export indices, base 1990.

Unit Value of Exports:
Source: Central Statistics Office. Annual unit value indices are Fisher ideal indices. Monthly unit value indices are Laspeyres indices using weights of the previous year. All indices are chained, weights reference period: 1990.

Unit Value of Imports:
Central Statistics Office data derived similarly to unit value of export indices, weights reference period: 1990.

Government Finance:

Quarterly and annual cash data on central government are derived from the Central Bank of Ireland. Data on general government are derived from Eurostat. The fiscal year ends December 31.

National Accounts:

Source: Central Statistics Office. As indicated by the country, data are compiled in accordance with the methodology of the *1995 ESA*. Prior to 1990, data are based on the *ESA 79*. Chain-linked GDP volume measures are expressed in the prices of the previous year and re-referenced to 2010.

Israel   436

Date of Fund Membership:

July 12, 1954

Standard Sources:

Bank of Israel
Central Bureau of Statistics of Israel

Exchange Rates:

On September 4, 1985 the new sheqel, equal to 1,000 old she-qalim, was introduced.

Market Rate (End of Period and Period Average):
Noon midpoint rate ascertained by the Bank of Israel.

International Liquidity:

† Beginning in January 1997, data for *line 1d.d* include accrued interest on securities. *Gold (National Valuation) (line 1and)* is equal to *Gold (Million Fine Troy Ounces) (line 1ad)*, valued at SDR 35 per fine troy ounce and converted into U.S. dollars at the dollar/SDR rate **sa** on the country page for the United States. Data for *lines 7a.d* and *7b.d* are taken from the Bank of Israel and are slightly different from the corresponding data in *lines 21* and *26c*.

Monetary Authorities:

Comprises Bank of Israel only. Significant amounts shown in *line 17r* are due mainly to the inclusion of redeposits by commercial banks of the full amount of private foreign currency deposits and of time deposits linked to the exchange rate.

Deposit Money Banks:

Comprises the 29 ordinary banking corporations which are fully subject to the liquidity regulations. † As of December 1992, data on *Claims on Other Banking Institutions (line 22f)* are included in *Claims on the Private Sector (line 22d)*. Data on claims include accrued interest and are net of provisions for losses. Beginning December 1992, other deposits, which were previously included in *Time and Savings Deposits (line 25)*, are included in *Demand Deposits (line 24)*. Earmarked government deposits, which were previously included in *Restricted Deposits (line 26b)*, are included in *Central Government Deposits (line 26d)*.
Claims on Other Banking Institutions comprise claims on mortgage banks.

Monetary Survey:

Line 34 is equal to the Bank of Israel measure of money supply.
Claims on Other Banking Institutions comprise claims on mortgage banks.

Interest Rates:

All rates are converted into annual rates by compounding the simple arithmetic averages of the monthly rates applicable on each day in the month.

Central Bank Policy Rate (End of Period):
Rate on monetary loans offered by tender by the Bank of Israel to commercial banks. Rate determined on a liquidity month, which is defined as the period from the last Thursday of the month to the last Thursday of the following month.

Discount Rate:
Average rate on monetary loans offered by tender by the Bank of Israel to commercial banks.

Treasury Bill Rate:
Yield to maturity on short-term treasury bills.

Deposit Rate:
Average rate offered by commercial banks on all short-term deposits up to one year. Prior to September 1988, the rate offered by commercial banks on 14-day fixed deposits of NIS 20,000 was used.

Lending Rate:
Average effective cost of all unindexed credit in Israeli currency, including overdraft credit. Prior to January 1989, the average rate charged by commercial banks on overdrafts.

Prices, Production, Labor:

Share Prices (End of Month):
Share price index, base, 1950. † Beginning in 1950, share price index, base 1960. † Beginning in January 1975, share price index, base 1974. † Beginning in January 1977, share price index, base 1976. † Beginning in December 1980, share price index, base December 31, 1980. † Beginning in December 1981, share price index, base December 31, 1981. † Beginning in December 1983, share price index, base December 29, 1983. † Beginning in January 1985, index covers all ordinary shares quoted on the Tel Aviv Exchange, base December 31, 1991.

Wholesale Prices: Industrial Products:
Source: Central Bureau of Statistics of Israel. Weights Reference Period: 2005; Sectoral Coverage: all establishments of the manufacturing divisions which include mining and quarrying industries, excluding the diamond industry; Number of Items in Basket: 1800; Basis for Calculation: weights for the present indices were obtained from the 2004–2005 monthly survey of manufacturing indices.

Consumer Prices:
Source: Central Bureau of Statistics of Israel. Weights Reference Period: January 2004-December 2005; Geographical Coverage: whole national territory; Number of Items in Basket: 1334; Basis for Calculation: weights are derived from the 2008–2009 Household Expenditure Surveys (HES).

Wages: Daily Earnings:
Source: Central Bureau of Statistics of Israel. Weights Reference Period: 2004; daily earnings covering total cash remuneration in manufacturing, mining, and quarrying. As of January 1978, the series is based on all employees. Prior to that date, it covered workers only. † The index excludes the diamond sector as of January 1979.

Industrial Production, Seasonally Adjusted:

Source: Central Bureau of Statistics of Israel. Weights Reference Period: 2004; Sectoral Coverage: manufacturing, mining and quarrying, excluding diamonds; Basis for Calculation: the weights used in the index are the gross value added at factor cost obtained from an annual survey of manufacturing. † The index excludes the diamond sector as of January 1979.

Industrial Employment:

Source: Central Bureau of Statistics of Israel. Weights Reference Period: 2004; Coverage: covering all employees engaged in manufacturing, mining, and quarrying. † The index excludes the diamond sector as of January 1979.

International Transactions:

Exports and Imports, c.i.f.:

Source: Central Bureau of Statistics of Israel. *Line 71..d* (imports including military goods) is compiled quarterly.

Export and Import Volume:

Source: Central Bureau of Statistics of Israel. Prior to 1980, they are Laspeyres indices obtained by dividing the value indices by the Paasche price indices. Beginning 1980, they are compiled using Fisher's ideal index.

Export and Import Unit Vaule:

Source: Central Bureau of Statistics of Israel. Prior to 1976, they are Paasche indices; beginning 1976, they are Laspeyres indices; from 1984 onwards they are compiled using Fisher's ideal index. The weights are revised every two years. For example, for 1981 the weights are calculated on the basis of Israel's trade in 1979. The weights reference period for volume and unit value indices of exports and imports is presently 2005=100. Export volume and unit value indices include ships, aircraft, and diamonds. Import volume and unit value indices exclude ships and aircraft.

Government Finance:

Data are derived from source S in collaboration with the Ministry of Finance and cover the operations of the consolidated budgetary central government institutions along with the National Insurance Institute (social security). The fiscal year ends December 31.

National Accounts:

Source: Central Bureau of Statistics of Israel. As indicated by the country, from 1995 onward, data are compiled according to the *1993 SNA.* Chain-linked GDP volume measures are expressed in the prices of the previous year and re-referenced to 2005.

Italy   136

Data are denominated in lire prior to January 1999 and in euros from January 1999 onward. An irrevocably fixed factor for converting lire to euros was established at 1,936.27 lire per euro. In 2002, the lira was retired from circulation and replaced by euro banknotes and coins. Beginning in January 1999, with the implementation of Stage Three of the European Economic and Monetary Union (EMU), a euro area-wide definition of residency was introduced: All positions with residents of other euro area (EA) countries, including the European Central Bank (ECB), are classi-fied as domestic positions, and foreign assets and foreign liabilities include only positions with non-euro area residents. Descriptions of the changes in the methodology and presentation of Italy's accounts following the introduction of the euro are shown in the introduction to *IFS* and in the notes on the euro area page.

Date of Fund Membership:

March 27, 1947

Standard Sources:

Bank of Italy
Central Institute of Statistics
Eurostat

Exchange Rates:

Market Rate (End of Period and Period Average):

Between September 1992 and December 1998, based on quotations of a sample of banks at 14.15 Central European Time polled by the Bank of Italy. In January 1999, the lira became a participating currency within the Eurosystem, and the euro market rate became applicable to all transactions. In 2002, the lira was retired from circulation and replaced by euro banknotes and coins. For additional information, refer to the section on Exchange Rates in the introduction to *IFS* and the notes on the euro area page.

International Liquidity:

Beginning in January 1999, *Total Reserves minus Gold (line 1l.d)* is defined in accordance with the Eurosystem's statistical definition of international reserves. The international reserves of Italy per the Eurosystem statistical definition at the start of the monetary union (January 1, 1999) in billions of U.S. dollars were as follows: *Total Reserves minus Gold,* $29,423; *Foreign Exchange,* $24,457; *SDR holdings,* $111; *Reserve Position in the Fund,* $4,314; *Other Reserve Assets,* $541; *Gold,* $23,991; *Gold (million fine troy ounces),* 83.363 ounces. *Foreign Exchange (line 1d.d)*: Between March 1979 and December 1998, gold and foreign exchange excluded deposits at the European Monetary Cooperation Fund (EMCF), and holdings of European currency units (ECUs) issued against these deposits were included in *line 1d.d. Gold (Eurosystem Valuation) (line 1and)*: Prior to January 1999, gold was valued according to national valuation practices, whereby gold was revalued quarterly on the basis of the average London market price in the preceding six months or the average price of the penultimate working day of the period, whichever was lower. From January 1999 onward, gold is revalued at the market price at the end of each month. Memorandum data are provided on *Non-Euro Claims on Euro Area Residents* and *Euro Claims on Non-Euro Area Residents,* which represent positions as of the last Friday in each month. For additional information, refer to the section on International Liquidity in the introduction to *IFS* and the notes on the euro area page.

Central Bank:

Consists of the Bank of Italy, which beginning in January 1999 is part of the Eurosystem, only. *Currency Issued* includes coins issued by the Treasury; also, beginning in January 1999, includes the equity of the Italian Foreign Exchange Office. For a description of the accounts, refer to the section on *Central Bank - Euro Area* in the introduction to *IFS*.

Other Depository Corporations:

Comprises all resident units classified as other monetary financial institutions (other MFIs), as defined by *1995 ESA* standards, including money market funds. Positions with residents of San Marino and the Vatican City are treated as nonresident positions. For a description of the accounts, refer to the section on *Other Depository Corporations - Euro Area* in the introduction to *IFS*.

Depository Corporations (National Residency):

For a description of the accounts and the methodology, refer to the section on *Depository Corporations (National Residency) - Euro Area* in the introduction to *IFS*.

Depository Corporations (Euro Area-wide Residency):

For a description of the methodology and accounts, refer to the section on *Depository Corporations (Euro Area-wide Residency)* in the introduction to *IFS*.

Interest Rates:

Discount Rate (End of Period):
Prior to January 1999, data refer to rate charged by the Bank of Italy for rediscounts on commercial bills; the same rate was also applied to the Bank of Italy's advances and was used as the base for "extraordinary" advances, on which penalties were applied. Beginning in January 1999, central bank policy rates are discontinued. See Eurosystem policy rate series on the euro area page.

Money Market Rate:
Three-month interbank rate. Beginning in February 1990, data represent arithmetic averages of daily rates, which are weighted averages of rates based on the volume of transactions for the day (data were compiled by the Bank of Italy).

Treasury Bill Rate:
Monthly average yield, before tax, on newly issued three-month, six-month, and twelve-month treasury bills, weighted by the respective volumes of the three maturities.

Deposit Rate:
Prior to August 1992, data referred to the average paid rate by banks on current accounts and savings accounts. † Beginning in August 1992, data refer to the rate paid by banks on current accounts, savings accounts, and certificates of deposits.

Deposit Rate (lines 60lhs, 60lhn, and 60lcr):
See notes in the introduction to *IFS* and *Euro-area Interest Rates*.

Lending Rate:
† Beginning in 1990, data refer to the average rate charged by credit institutions and specialized credit institutions on short-term loans.

Lending Rate (lines 60phs, 60pns, 60phm, 60phn, 60pcs, and 60pcn):
See notes in the introduction to *IFS* and *Euro-area Interest Rates*.

Government Bond Yield: Long-Term (line 61):
Average yields to maturity on bonds with original maturities of 15 to 20 years, issued on behalf of the Treasury by the Consortium of Credit for Public Works. † Beginning January 1980, average yields to maturity on bonds with residual maturities between 9 and 10 years. From January 1999 onward, monthly data are arithmetic averages of daily gross yields to maturity of the fixed-coupon ten-year treasury benchmark bond (last issued bond beginning from the date when it becomes the most traded issue among government securities with residual maturities between nine and ten years), based on prices in the official wholesale market. This rate is used to measure long-term interest rates for assessing convergence among the European Union member states.

Medium-Term (line 61b):
Prior to January 1991, the data are average yields to maturity on treasury bonds with maximum original maturities of nine years. Between January 1991 and December 1998, the data are average yields to maturity on bonds with residual maturity between four and six years. From January 1999 onward, monthly data are arithmetic averages of daily gross yields to maturity of the fixed-coupon five-year treasury benchmark bond (last issued bond beginning from the date when it becomes the most traded issue among government securities with residual maturities between four and five years), based on prices in the official wholesale market. For additional information, refer to the section on Interest Rates in the introduction to *IFS* and the notes on the euro area page.

Prices, Production, Labor:

Share Prices:
Share price index, base 1958. † Beginning in January 1975, MIB index calculated by the Milan Stock Exchange (MSE), base 1975. Data are based on the quoted prices of all stocks traded in the MSE.

Producer Prices:
Source: Central Institute of Statistics. Weights Reference Period: 2010; Sectoral Coverage: mining, manufacturing, and energy sectors, excluding construction. Number of Items in Basket: approximately 6,542 enterprises; Basis for Calculation: the main sources of weights for PPI are the ProdCom Survey (output sold value) and the Foreign Trade Statistics (export value) referred to year 2010.

Consumer Prices:
Source: Central Institute of Statistics. Weights Reference Period: 2010; Geographical Coverage: whole national territory; Number of Items in Basket: 597; Basis for Calculation: the weights are sources from the National Accounts, Household Budget Surveys and some ad-hoc sources.

Wages: Contractual:
Source: Central Institute of Statistics. Weights reference period: December 2005. Data refer to contractual hourly wages rate in the whole industry; Basis for Calculation: the index is based on results from the monthly survey on negotiated wages; they are calculated each month by averaging the increases set in each collective agreement signed in the national territory.

Industrial Production:
Data are sourced from the OECD database, weights reference period: 2005. The indices cover the whole industry.

Industrial Employment:
Central Institute of Statistics data on employees in industry in thousands of persons.

International Transactions:

Trade data are from the Central Institute of Statistics.
Volume and Unit Value indices, weights reference period: 2005. The *Unit* Value data are Fisher indices.

Government Finance:

Annual and quarterly noncash data are derived from Eurostat. Monthly and quarterly cash-based central government operations (the "State Sector") data are derived from the Ministry of Finance and Economy and cover the State Budget and Treasury operations, including transfers to finance the expenditure of local authorities and the deficit of the social security funds. The fiscal year ends December 31.

National Accounts:

Source: Central Institute of Statistics. Data include the underground economy as part of the reported figures. Data from 1988 onwards are in accordance with the *ESA 95*, as indicated by the country. Beginning in 1999, euro data are sourced from the Eurostat database. Eurostat introduced chain-linked GDP volume measures to both annual and quarterly data with the release of the third quarter 2005 on November 30, 2005. Chain-linked GDP volume measures are expressed in the prices of the previous year and re-referenced to 2005.

Jamaica   343

Date of Fund Membership:

February 21, 1963

Standard Sources:

Bank of Jamaica
Department of Statistics

Exchange Rates:

Market Rate (End of Period and Period Average):
The exchange rate of the Jamaica dollar is determined under the Interbank Foreign Exchange Trading System, which was introduced on September 17, 1990. The interbank foreign exchange market is operated by the commercial banks and the Bank of Jamaica.

International Liquidity:

Data for *line 1d.d* include small foreign exchange holdings by the government. Other official asset holdings reported in *line 3b.d* include the foreign assets held by the Capital Development Fund and the Sugar Industry Authority.

Central Bank:

Consists of the Bank of Jamaica (BOJ) only.
Data are based on a standardized report form (SRF) for central banks, which accords with the concepts and definitions of the IMF's *Monetary and Financial Statistics Manual (MFSM)*, 2000. Data in the SRF format are compiled from pre-SRF data which are not fully based on the *MFSM* methodology. Departures from the *MFSM* methodology are explained below.
Financial assets and liabilities for which economic sectorization is unavailable are allocated to the economic sector having the largest volume of transactions in the category.
Overdrafts to the central government are subtracted from *Liabilities to Central Government* rather than classified as loans to central government.

Claim on Other Financial Corporations includes loans net of provisions.
Securities Other than Shares Included in Broad Money includes all securities other than shares issued by the BOJ prior to January 2004, irrespective of the holder.
Shares and Other Equity includes the present value of excess funds of the pension scheme for the BOJ staff.
Accounts receivable and payable are included in *Other Items (Net)* rather than in the BOJ's claims on or liabilities to the corresponding sectors.
Accrued interest is included in *Other items (Net)* rather than in the outstanding amounts of the financial assets and liabilities.

Other Depository Corporations:

Comprises commercial banks, financial corporations established under the Financial Institutions Act (FIAs), and building societies. The FIAs comprise merchant banks, trust companies, and finance houses.
Data are based on a standardized report form (SRF) for other depository corporations, which accords with the concepts and definitions of the *Monetary and Financial Statistics Manual (MFSM)*. Data in the SRF format are compiled from data contained in the balance sheet of other depository corporations and are not fully based on the *MFSM* methodology. For other depository corporations in Jamaica, departures from the *MFSM* methodology are explained below.
Financial assets and liabilities for which economic sectorization is unavailable are allocated to the economic sector having the largest volume of transactions in the category.
Liabilities to Nonresidents includes a small portion of liabilities to residents in foreign currency.
Accounts receivable and payable are included in *Other Items (Net)* rather than in the other depository corporations' claims on or liabilities to the corresponding economic sectors.
Accrued interest is included in *Other items (Net)* rather than in the outstanding amounts of the financial assets and liabilities.

Depository Corporations:

See notes on central bank and other depository corporations.

Monetary Aggregates:

Broad Money:
Broad Money calculated from the liability data in the sections for the central bank and other depository corporations differs from *M2* described below as broad money includes demand, time, and savings deposits of other resident sectors and other nonfinancial corporations in national currency with FIAs and building societies and securities other than shares issued by the BOJ held outside other depository corporations.

Money (National Definitions):
Base Money comprises currency issued, statutory cash reserves, and current accounts of commercial banks with the BOJ in national currency.
M1 comprises notes and coins in circulation outside commercial banks and demand deposits of other resident sectors and other nonfinancial corporations in national currency with commercial banks.
M2 comprises M1 and quasi money. Quasi money comprises

time and savings deposits in national currency of other resident sectors and other nonfinancial corporations with commercial banks.

Interest Rates:

Money Market Rate:
Average rate on overnight interbank transactions in national currency.

Treasury Bill Rate:
Average yield of treasury bills issued during the month with maturities closest to 180 days.

Savings Rate:
Minimum rate offered by commercial banks on savings deposits.

Deposit Rate:
Weighted average rate offered by commercial banks on three- to six-month deposits. Rate is weighted by deposits amounts.

Lending Rate:
Weighted average rate offered by commercial banks on all loans, excluding staff loans. Rate is weighted by loan amounts.

Prices:

Industrial Share Prices:
Industrial share price index covering shares quoted in the Jamaican Stock Exchange, base 1969.

Consumer Prices:
Source: Bank of Jamaica. Weights Reference Period: December 2006; Geographical Coverage: all Jamaica; Number of Items in Basket: 480 items; Basis for Calculation: Household Expenditure Survey conducted from June 2004 to March 2005.

International Transactions:

Source: Bank of Jamaica.

Volume of Exports:
IFS average of alumina, bauxite, and sugar with a 1995 value of exports as weights.

National Accounts:

Source: Department of Statistics. As indicated by the country, from 1998 onward data are compiled and disseminated according to the recommendations of the *1993 SNA*. † From 2008 onward GDP volume data doesn't include taxes less subsidies on products.

Japan   158

Date of Fund Membership:
August 13, 1952

Standard Sources:
Bank of Japan
Cabinet Office
Ministry of Economy, Trade and Industry
Ministry of Finance
Statistics Bureau of Japan

Exchange Rates:

Market Rate (End of Period and Period Average):
Midpoint rate in the interbank foreign exchange market in Tokyo.

International Liquidity:

Gold (National Valuation) (line 1and) is the U.S. dollar value of official holdings of gold as reported in the country's standard sources. Beginning April 2000, gold is valued according to market prices, in U.S. dollars. Prior to April 2000, gold is valued at SDR 35 per fine troy ounce and converted into U.S. dollars at the U.S. dollar/SDR rate.

Data for *lines 7a.d* and *7b.d* include long-term foreign accounts and therefore are not the U.S. dollar equivalents of *lines 21* and *26c,* which comprise only short-term accounts; data are from the Bank for International Settlement's *Annual Report* and *Quarterly Press Release.*

Central Bank:

Consists of the Bank of Japan (BOJ) only.

Data in the SRF format are based on balance sheet data for the central bank published in the *Flow of Funds Accounts (FFA)* and other account information of the BOJ publicly available on a monthly basis, which are not fully based on the *Monetary and Financial Statistics Manual (MFSM)* methodology. Departures from the *MFSM* methodology are explained below.

Claims on Nonresidents includes the IMF accounts assigned to the central government. The portion of IMF accounts belonging to the Bank of Japan may be double counted in some periods.

Financial assets and liabilities for which economic sectorization is unavailable are allocated to the economic sector assumed to have a significant volume of transactions in the category.

Accrued interest is included in *Other items (Net)* rather than in the outstanding amounts of the financial assets and liabilities.

Accounts receivable and payable are included in *Other Items (Net)* rather than in the BOJ's claims on and liabilities to the corresponding sectors.

Currency in circulation includes coins circulated by BOJ on behalf of the government. The counter entry of this amount is included in *Other Items (Net).*

Shares and other equity comprises 100 million yen of funds contributed by owners. The figure is not significant in the publication which is expressed in trillion of yen.

Valuation adjustment is included in *Other Items (Net)* rather than in *Shares and Other Equity.*

Other Depository Corporations:

Comprises domestically licensed banks (including Japan Post Bank), foreign-owned banks in Japan, financial institutions for agriculture, forestry, and fisheries (Norinchukin Bank, Prefectural Credit Federations of Agricultural Cooperatives, agricultural cooperatives, Prefectural Credit Federations of Fishery Cooperatives, and fishery coops), financial institutions for small business (Shinkin banks, Shinkin Central Bank, Shoko Chukin Bank, Shinkumi Federation Bank, Shinkumi banks, Rokinren Bank, and labor banks), and collectively managed trusts.

Data in the SRF format are based on balance sheet data for other depository corporations published in the *FFA*, which are not fully based on the *Monetary and Financial Statistics Manual (MFSM)* methodology. For other depository corporations in Japan, departures from the *MFSM* methodology are explained below.

Data are available only on a quarterly basis. Data for the intervening months are estimated by interpolation. Data for the two months after the latest quarter are estimated by extrapolation.

Financial assets and liabilities for which economic sectorization is unavailable are allocated to the economic sector that assumed to have a significant volume of transactions in the category.

Commercial papers and bank debentures held by money holders are included in *Other Items (Net)* rather than in *Securities other than Shares Included in Broad Money*.

Accrued interest is included in *Other items (Net)* rather than in the outstanding amounts of the financial assets and liabilities.

Accounts receivable and payable are included in *Other Items (Net)* rather than in the other depository corporations' claim on and liabilities to the corresponding sectors.

Valuation adjustment is included in *Other Items (Net)* rather than in *Shares and Other Equity*.

Depository Corporations:

See notes on central bank and other depository corporations.

Other Financial Corporations:

Comprises life insurance companies, nonlife insurance companies, mutual aid insurance companies, pension funds, securities investment trusts, finance companies, structured-financing special purpose companies and trusts, public financial institutions, financial dealers and brokers, and financial auxiliaries.

Data in the SRF format are based on balance sheet data for other financial corporations published in the *FFA*, which are not fully based on the *Monetary and Financial Statistics Manual (MFSM)* methodology. Departures from the *MFSM* methodology are explained below.

Data for other financial corporations are available only on a quarterly basis.

Financial assets and liabilities for which economic sectorization is unavailable are allocated to the economic sector assumed having a significant volume of transaction in the category.

Accounts receivable and payable are included in *Other Items (Net)* rather than in the other financial corporations' claims on and liabilities to the corresponding sectors.

Accrued interest is included in *Other items (Net)* rather than in the outstanding amounts of the financial assets and liabilities.

Shares and other equity includes funds contributed by owners only. Retained earnings, current year result, general and special reserves, and valuation adjustment are included in the *Other Items (Net)*.

Financial Corporations:

See notes on central bank, other depository corporations, and other financial corporations.

Monetary Aggregates:

Broad Money:

Broad Money calculated from the liability data in the section for the central bank and other depository corporations differs from *L* described below mainly because broad money (i) excludes pecuniary trusts, investment trusts, bank debentures, commercial paper issued by financial institutions, repurchase agreements, securities lending with cash collateral, government bonds, and foreign bonds, (ii) is on an end-of-month basis while *L* is on a month average basis, and (iii) is estimated for the intervening months between end of each quarter and the most current two months. † Beginning in April 2003, L also excludes repurchase agreements and securities lending with cash collateral and includes privately placed investment trusts and straight bonds issued by banks.

Money (National Definitions):

M1 comprises notes and coins in circulation outside banking corporations and demand and savings deposits of households, nonfinancial corporations, local governments, securities companies, Tanshi companies, and some other financial corporations such as securities finance companies with banking corporations in national currency. The banking corporations surveyed comprise the BOJ, domestically licensed banks (excluding Japan Post Bank), foreign-owned banks in Japan, Shinkin Central Bank, Shinkin banks, Norinchukin Bank, and Shoko Chukin Bank. † Beginning in April 2003, M1 comprises notes and coins in circulation outside depository corporations and demand and savings deposits of households, nonfinancial corporations, local governments, and some other financial corporations such as securities finance companies with depository corporations in national currency. The depository corporations surveyed comprise the above-mentioned "banking corporations", Japan Post Bank, Shinkumi Federation Bank, Shinkumi banks, Rokinren Bank, labor banks, Prefectural Credit Federations of Agricultural Cooperatives, agricultural cooperatives, Prefectural Credit Federations of Fishery Cooperatives, and fishery coops.

M2 comprises notes and coins in circulation outside banking corporations; demand and savings deposits, fixed and installment savings deposits, time deposits, and certificates of deposit of households, nonfinancial corporations, local governments, securities companies, Tanshi companies, and some other financial corporations such as securities finance companies with banking corporations in national and foreign currency; and nonresident deposits with banking corporations in national currency. † Beginning in April 2003, M2 comprises notes and coins in circulation outside depository corporations and demand and savings deposits, fixed and installment savings deposits, time deposits, and certificates of deposit of households, nonfinancial corporations, local governments, and some other financial corporations such as securities finance companies with banking corporations in national and foreign currency.

M3 comprises notes and coins in circulation outside banking corporations; demand and savings deposits, fixed and installment savings deposits, time deposits, and certificates of deposit of households, nonfinancial corporations, local governments, securities companies, Tanshi companies, and some other financial corporations such as securities finance companies with depository corporations in national and foreign currency; and nonresident deposits with banking corporations in national currency. † Beginning in April 2003, M3 comprises notes and coins in circulation outside depository corporations and demand and savings deposits, fixed and installment savings deposits, time deposits, and certificates of deposit of households, nonfinancial corporations, local governments, and some other financial corporations such as securities finance companies with depository corporations in national and foreign currency.

L comprises M3, pecuniary trusts, investment trusts, bank debentures, commercial paper issued by financial institutions, repurchase agreements, securities lending with cash collateral, government bonds, and foreign bonds. † Beginning in April 2003, L excludes repurchase agreements and securities lending with cash collateral and includes privately placed investment trusts and straight bonds issued by banks.

M1 and M3 are an end-of-month basis while M2 and L are on a month average basis.

Interest Rates:

Discount Rate (End of Period):
Rate at which the BOJ discounts eligible commercial bills and loans secured by government bonds, specially designed securities, and eligible commercial bills. This rate is considered the key indicator of the BOJ's discount policy.

Money Market Rate:
Rate for collateral and overnight loans in the Tokyo Call Money Market.

Treasury Bill Rate:
Average yield on 3-month treasury discount bills.

Deposit Rate:
Average rate offered by banks on unregulated three-month time deposits, ranging in size from three million yen to under ten million yen.

Certificates of Deposit Rate:
Average rate on 90–179 day certificate of deposit issued by domestically licensed banks.

Lending Rate:
Weighted arithmetic average of contracted rates charged by banks on both short- and long-term loans, discounts, and overdrafts.

Government Bond Yield:
Arithmetic average yield on newly issued government bonds with ten-year maturity.

Prices, Production, Labor:

Share Prices:
The index, base January 4, 1968, refers to the average of daily closing prices for all shares listed on the Tokyo exchange.

Wholesale Price Indices:
The index, (Corporate Goods Price Index) weights reference period: 2005, covers 910 domestic products, weighted with 2000 transaction values.

Consumer Prices:
Source: Statistics Bureau of Japan. Weights Reference Period: 2010; Geographical Coverage: The entire country is divided into 167 strata and one municipality is selected from each stratum by using probability sampling method to represent the entire country; Number of Items in Basket: 588; Basis for Calculation: The weights are based on the 2010 Family Income and Expenditure Survey and are revised once every five years.

Wages: Monthly Earnings:
The series, weights reference period: 2010, refers to the monthly contract cash earnings of regular workers in all industries.

Industrial Production:
Source: Ministry of Economy, Trade and Industry, weights reference period: 2005. The index covers the whole industry.

Manufacturing Employment, Seasonally Adjusted:
The index, weights reference period: 2005, is from Bank of Japan. It refers to employment of regular workers only and covers all manufacturing establishments with 30 or more regular workers.

International Transactions:

Exports and *Imports, c.i.f.:* Ministry of Finance data.
Trade indices are from Bank of Japan, weights reference period: 2005. The unit value indices are Fisher Ideal indices. The volume indices are derived from the value indices divided by the unit value indices.

Export and Import Prices:
The series cover, in principle, all export and import commodities excluding used ships, jewelry, fresh fruits and vegetables, and works of art and are weighted with the value of exports and imports in 2010. The prices are contract prices, f.o.b. for exports and c.i.f. for imports.

International Investment Position:
The quarterly international investment position (IIP) data for Japan do not include financial derivatives. Japan intends to include financial derivatives in the quarterly IIP series (consistent with the end-year IIP series), when they convert to *BPM6* in 2014.

Government Finance:

Annual general government data are reported by the Bureau of Statistics. The general government data are not consolidated. Quarterly cash flow data for the budgetary central government data are reported by the Ministry of Finance. For quarterly data, expense includes the acquisition of nonfinancial assets. No further breakdowns of revenue and expense are available. The fiscal year ends March 31.

National Accounts:

Source: Cabinet Office. *Exports of Goods and Services (line 90c.c)* includes factor income received from abroad. *Imports of Goods and Services (line 98c.c)* includes factor income payments to abroad, and *lines 90c.c* through *98c.c* add up to *GNP (line 99a.c)*. *Line 98.nc* is not reported to *IFS* and is calculated for *IFS* as the difference between GNP and GDP. As indicated by the country, from 2000 onward data have been revised following the implementation of the *1993 SNA*. GDP chain-linked volume measures are calculated based on the prices and weights of the previous year, using Laspeyres formula in general. Quarterly data are seasonally adjusted at annual rates.

Jordan   439

Date of Fund Membership:
August 29, 1952

Standard Sources:
Central Bank of Jordan
Department of Statistics

Exchange Rates:

Official Rate: (End of Period and Period Average):
Central bank midpoint rate. Prior to 1988, the dinar was officially pegged to the SDR. Since May 1989, the dinar has been pegged to a basket of currencies.

International Liquidity:

Foreign Exchange (line 1d.d):
Prior to December 1993, foreign currency holdings included in *1d.d* are net of foreign currency deposits of licensed banks at the Central Bank of Jordan. Beginning this date, data include these foreign currency deposits. *Gold (National Valuation) (line 1and)* refers to gold valued at US$200 per ounce, in accordance with national valuation procedures.

Monetary Authorities:

Comprises the Central Bank of Jordan (CBJ) only. † Beginning in 1993, *lines 11, 14,* and *16c* reflect foreign currency deposits of licensed banks. Beginning in January 2001, data on the CBJ are on an accruals basis; data prior to January 2001 were on a cash basis.

Deposit Money Banks:

Comprises commercial banks and the Housing Bank. Data include estimates for bank branches in occupied territory. † Beginning in December 1993, *line 26d* includes deposits of the Social Security Corporation, which previously were included in *lines 24* and *25.*

Monetary Survey:

† See notes on monetary authorities and deposit money banks.

Other Banking Institutions:

Comprises the Industrial Development Bank, the Agriculture Credit Corporation, and the Municipal Loan Fund. † Beginning December 1993, comprises Cities and Villages Development Bank, Agricultural Credit Corporation, Industrial Development Bank, the Housing Corporation, and Jordan Co-operative Organization. *Line 45* includes some demand deposits.

Money (National Definitions):

Reserve Money comprises currency in circulation and legal reserve and excess deposits in national currency of commercial banks in national currency with the CBJ. Currency in circulation refers to notes and coins issued by the CBJ.
M1 comprises currency in circulation and transferable deposits. Currency in circulation refers to notes and coins issued by the CBJ less the amount held by commercial banks. Transferable deposits refer to current account deposits in national currency of nonbank financial institutions, state and local governments, public nonfinancial corporations, social security corporation, and private sector with the CBJ and commercial banks.
M2 comprises M1 and quasi-money. Quasi-money refers to time, savings, and foreign currency deposits of nonbank financial institutions, state and local governments, public nonfinancial corporations, social security corporation, and private sector with the CBJ and commercial banks.

Interest Rates:

Central Bank Policy Rate (End of Period):
Refers to the Overnight Deposit Window Rate which is the overnight rate on interbank money set by the CBJ.

Discount Rate (End of Period):
Rate charged by the Central Bank of Jordan on advances to licensed banks.

Money Market Rate:
Weighted average rate on loans between commercial banks. The rate is weighted by loan amounts.

Savings Rate:
Weighted average rate offered by commercial banks on savings deposits in national currency. Rate is weighted by deposit amounts.

Deposit Rate:
Weighted average rate offered by commercial banks on time deposits in national currency. The rate is weighted by deposit amounts.

Lending Rate:
Weighted average rate charged by commercial banks on loans and advances in national currency. The rate is weighted by loan amounts.

Prices and Production:

Wholesale Prices:
Central Bank, Laspeyres index, weights reference period: 1998. Weights from the 1992 Census of Wholesales. The prices are collected from 104 establishments with 142 products in three cities.

Producer Prices:
Central Bank, Laspeyres index, Weights Reference Period: 1999/2000; The weights are derived from the latest 1999 Survey of Industry at four digit level, and within each industry the weights were updated upon the 1999 Economic Establishment Census.

Consumer Prices:
Source: Central Bank. Weights Reference Period: 2006/2007; Geographical Coverage: whole national territory; Number of Items in Basket: 851; Basis for Calculation: weights are derived from the Quinquennial Household Income and Expenditure Survey and population estimates.

Industrial Production:
Central Bank index, weights reference period: 1999, covering selected manufactured commodities. Data refer to the East Bank only.

International Transactions:

All trade data are from the Central Bank.
Trade indices: Data are compiled with weights reference period 1994.

Government Finance:

Monthly, quarterly, and annual data are sourced from the Central Bank and cover budgetary central government. The fiscal year ends December 31.

National Accounts:

Source: Department of Statistics. As indicated by the country, beginning in 1992 data are compiled according to the *1993 SNA.*

Kazakhstan   916

Date of Fund Membership:

July 15, 1992

Standard Sources:

National Bank of Kazakhstan
National Statistical Agency

Exchange Rates:

The tenge was introduced in November 1993.

Official Rate: (End of Period and Period Average):
Prior to August 1995, the official rate was established at periodic interbank auctions. Between August and December 1995, the official rate was set at the beginning of each week by the central bank based on the auction rate for the previous week and taking into account market developments. Beginning in January 1996, the official weekly rate is a weighted average, by volume, of the interbank rates established at daily foreign exchange auctions and in the market outside of the auctions. Monthly data are averages of weekly data.

International Liquidity:

Gold (National Valuation) (line 1and) is equal to *Gold (Million Fine Troy Ounces) (line 1ad)* valued at the London fixing rate for the end of period. Beginning in December 2001, the National Bank of Kazakhstan values foreign currency operations on the basis of the market exchange rate.

Central Bank:

Comprises the National Bank of Kazakhstan (NBK) and custodian transactions of the NBK for the National Fund of the Republic of Kazakhstan. Beginning in January 2008, consists of the NBK only.
† Beginning in January 2003, data are based on a standardized report form (SRF) for central banks, which accords with the concepts and definitions of the IMF's *Monetary and Financial Statistics Manual (MFSM)*, 2000.
For December 2001 through December 2002 data have less conformity with the *MFSM* methodology and therefore are not strictly comparable to data for later periods.
Claims on Central Government and *Liabilities to Central Government* refer to positions with the general government, which comprises central and local government units and extrabudgetary funds.
Claims on Private sector includes financial assets with claims on public nonfinancial corporations.

Other Depository Corporations:

Comprises commercial banks. † Beginning in January 2003, data are based on a standardized report form (SRF) for other depository corporations, which accords with the concepts and definitions of the *Monetary and Financial Statistics Manual (MFSM)*. Departures from the *MFSM* methodology are explained below.
Holdings of securities for investment are valued at acquisition cost rather than at current market price or fair value.
Official rather than market exchange rates are used to convert foreign currency denominated accounts into tenge equivalents.
A legal rather than an economic criterion is used to delineate resident and nonresident units.
The recording of syndicated lending is not consistent among commercial banks.
For December 2001 through December 2002 data have less conformity with the *MFSM* methodology and therefore are not strictly comparable to data for later periods.
Holdings of securities for investment are valued at acquisition cost rather than at market price or fair value.
Official rather than markets exchange rates are used to convert foreign currency denominated accounts into tenge equivalents.
A legal rather than an economic criterion is used to delineate resident and nonresident units.
The recording of syndicated lending is not consistent among commercial banks.

Depository Corporations:

See notes on central bank and other depository corporations.

Monetary Aggregates:

Broad Money:
Broad Money is calculated from the liability data in the sections for the central bank and other depository corporations and is consistent with M3 described below.

Money (National Definitions):
M1 comprises currency in circulation and transferable deposits of households and nonbank legal entities in national currency with commercial banks.
M2 comprises *M1* and other deposits in national currency and transferable deposits in foreign currency of households and nonbank legal entities with commercial banks.
M3 comprises *M2* and other deposits in foreign currency of households and nonbank legal entities with commercial banks.

Interest Rates:

Central Bank Policy Rate (End of Period):
Rate determined by the Board of the NBK and is used for providing refinancing loans to banks. It is the standing facility rate and the upper boundary of the band of rates of the NBK.

Refinancing Rate (End of Period):
Annualized interest rate until June 1995; thereafter, compound annual rate, which is established as the minimum interest rate for NBK auctions of credit to commercial banks.

Treasury Bill Rate:
Yield based on treasury bill prices established at the last auction of the month.

Prices and Labor:

Producer Prices:
Source: National Statistical Agency. Weights Reference Period: 2001; Coverage: products from all economic activities, including mining, manufacturing, production, distribution of electric power, gas and water; Number of Items in Basket: some 230 commodity groups and 450 sub-groups coverage of activities within each main industrial group; Basis for Calculation: The value of the industrial output of Kazakhstan's enterprises in a base year is used to formulate basket weights. The base year is the year preceding the reference year. The weighting system follows the *1993 SNA* and concepts and definitions consistent with those contained in the *PPI Manual*.

Consumer Prices:
Source: National Statistical Agency. Weights Reference Period: 2002; Geographical Coverage: covers 14 oblasts, 27 districts, the capital at Astana, and three other large cities; Number of Items in Basket: includes 508 quotations of representative goods and services; Basis for Calculation: Chain-linked using the Laspeyres formula (1995=100), based on a Household Income Expenditure Survey (HIES, 2002) for the previous year of all resident households, both urban and rural.

Wages:
Information on average monthly wages is derived from monthly reports of large and medium enterprises and quarterly reports of small enterprises engaging in entrepreneurial activity.

International Transactions:

Source: National Statistical Agency. *Exports (line 70..d)* and *Imports, c.i.f. (line 71..d)* exclude informal trade.

Government Finance:

Data are derived from the Ministry of Finance monthly reports on the execution of the state budget. These data cover the general budget, which represents the consolidation of the republican and local budgets. The republican budget covers all the operations of central government entities. The fiscal year ends December 31.

National Accounts:

Source: National Statistical Agency. As indicated by the country, data are compiled according to the recommendations of the *1993 SNA*.

Kenya   664

Date of Fund Membership:

February 3, 1964

Standard Sources:

Central Bank of Kenya
National Bureau of Statistics

Exchange Rates:

Principal Rate (End of Period and Period Average):
Central bank midpoint rate. With the introduction of a foreign exchange bearer certificate scheme (FEBC) in October 1991, a dual exchange rate system is in effect.

International Liquidity:

Gold (National Valuation) (line 1and) is obtained by converting the value in national currency terms, as reported in the country's standard sources, using the prevailing exchange rate, as given in *line ae* or **we**. Data for *line 1d.d* include small foreign exchange holdings by the government.

Central Bank:

Consists of the Central Bank of Kenya (CBK) only. Data are based on a standardized report form (SRF) for central banks, which accords with the concepts and definitions of the IMF's *Monetary and Financial Statistics Manual (MFSM)*, 2000.

Other Depository Corporations:

Comprises commercial banks and nonbank financial institutions, namely the Housing Finance Company of Kenya and Savings and Loans Kenya. Data exclude savings and credit cooperative societies and Post Office Savings Bank. † Beginning in July 2008, data are based on a standardized report form (SRF) for other depository corporations, which accords with the concepts and definitions of the *Monetary and Financial Statistics Manual (MFSM)*. For the period December 2001 through June 2008, data in the SRF format are compiled from pre-SRF data which are not fully based on the *MFSM* methodology.
Financial assets and liabilities for which economic sectorization is unavailable are allocated to the economic sector having the largest volume of transactions in the category.
Foreign Assets includes deposits with the CBK.
Accrued interest is included in *Other Items (Net)* rather than in the outstanding amounts of the financial assets and liabilities.
While the majority of commercial banks value central government securities at acquisition cost plus accrued interest or amortized cost, a few locally owned commercial banks value them at face value.

Depository Corporations:

† See notes on central bank and other depository corporations.

Monetary Aggregates:

Broad Money:
Broad Money calculated from the liability data in the sections for the central bank and other depository corporations accords with the concepts and definitions of the *MFSM* and is consistent with M3 described below.

Money (National Definitions):
Reserve Money comprises currency in circulation and other depository corporations' deposits with the Central Bank of Kenya.
M0 comprises currency outside depository corporations and commercial banks' legal reserve requirements and clearing/settlement accounts with the CBK in national currency.
M1 comprises M0 and demand deposits in national currency of other financial corporations, public nonfinancial corporations, and private sector with other depository corporations.
M2 comprises M1 and time and savings deposits in the national currency of other financial corporations, public nonfinancial corporations, and private sector with other depository corporations.
M3 comprises M2 and foreign currency deposits of other financial corporations, public nonfinancial corporations, and private sector with other depository corporations.

Interest Rates:

Central Bank Policy Rate (End of Period):
Refers to the Central Bank Rate (CBR), which is the lowest rate that the CBK charges on loans to banks. The CBR is reviewed and announced by the Monetary policy Committee at least every two months.

Discount Rate:
Rate that the CBK charges on loans to commercial banks. Refers to the weighted average of interbank interest rates and repurchase agreements (REPO) rates.

Treasury Bill Rate:
Discount rate on three-month treasury bills. † Beginning in January 1990, weighted average rate on 91-day treasury bills.

Savings Rate:
Weighted average rate offered by commercial banks on savings deposits. The rate is weighted by deposit amounts.

Savings Rate (Foreign Currency):
Weighted average rate offered by commercial banks on savings deposits in foreign currency. The rate is weighted by deposit amounts.

Deposit Rate:
Weighted average rate offered by commercial banks on deposits of all maturities. The rate is weighted by deposit amounts.

Deposit Rate (Foreign Currency):
Weighted average rate offered by commercial banks on deposits of all maturities in foreign currency. The rate is weighted by deposit amounts.

Lending Rate:
Weighted average rate charged by commercial banks on loans of all maturities. The rate is weighted by loan amounts.

Lending Rate (Foreign Currency):
Weighted average rate charged by commercial banks on loans of all maturities in foreign currency. The rate is weighted by loan amounts.

Prices, Production, Labor:

Share Prices (End of Month):
Geometric mean of prices of all officially listed ordinary and preferred shares on the Nairobi Stock Exchange (NSE), base 1966.

Consumer Prices:
Source: National Bureau of Statistics. Weights Reference Period: 2005/2006; Geographical Coverage: whole national territory; Number of Items in Basket: 221; Basis for Calculation: 2005/2006 Kenyan Integrated Household Budget Survey (KIHBS). The CPI is computed using the standard Laspeyres index together with geometric averaging at the elementary level and arithmetic averaging at the higher level.

Industrial Production:
Source: National Bureau of Statistics. Quantum index, chained Laspeyers base year weighted index compiled at the 4-digit level of ISIC base 1976.

International Transactions:

Value data on *Exports* and total *Imports* are from source S.
Trade indices are compiled on weights reference period: 1982.

Government Finance:

Data cover the operations of the budgetary central government (including Appropriations-in-Aid) and are as reported by the Central Bank of Kenya. The data are derived from the monthly budget outturn statement prepared by the Ministry of Finance. Beginning in July 1996, revenue data include privatization proceeds, and the statistical discrepancy is identified separately. † Beginning in January 2001, domestic debt is reported on a gross basis and excludes government deposits and treasury advances to parastatals. The fiscal year ends June 30.

National Accounts:

Source: National Bureau of Statistics. From 1996 onward, data have been revised following the implementation of the *1993 SNA*.

Korea, Republic of   542

Date of Fund Membership:
August 26, 1955

Standard Sources:
Statistics Korea (KOSTAT)
Economic Statistics Department

Exchange Rates:

Market Rate (End of Period):
Market closing rate in the interbank foreign exchange market in Seoul.

Market Rate (Period Average):
Average market closing rate during the period in the interbank foreign exchange market in Seoul.

International Liquidity:

Line 1d.d refers only to the Bank of Korea's foreign exchange holdings and to the short-term foreign deposits of other domestic banks which are available to the Bank of Korea on demand. Hence, data exclude the bulk of other banks' foreign exchange holdings which are separately reported in *line 7a.d.* Furthermore, *line 7a.d* includes claims of foreign banks' branches on nonresidents.
Gold (National Valuation) (line 1and) is the U.S. dollar value of official holdings of gold as reported in the country's standard sources.

Central Bank:

Consists of the Bank of Korea (BOK) only. Data are based on a standardized report form (SRF) for central banks which accords with the concepts and definitions of the *Monetary and Financial Statistics Manual (MFSM)*, 2000. Departures from the *MFSM* methodology are explained below.
Financial assets and liabilities for which economic sectorization is unavailable are allocated to the economic sector having the largest volume of transactions in the category. *Claims on Private Sector* includes positions with public nonfinancial corporations. Settlement Accounts which do not have economic sectorization are included in *Other Items (Net)* rather than as claims on or liabilities to economic sectors.
Accrued interest is included in Other Items (Net), rather than in the outstanding amounts of the financial assets and liabilities.
Assets and liabilities denominated in foreign currencies are revalued twice a year, at the end of June and December. The accounting treatment is consistent with the BOK's accounting policies and cannot be amended for monetary statistics purposes unless the accounting rules are changed.

Other Depository Corporations:

Comprises domestically licensed commercial banks; branches of foreign banks; merchant banks; The Export-Import Bank of Korea (Korea Eximbank); financial institutions for agriculture, forestry, and fisheries (Financial group of National Agricultural Cooperative Federation, National Federation of Fisheries Cooperatives, and National Forestry Cooperative Federation); financial institutions for local small business (Savings Banks, Credit Unions, Community Credit Cooperatives); collective investment units which issue beneficiary certificates; and Postal Savings.
Data are based on a standardized report form (SRF) for other depository corporations which accords with the concepts and definitions of the *Monetary and Financial Statistics Manual (MFSM)*. For other depository corporations in Korea, departures from the *MFSM* methodology are explained below.
Financial assets and liabilities for which economic sectorization is unavailable are allocated to the economic sector having the largest volume of transactions in the category. *Claims on Private Sector* includes positions with public nonfinancial corporations.

Settlement Accounts which do not have economic sectorization are included in *Other Items (Net)* rather than as claims on or liabilities to economic sectors.

Depository Corporations:

See notes on central bank and other depository corporations.

Monetary Aggregates:

Broad Money calculated from the liabilities in the sections for the central bank and other depository corporations accords with the concepts and definitions of *Monetary and Financial Statistics Manual (MFSM)* and is consistent with M2 described below.

Money (National Definitions):

M1 (Narrow Money) comprises notes and coins in circulation outside depository corporations and demand and transferable savings deposits of households, nonfinancial corporations, local governments, social security institutions, and other financial corporations with other depository corporations.

M2 (Broad Money) comprises M1 , fixed and installment savings deposits, time deposits, marketable financial instruments(certificates of deposit, repurchase agreements, cover bills), retail money market funds, beneficiary certificates, financial debentures, money in trusts, cash management accounts, and foreign currency deposits of households, nonfinancial corporations, local governments, social security institutions, and other financial corporations with other depository corporations. All of the financial assets included in M2 are those with maturity of less than two years.

Lf (Liquidity of Financial Institutions) comprises M2, life insurance reserves, deposits with the Korea Securities Finance Corporations (money temporarily deposited by investors at financial investment firms for the purchase of equity or the settlement of futures transactions and then fully re-deposited with the Korea Securities Finance Corporation) of households, nonfinancial corporations, local governments, social security institutions, and other financial corporations.

L (Liquidity) comprises Lf, non-life insurance reserves, government bonds, commercial papers, corporate bonds, repurchase agreements issued by securities corporations, and financial debentures issued by Korea Deposit Insurance Corporation, Korea Asset Management Corporation, and credit specialized financial institutions.

Interest Rates:

Data are from Bank of Korea.

Discount Rate (End of Period):

Rate offered by Bank of Korea on eligible commercial paper presented by commercial banks.

Money Market Rate:

Average daily rate on call money, weighted by the volume of transactions.

Corporate Bond Rate:

Through January 1992, yields on 91-day bills issued by enterprises without collateral. Beginning February 1992, data refer to corporate bond rate.

Deposit Rate:

Beginning in July 1984, maximum guideline rate set by the Bank of Korea on time deposits of one year or more with deposit money banks. † From July 1996, the rate is an average, weighted

by the amount of deposits for periods of one year or more but less than two years at nationwide commercial banks.

Lending Rate:

Minimum rate charged to general enterprises by deposit money banks on loans of general funds for up to one year. † From July 1996, the rate is an average, weighted by new loans extended during the period by nationwide commercial banks.

Government Bond Yield:

Arithmetic average of yields, by maturity, on Type 1 National Housing Bonds.

Prices, Production, Labor:

Share Prices (Period Average and End of Month):

Dow Jones Average Index, base January 1975. † Beginning in January 1980, comprises stock prices weighted by total market values, base January 4, 1980.

Producer Prices:

Source: Bank of Korea. Data are disseminated on the Producer Price Index (PPI), a modified Laspeyres index (2010=100), covering all commodities and selected services traded in the domestic market. The index covers about 5,500 price quotes for 884 items, and about 2,000 firms. Commodity weights are based on shipment values and service weights are based on output values for domestic use.

Consumer Prices:

Source: Statistics Korea (KOSTAT). Weights Reference Period: 2010; Geographical Coverage: 37 cities; Number of Items in Basket: 481; Basis for Calculation: Weights are based on Household Income and Expenditure Survey and are updated at approximately five-yearly intervals.

Wages:

Data refer to monthly earnings expressed in won, covering wage earners and salaried employees in nonagricultural sectors. The data are taken from a monthly survey of establishments employing ten or more persons and cover persons working for 45 or more days during the past three-month reporting period.

Industrial Production:

Source: Statistics Korea (KOSTAT). Weights Reference Period: 2010; Sectoral Coverage: mining, manufacturing, electricity and gas, and publishing industries; Basis for Calculation: the weights and index based year are revised every five years.

Manufacturing Employment:

Data refer to persons employed in manufacturing, in thousands.

International Transactions:

Source: Bank of Korea data. The data for imports exclude goods financed by U.S. aid programs and by aid relief from private agencies and include goods for processing that do not come into Korean ownership. The data for exports include the value of these processed goods when they are exported.

Volume of Exports and Imports:

Bank of Korea indices, weights reference period 2010.

Unit Value of Exports and Imports:

Bank of Korea Paasche indices, weights reference period 2005, reported in U.S. dollars and converted to national currency by *IFS*.

Export and Import Prices:

Bank of Korea, all commodities contract basis, weights reference period 2010. The export price index includes 216 items, and the import price index includes 147 items. Prior to 1975, the Fisher ideal formula was used, and from 1975 onwards the Laspeyres formula was used.

Government Finance:

Monthly and quarterly data are derived from Bank of Korea. † Prior to 2001, to the extent possible, existing sub annual *IFS* data were converted to the main aggregates that are presented in the *GFSM 2001* Statement of Sources and Uses of Cash (see the Introduction of the monthly *IFS* publication for details). Beginning in 2001, annual data are as reported for the *Government Finance Statistics Yearbook (GFSY)* and cover the consolidated central government. The fiscal year ends December 31.

National Accounts:

Data are from the Bank of Korea and are seasonally adjusted. As indicated by the country, data follow the implementation of the *1993 SNA*. Annual overlap method is used for the compilation of quarterly real GDP.

Kosovo   967

Date of Fund Membership:

June 29, 2009

Standard Sources:

Central Bank of the Republic of Kosovo
Statistical Office of Kosovo

Exchange Rates:

Market Rate (End of Period and Period Average):
Euro market rate. Beginning on January 1, 2002, the euro is the legal tender and the unit of account in the Republic of Kosovo. The Central Bank of Kosovo does not issue currency. Prior to January 1, 2002, the Deutsche mark was the legal tender. Data prior to January 1, 2002 are converted to euros using the irrevocably fixed rate of 1.95583 Deutsche marks per euro.

International Liquidity:

Foreign Exchange (line 1d.d) comprises the Central Bank of the Republic of Kosovo's foreign currency holdings, liquid correspondent accounts with nonresident banks, and holdings of foreign securities.

Central Bank:

Consists of the Central Bank of the Republic of Kosovo (CBK) only.
Data are based on a standardized report form (SRF) for central banks, which accords with the concepts and definitions of the IMF's *Monetary and Financial Statistics Manual (MFSM)*, 2000. Departures from the *MFSM* methodology are explained below.
Securities other than shares are valued at acquisition cost and valuation to market price or fair value is conducted on an annual basis.

Other Depository Corporations:

Comprises commercial banks.

Data are based on a standardized report form (SRF) for other depository corporations, which accords with the concepts and definitions of the IMF's *Monetary and Financial Statistics Manual (MFSM)*. For other depository corporations in the Republic of Kosovo, departures from the *MFSM* methodology are explained below.
Prior to June 2004, *Transferable* and *Other Deposits Included in Broad Money* exclude deposits of other financial corporations. Held-to-maturity securities other than shares are valued at acquisition cost rather than at current market price or fair value.

Depository Corporations:

See notes on central bank and other depository corporations.

Other Financial Corporations:

Comprises insurance companies, pension funds, microfinance institutions, and assets managers. Data exclude money transfer agencies and exchange bureaus.
Data are based on a standardized report form (SRF) for other financial corporations, which accords with the concepts and definitions of the IMF's *Monetary and Financial Statistics Manual (MFSM)*. For other financial corporations in the Republic of Kosovo, departures from the *MFSM* methodology are listed below.
Data are only available on a quarterly basis.
Held-to-maturity securities other than shares are valued at acquisition cost rather than at current market price or fair value.

Financial Corporations:

See notes on central bank, other depository corporations, and other financial corporations.

Interest Rates:

Treasury Bill Rate:
Rate on short-term government securities issued in the primary market through single price auctions.

Deposit Rate:
Weighted average rate offered by commercial banks on deposits of nonfinancial corporations and households in euros. The rate is weighted by new nontransferable deposits issued during the reference period and by end-of-period outstanding amount of transferable and savings deposits of households.

Lending Rate:
Weighted average rate offered by commercial banks on loans in euros. The rate is weighted by new loans granted during the reference period and by end-of-period outstanding amount of overdrafts.

Prices:

Producer Prices:
Statistical Office of Kosovo. Weights reference period: 2007; Number of Items in Basket: 280 products; Sectoral Coverage: mining and quarrying, manufacturing, electricity, gas and water supply; Basis for Calculation: the index covers 11,066 monthly prices collected directly from more than 3,544 enterprises.

Consumer Prices:
Source: Statistical Office of Kosovo. Weight Reference Period: 2008; Geographical Coverage: in rural and urban areas of 13 municipalities; Number of Items in Basket: 198 articles and services; Basis for Calculation: weights are based on the concept and definitions of household consumption that are generally consistent with the CPI Manual 2004.

International Transactions:

Exports and Imports:
Source: Statistical Office of Kosovo, provided by Kosovo Customs Service and the Kosovo Energy Corporation. Export data are provided on an f.o.b. basis, Imports are provided on a c.i.f. basis.

National Accounts:

Source: Statistical Office of Kosovo. As indicated by the country, data are compiled in accordance with the methodology of the *1995 ESA* and the *1993 SNA*.

Kuwait   443

Date of Fund Membership:
September 13, 1962

Standard Sources:
Central Bank of Kuwait
Central Statistical Office

Exchange Rates:

Official Rate: (End of Period and Period Average):
Central bank midpoint rate. The exchange rate is determined on the basis of a fixed but adjustable relationship with a weighted basket of currencies.

International Liquidity:

Gold (National Valuation) (line 1and) is obtained by converting the value in national currency terms, as reported in the country's standard sources, using the prevailing exchange rate, as given in *line* **dg** or *line* **ag**.

Central Bank:

Consists of the Central Bank of Kuwait (CBK) only.
Data are based on a standardized report form (SRF) for central banks, which accords with the concepts and definitions of the IMF's *Monetary and Financial Statistics Manual (MFSM)*, 2000. Departures from the MFSM methodology are explained below.
Accrued interest is included in *Other Items (Net)* rather than in the outstanding amounts of the financial assets and liabilities.
Monetary gold is recorded at book value rather than at current market price.

Other Depository Corporations:

Comprises commercial, specialized, and Islamic banks. Data exclude investment companies (conventional investment companies and those working according to Islamic sharia), which accept deposits.
Data are based on a standardized report form (SRF) for other depository corporations, which accords with the concepts and definitions of the IMF's *Monetary and Financial Statistics Manual (MFSM)*. For other depository corporations in Kuwait, departures from the MFSM methodology are explained below.
Financial derivatives are excluded from the data.
Negotiable certificates of deposit issued by other depository corporations held by resident sectors, other than other depository corporations and central government., are included in *Other Deposits Included in Broad Money* rather than in *Securities Other than Shares Included in Broad Money*.
Accrued interest is included in *Other Items (Net)* rather than in the outstanding amounts of the financial assets and liabilities.

Depository Corporations:

See notes on central bank and other depository corporations.

Other Financial Corporations:

Comprises conventional and Islamic investment companies. Data include a number of investment companies that accept deposits from resident sectors, other than depository corporations and central government.

Monetary Aggregates:

Broad Money:
Broad Money calculated from the liability data in the sections for the central bank and other depository corporations accords with the concepts and definitions of the *MFSM* and differs from M3 as M3 includes deposits of the private sector with investment companies.

Money (National Definitions):
Monetary Base (M0) comprises currency issued, demand and time deposits of banks and other resident financial corporations with the CBK, and bonds issued by the CBK held by banks and investment companies.
M1 comprises currency in circulation with the public and sight deposits in national currency of resident sectors, other than depository corporations and central government, with banks.
Currency in circulation is the currency issued by the CBK less the currency in the vaults of banks.
M2 comprises M1 and Quasi-Money. *Quasi-Money* comprises time and savings deposits in national currency and foreign currency deposits of resident sectors, other than depository corporations and central government, with depository corporations and certificates of deposit in national currency issued by banks held by other resident sectors, other than depository corporations and central government. Certificates of deposit comprise negotiable financial papers.
M3 comprises M2 and deposits of the private sector with investment companies.

Interest Rates:

Discount Rate (End of Period):
CBK's discount rate on three-month commercial paper.

Money Market Rate:
Average of daily bid and offer quotations for the interbank rate on three-month deposits in national currency. The rate is freely determined by the market. The rate on certificates of deposit fluctuates in line with, but is generally slightly lower than, the interbank deposit rate. Rates on time deposits with commercial banks are market determined and also vary with the interbank rate.

Treasury Bill Rate:
Average of maximum acceptable interest rates set by the CBK for three-month treasury bills sold at weekly auctions.

Deposit Rate:
Weighted average rate offered by commercial and specialized banks on all deposits of residents and nonresidents in national currency. The rate is weighted by deposit amounts.

Lending Rate:

Weighted average rate charged by commercial and specialized banks on credit facilities extended to residents and nonresidents in national currency.

Prices, Production, Labor:

Share Prices (End of Month):

Share price index, base January 1, 1976. † Beginning in August 1985, share price index of the Kuwait Stock Exchange (KSE), base December 29, 1993. The index is the arithmetic average of each session's share prices as quoted by the KSE.

Consumer Prices:

Source: Central Bank of Kuwait. Weights Reference Period: 2000; Geographical Coverage: whole national territory; Basis for Calculation: weights are derived from the 1999–2000 Household Expenditure Surveys.

Producer Prices:

Source: Central Bank of Kuwait. Weights Reference Period: 1980–82; Coverage: Manufacturing, Agriculture, Mining and Quarrying; Number of Items in Basket: 469; Basis for Calculation: weights were determined on the basis of imports and domestic production for the years 1980–82.

Crude Petroleum Production:

Central Bank of Kuwait data updated for current periods using petroleum quantities as reported in the *Oil Market Intelligence*. Data include Kuwaiti share (50 percent) of Neutral Zone oil production.

International Transactions:

Exports and Imports, c.i.f.:

All data are from Central Bank of Kuwait. Data on oil exports exclude gas prior to 1970.

International Investment Position:

Data on IIP assets exclude the external assets held by the general government for which the dissemination is restricted due to legal constraints. However, loans granted by the Kuwaiti Fund for Arab Economic Development (KFAED) and general government trade credits are included.

Government Finance:

Data are derived from Central Bank of Kuwait and cover the operations of the budgetary central government. The fiscal year ends June 30.

National Accounts:

Source: Central Bank of Kuwait.

Kyrgyz Republic   917

Date of Fund Membership:

May 8, 1992

Standard Sources:

National Bank of the Kyrgyz Republic
Ministry of Finance
National Statistical Committee

Exchange Rates:

The som was introduced on May 10, 1993 and replaced the Russian ruble at the rate of SOM1=RR200.

Official Rate: (End of Period and Period Average):

All data in this section are from the National Bank of the Kyrgyz Republic. The official rate is determined as the average volume-weighted exchange rate recorded at foreign exchange auctions held by the National Bank of the Kyrgyz Republic. Auctions are held each business Friday (Wednesday and Friday during 1994–96). The end-of-period rate is determined at the last auction of the reference period. The period-average rate is equal to the simple average of the official exchange rates recorded during auctions held during the reference period.

International Liquidity:

Foreign Exchange (line 1d.d) comprises the National Bank of the Kyrgyz Republic's cash, liquid correspondent accounts with nonresident banks, and foreign government securities.

Monetary Authorities:

Comprises the National Bank of the Kyrgyz Republic only. General government comprises central and local governments and their extrabudgetary funds, excluding the state Social Fund.

Banking Institutions:

Consolidated accounts of the commercial banks and the Settlement Savings Corporation. General government comprises central and local governments and their extrabudgetary funds, except the state Social Fund.

Money (National Definitions):

M1 comprises currency in circulation and demand deposits in national currency of other financial corporations, state and local governments, public nonfinancial corporations, and private sector with commercial banks. Currency in circulation refers to notes and coins issued by the National Bank of the Kyrgyz Republic (NBKR) less the amount held by commercial banks.

M2 comprises M1 plus time and savings deposits in national currency of other financial corporations, state and local governments, public nonfinancial corporations, and private sector with commercial banks.

M2x comprises M2 plus foreign currency deposits of other financial corporations, state and local governments, public nonfinancial corporations, and private sector with commercial banks.

Interest Rates:

Central Bank Policy Rate (End of Period):

Discount rate used as a major benchmark when determining the value of monetary resources in the economy. The size of the discount rate is linked to the yield of the NBKR's last four auctions of 28-day notes established by weekly auctions of the NBKR's notes.

Lombard Rate (line 60.a):

Rate at which the National Bank of the Kyrgyz Republic extends overnight loans in soms to banks. Calculated on the basis of interest rates on short-term repurchase transactions in the secondary market.

Money Market Rate (line 60b):

Weighted-average rate on interbank loans in soms with maturities of 1 to 90 days. It does not reflect transactions in the interbank repurchase market.

Treasury Bill Rate (line 60c):

Weighted average rate on 3-month treasury bills sold in the primary market.

Deposit Rate (line 60l):

Weighted average rate offered on som time deposits of one- to three-month maturities.

Lending Rate (line 60p):

Weighted average rate on loans in soms for one- to three-month maturities.

Prices:

Producer Prices:

Source: National Statistical Committee. Weights Reference Period: updated annually; Coverage: covering 3 main sectors of industry, 16 subsectors, and 23 groups; Number of Items in the Basket: around 289 price quotes are obtained monthly for 263 selected items; Basis for Calculation: a Laspeyres index (2010=100) with the production volume of the previous year being used as weights. The weights are updated annually in June on the basis of the annual production survey of enterprises.

Consumer Prices:

Source: National Statistical Committee. Base Year: updated annually; Geographical Coverage: Covers eight main cities and one district (Moskovskiy); Number of Items in Basket: 348 items; Basis for Calculation: Laspeyres index (2009=100) based on yearly data from the household budget survey, the weights are updated annually in June. When the weights are updated, a recalculation is performed for previous years by means of a correction factor.

International Transactions:

The data in this section are from sources B and S. *Exports (line 70)* and *Imports, c.i.f. (line 71):* Exports and imports (c.i.f.) are compiled from the monthly customs statistics and from the monthly and quarterly report forms submitted by enterprises. Adjustments to the customs data are made to account for humanitarian aid, 'shuttle' trade, barter trade, and the exports and imports of electricity and gas.

Government Finance:

The data in this section are from the Ministry of Finance. The monthly and annual data are derived from the reports of the central treasury that cover the cumulative cash transactions of the budgetary central and local governments. The data exclude the transactions of the social fund (earlier the insurance, employment, and pension funds) and other extrabudgetary units. The fiscal year ends December 31.

National Accounts:

Source: National Statistical Committee. As indicated by the country, the data are compiled in accordance with *1993 SNA* methodology.

Lao People's Dem.Rep   544

Date of Fund Membership:

July 5, 1961

Standard Source:

Ministry of Finance
Bank of Lao P.D.R.

Exchange Rates:

Prior to September 1995, data refer to the midpoint between the buying and selling rates quoted by the Bank of Lao P.D.R. In September 1995, a floating exchange rate policy was adopted, and the commercial banks were allowed to set their rates. Data beginning in September 1995 refer to the simple average of midpoint rates reported by the commercial banks on a daily basis, covering their transactions for the previous day.

Monetary Authorities:

Comprises the Bank of Lao P.D.R., which undertakes all monetary authority functions.

Deposit Money Banks:

Comprises commercial banks, which include state-owned banks, joint venture banks, and branches of foreign banks.

Monetary Survey:

Money (line 34) is the sum of *lines 14a* and *24* and demand deposits of the nonfinancial public enterprises and private sector with the monetary authorities.

Interest Rates:

Discount Rate (End of Period):
The lending rate of the Bank of Lao P.D.R.

Treasury Bill Rate:
Weighted average auction rate for 6-month treasury bills during the last auction of the month. Beginning in December 1997, weighted average auction rate for treasury bills with 12-month maturity.

Deposit Rate:
Minimum rate fixed by the Bank of Lao P.D.R. on commercial banks' three-month domestic-currency time deposits.

Lending Rate:
Prior to August 1995, data refer to the maximum rate set by the Bank of Lao P.D.R. for commercial banks' nonagricultural loans. The lending rate was liberalized in July 1995; data beginning August 1995 refer to the highest rate quoted by the commercial banks on nonagricultural loans.

Prices:

Consumer Prices:
Source: Bank of Lao P.D.R. Weights Reference Period: December 2010; Geographical Coverage: prices for most of these items are collected on a daily basis in Vientiane; Number of Items in the Basket: 197 items classified in 9 goods components; Basis for Calculation: using weights derived from a household budget survey.

Government Finance:

Source: Ministry of Finance. Beginning October 2007 data cover the operations of the budgetary central government. Local governments are nonautonomous and their operations are included.

Latvia   941

Date of Fund Membership:

May 19, 1992

Standard Sources:

Bank of Latvia
Central Statistical Bureau of Latvia
Eurostat

Exchange Rates:

Official Rate: (End of Period and Period Average):
Bank of Latvia midpoint rate. Rates quoted by banks and moneychangers closely follow the Bank of Latvia rate. The official rate is pegged to the SDR.

International Liquidity:

Data for *Foreign Exchange (line 1d.d)* comprise the Bank of Latvia's external assets that are readily available to and controlled by the Bank of Latvia for direct financing of payment imbalances, for indirectly regulating the magnitude of such imbalances through intervention in exchange markets to affect the currency exchange rate, and/or for other purposes.

Gold (National Valuation) (line 1and): Gold reserves were valued at 175.50 lats per troy ounce between April 28, 1997 – March 30, 1999. As of March 31, 1999, gold reserves are valued at market price. The periodicity of gold revaluation is daily.

Central Bank:

Consists of the Bank of Latvia only.
† Beginning in March 2003, data are compiled in accordance with the European Central Bank's framework for monetary statistics using the national residency approach.
For December 2001 to February 2003, data do not fully conform with the European Central Bank's framework for monetary statistics and are not strictly comparable to the data for later periods.

Other Depository Corporations:

Comprises all resident units sectorized as other monetary financial institutions (MFIs), in accordance with *1995 ESA* standards (i.e. licensed banks with domestic headquarters, branches of foreign banks, and credit unions). Data exclude liquid investment companies (i.e. money market mutual funds).
† Beginning in March 2003, data are compiled in accordance with the European Central Bank's framework for monetary statistics using the national residency approach.
For December 2001 to February 2003, data do not fully conform with the European Central Bank's framework for monetary statistics and are not strictly comparable to the data for later periods.

Depository Corporations:

† See notes on central bank and other despository corporations.

Monetary Aggregates:

Broad Money:
Broad Money calculated from the liability data in the sections for the central bank and other depository corporations is consistent with M3 described below.

Money (National Definitions):
M1 comprises currency outside MFIs and overnight deposits with the MFIs.
M2 comprises M1, deposits with agreed maturity of up to two years, and deposits redeemable at notice of up to three months with the MFIs.
M3 comprises M2, repurchase agreements with the MFIs, money market fund shares/units, and debt securities issued by the MFIs with maturity of up to two years.

Interest Rates:

Discount Rate (End of Period):
The Bank of Latvia sets the refinancing rate as a reference rate for the banking system. This rate serves as a general guide for the money market and is not used in monetary operations.

Money Market Rate:
Weighted average rate on overnight loans in national currency transacted in the interbank market. The rate is weighted by loan amounts.

Treasury Bill Rate:
Weighted average auction rate on 91-day treasury bills. † Beginning in January 2000, weighted average auction rate on six-month treasury bills.

Deposit Rate:
Weighted average rate offered by other depository corporations on deposits of less than one year in national currency. Rate is weighted by deposit amounts.

Lending Rate:
Weighted average rate charged by other depository corporations on loans of less than one year in national currency to enterprises and individuals. Rate is weighted by loan amounts.

Government Bond Yield:
Secondary market yields of government bonds with a 10-year maturity. This rate is used to measure long-term interest rates for assessing convergence among the European Union member states.

Prices, Production, Labor:

Share Prices:
Dow Jones Riga Stock Exchange (RSE) index, base April 2, 1996. The index covers common shares traded in the RSE and is weighted by market capitalization. The index is limited to shares whose market value is greater than one million Latvian lats. However, the component companies are adjusted to ensure that only the largest and most actively traded shares are included. The monthly index is calculated from the average of the daily closing quotations. † Beginning January 2001, data refer to the OMX Riga Index, base January 1, 2000. The index is a capitalization weighted chain-linked total-return index calculated on a continuous basis from the most recent prices of all shares listed on the Riga Stock Exchange's Main list and I-List.

Producer Prices:

Source: Central Statistical Bureau of Latvia. Weights Reference Period: Calendar year 2011; Sectoral Coverage: Mining and quarrying, manufacturing, electricity, gas, steam and water supply, sewerage and waste management; Number of Items in Basket: 730 enterprises; Basis for Calculation: Weights are derived from the annual survey on enterprise economic activity and covers all economically active enterprises in 2011.

Consumer Prices:

Source: Central Statistical Bureau of Latvia. Weights Reference Period: 4th quarter of 2011 to the 3rd quarter of 2012; Geographical Coverage: Riga and 11 other towns and cities; Number of Items in Basket: 501; Basis for Calculation: weights are based on continuous Household Budget Survey and are updated at approximately one-yearly intervals.

Industrial Production:

Source: Central Statistical Bureau of Latvia. Weights Reference Period: Calendar year T–2; Sectoral Coverage: starting in 1996, mining and quarrying, manufacturing, electricity, gas and steam, and construction; Number of Items in Basket: 1.323 units; Basis for Calculation: weights are based on gross value added to factor costs derived from structural statistics and applied to quantity relatives or, in some cases, to deflated value relatives.

Industrial Employment and Wages:

Source: Central Statistical Bureau of Latvia. Data are based on information obtained from quarterly enterprise surveys. Industrial employment data cover employees in the main job. Wage data comprise wages and salaries to employees in the main job before personal income tax deductions and social security contributions. The latter are payable by employees, while being deducted and transferred to the state budget by the employer. Wage data exclude remuneration in kind. Data are obtained from all public sector institutions and enterprises and all private companies with 50 employees and more.

International Transactions:

Exports and Imports:

Source: Central Statistical Bureau of Latvia. The special trade system of recording trade transactions is used. Revisions to quarterly data are not apportioned among monthly data. Data include, in addition to those recorded in the customs statistics, estimates of imports of electricity and natural gas each month and quarterly estimates of extraterritorial trade from fishing vessels. Through 1994, the data also include quarterly information on supplies to Russian troops stationed in Latvia and adjustments (based on estimates of consumption) for mineral fuel imports that were not reflected in customs declarations. The volume index for exports is an annual chain-linked Laspeyres index for merchandise trade.

Government Finance:

Monthly, quarterly, and annual cash data are as reported by the Treasury. Data cover the consolidated central government. However, data on grants from some foreign assistance programs are excluded. † Data prior to 1996 cover the budgetary central government only. † From January through March 1996, data cover the budgetary central government and the Social Security Fund. † From 1997 onwards, expenditure on education and health

functions was shifted within components of central government and between local government and central government. † Prior to 1998, data reported for *IFS* are not consolidated. The data are consolidated beginning with the data for January 1998. Data on general government are derived from source V. The fiscal year ends December 31.

National Accounts:

Source: Eurostat. As indicated by the country, data are compiled in accordance with the methodology of the *1995 ESA*. Beginning in 1999, data are sourced from the Eurostat database. Chain linked GDP volume measures are expressed according to 2005 prices.

Lebanon   446

Date of Fund Membership:
April 14, 1947

Standard Source:
Bank of Lebanon
Central Administration for Statistics

Exchange Rates:
Market Rate (End of Period and Period Average):
Closing midpoint rate in Beirut.

International Liquidity:
Gold (National Valuation) (line 1and) is obtained by converting the value in national currency terms, as reported in the country's standard sources, using the prevailing exchange rate, as given in *line* **ae** or **we**.

Monetary Authorities:
Consolidates the Bank of Lebanon (BDL) and monetary authority functions undertaken by the central government. The contra-entry to Treasury IMF accounts is included in *line 12a.*

Deposit Money Banks:
Comprises approximately 70 operating commercial banks.

Money (National Definitions):
M1 refers to currency in circulation and demand deposits in national currency of the private sector with the BDL and commercial banks. Currency in circulation refers to notes and coins issued by the BDL less the amount held by commercial banks.
M2 refers to M1 plus time and savings deposits in national currency of the private sector with the BDL and commercial banks.
M3 refers to M2 plus foreign currency deposits of the private sector with the BDL and commercial banks and bonds issued by commercial banks held by the private sector.
M4 refers to M3 plus treasury bills held by the nonbank private sector.

Interest Rates:
Discount Rate (End of Period):
Rate charged by the BDL to discount advances and paper offered by the commercial banks. Since June 7, 1985, the discount rate

has been formally linked to treasury bill rates and commercial bill rates. The discount rate has not been used extensively as an instrument of monetary policy, because discounting by the commercial banks with the BDL occurs very rarely and in relatively small amounts.

Treasury Bill Rate:

Average yield on newly issued three-month treasury bills. † Beginning January 1987, secondary market yield on three-month treasury bills determined by the BDL.

Deposit Rate:

Average rate offered by commercial banks on fixed-term deposits.

Lending Rate:

Average rate charged by commercial banks on loans and advances.

Prices:

Share Prices (End of Month):

BDL index, base January 1996. The BDL index is a market value weighted index of all listed companies on the Beirut Stock Exchange.

Consumer Prices:

Source: Central Administration for Statistics. Weights Reference Period: 2007; Geographical Coverage: whole country; Number of items in basket: 334; Basis for calculation: Chained Laspeyres Index, the weighting structure is based on the household expenditure survey conducted in 2007.

International Transactions:

Prior to 1993, exports were taken from Statistical Office data on total exports minus *Government Finance Statistics Yearbook (GFSY)* data on bank notes and coin exports. Imports, c.i.f. were Statistical Office data on total imports minus *GFSY* data on bank notes and coin imports. Beginning in 1993, the source of the data is the Customs Directorate of the Ministry of Finance. Exports are based on the *official dollar rate,* which is the previous month's average for the U.S. dollar. Imports are calculated using the *customs dollar rate.* From January 1, 1991 though May 15, 1991, the customs dollar rate was equal to 6 Lebanese pounds (LL). From May 16, 1991 through December 31, 1991 the customs dollar rate was equal to 100 LL. From January 1, 1992 through July 15, 1992 it was equal to 200 LL. From July 1992 through July 1995 it was fixed at 800 LL, and since July 15, 1995 the customs dollar rate has been equalized to the official dollar rate. Export values exclude re-export data.

Government Finance:

Prior to 2000, annual data are as reported for the *Government Finance Statistics Yearbook (GFSY)* and cover budgetary central government. † Since 2000, to the extent possible, existing subannual *IFS* data were converted to the main aggregates that are presented in the *GFSM 2001* Statement of Sources and Uses of Cash (see the Introduction of the monthly *IFS* publication for details). The fiscal year ends December 31.

National Accounts:

Source: Central Administration for Statistics. As indicated by the country, the national accounts are compiled according to the recommendations of the *1993 SNA.*

Lesotho   666

Date of Fund Membership:
July 25, 1968

Standard Sources:
Central Bank of Lesotho
Bureau of Statistics

Exchange Rates:
The loti is at par with the South African rand (see notes on South Africa page for description of exchange rates).

Central Bank:
Consists of the Central Bank of Lesotho (CBL) only.

Data are based on a standardized report form (SRF) for central banks, which broadly accords with the concepts and definitions of the IMF's *Monetary and Financial Statistics Manual (MFSM)*, 2000.

Beginning in January 2011, data are based on improved source data better aligned to the *MFSM* methodology. Departures from the *MFSM* methodology are explained below.

Held-to-maturity securities are valued at amortized cost rather than current market price or fair value.

For December 2001 through December 2010, accrued interest is included in *Other Items (Net)* rather than in the outstanding amounts of the financial assets and liabilities. Beginning in January 2011, accrued interest not disaggregated by financial instrument and/or economic sector is allocated either to the position having the largest share in the category or distributed proportionally to all positions in the category.

Other Depository Corporations:
Comprises commercial banks.

Data are based on a standardized report form (SRF) for other depository corporations, which accords with the concepts and definitions of the *Monetary and Financial Statistics Manual (MFSM)*.

Beginning in January 2011, data are based on improved source data better aligned to the *MFSM* methodology. For other depository corporations in Lesotho, departures from the *MFSM* methodology are explained below.

Held-to-maturity securities are valued at amortized cost rather than current market price or fair value.

Financial assets for which economic sectorization is unavailable are allocated to the economic sector having the largest volume of transactions in that category.

For December 2001 through December 2010, accrued interest is included in *Other Items (Net)* rather than in the outstanding amounts of the financial assets and liabilities. Beginning in January 2011, accrued interest not disaggregated by financial instrument and/or economic sector is allocated either to the position having the largest volume of transactions in the category or distributed proportionally to all positions in the category.

Depository Corporations:
See notes on central bank and other depository corporations.

Monetary Aggregates:

Broad Money:

Broad Money calculated from the liability data in the sections for the central bank and other depository corporations is in accordance with the concepts and definitions of the *MFSM* and is consistent with M2, as described below.

Money (National Definitions):

M1 comprises notes and coins in circulation outside depository corporations, demand and call deposits of other financial corporations, local governments, public nonfinancial corporations, and private sector with depository corporations, and some demand deposits of the central government with the CBL. † Beginning in January 2011, comprises notes and coins in circulation outside depository corporations and demand deposits of other financial corporations, local governments, public nonfinancial corporations, and private sector with depository corporations.

Quasi-money comprises time and savings deposits of other financial corporations, local governments, public nonfinancial corporations, and private sector with depository corporations. † Beginning in January 2011, comprises call, time, and savings deposits of other financial corporations, local governments, public nonfinancial corporations, and private sector with depository corporations.

M2 (Money Supply) comprises M1 and quasi-money. † See notes on M1 and quasi-money.

Interest Rates:

Discount Rate (End of Period):

Basic rate at which the Central Bank of Lesotho lends to commercial banks.

Treasury Bill Rate:

Average rate on treasury bills. † Beginning in April 1993 average rate of three issues of 91-day treasury bills. The rate is determined through securities auctions by the CBL.

Savings Rate:

Maximum rate offered by commercial banks on savings deposits.

Deposit Rate:

Rate prevailing at or near the end of the month for 88-day deposits.

Lending Rate:

Rate charged by banks to most creditworthy customers at or near the end of the month.

Prices:

Consumer Prices:

Source: Bureau of Statistics. Weights Reference Period: March 2010; Geographical Coverage: twelve urban towns and forty-five selected rural areas. Number of items in basket: approximately 200; Basis for Calculation: Household Budget Surveys of 2002/03.

International Transactions:

All trade value data are from Central Bank of Lesotho. *Imports, c.i.f.* include customs duties and are therefore not comparable to corresponding balance of payments data.

Government Finance:

Quarterly data are as reported by the Ministry of Finance and cover the budgetary central government. The fiscal year ends March 31.

National Accounts:

Source: Bureau of Statistics. Data are prepared in accordance with the 1993 United Nations System of National Accounts.

Liberia   668

Date of Fund Membership:

March 28, 1962

Standard Sources:

Central Bank of Liberia
Ministry of Planning and Economic Affairs

Exchange Rates:

Market Rate (End of Period and Period Average):

Until December 1997, rates are based on a fixed relationship with the U.S. dollar. † Beginning in January 1998, rates are market determined.

International Liquidity:

Small holdings of gold, including commemorative coins, are not shown separately.

Monetary Authorities:

Consolidates the Central Bank of Liberia, which replaced the National Bank of Liberia in October 1999 and monetary authority functions undertaken by the central government. The contra-entry to Treasury IMF accounts is included in *line 12a.* † Beginning in December 1980, data are based on a new reporting system. † Beginning in January 2000, data are based on an improved sectorization and classification of the accounts.

Banking Institutions:

Comprises commercial banks. † See note on monetary authorities.

Banking Survey:

† See note on monetary authorities.

Money (National Definitions):

M1 comprises Liberian dollar notes and coins in circulation outside the banking system and demand deposits of the private sector, nonfinancial public corporations, and nonbank financial institutions at commercial banks in national and foreign currency. *M2* comprises M1 plus time and savings deposits of the private sector, nonfinancial public corporations, and nonbank financial institutions at commercial banks in national and foreign currency.

Interest Rates:

Savings Rate:

Average rate offered by commercial banks on saving deposits.

Deposit Rate:

Average rate offered by commercial banks on time deposits.

Lending Rate:

Average rate offered by commercial banks on overdrafts. † Beginning in January 1998, average rate offered by commercial banks on all loans.

Prices:

Consumer Prices:

Source: Ministry of Planning and Economic Affairs. Weights Reference Period: 1964; Geographical Coverage: Capital city of Monrovia (households composed of two or more persons and headed by urban wage earners and clerical workers whose monthly income do not exceed US$250.00); Number of Items in Basket: 235; Basis for Calculation: the weights are derived from the 1964 Household Budget Survey. The index does not incorporate the imputed rents of owner-occupied dwellings, but actual rents are included.

Libya   672

Data refer to the Socialist People's Libyan Arab Jamahiriya.

Date of Fund Membership:
September 17, 1958

Standard Sources:
General Directorate for Economic and Social Planning
Central Bank of Libya
Census and Statistics Directorate

Exchange Rates:

Official Rate (End of Period):
Central bank midpoint rate. The official rate is pegged to the SDR.

International Liquidity:

Gold (National Valuation) (line 1and) is obtained by converting the value in national currency terms, as reported in the country's standard sources, using the prevailing exchange rate, as given in *line* **ag** or *line* **wg**.
Foreign nonbank components of *lines 7a.d* and *7b.d* are small and are not reported separately.

Monetary Authorities:

Comprises the Central Bank of Libya (CBL). † Prior to March 2002, *Claims on Nonfinancial Public Enterprises (line 12c)* include positions arising from contingent operations such as issuance of letters of credit and guarantees; the contra-entries to these positions are in *Foreign Liabilities (line 16c), Time, and Foreign Currency Deposits (line 15),* and *Other Items (net) (line 17r).* † Beginning in June 1997, data are based on improved reporting and classification of accounts.

Deposit Money Banks:

Comprises commercial banks including, since December 2000, the regional (ahlia) banks. † From June 1997 to February 2002, *Claims on Nonfinancial Public Enterprises (line 22c)* include positions arising from contingent operations such as issuance of letters of credit and guarantees; the contra-entries to these positions are in *Foreign Liabilities (line 26c)* and *Other Items (net) (line 27r).* † Prior to January 1999, some central government time deposits are included in *Time and Foreign Currency Deposits (line 25).*

Monetary Survey:

† See notes on monetary authorities and deposit money banks.

Other Banking Institutions:

Comprise the Development Bank, the Agricultural Bank, and the Savings and Real Estate Investment Bank. † Prior to 1991, data refer to the National Agricultural Bank.

Money (National Definitions):

Monetary Base comprises currency issued by the CBL, banks' deposits and public enterprises' demand deposits with the CBL.
Money comprises currency in circulation and demand deposits of non-bank non-government resident sectors. Currency in circulation refers to currency issued by the CBL minus currency in banks' vaults.
Quasi-Money comprises time, saving and foreign currency deposits of non-bank non-government resident sectors, and margin deposits for letters of credit and letters of guarantee.

Interest Rates:

All interest rate data are from Central Bank of Libya. With the exception of *Discount Rate (End of Period),* all interest rate data are period averages.

Discount Rate (End of Period):
The rate applies to rediscounts of eligible commercial paper to banks by the Bank of Libya. Ceilings are established by the Bank of Libya for each commercial bank not exceeding 20 percent of its capital and reserves or 10 percent of its deposits, whichever is lower. Borrowing from the Bank is a privilege granted to banks at the discretion of the Central Bank, and the volume of discounts is limited.

Money Market Rate:
Maximum rate on interbank call loans.

Deposit Rate:
Maximum rate on six-month fixed deposits at commercial banks.

Lending Rate:
Maximum rate on secured loans and overdrafts.

Prices and Production:

Consumer Prices:
Source: Census and Statistics Directorate. Weights Reference Period: 2003; Geographical Coverage: Capital City Tripoli; Basis for Calculation: expenditure data collected during the 2003 Household Expenditure Survey (HES).

Crude Petroleum Production:
Index constructed from Central Bank of Libya data. If uncurrent, the index is calculated from production quantities reported in the *Oil Market Intelligence.*

International Transactions:

All trade data are from the Census and Statistics Directorate.

National Accounts:

Source: General Directorate for Economic and Social Planning.

Lithuania   946

Date of Fund Membership:
April 29, 1992

Standard Sources:
Bank of Lithuania
Lithuanian Department of Statistics

Exchange Rates:

The talons replaced the ruble in October 1992 at the rate of RUB 1 = LTT 1. The litas replaced the talonas in June 1993 at the rate of LTT 100 = LTL 1.

Official Rate: (End of Period and Period Average):
The official exchange rate of the litas is set by resolution of the Bank of Lithuania's Board. Until February 1, 2002, the anchor currency of the litas was the U.S. dollar. Effective February 2, 2002, the litas are pegged to the euro.

International Liquidity:

Until November 1997 gold was valued at US$333 per fine troy ounce. Between December 1997 and November 1998, gold was valued at US$283 per fine troy ounce. Beginning in December 1998, gold is valued at US$273.4 per fine troy ounce in national sources. Since December 2001, the gold holdings have been revalued once per month on the last working day at the value of London gold price fixing. Previously, gold was revalued once per year on the last working day at the lowest gold price fixing during the year, if that value was lower than the book value.

Central Bank:

Consists of the Bank of Lithuania only.
† Beginning in March 2004, data are compiled in accordance with the European Central Bank's framework for monetary statistics using the national residency approach.
Prior to March 2004, data do not fully conform with the European Central Bank's framework for monetary statistics and are not strictly comparable to the data for later periods.

Other Depository Corporations:

Comprises commercial banks, branches of foreign banks, and credit unions.
† Beginning in March 2004, data are compiled in accordance with the European Central Bank's framework for monetary statistics using the national residency approach. Prior to March 2004, data do not fully conform with the European Central Bank's framework for monetary statistics and are not strictly comparable to the data for later periods.

Depository Corporations:

† See notes on central bank and other depository corporations.

Monetary Aggregates:

Broad Money:
Broad Money is calculated from the liability data in the sections for the central bank and other depository corporations.

Money (National Definitions):
Base Money comprises currency in circulation and deposits of resident sectors at the Bank of Lithuania excluding deposits of central and other general government.
M1 comprises currency held by the public and demand deposits of the private sector, public nonfinancial corporations, and other financial corporations with the Bank of Lithuania and other depository corporations. † Beginning in March 2004, M1 comprises currency in circulation and overnight deposits with monetary financial institutions (MFIs) of the non-central government, non-MFI resident sectors.
M2 comprises M1 and time, savings, and foreign currency deposits of the private sector, public nonfinancial corporations, and other financial corporations with the Bank of Lithuania and other depository corporations. † Beginning in March 2004, M2

comprises M1and deposits with agreed maturity up to two years and deposits redeemable at notice up to three months of the non-central government, non-MFI resident sectors with resident MFIs.
M3 comprise M2 and marketable instruments issued by MFIs, namely repurchase agreements contracted by MFIs with non-central government non-MFI resident sectors, and money market fund shares/units and debt securities with maturity up to two years issued by MFIs to non-central government, non-MFI resident sectors.

Interest Rates:

Repurchase Agreement Rate (End of Period):
Bank of Lithuania rate on overnight repurchase agreements.

Money Market Rate:
Average rate on interbank credit with maturities of up to one month. † Beginning in January 1998, average rate on one-day contracts between resident banks in national currency.

Money Market Rate (Foreign Currency):
Average rate on one-day contracts between resident banks in foreign currency.

Savings Rate:
Average rate offered by banks on savings deposits in national currency.

Savings Rate (Foreign Currency):
Average rate offered by banks on savings deposits in foreign currency.

Treasury Bill Rate:
Average auction rate on 91-day treasury bills. † Beginning in January 2000, average auction rate on one-year treasury bills.

Deposit Rate:
Average of rates offered by banks on time deposits of residents in national currency weighted by volume. † Beginning in January 2005, average of rates on new time deposits of households and nonfinancial corporations in national currency weighted by volume.

Deposit Rate (Foreign Currency):
Average of rates offered by banks on time deposits of residents in foreign currency weighted by volume. † Beginning in January 2005, average of rates on new time deposits of households and nonfinancial corporations in euros weighted by volume.

Lending Rate:
Average of rates charged by banks on all loans and advances to residents in national currency weighted by volume. † Beginning in January 2005, average of rates on new loans to households and nonfinancial corporations in national currency weighted by volume.

Lending Rate (Foreign Currency):
Average of rates charged by banks on loans and advances to residents in foreign currency, weighted by volume. † Beginning in January 2005, average of rates on new loans to households and nonfinancial corporations in euros weighted by volume.

Government Bond Yield:
Primary market yields of government bonds with a 10-year maturity. Beginning October 1997, data refer to secondary market

yields on government bonds with a 10-year maturity. This rate is used to measure long-term interest rates for assessing convergence among the European Union member states.

Prices, Production, Labor:

Share Prices:

Market capitalization weighted chain-linked total-return index calculated on a continuous basis using the most recent prices of all shares listed on the Vilnius Stock Exchange's Main list and I-list, base January 1, 2000.

Producer Prices:

Source: Lithuanian Department of Statistics. Weights Reference Period: Calendar year t–2; Sectoral Coverage: Mining, quarrying, manufacturing, electricity, gas, steam and air conditioning supply, water supply, sewerage, waste management and remediation activities; Number of Items in Basket: 668 enterprises: Basis for Calculation: Weights are derived from statistical data on industrial production sales volume in value estimation when VAT and excises are excluded.

Consumer Prices:

Source: Lithuanian Department of Statistics. Weights Reference Period: December previous year; Geographical Coverage: entire country; Number of Items in Basket: 889; Basis for Calculation: Weights are based on Household Budget Survey (HBS) and are reviewed and updated each year.

Wages: Average Earnings:

Source: Lithuanian Department of Statistics. Annual survey on wages and salaries has been discontinued since 2004, and annual indicators on labour statistics have been calculated by mathematical methods using administrative sources and data of Quarterly Survey on Wages and Salaries by Statistics Lithuania.

Industrial Production:

Source: Lithuanian Department of Statistics. Weights Reference Period: 2005; Sectoral Coverage: Mining and quarrying, manufacturing, electricity, gas, steam and air conditioning, water supply; Number of items in Basket: about 2,400 enterprises: Basis for Calculation: the survey is a sample survey. Sampling design is stratified simple random sampling.

Manufacturing Employment:

Data are from the same survey as the manufacturing production data. Data on total hours worked in the period are divided by the standard work hours for the period to obtain the equivalent numbers employed.

International Transactions:

Exports and Imports:

Source: Lithuanian Department of Statistics. The special system of recording trade transactions is used.

Government Finance:

Monthly and quarterly cash data are as reported by the Ministry of Finance. All data cover the consolidated central government. However, not all extrabudgetary operations financed by foreign grants and loans are covered. † In 1997, expenditure on health functions and their financing was shifted from local to central government. † Prior to 2004, to the extent possible, existing sub-annual *IFS* data were converted to the main aggregates that are presented in the *GFSM 2001* Statement of Sources and Uses of

Cash (see the Introduction of the monthly *IFS* publication for details). Beginning in January 2004, monthly and quarterly data are reported in the *GFSM 2001* analytical framework The fiscal year ends December 31.

National Accounts:

Source: Lithuanian Department of Statistics. As indicated by the country, data are compiled in accordance with the methodology of the *1993 SNA*. The coverage of the private sector activity is incomplete. Beginning in 1999, data are sourced from the Eurostat database. Eurostat introduced chain-linked GDP volume measures to both annual and quarterly data with the release of the third quarter 2005 on November 30, 2005. Chain-linked GDP volume measures are expressed in the prices of the previous year and re-referenced to 2005.

Luxembourg   137

Data are denominated in Luxembourg francs prior to January 1999 and in euros from January 1999 onward. An irrevocably fixed factor for converting Luxembourg francs to euros was established at 40.3399 Luxembourg francs per euro. In 2002, the Luxembourg franc was retired from circulation and replaced by euro banknotes and coins. Beginning in January 1999, with the implementation of Stage Three of the European Economic and Monetary Union (EMU), a euro area-wide definition of residency was introduced: All positions with residents of other euro area (EA) countries, including the European Central Bank (ECB), are classified as domestic positions, and foreign assets and foreign liabilities include only positions with non-euro area residents. Descriptions of the changes in the methodology and presentation of Luxembourg's accounts following the introduction of the euro are shown in the introduction to *IFS* and in the notes on the euro area page.

Date of Fund Membership:

December 27, 1945

Standard Sources:

Central Bank of Luxembourg
Statec
Eurostat

Exchange Rates:

Prior to March 5, 1990, there was a dual exchange rate system in which the primary rate, maintained within the cooperative exchange arrangement under the European Monetary System (EMS), was applicable to most current transactions, and the secondary or free market rate was applicable to most capital transactions. Between March 1990 and December 1998, the market rate maintained within the EMS was applicable to all transactions. Prior to January 1999, *Market Rate (End of Period and Period Average)* was the midpoint rate of the Luxembourg franc in the official market in Brussels. In January 1999, the Luxembourg franc became a participating currency within the Eurosystem, and the euro market rate became applicable to all transactions. In 2002, the Luxembourg franc was retired from circulation and replaced by euro banknotes and coins. For additional information, refer to the section on Exchange Rates in the introduction to *IFS* and the notes on the euro area page.

International Liquidity:

Beginning in January 1999, *Total Reserves minus Gold (line 1l.d)* is defined in accordance with the Eurosystem's statistical definition of international reserves. The international reserves of Luxembourg per the Eurosystem statistical definition at the start of the monetary union (January 1, 1999) in billions of U.S. dollars were as follows: *Total Reserves minus Gold,* $174; *Foreign Exchange,* $78; *SDR holdings,* $12; *Reserve Position in the Fund,* $84; *Other Reserve Assets,* $0; *Gold, – $55; Gold (million fine troy ounces),* – .191 ounces. *Foreign Exchange (line 1d.d):* Between March 1979 and December 1998, gold and foreign exchange holdings excluded deposits at the European Monetary Cooperation Fund (EMCF), and the holdings of European currency units (ECUs) issued against these deposits were included in *line 1d.d. Gold (Eurosystem Valuation) (line 1and):* Prior to June 1998, data pertained to gold holdings of the Institut Monétaire Luxembourgeois (IML). The government of Luxembourg held a claim on the IML, covered at all times by the IML's gold holdings, which could include gold receivable from the European Monetary Institute (EMI). After June 1998, the gold retained by the Central Bank of Luxembourg (CBL)—the IML's successor—was sold (demonetized). Until December 1998, CBL's only gold account was for gold receivable from the ECB. The negative entries from January to May 1999 indicate a short position in the holdings of monetary gold, which was due to the delivery to the ECB of gold previously received under a gold loan from Belgium. Memorandum data are provided on *Non-Euro Claims on Euro Area Residents* and *Euro Claims on Non-Euro Area Residents,* which represent positions as of the last Friday in each month. For additional information, refer to the section on International Liquidity in the introduction to *IFS* and the notes on the euro area page.

Central Bank:

Consists of the Central Bank of Luxembourg, which beginning in January 1999 is part of the Eurosystem, only. For a description of the accounts, refer to the section on *Central Bank - Euro Area* in the introduction to *IFS.*

Other Depository Corporations:

Comprises all resident units classified as other monetary financial institutions (other MFIs), as defined in *1995 ESA* standards, including money market funds. For a description of the accounts, refer to the section on *Other Depository Corporations - Euro Area* in the Introduction to *IFS. Central Government Monetary Liabilities —* consists of post office deposit liabilities, which beginning in 1999 are a component of euro area monetary aggregates.

Depository Corporations (Euro Area-wide Residency):

For a description of the methodology and accounts, refer to the section on *Depository Corporations (Euro Area-wide Residency)* in the introduction to *IFS.*

Interest Rates:

Deposit Rate:
Rate on savings deposits with the Banque et Caisse d'Epargne de l'Etat.

Deposit Rate (lines 60lhs, 60lhn, 60lcs, and 60lcn):
See notes in the introduction to *IFS* and *Euro-area Interest Rates.*

Lending Rate:
Minimum rate on mortgage loans by the Banque et Caisse d'Epargne de l'Etat.

Lending Rate (lines 60phm, 60pcs, and 60pcn):
See notes in the introduction to *IFS* and *Euro-area Interest Rates.*

Government Bond Yield: Long-Term (line 61):
Weighted average yield to maturity on all government bonds quoted in the Luxembourg Stock Exchange. † Beginning July 1977, refers to the average weighted yield to average maturity as then calculated by the Luxembourg Stock Exchange. For additional information, refer to the section on interest rates in the introduction to *IFS* and the notes on the euro area page. † Beginning January 1985, refers to secondary market yields of a basket of long-term bonds issued by a private credit institution with a residual maturity of close to ten-years as the Luxembourg government no longer issues long-term debt securities. This rate is used to measure long-term interest rates for assessing convergence among the European Union member states, however its definition is not fully harmonized.

Prices, Production, Labor:

Share Prices:
Share price index, base December 1967, calculated by the Luxembourg Stock Exchange and covers national companies. † Beginning in January 1987, share price index, base January 1985.

Producer Prices:
Source: Statec. Weights Reference Period: 2005; Geographic Coverage: the Grand-Duchy of Luxembourg; Number of Items: around 1,200 products; Sectoral Coverage: around 100 production units KAUs in NACE Rev. 2. B to D; Basis for Calculation: weights are updated every five years.

Consumer Prices:
Source: Statec. Weights Reference Period: for the year Y is the year Y–2; Geographical Coverage: entire country; Number of Items in Basket: about 8000; Basis for Calculation: the source for the weights at all levels of aggregation are National Accounts. Household Budget Survey results are integrated in the NA results.

Industrial Production:
Data are sourced from the OECD database, weights reference period: 2005. Data cover all industries, except construction and civil engineering. New enterprises are included as soon as they are created.

Employment:
Source: Statec. Weights reference period: 2000. The index covers the whole economy.

International Transactions:

Luxembourg's trade with countries outside the Belgium-Luxembourg Economic Union (BLEU) is also part of the BLEU's foreign trade statistics which are shown on the page for Belgium. Beginning in 1997, trade data are for Luxembourg only, which includes trade between Belgium and Luxembourg.

Government Finance:

Preliminary data on general government are compiled by Eurostat. The fiscal year ends December 31.

National Accounts:

GDP in the Luxembourg version used to be higher than GDP according to the *SNA,* to the extent that, depending on the special characteristics of the financial market, a very considerable proportion of imputed bank services is reported as exports. As indicated by the country, from 1995 onwards data have been revised following the implementation of the *ESA 95.* Beginning in 1999, euro data are sourced from the Eurostat database. Eurostat introduced chain-linked GDP volume measures to both annual and quarterly data with the release of the third quarter 2005 on November 30, 2005. Chain linked GDP volume measures are expressed in the prices of the previous year and re-referenced to 2005.

Macedonia, FYR   962

Date of Fund Membership:

December 14, 1992

Standard Sources:

National Bank of the Republic of Macedonia
Statistical Office of Macedonia

Exchange Rates:

Market Rate (End of Period and Period Average):
Weighted average of daily transactions reported by commercial banks.

Central Bank:

Consists of the National Bank of the Republic of Macedonia (NBRM) only.
† Beginning in January 2003, data are based on a standardized report form (SRF) for central banks, which accords with the concepts and definitions of the IMF's *Monetary and Financial Statistics Manual (MFSM),* 2000.
For December 2001 through December 2002, data have less conformity with the *MFSM* methodology and therefore are not strictly comparable to data for later periods.

Other Depository Corporations:

Comprises commercial banks and savings houses.
† Beginning in January 2003, data are based on a standardized report form (SRF) for other depository corporations, which accords with the concepts and definitions of the IMF's *Monetary and Financial Statistics Manual (MFSM).*
For December 2001 through December 2002, data have less conformity with the *MFSM* methodology and therefore are not strictly comparable to data for later periods.

Depository Corporations:

† See notes on central bank and other depository corporations.

Monetary Aggregates:

Broad Money:
Broad Money calculated from the liability data in the sections for the central bank and other depository corporations accords with the concepts and definitions of the *MFSM* and corresponds to M4 described below.

Money (National Definitions):

M1 comprises currency in circulation and demand deposits of residents other than central government and depository corporations with depository corporations. Currency in circulation refers to bank notes and coins issued by the NBRM less the amount held by depository corporations and demand deposits refer to current accounts.
M2 comprises M1 and quasi-deposits of residents other than central government and depository corporations with depository corporations. Quasi-deposits consist of short-term sight deposits, time deposits with maturity of up to one year, and short-term credits from non-banking institutions to other depository corporations.
M4 comprises M2 and long-term deposits of residents other than central government and depository corporations with depository corporations. Long-term deposits consist of time deposits with maturity of over one year and deposits for specific purposes prescribed by regulations, such as for opening letters of credits in payment operations abroad, guarantees, and remittances abroad. Long-term deposits also include long-term credits from non-banking institutions to other depository corporations.

Interest Rates:

Discount Rate (End of Period):
Reference rate for determining other rates charged by the NBRM on discounting eligible commercial bills and loans. † Beginning in February 2010, refers to the reference rate for determining other rates charged by the NBRM. The rate is set biannually on the last auction of NBRM bills in each December and July.

Deposit Rate:
Lowest rate on household deposits with maturities of three to six months. † Beginning in January 2005, weighted average rate offered by commercial banks on deposits of households and enterprises in national currency. The rate is weighted by end-of-period outstanding amount of deposits.

Deposit Rate (Foreign Currency):
Weighted average rate offered by commercial banks on deposits of households and enterprises in foreign currency. The rate is weighted by end-of-period outstanding amount of deposits.

Lending Rate:
Lowest rate on short-term loans to the agricultural sector. † Beginning in July 1995, midpoint rate for short-term lending to all sectors.
† Beginning in January 2005, weighted average rate charged by commercial banks on loans to households and enterprises in national currency. The rate is weighted by end-of-period outstanding amount of loans.

Lending Rate (Foreign Currency):
Weighted average rate charged by commercial banks on loans to households and enterprises in foreign currency. The rate is weighted by end-of-period outstanding amount of loans.

Prices, Production, Labor:

Producer Prices:
Source: Statistical Office of Macedonia. Weights reference period: 2005; Sectoral Coverage: mining and quarrying, manufacturing industry, electricity, gas and water supply; Number of

Items in Basket: 486; Basis for Calculation: weights are derived from the composition of sales values in the domestic market in 2005 and are gathered using a monthly survey.

Consumer Prices:

Source: Statistical Office of Macedonia. Weights Reference Period: 2010, weights are revised every three years; Number of Items in Basket: 586; Geographic Coverage: 8 major cities; Basis for Calculation: weights are derived from the 2008 Household Budget Survey.

Wages, Average Monthly:

Source: Statistical Office of Macedonia. Data are based on a regular monthly sample survey covering 70 percent of all employees. Annual data represent an average of monthly data.

Industrial Production:

Source: Statistical Office of Macedonia. Weights Reference Period: previous year; Sectoral Coverage: mining and quarrying, manufacturing industry, electricity, gas and water supply; Basis for Calculation: the weights of products are calculated as a share of value of gross output of each product into total gross output; the latest weights were calculated based on the data from the Annual Survey for Industry conducted in 2005.

International Transactions:

Exports and Imports, c.i.f.:

Source: Statistical Office of Macedonia. The special system of recording trade transactions is used. Products intended for reprocessing or finishing are included.

Balance of Payments and International Investment Position:

Data are incomplete. Banking and official sector data are included. Private sector transactions are partially covered. The National Bank of the Republic of Macedonia (NBRM) is responsible for the compilation and dissemination of the balance of payments and the International Investment Position in accordance with the methodology of the IMF's *Balance of Payments Manual*. The main sources of data for compiling the balance of payments are (1) the single administrative document for foreign trade; (2) the international transactions reporting system (ITRS); (3) the external debt reporting system (credit indebtedness); (4) banks' reports on the stock of assets and liabilities; (5) the monthly reports on stocks and flows on the accounts abroad of residents other than banks and the monthly stock and flow data on settlement accounts; (6) additional NBRM reports on realized turnover in foreign exchange offices and on official foreign exchange reserves stock of the Republic of Macedonia; and (7) data from the annual direct investment survey.

National Accounts:

Source: Statistical Office of Macedonia. As indicated by the country, data are compiled in accordance with the methodology of the *1993 SNA*. As the production-based GDP *(line 99bp)* is the official measure of GDP, the statistical discrepancy *(line 99bs)* represents the difference between the production-based GDP and the sum of the expenditure components shown. GDP volume measures are expressed according to 2005 prices.

Madagascar   674

Date of Fund Membership:
September 25, 1963

Standard Sources:
Central Bank
National Institute of Statistics

Exchange Rates:
The ariary was introduced in January 2005 and replaced the Malagasy franc at the rate of Ar1=FMG5.

Official Rate: (End of Period and Period Average):
Central bank midpoint rate. The official rate is managed flexibly and is adjusted according to a set of indicators.

Monetary Authorities:
Consolidates the Central Bank of Madagascar and monetary authority functions undertaken by the central government. † Beginning in 1979, claims on public enterprises are separately identified. The contra-entry to government foreign assets is included in *line 12a. Foreign Liabilities (line 16c)* comprises both short-term and long-term liabilities to nonresidents.

Deposit Money Banks:
Comprises commercial banks. † Beginning in 1979, data are based on an improved classification; as a result, bonds, central government lending funds, and credit from the central bank are separately identified.

Monetary Survey:
† See notes on monetary authorities and deposit money banks.

Interest Rates:

Base Rate (End of Period):
Central Bank's reference rate representing a minimum rate on repurchase agreement operations and a minimum penalty rate on required reserve deficiencies, with the effective rates equal to the base rate plus the margins.

Money Market Rate:
Highest rate charged on overnight interbank loans.

Treasury Bill Rate:
Monthly average of interest rates on one-month, three-month, and six-month treasury bills sold at daily auctions.

Deposit Rate:
Highest rate offered on large three-month deposits at the commercial banks.

Lending Rate:
Highest rate charged on short-term loans.

Prices:

Consumer Prices:
Source: National Institute of Statistics. Weights Reference Period: 2000; Geographical Coverage: Antananarivo, Fianarantsoa, Toamasina, Mahajanga, Antsiranana and Toliara. Basis for Calculation: the weights are derived from a 2008 national household survey.

International Transactions:
Source: National Institute of Statistics.

Government Finance:
Annual data are as reported in the *Government Finance Statistics Yearbook (GFSY)* and cover the consolidated central government. The fiscal year ends December 31.

National Accounts:
Source: National Institute of Statistics. As indicated by the country, the data are compiled in accordance with the *1968 SNA* from 1984 to date. Data for 2001 were compiled experimentally according to the *1993 SNA*.

Malawi   676

Date of Fund Membership:
July 19, 1965

Standard Sources:
Reserve Bank of Malawi
National Statistical Office

Exchange Rates:
Official Rate: (End of Period and Period Average):
Central bank midpoint rate. The official rate is pegged to a basket of currencies. From February 1994, the official rate is market-determined.

For the purpose of calculating the real effective exchange rate index (*line rec*), the consumer price index used is a weighted average of six official price series for high-, medium-, and low-income groups in Lilongwe and Blantyre. The monthly data are derived by interpolating the weighted average of published quarterly data.

International Liquidity:
Data for *line 1d.d* include small foreign exchange holdings by the government.

Gold (National Valuation) (line 1and) is obtained by converting the value in national currency terms, as reported in the country's standard sources, into US dollars, using the prevailing exchange rate, as given in *line de, line ae,* or *line we.* Prior to February 2010, gold holdings were recorded at book value. † Beginning February 2010, gold holdings were recorded at book value. † Beginning February 2010, *Gold (National Valuation)* is based on prevailing market prices.

Monetary Authorities:
Consolidates the Reserve Bank of Malawi (RBM) and monetary authority functions undertaken by the central government. The contra-entry to government foreign assets and Treasury IMF accounts is included in *line 16d,* while that for Trust Fund loans is included in *line 12a.*

Deposit Money Banks:
Comprises National Bank of Malawi and Stanbic Bank. Beginning in January 1998, includes First Merchant Bank and Finance Bank of Malawi.

Other Banking Institutions:
Comprises New Building Society, National Finance Company, Investment and Development Bank of Malawi, and Post Office Savings Bank. † Beginning in March 1988, comprises Inde Bank, New Building Society, National Finance Company, Leasing and Finance Company, Fincom Bank, Malawi Savings Bank, and CBM Financial Services.

Banking Survey:
† See note to other banking institutions.

Nonbank Financial Institutions:
Comprises life insurance companies and non-life insurance companies. Beginning in March 2004, includes the Old Mutual Insurance Company.

Money (National Definitions):
Reserve Money comprises currency in circulation and banker's correspondent and other accounts with the RBM. Currency in circulation refers to notes and coins issued by the RBM.
M1 comprises currency in circulation and transferable deposits. Currency in circulation refers to notes and coins issued by the RBM less the amount held by commercial banks. Transferable deposits refer to current account deposits in national currency of the private sector with commercial banks.
M2 comprises M1, fixed term and savings deposits in national currency and foreign currency deposits of the private sector with commercial banks.

Interest Rates:
Discount Rate (End of Period):
Rate charged by the RBM on loans to commercial banks.
Treasury Bill Rate:
Rate for 91-day treasury bills.
Deposit Rate:
Rate offered by commercial banks on three- to five-month time deposits.
Lending Rate:
Maximum rate charged by commercial banks on unsecured loans.
Government Bond Yield:
Yield on new issues of bonds.

Prices, Production, Labor:
Consumer Prices:
Source: National Statistical Office. Weights Reference Period: September 1997- November 1998; Geographical Coverage: national territory; Basis for Calculation: Integrated Household Survey conducted from September 1997 to November 1998.

Industrial Production:
Source: National Statistical Office. Weights reference period: 1984. Basis for Calculation: the index is based on monthly production data of 50 large-scale firms from the manufacturing and utilities sectors.

International Transactions:
Value data on *Exports* and total *Imports* are from the National Statistical Office. Revisions are made to annual data only; consequently, monthly and quarterly figures may not add up to annual data.

National Accounts:

Source: National Statistical Office. Data are prepared in accordance with the SNA93.

Malaysia   548

Data refer to Malaysia, i.e., to West Malaysia (the former State of Malaya) and East Malaysia (the former Sabah and Sarawak). Data do not include Singapore. Exceptions are noted.

Date of Fund Membership:

March 7, 1958

Standard Sources:

Bank Negara
Department of Statistics

Exchange Rates:

Official Rate: (End of Period and Period Average):
Closing interbank rate in Kuala Lumpur. Effective September 2, 1998, the official rate of the ringgit was pegged to the U.S. dollar at a rate of RM 3.80 per dollar. Effective July 21, 2005, the exchange rate operates as a managed float, with its value being determined by economic fundamentals and maintained against a trade-weighted index of Malaysia's major trading partners.

International Liquidity:

Gold (National Valuation) (line 1and) is equal to *Gold (Million Fine Troy Ounces) (line 1ad),* valued at SDR 35 per fine troy ounce and converted into U.S. dollars at the dollar/SDR rate **sa** on the country page for the United States. † Beginning April 2000, *Gold (National Valuation)* is based on historical cost. † Beginning September 2009, *Gold (National Valuation)* is based on current market prices.

Central Bank:

Consists of the Bank Negara Malaysia (BNM) only.
† Beginning in December 2002, data are based on a standardized report form (SRF) for central banks, which accords with the concepts and definitions of the IMF's *Monetary and Financial Statistics Manual (MFSM),* 2000. Departures from the *MFSM* methodology are explained below.
Securities other than shares are valued at acquisition cost adjusted for any amortization of premium and accretion of discounts rather than at current market price or fair value and are revalued at the end of the fiscal year, only when market value is lower than acquisition cost. Foreign assets and foreign liabilities are revalued quarterly rather than on a monthly basis.
Accrued interest not disaggregated by economic sector is allocated to the economic sector having the largest volume of transactions in the category.
For December 2001 through November 2002, data in the SRF format are compiled from pre-SRF data not based on the *MFSM* methodology. Departures from the *MFSM* methodology are explained below.
Financial derivatives are excluded from the data.
Financial assets and liabilities not disaggregated by economic sector are allocated to the economic sector having the largest vol-

ume of transactions in the category.
Claims on Public Nonfinancial Corporations includes some claims on other financial corporations.
Liabilities to Central Government includes some deposits of other financial corporations.
All bills issued by the BNM are included in *Other Liabilities to Other Depository Corporations* in the absence of data on an individual economic sector's holdings, recognizing that other depository corporations are the principal holders of BNM bonds.
Securities other than shares are valued at acquisition cost adjusted for any amortization of premium and accretion of discounts rather than at current market price or fair value and are revalued at the end of the fiscal year, only when market value is lower than acquisition cost. Foreign assets and foreign liabilities are revalued quarterly rather than on a monthly basis.
Accrued interest is included in *Other Items (Net)* rather than in the outstanding amounts of the financial assets and liabilities.

Other Depository Corporations:

Comprises commercial banks, finance companies, merchant banks, Islamic banks, and discount houses. Beginning in January 2006, the finance companies merged operations with commercial banks. Data exclude the housing credit institutions, savings institutions, deposit-taking development financial institutions, and cooperative societies, which issue deposits or substitutes of deposits to money holding sectors.
† Beginning in December 2002, data are based on a standardized report form (SRF) for other depository corporations, which accords with the concepts and definitions of the *Monetary and Financial Statistics Manual (MFSM).* For other depository corporations in Malaysia, departures from the *MFSM* methodology are explained below.
Financial assets and liabilities for which economic sectorization is unavailable are allocated to the economic sector having the largest volume of transactions in the category.
Foreign Assets and *Foreign Liabilities* include some claims on and liabilities to other financial corporations, respectively.
Securities and shares held for trading are valued at the lower of acquisition cost and market price rather than at current market price or fair value. Securities other than shares held for investment are valued at either acquisition cost adjusted for amortization/accretion of discount or acquisition cost plus earned discount rather than at market price or fair value. Shares and other equity held for investment are valued at acquisition cost rather than at market price or fair value. Beginning in January 2005, securities and shares for trading are valued at fair value and any gain or loss arising from a change in the fair value is recognized as a profit or loss. Held-to-maturity securities and shares are valued at the amortized cost using the effective interest method and a gain or loss is recognized when the securities are derecognized or impaired and through the amortization process. Other securities that are not held for trading or held-to-maturity investments are measured at fair value. Investments in equity instruments that do not have a quoted market price in an active market and whose fair value cannot be reliably measured are valued at acquisition cost and any gain or loss arising from a change in the fair value is recognized directly in equity through the statement of changes in equity, except for impairment losses and foreign exchange gains and losses.

Accrued interest not disaggregated by economic sector is allocated to the economic sector having the largest volume of transactions in the category.

For December 2001 through November 2002, data in the SRF format are compiled from pre-SRF data not based on the *MFSM* methodology. Departures from the *MFSM* methodology are explained below.

Financial derivatives are excluded from the data.

Financial assets and liabilities for which economic sectorization is unavailable are allocated to the economic sector having the largest volume of transactions in the category.

Claims on Other Nonfinancial Corporations includes some holdings of securities issued by other financial corporations.

Other Deposits Included in Broad Money includes some deposits of the central government.

Securities and shares held for trading are valued at the lower of acquisition cost and market price rather than at current market price or fair value. Securities other than shares held for investment are valued at either acquisition cost adjusted for amortization/accretion of discount or acquisition cost plus earned discount rather than at market price or fair value. Shares and other equity held for investment are valued at acquisition cost rather than at market price or fair value.

Accrued interest is included in *Other Items (Net)* rather than in the outstanding amounts of the financial assets or liabilities.

Depository Corporations:

† See notes on central bank and other depository corporations.

Monetary Aggregates:

Broad Money:

Broad Money calculated from the liability data in the sections for the central bank and other depository corporations differs from M3 described below, because of the money holder/issuer classification used for M3.

Money (National Definitions):

Reserve Money comprises currency in circulation, bankers' required reserves, bankers' excess reserves, and deposits of the private sector. Currency in circulation refers to notes and coins issued by the BNM less the amount of notes and coins held by banking institutions (commercial banks, finance companies, merchant banks, Islamic banks, and discount houses). Required reserves refer to the amount placed by banking institutions, except discount houses, with the BNM in compliance with the Statutory Reserve Requirement. Excess reserves refer to cash in vault of the banking institutions and their demand deposits with the BNM. Deposits of the private sector refer to the demand and time deposits placed by other financial corporations and public agencies with the BNM.

Beginning in April 1997, *reserve money* excludes deposits of the private sector. As part of performing the role of banker to the government, the BNM had been providing retail banking services to the other financial corporations and public agencies. In April 1997, the BNM ceased to provide these services.

M1 comprises currency in circulation and transferable deposits. Currency in circulation refers to the notes and coins issued by the BNM less the amount held by commercial banks and Islamic banks. Transferable deposits refer to the current accounts in national currency of state and local governments, public nonfinan-

cial corporations, and private sector with commercial banks and Islamic banks.

M2 comprises *M1* and narrow quasi-money. Narrow quasi-money refers to savings, time, and other deposits, negotiable instruments of deposits, and repurchase agreements of state and local governments, public nonfinancial corporations, and private sector with commercial banks and Islamic banks and foreign currency deposits of state and local governments, public nonfinancial corporations, private sector, and foreign entities with commercial banks and Islamic banks.

M3 comprises *M2* and deposits placed with other banking institutions. Deposits with other banking institutions refer to savings, time, and other deposits, negotiable instruments of deposits, and repurchase agreements of state and local governments, public nonfinancial corporations, and private sector with finance companies, merchant banks, and discount houses and foreign currency deposits of state and local governments, public nonfinancial corporations, and private sector, and foreign entities with finance companies, merchant banks, and discount houses.

Interest Rates:

Central Bank Policy Rate (End of Period):

Refers to the overnight policy rate, which is set by BNM for monetary policy direction. It is the target rate for the day-to-day liquidity operations of the BNM.

Discount Rate (End of Period):

Rate of discount on three-month treasury bills.

Money Market Rate:

Weighted average overnight interbank rate. Monthly rates refer to the average for the trading days of the month. Daily rates are calculated as the average of interbank deposit rates for the day, with individual rates weighted by the volume of transactions.

Treasury Bill Rate:

Average discount rate on three-month treasury bills.

Savings Rate:

Weighted average rate offered by commercial banks on savings deposits in national currency. The rate is weighted by deposit amounts in single rate savings accounts as well as multi-tiered savings accounts.

Deposit Rate:

Average rate offered by commercial banks on three-month time deposits to the private sector in national currency.

Lending Rate:

Weighted average rate offered by commercial banks on all loans in national currency. The rate is weighted by loan amounts.

Government Bond Yield:

Market yield to maturity on five-year government bonds.

Prices, Production, Labor:

Share Prices (Period Average and End of Month):

Composite stock price index of the Kuala Lumpur Stock Exchange, weights reference period: 1977. The index is limited to 100 companies although the actual component companies can change from time to time and weighted by market capitalization. The monthly average index is calculated from the daily closing quotations.

Producer Prices:

Source: Department of Statistics. Weights Reference Period: 2005; Coverage: agriculture, fishing, mining, manufacturing, and water, gas, and electricity sectors; Number of Items in Basket: 2009 commodities; Basis for Calculation: weights used in the index are derived from the Census of Economy 2005, Final National Accounts 2005 and other alternative sources of data for the value of production imports.

Consumer Prices:

Source: Department of Statistics. Weights Reference Period: 2010; Geographical Coverage: whole national territory; Number of Items in Basket: 460; Basis for Calculation: weights are derived from the 2009–2010 Household Expenditure Survey.

Industrial Production:

Source S. Weights Reference Period: 2005; Sectoral Coverage: manufacturing, mining, and electricity sectors; Basis for Calculation: the weights are based on the group or industry's proportion of the total census of value added in the 2000 weights reference period.

International Transactions:

All trade data are from Bank Negara. Beginning 1965, imports of ships, aircraft, military weapons, bunkers, and ships' stores are excluded.

Government Finance:

Prior to 2000, quarterly and annual data on central government are derived from Bank Negara. † Beginning in 2000, annual data are as reported in the *Government Finance Statistics Yearbook (GFSY)* and cover the consolidated central government. The fiscal year ends December 31.

National Accounts:

Data are derived from Bank Negara.

Maldives   556

Date of Fund Membership:

January 13, 1978

Standard Sources:

Maldives Monetary Authority
Ministry of Planning and Development

Exchange Rates:

Official Rate: (End of Period and Period Average):
Commercial bank midpoint rate. Effective October 19, 1994, the official rate of the rufiyaa was pegged to the U.S. dollar at a rate of Rf 11.77 per dollar. Effective July 25, 2001, the rufiyaa was devalued and fixed at Rf 12.80 per US$1.

International Liquidity:

Data for *Gold (National Valuation) (line 1and)* are calculated on the basis of cost of acquisition as given in the accounts of the central bank.

Central Bank:

Consists of the Maldives Monetary Authority (MMA) only.

Data are based on a standardized report form (SRF) for central banks, which accords with the concepts and definitions of the IMF's *Monetary and Financial Statistics Manual (MFSM)*, 2000. Departures from the *MFSM* methodology are explained below.

Accounts receivable and payable for which economic sectorization is unavailable are included in *Other Items (Net)* rather than in the claims on or liabilities to the corresponding sectors.

Some accrued interest is included in *Other Items (Net)* rather than in the outstanding amounts of the financial assets and liabilities. Financial assets and liabilities denominated in foreign currency are converted to national currency units at the buying exchange rate rather than at the mid-point rate of the buying and selling exchange rates.

Securities other than shares issued by the MMA and holdings of central government bills are valued at acquisition cost or face value rather than at current market price or fair value.

Other Depository Corporations:

Comprises commercial banks. Beginning in January 2005, includes the government-owned Housing Development Finance Corporation (HDFC). Beginning in September 2007, the HDFC was reclassified as an other financial corporation as the corporation no longer issues short-term liabilities to money holding sectors. Data exclude banks in liquidation.

† Beginning in February 2007, data are based on a standardized report form (SRF) for other depository corporations, which accords with the concepts and definitions of the *Monetary and Financial Statistics Manual (MFSM)*. For other depository corporations in Maldives, departures from the *MFSM* methodology are explained below.

Financial assets and liabilities for which economic sectorization is unavailable are allocated to the economic sector having the largest volume of transactions in the category.

Held-to-maturity securities are valued at acquisition cost rather than at current market price or fair value. Holdings of equity shares not traded in active markets are valued at acquisition cost rather than at current market price or fair value.

For December 2001 through January 2007, data in the SRF format are compiled from pre-SRF data not based on the *MFSM* methodology. Departures from the *MFSM* methodology are explained below.

Financial assets and liabilities for which economic sectorization is unavailable are allocated to the economic sector having the largest volume of transactions in the category.

Accrued interest is included in *Other Items (Net)* rather than in the outstanding amounts of the financial assets and liabilities.

Depository Corporations:

† See notes on central banks and other depository corporations.

Other Financial Corporations:

Comprises Maldives Finance Leasing Company Private Limited. Beginning in March 2007, includes most insurance companies, Beginning in September 2007, includes the Housing Development Finance Corporation Public Limited Company. Beginning in December 2010, includes the Maldives Pension Administration Office. Data exclude one insurance company, money remittance companies, and insurance agents and brokers.

Data are based on a standardized report form (SRF) for other financial corporations, which accords with the concepts and definitions of the *Monetary and Financial Statistics Manual* (*MFSM*). Data in the SRF format are compiled from pre-SRF data which are not fully based on the *MFSM* methodology. For other financial corporations in Maldives, departures from the *MFSM* methodology are explained below.

Data for the insurance companies are available only on a quarterly basis. Data for the intervening months and the two months after the latest quarter are estimated by carrying forward the data for the last month of the previous quarter.

Financial assets and liabilities for which financial instrument breakdown is unavailable are allocated to the financial instrument having the largest volume of transactions in the category.

Financial assets and liabilities for which economic sectorization is unavailable are allocated to the economic sector having the largest volume of transactions in the category.

Held-to-maturity securities are valued at acquisition cost rather than at current market price or fair value. Holdings of equity shares not traded in active markets are valued at acquisition cost rather than at current market price or fair value.

Monetary Aggregates:

Broad Money:
Broad Money calculated from the liability data in the sections for the central bank and other depository corporations accords with the concepts and definitions of the *MFSM* and is consistent with M2 described below.

Money (National Definitions):
Reserve Money comprises currency in circulation, transferable deposits of commercial banks and public nonfinancial corporations with the MMA in national and foreign currency, and securities issued by the MMA held by public nonfinancial corporations. Currency in circulation refers to notes and coins issued by the MMA less the cash in the vault of the MMA. Commercial banks' deposits comprise minimum required reserves and other settlement balances with the MMA in national and foreign currency.

Narrow Money (*M1*) comprises currency outside depository corporations, transferable deposits of public nonfinancial corporations with the MMA in national currency, and transferable deposits of public nonfinancial corporations, other financial corporations, and private sector with commercial banks in national currency.

Quasi Money comprises transferable deposits of public nonfinancial corporations with the MMA in foreign currency and other deposits of public nonfinancial corporations, other financial corporations, and private sector with commercial banks in national and foreign currency. For January 2005 through August 2007, includes short-term securities issued by the HDFC held by public nonfinancial corporations.

Broad Money (*M2*) comprises narrow money and quasi money.

Interest Rates:

Discount Rate (End of Period):
Rate charged by the MMA on loans to commercial banks. Effective August 6, 2001, commercial banks have access to a Lombard window at the MMA with a maximum interest of five percentage points above the highest rate prevailing in the banking industry. † Beginning in November 2006, Repurchase Facility Rate offered by the MMA to commercial banks on short-term liquid-

ity loans collateralized by treasury bills in national currency. The rate corresponds to the 28-day treasury bill rate plus seven percentage points. † Beginning in May 2010, overnight Lombard facility rate.

Money Market Rate:
Average yield on overnight deposits in the interbank market.

Treasury Bill Rate:
Rate on 28-day treasury bills in national currency announced by the MMA.

Savings Rate:
Maximum rate offered by commercial banks on savings deposits in national and foreign currency. † Beginning in January 2004, maximum rate offered by commercial banks on savings deposits in national currency.

Savings Rate (Foreign Currency):
Maximum rate offered by commercial banks on savings deposits in foreign currency.

Deposit Rate:
Maximum rate offered by commercial banks on time deposits of six months to one year in national and foreign currency. † Beginning in January 2004, maximum rate offered by commercial banks on time deposits of six months to one year in national currency.

Deposit Rate (Foreign Currency):
Maximum rate offered by commercial banks on time deposits of six months to one year in foreign currency.

Lending Rate:
Maximum rate charged by commercial banks on loans of up to three months to the private sector in national and foreign currency. † Beginning in January 2004, maximum rate charged by commercial banks on loans of up to three months to the private sector in national currency.

Lending Rate (Foreign Currency):
Maximum rate charged by commercial banks on loans of up to three months to the private sector in foreign currency.

Prices, Production, Labor:

Consumer Prices:
Maldives Monetary Authority index, weights reference period: June 2004. Geographical coverage: whole country.

Fish Catch Index:
Maldives Monetary Authority data on live weight of total fish landings reported in metric tons.

Tourist Bed Night Index:
Maldives Monetary Authority data on monthly number of tourist bed nights based on receipt of tourist tax.

International Transactions:

Merchandise Exports f.o.b.:
The entries are derived from customs returns, supplemented by estimates of the purchases of consumer durables by travelers from India and Sri Lanka and other expenditures by all other tourists. Re-exports of ships not reported by customs are included.

Exports and Imports (f.o.b.):
Data are from "Customs, Male" as reported in sources B and S.

Government Finance:

Data for consolidated central government are as reported by the Maldives Monetary Authority. Beginning in 1990, annual data are as reported in the *Government Finance Statistics Yearbook (GFSY)* and cover the budgetary central government. The fiscal year ends December 31.

Mali   678

Date of Fund Membership:

September 27, 1963

Standard Sources:

Banque centrale des États de l'Afrique de l'Ouest (Central Bank of West African States)

Institut National de la Statistique

Mali became the seventh member of the West African Economic and Monetary Union on June 1, 1984, joining Benin, Burkina Faso, Côte d'Ivoire, Niger, Senegal, and Togo. The Union, which was established in 1962, has a common central bank, the Central Bank of West African States (BCEAO), with headquarters in Dakar, and national branches in the member states. Guinea-Bissau joined the Union on May 2, 1997.

Exchange Rates:

Official Rate: (End of Period and Period Average):

Prior to January 1999, the official rate was pegged to the French franc. On January 12, 1994, the CFA franc was devalued to CFAF 100 per French franc from CFAF 50 at which it had been fixed since 1948. From January 1, 1999, the CFAF is pegged to the euro at a rate of CFA franc 655.957 per euro.

International Liquidity:

Gold is revalued on a quarterly basis at the rate communicated by the BCEAO, which corresponds to the lowest average fixing in the London market.

Monetary Authorities:

Comprises the national branch of the BCEAO only. The amount of currency outside banks is estimated by subtracting from the amount of CFA franc notes issued by Mali the estimated amounts of Mali's currency in the cash held by the banks of all member countries of the Union.

Deposit Money Banks:

Comprises commercial banks and development banks and includes certain banking operations of the Treasury and the Post Office. The Treasury accepts customs duty bills (reported separately in *line 22d.i*). Through its many branches, the Postal Checking System acts as the main depository for the private sector in the interior of Mali. *Claims on the Private Sector (line 22d)* include doubtful and litigious debts. † Beginning in 1979, *Central Government Deposits (line 26d)* include the deposits of the public establishments of an administrative or social nature (EPAS) and exclude those of the savings bank; *Demand and Time Deposits (lines 24 and 25)* include deposits of the savings bank

and exclude deposits of EPAS; and *Claims on Private Sector (line 22d)* exclude claims on other financial institutions.

Monetary Survey:

The data reported agree with the Central Bank of West African States aggregates, as given in the table on the position of the monetary institutions. Valuation differences exist as a result of the *IFS* calculations of reserve position in the Fund and the SDR holdings, both components of *line 11,* based on Fund record. † Beginning in 1979, *Claims on Other Financial Institutions (line 32f)* includes claims of deposit money banks on other financial institutions; see deposit money bank notes for explanation of other break symbols.

Interest Rates:

Discount Rate (End of Period):

Basic discount rate offered by the BCEAO.

Repurchase Agreement Rate (End of Period):

Rate on repurchase agreements between the BCEAO and the banks.

Money Market Rate:

Rate paid on overnight interbank advances.

Deposit Rate:

Rate offered by banks on time deposits of CFAF 500,000–2,000,000 for under six months.

Prices:

Consumer Prices:

Source: Central Bank of West African States. Weights Reference Period: 2008; Geographical Coverage: Bamako metropolitan area; Number of Items in Basket: 321; Basis for Calculation: The weights are taken from a household expenditure survey conducted in 1996 in the Bamako metropolitan area.

International Transactions:

All trade data are from the National Institute of Statistics.

Government Finance:

Data are as reported by the Central Bank of West African States and cover budgetary central government as well as the budgets of special funds and annexed budgets. A statistical discrepancy results from the difference between the deficit and financing. † Beginning in 1980, data also cover extrabudgetary foreign grants and loans not recorded in the treasury accounts. † Data for 1980 and 1981 do not cover social security operations. † From 1989 to 1997, net lending and privatization receipts are included in revenue. The fiscal year ends December 31.

National Accounts:

Source: National Institute of Statistics. Data are prepared in accordance with the 1973 United Nations System of National Accounts.

Malta   181

Data are denominated in Maltese lira prior to January 2008 and in euros from January 2008 onward. An irrevocably fixed factor for converting lira to euros was established at 0.4293 lira per euro. With Malta's entry into Stage Three of the European Economic and Monetary Union (EMU) in January 2008, a euro area-wide definition of residency was introduced: all positions with residents of other euro area (EA) countries, including the European Central Bank (ECB), are classified as domestic positions, and foreign assets and foreign liabilities include only positions with non-EA residents. In 2008, the lira was retired from circulation and replaced by euro banknotes and coins. Descriptions of the methodology and presentation of Malta's accounts following the introduction of the euro are discussed under *European Economic and Monetary Union* in the introduction to *IFS* and in the notes on the euro area page.

Date of Fund Membership:
September 11, 1968

Standard Sources:
Central Bank
National Statistics Office

Exchange Rates:

Market Rate (End of Period and Period Average):
In January 2008, the Maltese lira became a participating currency within the Eurosystem, and the euro market rate became applicable to all transactions. In 2008, the lira was retired from circulation and replaced by euro banknotes and coins. For additional information, refer to the section on Exchange Rates in the *Introduction* to *IFS* and the notes on the euro area page. Prior to January 2008, closing central bank midpoint rate. The official rate was pegged to a weighted basket consisting of the pound sterling, the U.S. dollar, and the Euro. On May 1, 2005 the Maltese lira entered the Exchange Rate Mechanism II (ERM II) of the European Union at a central parity rate of MTL/EUR 0.4293. The average rates were calculated on the arithmetic mean of the daily opening and closing Central Bank of Malta middle rates.

International Liquidity:
Beginning in January 2008, *Total Reserves minus Gold (line 1l.d)* and *Foreign Exchange (line.1d.d)* are defined in accordance with the Eurosystem's statistical definition of international reserves. *Gold (Eurosystem Valuation) (line 1and)* is revalued monthly at market prices. Memorandum data are provided on *Non-Euro Claims on Euro Area Residents and Euro Claims on Non-Euro Area Residents.* Prior to January 2008, *line 1and* was obtained by converting the value in national currency as reported in the country's standard sources using the national currency/dollar conversion rates utilized for balance sheet purposes. The conversion rates prior to January 2008 differ from the prevailing exchange rates reported in *IFS*. For additional information, refer to the section on International Liquidity in the introduction to *IFS* and the notes on the euro area page.

Central Bank:
Consists of the Central Bank of Malta (CBM) only, which beginning in January 2008 is part of the Eurosystem (for a description of accounts refer to the section on *Central Bank - Euro Area* in the introduction to *IFS*). Beginning in January 2008, *Currency Issued* comprises euro banknotes and coins and unretired liri.

† Beginning in October 2003, data are compiled based on a new, more detailed reporting system. † Beginning in July 2004, data are compiled in accordance with the European Central Bank's framework for monetary statistics; however, presentation of data during July 2004-December 2007 is based on the national residency approach only. For a description of accounts refer to the section on *Central Bank - Euro Area* in the introduction to *IFS*. For December 2001 to June 2004, data do not fully conform with the European Central Bank's framework for monetary statistics and are not strictly comparable to data for later periods.

Other Depository Corporations:
Comprises commercial banks, specialized financial institutions, and international banking institutions (offshore banks). Beginning in July 2004, comprises all resident units classified as other monetary financial institutions (other MFIs), in accordance with *1995 ESA* standards, including money market funds.
† Beginning in October 2003, data are compiled based on a new, more detailed reporting system.† Beginning in July 2004, data are compiled in accordance with the European Central Bank's framework for monetary statistics; however, presentation of data during July 2004-December 2007 is based on the national residency approach only. For a description of accounts, refer to the section on *Other Depository Corporations - Euro Area* in the introduction to *IFS*. For December 2001 to June 2004, data do not fully conform with the European Central Bank's framework for monetary statistics and are not strictly comparable to data for later periods.

Depository Corporations (National Residency):
† See notes on central bank and other depository corporations. For a description of the methodology and accounts, refer to the section on *Depository Corporations (Based on National Residency) - Euro Area* in the introduction to *IFS*.

Depository Corporations (Euro Area-wide Residency):
See notes on central bank and other depository corporations. For a description of the methodology and accounts, refer to the section on *Depository Corporations (Based on Euro Area-wide Residency) - Euro Area* in the introduction to *IFS*.

Monetary Aggregates:

Broad Money:
Broad Money is calculated from the liability data in the sections for the central bank and other depository corporations.
Broad money differs from M3 described below because separate data on the issuance by monetary financial institutions (MFIs) of *money market funds/shares* and *debt securities with maturity up to two years* to the money holding sectors are not currently available under the ECB reporting framework.

Money (National Definitions):
Beginning in January 2008, national monetary aggregates series were discontinued. The euro area aggregates are presented on the euro area page.
M1 comprises currency in circulation and transferable deposits. Currency in circulation refers to notes and coins issued by the CBM less the amount held by other depository corporations. Transferable deposits refer to the demand deposits of the private sector, public nonfinancial corporations, state and local governments, and other financial corporations with the CBM and other

depository corporations. † Beginning in October 2003, M1 comprises currency in circulation and demand and savings deposits withdrawable on demand of the private sector, public nonfinancial corporations, state and local governments, and other financial corporations with other depository corporations.

M2 comprises M1 and savings deposits redeemable at notice up to three months and deposits with agreed maturity up to two years of the private sector, public nonfinancial corporations, state and local governments, and other financial corporations with other depository corporations.

M3 comprises M1 and time and savings deposits of the private sector, public nonfinancial corporations, state and local governments, and other financial corporations with other depository corporations. † Beginning October 2003, M3 comprises M2 and marketable instruments issued by MFIs, namely repurchase agreements contracted by MFIs with non-central government non-MFI resident sectors, money market fund shares/units, and debt securities with maturity up to two years issued by MFIs to non-central government, non-MFI resident sectors.

Interest Rates:

Discount Rate:
Rate at which the CBM lends to credit institutions. † Beginning in February 2003, data refer to the central intervention rate used by the CBM to manage liquidity in the banking system, as discount rates were no longer in use.

Treasury Bill Rate:
Weighted average rate on three-month Treasury bills sold through weekly auctions.

Deposit Rate:
Rate on six-month time deposits.

Deposit Rate (lines 60lhs, 60lhn, 60lcs, and 60lcn):
See notes in the introduction to *IFS* and *Euro-Area Interest Rates.*

Lending Rate:
Weighted average rate on loans and advances extended by other depository corporations. The rate is weighted by loan amounts.

Lending Rate (lines 60phm, 60pcs, and 60pcn):
See notes in the introduction to *IFS* and *Euro-area Interest Rates:*

Government Bond Yield (Line 61):
Average daily secondary market yield on ten-year fixed-rate government bonds. This rate is used to measure long-term interest rates for assessing convergence among the European Union member states.

Prices:

Consumer Prices:
Source: National Statistics Office. Weights Reference Period: December 2009; Geographical Coverage: Malta and Gozo; Number of Items in Basket: 355; Basis for Calculation: weights are derived from the 2008–2009 Household Budget Survey.

Producer Prices:
Source: National Statistics Office. Weights Reference Period: 2005; Sectoral Coverage: enterprises classified under NACE Rev. 2 B to E; Number of Items in the Basket: over 400 prices from 80 enterprises; Basis for Calculation: weights are based on total sale values from the annual manufacturing structural business statistics (SBS).

International Transactions:

Exports and Imports, c.i.f.:
Source: National Statistics Office. Since Accession to the EU on May 1, 2004 foreign trade statistics in Malta are made up of Extra and Intra trade statistics covering non-EU and EU trade respectively.

Government Finance:

Starting 2008, data include the operations of the Sinking Fund as well. Beginning in 1998, monthly and quarterly data are as reported by the Central Bank of Malta and cover the consolidated central government, except for a relatively small amount of own revenues and the corresponding expenditures of extrabudgetary funds. Beginning in 1999, expenditure data exclude lending minus repayments, which have been reclassified as domestic financing. † Prior to 1999, to the extent possible, existing subannual IFS data were converted to the main aggregates that are presented in the *GFSM 2001* Statement of Sources and Uses of Cash (see the Introduction of the monthly *IFS* publication for details). Beginning in 1999, annual data are as reported in the *Government Finance Statistics Yearbook (GFSY)* and cover the consolidated central government. The fiscal year ends December 31. Monthly data cover the central government operations from the Consolidated Fund only. Central government operations from the Treasury Clearance Fund are not included.

National Accounts:

Source: National Statistics Office. As indicated by the country, beginning in 1999, data are compiled in accordance with the methodology of the *1995 ESA* and the *1993 SNA*. GDP volume measures are expressed according to 2005 prices.

Mauritania   682

Date of Fund Membership:
September 10, 1963

Standard Sources:
Central Bank
National Statistics Office

Exchange Rates:

Official Rate: (End of Period and Period Average):
Central bank midpoint rate.

International Liquidity:

Gold (National Valuation) (line 1and) is obtained by converting the value in national currency terms, as reported in the country's standard sources, using the prevailing exchange rate, as given in *line de, line ae,* or *line we.*

Monetary Authorities:

Comprises the Central Bank of Mauritania. † The sectorization and classification of accounts have been revised from 1989 onwards. *Claims on Private Sector (line 12d)* includes loans to the Central Bank employees.

Deposit Money Banks:

Consolidates commercial banks and includes the accounts of the Islamic Bank. † The sectorization and classification of accounts have been revised from 1989 onwards. In addition, the following accounts are consolidated with the commercial banks' demand deposits, with a contra-entry in claims on central government demand deposits with the postal checking account and claims arising from the Treasury's function as a lender to the private sector in the form of custom bills accepted in payment of import and other indirect taxes.

Monetary Survey:

† See notes on monetary authorities.

Interest Rates:

Discount Rate (End of Period):
Rate charged by the Banque centrale de Mauritanie to commercial banks on repurchase agreement operations.

Treasury Bill Rate:
Weighted average rate of accepted bids on treasury bills at weekly auctions.

Deposit Rate (End of Period):
Minimum rate on saving passbooks at the commercial banks as set by the Banque centrale de Mauritanie.

Lending Rate (End of Period):
Maximum authorized rate charged by commercial banks on any loan as set by the Banque centrale de Mauritanie.

Prices:

Consumer Prices:
National Statistics Office index for Mauritanian households, weights reference period: July 2006-June 2007. Geographical Coverage: Nouakchott; Number of Items in Basket: 361; Basis for Calculation: weights are derived from a survey conducted in 2006–2007 from more than 1000 households.

Government Finance:

† Beginning in 1990, annual data are reported for publication by the Budget Directorate of the Ministry of Finance and cover the consolidated operations of the Treasury and operations financed with foreign resources not recorded in the treasury accounts. Revenue data are adjusted for uncashed checks. Expenditure data are reported on a payment order basis. Therefore, changes in domestic and foreign arrears are included in the financing. The fiscal year ends December 31.

National Accounts:

Data are from the National Statistics Office. National accounts are compiled according to the recommendations of the *1968 SNA*.

Mauritius   684

Date of Fund Membership:
September 23, 1968

Standard Sources:
Bank of Mauritius
Central Statistical Office

Exchange Rates:

Market Rate (End of Period and Period Average):
Average of opening midpoint rates in the interbank foreign exchange market in Mauritius.

International Liquidity:

Gold is revalued on the basis of the monthly average quotations in London over the three preceding years, less a discount of 25 percent. *Gold (National Valuation) (line 1and)* is obtained by converting the value in national currency terms, as reported in the country's standard sources, using the prevailing exchange rate, as given in *line* **de,** *line* **ae,** or *line* **we.**

Central Bank:

Consists of the Bank of Mauritius (BOM) only.
† Beginning in June 2003, data are based on a standardized report form (SRF) for central banks, which accords with the concepts and definitions of the IMF's *Monetary and Financial Statistics Manual (MFSM)*, 2000. Departures from the *MFSM* methodology are explained below.
Financial assets and liabilities not disaggregated by economic sector are allocated to the economic sector having the largest volume of transactions in that category.
For June 2003 through December 2009, some transferable deposits of the central government are included in *Liabilities to Other Sectors* rather than in *Liabilities to Central Government* and *Liabilities to Nonresidents* includes some transferable deposits of resident sectors.
Some accrued interest is included in *Other Items (Net)* rather than in the outstanding amounts of the financial assets and liabilities.
For December 2001 through May 2003, data in the SRF format are compiled from pre-SRF data not based on the *MFSM* methodology. Departures from the *MFSM* methodology are explained below.
Monetary gold is included in *Other Items (Net)* rather than in *Claims on Nonresidents.*
Financial assets and liabilities not disaggregated by economic sector are allocated to the economic sector having the largest volume of transactions in that category. Financial assets with the private sector are included in *Other Items (Net)* rather than in *Claims on the Private Sector.* Some transferable deposits of the central government are included in *Liabilities to Other Sectors* rather than in *Liabilities to Central Government* and *Liabilities to Nonresidents* includes some transferable deposits of resident sectors.
Restricted deposits are included in *Other Items (Net)* rather than in *Deposits Excluded from Broad Money.*
Some accrued interest is included in *Other Items (Net)* rather than in the outstanding amounts of the financial assets and liabilities.
Valuation adjustment and general and special reserves are included in *Other Items (Net)* rather than in *Shares and Other Equity.*

Other Depository Corporations:

Comprises state and private commercial banks, branches of foreign banks, and Mauritius Post Office Savings Bank. † Beginning in June 2003, includes deposit-taking nonbank financial institutions which comprise leasing and finance corporations, Mauritius Housing Company Ltd., SICOM Financial Services Ltd., and Mauritius Civil Service Mutual Aid Association Ltd. In August 2003, the Mauritius Post Office Savings Bank merged operations with the New Co-operative Bank Ltd. a commercial bank. Data exclude the Mauritius Development Bank.

† Beginning in June 2003, data are based on a standardized report form (SRF) for other depository corporations, which accords with the concepts and definitions of the *Monetary and Financial Statistics Manual (MFSM)*. For other depository corporations in Mauritius, departures from the *MFSM* methodology are explained below.

Financial assets and liabilities not disaggregated by economic sector are allocated to the economic sector having the largest volume of transactions in that category.

For June 2003 through December 2008, some transferable and other deposits of the central government are included in *Transferable Deposits Included in Broad Money* and *Other Deposits Included in Broad Money*, respectively, rather than in *Liabilities to Central Government*.

† For December 2001 through May 2003, data in the SRF format are compiled from pre-SRF data not based on the *MFSM* methodology. Departures from the *MFSM* methodology are explained below.

Financial assets and liabilities not disaggregated by economic sector are allocated to the economic sector having the largest volume of transactions in that category. Some transferable and other deposits of the central government are included in *Transferable Deposits Included in Broad Money* and *Other Deposits Included in Broad Money*, respectively, rather than in *Liabilities to Central Government*.

Claims on other financial corporations and claims on state and local government are not separately identified.

Claims on Public Nonfinancial Corporations excludes a significant portion of loans, securities other than shares, and shares and other equity.

Claims on Private Sector excludes financial derivatives and a significant portion of loans. Securities other than shares excluded from broad money, loans, and financial derivatives are included in *Other Items (Net)*.

Valuation adjustment and retained earnings are included in *Other Items (Net)* rather than in *Shares and Other Equity*.

Depository Corporations:

† See notes on central bank and other depository corporations.

Monetary Aggregates:

Broad Money:

Broad Money (line 59m) calculated from the liability data in the sections for the central bank and other depository corporations accords with the concepts and definitions of the MFSM and is consistent with Broad Money (line 59mea) described below.

Money (National Definitions):

Monetary Base comprises currency in circulation, reserve deposits of other depository corporations with the BOM, and deposits of the private sector, central government, local governments, public nonfinancial corporations, and other financial corporations with the BOM.

Beginning in January 2010, excludes deposits of the central government.

Reserve Money comprises currency in circulation, demand deposits with the BOM, and BOM bills held by banks.

M1 comprises notes and coins in circulation outside banks and demand deposits of the private sector, central government, local governments, public nonfinancial corporations, and other financial corporations with banks.

Narrow Money comprises notes and coins in circulation outside depository corporations, transferable deposits of the private sector, central government, local governments, public nonfinancial corporations, and other financial corporations in national currency with depository corporations. Beginning in January 2009, excludes transferable deposits of the central government.

M2 comprises M1 and time, savings, and foreign currency deposits of the private sector, central government, local governments, public nonfinancial corporations, and other financial corporations with banks.

Broad Money comprises notes and coins in circulation outside depository corporations; transferable, time, and savings deposits of the private sector, central government, local governments, public nonfinancial corporations, and other financial corporations with depository corporations; and securities other than shares issued by other depository corporations held by the private sector, local governments, public nonfinancial corporations, and other financial corporations. Beginning in January 2009, excludes deposits of the central government.

Interest Rates:

Discount Rate (End of Period):

Rate offered by the Bank of Mauritius on overnight collateralized loans to commercial banks.

Money Market Rate:

Interbank deposits at call.

Savings Rate:

Minimum rate offered by commercial banks on savings deposits.

Deposit Rate:

Maximum rate offered by commercial banks on three-month deposits.

Lending Rate:

Maximum rate charged by commercial banks on overdraft loans to prime customers.

Prices and Labor:

Share Prices:

Share price index, base July 5, 1989. Prices are the arithmetic average of each session's share prices as quoted by the Stock Exchange Commission of Mauritius.

Consumer Prices:

Source: Bank of Mauritius. Weights Reference Period: July 2006-June 2007; Geographical Coverage: whole national territory; Number of Items in Basket: 194; Basis for Calculation: weights are derived from the Household Budget Survey (HBS) conducted in 2006/07 on 6,720 households using the Laspeyres index.

Employment:

Figures prior to 2004 refer to employment in large establishments, employing 10 or more persons and include foreign workers. After 2004 data refer to all establishments but exclude foreign workers and are based on the Continuous Multi-Purpose Household Survey which is used to estimate labor force, employment, and unemployment on a quarterly basis.

International Transactions:

Value data on total *Exports, Imports, cif,* and *Imports, fob* are from the Central Statistical Office.

Trade indices are from source S data, weights reference period: 2003.

Balance of Payments:
Beginning 2010, quarterly data include cross border transactions of global business entities.

International Investment Position:
Beginning 2009, annual data include cross border positions of global business entities.

Government Finance:

Beginning in 1990, annual data are as reported for the *Government Finance Statistics Yearbook (GFSY)* and cover consolidated central government. † Changes in the coverage of the consolidated central government in 1992, 1993, 1994, and 1999 are as specified in *GFSY.* The fiscal year ends June 30.
Source: Central Statistical Office. Beginning in 2009, monthly data for the budgetary central government are reported on a non-cash basis-cash data are adjusted for accrued interest.

National Accounts:

† Source: Central Statistical Office. From 1998, the data are prepared in accordance with the *1993 SNA.*

Mexico   273

Date of Fund Membership:
December 31, 1945

Standard Sources:
Bank of Mexico
Instituto Nacional de Estadística Geográfia e Informática
Statistical Office

Exchange Rates:
On January 1, 1993, the new peso, equal to 1,000 old pesos, was introduced. The denomination "new" was transitory and was used only on bills issued in January 1993 (series B) and in October 1994 (series C), but has been eliminated on bills issued beginning in 1996; therefore, the currency has been redenominated as pesos.

Market Rate (End of Period and Period Average):
On November 11, 1991, foreign exchange surrender requirements were eliminated, along with related exchange control measures that originated in the dual exchange system. Until October 31, 1991, the dual exchange market consisted of (1) a controlled market rate that applied to specific transactions amounting to about 70 percent of commercial and payments transactions, and (2) a free market rate that applied to the remaining transactions. As of November 1991, a more flexible exchange regime was introduced under which the peso fluctuated within an intervention band. As of August 1, 1996, the Bank of Mexico introduced a system for buying foreign exchange on the market, without abandoning its commitment to the floating exchange rate. Under this system, the Bank of Mexico organized monthly auctions of options that give financial institutions the right to sell U.S. dollars to the Bank of Mexico in exchange for Mexican pesos.

International Liquidity:
The data on *line 1d.d* include interest accrued but not collected on deposits, securities, and other obligations payable outside the national territory, loans granted to central banks, and SDR holdings, as well as the difference in favor of the central bank between the value of foreign exchange receivable and payable on forex futures in currencies other than the domestic currency. The central bank values gold holdings daily at the equivalent in U.S. dollars based on the dollar/ounce rate; the dollar/ounce rate is the arithmetical average of the rates quoted at opening on that day in London and at closing the previous day in New York.

Central Bank:
Consists of the Bank of Mexico only.
Data are based on a standardized report form (SRF) for central banks, which accords with the concepts and definitions of the IMF's *Monetary and Financial Statistics Manual (MFSM),* 2000.

Other Depository Corporations:
Comprises commercial banks, development banks, credit unions, savings and loans associations, investment funds, financial leasing companies, and specialized lending institutions.
Data are based on a standardized report form (SRF) for other depository corporations, which accords with the concepts and definitions of the *Monetary and Financial Statistics Manual (MFSM).* Departures from the MFSM methodology are explained below. *Other Items (Net)* include the net balance of financial derivatives, due to lack of sectorization of the instruments.

Depository Corporations:
See notes on central bank and other depository corporations.

Other Financial Corporations:
Comprises insurance companies, pension funds, guarantee corporations, general deposit warehouses, economic development funds, and stock exchange houses.
Data are based on a standardized report form (SRF) for other financial corporations, which accords with the concepts and definitions of the *Monetary and Financial Statistics Manual (MFSM).*

Financial Corporations:
See notes on central bank, other depository corporations, and other financial corporations.

Monetary Aggregates:

Broad Money:
Broad Money calculated from the liability data in the sections for the central bank and other depository corporations accords with the concepts and definitions of the *MFSM.* Broad money differs from M2 described below as M2 includes securities issued by the entire public sector held by residents and other instruments held by pension funds, while broad money includes only central government bonds. Conversely, broad money includes deposits of local governments and public nonfinancial corporations, while M2 includes only deposits of the private sector.

Money (National Definitions):
Base Money comprises bills and coins outside the Bank of Mexico and demand deposits of commercial and development banks in the Bank of Mexico
M1 comprises banknotes and coins outside the depository corporations system and deposits in checking and current accounts, which can be withdrawn through debit cards, in national and foreign cur-

rency of the private sector in other depository corporations.

M2 comprises M1 plus demand (other than deposits in checking and current accounts) and time deposits in national and foreign currency of the private sector in other depository corporations, public securities (federal government, Banco de Mexico, Institute for the Protection of Bank Savings (IPAB), other public sector institutions, and local governments) held by residents, and other instruments held by pension funds.

M3 comprises M2 plus demand and time deposits of nonresidents in other depository corporations and public securities (federal government, Banco de Mexico, and IPAB) held by nonresidents.

M4 comprises M3 plus deposits of residents and nonresidents in branches abroad of domestic other depository corporations.

M4a comprises M4 plus deposits and instruments of the public sector (federal, municipal, and state governments, nonfinancial public enterprises, and development trust funds).

M4 National Currency comprises all the instruments denominated in national currency that are included in M4.

M4 Foreign Currency comprises all the instruments denominated in foreign currency that are included in M4.

Interest Rates:

Central Bank Policy Rate (End of Period):
Refers to the target rate. The Bank of Mexico implements monetary policy using a target for the overnight interest rate charged in the interbank market. With the rate target regime, open market operations aim to provide the incentives for banks to keep their accounts at the central bank with a balance of zero at the daily market closing, in an environment where the overnight rate equals the target rate.

Money Market Rate:
Average of rates quoted by commercial banks on six-month bankers' acceptances. † Beginning in July 1988, average of rates quoted by commercial banks on three-month bankers' acceptances. † Beginning in March 1995, weighted average rate on loans between financial corporations (TIIE). The rate is weighted by daily loan amounts.

Treasury Bill Rate:
Average yield on 90-day treasury bills. † Beginning in January 1988, average yield on 28-day treasury bills, calculated from the weighted average rate of discount on daily transactions among dealers on the Mexican Securities Exchange. For periods during which no auction of treasury bills were held, no data are published.

Savings Rate:
Weighted average of gross rates agreed on operations during the month, payable to individuals.

Deposit Rate:
Weighted average rate paid to individuals on 60-day time deposits.

Average Cost of Funds:
Weighted average percentage cost of deposit-taking (CPP), including time bank deposits, promissory notes with yield payable at maturity, other deposits (except sight and savings), bankers' acceptances, and commercial paper with bank guarantees. † Beginning in February 1996, weighted cost of deposit-taking (CPP), including time bank deposits, promissory notes with yield payable

at maturity, other deposits (except sight and savings), bankers' acceptances, and commercial paper with bank guarantee.

Lending Rate:
Lending rate indicator: Weighted average of amounts placed on the securities exchange at various terms with the yield curve calculated on commercial paper and stock certificates of qualified companies.

Government Bond Yield: Long-Term (line 61):
Weighted average yield on development bonds of 728 days. † Beginning in January 2000, weighted average yield on three-year fixed rate government bonds. † Beginning in December 2001, weighted average yield on ten-year fixed rate government bonds. The yield is weighted by issuance amounts.

Prices, Production, Labor:

Share Prices (Period Average and End of Month):
General share price index covering shares quoted on the Mexico City Stock Exchange, base October 30, 1978.

Producer Price Index:
Source: Bank of Mexico. Weights Reference Period: 2003, based on a monthly survey covering 15,000 direct prices at 2,000 enterprises making up a representative sample of all economic activities throughout the national territory; the basket for the index is made up of 600 generic products.

Consumer Prices:
Source: Bank of Mexico. Weights Reference Period: December 2010; Geographical Coverage: 46 cities; Number of Items in Basket: 308; Basis for Calculation: 2008 National Income and Expenditure Household Survey (NIEHS) consisting of a sample of 12,000 households and the 2000 Population Census.

Wages, Monthly:
Source: National Institute of Statistics and Geography. Index on average real remunerations in manufacturing, weights reference period: 2003.

Industrial Production:
Source: National Institute of Statistics and Geography. Weights Reference Period: 2012; Sectoral Coverage: mining, manufacturing, construction, and electricity, gas and water; Basis for Calculation: the weights are based on the 2012 GDP of each activity subgroup in the Sistema de Cuentas Nacionales de México (SCNM) "Mexico's National Accounts System" classification.

International Transactions:

All trade data are from the Statistical Office. Beginning in 1970, trade data exclude exports and imports of in-bond industries. Total exports are adjusted by the Bank of Mexico to reflect transaction values of certain commodities which are valued by Customs at administrative prices. Silver exports, which are not published by the Statistical Office, are directly reported by the national authorities and included in total exports by *IFS*.

Government Finance:

Data are as reported in *Estadisticas Oportunas de Finanzas Publicas y Deuda Publica,* published by the *Direccion de Estadistica Hacendaria,* and cover consolidated central government, post office, and telecommunications. The fiscal year ends December 31.

National Accounts:

Source: National Institute of Statistics and Geography. † As indicated by the country, beginning in 1988 data have been revised significantly following the implementation of the *1993 SNA*. Quarterly data are seasonally adjusted at annual rates.

Micronesia, Fed.Sts.   868

Date of Fund Membership:
June 24, 1993

Standard Source:
Federal States of Micronesia Banking Board

Exchange Rates:

Market Rate (End of Period):
There is no independent national currency in the Federated States of Micronesia (FSM). The U.S. dollar is legal tender that circulates freely.

International Liquidity:

Foreign Exchange (line 1d.d) comprises the government's (monetary authorities) holdings of foreign exchange.

Monetary Authorities:

Comprises the monetary authority functions of the government. The contra-entries to government foreign assets, Treasury IMF accounts, and SDR holdings are included in *line 16d*. There is no formal central bank in the FSM; the Bank of Hawaii (Pohnpei Branch) has been designated as the depository of the Fund's holdings of currency.

Banking Institutions:

Comprises commercial banks and the FSM Development Bank.

Interest Rates:

Savings Rate:
Average end-of-month rate on passbook savings deposits offered by banks.

Deposit Rate:
Average rate on six- to nine-month certificates of deposit offered by banks.

Lending Rate:
Average rate charged by banks on consumer loans.

Moldova   921

Date of Fund Membership:
August 12, 1992

Standard Sources:
National Bank of Moldova
Statistical Office

Exchange Rates:

Up to July 1993, the Russian ruble (supplemented by ruble denominated coupons) was the legal tender in Moldova. On Au-

gust 9, 1993 the Moldovan ruble was introduced. On November 29, 1993 the Moldovan leu, equal to 1,000 Moldovan rubles, was introduced.

Official Rate: (End of Period and Period Average):
The official rate is the rate used by the National Bank of Moldova (NBM). Effective June 30, 2002, the exchange regime was reclassified to the category managed floating, with no pre-announced path for the exchange rate.

International Liquidity:

Total Reserves Minus Gold (line 1l.d) comprises NBM's holdings of SDRs, reserve position in the Fund, and convertible foreign exchange.

Central Bank:

Consists of the National Bank of Moldova (NBM) only.
† Beginning in July 2005, data are based on a standardized report form (SRF) for central banks, which accords with the concepts and definitions of the IMF's *Monetary and Financial Statistics Manual (MFSM)*, 2000. Departures from the *MFSM* methodology are explained below.
Claims on Private Sector includes some positions with public non-financial corporations.
For December 2001 through June 2005, data in the SRF format are compiled from pre-SRF data not based on the *MFSM* methodology. Departures from the *MFSM* methodology are explained below.
Claims on Private Sector includes some positions with public non-financial corporations.

Other Depository Corporations:

Comprises commercial banks.
† Beginning in July 2005, data are based on a standardized report form (SRF) for other depository corporations, which accords with the concepts and definitions of the *Monetary and Financial Statistics Manual (MFSM)*. Departures from the *MFSM* methodology are explained below.
Claims on Private Sector includes some positions with public non-financial corporations.
For December 2001 through June 2005, data in the SRF format are compiled from pre-SRF data not based on the *MFSM* methodology. Departures from the *MFSM* methodology are explained below.
Claims on Private Sector includes some positions with public non-financial corporations.
Provisions for loan losses are included in *Shares and Other Equity* rather than in *Other Items (Net)*.

Depository Corporations:

† See notes on central bank and other depository corporations.

Monetary Aggregates:

Broad Money:
Broad Money calculated from the liability data in the sections for the central bank and other depository corporations accords with the concepts and definitions of the *MFSM* and is consistent with M3 described below.

Money (National Definitions):
Money Base comprises currency in circulation, bankers' reserves, and transferable deposits of other financial corporations, public nonfinancial corporations, and private sector with the NBM.

Currency in circulation refers to notes and coins issued by the NBM less cash at the NBM's vaults. Bankers' reserves comprise required reserves and other deposits in national currency with the NBM and cash in the banks' vaults.

Broad Monetary Base comprises monetary base, overnight deposits of commercial banks with the NBM, and all deposits of commercial banks with the NBM in foreign currency.

M1 comprises currency in circulation and transferable deposits. Currency in circulation refers to notes and coins issued by the NBM less cash at the NBM's vaults and currency held by other depository corporations. Transferable deposits refer to current account deposits in national currency of other financial corporations, public nonfinancial corporations, and private sector with the NBM and other depository corporations.

M2 comprises M1, time deposits, and money market instruments. Time deposits include time and savings deposits in national currency of other financial corporations, public nonfinancial corporations, and private sector with the NBM and other depository corporations. Money market instruments comprise securities other than shares issued by other depository corporations in national currency held by other financial corporations, public nonfinancial corporations, and private sector.

M3 comprises M2 and foreign currency deposits of other financial corporations, public nonfinancial corporations, and private sector with other depository corporations.

Interest Rates:

Central Bank Policy Rate (End of Period):
Refers to the NBM base rate that is the reference rate for the main short-term monetary policy operations. The base rate is used by the NBM to determine the interest rates attached to its overnight credits (highest rate) and overnight deposits (lowest rate) under the "corridor" method for interest rate policy. The base rate is set every month by the NBM Council of Administration taking into account the developments in the money and foreign exchange markets, developments in the economy, and inflation outlook, as well as the forecast of main macroeconomic indicators.

Overnight Deposit Rate (End of Period):
Rate that the NBM offers on overnight deposits to commercial banks in national currency. The overnight deposit rate is attached to the NBM base rate.

Central Bank Bill Rate:
Weighted average rate on NBM bills. The rate is determined through bill issuance auctions conducted by the NBM.

Money Market Rate:
Weighted average rate on funds obtained by commercial banks in the interbank market in national currency. The rate is weighted by loan amounts. † Beginning in January 2004, weighted average rate on interbank loans and deposits with maturities of up to one month in national currency. The rate is weighted by loan and deposit amounts.

Money Market Rate (Foreign Currency):
Weighted average rate on interbank loans in foreign currency. The rate is weighted by loan amounts.

Treasury Bill Rate:
Weighted average effective yield on all treasury bills sold through securities auctions conducted by the NBM.

Deposit Rate:
Weighted average rate offered by commercial banks on all newly accepted deposits in national currency. The rate is weighted by deposit amounts.

Deposit Rate (Foreign Currency):
Weighted average rate offered by commercial banks on all newly accepted deposits in foreign currency. The rate is weighted by deposit amounts.

Lending Rate:
Weighted average rate charged by commercial banks on new loans to customers in national currency. The rate is weighted by loan amounts.

Lending Rate (Foreign Currency):
Weighted average rate charged by commercial banks on new loans in foreign currency. The rate is weighted by loan amounts.

Government Bond Yield:
Weighted average effective yield on two-year government bonds sold through auctions conducted by the NBM.

Prices:

Consumer Prices:
Source: Statistical Office. Weights Reference Period: weights are updated every year; Geographical Coverage: 8 cities of Moldova but excludes the Transnistria region; Number of Items in Basket: over 1200 items; Basis for Calculation: weights are derived from the Household Budget and Expenditure Survey (HBS) and are updated every year.

International Transactions:

Source: Statistical Office. Compiled on the basis of customs declarations. The data do not cover the territory of Transnistria region.

Government Finance:

Annual data are as reported in the *Government Finance Statistics Yearbook (GFSY)* and cover the budgetary central government. The fiscal year ends December 31.

National Accounts:

Source: Statistical Office. As indicated by the country, data are compiled in accordance with the methodology of the *1993 SNA*.

Mongolia   948

Date of Fund Membership:
February 14, 1991

Standard Sources:
Bank of Mongolia
National Statistical Office of Mongolia

Exchange Rates:

Official Rate: (End of Period and Period Average):
Beginning on May 27, 1993, the midpoint of the average buying and selling rates that was freely determined on the basis of market transactions between commercial banks and the nonbank public. Also beginning on May 27, 1993, all exchange rates were unified in the context of the floating exchange rate system. Beginning on July 21, 2009, the exchange rate is determined as a weighted average of banks' buying and selling quotes for noncash transactions.

International Liquidity:

Gold (National Valuation) (line 1and) is valued at 4300 togrogs per gram since June 6, 1993; it was valued at 1600 Tog/gram from November 19, 1992; at 450 Tog/gram from September 12, 1991; at 60 Tog/gram from October 23, 1986; at 52 Tog/gram from March 27, 1985; at 40 Tog/gram from November 1, 1983; and at 32.03 Tog/gram from December 15, 1980.

Line 1d.d comprises balances held by the Mongolbank and small holdings by the Ministry of Finance since April 1993. Prior to April 1993, the State Bank (International) also held part of the official international reserves.

Central Bank:

Consists of the Bank of Mongolia (BOM) only.

Data are based on a standardized report form (SRF) for central banks, which accords with the concepts and definitions of the IMF's *Monetary and Financial Statistics Manual (MFSM)*, 2000. Departures from the *MFSM* methodology are explained below.

For December 2001 through December 2007, financial derivatives are reported on a net basis.

Other Depository Corporations:

Comprises commercial banks. Beginning in February 2010, includes savings and credit cooperatives.

Data are based on a standardized report form (SRF) for other depository corporations, which accords with the concepts and definitions of the IMF's *Monetary and Financial Statistics Manual (MFSM)*. For other depository corporations in Mongolia, departures from the *MFSM* methodology are explained below.

For December 2001 through February 2004, *Claims on Private Sector* includes positions with other financial corporations.

Holdings of securities other then shares (except for tradable certificates of deposits since January 2003) and shares and other equity are allocated to the economic sector having the largest transactions in the category.

For December 2001 through December 2007, financial derivatives were reported by some commercial banks on a net basis.

Accrued interest on loans, deposits, and securities other than shares (except for holdings of government securities) is included in *Other Items (Net)* rather than in the outstanding amounts of the financial instruments.

Depository Corporations:

See notes on central bank and other depository corporations.

Monetary Aggregates:

Broad Money:

Broad Money calculated from the liability data in the sections for the central bank and other depository corporations accords with the concepts and definitions of the *MFSM* and is consistent with M2 described below.

Money (National Definitions):

M1 comprises currency in circulation outside depository corporations and demand deposits in national currency of other financial corporations, public nonfinancial corporations, and private sector with commercial banks.

M2 comprises M1, time and savings deposits in national currency, all deposits in foreign currency, and certificates of deposit in national and foreign currency of other financial corporations, public nonfinancial corporations, and private sector with commercial banks.

Interest Rates:

Central Bank Policy Rate (End of Period)

Rate on seven-day BOM bills, which is the main monetary policy rate.

Discount Rate (End of Period):

Minimum rate charged by the BOM on automatic loans to banks to settle overdrafts in their clearing accounts.

Central Bank Bill Rate:

Weighted average rate on BOM bills of all maturities. The rate is weighted by the amount of bills.

Treasury Bill Rate:

Weighted average rate on treasury bills of all maturities in national currency. The rate is weighted by the amount of securities outstanding.

Deposit Rate:

Minimum rate offered by commercial banks on time deposits of three months and over in national currency. Beginning in May 1993, average of the minimum and maximum rates offered by commercial banks on time deposits up to one year in national currency. † Beginning in December 2008, weighted average rate offered by commercial banks on all deposits in national currency. The rate is weighted by deposit amounts.

Deposit Rate (Foreign Currency):

Average of the minimum and maximum rates offered by commercial banks on time deposits up to one year in foreign currency. † Beginning in December 2008, weighted average rate offered by commercial banks on all deposits in foreign currency. The rate is weighted by deposit amounts.

Lending Rate:

Weighted average rate on commercial loans in national and foreign currency to prime borrowers. † Beginning in February 1998, weighted average rate charged by commercial banks on loans in national currency. The rate is weighted by loan amounts.

Lending Rate (Foreign Currency):

Weighted average rate charged by commercial banks on loans in foreign currency. The rate is weighted by loan amounts.

Prices:

Data are from the National Statistical Office of Mongolia.

Consumer Prices:

Source: National Statistical Office of Mongolia. Weights Reference Period: December 2010; Geographical Coverage: covers the capital city, Ulaanbaatar, and the 21 aimags (provinces); Number of Items in the Basket: 287 items in eight main item categories.

International Transactions:

National Statistical Office of Mongolia data; trade in convertible currencies was valued at the commercial rate from 1990 to May 1993. Trade in nonconvertible currencies valued at official exchange rates.

Balance of Payments:

Data include transactions in nonconvertible currencies at the official cross rates.

Government Finance:

Monthly data are provided by the Ministry of Finance and cover the consolidated central and local government. The fiscal year ends December 31.

National Accounts:

Source: National Statistical Office of Mongolia. As indicated by the country, data are compiled according to the *1993 SNA*.

Montenegro   943

Date of Fund Membership:

January 18, 2007

Standard Sources:

Central Bank of Montenegro
Statistical Office

Exchange Rates:

Market Rate (End of Period and Period Average):
Euro market rate. Since April 1, 2002, euro is the legal tender and the unit of account in Montenegro. During the transition period January - March 2002, the deutsche mark and the euro were the parallel legal tender.

Monetary Authorities:

Comprises Central Bank of Montenegro. Central Bank of Montenegro does not issue currency. Euro is the legal tender and the unit of account in Montenegro. See notes on Exchange Rates. *Other general government* comprises municipalities, social security funds, and the Development fund.

Banking Institutions:

Comprises commercial banks; banks in liquidation are excluded. *Other general government* comprises municipalities, social security funds, and the Development fund.

Banking Survey:

Deposit Money (line 34) and *Time, Savings, and Foreign Currency Deposits (line 35)* comprise depository liabilities only. Euro notes and coins are used as a domestic medium of exchange or for payments abroad; their amount in circulation, however, is not precisely known, and hence no attempt was made to calculate *Money* for Montenegro. See notes for Monetary Authorities and Banking Institutions.

Interest Rates:

Treasury Bill Rate:
Yield on newly issued 182-day Treasury bills from the latest auction.

Deposit Rate:
Average rate on euro deposits weighted by volume. † Prior to December 2007, simple average of midpoints between maximum and minimum rates on euro deposits with maturity of 3–12 months offered by four largest banks.

Lending Rate:
Average rate on loans weighted by volume.

Prices and Production:

Share Prices (End of Month):
NEX Montenegro Stock Exchange index of the basket of share prices of 20 largest companies weighted by capitalization, turnover, and the number of transactions, base March 1, 2003.

Producer Prices:
Statistical Office. Weights Reference Period: 2005; Sectoral Coverage: mining, quarrying, electricity, gas and water supply; Number of Items in Basket: prices are collected for the 19 divisions of industrial activity; Basis for Calculation: the structure of weights is based on the sales value in the domestic market.

Consumer Prices:
Statistical Office. Weights Reference Period: weights are used from the annual Household Budget survey in year n–2 with prices from year n–1; Geographical Coverage: 4 towns; Number of Items in Basket: 502; Basis for Calculation: The 2010 CPI weight system was developed by the Household Budget Survey for 2008.

Industrial Production:
Statistical Office. Base year: 2010; Sectoral Coverage: mining and quarrying, manufacturing, electricity, gas and water supply; Basis for Calculation: weights are obtained from the Complex Annual Survey and the Annual Industrial Report.

Population:

Source: Statistical Office.

Montserrat   351

Standard Sources:

Eastern Caribbean Central Bank

Exchange Rates:

Official Rate: (End of Period and Period Average):
The official rate is pegged to the U.S. dollar.

Central Bank:

Data are based on a standardized report form (SRF) for central banks, which accords with the concepts and definitions of the IMF's *Monetary and Financial Statistics Manual (MFSM)*, 2000. Departures from the *MFSM* methodology are explained below.

Data refer to accounts in the balance sheet of the East Caribbean Central Bank (ECCB) attributable to Montserrat.

Financial derivatives are excluded from the data.

Claims on Nonresident comprises estimates of Montserrat's notional share of the ECCB's foreign assets.

Claims on Other Depository Corporations comprises the portion of the ECCB's claims on resident other depository corporations attributable to Montserrat.

Claims on Central Government and *Liabilities to Central Government* comprise the portion of the ECCB's claims on and liabilities to the central government attributable to Montserrat.

Financial assets with other financial corporations, state and local governments, public nonfinancial corporations, and private sector attributable to Montserrat are not included in the data in the absence of a country of these accounts in the balance sheet of the ECCB.

Currency in circulation comprises the portion of currency in circulation attributable to Montserrat less vault cash held by other depository corporations.

Some portion of other deposits to other depository corporations and interest accrued from these deposits are included in *Other Items (Net)*.

Share and other equity is not applicable to the member countries of the ECCU because the shares and other equity in the balance sheet of the ECCB exclusively belong to the ECCB.

Other Depository Corporations:

Comprises commercial banks. Data exclude building societies and credit unions, which accept deposits.

Data are based on a standardized report form (SRF) for other depository corporations, which accords with the concepts and definitions of the *Monetary and Financial Statistics Manual (MFSM)*. For resident other depository corporations in the member countries of the ECCU, departures from the *MFSM* methodology are explained below.

Financial derivatives and insurance technical reserves are excluded from the data.

Financial assets and liabilities for which economic sectorization is unavailable are allocated to the economic sector having the largest volume of transactions in the category.

Transferable Deposits Included in Broad Money includes all deposits of the private sector denominated in foreign currency.

Accounts receivable and payable are included in *Other Items (Net)* rather than in other depository corporations' claims or liabilities to the corresponding economic sectors.

Accrued interest on transactions with nonresidents is included in *Other Items (Net)* rather than in the outstanding amount of foreign assets and liabilities.

Depository Corporations:

See notes on central bank and other depository corporations.

Monetary Aggregates:

Broad Money:

Broad Money is calculated from the liability data in the sections for the central bank and other depository corporations. Broad money differs from M2 described below as broad money includes the deposits of money holding sectors with the ECCB attributable to Montserrat and deposits of other financial corporations, state and local government, and public nonfinancial corporations in national and foreign currencies with commercial banks.

Money (National Definitions):

M1 comprises notes and coins held by the public and demand deposits in national currency of the private sector with commercial banks.

M2 comprises M1 plus time, savings, and foreign currency deposits of the private sector with commercial banks.

Interest Rates:

Discount Rate (End of Period):

Rate charged by the ECCB on loans of last resort to commercial banks.

Money Market Rate:

Fixed rate on loans between commercial banks. The rate includes the commission charged by the ECCB as agent. † Beginning in October 2001, weighted average rate on loans between commercial banks. The rate is weighted by loans amounts.

Savings Rate:

Maximum rate offered by commercial banks on savings deposits in national currency. † Beginning in June 2003, weighted average

rate offered by commercial banks on savings deposits in national currency. The rate is weighted by deposit amounts.

Deposit Rate:

Maximum rate offered by commercial banks on three-month time deposits. The rate is weighted by deposit amounts.

Deposit Rate (Foreign currency):

Weighted average rate offered by commercial banks on deposits in foreign currency. The rate is weighted by deposit amounts.

Lending Rate:

Maximum rate charged by commercial banks on prime loans. The rate is weighted by loan amounts.

National Accounts:

Source: Eastern Caribbean Central Bank.

Morocco   686

Date of Fund Membership:

April 25, 1958

Standard Sources:

Bank Al-Maghrib
Ministry of Finance
Division of Statistics

Exchange Rates:

Official Rate: (End of Period and Period Average):

Central bank midpoint rate. Prior to January 1999, the official rate is fixed daily in terms of the French franc. From January 1, 1999, the official rate is fixed daily on the basis of a basket of currencies (80 percent euro and 20 percent U.S. dollar).

The weighting scheme used to calculate indices of nominal and real effective exchange rates (*lines* **nec** and **rec**) is based on data for tourism receipts as well as on data for merchandise trade.

International Liquidity:

Gold (National Valuation) (line 1and) is obtained by converting the value in national currency terms, as reported in the country's standard sources, using the prevailing exchange rate, as given in *line* **de**, *line* **ae**, or *line* **we**.

Central Bank:

Consists of the Bank Al-Maghrib (BAM) only.

Data are based on a standardized report form for central banks, which accords with the concepts and definitions of the IMF's *Monetary and Financial Statistics Manual (MFSM)*, 2000.

Other Depository Corporations:

Comprises commercial banks and a network of cooperative banks (Groupe Banques Populaires). Beginning in January 2005, includes money market mutual funds. Data exclude offshore banks.

Data are based on a standardized report form for other depository corporations, which accords with the concepts and definitions of the *Monetary and Financial Statistics Manual (MFSM)*. For other depository corporations in Morocco, departures from the *MFSM* methodology are explained below.

Transferable and *Other Deposits Included in Broad Money* include deposits of nonresidents, namely Moroccan citizens living abroad.

Securities held for purposes other than for sale are valued at amortized cost rather than at market price or fair value.

Depository Corporations:
See notes on central bank and other depository corporations.

Monetary Aggregates:

Broad Money:

Broad Money calculated from the liability data in the sections for the central bank and other depository corporations accords with the concepts and definitions of the *MFSM*. Broad money includes demand and saving deposits of nonfinancial corporations and households with the postal administration (Comptes de Chèques Postaux and Caisse d'Épargne Nationale) and Treasury. Broad money is consistent with M3 described below.

Money (National Definitions):

M1 (means of payment) comprises banknotes and coins issued by BAM less the amount held by other depository corporations; demand deposits in national currency of nonfinancial corporations, households, other financial corporations, local governments, and Moroccan citizens living abroad with depository corporations, the postal administration (Comptes de Chèques Postaux), and Treasury.

M2 comprises M1 and savings deposits with other depository corporations, and saving passbooks with the postal administration (Caisse d'Épargne Nationale) in national currency of households and Moroccan citizens living abroad.

M3 (money stock in national and foreign currency) comprises M2 and time deposits in national currency, certificates of deposit up to two-year residual maturity, deposits in foreign currency, and deposits in the form of repurchase agreements issued by other depository corporations, shares in money market mutual funds, and time deposits with the Treasury of nonfinancial corporations, households, other financial corporations, local governments, and Moroccan citizens living abroad.

Interest Rates:

Discount Rate (End of Period):
Offer rate on seven-day credit auctions.

Money Market Rate:
Data refer to the interbank lending rate.

Deposit Rate:
Rate offered by commercial banks on 12-month time deposits in national currency.

Lending Rate:
Maximum rate charged by commercial banks on short-term loans.

Government Bond Yield:
Medium-term series refers to rate on 5-year treasury bonds. Long-term series refers to rate on 15-year treasury bonds.

Prices, Production, Labor:

Share Prices (End of Month):
The Moroccan All Shares Index (MASI) is a global capitalization weighted index comprised of all securities of the share type listed on the Casablanca Stock Exchange list, base December 31, 1991.

Wholesale Prices:
Division of Statistics, national index, weights reference period: 1977, covers 231 final products available in local markets (in nine

important cities), including 77 items from the agricultural sector and 154 items from the industrial and energy sectors.

Producer Prices:
Source: Division of Statistics. Weights Reference Period: 1997; Coverage: goods manufactured in Morocco covering all the mining, industrial, and energy sectors; Number of items in Basket: 301; Basis for Calculation: The weights were calculated on the basis of the production values for base year 1997.

Consumer Prices:
Source: Division of Statistics. Weights Reference Period: 2006; Geographical Coverage: the entire urban environment, represented by the 17 largest cities: Agadir, Casablanca, Fez, Kénitra, Marrakesh, Oujda, Rabat, Tétouan, Meknès, Tangier, and Laâyoune. Number of Items in Basket: 478; Basis for Calculation: weights are derived from a 2001 national household consumption and expenditure survey and 2007 household living standards surveys.

Manufacturing Production:
Division of Statistics index, weights reference period: 1992–1998. It includes 3000 enterprises from among 14 branches of manufacturing.

Mining Production:
Division of Statistics index, weights reference period: 1992–1998. It includes 10 branches of mining.

Employment:
Urban and rural population for ages 15 and older.

International Transactions:

All trade value data are from the Division of Statistics. Trade indices are compiled on weights reference period: 1976 and supplied directly by the Bank Al-Maghrib.

Government Finance:

Monthly data are from Bank Al-Maghrib and cover the operations of the consolidated central government. Beginning in 2006, monthly budgetary central government data are reported according to the GFSM 2001 analytical framework. Liabilities are all debt and at nominal value. The fiscal year ends December 31.

National Accounts:

Source: Bank Al-Maghrib.

Mozambique   688

Date of Fund Membership:
September 24, 1984

Standard Source:
Bank of Mozambique

Instituto Nacional de Estatística

Exchange Rates:

On July 1, 2006, the new metical (MT), equivalent to 1,000 of the old metical (MT) was introduced.

Market Rate (End of Period and Period Average):
Before April 1, 1992, the market rate referred to the official rate set by the Central Bank and covered most transactions. Between

1992 and January 5, 2005, rate refers to the average buying and selling exchange rates of commercial banks' transactions with the public. Beginning on January 5, 2005, the exchange rate is determined as the weighted average of buying and selling exchange rates of all transactions of commercial banks and foreign exchange dealers, including interbank transactions, and any transactions in foreign exchange auctions undertaken by the Bank of Mozambique.

Central Bank:

Comprises the Bank of Mozambique (BOM) only.

† Beginning in December 2002, data are based on a standardized report form (SRF) for central banks, which accords with the concepts and definitions of the IMF's *Monetary and Financial Statistics Manual* (*MFSM*), 2000. Departures from the *MFSM* methodology are explained below.

Financial assets and liabilities for which economic sectorization is unavailable are allocated to the economic sector having the largest volume of transactions in the category.

Financial assets and liabilities are not valued at market prices or fair values.

Accrual accounting is not yet fully applied to all assets and liabilities. Beginning in April 2004, securities other than shares are recorded on an accrual basis.

For December 2001 through November 2002, data in the SRF format are compiled from pre-SRF data not based on the *MFSM* methodology. Departures from the *MFSM* methodology are explained below.

Financial assets and liabilities of the resident sector for which the currency of denomination is unavailable are allocated to the national currency.

Financial assets and liabilities for which economic sectorization is unavailable are allocated to the economic sector having the largest volume of transactions in the category.

Accrual accounting is not applied and financial assets and liabilities are not valued at market prices or fair values.

Where data for other depository corporations were not directly distinguished from data for other financial corporations, separation of the data was based on the characteristics of the financial asset or liability.

Other Depository Corporations:

Comprises commercial banks. Beginning in January 2003, includes credit cooperatives.

†Beginning in December 2002, data are based on a standardized report form (SRF) for other depository corporations, which accords with the concepts and definitions of the *Monetary and Financial Statistics Manual* (*MFSM*). For other depository corporations in Mozambique, departures from the *MFSM* methodology are explained below.

Financial derivatives are excluded from the data.

Financial assets and liabilities for which the residency is unavailable are allocated to nonresidents when denominated in foreign currency and to residents when denominated in national currency.

The sectorization of financial assets and liabilities between public nonfinancial corporations and other nonfinancial corporation is estimated based on information collected from a representative sample. Accrued interest on these assets and liabilities was allocated following the same criteria.

For December 2001 through November 2002, data in the SRF format are compiled from pre-SRF data not based on the *MFSM*

methodology. Departures from the *MFSM* methodology are explained below.

Financial assets and liabilities for which economic sectorization is unavailable are allocated to the economic sector having the largest volume of transactions in the category. Where data for other depository corporations were not directly distinguished from data for other financial corporations, separation of the data was based on the characteristics of the financial asset or liability. Accrued interest is included in *Other Items (Net)* rather than in the outstanding amounts of the financial assets and liabilities.

Depository Corporations:

† See notes on central bank and other depository corporations.

Monetary Aggregates:

Broad Money:
Broad Money calculated from the liability data in the sections for the central bank and other depository corporations accords with the concepts and definitions of the *MFSM* and mainly differs from M2 described below as M2 excludes accrued interest. Beginning in December 2007, broad money is consistent with *M2* described below.

Money (National Definitions):
Base Money comprises notes and coins in circulation outside the BOM and other depository corporations' deposits with the BOM in national currency, including central bank securities.

M1 comprises notes and coins in circulation outside the depository corporations and transferable deposits of other financial corporations, local governments, public nonfinancial corporations, other nonfinancial corporations, and other resident sectors in national and foreign currency with depository corporations.

M2 comprises M1; time and saving deposits in national and foreign currency of other financial corporations, local governments, public nonfinancial corporations, other nonfinancial corporations, and other resident sectors with depository corporations; repurchase agreements in national currency between depository corporations and other financial corporations, local governments, public nonfinancial corporations, other nonfinancial corporations, and other resident sectors; and certificates of deposit issued by depository corporations held by other financial corporations, local governments, public nonfinancial corporations, other nonfinancial corporations, and other resident sectors.

Interest Rates:

Discount Rate (End of Period):
Rate at which the BOM lends in national currency to commercial banks.

Money Market Rate:
Average loan rate on loans up to seven days in national currency between commercial banks.

Treasury Bill Rate:
Average yield on 91-day treasury bills denominated in national currency.

Deposit Rate:
Average rate offered by commercial banks on deposits of up to 365 days in national currency.

Lending Rate:
Average rate charged by commercial banks on loans of up to 365 days in national currency.

Prices:

Consumer Prices:
Source: Instituto Nacional de Estatística. Weights Reference Period: December 2004; Geographical Coverage: Maputo City; Number of Items in the Basket: 210 items; Basis for Calculation: The weights are derived from a national Survey of Household Units (IAF) conducted between July 2002 to June 2003.

International Transactions:
Source: Instituto Nacional de Estatística.

National Accounts:
Source: Instituto Nacional de Estatística. As indicated by the country, beginning in 1991, data are compiled according to the *1993 SNA*.

Myanmar 518

Date of Fund Membership:
January 3, 1952

Standard Sources:
Central Bank of Myanmar
Central Statistical Organization

Exchange Rates:

Official Rate: (End of Period and Period Average):
Beginning January 1975, the official rate is pegged to the SDR. †
Beginning on April 1, 2012, the Central Bank of Myanmar adopted the managed float exchange rate regime for Kyat vis-à-vis the U.S. dollar.

International Liquidity:
Gold (National Valuation) (line 1and) is equal to *Gold (Million Fine Troy Ounces) (line 1ad),* valued at SDR 35 per fine troy ounce and converted into U.S. dollars at the dollar/SDR rate **sa** on the country page for the United States. Source: OECD

Central Bank:
Consists of the Central Bank of Myanmar (CBM) only.
Data are based on a standardized report form (SRF) for central banks, which accords with the concepts and definitions of the IMF's *Monetary and Financial Statistics Manual (MFSM)*, 2000. Departures from the *MFSM* methodology are explained below.
Monetary gold is valued at a historical price rather than at market price or fair value. Securities other than shares are valued at face value rather than at market price or fair value.
Accrued interest is recognized only at the end fiscal year (end-March) rather than during the year. Accrued interest is included in *Other Items (Net)* rather than in the outstanding amounts of the financial assets and liabilities.

Other Depository Corporations:
Comprises state and private commercial banks.
Claims on Central Government and *Liabilities to Central Government* include positions with local governments because they are not financially independent from central government.
Data are based on a standardized report form (SRF) for other depository corporations, which accords with the concepts and def-

initions of the IMF's *Monetary and Financial Statistics Manual (MFSM)*, 2000. For other depository corporations in Myanmar, departures from the *MFSM* methodology are explained below.
Securities other than shares are valued at face value rather than at market price or fair value. Foreign currency denominated positions are revalued on a semi-annual basis (at end-September and end-March) rather than on a monthly basis.
Accrued interest is recognized on a quarterly, semi-annual, or annual basis rather than on a monthly basis. Accrued interest is included in *Other Items (Net)* rather than in the outstanding amounts of the financial assets and liabilities.
Central government overdrafts that have been reported as deposits with negative values are included in *Liabilities to Central Government* rather than in *Claims on Central Government*.
Beginning in October 2011, foreign currency positions of private banks authorized for foreign currency operations are valued at the *retail counter exchange rate* (approximately 800 kyat per U.S. dollar) instead of at the official rate used by all other banks. For April 2012 through August 2012, some commercial banks valued their foreign currency accounts using the official exchange rate that was in effect until April 1, 2012 rather than the exchange rate under the managed float in effect since April 1, 2012.
Financial assets and liabilities for which economic sectorization is unavailable are allocated to the economic sector having the largest volume of transactions in the category.

Depository Corporations:
See notes on central bank and other depository corporations.

Monetary Aggregates:

Broad Money:
Broad Money (line 59m) calculated from the liability data in the sections for the central bank and other depository corporations accords with the concepts and definitions of the *MFSM* and is consistent with broad money (line 59mea) described below.

Money (National Definitions):
Reserve Money comprises notes and coins in kyat and Foreign Exchange Certificates (FECs) issued by the CBM; commercial banks' deposits with the CBM in national currency, FECs and foreign currency; and demand deposits of other financial corporations, public nonfinancial corporations, and private sector with the CBM in national currency.
Broad Money comprises currency in circulation and demand, time, and savings deposits of other financial corporations, public nonfinancial corporations and private sector with depository corporations in national currency, FECs, and foreign currency. Currency in circulation refers to notes and coins in kyat and FECs issued by the CBM less the amounts held by commercial banks.

Interest Rates:

Discount Rate (End of Period):
Rediscount rate of the Central Bank of Myanmar.

Deposit Rate:
Rate offered on six-month fixed deposits. Beginning in September 2011, maximum rate on six-month fixed deposits.

Lending Rate:
Rate charged on loans to private sector for financing working capital.

Government Bond Yield:
Rate on five-year government treasury bonds. † Beginning in September 2011, maximum rate on five-year government treasury bonds.

Prices:

Consumer Prices:
Source: Central Statistical Organization. Weights Reference Period: 1997; Geographical Coverage: Yangon; Number of Items in Basket: 135; Basis for Calculation: the weights are derived from the 1997 household income and expenditure survey.

International Transactions:
All trade data are from the Central Statistical Organization.

Exports:
Data include re-exports.

Imports:
Current data are provisional, as they exclude government imports under special order and military goods.

Government Finance:
Annual data are as reported in the *Government Finance Statistics Yearbook* (*GFSY*) and cover the consolidated central government. The fiscal year ends March 31.

National Accounts:
† Data prior to 1974 refer to fiscal years ending September 30. Data from 1974 onward relate to the new fiscal year, ending March 31. For the year ending September 1974, that is, based on the old fiscal year, GDP at current market prices was estimated to be 14,852 million kyats. Data for *line 96f* comprise government and private consumption, when those data are not shown separately.

Namibia   728

Date of Fund Membership:
September 25, 1990

Standard Sources:
Ministry of Finance
Bank of Namibia
Central Bureau of Statistics

Exchange Rates:

Market Rate (End of Period and Period Average):
The Namibian dollar is at par with the South African rand (see note on the page for South Africa for a description of the exchange rates).

International Liquidity:
Gold (National Valuation) (line 1and) is obtained by converting the value in national currency terms, as reported in the country's standard sources and as given in line **ae**. Gold is revalued at the end of each month.

Central Bank:
Consists of the Bank of Namibia (BON) only.
† Beginning in April 2002, data are based on a standardized re-

port form (SRF) for central banks, which accords with the concepts and definitions of the IMF's *Monetary and Financial Statistics Manual* (*MFSM*), 2000. Departures from the *MFSM* methodology are explained below.

Accrued interest on financial assets is included in *Claims on Nonresidents*.

For December 2001 through March 2002, data in the SRF format are compiled from pre-SRF data not based on the *MFSM* methodology. Departures from the *MFSM* methodology are explained below.

Financial assets with the private sector are included in *Other Items (Net)* rather than in *Claims on Private Sector*.

Accrued interest is included in *Other Items (Net)* rather than in the outstanding amounts of the financial assets and liabilities.

Other Depository Corporations:
Comprises commercial banks, Namibia Post Office Savings Bank, Agricultural Bank of Namibia, and National Housing Enterprise. Beginning in August 2003, data include the SWABOU Building Society which merged operations with a commercial bank.

† Beginning in April 2002, data are based on a standardized report form (SRF) for other depository corporations, which accords with the concepts and definitions of the *Monetary and Financial Statistics Manual* (*MFSM*). For other depository corporations in Namibia, departures from the *MFSM* methodology are explained below.

For April 2002 through May 2003, financial assets and liabilities not disaggregated by economic sector are allocated to the economic sector having the largest volume of transactions in that category.

Holdings of domestic securities are recorded at book value (principal plus accrued interest) rather than at market prices or fair value. Some loans are reported net of provisions.

For December 2001 through May 2002, data in the SRF format are compiled from pre-SRF data not based on the *MFSM* methodology. Departures from the *MFSM* methodology are explained below.

Financial assets and liabilities not disaggregated by economic sector are allocated to the economic sector having the largest volume of transactions in that category.

Securities than other than shares issued and loans received by other depository corporations are included in *Other items (Net)*.

Holdings of domestic securities are recorded at book value (principal plus accrued interest) rather than at market prices or fair value. Some loans are reported net of provisions.

Depository Corporations:
† See notes on central bank and other depository corporations.

Monetary Aggregates:

Broad Money:
Broad Money calculated from the liability data in the sections for the central bank and other depository corporations accords with the concepts and definitions of the *MFSM* and is consistent with M2 described below.

Money (National Definitions):
M1 comprises notes and coins in circulation outside the depository corporations and transferable deposits in national and foreign currency of the other financial corporations, state and local

governments, public nonfinancial corporations, other nonfinancial corporations, and other resident sectors with the depository corporations.

M2 comprises M1 and other deposits in national currency of the other financial corporations, state and local governments, public nonfinancial corporations, other nonfinancial corporations, and other resident sectors with the depository corporations.

Interest Rates:

Overdraft Rate:
Rate charged by the BON on overdrafts to commercial banks.

Money Market Rate:
Average rate on loans between banks. † Prior to 1996 refers to the rate charged in the South Africa interbank market.

Treasury Bill Rate:
Tender rate on three-month treasury bills.

Deposit Rate:
Weighted average rate offered by other depository corporations on three-month time deposits. Rate is weighted by deposit amounts.

Lending Rate:
Weighted average rate charged by other depository corporations on loans. Rate is weighted by loan amounts.

Government Bond Yield: Long-Term:
Yield on five-year government bonds. † Beginning in April 2002, yield on 15-year government bonds.

Prices:

Consumer Prices:
Source: Central Bureau of Statistics. Weights Reference Period: 1993–1994; Geographical Coverage: Whole national territory; Basis for Calculation: The Namibia Income and Expenditure Survey was conducted by the National Planning Commission, covering the period of September 1993-August 1994.

International Transactions:

All trade data are from the Central Bureau of Statistics.

Balance of Payments:
The source of data is the Bank of Namibia. For explanatory information see *Balance of Payments, Namibia* published by the Bank of Namibia.

Government Finance:

Annual data are as reported in the *Government Finance Statistics Yearbook (GFSY)* and cover budgetary central government from 1990 onwards. The fiscal year ends March 31.

National Accounts:

Source: Central Bureau of Statistics. Data are prepared in accordance with the 1993 United Nations System of National Accounts.

Nepal   558

Unless otherwise indicated, monthly data refer to Nepalese months ending in the middle of the calendar months shown.

Date of Fund Membership:

September 6, 1961

Standard Sources:

Nepal Rastra Bank
Central Bureau of Statistics

Exchange Rates:

Market Rate (End of Period and Period Average):
Effective February 12, 1993, the dual exchange rate system was unified, and the exchange rate of the Nepali rupee (NR) was set at NR 1.6 to 1 Indian rupee, with cross rates against other currencies determined by the market rate of the Indian rupee against other currencies.

International Liquidity:

Central bank gold and foreign exchange holdings are as of the middle of the month while *lines 1b.d* and *1c.d* are at the end of the month.

Gold (National Valuation) (line 1and): Official gold is valued at US$42.22 per fine troy ounce.

Central Bank:

Consists of the Nepal Rastra Bank (NRB) only.

† Beginning in July 2004, data are based on a standardized report form (SRF) for central banks, which accords with the concepts and definitions of the IMF's *Monetary and Financial Statistics Manual (MFSM)*, 2000. Departures from the *MFSM* methodology are explained below.

Accrued interest is included in *Other Items (Net)* rather than in the outstanding amounts of the financial asset or liability.

Nonmonetary gold is valued at acquisition cost rather than at end-month market price or fair value.

Securities other than shares are valued at acquisition cost rather than at market price or fair value.

Securities other than shares issued by the NRB are valued at face value rather than at market price or fair value.

Shares and other equity are valued at acquisition cost rather than at market price or fair value.

For December 2001 through June 2004, data have less conformity with the *MFSM* methodology and therefore are not strictly comparable to data for later periods. For December 2001, securities repurchase agreements are treated as sales of securities rather than as collateralized loans.

Other Depository Corporations:

Comprises commercial banks. Beginning in April 2008 comprises commercial banks, development banks, and finance companies, which accept deposits. Monthly data for development banks and finance companies for January, April, July, and October (which are end-quarter months in Nepali calendar) are based on accounting records and are estimates for other months.

† Beginning in February 2002, data are based on a standardized report form (SRF) for other depository corporations, which accords with the concepts and definitions of the IMF's *Monetary and Financial Statistics Manual (MFSM)*. For other depository corporations in Nepal, departures from the *MFSM* methodology are explained below.

Accrued interest is included in *Other Items (Net)* rather than in the outstanding amounts of the financial asset or liability.

Securities other than shares are valued at acquisition cost rather than at market price or fair value.

Securities other than shares issued by other depository corporations are recorded at face value rather than at market price or fair value.

Shares and other equity are valued at acquisition cost rather than at market price or fair value.

For December 2001 through January 2002, data have less conformity with the *MFSM* methodology and therefore are not strictly comparable to data for later periods. For December 2001, securities repurchase agreements are treated as sales of securities rather than as collateralized loans.

Depository Corporations:

† See notes on central bank and other depository corporations.

Monetary Aggregates:

Broad Money:

Broad Money (line 59m) calculated from the liability data in the sections for the central bank and other depository corporations differs from M2 described below as M2 includes deposits of development banks and finance companies with commercial banks. Beginning in April 2008, *Broad Money* (line *59m*) calculated from the liability data in the sections for the central bank and other depository corporations (see notes on other depository corporations) accords with the concepts and definitions of the *MFSM* and is consistent with Broad Money (*line 59mea*) described below.

Money (National Definitions):

Reserve Money comprises notes and coins issued by the NRB, commercial banks' deposits in national and foreign currency with the NRB, and demand deposits in national currency of other non-government resident sectors with the NRB.

M1 comprises currency in circulation and demand deposits in national currency of other financial corporations, public nonfinancial corporations, and private sector with the NRB and commercial banks only. Currency in circulation refers to notes and coins issued by the NRB less the amount held by commercial banks only.

M2 comprises M1 and time, savings, and margin deposits in national currency of the private sector with commercial banks only. *Broad Money* comprises currency in circulation, demand, time, savings, and margin deposits in national and foreign currency of other financial corporations, public nonfinancial corporations, and private sector with the NRB, the commercial banks, development banks, and finance companies. Currency in circulation refers to notes and coins issued by the NRB less the amount held by commercial banks, development banks, and finance companies.

Interest Rates:

Central Bank Policy Rate (End of Period):

Rate charged by the NRB on loans to commercial banks for refinance purpose.

Treasury Bill Rate:

Weighted average yield on 91-day treasury bills.

Deposit Rate:

Minimum rate offered by commercial banks on twelve-month time deposits to private sector in national currency.

Lending Rate:

Minimum rate charged by commercial banks on working capital loans to private sector in national currency.

Government Bond Yield:

Yield on government development bonds. † Beginning in March 1984, annual coupon rate on five-year national/citizen savings certificates issued by the government to mobilize funds from nonbank sources.

Prices:

Consumer Prices:

Source: Nepal Rastra Bank. Weights Reference Period: fiscal year 1995–96 (starts in mid-July); Geographical Coverage: urban areas defined as government municipalities (about 13 percent of total population); Number of Items in the Basket: 301 items; Basis for Calculation: 1995–1996 Household Budget Survey in urban areas conducted over the 12-month period.

International Transactions:

All trade data are from Nepal Rastra Bank and are based on customs data.

Government Finance:

Annual data are derived from Nepal Rastra Bank and cover budgetary central government. Debt service payments and grants include foreign transaction in kind. The fiscal year ends July 15.

National Accounts:

Source: Nepal Rastra Bank. As indicated by the country, the data are compiled in the framework of the *1993 SNA*.

Netherlands   138

Data are denominated in guilders prior to January 1999 and in euros from January 1999 onward. The guilder's irrevocable fixed conversion factor to the euro is 2.20371 guilders per euro. In 2002, the guilder was retired from circulation and replaced by euro banknotes and coins. Beginning in January 1999, with the implementation of Stage Three of the European Economic and Monetary Union (EMU), an alternative euro area-wide definition of residency was introduced: All positions with residents of other euro area (EA) countries, including the European Central Bank (ECB), are classified as domestic positions, and foreign assets and foreign liabilities include only positions with non-euro area residents. Descriptions of the changes in the methodology and presentation of the Netherlands' accounts following the introduction of the euro are shown in the introduction to *IFS* and in the footnotes on the euro area page.

Date of Fund Membership:

December 27, 1945

Standard Sources:

Netherlands Bank
Statistics Netherlands
Eurostat

Exchange Rates:

Market Rate (End of Period and Period Average):

Prior to January 1999, the market rate refers to guilder midpoint rate in the Amsterdam market at 2:15 p.m. In January 1999, the guilder became a participating currency with the Eurosystem, and the euro market rate became applicable to all transactions. In 2002, the guilder was retired from circulation and replaced by euro banknotes and coins. For additional information, refer to the section on Exchange Rates in the introduction to *IFS* and the footnotes on the euro area page.

International Liquidity:

Beginning in January 1999, *Total Reserves minus Gold (line 1l.d)* is defined in accordance with the Eurosystem's statistical definition of international reserves. The international reserves of the Netherlands per the Eurosystem statistical definition at the start of the monetary union (January 1, 1999) in billions of U.S. dollars were as follows: *Total Reserves minus Gold,* $13,641; *Foreign Exchange,* $9,766; *SDR holdings,* $905; *Reserve Position in the Fund,* $2,969; *Other Reserve Assets,* $0; *Gold,* $9,726; *Gold (million fine troy ounces),* 33.835 ounces. *Foreign Exchange (line 1d.d):* From March 1979 through December 1998, gold and foreign exchange holdings excluded deposits at the European Monetary Cooperation Fund (EMCF), and the holdings of European currency units (ECUs) issued against these deposits were included in *line 1d.d. Gold (Eurosystem Valuation) (line 1and)* is obtained by converting the value in national currency terms, as reported in the country's standard sources, using the prevailing exchange rate, as given in *line* **ae**. During August 1978-December 1998, gold was revalued every three years at 70 percent of the lowest annual average of the daily noon market prices in Amsterdam in the preceding three years. From January 1999 onward, gold is revalued at market rate at the end of each month. Memorandum data are provided on *Non-Euro Claims on Euro Area Residents* and *Euro Claims on Non-Euro Area Residents,* which represent positions as of the last working day of each month. For additional information, refer to the section on International Liquidity in the introduction to *IFS* and on the euro area page.

Central Bank:

Consists of the Netherlands Bank, which is part of the Eurosystem beginning in January 1999, only. *Currency Issued* includes coins issued by the general government. For a description of the accounts, refer to the section on *Central Bank - Euro Area* in the introduction to *IFS.*

Other Depository Corporations:

Comprises all resident units classified as other monetary financial institutions (other MFIs), as defined in *1995 ESA* standards, including money market funds. For a description of the accounts, refer to the section on *Other Depository Corporations - Euro Area* in the introduction to *IFS.*

Depository Corporations (National Residency):

For a description of the methodology and accounts, refer to the section on *Depository Corporations (National Residency) - Euro Area* in the introduction to *IFS.*

Depository Corporations (Euro Area-wide Residency):

For a description of the methodology and accounts, refer to the section on *Depository Corporations (Euro Area-wide Residency)* in the introduction to *IFS.*

Interest Rates:

Bank Rate (End of Period):
Interest rate charged by the Netherlands Bank on advances to credit institutions. Beginning in January 1999, central bank policy rates are discontinued. See Eurosystem policy rate series on the Euro Area page.

Money Market Rate:
Average market rate paid on bankers' call loans.

Deposit Rate:
Interest rate on savings deposits with minimum balance of five thousand euros. † Prior to December 1993, interest offered by banks on time deposits with three months' notice.

Deposit Rate (lines 60lhs, 60lhn, 60lcs, and 60lcn):
See notes in the introduction to *IFS* and *Euro-area Interest Rates.*

Lending Rate:
Prior to January 1999, referred to midpoint of the minimum and maximum interest charged on current account advances. Beginning in January 1999, represents base rate charged by commercial banks on advances.

Lending Rate (lines 60phs, 60pns, 60phm, 60phn, 60pcs, and 60pcn):
See notes in the introduction to *IFS* and *Euro-area Interest Rates.*

Government Bond Yield:
The data refer to secondary market yields of the most recent 10-year government bond. For additional information, refer to the section on interest rates in the introduction to *IFS* and on the euro area page. This rate is used to measure long-term interest rates for assessing convergence among the European Union member states.

Prices, Production, Labor:

Share Prices:
Share price index, base 1953. † Beginning in August 1968, share price index, base 1963. † Beginning in January 1973, share price index, base 1970. † Beginning in January 1975, share price index, base 1976. † Beginning in January 1983, the AEX Index, base January 3, 1983, covers 25 shares quoted on the Amsterdam Exchange.

Share Prices: Manufacturing:
Manufacturing share price index, base 1953. † Beginning in August 1963, manufacturing share price index, base 1963. † Beginning in January 1973, share price index, base 1970. † Beginning in January 1975, manufacturing share price index, base 1985, comprised a sample of 127 shares; the index was discontinued at the end of 2002.

Producer Prices: Final Products:
Source: Statistics Netherlands. Weights Reference Period: 2006; Sectoral Coverage: mining and quarrying, industry, electricity, gas and water; Number of Items in the Basket: about 23,000 prices from about 4,000 commodities; Basis for Calculation: the indices are computed as base-weighted arithmetic averages of price relatives using the Laspeyres formula. Base year is revised at least every five years.

Consumer Prices:
Source: Statistics Netherlands. Weights Reference Period: 2010; Geographical Coverage: covering all private households in the country; Number of Items in Basket: over 1,300 items and services; Basis for Calculation: the weights are derived primarily from National Accounts results on private consumption. Additional information at a more detailed level is taken from a Household Budget Survey.

Wages: Hourly Rates:
Source: Statistics Netherlands. Weights Reference Period: 2000; The wages used refer to gross basis wage rates for hours normally worked including guaranteed allowances. The indices are mainly based on information laid down in collective labor agreements; Covers wages in manufacturing only.

Industrial Production:

Source: Statistics Netherlands. Weights Reference Period: 2005; Sectoral Coverage: mining and quarrying, manufacturing, electricity, gas, steam and air conditioning supply and water supply; sewerage, waste management and remediation activities; Basis for Calculation: the relative weight is derived from the value added from a monthly survey covering about 6600 establishments.

Industrial Employment:

Statistics Netherlands index. The data refer to the average number of employed at the beginning and the end of the quarter in manufacturing industries, mining, and public utilities.

International Transactions:

Data on exports and imports and trade indices are from Statistics Netherlands.

Government Finance:

Cash data on central government are derived from unpublished sources of the "Rijkshoofdboekhouding" (Accounts Department of the Ministry of Finance) and cover the consolidated central government, excluding the social security funds. Data on general government are derived from Eurostat. The fiscal year ends December 31.

National Accounts:

Source: Statistics Netherlands. As indicated by the country, data are compiled in accordance with the methodology of the *1995 ESA* and the *1993 SNA*. Beginning in 1999, euro data are sourced from the Eurostat database. Chain linked GDP volume measures are expressed in the prices of the previous year and re-referenced to 2005.

Netherlands Antilles 353

See page for Netherlands

The Netherlands Antilles was dissolved on October 10, 2010. After dissolution, the BES Islands (Bonaire, Sint Eustatius, and Saba) became special municipalities of the Netherlands, while Curaçao and Sint Maarten became autonomous countries within the Kingdom of the Netherlands, similar to Aruba, which separated from Netherlands Antilles in 1986.

Standard Sources:

Bank of the Netherlands Antilles
Bureau of Statistics

Exchange Rates:

Official Rate: (End of Period and Period Average):
Central bank midpoint rate. The official rate is pegged to the U.S. dollar.

The weighting scheme used to calculate indices of nominal and real effective exchange rates (*lines* **nec** and **rec**) is based on data for aggregate bilateral non-oil trade flows for 1980.

International Liquidity:

Data include the offshore departments of commercial banks but exclude the transactions of banks operating in Aruba. Data for *line*

1d.d include small foreign exchange holdings by the government. *Gold (National Valuation) (line 1and)* is obtained by converting the value in national currency terms, as reported in the country's standard sources, using the prevailing exchange rate, as given in *line* **ae** or **we.**

Lines 7a.d and *7b.d* refer to the U.S. dollar equivalents of *lines 21* and *26c,* respectively. They include accounts of the special offshore departments of commercial banks. The accounts of a number of other financial institutions dealing exclusively offshore are not included. *Line 7k.d* measures the balance sheet total for most of the offshore banking units (OBUs) licensed to offer a full range of banking facilities to nonresidents. Data agree with Bank of the Netherlands Antilles and are directly reported to *IFS.*

Monetary Authorities:

Consolidates the Bank of the Netherlands Antilles and monetary authority functions undertaken by the central government. The contra-entry to government foreign assets and coin issues is included in *line 12a.* Data include the offshore departments of commercial banks but exclude the transactions of banks operating in Aruba.

Monetary authorities data agree with Bank of the Netherlands Antilles table "Monetary Authorities Summary Account." Exceptions are as follows:

Claims on Private Sector in Bank of the Netherlands Antilles is net of long-term special foreign borrowing.

Reserve Money equals Bank of the Netherlands Antilles data on money base minus Island Government time deposits.

Deposit Money Banks:

Consolidates commercial banks. Data include the offshore departments of commercial banks, excluding banks in Aruba.

Monetary Survey:

Data include the offshore departments of commercial banks but exclude the transactions of banks operating in Aruba. Data agree with the Bank of the Netherlands Antilles table "Money-Creating Institutions Summary Account." The exception is as follows: *Claims on Private Sector* in Bank of the Netherlands Antilles is net of long-term special foreign borrowing by the monetary authorities and commercial banks.

In the monetary survey (see introduction for the standard method of calculation), *line 32an* includes *Central Government Deposits* with Girosystem Curacao (*line 26d.i*), and *line 34* includes *Private Sector Deposits* with Girosystem Curacao (*line 24..i*). *Line 32b* includes the contra-entries for *lines 24..i* and *26d.i. Line 35* is equal to *Time and Savings* plus *Foreign Currency Deposits* (*lines 25a* and *25b,* respectively).

Interest Rates:

Discount Rate (End of Period):
Central bank official discount rate.

Treasury Bill Rate:
Interest rate on three-month treasury bills.

Deposit Rate:
Rate offered by commercial banks on passbook deposits.

Lending Rate:
Rate charged by commercial banks on prime loans.

Government Bond Yield:
Yield on medium- and long-term Government bonds.

Prices:

Consumer Prices:
Source: Bureau of Statistics. Weights Reference Period: October 2006; Geographical Coverage: Curaçao.

International Transactions:

Exports and Imports:
Bureau of Statistics data; also published in Bank of the Netherlands Antilles. *Imports* are reported on a c.i.f. basis beginning 1971. † As of January 1986, data exclude Aruba. Current data for total exports and imports are on a payments basis.

Government Finance:

Annual data are as reported for the *Government Finance Statistics Yearbook (GFSY)* and cover the budgetary central government. † Beginning in 1980, data also cover social security operations. † In 1986, the island government of Aruba became independent of the Netherlands Antilles. † Provisional data for 1995 do not include social security operations. The fiscal year ends December 31.

New Zealand   196

Date of Fund Membership:
August 31, 1961

Standard Sources:
Reserve Bank of New Zealand
Statistics New Zealand

Exchange Rates:

Market Rate (End of Period and Period Average):
Beginning in April 1991, figures are market midrates at 11 a.m., which the Reserve Bank republishes on its website. Prior to that date, figures were established at 3 p.m.

International Liquidity:
Gold (National Valuation) (line 1and) is equal to *Gold (Million Fine Troy Ounces) (line 1ad)*, valued at SDR 35 per fine troy ounce and converted into U.S. dollars at the dollar/SDR rate **sa** on the country page for the United States. Source: OECD

Monetary Authorities:
Consolidates the Reserve Bank of New Zealand and monetary functions undertaken by the central government. The contra-entry to government foreign assets is included in *line 16d;* the contra-entry to Treasury coin issues and the adjustment for Treasury IMF accounts are included in *line 12a.* † Beginning in September 1988, data are based on an improved sectorization of the accounts.

Banking Institutions:
Comprises trading banks. † From September 1988, comprised monetary financial institutions (MFI) whose deposits and private sector loans comprise more than 95 percent of the estimated total MFI market. Data are based on an improved sectorization of the accounts.

Banking Survey:
† See notes on monetary authorities and banking institutions.

Money (National Definitions):
M1 comprises currency outside M3 financial institutions plus check balances, less interinstitutional transaction balances and central government demand deposits. M3 financial institutions include the Reserve Bank of New Zealand, most registered banks, and other financial intermediaries of significant size.
M2 comprises M1 and all other call deposits not included in M1, less interinstitutional call balances.
M3R comprises currency outside M3 institutions and their total New Zealand dollar deposits, less interinstitutional deposits, central government deposits, and deposits from nonresidents. The national official measure of broad money M3 includes NZ dollar deposits from nonresidents.

Other Banking Institutions:
Comprises finance companies and savings banks. The data on finance companies relate to companies with outstanding loans and advances exceeding $NZ200,000 and with assets constituting about 90 percent of the total assets of all finance companies.

Nonbank Financial Institutions:
Comprises life insurance and reassurance companies.

Interest Rates:

Central Bank Policy Rate (End of Period):
Official Cash Rate (OCR) around which the Reserve Bank transacts with the market. The OCR is reviewed eight times a year (every six and a half weeks).

Discount Rate (End of Period):
Rate at which the Reserve Bank discounts eligible 28-day Reserve Bank bills to the market.

Money Market Rate:
Refers to the New Zealand Overnight Interbank Cash Average rate on secured and unsecured overnight transactions, direct or through brokers, between banks, which are price makers in the New Zealand cash market.

Treasury Bill Rate:
Tender rate on three-month treasury bills.

Deposit Rate:
Maximum rate offered by banks on 31- to 89-day small deposits. † Beginning in March 1988, quarterly weighted averages for registered banks' total deposits in national currency. † Beginning in January 1990, weighted average rate offered by New Zealand's six largest banks on six-month deposits of $NZ10,000 or more, each bank's rate being weighted according to its share of the group's total New Zealand dollar deposits.

Lending Rate:
Weighted average interest rate charged by registered banks on loans to New Zealand residents, includes households, business and agriculture. The rate is weighted by loan amounts.

Government Bond Yield:

Yield on government bonds. † Beginning in January 1987, rate on the five-year 'benchmark' bond, a specific bond selected by the Reserve Bank to provide a representative five-year government bond rate.

Prices, Production, Labor:

Share Prices (End of Period):

Share price index, base 1960. † Beginning in January 1961, share price index, base November 1978. † Beginning in January 1967, general index on shares, base January 1968. † Beginning in June 1986, gross index calculated by the New Zealand Stock Exchange, base June 1986. All shares of all public companies listed on the New Zealand Stock Exchange are contained within the index. Payments of a dividend, rights issues, cash issues, and the flotation of new companies each have a neutral effect on the index.

Producer Prices:

Source: Statistics New Zealand. Weight Reference Period: fourth quarter 2010; Coverage: has two types of indexes: the *outputs indexes* which measure changes in the prices received by producers and the *inputs indexes* which measure changes in the cost of production (excluding labor and capital costs); Number of Items in the Basket: approximately 13,000 individual commodity items are surveyed from about 3,000 respondents; Basis for Calculation: since March 1996, the PPI has been produced using industry groups defined by the Australian and New Zealand Standard Industrial Classification (ANZSIC).

Consumer Prices:

Source: Statistics New Zealand. Weight Reference Period: second quarter 2006; Geographical Coverage: all resident households living in permanent dwellings; Number of Items in the Basket: expenditure weight index are derived from 2300 HES expenditure items group to about 360 items in the CPI regimen; Basis for Calculation: the annual Household Economic Survey (HES).

Labor Cost Index:

The index includes salaries and wage rates, overtime wage rates, and some nonwage labor-related costs like annual leave, medical insurance, and low-interest loans. It covers all employees aged 15 years and over in all occupations and all industries except domestic services.

Manufacturing Production:

Data are sourced from the OECD database. Index of manufacturing gross domestic product, base 1995–96, year beginning April 1.

Manufacturing Employment:

Statistics New Zealand data on persons employed in manufacturing.

International Transactions:

All data on trade are from Statistics New Zealand. The index series are of the chain-linked Fisher Ideal type, base second quarter 2002. The merchandise export indexes are calculated using NZ dollar f.o.b.-values. The merchandise import indexes use NZ dollar v.f.d.-values (represent the value of goods excluding the cost of freight and insurance). Prior to the September 2003 quarter, the merchandise import indexes used c.i.f.-values.

Volume of Exports:

Statistics New Zealand Fisher index of volume of exports, base July 1988-June 1989. *Butter:* Statistics New Zealand data reported in thousand metric tons.

Volume of Imports:

Statistics New Zealand Fisher index of volume of imports, base July 1988-June 1989.

Balance of Payments:

Annual balance of payments data for years prior to 1980 are compiled on the basis of fiscal years ending March 31. From 1980 onwards, the data are on a calendar year basis.

International Investment Position:

Data are compiled as at March 31 each year until March 31, 1999. From March 31, 2000, data are available quarterly.

Government Finance:

Annual data are as reported for the *Government Finance Statistics Yearbook (GFSY)* and cover budgetary central government. Annual data refer to a fiscal year different from calendar year (fiscal year ends June 30 from 1990 onwards; fiscal year begins April 1 through 1988). Beginning in 1990, annual data are as reported in the *Government Finance Statistics Yearbook (GFSY)* and cover the budgetary central government. The fiscal year ends June 30.

National Accounts:

Source: Statistics New Zealand. *Lines 99a.c* and *99b.c* include a statistical discrepancy. As indicated by the country, from 1987 onwards data have been revised according to the *1993 SNA*.

Nicaragua   278

Date of Fund Membership:

March 14, 1946

Standard Sources:

Central Bank of Nicaragua

Exchange Rates:

On February 15, 1988 the new cordoba, equal to 1,000 old cordobas, was introduced. A new currency unit called córdoba oro, equivalent to one U.S. dollar, was introduced as a unit of account on May 1, 1990 and began to be circulated in August 1990. On March 4, 1991, the gold córdoba was devalued to US$0.2 per gold córdoba, equal to five million old córdobas. On April 30, 1991 the córdoba completely replaced the gold and the old córdoba as the sole legal tender. *IFS* money and banking accounts are now expressed in gold córdobas.

Principal Rate (End of Period and Period Average):

The córdoba is pegged to the U.S. dollar.

For the purpose of calculating effective exchange rates (*lines* **nec** and **rec**), a weighted average exchange rate index for U.S. dollars per cordoba is based on trade at the rates applicable for exports and imports.

Central Bank:

Consists of the Central Bank of Nicaragua (CBN) only.

Data are based on a standardized report form (SRF) for central banks, which accords with the concepts and definitions of the IMF's *Monetary and Financial Statistics Manual (MFSM)*, 2000. Departures from the *MFSM* methodology are explained below. Financial instruments that cannot be valued at market prices are valued at acquisition cost-as in the case of CBN securities.

For December 2001 to August 2003, accrued interest is included in *Other Items (Net)* rather than in the outstanding amounts of the financial assets and liabilities. Beginning in September 2003, the open market operations system (OMAS) allows the regular calculation of accrued interest.

Other Depository Corporations:

Comprises commercial banks and finance companies. Data exclude microfinance institutions, which accept deposits.

Data are based on a standardized report form (SRF) for other depository corporations, which accords with the concepts and definitions of the *Monetary and Financial Statistics Manual (MFSM)*. For other depository corporations in Nicaragua, departures from the *MFSM* methodology are explained below.

The lack of proper sectorization due to insufficient detail in the source data of other depository corporations, mainly for claims and deposits of the nonfinancial public sector)-i.e., central government, local government, and public nonfinancial corporations-detract from the ability to accurately compile the net credit to central government and the rest of the nonfinancial public sector.

Financial assets and liabilities are valued at market prices, if possible, otherwise, at the acquisition cost.

Depository Corporations:

See notes on central bank and other depository corporations.

Other Financial Corporations:

Consists of the Banco Produzcamos only. Data exclude insurance corporations, pension funds, and financial auxiliaries.

Data are based on a standardized report form (SRF) for other financial corporations, which accords with the concepts and definitions of the *Monetary and Financial Statistics Manual (MFSM)*. For other financial corporations in Nicaragua, departures from the *MFSM* methodology are explained below.

The lack of proper sectorization due to insufficient detail in the source data of other financial corporations, mainly for claims and deposits of the nonfinancial public sector)-i.e., central government, local government, and public nonfinancial corporations-detract from the ability to accurately compile the net credit to central government and the rest of the nonfinancial public sector.

Financial assets and liabilities are valued at market prices, if possible, otherwise, at the acquisition cost.

Monetary Aggregates:

Broad Money:

Broad Money calculated from the liability data in the sections for the central bank and other depository corporations accords with the concepts and definitions of the *MFSM*. Broad money differs from M3A described below as M3A includes deposits of the central government with other depository corporations.

Money (National Definitions):

Base money comprises notes and coins in circulation and deposits in national currency of other depository corporations with the CBN.

M1 comprises notes and coins in circulation outside the banking system and demand deposits in national currency of the private sector with other depository corporations.

M1A comprises M1 and demand deposits in national currency of the nonfinancial public sector with other depository corporations.

M2 comprises M1 and savings and time deposits in national currency of the private sector with other depository corporations.

M2A comprises M2 and savings and time deposits in national currency of the nonfinancial public sector with other depository corporations.

M3 comprises M2 and foreign currency deposits of the private sector with other depository corporations.

M3A comprises M3 and foreign currency deposits of the nonfinancial public sector with other depository corporations.

Interest Rates:

Discount Rate (End of Period):

Rediscount rate charged by the CBN on short-term loans to commercial banks.

Savings Rate:

Rate offered by commercial banks on savings deposits in national currency. † Beginning in January 1999, weighted average rate offered by commercial banks on savings deposits in national currency. The rate is weighted by deposit amounts.

Savings Rate (Foreign Currency):

Rate offered by commercial banks on savings deposits in foreign currency. † Beginning in January 1999, weighted average rate offered by commercial banks on savings deposits in foreign currency. The rate is weighted by deposit amounts.

Deposit Rate:

Average rate offered by commercial banks on one-month deposits in national currency. † Beginning in January 1999, weighted average rate offered by commercial banks on one-month deposits in national currency. The rate is weighted by deposit amounts.

Deposit Rate (Foreign currency):

Average rate offered by commercial banks on one-month deposits in foreign currency. † Beginning in January 1999, weighted average rate offered by commercial banks on one-month deposits in foreign currency. The rate is weighted by deposit amounts.

Lending Rate:

Average rate charged by commercial banks on loans of up to 18 months in national currency. † Beginning in January 1999, weighted average rate charged by commercial banks on loans of up to 18 months in national currency. The rate is weighted by loan amounts.

Lending Rate (Foreign Currency):

Average rate charged by commercial banks on loans of up to 18 months in foreign currency. † Beginning in January 1999, weighted average rate charged by commercial banks on loans of up to 18 months in foreign currency. The rate is weighted by loan amounts.

Prices:

Consumer Prices:

Source: Central Bank of Nicaragua. Weights Reference Period: 2006–2007; Geographical Coverage: Urban areas, Managua and the rest of the departments and autonomous regions; Number of

Items in Basket: 489; Basis for Calculation: The weights are derived from the Household Income and Expenditure Survey (EIGH) carried out in March 2006-February 2007.

Industrial Production:

Source: Central Bank of Nicaragua. Weights Reference Period: January 1992-December 1997; Sectoral Coverage: manufacturing; Basis for Calculation: Laspeyres-type index, Base-year sales are used as weights, and sales of product i are calculated relative to the total sales of activity sector j, as well as total sales of activity sector j relative to total industry sales.

International Transactions:

Central Bank of Nicaragua trade data in U.S. dollars.

Government Finance:

Monthly, quarterly, and annual data are derived from the Central Bank of Nicaragua and information provided by the Central Bank cover budgetary central government. The fiscal year ends December 31.

National Accounts:

Source: Central Bank of Nicaragua.

Niger   692

Date of Fund Membership:

April 24, 1963

Standard Source:

Banque Centrale des Etats de l'Afrique de l'Ouest (Central Bank of West African States)
Institut National de la Statistique
Niger is a member of the West African Economic and Monetary Union, together with Benin, Burkina Faso, Côte d'Ivoire, Guinea-Bissau, Mali, Senegal, and Togo. The Union, which was established in 1962, has a common central bank, the Central Bank of West African States (BCEAO), with headquarters in Dakar, and national branches in the member states. Mali and Guinea-Bissau joined the Union on June 1, 1984 and May 2, 1997, respectively.

Exchange Rates:

Official Rate: (End of Period and Period Average):
Prior to January 1999, the official rate was pegged to the French franc. On January 12, 1994, the CFA franc was devalued to CFAF 100 per French franc from CFAF 50 at which it had been fixed since 1948. From January 1, 1999, the CFAF is pegged to the euro at a rate of CFA franc 655.957 per euro.

International Liquidity:

Gold is revalued on a quarterly basis at the rate communicated by the BCEAO, which corresponds to the lowest average fixing in the London market.

Monetary Authorities:

Comprises the national branch of the BCEAO only. The amount of currency outside banks is estimated by subtracting from the amount of CFA franc notes issued by Niger the estimated amounts of Niger's currency in the cash held by the banks of all member countries of the Union.

Deposit Money Banks:

Comprises commercial banks, the Development Bank, and the Credit du Niger, and includes certain banking operations of the Treasury and the Post Office. The Treasury accepts customs duty bills (reported separately in *line 22d.i*). Through its many branches, the Postal Checking System acts as the main depository for the private sector in the interior of Niger. *Claims on the Private Sector (line 22d)* include doubtful and litigious debts.

† Beginning in 1979, *Central Government Deposits (line 26d)* include the deposits of the public establishments of an administrative or social nature (EPAS) and exclude those of the savings bank; *Demand and Time Deposits (lines 24 and 25)* include deposits of the savings bank and exclude deposits of EPAS; and *Claims on Private Sector (line 22d)* exclude claims on other financial institutions.

Monetary Survey:

The data reported agree with Central Bank of West African States aggregates, as given in the table on the position of the monetary institutions. Valuation differences exist as a result of the IFS calculations of reserve position in the Fund and the SDR holdings, both components of *line 11*, based on Fund record.† Beginning in 1979, *Claims on Other Financial Institutions (line 32f)* includes claims of deposit money banks on other financial institutions; see deposit money bank notes for explanation of other break symbols.

Interest Rates:

Discount Rate (End of Period):
Basic discount rate offered by the BCEAO.

Repurchase Agreement Rate (End of Period):
Rate on repurchase agreements between the BCEAO and the banks.

Money Market Rate:
Rate paid on overnight interbank advances.

Deposit Rate:
Rate offered by banks on time deposits of CFAF 500,000–2,000,000 for under six months.

Prices:

Consumer Prices:
Source: Institut National de la Statistique. Weights Reference Period: 2008; Geographical Coverage: Niamey metropolitan area; Number of Items in Basket: 657; Basis for Calculation: The weights are derived from the survey "WAEMU Prices" of 1996.

International Transactions:

All trade value data are from the Central Bank of West African States .

National Accounts:

Source: Institut National de la Statistique. Data are prepared in accordance with the 1993 United Nations System of National Accounts.

Nigeria   694

Date of Fund Membership:
March 30, 1961

Standard Sources:
Central Bank
National Bureau of Statistics

Exchange Rates:

Principal Rate (End of Period and Period Average):
Central bank midpoint rate. The official exchange rate is based on an allocation by the Central Bank of Nigeria of official foreign exchange receipts to the authorized dealers through a Dutch auction system. Between March 1992 and January 1993 the auction system was replaced by an interbank system under which the official exchange rate was freely determined in the interbank market.

International Liquidity:

Line 1d.d includes small holdings of foreign exchange by the Federal Government.
Gold (National Valuation) (line 1and) is obtained by converting the value in national currency terms, as reported in the country's standard sources, using the prevailing exchange rate, as given in *line* **ae** or **we**.

Central Bank:

Consists of the Central Bank of Nigeria (CBN) only.
† Beginning in December 2007, data are based on the standardized report form (SRF) for central banks, which accords with the concepts and definitions of the IMF's *Monetary and Financial Statistics Manual (MFSM), 2000.* Departures from the *MFSM* methodology are explained below.
Financial derivatives are excluded from the data.
Monetary gold is valued at a fixed price rather than at current market price.
Held-to-maturity securities are valued at acquisition cost rather than at current market price or fair value.
Holdings of equity shares are valued at acquisition cost rather than at current market price or fair value.
For December 2001 through November 2007, data in the SRF format are compiled from pre-SRF data not based on the *MFSM* methodology. Departures from the *MFSM* methodology are explained below.
Financial derivatives are excluded from the data.
Financial assets and liabilities for which financial instrument breakdown is unavailable are allocated to the financial instrument having the largest volume of transactions in the category.
Accrued interest is included in *Other Items (Net) rather than* in the outstanding amounts of the financial assets and liabilities.
Held-to-maturity securities are valued at acquisition cost rather than at current market price or fair value.
Holdings of equity shares are valued at acquisition cost rather than at current market price or fair value.
Some positions with domestic units are recorded on a net basis.

Other Depository Corporations:

Comprises commercial banks, including branches of foreign banks, and nonbank deposit-taking financial institutions, consisting of mi-

crofinance banks and primary mortgage institutions. Data exclude discount houses, development finance institutions, finance companies, and credit unions, which issue short-term liabilities.
† Beginning December 2007, data are based on the standardized report form (SRF) for other depository corporations, which accords with the concepts and definitions of the *Monetary and Financial Statistics Manual (MFSM).* For other depository corporations in Nigeria, departures from the *MFSM* methodology are explained below. Financial derivatives are excluded from the data.
Financial assets and liabilities for which financial instrument breakdown is unavailable are allocated to the financial instrument having the largest volume of transactions in the category.
Accrued interest is included in *Other Items (Net) rather* than in the outstanding amounts of the financial assets and liabilities.
Held-to-maturity securities are valued at acquisition cost rather than at current market price or fair value.
Holdings of equity shares are valued at acquisition cost rather than at current market price or fair value.
Holdings of foreign currency are not converted into national currency using the mid-point exchange rate.
† For December 2001 through November 2007, data in the SRF format are compiled from pre-SRF data not based on the *MFSM* methodology. Departures from the *MFSM* methodology are explained below.
Financial derivatives are excluded from the data.
Financial assets and liabilities for which financial instrument breakdown is unavailable are allocated to the financial instrument having the largest volume of transactions in the category.
Trade credit/advances and settlement accounts are included in *Other Items (Net)* rather than as claims on or liabilities to the corresponding subsectors of the economy.
Financial assets and liabilities for which economic sectorization is unavailable are allocated to the economic sector having the largest volume of transactions in the category.
Claims on Central Government and *Liabilities to Central Government* include positions with state and local governments.
Other Items (Net) includes positions with other financial corporations.
Some positions with domestic units are recorded on a net basis.
Accrued interest is included in *Other Items (Net)* rather than in the outstanding amounts of the financial assets and liabilities.
Held-to-maturity securities are valued at acquisition cost rather than at current market price or fair value.
Holdings of equity shares are valued at acquisition cost rather than at current market price or fair value.
Holdings of foreign currency are not converted into national currency using the mid-point exchange rate.

Depository Corporations:

† See notes on central bank and other depository corporations.

Monetary Aggregates:

Broad Money:
Broad Money calculated from the liability data in the sections for the central bank and other depository corporations accords with the concepts and definitions of the *MFSM* and differs slightly from M2 mainly because of a better economic sectorization used in broad money.

Money (National Definitions):

Narrow Money (M1) comprises currency outside depository corporations; demand deposits of state and local governments and public nonfinancial corporations with the CBN; deposits of state and local governments, public nonfinancial corporations, and private sector with depository corporations.

Quasi Money comprises time and savings deposits of state and local governments and public nonfinancial corporations with the CBN; deposits of state and local governments, public nonfinancial corporations, and private sector with other depository corporations.

Broad Money (M2) comprises M1 and quasi-money.

Interest Rates:

Discount Rate (End of Period):
Minimum rediscount rate offered by the CBN.

Treasury Bill Rate:
Rate on new issues of treasury bills.

Savings Rate:
Weighted average rate offered by commercial banks on savings deposits. The rate is weighted by deposits amounts.

Deposit Rate:
Weighted average rate offered by commercial banks on three-month deposits. The rate is weighted by deposits amounts.

Lending Rate:
Prime lending rate charged by commercial banks on first-class advances.

Prices and Production:

Consumer Prices:
Source: National Bureau of Statistics. Weights Reference Period: November 2009; Geographical Coverage: whole national territory; Number of Items in Basket: 512; Basis for Calculation: weights are determined based on the Nigeria Living Survey 2003/04 updated to 2009.

Industrial Production:
Central Bank index, weights reference period 1990 covering mining (mainly crude petroleum), manufacturing, and electricity.

Crude Petroleum Production:
Central Bank data.

Manufacturing Production in the eastern states was not included prior to the third quarter of 1971. The manufacturing production index is a component of the industrial production index.

International Transactions:

Data are from the Central Bank.

Government Finance:

Data are derived from the Central Bank and cover the operations of the budgetary central government. The fiscal year ends December 31.

National Accounts:

Source: National Bureau of Statistics. *Lines 99a* and *99b* include a statistical discrepancy. *Line 96f* includes increases and/or decreases in stocks. Prior to May 1981, national accounts data were reported in years beginning on April 1. The large fluctuations in 1995 were due to a movement away from a pegged exchange rate in 1994 to a market-determined exchange rate in 1995. The data are compiled in the framework of the *1993 SNA*.

Norway   142

Date of Fund Membership:
December 27, 1945

Standard Sources:
Bank of Norway
Statistics Norway

Exchange Rates:

Official Rate: (End of Period and Period Average):
The Norwegian kroner was floated on December 10, 1992, with the aim of maintaining a stable krone exchange rate against European currencies.

International Liquidity:

Gold (National Valuation) (line 1and) is revalued monthly using the end-of-period London Gold Market Fixing price. In the period December 1999 to December 2001, gold was valued at 20 percent below market value as gold was traded in an illiquid market. Prior to this period, gold was valued according to historical cost. Data for *Foreign Exchange (line 1d.d)* do not include Government Petroleum Fund investments.

Monetary Authorities:

Beginning in 1976, data for the Bank of Norway are based on improved sectorization in national source data. From May 1996 to June 1999, the Government Petroleum Fund investments are included in *Foreign Assets (line 11)*, and the Government Petroleum Fund deposits are included in *Central Government Deposits (line 16d)*.

Deposit Money Banks:

Comprises the commercial and savings banks and the Postal Bank. † Beginning in 1976, data for state banks are based on improved sectorization in national source data.

Beginning in 1995, the P.O. Savings Bank and Postal Giro, the accounts of which were previously published under a separate subsection of the deposit money banks, merged into the Postal Bank.

Monetary Survey:

See Introduction for the standard method of calculation.

Money (National Definitions):

Broad Money (line 39m) is defined as the money holding sector's possession of notes and coins, bank deposits (both in Norwegian kroner and foreign currencies), and certificates of deposits. Restricted deposits are not included in *Broad Money*. The money holding sector consists of local government, nonfinancial corporations, households, and other financial corporations (other than banks and state lending institutions).

Other Banking Institutions:

Comprises state lending institutions and mortgage institutions. Beginning in January 1984, data for *State Lending Institutions* include two additional banks. Beginning in 1988, data for *Mortgage Institutions* are based on a more detailed reporting of accounts.

Nonbank Financial Institutions:

Comprises life insurance companies.

Interest Rates:

Central Bank Policy Rate (End of Period):
Marginal lending rate of the Bank of Norway.

Average Cost for Central Bank Funding:
Weighted average rate of interest on the Bank of Norway's overnight, fixed-rate, and subsidized loans to banks.

Deposit Rate:
Average rate on all time deposits with deposit money banks. Beginning in the second quarter of 2001, statistics for deposit rates have been revised in keeping with new specifications for banks' monthly balance sheets. As a result the deposit rate refers to deposits other than deposits on transaction accounts.

Lending Rate:
Average rate of interest on all loans extended by deposit money banks.

Three-Month Interbank Rate (Norwegian Interbank Offered Rate—NIBOR):
Norwegian kroner rate in the foreign exchange market, based on forward rates.

Government Bond Yield:
Yield to maturity on five-year government bonds.

Prices, Production, Labor:

Share Prices:
Share price index, base 1937. † Beginning In January 1970, share price index, base January 1, 1972. † Beginning in January 1983, share price index, base January 1, 1983. The index refers to mid-month prices of manufacturing and mining shares quoted on the Oslo Exchange. † Beginning in January 1996, data refer to the Oslo All-Share Index, base December 29, 1995. The Oslo All-Share Index is a market capitalization weighted index tracking all shares listed on the exchange.

Producer Prices:
Source: Statistics Norway. Weights reference period: weights are updated annually; Sectoral Coverage: selling prices for the domestic market and for the exports of goods in the oil and gas extraction, mining, manufacturing (most activities), and electricity supply production sectors; Number of Items in Basket: approximately 1250 establishments; Basis for Calculation: weights are based on output and export values from the year t–1 national accounts, and the data obtained from the sample survey are subsequently weighted by market share indices to arrive at the producer price index.

Consumer Prices:
Source: Statistics Norway. Weights reference period: weights are updated annually; Geographical Coverage: whole national territory; Number of Items in Basket: 810; Basis for Calculation: the weights used in the index are derived from the annual Household Budget Surveys (HBS).

Wages: Monthly Earnings:
Source: Statistics Norway. Weights reference period: 2005. Data refer to total average monthly earnings. The index is prepared on the basis of reports from a representative sample of companies.

Industrial Production:
Source: Statistics Norway. Weights Reference Period: weights are updated annually; Sectoral Coverage: oil and gas extraction, mining and quarrying, manufacturing, and electricity supply in-dustries; Basis for Calculation: the weights are based on the value added at factor cost of the different industries.

Crude Petroleum Production:
Bank of Norway data in thousand metric tons.

International Transactions:

All trade data are from the *Monthly Bulletin of External Trade.*
Trade indices are from Statistics Norway, weights reference period: 2000. Volume data are Laspeyres indices, and unit value data are Paasche indices. The coverage of the trade data is slightly less comprehensive than in the national accounts and balance of payments. Items not included in the merchandise trade data are primarily certain goods shipped directly to and from oil fields, shipping and air companies' expenditures on fuel abroad, and direct export to foreign ships, oil rigs and air companies' expenditures abroad.

Government Finance:

Annual consolidated central government cash data are as reported for the *Government Finance Statistics Yearbook (GFSY).* † Beginning in 1996, quarterly general government data are reported according to the *GFSM 2001* analytical framework. † Beginning in 2003, monthly budgetary central government data also are reported according to the *GFSM 2001* analytical framework. The fiscal year ends December 31.

National Accounts:

Source: Statistics Norway. As indicated by the country, beginning in 1970, data are compiled in accordance with the methodology of the *1995 ESA* and the *1993 SNA.* Chain linked GDP volume measures are expressed according to 2010 prices.

Oman 449

Date of Fund Membership:
December 23, 1971

Standard Sources:
Central Bank of Oman
Ministry of Development

Exchange Rates:

Official Rate: (End of Period and Period Average):
The official rate is pegged to the U.S. dollar.

International Liquidity:

Gold (National Valuation) (line 1and) is obtained by converting the value in national currency terms, as reported in the country's standard sources, using the prevailing exchange rate, as given in line **de,** line **ae,** or line **we.**
Line 3..d reports the foreign currency deposits of the State General Reserve Fund with the Central Bank.
Lines 7a.d and *7b.d* are based on balance sheet data which report gross claims on and liabilities to head offices, branches, and other banks abroad. Prior data included net figures.

Central Bank:

Consists of the Central Bank of Oman (CBO) only.

† Beginning in January 2007, data are based on a standardized report form (SRF) for central banks, which accords with the concepts and definitions of the IMF's *Monetary and Financial Statistics Manual (MFSM)*, 2000. Departures from the *MFSM* methodology are explained below.

Accrued interest on deposits and certificates of deposit issued by the CBO is included in *Other Items (Net)* rather than in the outstanding amounts of the financial liability.

For December 2001 through December 2006, data have less conformity with the *MFSM* methodology and therefore are not strictly comparable to data for later periods.

Other Items (Net) includes claims on private sector, holdings of securities issued by commercial banks, holdings of shares issued by other financial corporations, and valuation adjustment.

Prior to January 2003, certificates of deposit issued by the CBO held by other depository corporations are included in *Monetary Base* (specifically in *Liabilities to Other Depository Corporations*) rather than in *Other Liabilities to Other Depository Corporations*.

Other Depository Corporations:

Comprises commercial banks.

† Beginning in January 2007, data are based on a standardized report form (SRF) for other depository corporations, which accords with the concepts and definitions of the IMF's *Monetary and Financial Statistics Manual (MFSM)*. For other depository corporations in Oman, departures from the *MFSM* methodology are explained below.

Financial derivatives are included in *Other Items (Net)* rather than classified in claims or liabilities to the counterpart sector.

Accrued interest on holdings of central government securities and certificates of deposits issued by other depository corporations is included in *Other Items (Net)* rather than in the outstanding amounts of the financial asset or liability.

Central government securities are recorded at face value rather than at current market price or fair value.

For December 2001 through December 2006, data have less conformity with the *MFSM* methodology and therefore are not strictly comparable to data for later periods.

Claims on Private Sector includes claims on other financial corporations.

Securities issued by commercial banks held by nonresidents are included in *Other Items (Net)*.

Prior to January 2003, holdings of certificates of deposit issued by the CBO are included in *Other Items (Net)*.

Depository Corporations:

† See notes on central bank and other depository corporations.

Monetary Aggregates:

Broad Money:
Broad Money calculated from the liability data in the sections for the central bank and other depository corporations accords with the concepts and definitions of the *MFSM* and is consistent with M2 described below.

Money (National Definitions):
Reserve Money comprises currency issued by the CBO and deposits of commercial banks with the CBO.

M1 comprises currency in circulation and transferable deposits of resident non-bank non-central government sectors in national

currency with commercial banks. Currency in circulation refers to notes and coins issued by the CBO less the amount held by commercial banks.

M2 comprises M1, savings and time deposits in national currency, import deposits, and foreign currency deposits of nonbank non-central government sectors with commercial banks.

Interest Rates:

Discount Rate (End of Period):
Rate Charged by the CBO on loans to commercial banks.

Central Bank Bill Rate:
Weighted average rate on 28-day certificates of deposit issued by the CBO.

Money Market Rate:
Rate charged on overnight inter-bank lending in national currency.

Deposit Rate:
Weighted average rate offered by commercial banks on time deposits of the private sector in national currency. The rate is weighted by deposit amounts.

Deposit Rate (Foreign Currency):
Weighted average rate offered by commercial banks on time deposits of the private sector in foreign currency. The rate is weighted by deposit amounts.

Lending Rate:
Weighted average rate charged by commercial banks on all loans in national currency. The rate is weighted by loan amounts.

Lending Rate (Foreign Currency):
Weighted average rate charged by commercial banks on all loans in foreign currency. The rate is weighted by loan amounts.

Prices and Production:

Consumer Prices:
Source: Ministry of Development. Weights reference period: 1999–2000; Geographical coverage: all regions and governorates, except Musandam Governorate and Al-Wusta region; *Number of items in basket: 304;* Basis for calculation: Laspeyres type index that uses the annual base year expenditure weights from the 1999–2000 Household Expenditure Survey of the Sultanate.

Crude Petroleum Production:
Index calculated from Central Bank of Oman.

International Transactions:

Exports:
Ministry of Development data, except for the value of *Crude Petroleum* exports. The value of crude petroleum exports is obtained by multiplying the volume by the export price. Volume exports and the export prices of crude petroleum are from the Ministry of Development. Data are based on monthly average government sales prices in U.S. dollars per barrel.

Imports, c.i.f.:
Ministry of Development data, excluding public sector imports and, prior to mid–1973, petroleum company imports and imports of contractors undertaking public development projects.

Government Finance:

Annual data are as reported in the *Government Finance Statistics Yearbook (GFSY)* and cover transactions or recurrent and capital budgets of central government (the operations of the State General Reserve Fund are not included). The fiscal year ends December 31.

Pakistan 564

Data on international liquidity prior to July 1977 refer to last Friday of the period.

Date of Fund Membership:
July 11, 1950

Standard Sources:
State Bank of Pakistan
Federal Bureau of Statistics

Exchange Rates:

Market Rate (End of Period and Period Average):
Prior to July 22, 1998, the State Bank of Pakistan buying rate. †
From July 22, 1998 to May 18, 1999, the rate established by the State Bank of Pakistan. † Beginning in May 19, 1999, Free Interbank Exchange rate, as determined in the interbank foreign exchange market.

International Liquidity:

Gold (National Valuation) (line 1and) is obtained by converting the value in national currency terms, as reported in the country's standard sources, using the prevailing exchange rate, as given in *line ae*. Gold is revalued annually on the last working day of June on the basis of the closing market rates fixed in London. Beginning in June 2007, gold is revalued at the end of each month on the basis of the closing market rates fixed in London.

Central Bank:

Consists of the State Bank of Pakistan (SBP) only.
† Beginning in June 2008, data are based on a standardized report form (SRF) for central banks, which accords with the concepts and definitions of the IMF's *Monetary and Financial Statistics Manual (MFSM)*, 2000. Departures from the *MFSM* methodology are explained below.
For June 2008 through August 2009, financial derivatives record the full amount of the underlying instrument on both assets and liabilities rather than only those asset and liability positions resulting from price changes in the underlying instrument.
† For September 2006 through May 2008, even though data are based on a SRF for central banks, they have less conformity with the *MFSM* methodology and therefore are not strictly comparable to data for later periods. Departures from the *MFSM* methodology are explained below.
Repurchase agreements (repos) are treated as outright sales of securities rather than as collateralized loans.
Overdrafts of the provincial governments are deducted from *Deposits Excluded from Broad Money* rather than included in *Claims on State and Local Governments*.
For September 2006 through May 2007, monetary gold is revalued on an annual basis rather than monthly.
For December 2001 through August 2006, data in the SRF format are compiled from pre-SRF data not based on the *MFSM*

methodology. Departures from the *MFSM* methodology are explained below.
Financial assets and liabilities not disaggregated by economic sector are allocated to the economic sector having the largest share in the category.
Repurchase agreements (repos) are treated as outright sales of securities rather than as collateralized loans.
Overdrafts of the provincial governments are deducted from *Deposits Excluded from Broad Money* rather than included in *Claims on State and Local Governments*.
Monetary gold is revalued on an annual basis rather than monthly.
Financial derivatives are excluded from the data.
Accrued interest is included in *Other Items (Net)* rather than in the outstanding amounts of the financial assets and liabilities.

Other Depository Corporations:

Comprises scheduled banks. Beginning in June 2008, includes depository development financial institutions, leasing companies, investment banks, modarabas, housing finance companies, and cooperative banks. Beginning in April 2009, includes microfinance institutions. Data exclude other depository corporations in liquidation, whose total assets are small.
† Beginning in June 2008, data are based on a standardized report form (SRF) for other depository corporations, which accords with the concepts and definitions of the *Monetary and Financial Statistics Manual (MFSM)*. For other depository corporations in Pakistan, departures from the *MFSM* methodology are explained below.
Some accrued interest not disaggregated by economic sector is allocated to the economic sector proportionally, based on its share in the category.
† For September 2006 through May 2008, even though data are based on a SRF for other depository corporations, they have less conformity with the *MFSM* methodology and therefore are not strictly comparable to data for later periods. Departures from the *MFSM* methodology are explained below.
Securities issued by scheduled banks are not separately identified and are mostly included in *Other Items (Net)*.
Repurchase agreements (repos) are treated as outright sales of securities rather than as collateralized loans.
Financial derivatives are included in *Other Items (Net)* rather than shown separately as claims on or liabilities to the corresponding subsectors of the economy resulting from price changes in the underlying instrument.
Some accrued interest is included in *Other Items (Net)* rather than in the outstanding amounts of the financial assets and liabilities.
For December 2001 through August 2006, data in the SRF format are compiled from pre-SRF data not based on the *MFSM* methodology. Departures from the *MFSM* methodology are explained below.
Financial assets and liabilities not disaggregated by economic sector are allocated to the economic sector having the largest share in the category.
Securities issued by scheduled banks are not separately identified and are mostly included in *Other Items (Net)*.
Repurchase agreements (repos) are treated as outright sales of securities rather than as collateralized loans.
Financial derivatives are included in *Other Items (Net)* rather than

shown separately as claims on or liabilities to the corresponding subsectors of the economy resulting from price changes in the underlying instrument.

Accrued interest is included in *Other Items (Net)* rather than in the outstanding amounts of the financial assets and liabilities.

Depository Corporations:

† See notes on central bank and other depository corporations.

Monetary Aggregates:

Broad Money:

Broad Money calculated from the liability data in the sections for the central bank and other depository corporations accords with the concepts and definitions of the *MFSM*. Broad money includes coins issued by the central government, Post Office deposits, and households' savings through government schemes, including Special Savings Certificates (SSCs), Defence Savings Certificates (DSCs), Prize Bonds, and National Saving accounts. Broad Money is consistent with M3 described below.

For December 2001 through May 2006, broad money excludes households' savings through government schemes and differs from M2 described below as M2 excludes Post Office deposits.

Money (National Definitions):

Reserve Money comprises currency in circulation, transferable deposits in national and foreign currency of other depository corporations with the SBP, and transferable and other deposits in national currency of other financial corporations, public nonfinancial corporations, and private sector with the SBP. Currency in circulation refers to notes issued by the SBP less note holdings of the SBP.

M1 comprises currency in circulation outside depository corporations and transferable deposits in national and foreign currency of other financial corporations, public nonfinancial corporations, and private sector with depository corporations. Currency in circulation outside depository corporations refers to the notes in circulation less the note and coin holdings of other depository corporations.

M2 comprises M1, coins in circulation outside depository corporations issued by the central government, other deposits in national and foreign currency of other financial corporations, public nonfinancial corporations, and private sector with depository corporations, and securities other than shares issued by other depository corporations held by other financial corporations, public nonfinancial corporations, and private sector.

M3 comprises M2, Post Office deposits, and households' savings through government schemes, including SSCs, DSCs, Prize Bonds, and National Saving accounts.

Interest Rates:

Discount Rate (End of Period):

The State Bank of Pakistan rate on its repurchase facility. † Prior to January 1994, rate at which the State Bank of Pakistan made advances to scheduled banks against acceptable securities. Beginning in 1994, data refer to the State Bank of Pakistan discount rate for its reverse repo facility.

Money Market Rate:

Monthly average of daily minimum and maximum call-money rates.

Treasury Bill Rate:

Weighted average yield on six-month treasury securities. † Prior to July 1996, rate on six-month Federal Treasury Bill. Since July 1996, rate on six-month Federal Treasury Bond (STFB), which replaced the six-month Federal Treasury Bill.

Government Bond Yield:

Beginning in June 1989, data relate to monthly yields based on average prices quoted on the last Wednesday of the month for the 113/4 percent bond due for redemption in 2002.

Prices, Production, Labor:

Share Prices (End of Month):

Share price index, base 1969–70. † Beginning in July 1976, share price index, base 1975–76. † Beginning in July 1981, share price index, base 1980–81. † Beginning in July 1991, share price index refers to midday quotes for the last Friday of the month for 242 common shares on the Karachi Exchange, base 2000–2001. The index is chained. † Beginning in September 1997, share price index refers to midday quotes for the last day of the month for 100 common shares on the Karachi Exchange, base November 1991.

Wholesale Prices:

Source: Federal Bureau of Statistics. † Weights reference period: 2007–2008; Coverage: food, raw material, fuel, lighting, lubricants, and manufactures; Number of items in basket: 463 commodities; Basis for calculation: Weights are based on 1990/91 national marketable surpluses (total value of output less use by the producers themselves plus imports minus exports if any).

Consumer Prices:

Source: Federal Bureau of Statistics. Weights reference period: 2007–2008; Geographical Coverage: 40 urban centers of Pakistan; Number of Items in Basket: 487; Basis for Calculation: weights are derived from the Family Budget Survey conducted in 2007–2008.

Manufacturing Production:

Source: Federal Bureau of Statistics. Weights Reference Period: 1999–2000; Coverage: manufacturing; Number of Items in Basket: 100; Basis for Calculation: quantum index numbers of manufacturing.

International Transactions:

All trade data are from the Federal Bureau of Statistics.

Value of Exports and Imports:

Export data include re-exports. Trade in military goods and silver bullions are excluded.

Volume and Unit Value of Exports and Imports:

Laspeyres indices, weights reference period: 1990–91. The export indices cover 96.5 percent of total exports, and the import indices cover 86.7 percent of total imports.

Government Finance:

Annual data are as reported for the *Government Finance Statistics Yearbook (GFSY)* and cover budgetary central government. The fiscal year ends June 30.

National Accounts:

Source: Federal Bureau of Statistics.

Panama 283

Date of Fund Membership:
March 14, 1946

Standard Sources:
Directorate of Statistics and Census

Exchange Rates:

Official Rate: (End of Period and Period Average):
Rates are based on a fixed relationship to the U.S. dollar.

International Liquidity:

Lines 7a.d and *7b.d* relate to foreign accounts of deposit money banks operating under general licenses, as reported in section 20. In addition, there are international license banks (ILB) that deal freely with the foreign sector but are limited locally to interbank markets.

Central Bank:

Consists of the National Bank of Panama (NBP) only. The NBP performs some central banking functions, i.e., fiscal agent for the Government, a clearing house for commercial banks, and holder of international reserves and positions vis-à-vis the IMF.

† Beginning in December 2002, data are based on a standardized report form (SRF) for central banks, which accords with the concepts and definitions of the IMF's *Monetary and Financial Statistics Manual (MFSM)*, 2000. All assets and liabilities with a resident unit are classified as if in national currency (the U.S. dollar is assumed to be the national currency for officially dollarized countries in *IFS*). Departures from the *MFSM* methodology are explained below.

Assets and liabilities denominated in foreign currencies other than the U.S. dollar cannot be identified and are included as if in national currency.

Claims on Central Government and *Liabilities to Central Government* generally include assets and liabilities with the state or local governments, respectively.

Assets and liabilities with nonfinancial public corporations are generally not separately identified and included as with other nonfinancial corporations.

Assets and liabilities with other depository corporations include those with commercial banks only. Positions with the rest of other depository corporations are classified as with other financial corporations.

Deposits Included in Broad Money and *Securities Other than Shares Included in Broad Money* include long-term deposits and securities other than shares, respectively. Held-to-maturity securities are valued at acquisition cost rather than at current market price or fair value.

Holdings of equity shares not traded in active markets are valued at acquisition cost rather than at market price or fair value.

For December 2001 through November 2002, data have less conformity with the *MFSM* methodology and therefore are not strictly comparable to data for later periods.

Other Depository Corporations:

Comprises commercial banks and savings houses. Data exclude credit and savings corporations, money market mutual funds, and savings and loans mortgage associations.

† Beginning in December 2002, data are based on a standardized report form (SRF) for other depository corporations, which accords with the concepts and definitions of the IMF's *Monetary and Financial Statistics Manual (MFSM)*. All assets and liabilities with a resident unit are classified as if in national currency (the U.S. dollar is assumed to be the national currency for officially dollarized countries in *IFS*). Departures from the *MFSM* methodology are explained below.

Assets and liabilities denominated in foreign currencies other than the U.S. dollar cannot be identified and are included as if in national currency.

Claims on Central Government and *Liabilities to Central Government* generally include assets and liabilities with the state or local governments, respectively.

Assets and liabilities with nonfinancial public corporations are generally not separately identified and included as with other nonfinancial corporations.

Assets and liabilities with other depository corporations include those with commercial banks only. Positions with the rest of other depository corporations are classified as with other financial corporations.

Other Deposits Included in Broad Money and *Securities Other than Shares Included in Broad Money* include long-term deposits and securities other than shares, respectively.

Held-to-maturity securities are valued at acquisition cost rather than at current market price or fair value.

Holdings of equity shares not traded in active markets are valued at acquisition cost rather than at market price or fair value.

For December 2001 through November 2002, data have less conformity with the *MFSM* methodology and therefore are not strictly comparable to data for later periods.

Depository Corporations:

† See notes on central bank and other depository corporations.

Interest Rates:

Money Market Rate:
Rate on funds obtained by commercial banks on one-month deposits in the interbank market. † Beginning in February 2006, the rate is calculated as an average of the rates paid during the month.

Savings Rate:
Rate offered by commercial banks on savings deposits to nonfinancial corporations.

Deposit Rate:
Average rate offered by domestic banks on six-month time deposits. † Beginning in December 1992, weighted average rate offered by domestic banks on six-month time deposits. The rate is weighted by deposit amounts.

Lending Rate:
Average rate charged by banks on one- to five-year loans for trading activities. † Beginning in June 1990, weighted average rate charged by banks on one- to five-year loans for trading activities. † Beginning in December 2000, weighted average rate charged by domestic banks on one- to five-year loans for trading activities. The rate is weighted by loan amounts.

Prices and Production:

Wholesale Prices:

Source: Directorate of Statistics and Census. Index of wholesale prices for the entire country, covering the agricultural, industrial, and import sectors, base 1987.

Consumer Prices:

Source: Directorate of Statistics and Census. Weights Reference Period: October 2002; Geographical Coverage: Urban areas of the whole country; Number of Items in Basket: 211; Basis for Calculation: The data source is retail merchants.

International Transactions:

All trade data are from the Directorate of Statistics and Census. Exports include re-exports and petroleum products.

Volume of Exports:

IFS average of commodities with a 1985 value of exports as weights.

Government Finance:

Monthly and quarterly data cover budgetary central government only. Data on outstanding debt are derived from the annual bulletin published by "Contraloría General de la República," entitled *Situacion Economica.* The fiscal year ends December 31.

National Accounts:

Source: Directorate of Statistics and Census. As indicated by the authorities, concepts and definitions are in accordance with the *1993 SNA.*

Papua New Guinea   853

Date of Fund Membership:

October 9, 1975

Standard Sources:

Bank of Papua New Guinea
National Statistics Office

Exchange Rates:

Market Rate (End of Period and Period Average):

Prior to 1994, central bank midpoint rate. Beginning in 1994, closing rate set at the foreign exchange auction in which commercial banks, the only authorized foreign exchange dealers, participate. The exchange rate floats independently with respect to the U.S. dollar and is determined in the interbank market.

International Liquidity:

Gold (National Valuation) (line 1and) was revalued at the end of December 2001 to reflect the market price of gold instead of the historical cost.

Central Bank:

Consists of the Bank of Papua New Guinea (BPNG) only.
Data are based on a standardized report form (SRF) for central banks, which accords with the concepts and definitions of the IMF's *Monetary and Financial Statistics Manual (MFSM),* 2000. Departures from the *MFSM* methodology are explained below.

Accrued interest not disaggregated by economic sector is allocated to the economic sector having the largest volume of transactions in the category.

For September 2004 through August 2005, all central bank bills issued by the BPNG are included in *Other Liabilities to Other Depository Corporations* in the absence of data on an individual economic sector's holdings, recognizing that other depository corporations are the principal holders of central bank bills.

Other Depository Corporations:

Comprises commercial banks, finance companies, merchant banks, savings and loan societies, and a microfinance company. Beginning in March 2008, includes the other microfinance company and excludes some savings and loans societies.

† Beginning in March 2008, data are based on a standardized report form (SRF) for other depository corporations, which accords with the concepts and definitions of the *Monetary and Financial Statistics Manual (MFSM).* For other depository corporations in Papua New Guinea, departures from the *MFSM* methodology are explained below.

Some financial derivatives are excluded from the data.

Some accrued interest and trade credit are included in *Other Items (Net)* rather than in the outstanding amounts of the financial assets and liabilities.

For December 2001 through February 2008, data in the SRF format are compiled from pre-SRF data which are not fully based on the *MFSM* methodology. Departures from the *MFSM* methodology are explained below.

Financial derivatives are excluded from the data.

Financial assets and liabilities for which economic sectorization is unavailable are allocated to the economic sector having the largest volume of transactions in the category.

Though data for other depository corporations were not directly distinguished from data for other financial corporations, separation of the data was based on the characteristics of the financial asset or liability. *Transferable Deposits Included in Broad Money* and *Other Deposits Included in Broad Money* include some deposits of other depository corporations other than commercial banks. *Other Items (Net)* includes some claims on other financial corporations.

For September 2004 through August 2005, *Other Claims on Central Bank* includes the holdings of all central bank bills issued by the BPNG, even though some central bank bills were held by other sectors.

Claims on Central Government is understated by the amount of central bank bills that, though held by other sectors, were treated as being held by other depository corporations.

Claims on Private Sector includes some fixed assets in the form of real estate.

Accrued interest is included in *Other Items (Net)* rather than in the outstanding amounts of the financial assets and liabilities.

Securities other than shares are valued at acquisition cost rather than at current market price or fair value. Shares and other equity are valued at lower of acquisition cost or market price rather than at market price or fair value.

Depository Corporations:

† See notes on central bank and other depository corporations.

Other Financial Corporations:

Comprises superannuation funds, life insurance companies, National Development Bank, investment managers, and fund administrators. Beginning in June 2011, includes life insurance brokers. Beginning in December 2011, includes general insurance companies. Data exclude some general insurance companies, private money lenders, trustees, one life insurance broker, general insurance brokers, and other financial auxiliaries.

Data are based on a standardized report form (SRF) for other financial corporations, which accords with the concepts and definitions of the *Monetary and Financial Statistics Manual (MFSM)*. For other financial corporations in Papua New Guinea, departures from the *MFSM* methodology are explained below.

Financial assets and liabilities for which financial instrument breakdown is unavailable are allocated to the financial instrument having the largest volume of transactions in the category.

Financial assets and liabilities for which economic sectorization is unavailable are allocated to the economic sector having the largest volume of transactions in the category.

Accrued interest is included in *Other Items (Net)* rather than in the outstanding amounts of the financial assets and liabilities.

Securities other than shares and shares and other equity are valued at acquisition cost rather than at current market price or fair value.

Financial Corporations:

See notes on central bank, other depository corporations, and other financial corporations.

Monetary Aggregates:

Broad Money:

Broad Money calculated from the liability data in the sections for the central bank and other depository corporations accords with the concepts and definitions of the *MFSM* and is consistent with M3* described below.

Money (National Definitions):

Reserve Money comprises currency in circulation, deposits of other depository corporations with the BPNG, and transferable deposits of other financial corporations and private sector with the BPNG.

M1* comprises currency outside other depository corporations and transferable deposits of other financial corporations, provincial and local governments, public nonfinancial corporations, and private sector (other nonfinancial corporations and other resident sectors) with the BPNG and other depository corporations.

M3* comprises M1* and quasi-money. Quasi-money comprises savings and term deposits of other financial corporations, provincial and local governments, public nonfinancial corporations, and private sector (other nonfinancial corporations and other resident sectors) with the BPNG and other depository corporations.

Interest Rates:

Central Bank Policy Rate (End of Period):

The Kina Facility Rate (KFR) provides a signal to the market of the BPNG's monetary stance and is announced monthly.

Discount Rate (End of Period):

Rate charged by the Bank of Papua New Guinea (BPNG) on loans to commercial banks. † Beginning in January 1993, maximum rate charged by the BPNG on loans to commercial banks against acceptable commercial paper. † Beginning in May 1995, rate refers to the Kina Auction Facility and is the weighted average of bids in national currency placed by commercial banks at the auction. On February 5, 2001, the Kina Auction Facility was replaced with the (KFR) and an overnight REPO facility. Both the Kina Auction and the overnight REPO facilities were offered at fixed rates based on the KFR. The Kina Auction Facility was abolished on April 14, 2003. † Beginning in April 2003, term REPOs were introduced and is the rate charged by the BPNG on overnight and term repurchase agreements in national currency with commercial banks. Margins on trading under the REPO facility are changed periodically by the BPNG. Trading under the REPO facility in unsecuritized.

Repo Rate:

Rate charged by the BPNG on overnight and term repurchase agreements with commercial banks.

Reverse Repo Rate:

Rate offered by the BPNG on overnight and term repurchase agreements with commercial banks.

Central Bank Bill Rate:

Weighted average rate offered by the BPNG on 28-day bills in national currency. The rate is weighted by the value of successful bids.

Money Market Rate:

Average rate on loans between commercial banks.

Treasury Bill Rate:

Rate on 182-day treasury bills. Data refer to the second Thursday of the month. † Beginning in August 1994, weighted average rate on 182-day treasury bills in national currency at the last auction of the month.

Savings Rate:

Average rate offered by commercial banks on savings deposits in national currency.

Deposit Rate:

Weighted average rate offered by commercial banks on three- to six-month term deposits in national currency. † Beginning in January 1995, weighted average rate offered by commercial banks on deposits in national currency. Rate is weighted by deposit amounts.

Lending Rate:

Weighted average rate charged by commercial banks on loans in national currency. Rate is weighted by loan amounts.

Government Bond Yield:

Weighted average yield on all bonds (inscribed stock).

Prices and Labor:

Share Prices:

Kina Securities Share Index (KSi), base January 2, 2001. The index covers shares quoted on the Port Moresby Stock Exchange. Beginning in March 2006, the KSi includes debt securities.

Consumer Prices:

Source: National Statistics Office. Weights Reference Period: 1977; Geographical Coverage: Urban Households in Papua New Guinea; Number of Items in the Basket: This regimen(list) is used in compilation of the index. The prices of the regimen are collected from a total of 240 specifications, which represented 124 items; Basis for Calculation: the weights are derived from the Household Expenditure Survey (HES).

Total Employment:
Source: Bank of Papua New Guinea. Data refer to employment in trade, building and construction, transport, agriculture, forestry and fisheries, financial and business services, and manufacturing industries. Employment data are presented as an index with March 2002 as a base.

International Transactions:

All trade data are from Bank of Papua New Guinea.

Volume of Exports:
Bank of Papua New Guinea, weights reference period: 1994.
Export Unit Value index is from Bank of Papua New Guinea, weights reference period: 1994.

Government Finance:

Monthly data are from unpublished sources, as provided by Bank of Papua New Guinea and cover the operations of the budgetary central government. The fiscal year ends December 31.

National Accounts:

Source: National Statistics Office. The structure of the accounts follows more closely to the *1968 SNA*. Prior to 1977, data relate to fiscal years ending June 30. Since this date, data refer to calendar years.

Paraguay   288

Date of Fund Membership:

December 28, 1945

Standard Source:

Central Bank of Paraguay

Exchange Rates:

Market Rate (End of Period and Period Average):
From early 1998 onwards, the exchange rate is operated as a managed float. Prior to that, the exchange rate was determined freely in the market. The exchange rate is determined as the average of sales and purchases weighted by the volume of transactions of the main banks and exchange houses.
For the purpose of calculating effective exchange rates (*lines* **nec** and **rec**), a weighted average exchange rate index for U.S. dollars per guarani is based on trade for non-oil imports.

International Liquidity:

Gold (National Valuation) (line 1and) is valued on the basis of the international market price of the period in reference. *Monetary Authorities: Other Assets (line 3..d)* includes holdings of shares from the Latin American Export Bank.

Central Bank:

Consists of the Central Bank of Paraguay (CBP) only.
Data are based on a standardized report form (SRF) for central

banks, which accords with the concepts and definitions of the IMF's *Monetary and Financial Statistics Manual (MFSM)*, 2000. Departures from the *MFSM* methodology are explained below. Held-to-maturity securities are valued at acquisition cost rather than at current market price or fair value.

Other Depository Corporations:

Comprises commercial banks, finance companies, and savings and loans associations. Beginning in January 2006, the two remaining savings and loan associations were absorbed by finance companies. Beginning in December 2008, includes Type A credit unions, which account 80 percent of credit unions. Data exclude banks and finance companies in liquidation and the rest of the credit unions.
Data are based on a standardized report form (SRF) for other depository corporations, which accords with the concepts and definitions of the *Monetary and Financial Statistics Manual (MFSM)*. For other depository corporations in Paraguay, departures from the *MFSM* methodology are explained below.
For December 2008 through November 2010, data for the credit unions are only available on a quarterly basis. Data for the intervening months have been estimated by carrying forward the data from the last quarter.
Held-to-maturity securities are valued at acquisition cost rather than at current market price or fair value.

Depository Corporations:

See notes on central bank and other depository corporations.

Monetary Aggregates:

Broad Money:
Broad Money calculated from the liability data in the sections for the central bank and other depository corporations accords with the concepts and definitions of the *MFSM*. Broad money differs from M5 described below as M5 does not include deposits with the CBP, nor deposits of local governments and public nonfinancial corporations with other depository corporations.

Money (National Definitions):
Base money comprises notes and coins in circulation and legal reserve requirements and demand deposits in national currency of commercial banks and finance companies with the CBP.
M1 comprises notes and coins held by the public and demand deposits in national currency of the private sector with commercial banks.
M2 comprises M1, savings and time deposits in national currency of the private sector with commercial banks and finance companies, and savings certificates issued by commercial banks and finance companies held by the private sector. Beginning in December 2008, includes savings and time deposits of the private sector with credit unions in national currency.
M3 comprises M2, deposits in foreign currency of the private sector with commercial banks and finance companies, and savings certificates in foreign currency issued by commercial banks and finance companies held by the private sector.
M4 comprises M3 and bonds and other securities in circulation issued by commercial banks held by the private sector.
M5 comprises M4 and trust funds and mutual funds of the private sector in commercial banks.

Interest Rates:

Central Bank Policy Rate (End of Period):
Rate charged by the CBP on 14-day loans to the commercial banks.

Discount Rate (End of Period):
Rediscount rate charged by the CBP. † Beginning in September 1990, rate charged by the CBP for short-term liquidity loans to commercial banks.

Money Market Rate:
Average rate on loans between financial corporations in national currency.

Savings Rate:
Rate offered by commercial banks on savings deposits in national currency. † Beginning in January 1994, weighted average rate paid by commercial banks on savings deposits in national currency.

Savings Rate (Foreign Currency):
Weighted average rate paid by commercial banks on savings deposits in foreign currency.

Deposit Rate:
Rate offered by commercial banks on 180-day certificates of deposits in national currency. † Beginning in March 1998, weighted average rate paid by commercial banks on 90- to 180-day time deposits in national currency. The rate is weighted by deposit amounts.

Deposit Rate (Foreign Currency):
Weighted average rate paid by commercial banks on 90- to 180-day time deposits in foreign currency. The rate is weighted by deposit amounts.

Lending Rate:
Rate charged by commercial banks on loans in national currency. † Beginning in January 1994, weighted average rate charged by commercial banks on commercial, developmental, personal, and various loans in national currency. The rate is weighted by loan amounts.

Lending Rate (Foreign Currency):
Weighted average rate charged by commercial banks on commercial, developmental, personal, and various loans in foreign currency. The rate is weighted by loan amounts.

Prices:

Producer Prices:
Source: Central Bank of Paraguay. Weights Reference Period: June 2011; Sectoral Coverage: agricultural products, fisheries, livestock, forestry, mining, and manufacturing; Number of Items in the Basket: 341 products; Basis for Calculation: two indices are calculated: one for local goods and another for imported goods.

Consumer Prices:
Source: Central Bank of Paraguay. Weights Reference Period: December 2007; Geographical Coverage: urban households at the national level; Number of Items in the Basket: 450 products (goods and services); Basis for Calculation: June 2005-June 2006 Household Budget Survey.

International Transactions:

All trade data are from the Central Bank of Paraguay.

Government Finance:

Data are as reported in the *Government Finance Statistics Yearbook (GFSY)* and cover the budgetary central government. † The fiscal year ends December 31.

National Accounts:

Source: Central Bank of Paraguay. As indicated by the country, concepts and definitions are in accordance with the *1953 SNA*.

Peru   293

Date of Fund Membership:
December 31, 1945

Standard Source:
Central Reserve Bank of Peru

Exchange Rates:

On February 1, 1985, the inti, equal to 1,000 soles, was introduced. On July 1, 1991, the nuevo sol, equal to one million intis, replaced the inti as the currency unit of Peru.

Market Rate (End of Period and Period Average):
Midpoint rate of interbank operations as published by the Superintendency of Banks and Insurance Corporations.

International Liquidity:

Line 1and is equal to *line 1ad,* converted into U.S. dollars at the dollar price of gold used by national sources, as reported to *IFS.* Gold acquired prior to June 1979 is valued at SDR 35 per ounce. Gold acquired from this date onwards is revalued once a month based on an accounting value equal to 85 percent of the international price shown in the London, New York, and Zurich markets.

Monetary Authorities:

Comprises the Central Reserve Bank of Peru (CRBP) only.

Deposit Money Banks:

Comprises the Bank of the Nation and private commercial banks. Beginning in May 1994, the new charter of the Bank of the Nation establishes its role as fiscal agent of the government.

Other Banking Institutions:

Comprises development banks, which were under liquidation until December 2000. Beginning in January 2001, the institutional coverage of the other banking institutions sector ends.

Money (National Definitions):

Monetary Base comprises notes and coins issued and demand deposits in national currency of deposit money banks and other banking institutions at the CRBP. Beginning in January 1994, excludes deposits of the Bank of the Nation and development banks.
Money comprises notes and coins held by the public and demand deposits in national currency of the private sector in deposit money banks and other banking institutions.
Quasi-Money in National Currency comprises time and savings deposits in national currency of the private sector in deposit money banks and other banking institutions and bonds and other securities

in national currency issued by deposit money banks and other banking institutions which are held by the private sector.

Quasi-Money in Foreign Currency comprises time and savings deposits in foreign currency of the private sector in deposit money banks and other banking institutions and bonds and other securities in foreign currency issued by deposit money banks and other banking institutions which are held by the private sector.

Liquidity in National Currency comprises money and quasi-money in national currency.

Liquidity comprises money and quasi-money in national and foreign currency.

Interest Rates:

Central Bank Policy Rate (End of Period):
Reference rate determined by CRBP to establish a benchmark interest rate for interbank transactions, impacting operations of the financial institutions with the public.

Discount Rate (End of Period):
Central Reserve Bank of Peru's rediscount rate on short-term monetary regulation loans to commercial banks in national currency.

Discount Rate (Foreign Currency) (End of Period):
Central Reserve Bank of Peru's rediscount rate on short-term monetary regulation loans to commercial banks in foreign currency.

Money Market Rate:
Weighted average rate on noncollateralized loans between commercial banks in national currency. The rate is the arithmetic average of daily rates and is weighted by the individual banks' participation in total loans.

Money Market Rate (Foreign Currency):
Weighted average rate on noncollateralized loans between commercial banks in foreign currency. The rate is the arithmetic average of daily rates and is weighted by the individual banks' participation in total loans.

Savings Rate:
Average rate offered by commercial banks on savings deposits in national currency. The rate is converted to percent per annum by compounding monthly rates of interest.

Savings Rate (Foreign Currency):
Average rate offered by commercial banks on savings deposits in foreign currency.

Deposit Rate:
Weighted average rate offered by commercial banks on 31- to 179-day time deposits in national currency. † Beginning in February 1992, weighted average rate offered by commercial banks on all deposits in national currency. The rate is the arithmetic average of daily rates and is weighted by the individual banks' participation in total deposits.

Deposit Rate (Foreign Currency):
Weighted average rate offered by commercial banks on all deposits in foreign currency. The rate is the arithmetic average of daily rates and is weighted by the individual banks' participation in total deposits.

Lending Rate:
Weighted average rate charged by commercial banks on loans in national currency of 360 days or less. The rate is the arithmetic average of daily rates and is weighted by the individual banks'

participation in total loans. † Beginning in February 1992, weighted average rate charged by the eight most important commercial banks on overdrafts and advances on current accounts, credit cards, discounts, and loans up to 360 days and mortgage loans in national currency. The rate is the geometric average of daily rates and is weighted by the individual banks' participation in total loans.

Lending Rate (Foreign Currency):
Weighted average rate charged by the eight most important commercial banks on overdrafts and advances on current accounts, credit cards, discounts, and loans up to 360 days and mortgage loans in foreign currency. The rate is the geometric average of daily rates and is weighted by the individual banks' participation in total loans.

Prices, Production, Labor:

Share Prices (End of Month):
General share price index covering industrial and mining shares quoted in the Lima Stock Exchange, base December 31, 1991.

Wholesale Prices:
Source: Central Reserve Bank of Peru. Weights Reference Period: 1994. A Laspeyres index that measures the evolution of prices of a representative group of goods traded in the wholesale markets in the Lima metropolitan area and 25 other cities. The index covers 394 products.

Consumer Prices:
Source: Central Reserve Bank of Peru. Weights Reference Period: January 2009; Geographical Coverage: Metropolitan Lima; Number of Items in Basket: 532; Basis for Calculation: The weights used to calculate the CPI are derived from the national family budget survey (ENAPREF), carried out between May 2008 and April 2009 and consisting of a sample of 6900 single-family homes in Lima.

Industrial Production:
Source: Central Reserve Bank of Peru. Weights Reference Period: 1994; Sectoral Coverage: Agriculture and livestock, fishing, mining and fuel, manufacturing, construction, trade and other services sectors; Basis for Calculation: The weighting factor is the annual percentage structure of the 1994 base year value added.

Industrial Employment:
Source: Central Reserve Bank of Peru. Monthly index of industrial employment in metropolitan Lima, weights reference period: October 1997. The index covers all registered enterprises employing at least 100 workers.

International Transactions:

All trade data are from Central Reserve Bank of Peru. Prior to 1975, data on exports and imports in U.S. dollars were derived by conversion of national currency data into U.S. dollars. Annual figures include grants and other adjustments.

Volume of Exports:
IFS average of copper, crude petroleum, fishmeal, iron ore, silver, zinc, and lead with a 1995 value of exports as weights.

Unit Value of Exports:
IFS average of copper, crude petroleum, fishmeal, iron ore, silver, zinc, and lead with a 1995 value of exports as weights.

Government Finance:

Monthly and quarterly data are derived from Central Reserve Bank of Peru and cover the budgetary central government. The fiscal year ends December 31.

National Accounts:

As indicated by the country, from 1990 onward data have been revised following the implementation of the *1993 SNA*.

Philippines 566

Date of Fund Membership:
December 27, 1945

Standard Source:
Central Bank of Philippines
National Statistics Office

Exchange Rates:

Market Rate (End of Period and Period Average):
Bankers' Association reference rate, which is the weighted average rate of all transactions conducted through the Philippines Dealing System during the previous day.

International Liquidity:

Gold (National Valuation) (line 1and) is the U.S. dollar value of official holdings of gold as reported in the country's standard sources. In early 1977 a number of offshore banking units (OBUs) and foreign currency deposit units (FCDUs) were established. OBUs deal freely with nonresidents but are permitted to undertake only limited domestic operations, essentially with the monetary system and Government. FCDUs are allowed to undertake longer-term foreign currency operations with residents. *Lines 7a.d* and *7b.d* are derived from the accounts of commercial banks (see section 20). They exclude OBU accounts but include most FCDU accounts as well as claims on and liabilities to OBUs. *Lines 7k.d* and *7m.d* relate to the foreign assets and foreign liabilities of OBUs. Their assets and liabilities with the monetary system are classified as part of the foreign sector accounts in sections monetary authorities, deposit money banks, and monetary survey.

Central Bank:

Consists of the Central Bank of the Philippines (CBP) only.
Data are based on a standardized report form (SRF) for central banks, which accords with the concepts and definitions of the IMF's *Monetary and Financial Statistics Manual (MFSM)*, 2000.

Other Depository Corporations:

Comprises universal and commercial banks, thrift banks, rural banks, nonbanks with quasi-banking functions, nonstock savings and loan associations, and banks in liquidation.
† Beginning in January 2006, data are based on a standardized report form (SRF) for other depository corporations, which accords with the concepts and definitions of the *Monetary and Financial Statistics Manual (MFSM)*. For other depository corporations in Philippines, departures from the *MFSM* methodology are explained below.

For January 2006 through February 2008, financial assets and liabilities, including accrued interest, for which economic sectorization is unavailable are allocated to the economic sector using percent distribution. Beginning in March 2008, financial assets and liabilities, including accrued interest, for which economic sectorization is unavailable are allocated to the economic sector having the largest volume of transactions in the category.

For December 2001 through December 2005, data in the SRF format are compiled from pre-SRF data not based on the *MFSM* methodology. Departures from the *MFSM* methodology are explained below.

Financial assets and liabilities, including accrued interest, for which economic sectorization is unavailable are allocated to the economic sector using percent distribution.

Prepayments required by banks for letters of credit and small amounts of foreign currency deposits held by residents are included in *Other Deposits Included in Broad Money* rather than in *Deposits Excluded from Broad Money*.

Depository Corporations:

† See notes on central bank and other depository corporations.

Monetary Aggregates:

Broad Money:
Broad Money calculated from the liability data in the sections for the central bank and other depository corporation accords with the concepts and definitions of the *MFSM* and is consistent with M4 described below.

Money (National Definitions):
Reserve Money comprises currency notes and coins issued by the CBP and required and excess reserves, including accrued interest, in national currency of universal and commercial banks, thrift banks, rural banks, nonbanks with quasi-banking functions, and trust entities.

Narrow Money comprises currency outside depository corporations and transferable deposits of other financial corporations, state and local governments, public nonfinancial corporations, and private sector with other depository corporations. Currency outside depository corporations refers to currency in circulation and peso deposits subject to check of the monetary system or transferable deposits. Currency in circulation is obtained by deducting from the currency issue of the CBP, cash in the vaults of the Bureau of the Treasury and other depository corporations. Peso deposits subject to check of the monetary system or transferable deposits refers to managers and cashiers' checks and deposits automatically transferred from savings to demand deposits.

M3 comprises narrow money, quasi-money, and deposit substitutes. Quasi-money or other deposits refers to interest-bearing deposits of other financial corporations, state and local governments, public nonfinancial corporations, and private sector with universal and commercial banks, thrift banks, rural banks, and nonstock savings and loan associations. Interest-bearing deposits comprise those which can be withdrawn upon presentation of properly completed withdrawal slips together with the corresponding passbooks or by means of negotiable orders of withdrawal (for NOW accounts), and those with specific maturity dates and evidenced by certificates issued by the bank.

Deposit substitutes refer to money market borrowings by

commercial banks and nonbanks with quasi-banking functions such as promissory notes, repurchase agreements, commercial paper, and certificates of assignment with recourse.

M4 comprises M3 and foreign currency deposits of other financial corporations, state and local governments, public nonfinancial corporations, and private sector with universal and commercial banks, thrift banks, and rural banks.

Interest Rates:

Discount Rate (End of Period):
Rediscount rate for loans for traditional exports, which account for a large part of total rediscount credits. † Beginning in December 1985, the rediscount facility was unified and refers to the rediscount rate charged by the CBP on loans to banks in national currency.

Money Market Rate:
Weighted average rate on overnight loans between universal and commercial banks, thrift banks, savings banks, and nonbanks with quasi-banking functions to cover reserve deficiencies. The rate is weighted by loan amounts.

Treasury Bill Rate:
Weighted average rate on 91-day treasury bills denominated in national currency. Rate is weighted by the volume of bills sold.

Savings Rate:
Rate offered by universal and commercial banks on savings deposits in national currency. Rate is calculated as the ratio of the amount of interest on the deposits of universal and commercial banks and the total outstanding amount of these deposits.

Savings Rate (Foreign Currency):
Rate offered by universal and commercial banks on savings deposits in foreign currency. Rate is calculated as the ratio of the amount of interest on the deposits of universal and commercial banks and the total outstanding amount of these deposits.

Deposit Rate:
Weighted average rate offered by universal and commercial banks on 61- to 90-day time deposits in national currency. Rate is weighted by deposit amounts.

Deposit Rate (Foreign Currency):
Weighted average rate offered by universal and commercial banks on 61- to 90-day time deposits in foreign currency. Rate is weighted by deposit amounts.

Lending Rate:
Weighted average rate charged by universal commercial banks on loans in national currency. Rate is weighted by loan amounts and is calculated as the ratio of the amount of interest on the loans of universal and commercial banks and the total outstanding amount of these loans.

Government Bond Yield:
Yield on two-year treasury notes. † Beginning in March 1998, average bid rate of the last issue of the month on two-year treasury notes.

Prices and Production:

Share Prices:
Index of the Manila Stock Exchange on commercial and industrial shares, base 1953. † Beginning in 1955, index of the Manila

Stock Exchange on commercial and industrial shares, base 1955. † Beginning in December 1962, index of the Manila Stock Exchange on commercial and industrial shares, base 1965. † Beginning in December 1972, stock price index of the Manila and Makati stock exchanges, base 1972.† Beginning in January 1978, stock price index of the Manila and Makati stock exchanges, base 1985.

Mining:
Mining share price index, base 1965. † Beginning in April 1981, average of daily quotations of mining share price indices in the Manila and Makati stock exchanges, base 1972.

Sugar:
Sugar share price index, base 1965.

Share Prices (End of Month):
All Shares Index, base November 14, 1996, covering all common stocks of companies listed on the Philippine Stock Exchange. The full market capitalization method is used in computing the index, using the daily closing prices. The index excludes those listed in the Small and Medium Enterprises (SME) Board.

Producer Prices:
Source: National Statistics Office. Weights Reference Period: 2000; Coverage: covers 237 sample manufacturing establishments ; Number of Items in the Basket: 548 manufactured goods; Basis for Calculation: the weights are revised every year based on the latest data available from the Annual Survey of Establishments/Census of Establishments (ASE/CE).

Consumer Prices:
Source: National Statistics Office. Weights Reference Period: 2006; Geographical Coverage: covers about 9,500 outlets nationwide; Number of Items in the Basket: covers between 285 and 750 items, the number varying by province; Basis for Calculation: the weights are derived from the 2000 Family Income and Expenditures (FIES) data.

Manufacturing Production:
Source: National Statistics Office. Weights Reference Period: 1994; Sectoral Coverage: manufacturing sector; Basis for Calculation: the weights used for the index are based on the 1994 Census of Establishments (CE).

International Transactions:
All trade data are from Central Bank of Philippines.

Government Finance:
Monthly, quarterly, and annual data are reported by Central Bank of Philippines and are derived from *Cash Operations Statements,* Bureau of Treasury. Data cover operations of the budgetary central government. The fiscal year ends December 31.

National Accounts:
Source: Central Bank of Philippines.

Poland   964

Date of Fund Membership:
June 12, 1986

Standard Sources:

National Bank
Central Statistical Office
Eurostat

Exchange Rates:

The post-January 1, 1995 zloty is equal to 10,000 of the pre-January 1, 1995 zlotys.

Market Rate (End of Period and Period Average):
National Bank midpoint rate.

International Liquidity:

Gold (National Valuation) (line 1and): Gold is valued at US$400 per ounce.

An accurate bank/nonbank distinction of foreign accounts of deposit money banks is not available, in particular because on the liabilities side certain debts originally owed to foreign bank creditors have been taken over by foreign governments in the context of debt rescheduling. Deposit money banks' liabilities do not include interest payments in arrears, defined to cover also those rescheduled but not booked.

Central Bank:

Consists of the National Bank of Poland (NBP) only.
† Beginning in January 2004, data are compiled in accordance with the European Central Bank's framework for monetary statistics using the national residency approach.
Prior to January 2004, data do not fully conform with the European Central Bank's framework for monetary statistics and are not strictly comparable to data for later periods.
Claims on General Government and *Liabilities to Central Government* include positions with local government.

Other Depository Corporations:

Comprises all resident units classified as other monetary financial institutions (other MFIs) in accordance with *1995 ESA* standards.
† Beginning in January 2004, data are compiled in broad conformity with the European Central Bank's framework for monetary statistics using the national residency approach. Departures from the framework are explained below.
Securities Other than Shares Included in Broad Money includes debt securities with maturity of up to two years issued by MFIs and held by nonresident non-MFIs, other than central government. However, the amount of debt securities issued by MFIs and sold to nonresidents is minor and assumed to be zero in calculating M3.
Prior to January 2004, data do not fully conform with the European Central Bank's framework for monetary statistics and are not strictly comparable to data for later periods.
Claims on General Government and *Liabilities to Central Government* include positions with local government.

Depository Corporations:

† See notes on central bank and other depository corporations.

Monetary Aggregates:

Broad Money:
Broad Money calculated from the liability data in the sections for the central bank and other depository corporations. Broad money differs from M3 described below because separate data on the is-

suance by MFIs of money market funds/shares and debt securities with maturity up to two years to the money holding sectors are not currently available under the ECB reporting framework.
Money (National Definition):
M0 comprises currency in circulation (including vault cash) and current account balances of other MFIs with the NBP in national currency.
M1 comprises currency outside MFIs, overnight deposits in national and foreign currency of resident non-MFIs, other than central government, with MFIs, and deposits without an agreed term among all reporting MFIs. † Beginning in April 2001, comprises currency outside MFIs and overnight deposits in national and foreign currency of resident non-MFIs, other than central government, with MFIs.
M2 comprises M1 and deposits with agreed maturity of up to two years and deposits redeemable at notice of up to three months of resident non-MFIs, other than central government, with MFIs.
M3 comprises M2, money market fund shares/units, repurchase agreements, and debt securities with maturity of up to two years issued by MFIs and held by resident non-MFIs, other than central government. † Beginning in April 2001, includes deposits without an agreed term among all reporting MFIs, which meet the definition of demand deposits. † Beginning in January 2004, comprises M2, money market fund shares/units, repurchase agreements, and debt securities with maturity of up to two years issued by MFIs and held by resident and nonresident non-MFIs, other than central government.

Interest Rates:

Repo Rate (End of Period):
Reference rate (minimum money market intervention rate) quoted by the NBP on 28-day open market operations (reverse repo rate). Beginning in January 2003, reference rate on 14-day open market operations. Beginning in January 2005, reference rate on 7-day open market operations.
Refinancing Rate (End of Period):
Refinancing credit rate. † Beginning in December 1989, basic rate at which the NBP rediscount bills of exchange to commercial banks.
Money Market Rate:
Weighted average rate on outstanding one-month deposits in the interbank market. † Beginning in January 1992, weighted average rate on outstanding deposits of one month or less in the interbank market. † Beginning in August 2002, average rate on outstanding overnight deposits in the interbank market.
Treasury Bill Rate:
Weighted average yield on 13-week Treasury bills sold at auctions. † Beginning in December 2002, weighted average yield on all treasury bills offered on the primary market. The rate is weighted by the purchase of outstanding bill amount.
Deposit Rate:
Rate offered by commercial banks on short-term deposits in national currency. † Beginning in January 1991, rate offered by commercial banks on 12-month time deposits in national currency. † Beginning in March 1993, weighted average rate offered by commercial banks on households' deposits in national currency. This rate was discontinued in January 2007 and replaced

with harmonized interest rates in line with the requirements of the European Central Bank (Regulation ECB/2001/18).

Deposit Rate (lines 60lhs, 60lhn, 60lcs, 60lcn, 60lcr, and 60l.f):

For lines *60lhs*, *60lcs*, and *60lcr*, see notes in the introduction to *IFS* and *Euro-area Interest Rates*. Deposit Rate, Households-New Business (*line 60lhn*) and *Deposit Rate, Corporations-New Business* (*line 60lcn*) are the rates for new business with an agreed maturity of over six months up to and including one year. *Deposit Rate, in Euro, New Business* (*line 60l.f*) is the weighted average rate of all new business in Euro denomination. The rate is weighted by deposit amounts.

Lending Rate:

Rate charged by commercial banks on loans of lowest risk. † Beginning in January 1995, weighted average rate charged by commercial banks on minimum risk loans. This rate was discontinued in January 2007 and replaced with harmonized interest rates in line with the requirements of the European Central Bank (Regulation ECB/2001/18).

Lending Rate (60phs, 60pns, 60phm, 60phn, 60pcs, 60pcn, and 60p.f):

For lines *60phs*, *60phm*, *60phn*, and *60pcs*, see notes in the introduction to *IFS* and *Euro-area Interest Rates*. *Lending Rate, Households-New Business* (*line 60pns*) is the rate for new business loans with an agreed maturity of over three months and up to one year initial rate fixation. *Lending Rate, Corporations-New Business* (*line 60pcn*) is the rate for new business loans over four million zlotys with an agreed maturity of over three months and up to one year initial rate fixation. *Lending Rate, in Euro, New Business* (*line 60p.f*) is the weighted average rate of all new business loans in Euro denomination. The rate is weighted by loan amounts.

Government Bond Yield:

Yield of government bonds in secondary markets with a ten-year maturity. This rate is used to measure long-term interest rates for assessing convergence among the European Union member states.

Prices, Production, Labor:

Share Prices (Period Average and End of Month):

Warsaw Stock Exchange Price Index (WIG Index), base April 16, 1991. Total return index which includes dividends and pre-emptive rights (subscription rights). Index includes all companies listed on the main market, excluding foreign companies and investment funds.

WIG–20 (Period Average and End of Month):

Warsaw Stock Exchange Price Index 20 (WIG 20 Index), base April 16, 1994. Modified capitalization-weighted index of 20 Polish stocks which are listed on the main market. The index is the underlying instrument for futures transactions listed on the Warsaw Stock Exchange.

Producer Prices:

Source: Central Statistical Office. Weights reference period: weights are generally updated every 5 years; Sectoral Coverage: mining and quarrying, manufacturing, electricity, gas, steam and air conditioning supply and water supply, sewerage, waste management and remediation activities; Number of Items in Basket: about 30,000 individual price observations; Basis for Calculation: weights are derived from annual sold production net-data obtained from the industrial survey.

Consumer Prices:

Source: Central Statistical Office. Weights Reference Period: previous calendar year; Geographical Coverage: the entire country; Number of Items in Basket: 1400 items; Basis for Calculation: weights are derived from average annual expenditures primarily taken from the monthly Household Budget Survey.

Wages: Average Earnings:

Source: Central Statistical Office. The index, weights reference period: 2010, covers the socialized sector and excludes apprentices and outworkers (employees who contract for outside work).

Industrial Production:

Source: Central Statistical Office. Weights Reference Period: 2005; Sectoral Coverage: mining and quarrying, manufacturing, electricity, gas, steam and air conditioning supply and water supply; Number of Items in Basket: about 12,900 enterprises. Data are sourced from the OECD database.

Industrial Employment:

Weights reference period: 2005. † Before 1991, the data covered only the socialized sector. Since 1991, covers both private and socialized units where the number of employed persons exceeds five.

International Transactions:

Exports and Imports:

Data in zlotys since 1982 are not comparable to previous yearly data which are in foreign exchange zlotys. Index numbers are on weights reference period: 1990. Since 1991, data include import and export invoices as well as customs declarations. Monthly and quarterly data on prices are derived as a ratio of turnover in zlotys to turnover volume. Annual data are obtained on the basis of direct surveys of price changes.

Balance of Payments:

The annual and quarterly data for the balance of payments are not fully compatible. Quarterly data are compiled, primarily, from records of cash settlement, with only restricted detail and limited adjustment to bring the statistics closer to the recommendations for coverage and timing contained in the IMF's *Balance of Payments Manual (Manual)*. The annual data, however, are compiled incorporating additional data, available only annually, to improve compliance with the recommendations contained in the *Manual* for the coverage, timing, and classification of transactions in the balance of payments.

Government Finance:

Monthly and quarterly data are as reported by the Ministry of Finance and cover, through July 1999, the consolidated central government, namely, the state budget, the Labor Fund, the Pension and Disability Fund, and the Social Insurance Fund. From August 1999, data on consolidated core operations of central government do not cover the Social Insurance Fund. † Beginning in 2007, data are reported in the GFSM 2001 analytical framework. Preliminary data on general government are compiled by Eurostat. The fiscal year ends December 31.

National Accounts:

Source: Central Statistical Office. As indicated by the country, data are compiled in accordance with the methodology of the

1995 ESA and the 1993 SNA. Beginning in 1994, data at previous year prices are used to construct line 99bvpzf. Beginning in 1999, data are sourced from the Eurostat database. Eurostat introduced chain-linked GDP volume measures to both annual and quarterly data with the release of the third quarter 2005 on November 30, 2005. Chain-linked GDP volume measures are expressed in the prices of the previous year and re-referenced to 2005.

Portugal 182

Data are denominated in Portuguese escudos prior to January 1999 and in euros from January 1999 onward. An irrevocably fixed factor for converting escudos to euros was established at 200.482 escudos per euro. In 2002, the escudo was retired from circulation and replaced by euro banknotes and coins. Beginning in January 1999, with the implementation of Stage Three of the European Economic and Monetary Union (EMU), an alternative euro area-wide definition of residency was introduced: All positions with residents of other euro area (EA) countries, including the European Central Bank (ECB), are classified as domestic positions, and foreign assets and foreign liabilities include only positions with non-euro area residents. Descriptions of the changes in the methodology and presentation of Portugal's accounts following the introduction of the euro are shown in the introduction to IFS and in the notes on the euro area page.

Date of Fund Membership:
March 29, 1961

Standard Sources:
Banco de Portugal
National Institute of Statistics
Eurostat

Exchange Rates:
Market Rate (End of Period and Period Average):
Central bank midpoint rate. Central Bank indicative midpoint rate. Prior to January 1999, the official indicative rates for the U.S. dollar and other currencies were determined by the Banco de Portugal on the basis of market exchange rates data received by 12:00 p.m. from the main foreign exchange market-makers. These rates were a reference for bank bid-offer rates, which were freely determined. In January 1999, the escudo became a participating currency within the Eurosystem, and the euro market rate became applicable to all transactions. In 2002, the escudo was retired from circulation and replaced by euro banknotes and coins. For additional information, refer to the section on Exchange Rates in the introduction to IFS and the notes for the euro area page. *Real Effective Exchange Rates:* Prior to January 1998, calculations are based on a consumer price index that excludes rents.

International Liquidity:
Beginning in January 1999, *Total Reserves minus Gold (line 1l.d)* is defined in accordance with the Eurosystem's statistical definition of international reserves. The international reserves of Portugal per the Eurosystem statistical definition at the start of the mone-

tary union (January 1, 1999) in billions of U.S. dollars were as follows: *Total Reserves minus Gold,* $9,087; *Foreign Exchange,* $8,273; *SDRs,* $135; *Reserve Position in the Fund,* $621; *Other Reserve Assets,* $60; *Gold,* $5,774 *Gold (million fine troy ounces),* 20.089 ounces. *Foreign Exchange (line 1d.d):* Foreign exchange holdings of the Treasury Department of the government of Portugal are included in reserves *(line 1dbd).* Beginning in January 1988, *line 1d.d* excludes deposits made with the European Monetary Cooperation Fund (EMCF); the holdings of European currency units (ECUs) issued by the EMCF against those deposits (and similar deposits of gold) are included in *line 1d.d. Gold (Eurosystem Valuation) (line 1and):* Prior to January 1980, *Gold (Million Fine Troy Ounces) (line 1ad)* was valued at SDR 35 per ounce and converted into U.S. dollars at the U.S. dollar/SDR exchange rate **sa** on the *IFS* page for the United States. From January 1980 to December 1987, *line 1and* was revalued at 70 percent of the average price of gold in the London market during the second half of 1979. From January 1988 to November 1998, *line 1and* excluded deposits of gold. From January 1999 onward, *line 1and* is revalued at market prices at the end of each month. Gold swaps within *line 1and* are treated as repurchase transactions that do not affect the volume of gold held. Memorandum data are provided on *Non-Euro Claims on Euro Area Residents* and *Euro Claims on Non-Euro Area Residents,* which represent positions as of the last Friday in each month. For additional information, see the section on International Liquidity in the introduction to *IFS* and on the euro area page.

Central Bank:
Consists of the Banco de Portugal, which is part of the Eurosystem beginning in January 1999, only. *Currency Issued* includes coins issued by the Treasury. For a description of the accounts, refer to the section on *Central Bank - Euro Area* in the introduction to *IFS.*

Other Depository Corporations:
Comprises all resident units classified as other monetary financial institutions (other MFIs), defined in accordance with *1995 ESA* standards. Deposit accounts of emigrants that can be accessed by residents are classified as deposits of residents in *Demand Deposits* or *Other Deposits.* For a description of the accounts, refer to the section on *Other Depository Corporations - Euro Area* in the introduction to *IFS.*

Depository Corporations (National Residency):
For a description of the methodology and accounts, refer to the section on *Depository Corporations (National Residency) - Euro Area* in the introduction to *IFS.*

Depository Corporations (Euro Area-wide Residency):
For a description of the methodology and accounts, refer to the section on *Depository Corporations (Euro Area-wide Residency)* in the introduction to *IFS.*

Interest Rates:
Discount Rate (End of Period):
† Prior to 1987, the end-of-year rate on first tranche rate at which the Banco de Portugal rediscounted the financial claims held by the banking system. From 1987 until May 1991, first tranche rate at which the Banco de Portugal rediscounted the financial claims

held by the banking system. From May 1991 to January 1999, the rate on regular provision of liquidity announced by the Banco de Portugal. For months when no announcements were made, the rate corresponded to the weighted average of various auction rates for repurchase agreements used for provision of liquidity by the Banco de Portugal. Data were those from the last reserve maintenance period for the month on which an announcement or auction took place. Beginning in January 1999, the central bank rates are discontinued. Refer to Eurosystem policy rate series on the euro area page.

Money Market Rate:
† Prior to 1986, weighted average rate for interbank deposits up to three days. From 1986 to 1991, weighted average rate for interbank deposits up to five days. † Beginning in 1992, weighted monthly average rate for interbank overnight transactions.

Treasury Bill Rate:
Weighted monthly average rate on three-month treasury bills in the primary market, excluding underwriting by the Banco de Portugal (when it was allowed). † Prior to 1986, average rate of all treasury bills issued.

Deposit Rate:
† Prior to 1990, administrative minimum rate offered by commercial banks on time deposits with maturities of 180 days to one year. Beginning in January 1990, weighted monthly average rate offered by commercial banks on time deposits with maturities of 181 days to one year.

Deposit Rate (lines 60lhs, 60lhn, 60lcs, and 60lcn):
See notes in the introduction to *IFS* and *Euro-area Interest Rates*.

Lending Rate:
† Prior to January 1990, administrative maximum rate on 91- to 180-day loans. Beginning in January 1990, weighted monthly average rate charged by commercial banks on 91- to 180-day loans and advances to nonfinancial private enterprises.

Lending Rate (lines 60phs, 60pns, 60phm, 60phn, 60pcs, and 60pcn):
See notes in the introduction to *IFS* and *Euro-area Interest Rates*.

Government Bond Yield:
Weighted monthly average of daily yields on floating rate ten-year government bonds. Beginning in July 1993, simple monthly average of daily yields on ten-year floating rate government bonds in the secondary market. For additional information, refer to the section on interest rates in the introduction to *IFS* and on the euro area page. This rate is used to measure long-term interest rates for assessing convergence among the European Union member states.

Prices and Production:

Share Prices (End of Month):
Data refer to the Lisbon Stock Exchange Share Prices Index including all shares listed on the official market, base 1988. † Beginning in December 1992, data refer to the Portugal PSI–20 Index, base December 31, 1992. The PSI–20 is a capitalization weighted index of the top 20 stocks listed on the Lisbon Stock Exchange. The equities use free float shares in the index calculation.

Producer Prices:
Source: National Institute of Statistics. Weights Reference Period: weights are revised approximately every five years; Sectoral Coverage: mining and quarrying, manufacturing, and electricity, gas, and water; Number of Items in Basket: 2498 units;

Basis for Calculation: weights used for the index are from the surveys conducted by the National Statistics Institute (INE).

Consumer Prices:
Source: National Institute of Statistics. Weights Reference Period: weights are revised every five years; Geographical Coverage: entire country; Number of Items in Basket: 1206 products; Basis for Calculation: weights are derived from a Household Budget Survey (HBS).

Industrial Production:
Source: National Institute of Statistics. Weights Reference Period: 2005; Sectoral Coverage: mining and quarrying, manufacturing, electricity, gas and water industrial sectors; Number of Items in Basket: 2000 industrial enterprises; Basis for Calculation: weights are based on Industry surveys conducted by the National Statistics Institute (INE).

International Transactions:

All trade data are from the National Institute of Statistics.

Balance of Payments:
As only a net figure is available for transactions in *Other Goods, Services, and Income* for the fourth quarter of 1978, this is entered in the line for gross debits. In line with this treatment, the gross debit for the full year 1978 is calculated as the sum of the gross debits for the first three quarters and the net debit for the final quarter, while the gross credit shows the sum of the gross credits for the first three quarters. *Merchandise: Exports f.o.b. (line 77aad)* include exports of nonmonetary gold in the amount of (in millions of U.S. dollars) 531 for 1977, 370 for 1978, 197 for 1983 second quarter, 440 for 1983 third quarter, and 37 for 1983 fourth quarter.

Government Finance:

Data on general government are derived from Eurostat. The fiscal year ends December 31.

National Accounts:

Source: National Institute of Statistics. As indicated by the country, data are compiled in accordance with the methodology of the *1995 ESA* . Beginning in 1999, euro data are sourced from the Eurostat database. Eurostat introduced chain-linked GDP volume measures to annual data with the release of the third quarter 2005 on November 30, 2005. Chain linked GDP volume measures are expressed in the prices of the previous year and re-referenced to 2005.

Qatar   453

Date of Fund Membership:
September 8, 1972

Standard Sources:
Qatar Central Bank
Customs Department

Exchange Rates:

Official Rate: (End of Period and Period Average):
The Qatar Central Bank midpoint rate. The official rate shows limited flexibility against the U.S. dollar.

International Liquidity:

Gold (National Valuation) (line 1and) is obtained by converting the value in national currency terms, as reported in the country's standard sources, using the prevailing exchange rate, as given in *line* **ae** or **we.**

Central Bank:

Consists of the Qatar Central Bank (QCB) only.

Data are based on a standardized report form (SRF) for central banks, which accords with the concepts and definitions of the IMF's *Monetary and Financial Statistics Manual (MFSM)*, 2000.

Other Depository Corporations:

Comprises commercial banks (including Islamic banks) and Industrial Development Bank. Beginning in January 2006, excludes the Industrial Development Bank, when it was reclassified as an other financial corporation as it no longer accepts deposits. Data exclude banks registered and operating in the Qatar International Financial and Bank Center.

† Beginning in August 2012, data are based on a standardized report form (SRF) for other depository corporations, which accords with the concepts and definitions of the *Monetary and Financial Statistics Manual (MFSM)*. For other depository corporations in Qatar, departures from *MFSM* methodology are explained below.

Accrued interest is included in *Other Items (Net)* rather than in the outstanding amounts of the financial assets and liabilities.

Held-to-maturity securities other than shares are valued at acquisition cost rather than at current market price or fair value.

For December 2001 through July 2012, data in the SRF format are compiled from pre-SRF data which are not fully based on the *MFSM* methodology. Departures from the *MFSM* methodology are explained below.

Transferable deposits of other financial corporations are included in *Deposits Excluded from Broad Money* rather than in *Transferable Deposits Included in Broad Money*.

Financial assets and liabilities for which financial instrument breakdown is unavailable are allocated to the financial instrument having the largest volume of transactions in the category. Some other deposits are included in transferable deposits and securities other than shares are included in other deposits.

Positions with financial derivatives are included in *Other Items (Net)* rather than as claims on or liabilities to the corresponding sectors of the economy.

Accrued interest is included in *Other Items (Net)* rather than in the outstanding amounts of the financial assets and liabilities.

Held-to-maturity securities other than shares are valued at acquisition cost rather than at current market price or fair value.

Depository Corporations:

† See notes on central bank and other depository corporations.

Monetary Aggregates:

Broad Money:

Broad Money calculated from the liability data in the sections for the central bank and other depository corporations accords with the concepts and definitions of the *MFSM* and is consistent with M2 described below. Prior to January 2007, broad money differs from M2 as M2 includes deposits of public nonfinancial corporations.

Money (National Definitions):

Reserve Money comprises currency issued by the QCB and required reserves, clearing balances, and short-term deposits of commercial banks with the QCB.

M1 comprises currency in circulation (notes and coins held by the public) and demand deposits of the private sector in national currency with commercial banks.

Quasi-Money comprises time and savings deposits of the private sector in national currency with commercial banks and foreign currency deposits of the private sector with commercial banks.

M2 comprises M1 and quasi-money.

M3 comprises M2 and deposits of the central government and public nonfinancial corporations with commercial banks.

Interest Rates:

Central Bank Policy Rate (End of Period):

The QCB Policy Lending Rate, the key rate used to signal the monetary policy stance, is the rate announced by the QCB on overnight loans to local commercial banks through the Qatar Money Market Rate Standing Facility.

Deposit Facility Rate (End of Period):

The QCB Policy Deposit Rate is the rate announced by the QCB for overnight deposits of local commercial banks through the Qatar Money Market Rate Standing Facility.

Reverse Repo Rate (End of Period):

Repurchase Rate for QCB repurchase operations conducted with domestic government securities of two-week or one-month maturity.

Money Market Rate:

Weighted average of rates on overnight balances in national currency between commercial banks.

Savings Rate:

Weighted average rate offered by commercial banks on savings deposits in national currency. The rate is weighted by deposit amounts.

Deposit Rate:

Rate offered by commercial banks on one-year time deposits in national currency. Beginning in mid-December 1993, statutory base rates on deposits of different maturities were unified, and data refer to the uniform base rate offered by commercial banks on one-year time deposits in national currency.

Lending Rate:

Weighted averages of rates charged by commercial banks on loans up to one year. The rate is weighted by loan amounts.

Prices and Production:

Share Prices (End of Month):

Market capitalization weighted index covering 20 listed companies in the banking and financial, insurance, industrial, and services sectors quoted on the Doha Securities Market (DSM), base December 31, 1997.

Consumer Prices:

Data are from Qatar Central Bank, weight reference period: 2007. Geographical coverage: whole country; Number of items in basket: 1100 ; Basis for calculation: The weights have been derived from a household budget survey (HBS) that was undertaken in 2006.

Crude Petroleum Production:

Index is calculated from annual data through 1983 from Qatar Central Bank, and monthly data through June 1984 supplied directly by the Monetary Agency (now the Central Bank). The data covered onshore and offshore production as well as production of the Al Bunduq field. Data for July 1984 onwards are based on production quantities as reported in the *Oil Market Intelligence.*

International Transactions:

Imports, c.i.f.:

Annual data are from Qatar Central Bank, and monthly data are supplied directly by the Central Bank. Defense imports are excluded.

National Accounts:

Source: Qatar Central Bank.

Romania   968

Date of Fund Membership:

December 15, 1972

Standard Sources:

National Bank of Romania
National Institute of Statistics

Exchange Rates:

On July 1, 2005, the new currency leu (RON), equal to 10,000 units of the old currency leu (ROL) was introduced.
Market Rate:
In February 1991 an interbank rate was implemented, which was applicable to an increasing number of commercial and individual transactions. Effective November 1991, the *principal rate* and *secondary rate* were eliminated, and all foreign exchange transactions are effected through the free market.

International Liquidity:

Gold (National Valuation): Gold is valued using the average cost method and is revalued monthly at market price. Prior to 2005, gold was valued using a fixed domestic price, revalued at the end of the year only. *Foreign Exchange:* Comprises gross balances held by the National Bank of Romania. For periods prior to November 1999, comprises gross balances held by the National Bank of Romania and the Romanian Foreign Trade Bank. The latter's holdings include a large part of Romania's foreign exchange reserves held for balance of payments purposes, but they also comprise working balances as well.

Central Bank:

Consists of the National Bank of Romania (NBR) only.
Data are based on a standardized report form (SRF) for central banks, which accords with the concepts and definitions of the IMF's *Monetary and Financial Statistics Manual (MFSM),* 2000. Departures from the *MFSM* methodology are explained below.
Accrued interest is included in *Other Items (Net)* rather than in the outstanding amounts of the financial assets and liabilities.

Other Depository Corporations:

Comprises commercial banks and banks in liquidation. Beginning in May 2003, the data include credit cooperatives .
Data are based on a standardized report form (SRF) for other depository corporations, which accords with the concepts and definitions of the *Monetary and Financial Statistics Manual (MFSM).* For other depository corporations, departures from the *MFSM* methodology are explained below.
Accrued interest is included in *Other Items (Net)* rather than in the outstanding amounts of the financial assets and liabilities.
Market traded securities are valued at acquisition cost rather than at the current market price or fair value.
Other Deposits included in Broad Money include deposit liabilities of banks in liquidation.

Depository Corporations:

See notes on central bank and other depository corporations.

Other Financial Corporations:

Comprises investment funds, financial leasing corporations, consumer credit corporations, mortgage loan associations, corporations having legal status that issue credit cards, factoring corporations, mutual benefit societies, microfinance corporations, and loan-guarantee funds. Data exclude insurance corporations, pension funds, securities and derivates dealers, financial vehicle corporations, financial holding corporations, and central clearing counterparties.
Data are based on a standardized report form (SRF) for other financial corporations, which accords with the concepts and definitions of the *Monetary and Financial Statistics Manual (MFSM).* For other financial corporations in Romania, departures from the *MFSM* methodology are explained below.
Accrued interest is included in *Other Items (Net)* rather than in outstanding amounts of the financial assets and liabilities.

Monetary Aggregates:

Broad Money:
Broad Money is calculated from the liability data in the sections for the central bank and other depository corporations.

Money (National Definitions):
M1 comprises currency outside depository corporations and demand deposits in national currency of resident non-bank non-central government sectors with banking institutions.
M2 comprises M1 and time, saving deposits and foreign currency deposits of resident non-bank non-central government sectors with banking institutions and banks in liquidation.
M3 comprises M2, money market fund shares/units, repurchase agreements, and debt securities with original maturity of up to two years issued by banking institutions to residents other than banking institutions and central government.

Interest Rates:

Discount Rate (End of Period):
Structural Credit Rate, which is the predominant rate on central bank loans to commercial banks. Since February 2002, reference rate is calculated as a weighted average of the interest rates on NBR's deposit-taking and reverse-repo operations in the month prior to that of the announcement.

Money Market Rate:

Daily average rate on deposits between commercial banks in national currency.

Treasury Bill Rate:

Rate on 91-day Treasury bills.

Deposit Rate:

Average rate offered by credit institutions on outstanding time deposits of nonfinancial corporations and households in national currency.

Lending Rate:

Average rate charged by credit institutions on outstanding loans to nonfinancial corporations and households in national currency.

Government Bond Yield:

Weighted average yield of the newly issued government bonds with terms over one year sold at primary auctions. Beginning January 2006, refers to secondary market yields. This rate is used to measure long-term interest rates for assessing convergence among the European Union member states.

Prices, Production, Labor:

Producer Prices:

Source: National Institute of Statistics. Weights Reference Period: weights are updated every five years; Sectoral Coverage: mining, quarrying and manufacturing sectors, energy sectors and water supply, sewerage, waste management; Number of Items in Basket: about 2,000 economic operators; Basis for Calculation: the weights are obtained from Annual Business Statistical Survey and are represented by the turnover.

Consumer Prices:

Source: National Institute of Statistics. Weights Reference Period: 2011; Geographical Coverage: entire country; Number of Items in the Basket: about 1,822 goods and services items; Basis for Calculation: the weights are obtained from Household Budget Survey. Starting in 1999 the weights are updated annually using HBS data from year t–2.

Wages, Average Earnings:

Source: National Institute of Statistics. Geographical Coverage: entire country; Basis for Calculation: monthly sample survey enterprises and public authorities.

Industrial Production:

Source: National Institute of Statistics. Weights Reference Period: 2005; Sectoral Coverage: mining and quarrying, manufacturing and electricity, gas, steam and air contioning; Number of Items in the Basket: approximately 3,500 products; Basis for Calculation: weights are obtained from the production survey and Structural Business Survey and are updated every 5 years.

International Transactions:

Source S. Based on the trade statistics compiled by the National Institute of Statistics (NIS) from customs documents and makes adjustments regarding timing coverage and valuation in respect of BOP purposes.

Balance of Payments:

Since April 2003, Romania's Balance of Payments has been expressed and disseminated in national publications in euro. While transactions denominated in other currencies are converted in euro at the rate prevailing at the time of the transactions, for data deriving from balance sheets of reporters, the exchange rate at the end of the reporting period is used. To the extent possible for those data derived from balance sheets, foreign exchange valuation changes are excluded from the Balance of Payments (Reserve Assets, Medium- and Long-Term Loans—Liabilities etc.). BOP and IIP data reported to the IMF to be published in the *IFSY* are converted from euro in U.S. dollars using the average quarterly EUR/USD rate.

Government Finance:

Quarterly data cover the general government. The fiscal year ends December 31.

National Accounts:

Source: National Institute of Statistics. As indicated by the country, data are compiled in accordance with the methodology of the *1995 ESA* and the *1993 SNA*. Chain linked GDP volume measures are expressed according to 2005 prices.

Russian Federation   922

Date of Fund Membership:

June 1, 1992

Standard Sources:

Central Bank of Russia

State Statistical Office

Exchange Rates:

The post-January 1, 1998 ruble is equal to 1,000 of the pre-January 1, 1998 rubles.

Official Rate: (End of Period and Period Average):

Central Bank of Russia rate based on the Moscow Interbank Currency Exchange (MICEX) rate.

International Liquidity:

Gold (National Valuation) (line 1and) is valued at current quotations fixed by the Bank of Russia. † Prior to December 2005, gold was valued at US$300 per fine troy ounce.

Central Bank:

Consolidates the accounts of the Central Bank of Russia (CBR) and monetary authority functions conducted by the central government.

Data are based on summarized survey information that closely follows the format of the Central Bank Survey of the IMF's *Monetary and Financial Statistics Manual (MFSM)*. Departures from the *MFSM* methodology are explained below.

Claims on Central Government and *Liabilities to Central Government* include positions with local governments and their extrabudgetary funds.

Financial derivatives are excluded from the data.

Current year result, retained earnings, and gold and other unrealized revaluations are included in *Other Items (Net)* rather than in *Shares and Other Equity*.

Shares are valued at acquisition cost rather than at current market price

Other Depository Corporations:

Comprises commercial banks (including branches of foreign banks) and Vneshekonombank.

Data are based on summarized survey information that closely follows the format of the Other Depository Corporations Survey of the IMF's *Monetary and Financial Statistics Manual* (*MFSM*). For other depository corporations in the Russian Federation, departures from the *MFSM* methodology are explained below.

Claims on Central Government and *Liabilities to Central Government* include positions with local governments and their extrabudgetary funds.

Financial derivatives are excluded from the data.

Securities held to maturity are valued at amortized cost rather than at current market price or fair value.

Shares held for investment are valued at acquisition cost rather than at current market price

Depository Corporations:

See notes on central bank and other depository corporations.

Other Financial Corporations:

Comprises insurance companies and private pension funds. Data exclude investment funds, mutual funds, general funds of bank management, financial leasing companies, asset management companies, and financial auxiliaries.

Data are available only on a quarterly basis.

Data are based on summarized survey information (*IFS* publication aggregates) for other financial corporations.

Claims on Central Government and *Liabilities to Central Government* include positions with local governments.

Accrued interest is included in *Other Items (Net)* rather than in the outstanding amounts of the financial assets and liabilities.

Other Items (Net) include insurance companies' and private pension funds' claims on other financial corporations not yet covered, resulting in a large negative balance.

Monetary Aggregates:

Broad Money:

Broad Money calculated from the liability data in the sections for the central bank and other depository corporations accords with the concepts and definitions of the *MFSM* and is consistent with *Broad Money Liabilities* described below.

Money (National Definitions):

Broad Monetary Base comprises currency issued by the CBR (excluding cash in its vaults), other depository corporations' required reserves and correspondent accounts in national currency with the CBR, CBR bonds held by other depository corporations valued at market price, and other funds on operations of other depository corporations with the CBR.

M0 comprises currency in circulation outside depository corporations.

M1 comprises currency in circulation outside depository corporations and demand deposits (current, settlement and other transferable accounts) in national currency of public and private nonfinancial corporations, other financial corporations, and households with the CBR and other depository corporations.

M2 comprises M1 and time deposits in national currency of other financial corporations, public nonfinancial corporations, private nonfinancial corporations, and households with the

CBR and other depository corporations.

Broad Money Liabilities comprises currency in circulation and demand, time, and savings deposits in national and foreign currency, including accrued interest on deposits, of other financial corporations, public nonfinancial corporations, private nonfinancial corporations, and households with the CBR and other depository corporations.

Interest Rates:

Central Bank Policy Rate (End of Period):
Minimum bid rate for one-day repurchase agreements auction of CBR with credit institutions.

Refinancing Rate (End of Period):
Monetary policy instrument used by the CBR to influence interest rates in various segments of the financial market. The rate is set by the Board of Directors of the CBR.

Money Market Rate:
Weighted average rate on one-day loans in national currency of the Moscow interbank market. The rate is weighted by loan amounts.

Treasury Bill Rate:
Weighted average rate on government short-term obligations ("GKO") with maturities of up to 90 days.
Beginning in September 2004, the "GKO" don't circulate in the market.

Deposit Rate:
Prevailing rate for one-month time deposits in denominations of more than Rub 300,000. † Beginning in January 1997, weighted average rate offered by other depository corporations on deposits of households in national currency with maturity of up to one year. The rate is weighted by deposit amounts.

Lending Rate:
Weighted average rate on various regional commercial banks' loans of up to one year in national currency to legal entities (companies and organizations). † Beginning in January 1997, weighted average rate charged by other depository corporations on loans to nonfinancial institutions in national currency with maturity of up to one year. The rate is weighted by loan amounts.

Government Bond Yield:
Average yield on 15-year government bonds.

Prices, Production, Labor:

Share Prices:
The effective capitalization-weighted market index of Russian issuers' most liquid stocks listed on the MICEX stock exchange, base September 22, 1997.
The *Russian Trading System (RTS)* index is the ratio of the aggregate effective capitalization of the stocks included in the index calculation list to the aggregate effective capitalization of the same stocks as of the initial trading date multiplied by the index value as of the initial trading date and a correction factor for changes made to the stock index calculation list, base September 1, 1995.

Producer Prices:
Source: State Statistical Office. Weights Reference Period: weights are revised annually; Number of Items in Basket: approximately 800; Sectoral Coverage: mining, manufacturing, production and distribution of electricity, gas, and water; Basis for Calculation:

weights are derived from industry survey data on production output in value terms at current prices for the base year.

Consumer Prices:
Source: State Statistical Office. Weights Reference Period: September of previous year; Geographic Coverage: entire country; Number of Items in Basket: 445; Basis for Calculation: data on consumer spending by the population, derived from household budget surveys, are used as weights.

International Transactions:
Source: State Statistical Office. *Exports (line 70..d)* and *Imports (line 71..d)* include adjustments for barter trade and for shuttle trade but exclude humanitarian aid and trade in fish and other marine products by Russian vessels operating overseas. † Data prior to 1994 exclude trade with the Baltic countries and the other countries of the former Soviet Union. Beginning in January 1994, data for imports c.i.f. are obtained by conversion from reported imports f.o.b. data using 10 percent c.i.f./f.o.b. factor.

Government Finance:
Data are as reported by the Federal Treasury and cover operations of the budgetary central (federal) government. † From January 2002, budget accounts balances in foreign currency are included under net domestic financing. Beginning in January 2007, budgetary central government data are presented in the GFSM 2001 Statement of Sources and Uses of Cash. The fiscal year ends December 31.

National Accounts:
Source: State Statistical Office. As indicated by the country, data are compiled in accordance with the methodology of the *1993 SNA. Gross Domestic Product, Production Based (line 99bp)* is compiled from the production approach using data on gross output and intermediate consumption from production surveys, adjusted to exclude holding gains in inventories. The statistical discrepancy *(line 99bs)* represents the difference between the GDP from the production approach *(line 99bp)* and the sum of the expenditure components shown. Chain linked GDP volume measures are expressed according to 2008 prices.

Rwanda 714

Date of Fund Membership:
September 30, 1963

Standard Sources:
National Bank of Rwanda
National Institute of Statistics of Rwanda

Exchange Rates:
Market Rate (End of Period and Period Average):
On March 6, 1995, Rwanda adopted a market-determined exchange rate system. Before then, the official rate was pegged to the SDR.

Monetary Authorities:
Comprises the National Bank of Rwanda only.

Deposit Money Banks:
Comprises the commercial banks. Excludes demand deposits with the Centre des Chèques Postaux (Postal System). Excludes the Caisse d'Epargne (Savings Bank), liquidated in 2000. † Beginning in 1981, the classification of external and government accounts has been improved.

Monetary Survey:
† See note on deposit money banks.

Other Banking Institutions:
Comprises the Development Bank and the Mortgage Loan Fund. Excludes the Union des Banques Populaires (Cooperative Bank) and Saving and Credit Cooperatives.

Interest Rates:
Discount Rate (End of Period):
Rate at which banks may obtain refinancing from the National Bank of Rwanda through repurchase agreement transactions.

Interbank Market Rate:
Volume-weighted monthly average rate on loans between banks. The rate is compiled every month by the National Bank of Rwanda on the basis of declarations made by operators. When no transaction occurs during one month, the National Bank of Rwanda carries forward data from the preceding month.

Treasury Bill Rate:
Volume-weighted monthly average yield at issuance on four-week Treasury bills sold at auctions by the National bank of Rwanda on behalf of the central government. † Beginning in January 2007, volume-weighted monthly average yield at issuance on 13-week Treasury bills sold at auctions.

Deposit Rate:
Volume-weighted average rate across all banks of term deposit rate at 1-month, 3-month, 6-month, and 12-month maturities. Average rates on term deposits are compiled by the National bank of Rwanda monthly. For each maturity and each bank, the National Bank of Rwanda collects the rate applied at the end of each week, then compile a simple average monthly rate for each maturity; subsequently, the National Bank of Rwanda compiles for each maturity an average rate across all banks weighted by the volume of such term deposit at the end of the month in each bank.

Lending Rate:
Volume-weighted average rate of new loans at all maturities granted by banks during the reference month. Volume-weighted average rates are compiled monthly by the National Bank of Rwanda for short-, medium-, and long-term maturities on the basis of individual declarations by banks.

Prices:
Consumer Prices:
Source: National Institute of Statistics of Rwanda. Weights Reference Period: 2005–2006; Geographical Coverage: whole national territory; Number of Items in the Basket: 1136; Basis for Calculation: the weights were based on national household budget-consumption surveys conducted in 2005–2006 with a sample of 6900 households.

International Transactions:
Source: National Bank of Rwanda.

Government Finance:

From 1992 onwards, data are as reported by National Bank of Rwanda and cover consolidated central government. The fiscal year ends December 31.

National Accounts:

Source: National Institute of Statistics of Rwanda. As indicated by the country, the data are compiled in the framework of the *1993 SNA*.

St. Kitts and Nevis 361

Date of Fund Membership:
August 15, 1984

Standard Sources:
Eastern Caribbean Central Bank
Statistical Office

Exchange Rates:

Official Rate: (End of Period and Period Average):
Rates are based on a fixed relationship to the U.S. dollar.

Central Bank:

Data are based on a standardized report form (SRF) for central banks, which accords with the concepts and definitions of the IMF's *Monetary and Financial Statistics Manual (MFSM)*, 2000. Departures from the *MFSM* methodology are explained below.
Data refer to accounts in the balance sheet of the East Caribbean Central Bank (ECCB) attributable to St. Kitts and Nevis.
Financial derivatives are excluded from the data.
Claims on Nonresident comprises estimates of St. Kitts and Nevis' notional share of the ECCB's foreign assets.
Claims on Other Depository Corporations comprises the portion of the ECCB's claims on resident other depository corporations attributable to St. Kitts and Nevis.
Claims on Central Government and *Liabilities to Central Government* comprise the portion of the ECCB's claims on and liabilities to the central government attributable to St. Kitts and Nevis.
Financial assets with other financial corporations, state and local governments, public nonfinancial corporations, and private sector attributable to St. Kitts and Nevis are not included in the data in the absence of a country of these accounts in the balance sheet of the ECCB.
Currency in circulation comprises the portion of currency in circulation attributable to St. Kitts and Nevis less vault cash held by other depository corporations.
Some portion of other deposits to other depository corporations and interest accrued from these deposits are included in *Other Items (Net)*.
Share and other equity is not applicable to the member countries of the ECCU because the shares and other equity in the balance sheet of the ECCB exclusively belong to the ECCB.

Other Depository Corporations:

Comprises commercial banks. Data exclude finance companies and credit unions, which accept deposits.
Data are based on a standardized report form (SRF) for other de-

pository corporations, which accords with the concepts and definitions of the *Monetary and Financial Statistics Manual (MFSM)*. For resident other depository corporations in the member countries of the ECCU, departures from the *MFSM* methodology are explained below.
Financial derivatives and insurance technical reserves are excluded from the data.
Financial assets and liabilities for which economic sectorization is unavailable are allocated to the economic sector having the largest volume of transactions in the category.
Transferable Deposits Included in Broad Money includes all deposits of the private sector denominated in foreign currency.
Accounts receivable and payable are included in *Other Items (Net)* rather than in other depository corporations' claims or liabilities to the corresponding economic sectors.
Accrued interest on transactions with nonresidents is included in *Other Items (Net)* rather than in the outstanding amount of foreign assets and liabilities.

Depository Corporations:

See notes on central bank and other depository corporations.

Monetary Aggregates:

Broad Money:
Broad Money is calculated from the liability data in the sections for the central bank and other depository corporations. Broad money differs from M2 described below as broad money includes the deposits of money holding sectors with the ECCB attributable to St. Kitts and Nevis and deposits of other financial corporations, state and local government, and public nonfinancial corporations in national and foreign currencies with commercial banks.

Money (National Definitions):
M1 comprises notes and coins held by the public and demand deposits in national currency of the private sector with commercial banks.
M2 comprises M1 plus time, savings, and foreign currency deposits of the private sector with commercial banks.

Interest Rates:

Discount Rate (End of Period):
Rate charged by the ECCB on loans of last resort to commercial banks.

Money Market Rate:
Fixed rate on loans between commercial banks. The rate includes the commission charged by the ECCB as agent. † Beginning in October 2001, weighted average rate on loans between commercial banks. The rate is weighted by loans amounts.

Treasury Bill Rate:
Rate on three-month treasury bills.

Savings Rate:
Maximum rate offered by commercial banks on savings deposits in national currency. † Beginning in June 1993, weighted average rate offered by commercial banks on savings deposits in national currency. The rate is weighted by deposit amounts.

Savings Rate (Foreign Currency):
Weighted average rate offered by commercial banks on savings deposits in foreign currency. The rate is weighted by deposit amounts.

Deposit Rate:
Maximum rate offered by commercial banks on three-month time deposits. The rate is weighted by deposit amounts.

Deposit Rate (Foreign Currency):
Weighted average rate offered by commercial banks on time deposits in foreign currency. The rate is weighted by deposit amounts.

Lending Rate:
Maximum rate charged by commercial banks on prime loans. The rate is weighted by loan amounts.

Lending Rate (Foreign Currency):
Weighted average rate charged by commercial banks on loans in foreign currency. The rate is weighted by loan amounts.

Prices:

Consumer Prices:
Source: Statistical Office. Weights Reference Period: 2001; Geographical Coverage: Basseterre and Sandy Point; Number of Items in Basket: 329; Basis for Calculation: weights are derived from the 1998 Household Income and Expenditure Survey.

International Transactions:

Source: Statistical Office.

Government Finance:

Data cover budgetary central government. The fiscal year ends December 31.

National Accounts:

Source: Eastern Caribbean Central Bank. There are no data for Increase/Decrease in Stocks. As indicated by the country, data have been revised following the implementation of the *1993 SNA*.

St. Lucia   362

Date of Fund Membership:
November 15, 1979

Standard Sources:
Eastern Caribbean Central Bank
Statistical Office, Government of St. Lucia

Exchange Rates:

Official Rate: (End of Period and Period Average):
Rates are based on a fixed relationship to the U.S. dollar.

Central Bank:

Data are based on a standardized report form (SRF) for central banks, which accords with the concepts and definitions of the IMF's *Monetary and Financial Statistics Manual (MFSM)*, 2000. Departures from the *MFSM* methodology are explained below.

Data refer to accounts in the balance sheet of the East Caribbean Central Bank (ECCB) attributable to St. Lucia.

Financial derivatives are excluded from the data.

Claims on Nonresident comprises estimates of St. Lucia' notional share of the ECCB's foreign assets.

Claims on Other Depository Corporations comprises the portion of

the ECCB's claims on resident other depository corporations attributable to St. Lucia.

Claims on Central Government and *Liabilities to Central Government* comprise the portion of the ECCB's claims on and liabilities to the central government attributable to St. Lucia.

Financial assets with *other* financial corporations, state and local governments, public nonfinancial corporations, and private sector attributable to St. Lucia are not included in the data in the absence of a country of these accounts in the balance sheet of the ECCB.

Currency in circulation comprises the portion of currency in circulation attributable to St. Lucia less vault cash held by other depository corporations.

Some portion of other deposits to other depository corporations and interest accrued from these deposits are included in *Other Items (Net)*.

Share and other equity is not applicable to the member countries of the ECCU because the shares and other equity in the balance sheet of the ECCB exclusively belong to the ECCB.

Other Depository Corporations:

Comprises commercial banks. Data exclude finance companies, mortgage companies, and credit unions, which accept deposits. Data are based on a standardized report form (SRF) for other depository corporations, which accords with the concepts and definitions of the *Monetary and Financial Statistics Manual (MFSM)*. For resident other depository corporations in the member countries of the ECCU, departures from the *MFSM* methodology are explained below.

Financial derivatives and insurance technical reserves are excluded from the data.

Financial assets and liabilities for which economic sectorization is unavailable are allocated to the economic sector having the largest volume of transactions in the category.

Transferable Deposits Included in Broad Money includes all deposits of the private sector denominated in foreign currency.

Accounts receivable and payable are included in *Other Items (Net)* rather than in other depository corporations' claims or liabilities to the corresponding economic sectors.

Accrued interest on transactions with nonresidents is included in *Other Items (Net)* rather than in the outstanding amount of foreign assets and liabilities.

Depository Corporations:

See notes on central bank and other depository corporations.

Monetary Aggregates:

Broad Money:
Broad Money is calculated from the liability data in the sections for the central bank and other depository corporations. Broad money differs from M2 described below as broad money includes the deposits of money holding sectors with the ECCB attributable to St. Lucia and deposits of other financial corporations, state and local government, and public nonfinancial corporations in national and foreign currencies with commercial banks.

Money (National Definitions):
M1 comprises notes and coins held by the public and demand deposits in national currency of the private sector with commercial banks.

M2 comprises M1 plus time, savings, and foreign currency deposits of the private sector with commercial banks.

Interest Rates:

Discount Rate (End of Period):
Rate charged by the ECCB on loans of last resort to commercial banks.

Money Market Rate:
Fixed rate on loans between commercial banks. The rate includes the commission charged by the ECCB as agent. † Beginning in October 2001, weighted average rate on loans between commercial banks. The rate is weighted by loans amounts.

Treasury Bill Rate:
Rate on three-month treasury bills. † Beginning in January 2004, rate on one-year treasury bills. † Beginning in July 2007, rate on six-month treasury bills.

Savings Rate:
Maximum rate offered by commercial banks on savings deposits in national currency. † Beginning in June 2003, weighted average rate offered by commercial banks on savings deposits in national currency. The rate is weighted by deposit amounts.

Deposit Rate:
Maximum rate offered by commercial banks on three-month time deposits. The rate is weighted by deposit amounts.

Deposit Rate (Foreign currency):
Weighted average rate offered by commercial banks on deposits in foreign currency. The rate is weighted by deposit amounts.

Lending Rate:
Maximum rate charged by commercial banks on prime loans. The rate is weighted by loan amounts.

Lending Rate (Foreign Currency):
Weighted average rate charged by commercial banks on loans in foreign currency. The rate is weighted by loan amounts.

Prices:

Consumer Prices:
Source: Statistical Office. Weights Reference Period: January 2008.

International Transactions:

All trade data are from the Statistical Office. *Exports* include re-exports.

National Accounts:

Data are as reported by national authorities. Data differ from earlier estimates published in the *UN Monthly Bulletin of Statistics.*

St. Vincent & Grens.   364

Date of Fund Membership:

December 28, 1979

Standard Sources:

Eastern Caribbean Central Bank
Statistical Unit, St. Vincent and the Grenadines

Exchange Rates:

Official Rate: (End of Period and Period Average):
Rates are based on a fixed relationship to the U.S. dollar.

Central Bank:

Data are based on a standardized report form (SRF) for central banks, which accords with the concepts and definitions of the IMF's *Monetary and Financial Statistics Manual (MFSM),* 2000. Departures from the *MFSM* methodology are explained below. Data refer to accounts in the balance sheet of the East Caribbean Central Bank (ECCB) attributable to St. Vincent and the Grenadines.

Financial derivatives are excluded from the data.

Claims on Nonresident comprises estimates of St. Vincent and the Grenadines' notional share of the ECCB's foreign assets.

Claims on Other Depository Corporations comprises the portion of the ECCB's claims on resident other depository corporations attributable to St. Vincent and the Grenadines.

Claims on Central Government and *Liabilities to Central Government* comprise the portion of the ECCB's claims on and liabilities to the central government attributable to St. Vincent and the Grenadines. Financial assets with other financial corporations, state and local governments, public nonfinancial corporations, and private sector attributable to St. Vincent and the Grenadines are not included in the data in the absence of a country of these accounts in the balance sheet of the ECCB.

Currency in circulation comprises the portion of currency in circulation attributable to St. Vincent and the Grenadines less vault cash held by other depository corporations.

Some portion of other deposits to other depository corporations and interest accrued from these deposits are included in *Other Items (Net).*

Share and other equity is not applicable to the member countries of the ECCU because the shares and other equity in the balance sheet of the ECCB exclusively belong to the ECCB.

Other Depository Corporations:

Comprises commercial banks. Data exclude finance companies, mortgage companies, and credit unions, which accept deposits.

Data are based on a standardized report form (SRF) for other depository corporations, which accords with the concepts and definitions of the *Monetary and Financial Statistics Manual (MFSM).* For resident other depository corporations in the member countries of the ECCU, departures from the *MFSM* methodology are explained below.

Financial derivatives and insurance technical reserves are excluded from the data.

Financial assets and liabilities for which economic sectorization is unavailable are allocated to the economic sector having the largest volume of transactions in the category.

Transferable Deposits Included in Broad Money includes all deposits of the private sector denominated in foreign currency.

Accounts receivable and payable are included in *Other Items (Net)* rather than in other depository corporations' claims or liabilities to the corresponding economic sectors.

Accrued interest on transactions with nonresidents is included in *Other Items (Net)* rather than in the outstanding amount of foreign assets and liabilities.

Depository Corporations:

See notes on central bank and other depository corporations.

Monetary Aggregates:

Broad Money:

Broad Money is calculated from the liability data in the sections for the central bank and other depository corporations. Broad money differs from M2 described below as broad money includes the deposits of money holding sectors with the ECCB attributable to St. Vincent and the Grenadines and deposits of other financial corporations, state and local government, and public nonfinancial corporations in national and foreign currencies with commercial banks.

Money (National Definitions):

M1 comprises notes and coins held by the public and demand deposits in national currency of the private sector with commercial banks.

M2 comprises M1 plus time, savings, and foreign currency deposits of the private sector with commercial banks.

Interest Rates:

Discount Rate (End of Period):

Rate charged by the ECCB on loans of last resort to commercial banks.

Money Market Rate:

Fixed rate on loans between commercial banks. The rate includes the commission charged by the ECCB as agent. † Beginning in October 2001, weighted average rate on loans between commercial banks. The rate is weighted by loans amounts.

Treasury Bill Rate:

Rate on three-month treasury bills.

Savings Rate:

Maximum rate offered by commercial banks on savings deposits in national currency. † Beginning in June 2003, weighted average rate offered by commercial banks on savings deposits in national currency. The rate is weighted by deposit amounts.

Deposit Rate:

Maximum rate offered by commercial banks on three-month time deposits. The rate is weighted by deposit amounts.

Deposit Rate (Foreign currency):

Weighted average rate offered by commercial banks on deposits in foreign currency. The rate is weighted by deposit amounts.

Lending Rate:

Maximum rate charged by commercial banks on prime loans. The rate is weighted by loan amounts.

Lending Rate (Foreign Currency):

Weighted average rate charged by commercial banks on loans in foreign currency. The rate is weighted by loan amounts.

Prices:

Consumer Prices:

Source: Statistical Unit. Weights Reference Period: January 2001; Geographical Coverage: whole national territory; Number of Items in Basket: 256; Basis for Calculation: weights are based on the 1996–1997 Household Budget and Expenditure Survey.

International Transactions:

All trade data are from the Statistical Unit.

Government Finance:

Annual data are as reported for the *Government Finance Statistics Yearbook (GFSY)* and cover budgetary central government. The fiscal year ends December 31.

National Accounts:

Data are as reported by national authorities. Data differ from earlier estimates published in the *UN Monthly Bulletin of Statistics.* As indicated by the country, data have been revised following the implementation of the *1993 SNA.*

Samoa   862

Date of Fund Membership:

December 28, 1971

Standard Sources:

Central Bank of Samoa
Bureau of Statistics

Exchange Rates:

Official Rate: (End of Period and Period Average):

The exchange rate is operated as a fixed peg arrangement against a composite of currencies. Central bank midpoint rate.

International Liquidity:

Foreign Exchange (line 1d.d) comprises holdings of the Bank of Samoa, the government, and the commercial banks.

Central Bank:

Consists of the Central Bank of Samoa (CBS) only.
† Beginning in December 2006, data are based on a standardized report form (SRF) for central banks, which accords with the concepts and definitions of the IMF's *Monetary and Financial Statistics Manual (MFSM)*, 2000.
For December 2001 through November 2006, data in the SRF format are compiled from pre-SRF data not based on the *MFSM* methodology. Departures from the *MFSM* methodology are explained below.
Financial assets and liabilities for which economic sectorization is unavailable are allocated to the economic sector having the largest volume of transactions in the category.
Accrued interest is included in *Other Items (Net)* rather than in the outstanding amounts of the financial assets and liabilities.
Valuation adjustment is included in *Other Items (Net)* rather than in *Shares and Other Equity.*

Other Depository Corporations:

Comprises commercial banks. Data exclude credit unions.
† Beginning in December 2006, data are based on a standardized report form (SRF) for other depository corporations, which accords with the concepts and definitions of the *Monetary and Financial Statistics Manual (MFSM)*. For other depository corporations in Samoa, departures from the *MFSM* methodology are explained below.
Deposits Included in Broad Money include deposits of credit unions.
For December 2001 through November 2006, data in the SRF

format are compiled from pre-SRF data not based on the *MFSM* methodology. Departures from the *MFSM* methodology are explained below.

Financial assets and liabilities for which economic sectorization is unavailable are allocated to the economic sector having the largest volume of transactions in the category.

Accrued interest is included in *Other Items (Net)* rather than in the outstanding amounts of the financial assets and liabilities.

Valuation adjustment is included in *Other Items (Net)* rather than in *Shares and Other Equity*.

Depository Corporations:

† See notes on central bank and other depository corporations.

Monetary Aggregates:

Broad Money:

Broad Money is calculated from the liability data in the sections for the central bank and other depository corporations and is consistent with M2 described below.

Money (National Definitions):

M1 comprises currency in circulation outside depository corporations and demand deposits of other financial corporations, public nonfinancial corporations, and private sector with commercial banks in national currency.

Quasi Money comprises saving and time deposits of other financial corporations, public nonfinancial corporations, and private sector with commercial banks in national currency and demand deposits of other financial corporations, public nonfinancial corporations, and private sector with commercial banks in foreign currency.

M2 comprises M1 and quasi money.

Interest Rates:

Savings Rate:

Maximum rate offered by commercial banks on savings deposits.

Deposit Rate:

Weighted average of rates offered by commercial banks on deposits. The rate is weighted by deposit amounts.

Lending Rate:

Weighted average of rates charged by commercial banks on loans and advances. The rates is weighted by loan amounts.

Government Bond Yield:

Yield to maturity on seven-year government bonds.

Prices:

Consumer Prices:

Source: Bureau of Statistics. Weights reference period August 2010. Geographical coverage: Samoan households in Apia, the capital city, and the surrounding region. Number of Items in the Basket: 188. Basis for Calculation: The weights are based on a Household Income and Expenditure Survey (HIES) conducted in 2008.

International Transactions:

† Prior to January 1977, data are based on customs clearances; diplomatic imports are included in total imports. After January 1977, data refer to actual imports landed in Samoa. All value data on trade are from source S. † October tala 1985 re-export value data include the sale proceeds of an aircraft by the government for 2.54 million tala (equivalent to US $1.1 million). † Imports for August 1986 include the engine for a damaged aircraft valued at

3,676,019 tala. Effective May 2005, figures for imports, petroleum and petrol products have been revised since 2000 to exclude freight and insurance. Beginning with August 2011 figures, exports and re-exports include fuel sold to foreign-owned carriers (sea and air), in line with the Sixth Edition of the *Balance of Payments and International Investment Position Manual (BPM6).*

San Marino   135

Data are denominated in Italian lire prior to January 1999 as the currency of San Marino was the Italian lire under a monetary union agreement between Italy and San Marino. With the authority of the Council of the European Union (EU), Italy was empowered to negotiate agreements with San Marino to replace the monetary union agreement between itself and San Marino, making the euro the official currency of San Marino, providing access to payment systems and covering other monetary conditions. Pursuant to the new monetary agreement, San Marino adopted the euro and all data are denominated in euros from January 1999 onward. An irrevocably fixed factor for converting lire to euros was established at 1,936.27 lire per euro. In 2002, Italian lire banknotes and Sammarinese lire coins were retired from circulation and replaced by euro banknotes and coins. San Marino is obligated to apply EU rules regarding banknotes and coins.

Date of Fund Membership:

September 23, 1992

Standard Source:

Central Bank of the Republic of San Marino
Office of Economic Planning and Data Processing Center and Statistics

Exchange Rates:

Market Rate (End of Period and Period Average):

Refer to the section on exchange rates in the notes for the pages for Italy and for the euro area.

Monetary Authorities:

Comprises Banca Centrale della Repubblica di San Marino (Central Bank of the Republic of San Marino).

Deposit Money Banks:

Comprises private commercial and savings banks. Commercial banks are not subject to a legal reserve requirement, but instead to a liquidity requirement, under which banks must hold at least 10 percent of their deposits, less 10 times their capital, in the form of cash or bonds issued or guaranteed by the Sammarinese government, the Italian government, and/or international organizations. The reported data cover all of the asset management activities of banks but do not include custodial securities activities.

Monetary Survey:

Deposit Money (line 34) comprises *Demand Deposits in Monetary Authorities (line 14d)*, and *Demand Deposits in Deposit Money Banks (line 24).*

Interest Rates:

Deposit Rate:

Data pertains to average rates weighted by the outstanding level of all time deposits.

Lending Rate:

Data pertains to average lending rates weighted by the outstanding level of all loans of more than 10,000 euros.

Prices and Production:

Consumer Prices:

Source: Office of Economic Planning and Data Processing Center and Statistics. Weights Reference Period: weights are updated annually; Number of Items in Basket: 1,101.

National Accounts:

Source: Office of Economic Planning and Data Processing Center and Statistics. As indicated by the country, data are compiled in accordance with the methodology of the *1995 ESA*. GDP volume measures are expressed according to 1995 prices.

São Tomé & Príncipe   716

Date of Fund Membership:

September 30, 1977

Standard Source:

Central Bank of São Tomé and Príncipe
Instituto Nacional de Estatística

Exchange Rates:

Market Rate (End of Period and Period Average):

Between July 22, 1987 and December 2, 1994, São Tomé and Príncipe's currency, the dobra, was pegged to a basket of currencies of the country's seven major trading partners. Beginning in December 1994, the official exchange rate is determined daily as a weighted average of exchange rates in commercial banks, exchange bureaus, and the parallel market. The weights are based on the U.S. dollar value of the previous day's transactions reported by commercial banks and exchange bureaus and an estimate of the U.S. dollar value of transactions in the parallel market. Beginning in January 2004, the official exchange rate is determined daily based 40 percent on the U.S. dollar value of the previous day's transactions reported by commercial banks, and 60 percent on the U.S. dollar value of the last auction rate regarding the sale of foreign exchange made by the central bank. Beginning in January 2010, the dobra was pegged to the euro, at an exchange rate of 24,500 dobras per euro.

International Liquidity:

Foreign Exchange (line 1d.d) is the U.S. dollar value of deposits in foreign banks and holdings of foreign currency of the Central Bank of São Tomé and Príncipe.

Central Bank:

Comprises the Central Bank of São Tomé and Príncipe (CBSTP) only.

† Beginning in December 2006, data are based on a standardized report form (SRF) for central banks, which accords with the concepts and definitions of the IMF's *Monetary and Financial Statistics Manual (MFSM)*, 2000. Departures from the *MFSM* methodology are explained below.

Financial assets and liabilities for which economic sectorization is unavailable are allocated to the economic sector having the largest volume of transactions in the category.

Not all financial assets and liabilities are valued at market prices or fair values.

Most accounts receivable and payable are included in *Other Items (Net)* rather than in the CBSTP's claims on or liabilities to the corresponding sectors.

For December 2001 through November 2006 data in the SRF format are compiled form pre-SRF data not compiled based on the *MFSM* methodology. Departures from the *MFSM* methodology are explained below.

Financial assets and liabilities for which economic sectorization is unavailable are allocated to the economic sector having the largest volume of transactions in the category.

Accrual accounting is not fully applied and accrued interest is included in *Other Items (Net)* rather in the outstanding amounts of the financial assets and liabilities.

Financial assets and liabilities are not all valued at market prices or fair values.

Accounts receivable and payable are included in *Other Items (Net)* rather than in the CBSTP's claims on or liabilities to the corresponding sectors.

Other Depository Corporations:

Comprises commercial banks only.

†Beginning in December 2006, data are based on a standardized report form (SRF) for other depository corporations, which accords with the concepts and definitions of the *Monetary and Financial Statistics Manual (MFSM)*. For other depository corporations in São Tomé and Principe, departures from the *MFSM* methodology are explained below.

Financial assets and liabilities for which economic sectorization is unavailable are allocated to the economic sector having the largest volume of transactions in the category.

Where data for other depository corporations are not directly distinguished from data for other financial corporations, separation of the data is based on the characteristics of the financial asset or liability.

Most accounts receivable and payable are included in *Other Items (Net)* rather than in the other depository corporations' claims on or liabilities to the corresponding sectors.

For December 2001 trough November 2006 data in the SRF format are compiled form pre-SRF data not compiled based on the *MFSM* methodology. Departures from the *MFSM* methodology are explained below.

Financial assets and liabilities for which economic sectorization is unavailable are allocated to the economic sector having the largest volume of transactions in the category.

Accrual accounting is not fully applied and accrued interest is included in *Other Items (Net)* rather in the outstanding amounts of the financial assets and liabilities.

Financial assets and liabilities are not all valued at market prices or fair values.

Accounts receivable and payable are included in *Other Items (Net)* rather than in the ODC's claims on or liabilities to the corresponding sectors.

† Beginning in January 2010, data are based on a new plan of accounts, which fully complies with the *MFSM* methodology regarding classificatiion and valuation of financial instruments and sectorization of institutional units.

Depository Corporations:

† See notes on central bank and other depository corporations.

Monetary Aggregates:

Broad Money:

Broad Money calculated from the liability data in the sections for the central bank and other depository corporations accords with the concepts and definitions of the MFSM and is consistent with M3 described below.

Money (National Definitions):

Base Money comprises notes and coins in circulation outside the CBSTP and other depository corporations' deposits with the CBSTP in national and foreign currency.

M1 comprises notes and coins in circulation outside depository corporations and transferable deposits in national currency of other financial corporations, public nonfinancial corporations, and private sector with depository corporations.

M2 comprises M1 and other deposits in national currency of other financial corporations, local governments, public nonfinancial corporations, and private sector with depository corporations.

M3 comprises M2 and deposits in foreign currency of other financial corporations, local governments, public nonfinancial corporations, and private sector with depository corporations.

Interest Rates:

Central Bank Policy Rate (End of Period):

Rate at which the CBSTP lends in national currency to commercial banks.

Deposit Rate:

Rate offered by commercial banks on deposits of 31 to 90 days in national currency. † Beginning in August 2000, average rate offered by commercial banks on one-year time deposits. † Beginning in March 2005, simple average of minimum rates offered by commercial banks on deposits up to 90 days, up to 180 days, and up to a year.

Lending Rate:

Rate charged by commercial banks on 180-day loans in national currency. † Beginning in August 2000, average rate charged by commercial banks on one-year loans. † Beginning in March 2005, simple average of maximum rates charged by commercial banks on loans from 91 to 180 days, 181 days to a year, and over one year.

Prices and Production:

Consumer Prices:

Source: National Institute of Statistics. Weight Reference Period: 1995; Geographical Coverage: city of São Tomé; Number of Items in the Basket:190 items; Basis of Calculation: Household Cluster Survey (IAF) conducted between June and August of 1995 in the city of São Tomé.

International Transactions:

Source: National Institute of Statistics.

Government Finance:

Statistical data relating to budget execution are produced and disseminated by the Ministry of Planning and Finance. The data on budget execution in *GFSM 2001* format are derived from data compiled according to the Government Financial Operations Table (TOFE). The fiscal year ends December 31.

National Accounts:

Source: National Institute of Statistics. The data are compiled in the framework of the *1993 SNA*.

Saudi Arabia   456

Calendar:

The Islamic lunar year (Hijra year) is about eleven days shorter than the Gregorian year. The Gregorian calendar equivalent of the lunar year changes annually. Hence, after three years the difference amounts to one lunar month which must be skipped in the Gregorian calendar. The data in the monetary sections are compiled on the basis of the lunar calendar, and the end of lunar month data are allocated to the approximate equivalent of the Gregorian dates.

Date of Fund Membership:

August 26, 1957

Standard Sources:

Saudi Arabian Monetary Agency

Exchange Rates:

Official Rate: (End of Period and Period Average):

The exchange rate of the Saudi Riyal is fixed at SR 3.75 per U.S. dollar.

International Liquidity:

† Beginning April 1978, *line 1d.d* excludes the foreign exchange cover against the note issue which together with *Monetary Authorities: Other Assets* are included in *line 11*. As of March 1978, this foreign exchange cover amounted to about US$5.3 billion. The authorities revised their methodology for classifying foreign assets to include the foreign exchange cover against the note issue, and provided revised data on *Foreign Exchange (line 1d.d)* for 1996 onward. Prior to 2005, data on foreign exchange excluded SAMA's investments and deposits abroad. As a result, the classification of published data for prior periods may differ, resulting in a break in time series data. Beginning in March 1975, *Gold (National Valuation) (line 1and)* is equal to *line 1ad* valued at SDR 35 per fine troy ounce and converted into U.S. dollars at the dollar/SDR rate *line **sa*** on the *IFS* page for the United States. Beginning in February 2008, *Gold (Million Fine Troy Ounces)* is revised as a result of an adjustment in SAMA's gold accounts, and is valued according to national practice.

Monetary Authorities:

Comprises the Saudi Arabian Monetary Agency (SAMA) only.

Deposit Money Banks:

Comprises commercial banks.

† Beginning in 1983, data are based on improved classification. † Beginning December 1992, claims on public enterprises *(line 22c)* include claims on financial and nonfinancial public enterprises, and may include a small amount of loans and advances to central government. Demand deposits *(line 24)*, quasi-monetary deposits *(line 25a)*, and foreign currency deposits *(line 25b)* may include some central government deposits.

Monetary Survey:

In the monetary survey (see Introduction for the standard method of calculation), *line 35* equals *Quasi-Monetary* and *Foreign Currency Deposits (lines 25a* and *25b)*, respectively. † See note on deposit money banks.

Other Banking Institutions:

† Prior to 1976, data refer to the Saudi Agricultural Bank. Thereafter, consolidates the Saudi Agricultural Bank, the Saudi Indus-

trial Development Fund, the Public Investment Fund, the Real Estate Development Fund, and the Saudi Credit Bank. Foreign accounts relate solely to the Public Investment Fund.

Money (National Definitions):

Monetary Base comprises currency in circulation and bankers' deposits with SAMA. Currency in circulation refers to notes and coins issued by SAMA.

M1 comprises currency outside banks and demand deposits of businesses, individuals, and government entities in national currency with commercial banks. Currency in circulation refers to notes and coins issued by SAMA less the amount held by commercial banks.

M2 comprises M1 and time and savings deposits of businesses, individuals, and government entities in national currency with commercial banks.

M3 comprises M2 and other quasi-monetary liabilities of commercial banks. Other quasi-monetary liabilities comprise foreign currency deposits of businesses, individuals, and government entities; marginal deposits for letters of credit, outstanding remittances; and banks' repurchase agreements with the private sector.

Interest Rates:

Central Bank Policy Rate (End of Period):
Rate offered by SAMA on overnight reverse repurchase agreements.

Central Bank Repo Rate:
Rate charged by SAMA on overnight repurchase agreements.

Money Market Rate:
Rate offered by commercial banks on three-month funding in the interbank market. The rate is an average derived from the quotations provided by ten commercial banks. The rate is known as the Saudi Interbank Offered Rate (SIBOR).

Money Market Rate (Foreign Currency):
Simple average of daily interest rates on three-month interbank deposits in US Dollars.

Treasury Bill Rate:
Rate on thirteen-week treasury bills. The target price set in the wholesome market auction for treasury bills is based on the interest rates offered by commercial banks on thirteen-week interbank deposits.

Prices, Production, Labor:

Share Prices (End of Month):
Domestic Share Index covering agriculture, cement, electricity, other industry, banking, and other services, base 1985.

Wholesale Prices:
Source: Saudi Arabian Monetary Agency. Weights reference period: 1988; Coverage: imported items sold in domestic markets, export items up to the customs frontiers, and domestic products of both agricultural and industrial origin; Number of items in basket: 160.

Consumer Prices:
Source: Saudi Arabian Monetary Agency. Weights reference period: 1999; Geographical coverage: all-income population of 16 cities; Number of items in basket: 406; Basis for calculation: The expenditure weights for the index are derived from the *Household Expenditure and Income Survey* (HEIS) conducted in 1999.

Crude Petroleum Production:
Calculated from production quantities reported in the *Oil Market Intelligence.*

International Transactions:

Exports:
Data are from the Saudi Arabian Monetary Agency. The volume index of petroleum exports is calculated as an average of crude and refined petroleum volumes with 1985 export values as weights. If actual data is uncurrent, the index is projected forward using total petroleum production. The crude petroleum price index *(line 76aad)* is calculated by *IFS* as the weighted average of official state sales prices of Light, Medium, and Heavy grade crudes. The weights are the average of estimated supply figures published in *Petroleum Intelligence Weekly (PIW)* from Dec. 6, 1982 through June 24, 1985.

Imports, c.i.f.:
Saudi Arabian Monetary Agency data. Defense imports are excluded.

Balance of Payments:
Starting in 2009, SAMA published balance of payments data for 2005–2008 in *BPM5* format. As a result, the classification of published data for prior periods may differ, resulting in a break in time series data.
Reserve assets: Prior to 2005, data on reserve assets excluded SAMA's investments and deposits abroad.

National Accounts:

Data are published for Gregorian years.

Senegal 722

Date of Fund Membership:
August 31, 1962

Standard Source:
Banque Centrale des Etats de l'Afrique de l'Ouest (Central Bank of West African States)
Agence Nationale de la Statistique et de la Démographie
Senegal is a member of the West African Economic and Monetary Union, together with Benin, Burkina Faso, Côte d'Ivoire, Guinea-Bissau, Mali, Niger, and Togo. The Union, which was established in 1962, has a common central bank, the Central Bank of West African States (BCEAO), with headquarters in Dakar, and national branches in the member states. Mali and Guinea-Bissau joined the Union on June 1, 1984 and May 2, 1997, respectively.

Exchange Rates:

Official Rate: (End of Period and Period Average):
Prior to January 1999, the official rate was pegged to the French franc. On January 12, 1994, the CFA franc was devalued to CFAF 100 per French franc from CFAF 50 at which it had been fixed since 1948. From January 1, 1999, the CFAF is pegged to the euro at a rate of CFA franc 655.957 per euro.

International Liquidity:

Gold is revalued on a quarterly basis at the rate communicated by the BCEAO, which corresponds to the lowest average fixing in the London market.

Monetary Authorities:

Comprises the national branch of the BCEAO only. The amount of currency outside banks is estimated by subtracting from the amount of CFA franc notes issued by Senegal the estimated amounts of Senegal's currency in the cash held by the banks of all member countries of the Union. The data reported agree with Central Bank of West African States aggregates, as given in the table on the position of the monetary institutions. Valuation differences exist as a result of the *IFS* calculations of reserve position in the Fund and the SDR holdings, both components of *line 11,* based on Fund record. † Beginning in 1979, *Claims on Other Financial Institutions (line 32f)* includes claims of deposit money banks on other financial institutions; see deposit money bank notes for explanation of other break symbols.

Deposit Money Banks:

Comprises commercial banks and development banks, and includes certain banking operations of the Treasury and the Post Office. The Treasury accepts customs duty bills (reported separately in *line 22d.i*). Through its many branches, the Postal Checking System acts as the main depository for the private sector in the interior of Senegal. *Claims on the Private Sector (line 22d)* include doubtful and litigious debts. † Beginning in 1979, *Central Government Deposits (line 26d)* include the deposits of the public establishments of an administrative or social nature (EPAS) and exclude those of the savings bank; *Demand and Time Deposits (lines 24 and 25)* include deposits of the savings bank and exclude deposits of EPAS; and *Claims on Private Sector (line 22d)* exclude claims on other financial institutions.

Monetary Survey:

The data reported agree with source B aggregates, as given in the table on the position of the monetary institutions. Valuation differences exist as a result of the *IFS* calculations of reserve position in the Fund and the SDR holdings, both components of *line 11,* based on Fund record. † Beginning in 1979, *Claims on Other Financial Institutions (line 32f)* includes claims of deposit money banks on other financial institutions; see deposit money bank notes for explanation of other break symbols.

Interest Rates:

Discount Rate (End of Period):
Basic discount rate offered by the BCEAO.

Repurchase Agreement Rate (End of Period):
Rate on repurchase agreements between the BCEAO and the banks.

Money Market Rate:
Rate paid on overnight interbank advances.

Deposit Rate:
Rate offered by banks on time deposits of CFAF 500,000–2,000,000 for under six months.

Prices and Production:

Consumer Prices:
Source: Agence Nationale de la Statistique et de la Démographie. Weights Reference Period: 2008; Geographical Coverage: Dakar metropolitan area; Number of Items in Basket: 650; Basis for Cal-

culation: The weights are derived from a household expenditure survey of Dakar in 2008.

Industrial Production:
Source: Agence Nationale de la Statistique et de la Démographie. Weights reference period: 2006. The index is based on a sample of 69 companies representing 89.8% of the country's industrial value added.

International Transactions:

All trade data are from the Central Bank of West African States.

National Accounts:

Source: Agence Nationale de la Statistique et de la Démographie. Data are prepared in accordance with the 1993 United Nations System of National Accounts.

Serbia, Republic of   942

Date of Fund Membership:
December 14, 1992

Standard Sources:
National Bank of Serbia
Statistical Office of the Republic of Serbia

Exchange Rates:

Official Rate: (End of Period and Period Average):
From October 2000, the dinar exchange rate is set within the managed float regime. The dinar exchange rate against the euro is formed at the fixing session organized every business day by the commercial banks in Serbia and the National Bank of Serbia. The mid-point between the buy and sell rate formed at the session is the official dinar/euro mid-point exchange rate. The official exchange rates for the dinar against other currencies are computed using the dinar/euro rate and the cross rates for the euro against other currencies as provided by the Reuters service. Prior to October 2000, data are based on the fixed exchange rate of the dinar against the deutsche mark.

International Liquidity:

Gold (National Valuation) (line *1and*) is valued at the average price in three international markets prevailing at the end of the previous year.

Central Bank:

Consists of the National Bank of Serbia (NBS) only.
† Beginning in December 2003, data are based on a standardized report form (SRF) for central banks, which accords with the concepts and definitions of the IMF's *Monetary and Financial Statistics Manual (MFSM),* 2000. Departures from the *MFSM* methodology are explained below.
Claims on and *Liabilities to Central Government* include positions with the federal government of the former State Union of Serbia and Montenegro.
Holdings of securities and equity shares that are not actively traded are valued at acquisition cost rather than at current market price or fair value. Securities issued by the NBS are valued at

face value rather than at the current market price or fair value. For December 2001 through November 2003, data have less conformity with the *MFSM* methodology and therefore are not strictly comparable to data for later periods.

Other Depository Corporations:

Comprises commercial banks.

† Beginning in December 2003, data are based on a standardized report form (SRF) for other depository corporations, which accords with the concepts and definitions of the IMF's *Monetary and Financial Statistics Manual (MFSM)*. Departures from the *MFSM* methodology are explained below.

Claims on and *Liabilities to Central Government* include positions with the federal government of the former State Union of Serbia and Montenegro.

Claims on Central Government includes claims for frozen foreign-currency deposits. Restricted deposits include frozen foreign-currency deposits of the households; in July 2002 the liability for these deposits was assumed by the central government.

Holdings of securities and equity shares that are not actively traded are valued at acquisition cost rather than at current market price or fair value. Securities issued by the banks are valued at face value rather than at the current market price or fair value. For December 2001 through November 2003, data have less conformity with the *MFSM* methodology and therefore are not strictly comparable to data for later periods.

Depository Corporations:

† See notes on central bank and other depository corporations.

Monetary Aggregates:

Broad Money:
Broad Money calculated from the liability data in the sections for the central bank and other depository corporations accords with the concepts and definitions of the *MFSM* and is consistent with the M3 described below.

Money (National Definitions):
M1 comprises currency in circulation and dinar-denominated demand deposits of resident nonbank non-central government sectors with the commercial banks.
M2 comprises M1 and dinar-denominated time deposits of resident nonbank non-central government sectors with the commercial banks.
M3 comprises M2 and foreign currency deposits of resident nonbank non-central government sectors with the commercial banks.

Interest Rates:

Repurchase Agreement Rate (End of Period):
Average monthly rate on the 14-day NBS repurchase agreements weighted by volume.

Central Bank Bill Rate (End of Period):
Monthly average rate on the NBS bills of all maturities weighted by volume.

Money Market Rate:
Average monthly rate on the three-month interbank deposits (three-months Belgrade Interbank Offer Rate (BELIBOR)) weighted by volume.

Treasury Bill Rate:
Average monthly yield on three-month Treasury bills weighted by volume.

Deposit Rate:
Weighted average rate offered by commercial banks on deposits, excluding overnight deposits, of households, nonprofit institutions, and nonfinancial corporations in national currency. The rate is weighted by the volume of new deposits received during the month. Beginning in September 2010, the European Central Bank's (ECB) new methodology on interest rates statistics was implemented.

Deposit Rate (Indexed to Foreign Currency):
Weighted average rate offered by commercial banks deposits, excluding overnight deposits, of households, nonprofit institutions, and nonfinancial corporations in national currency indexed to foreign currency. The rate is weighted by volume of new deposits received during the month. Beginning in September 2010, the ECB's new methodology on interest rates statistics was implemented.

Deposit Rate (Foreign Currency):
Weighted average rate offered by commercial banks deposits, excluding overnight deposits, of households, nonprofit institutions, and nonfinancial corporations in foreign currency. The rate is weighted by volume of new deposits received during the month. Beginning in September 2010, the ECB's new methodology on interest rates statistics was implemented.

Lending Rate:
Average rate charged by commercial banks on credits, excluding overdrafts, to households, nonprofit institutions, and nonfinancial corporations in national currency. The rate is weighted by volume of new credits granted during the month. Beginning in September 2010, the ECB's new methodology on interest rates statistics was implemented.

Lending Rate (Indexed to Foreign Currency):
Average rate charged by commercial banks on credits, excluding overdrafts, of households, nonprofit institutions, and nonfinancial corporations in national currency indexed to foreign currency. The rate is weighted by the volume of new credits granted during the month. Beginning in September 2010, the ECB's new methodology on interest rates statistics was implemented.

Lending Rate (Foreign Currency):
Average rate charged by commercial banks on credits, excluding overdrafts, of households, nonprofit institutions, and nonfinancial corporations in foreign currency. The rate is weighted by the volume of new credits granted during the month. Beginning in September 2010, the ECB's new methodology on interest rates statistics was implemented.

Prices and Production:

Share Prices:
BELEX–15 index of the Belgrade Stock Exchange, base October 1, 2010.

Consumer Price Index:
Source: Statistical Office of the Republic of Serbia. Weights Reference Period: 2005; Geographic Coverage: all economic territory of the country; Number of Items in Basket: 582; Basis for

Calculation: main source of weights is the Household Budget Survey and the structure of the final consumption of households, taken from the GDP. When calculating the CPI for 2009, consumption structure of 2007, revised by prices growth in 2008, is used.

Industrial Production:
Source: Statistical Office of the Republic of Serbia. Weights Reference Year: 2008; Sectoral Coverage: mining and quarrying, manufacturing industry, electricity, gas and water supply. Weights are derived as value added shares.

International Transactions:
Source: Statistical Office of the Republic of Serbia. Data exclude transactions with Montenegro.

National Accounts:
Source: Statistical Office of the Republic of Serbia. As indicated by the country, data are compiled in accordance with the methodology of the *1993 SNA*. As the production-based GDP (*line 99bp*) is the official measure of GDP, the statistical discrepancy (*line 99bs*) represents the difference between the production-based GDP and the sum of the expenditure components shown. GDP volume measures are expressed according to 2005 prices.

Population:
Source: Statistical Office of the Republic of Serbia.

Seychelles 718

Date of Fund Membership:
June 30, 1977

Standard Sources:
Central Bank of Seychelles
National Bureau of Statistics of Seychelles

Exchange Rates:

Official Rate: (End of Period and Period Average):
Prior to May 13, 1996, rates were based on a fixed relationship to the SDR. Beginning May 13, 1996, the Seychelles rupee is pegged to the Seychelles Trade and Tourism weighted basket. Beginning in September 2003, the Seychelles rupee is pegged to the U.S. dollar. Beginning in November 2008, the exchange rate regime changed from a basket peg to a float.

Central Bank:
Consists of the Central Bank of Seychelles (CBS) only.
Data are based on a standardized report form (SRF) for central banks, which accords with the concepts and definitions of the IMF's *Monetary and Financial Statistics Manual (MFSM)*, 2000. Departures from the *MFSM* methodology are explained below.
Accrued interest on holdings of central government securities is included in *Other Item (Net)* rather than in *Claims on Central Government*.
Holdings of treasury bills, both foreign and domestic, and other central government securities are valued at acquisition cost or face value rather than at market price or fair value.

Other Depository Corporations:
Comprises commercial banks, including the Seychelles Savings Bank. Data exclude the Seychelles Credit Union.

Data are based on a SRF for other depository corporations, which accords with the concepts and definitions of the *Monetary and Financial Statistics Manual (MFSM)*. Departures from the *MFSM* methodology are explained below.
Accrued interest on holdings of central government securities is included in *Other Item (Net)* rather than in *Claims on Central Government*.
Accrued interest on the deposits with commercial banks are included in *Other Items (Net)* rather than in the outstanding amounts of the deposits.
Holdings of central government securities are valued at acquisition cost or face value rather than at market price or fair value.
Holdings or other securities are valued at the lower of acquisition cost or market value rather than at market price or fair value.

Depository Corporations:
See notes on central bank and other depository corporations.

Other Financial Corporations:
Comprises the Development Bank of Seychelles. Data are based on a SRF for other financial corporations, which accords with the concepts and definitions of the *Monetary and Financial Statistics Manual (MFSM)*. Departures from the *MFSM* methodology are explained below.
Accrued interest on holdings of central government securities is included in *Other Item (Net)* rather than in *Claims on Central Government*.
Holdings of central government securities are valued at acquisition cost or face value rather than at market price or fair value.
Holdings or other securities are valued at the lower of acquisition cost or market value rather than at market price or fair value.

Monetary Aggregates:

Broad Money:
Broad Money calculated from the liability data in the sections for the central bank and other depository corporations accords with the concepts and definitions of the *MFSM* and is consistent with M2(p) described below.

Money (National Definitions):
M1 comprises currency in circulation and transferable deposits. Currency in circulation refers to notes and coins issued by the CBS less the amount held by the CBS and commercial banks. Transferable deposits refer to the current account deposits in national and foreign currency of public nonfinancial corporations and private sector with commercial banks.
M2 comprises M1 and other deposits in national and foreign currency of public nonfinancial corporations and private sector with commercial banks.
M2(p) comprises M2 and pipeline deposits (rupee deposits held at the CBS by other nonfinancial corporations to be withdrawn in foreign currency).

Interest Rates:

Discount Rate (End of Period):
Rate charged by the CBS on temporary advances to other depository corporations for liquidity purposes using treasury bills, treasury bonds, and government stocks as collateral. The rate for the advances against treasury bills is the simple average of the outstanding treasury bills plus five points whilst the rate on treasury bonds and government stocks is the same as that payable on the securities against which the advance is made.

Treasury Bill Rate:
Average rate on 91- and 365-day treasury bills.

Savings Rate:
Weighted average rate offered by other depository corporations on savings deposits in national and foreign currency. The rate is weighted by deposit amounts.

Deposit Rate:
Weighted average rate offered by other depository corporations on three-month time deposits in national and foreign currency. The rate is weighted by deposit amounts.

Lending Rate:
Weighted average rate charged by other depository corporations on loans in national and foreign currency. The rate is weighted by loan amounts.

Government Bond Yield:
Average yield on one-, two-, three-, five-, seven-, and ten-year government bonds.

Prices and Labor:

Consumer Prices:
Source: National Bureau of Statistics of Seychelles. Weights reference period: July 2007. Geographical coverage: whole country. Number of items in basket: over 300 specific goods and services. Basis for Calculation: 2006/2007 Household Budget Survey conducted on the islands of Mahe, Praslin and La Digue.

International Transactions:

All trade value and volume data are from the National Bureau of Statistics of Seychelles.

Government Finance:

Data are as reported by the Ministry of Finance and cover the budgetary central government. The fiscal year ends December 31.

National Accounts:

Source: National Bureau of Statistics of Seychelles. Data are prepared in accordance with the *SNA93*.

Sierra Leone   724

Date of Fund Membership:
September 10, 1962

Standard Source:
Bank of Sierra Leone
Central Office of Statistics — Statistics Sierra Leone

Exchange Rates:

Market Rate (End of Period and Period Average):
The central bank determines the exchange rate every Wednesday, based on the weighted-average rates of the commercial banks' transactions in that week for customs valuations and official transactions.

Central Bank:
Consists of the Bank of Sierra Leone (BSL) only.
Data are based on a standardized report form (SRF) for central banks, which accords with the concepts and definitions of the IMF's *Monetary and Financial Statistics Manual (MFSM)*, 2000. De-

partures from the *MFSM* methodology are explained below.
Deposits of rural banks are included in *Deposits Included in Broad Money* rather than in *Other Liabilities to Other Depository Corporations*.
Treasury bonds and, for December 2001 through December 2011, treasury bills are recorded at face value rather at current market price or fair value. Beginning in January 2012, treasury bills are recorded at amortized cost rather than at current market price or fair value.

Other Depository Corporations:
Comprises commercial banks, including branches of foreign banks. Beginning in December 2007, includes discount houses. Data exclude rural banks, mortgage banks, community banks, and deposit-taking microfinance institutions.
† Beginning in August 2007, data are based on a standardized report form (SRF) for other depository corporations, which accords with the concepts and definitions of the *Monetary and Financial Statistics Manual (MFSM)*. For other depository corporations in Sierra Leone, departures from the *MFSM* methodology are explained below.
Deposits of rural banks are included in *Transferable Deposits Included in Broad Money* and *Other Deposits Included in Broad Money* rather than in *Other Items (Net)*.
Beginning in December 2001 through July 2007, data in SRF are compiled from pre-SRF data not based on the *MFSM* methodology. Departures from the *MFSM* methodology are explained below.
For December 2001 through January 2004, positions with nonresidents are included as claims on/liabilities to the domestic sectors rather than as *Claims on Nonresidents/Liabilities to Nonresidents*. The currency of denomination was used to determine the residency.
Financial assets and liabilities for which economic sectorization is unavailable are allocated to the economic sector having the largest volume of transactions in the category. Deposits of rural banks are included in *Transferable Deposits Included in Broad Money* and *Other Deposits Included in Broad Money* rather than in *Other Items (Net)*.
Some accrued interest is included in *Other Items (Net)* rather than in the outstanding amounts of the financial assets or liabilities.

Depository Corporations:
† See notes on central bank and other depository corporations.

Monetary Aggregates:

Broad Money:
Broad Money calculated from the liability data in the sections for the central bank and other depository corporations accords with the concepts and definitions of the *MFSM* and is consistent with M2 described below.

Money (National Definitions):
Reserve Money comprises currency in circulation, commercial banks' correspondent and other accounts, and transferable deposits in national currency of rural banks, other financial corporations, public nonfinancial corporations, and private sector with the BSL. Currency in circulation refers to notes and coins issued by the BSL.
M0 comprises currency in circulation.
M1 comprises currency in circulation and transferable deposits of the private sector with other depository corporations in national currency. Currency in circulation refers to notes and coins

issued by the BSL less the amount held by other depository corporations. Transferable deposits refer to current account deposits of rural banks, other financial corporations, public nonfinancial corporations, and the private sector with the BSL and other depository corporations in national currency.

M2 comprises *M1* and time and savings deposits in national currency and foreign currency deposits of other financial corporations, public nonfinancial corporations, and the private sector with the BSL and other depository corporations.

Interest Rates:

Central Bank Policy Rate (End of Period):
Monetary Policy Rate determined at the Monetary Policy Committee based on recent and outlook on macroeconomic fundamentals.

Repurchase Agreement Rate (End of Period):
Used mainly in secondary market for repurchase agreements between the BSL and other depository corporations, and set at some basis points above the Monetary Policy Rate.

Treasury Bill Rate:
Yield on 91-day treasury bills auctioned by the BSL.

Savings Rate:
Average rate offered by commercial banks on savings deposits in national currency.

Deposit Rate:
Average rate offered by commercial banks on three- to six-months time deposits in national currency.

Lending Rate:
Average minimum rate charged by commercial banks on overdrafts in national currency.

Prices:

Consumer Prices:
Source: Statistics Sierra Leone. Weights Reference Period: 2007; Geographical Coverage: Freetown, Bo, Kenema, Koidu and Makeni; Number of Items in the Basket: 251; Basis for Calculation: 2003/04 Household Expenditure Survey Report.

International Transactions:

All trade data are from Bank of Sierra Leone.

Government Finance:

Data cover the consolidated central government † Prior to 1998, the fiscal year ends June 30. The fiscal year ends December 31.

National Accounts:

Source: Statistics Sierra Leone. Data are prepared in accordance with the 1993 United Nations System of National Accounts. The series "changes in inventories" also include statistical discrepancies.

Singapore   576

Date of Fund Membership:
August 3, 1966

Standard Sources:
Monetary Authority of Singapore
Department of Statistics

Exchange Rates:

Market Rate (End of Period and Period Average):
Midpoint interbank rate at noon. Real effective exchange rates, based on consumer price indices for the Singapore dollar, reflect imperfect underlying movements in competitiveness.

International Liquidity:

Data for foreign exchange include gold and government foreign exchange holdings. Beginning August 2000, foreign exchange data exclude gold holdings.

Asian currency units (ACUs), which began operations in 1968, deal extensively with nonresidents but perform only limited domestic operations, primarily with deposit money banks. Their assets and liabilities with the monetary system are regarded as part of the foreign sector in data reported in sections 10, 20, and 30. Hence, *lines 7a.d* and *7b.d* include commercial bank accounts with ACUs. *Lines 7k.d.* and *7m.d* relate to the foreign assets and foreign liabilities, respectively, of ACUs and exclude both their accounts with the monetary system and inter-ACU accounts.

Monetary Authorities:

Consolidates the Monetary Authority of Singapore (MAS) and monetary authority functions undertaken by the central government. The contra-entry to Treasury IMF accounts and government foreign assets is included in *line 16d.*

Currency Outside Deposit Money Banks (line 14a) excludes Singapore's estimated share of the currency issued by Malaya/British Borneo Currency Board and commemorative coins issued by the Board of Commissioners of Currency, Singapore.

Deposit Money Banks:

Comprises commercial banks and discount houses. † Beginning in April 1971, data are based on an improved sectorization of resident and nonresident accounts. Beginning in November 1998, includes Post Office savings deposits, previously classified within the other banking institutions.

Monetary Survey:

† See note on deposit money banks.

Other Banking Institutions:

Comprises finance companies and Post Office savings deposits. Beginning in November 1998, excludes Post Office savings deposits; they were reclassified within the deposit money banks.

Nonbank Financial Institutions:

Comprises life insurance offices.

Money (National Definitions):

M1 comprises currency in circulation (excludes commemorative, numismatic, and bullion coins issued by the Monetary Authority of Singapore and cash held by commercial banks and non-bank financial institutions) and demand deposits of the private sector in commercial banks in national and foreign currency.

M2 comprises M1 plus fixed, savings, and other deposits of the private sector in commercial banks in national and foreign currency and negotiable certificates of deposits in national currency.

M3 comprises M2 plus net deposits with non-bank financial institutions. Net deposits of non-bank financial institutions excludes these institutions' deposits with banks. Beginning in November 1998, with the acquisition of the Post Office Savings

Bank by DBS Bank, Ltd., Post Office Savings Bank's data has been incorporated as part of the banking system in M1 and M2, and not as a non-bank financial institution in M3.

Interest Rates:

Central Bank Policy Rate (End of Period):
Rate charged by the MAS on overnight repurchase agreements using government securities. The daily rates are determined by taking the prior day's weighted average rate on successful bids by Primary Dealers for $500 million of overnight interbank deposits. This repurchase rate is used to set the rates for the MAS' Standing Facilities. These facilities are not a mechanism for interest rate targeting and are purely for the purpose of containing intra-day interest rate volatility.

Money Market Rate:
Rate refers to the modes of the three-month interbank rates quoted by money brokers. Monthly data refer to the rates on the last Friday (or working day closest to the last Friday) of the month.

Money Market Rate (Foreign Currency):
Three-month rate offered by commercial banks on unsecured funds in the Singapore wholesale interbank market in US Dollars. Monthly data refer to the rates on the last Friday (or working day closest to the last Friday) of the month. The rate is also known as the Singapore InterBank Offer Rate (SIBOR).

Treasury Bill Rate:
Rate refers to modes of closing bid prices quoted by the Singapore Government Securities (SGS) primary dealers on three-month treasury bills. Beginning in January 2001, the average bid rate quoted by the SGS primary dealers. Monthly data refer to the rates on the last Friday, or working day closest to the last Friday, of the month.

Savings Rate:
Average rate offered by the ten leading commercial banks on savings deposits. Savings deposits are payable on demand or by notice but cannot be withdrawn by checks.

Deposit Rate:
Average rate offered by the ten leading commercial banks on three-month time deposits.

Lending Rate:
Average minimum rate charged by the ten leading commercial banks.

Government Bond Yield:
Rate refers to modes of closing bid prices quoted by the Singapore Government Securities (SGS) primary dealers on ten-year government bonds. Beginning in January 2001, the average bid rate quoted by the SGS primary dealers. Monthly data refer to the rates on the last Friday, or working day closest to the last Friday, of the month.

Prices, Production, Labor:

Share Prices (Period Average and End of Month):
Straits Times index, base January 10, 2008. The index covers common stocks, although not all components stocks are 100 percent represented and is weighted by market capitalization.

Wholesale Prices:
Data refer to all items of the domestic supply price index (DSPI), which covers goods manufactured locally (excluding exports) and imported goods retained for domestic use, weights reference period 2006. The weight for each commodity item in the DSPI is proportional to the value of its total supply or availability in the domestic market.

Consumer Prices:
Source: Department of Statistics. Weights Reference Period: 2009; Geographical Coverage: Whole of Singapore; Number of Items in Basket: 990; Basis for Calculation: The weights are derived from the results of the Household Expenditure Survey.

Manufacturing Production:
Source: Department of Statistics. Weights Reference Period: 2011; Sectoral Coverage: manufacturing sector; Basis for Calculation: the weights used in the index are based on the Census of Manufacturing Activities.

Employment:
Data refer to registered unemployment.

International Transactions:

All trade data are from the Department of Statistics.
Export and *Imports Volume* indices are calculated by *IFS* from export and import values and export and import price indices. The export volume index prior to 1978 and import volume index prior to 1975 were calculated by the Department of Statistics. *Exports* and *Imports (Direct Prices)* (Department of Statistics) are based on sample surveys of exporters and importers; for exports, and imports, weights reference period 2012.

Government Finance:

Data are derived from unpublished reports and reported by the Monetary Authority of Singapore. Data cover the budgetary central government. The fiscal year ends March 31.

National Accounts:

Data are as reported by the Department of Statistics. *Lines 99a* and *99b* include a statistical discrepancy. As indicated by the country, data follow the implementation of the *1993 SNA*.

Sint Maarten   352

Following the dissolution of the Netherlands Antilles on October 10, 2010, Sint Maarten became an autonomous country within the Kingdom of the Netherlands.

Standard Sources:

Central Bank of Curaçao and Sint Maarten
Bureau of Statistics

Exchange Rates:

Official Rate: (End of Period and Period Average):
Central bank midpoint rate. The official rate is pegged to the U.S. dollar.

Prices:

Consumer Prices:
Source: Bureau of Statistics. Weights Reference Period: October 2006; Geographical Coverage: Sint Maarten.

Slovak Republic 936

Data are denominated in Slovak koruny prior to January 2009 and in euros from January 2009 onward. An irrevocably fixed factor for converting Slovak koruny to euros was established at 30.1260 Slovak koruny per euro. With Slovak Republic's entry into Stage Three of the European Economic and Monetary Union (EMU) in January 2009, a euro area-wide definition of residency was introduced: all positions with residents of other euro area (EA) countries, including the European Central Bank (ECB), are classified as domestic positions, and foreign assets and foreign liabilities include only positions with non-EA residents. In 2009, the Slovak koruna was retired from circulation and replaced by euro banknotes and coins. Descriptions of the methodology and presentation of Slovak Republic's accounts following the introduction of the euro are discussed under *European Economic and Monetary Union* in the introduction to *IFS* and in the notes on the euro area page.

Date of Fund Membership:
January 1, 1993

Standard Sources:
National Bank of Slovakia (NBS)
Statistical Office of the Slovak Republic
Eurostat

Exchange Rates:

Official Rate: (End of Period and Period Average):
Prior to January 2009, the official rate was the National Bank of Slovakia's midpoint rate. In January 2009, the euro, which has a market determined exchange rate, was adopted.

Market Rate (End of Period and Period Average):
Beginning in January 2009, the Slovak Republic adopted the euro and the koruna was retired after a brief dual circulation period. The euro market rate became applicable to all transactions. For additional information, refer to the section on Exchange Rates in the introduction to *IFS* and the notes on the Euro Area page.

International Liquidity:
Beginning in January 2009, *Total Reserves minus Gold (line 1l.d)* and *Foreign Exchange (line.1d.d)* are defined in accordance with the Eurosystem's statistical definition of international reserves. *Gold (Eurosystem Valuation) (line 1and)* is revalued monthly at market prices. Memorandum data are provided on *Non-Euro Claims on Euro Area Residents and Euro Claims on Non-Euro Area Residents*. Prior to January 2009, *line 1and* was obtained by converting the value in national currency as reported in the country's standard sources using the national currency/dollar conversion rates utilized for balance sheet purposes. The conversion rates prior to January 2009 differ from the prevailing exchange rates reported in *IFS*. For additional information, refer to the section on International Liquidity in the introduction to *IFS* and the notes on the euro area page. † Prior to January 2002, *(Gold (National Valuation) (line 1and)* is valued at US$42.22 per ounce. *Monetary Authorities: Other Liabilities (line 4..d)* relate mainly to obligations to the Czech Republic in nonconvertible currencies.

Central Bank:
Consists of the National Bank of Slovakia only. In January 2009, the NBS became part of the Eurosystem. (For a description of its accounts refer to the section on *Central Bank - Euro Area* in the introduction to *IFS*. † Beginning in August 2003, data are compiled in accordance with the European Central Bank's framework for monetary statistics using the national residency approach.

For December 2001 to July 2003, data do not fully conform with the European Central Bank's framework for monetary statistics and are not strictly comparable to data for later periods.

Other Depository Corporations:
Comprises commercial banks including branches of foreign banks. Beginning in January 2004, comprises all resident units classified as other monetary financial institutions (other MFIs) in accordance with *1995 ESA* standards, including money market funds.

† Beginning in August 2003, data are compiled in accordance with the European Central Bank's framework for monetary statistics using the national residency approach.

For December 2001 to July 2003, data do not fully conform with the European Central Bank's framework for monetary statistics and are not strictly comparable to data for later periods † Beginning in January 2003, data are based on an improved classification of accounts due to availability of more detailed information. Prior to January 2003 *Claims on Central Government* and *Liabilities to Central Government* include positions with local governments and the National Property Fund.

Depository Corporations:

Depository Corporations (National Residency):
Beginning January 2009, see section on *Depository Corporations (Based on National Residency)* in the introduction to *IFS*.

Depository Corporations (Euro Area-wide Residency):
Beginning January 2009, see section on *Depository Corporations (based on Euro Area-wide Residency)* in the introduction to *IFS*.

For periods prior to January 2009, see notes on central bank and other depository corporations. † Prior to January 2003, *Net Claims on Central Government*, *Claims on Central Government*, and *Liabilities to Central Government* include positions with local governments and the National Property Fund.

Monetary Aggregates:
Beginning January 2009, national monetary aggregate series were discontinued. The Euro Area aggregates are presented on the Euro Area page. For periods prior to January 2009, monetary aggregates included:

Broad Money is calculated from the liability data in the sections for the central bank and other depository corporations.

Money (National Definitions):
M1 comprises currency outside banks and demand deposits of households, enterprises, and insurance companies with commercial banks. Beginning in January 2003, comprises currency outside banks and overnight deposits of resident non-MFI, noncentral government sectors with MFIs.

M2 comprises M1 and quasi-money. Quasi-money consists of time and savings deposits of households, enterprises, and insurance companies and foreign currency deposits of households and enterprises with commercial banks. Beginning in January 2003, comprises M1, deposits with agreed maturity up to two years, and deposits redeemable at notice up to three months of resident non-MFI, noncentral government sectors with MFIs.

M3 comprises M2, repurchase agreements contracted by MFIs

with other (non-MFI, nongovernmental) resident sectors, money market fund shares/units, and debt securities issued by commercial banks with maturity up to two years.

Interest Rates:

Beginning January 2009, Euro Area policy rates became applicable, and national policy rates were discontinued. See *Interest Rates* in the notes for the Euro Area page. For periods prior to January 2009.

Bank Rate (End of Period):
National Bank of Slovakia's main policy rate. Starting in May 2001, the data refer to the rate on two-week repurchase agreements. Prior to May 2001, the data refer to the discount rate.

Money Market Rate:
Rate on one-month interbank deposits.

Deposit Rate:
Beginning in January 2005, weighted average interest rate offered on short-term (up to one year) deposits of non-financial corporations (S.11). From January 1996 to December 2004, weighted average interest rate offered on short-term (up to one year) deposits of the private sector during the reference period. During 1993–95, weighted average rate offered by commercial banks on all accepted deposits.

Deposit Rate (lines 60lhs, 60lhn, 60lcs, and 60lcn):
See notes in the introduction to IFS and Euro-area Interest Rates.

Lending Rate:
Beginning in January 2005, weighted average interest rate on short-term loans drawn by non-financial corporations (S.11). From January 1995 to December 2004, weighted average interest rate on short-term loans granted to the private corporate sector during the reference period. During 1993–94, weighted average rate charged by commercial banks on all outstanding credits.

Lending Rate (lines 60phm, 60pcs, and 60pcn):
See notes in the introduction to IFS and *Euro-area Interest Rates*:

Government Bond Yield:
Monthly average of secondary market yields on 10-year government bonds. This rate is used to measure long-term interest rates for assessing convergence among the European Union member states.

Prices, Production, Labor:

Share Prices:
Data refer to the Slovak share index (SAX), base September 14, 1993. The SAX is a capital-weighted total return index that compares the market capitalization of a selected set of shares with the market capitalization of the same set of shares as of a given reference day.

Producer Prices:
Source: Statistical Office of the Slovak Republic. Weights Reference Period: 2010; Sectoral Coverage: mining and quarrying, manufacturing, electricity, gas, steam and water supply sectors; Number of Items in Basket: approximately 7000 products; Basis for Calculation: the prices are collected from monthly statistical statements. The selection includes industrial enterprises with a relatively important share in the 2010 industry production turnover.

Consumer Prices:
Source: Statistical Office of the Slovak Republic. Weights Reference Period: 2011; Geographical Coverage: the entire territory;

Number of Items in Basket: 713; Basis for Calculation: weights are derived from the household budget survey, adjusted for the results of the national accounts data and other administrative sources.

Wages:
Source: Statistical Office of the Slovak Republic. Coverage: all industries; Managers, entrepreneurs and their partners, persons on maternity and additional maternity leave are excluded.

Industrial Production:
Source: Statistical Office of the Slovak Republic. Weights Reference Period: weights are updated every five years; Sectoral Coverage: mining and quarrying, manufacturing, electricity, gas, steam, air conditioning and water supply, waste management sectors; Basis for Calculation: weights are based on annual survey of the production structure of enterprises, supplemented by cumulative data from monthly industrial surveys.

Industrial Employment:
Index of number of workers employed in all enterprises, reported in thousands.

International Transactions:

Data are from Statistical Office of the Slovak Republic.

Government Finance:

Starting January 2007, monthly data are reported by Ministry of Finance and cover the Budgetary Central Government and are in Millions of Koruny. Starting in January 2009, monthly data are reported in Millions of Euros. Data on general government (Operations Statement) are derived from source V and also provided by the Ministry of Finance (Cash Flow Statement). † Prior to 2004, to the extent possible, existing subannual *IFS* data were converted to the main aggregates that are presented in the *GFSM 2001* Statement of Sources and Uses of Cash (see the introduction of the monthly *IFS* publication for details). Beginning in 2004, annual data are as reported in the *Government Finance Statistics Yearbook (GFSY)* and cover the consolidated central government. The fiscal year ends December 31.

National Accounts:

Source: Statistical Office of the Slovak Republic. As indicated by the country, data are compiled in accordance with the methodology of the *1995 ESA*. Beginning in 2009, euro data are sourced from the Eurostat database. Eurostat introduced chain-linked GDP volume measures to both annual and quarterly data. Chain-linked GDP volume measures are expressed in the prices of the previous year and re-referenced to 2005.

Slovenia   961

Data are denominated in Slovenian tolars prior to January 2007 and in euros from January 2007 onward. An irrevocably fixed factor for converting tolars to euros was established at 239.640 tolars per euro. With Slovenia's entry into Stage Three of the European Economic and Monetary Union (EMU) in January 2007, a euro area-wide definition of residency was introduced: all positions with residents of other euro area (EA) countries, including the European Central Bank (ECB), are classified as domestic positions, and foreign assets and foreign liabilities include only positions with non-EA residents. In 2007, the tolar was retired from circulation and replaced by euro banknotes and coins. Descriptions of the methodology and presentation of Slovenia's accounts following the introduction of the euro are discussed under *European Economic and Monetary Union* in the introduction to *IFS* and in the notes on the euro area page.

Date of Fund Membership:
December 14, 1992

Standard Sources:
Ministry of Finance
Bank of Slovenia
Statistical Office of the Republic of Slovenia
Eurostat

Exchange Rates:
Market Rate (End of Period and Period Average):
In January 2007, the Slovenian tolar became a participating currency within the Eurosystem, and the euro market rate became applicable to all transactions. In 2007, the tolar was retired from circulation and replaced by euro banknotes and coins. For additional information, refer to the section on exchange rates in the introduction to *IFS* and the notes on the euro area page. Prior to January 2007, midpoint of the official tolar/U.S. dollar exchange rate, which was computed using the official tolar/Euro exchange rate and the market Euro/U.S. dollar exchange rate. The official tolar/Euro exchange rate was calculated daily by the Bank of Slovenia using a moving average of the daily market rates on the foreign exchange market over the preceding 14 days' interval.

International Liquidity:
Beginning in January 2007, *Total Reserves minus Gold (line 1l.d)* and *Foreign Exchange (line.1d.d)* are defined in accordance with the Eurosystem's statistical definition of international reserves. *Gold (Eurosystem Valuation) (line 1and)* is revalued monthly at market prices. The international reserves of Slovenia per the Eurosystem statistical definition as of January 2007 in millions of U.S. dollars were as follows: Total Reserves minus gold, $890.22; Foreign Exchange, $847.00, SDRs, $12.30; Reserve Position in the Fund, $30.93; Other Reserve Assets, $0; Gold, $66,95; Gold (million fine troy ounces), 0,10. In the period June 2001 to December 2006, gold was revalued monthly using end-of-month London gold market price; in the period 1999 to May 2001, gold was revalued quarterly; in the period 1995 through 1999, gold was revalued annually (at end-December); prior to 1995, gold was revalued semi-annually (at end-June and end-December). End-period London gold market price was used as the basis for revaluations. Memorandum data are provided on *Non-Euro Claims on Euro Area Residents and Euro Claims on Non-Euro Area Residents*. For additional information, refer to the section on International Liquidity in the introduction to *IFS* and the notes on the euro area page.

Central Bank:
Consists of the Bank of Slovenia only, which beginning in January 2007 is part of the Eurosystem. For a description of accounts refer to the section on *Central Bank - Euro Area* in the introduction to *IFS*. *Currency Issued* includes coins issued by the Treasury. Be-

ginning in January 2007, *Currency Issued* comprises euro banknotes and coins and unretired tolars. Prior to January 2007, the contra-entry to Treasury coin issue was included in *Claims on General Government*. From January 2007 onward, the contra-entry is included in *Other Items (Net)*.
† Beginning in January 2004, data are compiled in accordance with the European Central Bank's framework for monetary statistics; however, presentation of data during January 2004–December 2006 is based on the national residency approach only. Prior to January 2004, data do not fully conform with the European Central Bank's framework for monetary statistics and are not strictly comparable to data for later periods.

Other Depository Corporations:
Comprises commercial banks. Beginning in January 2004, comprises all resident units classified as other monetary financial institutions (other MFIs), in accordance with *1995 ESA* standards, including money market funds. For a description of accounts, refer to the section on *Other Depository Corporations - Euro Area* in the introduction to *IFS*.
† Beginning in January 2004, data are compiled in accordance with the European Central Bank's framework for monetary statistics; however, presentation of data during January 2004-December 2006 is based on the national residency approach only. Prior to January 2004, data do not fully conform with the European Central Bank's framework for monetary statistics and are not strictly comparable to data for later periods.

Depository Corporations (National Residency):
See notes on central bank and other depository corporations. For a description of the methodology and accounts, refer to the section on *Depository Corporations (Based on National Residency) - Euro Area* in the introduction to *IFS*.

Depository Corporations (Euro Area-wide Residency):
See notes on central bank and other depository corporations. For a description of the methodology and accounts, refer to the section on *Depository Corporations (Based on Euro Area-wide Residency)* in the introduction to *IFS*.

Money (National Definitions):
Beginning in January 2007, national monetary aggregates series were discontinued. The euro area aggregates are presented on the euro area page.
M1 comprises currency in circulation and demand deposits, including demand deposits of the central government, enterprises, and non-monetary financial institutions with the Bank of Slovenia. Currency in circulation is equal to currency issued by the central bank less currency in the central bank vault. † Beginning in January 2005, *M1* comprises currency in circulation and overnight deposits of non-central government, non-MFI resident sectors with resident MFIs.
M2 comprises *M1*, securities in tolar, central government time deposits at Bank of Slovenia, and tolar time deposits of non-central government non-bank residents at commercial banks and Bank of Slovenia. † Beginning in January 2005, *M2* comprises *M1*, deposits with agreed maturity up to two years, and deposits redeemable at notice up to three months of non-central government, non-MFI resident sectors with resident MFIs.

M3 comprises *M2*, foreign currency deposits at commercial banks, and foreign currency securities issued by commercial banks and held by non-banks. †Beginning in January 2005, *M3* comprises *M2*, repurchase agreements contracted with other (non-MFI) resident sectors, money market fund shares/units, and debt securities with maturity up to two years issued to non-central government, non-MFI resident sectors.

Interest Rates:

Central Bank Rate (End of Period):
Rate on one-day lombard loans by Bank of Slovenia to banks, with the Bank of Slovenia bills or government securities used as collateral. In January 2007, the central bank rate was discontinued. See Eurosystem policy rate series on the euro area page.

Money Market Rate:
Average interest rate in the Slovenian interbank market on the unsecured tolar deposits with a maturity up to 30 days, weighted by turnover. Beginning in January 2007, data refer to EURIBOR1M rate.

Treasury Bill Rate:
Rate on three-month treasury bills.

Deposit Rate (line 60l):
Prior to January 2007, period average rate on 31- to 90-day time deposits at commercial banks, weighted by stocks. Beginning in January 2007, rate on new deposits redeemable at notice with maturity up to three months calculated in accordance with the ECB's methodology.

Deposit Rate (lines 60lhs, 60lhn, 60lcs, and 60lcn):
See notes in the introduction to *IFS* and *Euro-area Interest Rates*.

Lending Rate (line 60p):
Prior to January 2007, period average rate on short-term commercial bank loans weighted by stocks. Beginning in January 2007, rate on new loans of up to EUR 1 million to non-financial corporations with maturity up to one year calculated in accordance with the ECB's methodology.

Lending Rate (lines 60phs, 60pns, 60phm, 60phn, 60pcs, and 60pcn):
See notes in the introduction to *IFS* and *Euro-area Interest Rates*.

Government Bond Yield:
Period average yield on government bonds with a 10-year residual maturity in the primary market. Beginning October 2003, refers to secondary market yields of government bonds with a ten-year maturity. This rate is used to measure long-term interest rates for assessing convergence among the European Union member states.

Prices, Production, Labor:

Share Prices (End of Month):
Slovenian Stock Exchange Index (SBI 20) of the Ljubljana Stocks Exchange, base December 31, 1993. † Beginning in April 2003, SBI TOP, the Slovenian blue chip index, base March 31, 2006. The SBI TOP is a free float capitalization weighted idex comprising the most liquid shares traded at Ljubljana Stock Exchange. Each stock's weighting is capped at 30 percent.

Producer Prices:
Source: Statistical Office of the Republic of Slovenia. Weights Reference Period: Calendar t–2, Recalculated to December t–1;

Sectoral Coverage: mining and quarrying, manufacturing, electricity, and water supply; Number of Items in Basket: 2640 price quotations; Basis for Calculation: the main source of weights is the annual industrial survey (IND-L) in t–2 and recalculated on the price base month — December t–1.

Consumer Prices:
Source: Statistical Office of the Republic of Slovenia. Weights Reference Period: weights are updated every year; Geographical Coverage: whole national territory; Number of Items in Basket: 663; Basis for Calculation: in 2012 weights are based on the average of expenditure data for consumer goods from HBS surveys for 2010 recalculated to the prices of December 2011, which is also the index base month.

Wages:
Data refer to average monthly gross wages in euros. Data are obtained from a census survey conducted every month of all establishments in the public sector and of those in the private sector. Individual private entrepreneurs and persons employed by them, own account workers, workers in employment promotion schemes, posted workers and farmers are not covered. Before January 2005, establishments in the private sector with one or two employees were not taken into account.

Industrial Production:
Source: Statistical Office of the Republic of Slovenia. Weights Reference Period: previous year; Sectoral Coverage: mining and quarrying, manufacturing and electricity, gas, steam and air conditioning supply; Number of Items in Basket: 2050 units; Basis for Calculation: weights are based on value added for the year 2008 and are replaced every year with the latest available data on value added.

Employment:
Persons in employment are persons in paid employment and self-employed persons. The registered unemployment rate is the percent of registered employed persons in the labor force.

International Transactions:

All trade data are from Statistical Office of the Republic of Slovenia. Prior to 1992, excludes exports and imports for processing and trade with former Yugoslav republics.

Government Finance:

Monthly data are derived from the Ministry of Finance and cover budgetary central government. Prior to 2006, annual data are as reported for the *Government Finance Statistics Yearbook (GFSY)*. Beginning in 2006, data are reported in the *GFSM 2001* analytical framework. Preliminary data on general government are compiled by Eurostat. The fiscal year ends December 31.

National Accounts:

Source: Statistical Office of the Republic of Slovenia. As indicated by the country, data are compiled in accordance with the methodology of the 1995 ESA. Beginning in 1999, data are sourced from the Eurostat database. Eurostat introduced chain-linked GDP volume measures to both annual and quarterly data. Chain-linked GDP volume measures are expressed in the prices of the previous year and re-referenced to 2005.

Solomon Islands   813

Date of Fund Membership:
September 22, 1978

Standard Sources:
Central Bank of Solomon Islands
Ministry of Finance
Statistical Office, Ministry of Finance

Exchange Rates:
Official Rate: (End of Period and Period Average):
Central bank midpoint rate. The exchange rate of the Solomon Islands dollar is determined on the basis of a trade-weighted basket of the currencies of Solomon Islands' four major trading partners.

International Liquidity:
Foreign Exchange (line 1d.d) comprises holdings of the central bank and the central government.

Central Bank:
Consists of the Central Bank of the Solomon Islands (CBSI) only.
† Beginning in December 2006, data are based on a standardized report form (SRF) for central banks, which accords with the concepts and definitions of the IMF's *Monetary and Financial Statistics Manual (MFSM)*, 2000. Departures from the *MFSM* methodology are explained below.
Monetary gold is valued at acquisition cost rather than at current market price. It is revalued annually or when it is traded or sold.
Held-to-maturity securities and equity shares are valued at acquisition cost rather than at current market price or fair value.
Some positions with domestic units are recorded on a net basis.
For January 2007 through November 2010, accrued interest on assets with nonresidents is included in *Other Items (Net)* in all the months with the exception of December.
For December 2001 through November 2006, data in the SRF format are compiled from pre-SRF data not based on the *MFSM* methodology. Departures from the *MFSM* methodology are explained below.
Financial assets and liabilities for which financial instrument breakdown is unavailable are allocated to the financial instrument having the largest volume of transactions in the category.
Other Items (Net) includes holdings of shares issued by other financial corporations.
For December 2001 through February 2007, *Other Items (Net)* includes holdings of treasury bills by credit unions.
Trade credit/advances and settlement accounts are included in *Other Items (Net)* rather than as claims on or liabilities to the corresponding subsectors of the economy.
Financial assets and liabilities not disaggregated by economic sector are allocated to the economic sector having the largest volume of transactions in the category.
Accrued interest is included in *Other Items (Net)* rather than in the outstanding amounts of the financial assets and liabilities.
Held-to-maturity securities and equity shares are valued at acquisition cost rather than at current market price or fair value.
Some positions with domestic units are recorded on a net basis.

Other Depository Corporations:
Comprises commercial banks and credit unions. Beginning in January 2006, includes the Credit Corporation of Solomon Islands (CCSI). Data exclude the savings clubs, which have small amounts of deposits.
† Beginning in January 2012, data are based on a standardized report form (SRF) for other depository corporations, which accords with the concepts and definitions of the *Monetary and Financial Statistics Manual (MFSM)*. For other depository corporations in Solomon Islands, departures from the *MFSM* methodology are explained below.
Data for the credit unions are only available on a quarterly basis. Data for intervening months have been estimated by carrying forward the data from the last quarter.
† For January 2010 through December 2011, data in the SRF format are compiled from improved source data for commercial banks and CCSI and pre-SRF data for credit unions which are not fully based on the *MFSM* methodology. Departures from the *MFSM* methodology are explained below.
Data for the credit unions are only available on a quarterly basis. Data for intervening months have been estimated by carrying forward the data from the last quarter.
Trade credit/advances and settlement accounts are included in *Other Items (Net)* rather than as claims on or liabilities to the corresponding subsectors of the economy.
Held-to-maturity securities and shares are valued at acquisition cost rather than at current market price or fair value.
For December 2001 through December 2009, data in the SRF format are compiled from pre-SRF data which are not fully based on the *MFSM* methodology. Departures from the *MFSM* methodology are explained below.
Data for the credit unions are only available on a quarterly basis. Data for intervening months have been estimated by carrying forward the data from the last quarter.
Financial assets and liabilities for which financial instrument breakdown is unavailable are allocated to the financial instrument having the largest volume of transactions in the category.
Trade credit/advances and settlement accounts are included in *Other Items (Net)* rather than as claims on or liabilities to the corresponding subsectors of the economy.
Financial assets and liabilities not disaggregated by economic sector are allocated to the economic sector having the largest volume of transactions in the category.
Transferable Deposits Included in Broad Money and *Other Deposits Included in Broad Money* include deposits of the Credit Corporation of Solomon Islands, credit unions, and savings clubs.
Accrued interest is included in *Other Items (Net)* rather than in the outstanding amounts of the financial assets and liabilities.
Held-to-maturity securities are valued at acquisition cost rather than at current market price or fair value.

Depository Corporations:
† See notes on central bank and other depository corporations.

Other Financial Corporations:
Comprises the National Provident Fund (NPF), Development Bank of Solomon Islands (DBSI) and Investment Corporation of Solomon Islands (ICSI). Beginning in March 2009, includes insur-

ance companies. Beginning in January 2011, includes Solomon Islands Home Finance Limited. Beginning in March 2012, includes insurance brokers. Data exclude insurance agents.

† Beginning in June 2012, data are based on a standardized report form (SRF) for other financial corporations, which accords with the concepts and definitions of the *Monetary and Financial Statistics Manual (MFSM)*. Data in the SRF format for insurance companies, DBSI, and ICSI are compiled from pre-SRF data which are not fully based on the *MFSM* methodology. For other financial corporations in Solomon Islands, departures from the *MFSM* methodology have decreased with the introduction of improved source data for the NPF but remain as explained below.

For December 2001 through May 2012, data in the SRF format are compiled from pre-SRF data which are not fully based on the *MFSM* methodology. Departures from the *MFSM* methodology are explained below.

Data for insurance companies and brokers are only available on a quarterly basis. Data for intervening and current months have been estimated by carrying forward the data from the last quarter. Data for the DBSI are only available through May 2011. Data for current months have been estimated by carrying forward the data from the last available month.

Financial assets and liabilities for which financial instrument breakdown is unavailable are allocated to the financial instrument having the largest volume of transactions in the category.

Trade credit/advances and settlement accounts are included in *Other Items (Net)* rather than as claims on or liabilities to the corresponding subsectors of the economy.

Financial assets and liabilities not disaggregated by economic sector are allocated to the economic sector having the largest volume of transactions in the category.

Prior to April 2006, *Claims on Depository Corporations* include some deposits of other financial corporations.

Accrued interest is included in *Other Items (Net)* rather than in the outstanding amounts of the financial assets and liabilities.

Held-to-maturity securities are valued at acquisition cost rather than at current market price or fair value.

Financial Corporations:

† See note on central bank, other depository corporations, and other financial corporations.

Monetary Aggregates:

Broad Money:

Broad Money calculated from the liability data in the sections for the central bank and other depository corporations accords with the concepts and definitions of the *MFSM* and is consistent with M3 described below.

Money (National Definitions):

M1 comprises of currency outside depository corporations and demand deposits of other financial corporations, state and local governments, public nonfinancial corporations, and private sector with depository corporations.

M2 comprises M1 and savings deposits of other financial corporations, state and local governments, public nonfinancial corporations, and private sector with other depository corporations.

M3 comprises M2 and time deposits of other financial corpora-

tions, state and local governments, public nonfinancial corporations, and private sector with other depository corporations.

Interest Rates:

Treasury Bill Rate:

End-month yield on 91-day treasury bills in national currency. † Beginning in January 2006, average of weekly weighted average rates on accepted bids on 91-day treasury bills in national currency.

Savings Rate:

Weighted average rate offered by commercial banks on savings deposits in national currency. The rate is weighted by deposit amounts. † Beginning in January 2010, weighted average rate offered by commercial banks and Credit Corporation of Solomon Islands on savings deposits in national currency. The rate is weighted by deposit amounts.

Deposit Rate:

Weighted average rate offered by commercial banks on three-month deposits of up to SI$25,000 in national currency. † Beginning in January 2010, weighted average rate offered by commercial banks and Credit Corporation of Solomon Islands on all deposits in national currency. The rate is weighted by deposit amounts.

Lending Rate:

Minimum rate charged by commercial banks on advances and overdrafts in national currency. † Beginning in January 1995, weighted average rate charged by commercial banks on overdrafts and loans in national currency. The rate is weighted by loan amounts. † Beginning in January 2010, weighted average rate charged by commercial banks and Credit Corporation of Solomon Islands on all loans and advances in national currency. The rate is weighted by loan amounts.

Government Bond Yield:

Coupon rate offered on long-term development bonds issued by the central government in national currency. † Beginning in April 1998, weighted average rate on restructuring bonds issued to replace defaulted treasury bills. † Beginning in July 2004, weighted average rate on amortized bonds issued to replace development, restructuring, and treasury bonds.

Prices, Production, Labor:

Consumer Prices:

Statistical Office retail price index, weights reference period: fourth quarter 2005, covering lower- and middle-income households in Honiara. The index includes 166 items. † Prior to 1990, weights reference period: fourth quarter 1984.

Copra Production and *Fish Catch:*

Indices calculated from Statistical Office data, expressed in metric tons.

South Africa   199

Date of Fund Membership:

December 27, 1945

Standard Sources:

South Africa Reserve Bank
Department of Customs and Excise
Statistics South Africa

Exchange Rates:

Principal Rate (End of Period and Period Average):
A dual exchange rate system, consisting of a commercial rand rate and a financial rand rate, was in effect until February 7, 1983 and again between September 1985 and March 1995. The exchange rate of the commercial rand was determined in a managed floating system and applied to all current transactions. The financial rand applied to the local sale or redemption proceeds of South African securities and other investments in South Africa owned by nonresidents (other than former residents of South Africa), capital remittances by emigrants and immigrants, and approved outward capital transfers by residents. The exchange rate of the financial rand was determined freely by the supply and demand for financial rand balances. Beginning March 13, 1995, the government abolished the financial rand system and repealed all exchange control restrictions on the free convertibility and repatriation of the local sale proceeds on investments in South Africa owned by nonresidents. Thus, beginning March 13, 1995, a unitary exchange rate that applies to both current and capital transactions between residents and nonresidents is in effect. Data prior to that date refer to the commercial rand rate.

International Liquidity:

Data for *line 1d.d* include small foreign exchange holdings by the government.
Gold (National Valuation) (line 1and) is obtained by converting the value in national currency terms, as reported in the country's standard sources, using the prevailing exchange rate, as given in *line* **ag** or *line* **wg**. Data on gold in national sources revalue gold at the end of each month at the average of the last ten gold fixings during the relevant month on the London market, less 10 percent. *Line 3..d* comprises long-term loans to foreign countries, mainly for development purposes.

Central Bank:

Consolidates the South Africa Reserve Bank (SARB) and the Corporation for Public Deposits (CPD), a full subsidiary of SARB. The CPD is a specialized financial institution that pools short-term public sector deposits and invests mainly in short-term government paper, public corporations paper, and bank instruments. Although a full subsidiary of the SARB it produces its own set of financial statements.
† Beginning in June 2002, the data are based on a standardized report form (SRF) for central banks, which accords with the concepts and definitions of the IMF's *Monetary and Financial Statistics Manual (MFSM),* 2000.
For December 2001 through May 2002, data in the SRF format are compiled from pre-SRF data not based on the *MFSM* methodology. Departures from the *MFSM* methodology are explained below.
Financial assets and liabilities not disaggregated by economic sector are allocated to the economic sector having the largest volume of transactions in that category.

Holdings of securities issued by other depository corporations held by the CPD are included in *Other Items (Net).*
Some claims on the central government are included in *Other Items (Net).*
Deposits excluded from broad money are included in *Other Items (Net).*
General and special reserves are included in *Other Items (Net)* rather than in *Shares and Other Equity.*
The assets and liabilities of the SARB and CPD are recorded on an aggregated rather than consolidated basis.

Other Depository Corporations:

Comprises private banking institutions (including the former commercial banks, discount houses, and equity building societies), mutual banks, the Land Bank, and the Postbank.
† Beginning in June 2002, data are based on a standardized report form (SRF) for other depository corporations, which accords with the concepts and definitions of the IMF's *Monetary and Financial Statistics Manual (MFSM),* 2000. For other depository corporations in South Africa, departures from the *MFSM* methodology are explained below.
Financial assets and liabilities not disaggregated by economic sector are estimated based on information available from other sources, including from other financial corporations, or allocated to the economic sector having the largest volume of transactions in that category.
For December 2001 through May 2002, data in the SRF format are compiled from pre-SRF data not based on the *MFSM* methodology. Departures from the *MFSM* methodology are explained below.
Financial derivatives are excluded form the data.
Financial assets and liabilities not disaggregated by economic sector are allocated to the economic sector having the largest volume of transactions in that category.
Securities issued by the SARB held by other depository corporations and loans to the SARB are included in *Other Items (Net).*
Some loans to other financial corporations and securities other than shares excluded from broad money issued by other depository corporations held by the CPD are included in *Other Items (Net).*
General and special reserves are included in *Other Items (Net)* rather than in *Shares and Other Equity.*
The assets and liabilities of the other depository corporations are recorded on an aggregated rather than consolidated basis.

Depository Corporations:

† See notes on central bank and other depository corporations.

Other Financial Corporations:

Comprises insurance companies (short- and long-term insurers), pension and provident funds, , the Public Investment Corporation (PIC), finance companies, and collective investment schemes (money market unit trusts, non-money market unit trusts, property unit trusts, and participation bond schemes).
† Beginning in June 2002, data are based on a standardized report form (SRF) for other depository corporations, which accords with the concepts and definitions of the IMF's *Monetary and Financial Statistics Manual (MFSM),* 2000.
Data are compiled on a quarterly basis and data for the interme-

diate months are maintained constant from the previous quarter. For other financial corporations in South Africa, departures from the *MFSM* methodology are explained below.

Financial assets and liabilities not disaggregated by economic sector are estimated based on counterpart data available from the other depository corporations or allocated to the economic sector having the largest volume of transactions in that category. Accrued interest of collective investment schemes is included in *Other Items (Net)* rather than in the outstanding amounts of the financial assets or liabilities.

Financial Corporations:

† See notes on central bank, other depository corporations, and other financial corporations.

Monetary Aggregates:

Broad Money:
Broad Money calculated from the liability data in the sections for the central bank and other depository corporations accords with the concepts and definitions of the *MFSM* and differs from M3 described below as M3 includes an adjustment for the difference between the certificates of deposits issued and held by other depository corporations.

Money (National Definitions):
M0 comprises notes and coins in circulation outside the SARB and other depository corporations' deposits with the SARB in national currency.
M1A comprises notes and coins in circulation outside the depository corporations and check and transferable deposits of households, local governments, public and private nonfinancial corporations, and other financial corporations (including the PIC beginning in January 1996) with the depository corporations.
M1 comprises M1A and other demand deposits of households, local governments, public and private nonfinancial corporations, and other financial corporations (including the PIC beginning in January 1996) with the depository corporations.
M2 comprises M1, other short- and medium-term deposits of households, local governments, public and private nonfinancial corporations, and other financial corporations (including the PIC beginning in January 1996) with the depository corporations, and negotiable certificates of deposits and promissory notes issued by other depository corporations held by households, local governments, public and private nonfinancial corporations, other financial corporations (including the PIC beginning in January 1996), and nonresidents. Short- and medium-term (up to six month's unexpired maturity) deposits include time and savings deposits and savings bank certificates issued by the Postbank.
M3 comprises M2 and long-term deposits of households, local governments, public and private nonfinancial corporations, and other financial corporations (including the PIC beginning in January 1996) with the depository corporations, and negotiable certificates of deposits and promissory notes (more than six month's unexpired maturity) issued by other depository corporations held by households, local governments, public and private nonfinancial corporations, other financial corporations (including the PIC beginning in January 1996), and nonresidents. Long-term deposits include national savings certificates issued by the Postbank.

Interest Rates:

Central Bank Policy Rate (End of Period):
Rate determined by the SARB on repurchase agreements in national currency between the SARB and private sector banks. The repo rate was introduced on March 9, 1998.

Discount Rate (End of Period):
Lowest rate at which the SARB discounts treasury bills to commercial banks.

Money Market Rate:
Rate on loans between banks. † Beginning in March 1976, predominant quoted rate on interbank deposits at call. † Beginning in September 2001, refers to the South African overnight interbank average rate (SAONIA) which is the weighted average rate of unsecured interbank overnight transactions at market rates in national currency. The rate is weighted by loan amounts. † Beginning in March 2007, the SAONIA rate was discontinued and replaced by the South African Benchmark Overnight Rate (SABOR). SABOR is the volume-weighted average of interbank funding at a rate other than the current repo rate and the twenty highest rates paid by banks on their overnight and call deposits, plus a five percent weight for funding through foreign exchange swaps.

Treasury Bill Rate:
Tender rate on 91-day treasury bills in national currency. Monthly data are averages of each Friday of the month.

Savings Rate:
Weighted average rate offered by banks on savings deposits in national currency. The rate is weighted by deposit amounts. † Beginning in January 2008, reflects banks' reclassifications and changed reporting methods and procedures.

Deposit Rate:
Predominant quoted rate on wholesale 88–91 day time deposits with clearing banks in national currency. † Beginning in January 2001, weighted average rate offered by banks on wholesale 88–91 day time deposits in national currency. The rate is weighted by deposit amounts. † Beginning in January 2008, weighted average rate offered by banks on wholesale 32–91 day notice deposits in national currency. The rate is weighted by deposit amounts.

Lending Rate:
Predominant prime overdraft rate charged by banks.

Government Bond Yield: Long-Term:
Yield on bonds with maturities of ten years and longer traded on the bond exchange.

Prices, Production, Labor:

Share Prices All Shares:
Weighted index of monthly average prices of all ordinary shares listed on the Securities Exchange South Africa, base 2000.

Share Prices Industrial:
Weighted index of monthly average prices of industrial shares listed on the Securities Exchange South Africa, base 2000.

Share Prices Gold Mining:
Weighted index of monthly average prices of gold mining shares listed on the Securities Exchange South Africa, base 2000.

Producer Prices:

Source: Statistics South Africa. Weights Reference Period: 2011; Coverage: output of all producers, importers and exporters; Number of Items in Basket: 274 products consisting of locally produced and sold goods, exports and imports; Basis for Calculation: value added up to the 3-digit level of ISIC, and on total sale values from the 4-digit level up to the 9-digit level for domestic output. For imports and exports, the weights are based total sale values only drawn from annual foreign trade statistics.

Consumer Prices:

Source: Statistics South Africa. Weights Reference Period: 2010/2011; Laspeyres index; Geographical Coverage: whole country; Number of Items in Basket: 393; Basis for Calculation: 2010/11 Household Expenditure Survey.

Manufacturing Production:

Source: Statistics South Africa. Weights Reference Period: 2005; Sectoral Coverage: all the major manufacturing groups as well as total manufacturing; Basis for Calculation: stratified simple random sample covering approximately 3,050 manufacturing enterprises, drawn in April 2010 from a population then of approximately 57,398 manufacturing enterprises.

Labor Force, Employment, Unemployment, and Unemployment Rate:

Source: Statistics South Africa. 1994–1999 annual data comes from the October Household Survey. 2000–2007 quarterly data comes from the Biannual Labour Force Survey. From 2008 onwards, quarterly data comes from the Quarterly Labour Force Survey.

International Transactions:

† Beginning in January 1998, foreign trade data refer to South Africa only, excluding intra-trade of the South African Common Customs Area. Prior to January 1998, trade data refer to the South African Common Customs Area, which includes Botswana, Lesotho, Namibia, South Africa, and Swaziland.

Exports:

Sources: Department of Customs and Excise and Statistics South Africa. Value of exports, f.o.b., including gold exports. From January 1973 to February 1980, export data excluded certain mineral oils.

Gold Output (Net):

South Africa Reserve Bank value of net gold output (balance of payments table).

† Imports c.i.f. and f.o.b.:

Data are from the Department of Customs and Excise and Statistics South Africa. Prior to March 1980, petroleum products and defense equipment were excluded.

Volume of Exports:

Source: Statistics South Africa. Laspeyres index of volume of domestic merchandise exports, weights reference period: 2000.

Volume of Imports:

Source: Statistics South Africa. Laspeyres index of volume of imports, f.o.b., base 2000.

Unit Value of Exports:

Source: Statistics South Africa. Paasche index of unit value of imports, f.o.b., base 2000.

Unit Value of Imports:

Source: Statistics South Africa. Paasche index of unit value of imports, f.o.b., base 2000.

Government Finance:

Monthly, quarterly, and annual data are as reported by the South Africa Reserve Bank. Data cover the budgetary central government channeled through the consolidated Exchequer and Paymaster Accounts. † From January 1991 onward, data include the revenue, expenditure, and financing of the former Transkei, Bophuthatswana, Venda, and Ciskei (TBVC) and self-governing states. † From April 1994 onward, outstanding debt data include debt of the former TBVC countries and self-governing states. This debt was assumed by the national government in terms of Section 239 of the Second Amendment Bill of the Constitution of the Republic of South Africa. † From May 1997, outstanding debt data include part of Namibia's debt, guaranteed by South Africa before Namibia's independence and subsequently assumed by South Africa. † Prior to 2004, to the extent possible, existing subannual *IFS* data were converted to the main aggregates that are presented in the *GFSM 2001* Statement of Sources and Uses of Cash (see the Introduction of the monthly *IFS* publication for details). Beginning in 2004, data are reported in the *GFSM 2001* analytical framework. The fiscal year ends March 31.

National Accounts:

Source: Statistics South Africa. † Since 1985, national accounts data correspond to the new set of national accounts estimates first published in the first quarter of 1994 by the Reserve Bank. *Lines 99a* and *99b.c* include a statistical discrepancy. As indicated by the country, data from 1993 onward are compiled according to the *1993 SNA*. Quarterly data are seasonally adjusted at annual rates.

Spain   184

Data are denominated in Spanish pesetas prior to January 1999 and in euros from January 1999 onward. An irrevocably fixed factor for converting pesetas to euros was established at 166.386 pesetas per euro. In 2002, the peseta was retired from circulation and replaced by the euro banknotes and coins. Beginning in January 1999, with the implementation of Stage Three of the European Economic and Monetary Union (EMU), an alternative euro area-wide definition of residency was introduced: All positions with residents of other euro area (EA) countries, including the European Central Bank (ECB), are classified as domestic positions, and foreign assets and foreign liabilities include only positions with non-euro area residents. Descriptions of the changes in the methodology and presentation of Spain's accounts following the introduction of the euro are shown in the introduction to *IFS* and in the notes on the euro area page.

Date of Fund Membership:

September 15, 1958

Standard Sources:

Bank of Spain
National Statistical Institute
Eurostat

Exchange Rates:

Prior to 1999, the market rate was the midpoint rate established each business day in the Madrid exchange market by the Bank of

Spain. In January 1999, the peseta became a participating currency within the Eurosystem, and the euro market rate became applicable to all transactions. In 2002, the peseta was retired from circulation and replaced by euro banknotes and coins. For additional information, see the section on Exchange Rates in the introduction to *IFS* and the notes for the euro area page.

International Liquidity:

Beginning in January 1999, *Total Reserves minus Gold (line 1l.d)* is defined in accordance with the Eurosystem's statistical definition of international reserves. The international reserves of Spain per the Eurosystem statistical definition at the start of the monetary union (January 1, 1999) in billions of U.S. dollars were as follows: *Total Reserves minus Gold,* $55,167; *Foreign Exchange,* $52,186; *SDR holdings,* $574; *Reserve Position in the Fund,* $2,189; *Other Reserve Assets,* $219; *Gold,* $5,617 *Gold (million fine troy ounces),* 19.539 ounces. *Foreign Exchange (line 1d.d):* Beginning in July 1988, excludes deposits made with the European Monetary Cooperation Fund (EMCF); the holdings of European currency units (ECUs) issued by the EMCF against those deposits (and similar deposits of gold) are included in *line 1d.d. Gold (Eurosystem Valuation) (line 1and):* In December 1981, gold was revalued from US $42.22 per ounce to US $298 per ounce. From March 1979 to December 1998, excludes deposits of gold at the EMCF. Prior to January 1999, *line 1and* was revalued based on the following formula: If the average market price for the calendar year (or the fourth quarter, if lower) was greater than 150 percent of the current book price, the book price was increased by an amount equal to the difference between the average market price and 150 percent of the book price. Conversely, if the book price was more than 80 percent of the average market price during any number of months since the last price adjustment, then the book price was lowered to 80 percent of the average market price for that period. From January 1999 onward, gold is revalued at market prices at the end of each month. Gold swaps within *line 1and* are treated as repurchase transactions that do not affect the volume of gold held. Memorandum data are provided on *Non-Euro Claims on Euro Area Residents* and *Euro Claims on Non-Euro Area Residents,* which represent positions as of the last day in each month. For additional information, see the section on International Liquidity in the introduction to *IFS* and the notes to the euro area page.

Central Bank:

Consists of the Bank of Spain, which is part of the Eurosystem beginning in January 1999, only. *Currency Issued* includes coins issued by the government. For a description of the accounts, refer to the section on *Central Bank - Euro Area* in the introduction to *IFS*.

Other Depository Corporations:

Comprises all resident units classified as other MFIs, defined in accordance with *1995 ESA* standards, including money market funds and the Instituto de Crédito Oficial (ICO). For a description of the accounts, refer to the section on *Other Depository Corporations - Euro Area* in the introduction to *IFS*.

Depository Corporations (National Residency):

For a description of the methodology and accounts, refer to the section on *Depository Corporations (National Residency) - Euro Area* in the introduction to *IFS*.

Depository Corporations (Euro Area-wide Residency):

For a description of the methodology and accounts, refer to the section on *Depository Corporations (Euro Area-wide Residency)* in the introduction to *IFS*.

Interest Rates:

Discount Rate (End of Period):
Prior to September 1977, rate at which the Bank of Spain discounted financial paper for commercial and saving banks. From September 1977 to January 1999, the weighted average of the interest rate on loans granted to the banking system, through auction, by the Bank of Spain. Data were for the last day of the month in which an auction took place. Beginning in January 1999, central bank policy rate series are discontinued. See Eurosystem policy rate series on the euro area page.

Money Market Rate:
Daily average rate on interbank operations effected through the Bank of Spain's cable service.

Treasury Bill Rate:
Prior to July 1987, the discount rate on three-month treasury bills. Beginning in July 1987, the discount rate on one-year treasury bills.

Deposit Rate:
Rate offered by banks on six- to 12-month time deposits.

Deposit Rate (lines 60lhs, 60lhn, 60lcs, 60lcn, and 60lcr):
See notes in the introduction to *IFS* and *Euro-area Interest Rates*.

Lending Rate:
Rate charged by banks to discount three-month commercial bills.

Lending Rate (lines 60phs, 60pns, 60phm, 60phn, 60pcs, and 60pcn):
See notes in the introduction to *IFS* and *Euro-area Interest Rates*.

Government Bond Yield:
Simple monthly average of daily yields on bonds with over two years maturity included in the government's Sistema de Anotaciones de Cuenta de Deuda del Estado (SACDE). For additional information, refer to the introduction to *IFS* and on the notes on the euro area page. † Beginning January 1980, refers to secondary market yields of government bonds traded in the book entry system with maturities close to ten years. This rate is used to measure long-term interest rates for assessing convergence among the European Union member states.

Prices, Production, Labor:

Share Prices (End of Month):
Share price index, base December 1968. † Beginning in January 1971, share price index of the Madrid Stock Exchange, base December 1970. † Beginning in January 1986, share price index of the Madrid Stock Exchange, base December 31, 1985.

Industrial Prices:
Source: National Statistical Institute. Weights Reference Period: 2005; Sectoral Coverage: all industrial sectors except building, thus surveying energy, mining and manufactures; Number of Items in Basket: 1,400 products; Basis for Calculation: weights are based on the information provided by the annual Industrial Survey.

Consumer Prices:
Source: National Statistical Institute. Weights Reference Period: weights are updated every five years; Geographical Coverage:

the entire country; Number of Items in Basket: 489; Basis for Calculation: weights are based on the Household Budget Survey (HBS), which is conducted by the National Statistical Institute.

Wages:
Source: National Statistical Institute. Index of hourly wages, weights reference period: 2005. The index covers all establishments with 500 or more employees. For units with less than 500 employees, a probability sample method is used.

Industrial Production:
Source: National Statistical Institute. Weights Reference Period: 2005; Sectoral Coverage: measures the production activity of industrial branches, except building; Number of Items in Basket: 1100; Basis for Calculation: Weights are based on the information provided by the Annual Industrial Survey.

Employment:
Source: National Statistical Institute. Data refer to the average number of employed persons for the quarter.

International Transactions:

All data on prices are from the National Statistical Institute.

Volume of Exports and Imports:
National Statistical Institute, Laspeyres type indices, weights reference period: 2000. *Export* and *Import Unit Values* are published by the country as export and import prices: National Statistical Institute, Paasche type indices, weights reference period: 2000.

Balance of Payments:
Beginning in 1990, the annual and quarterly balance of payments data have been compiled by the Bank of Spain, on a transaction basis, in accordance with the methodology set forth in the *Balance of Payments Manual*, fifth edition. Balance of payments data for earlier periods were compiled by the Ministry of Economy and Finance in accordance with the methodology set forth in the *Balance of Payments Manual*, fourth edition, and have been converted to the presentation recommended in the fifth edition of the *Manual*.

Government Finance:

Data on general government are derived from Eurostat. Monthly cash data are provided by the Bank of Spain and cover the budgetary central government. Privatization receipts are included in revenue. The fiscal year ends December 31.

National Accounts:

Source: National Statistical Institute. As indicated by the country, beginning in 1998, data are compiled in accordance with the methodology of the *1995 ESA*. Beginning in 1999, euro data are sourced from the Eurostat database. Eurostat introduced chain-linked GDP volume measures to both annual and quarterly data with the release of the third quarter 2005 on November 30, 2005. Chain linked GDP volume measures are expressed in the prices of the previous year and re-referenced to 2005.

Sri Lanka   524

Date of Fund Membership:
August 29, 1950

Standard Sources:
Central Bank of Sri Lanka
Department of Census and Statistics

Exchange Rates:
Market Rate (End of Period and Period Average):
Commercial bank midpoint rate.

International Liquidity:
Data for *line 1d.d* include small foreign exchange holdings by the government.

Gold (National Valuation) (line 1and) is obtained by converting the value in national currency terms, as reported in the national sources, and is calculated on the basis of the cost of acquisition at the prevailing exchange rate, as given in *line* **ae**. † For 2000–2002, data on the volume of gold include the balances in the Gold Trading Account, the Gold Stock Account, and the Gold Fixed Deposit Account of the Central Bank of Sri Lanka. Beginning in 2003, the outstanding balance on the Gold Stock Account is excluded as this item is no longer classified as foreign reserves by the Central Bank of Sri Lank. Beginning in January 2000, gold valuation is based on market price.

Lines 7a.d and *7b.d* are the U.S. dollar equivalents of *lines 21* and *26c,* respectively. † Beginning in January 1999, they include the foreign currency accounts of the commercial banks' offshore banking units (see notes on Deposit Money Banks). Through their offshore banking units, commercial banks may undertake foreign currency transactions with any nonresident and with designated residents, notably enterprises operating in the free trade zone of the Greater Colombo Economic Commission.

Monetary Authorities:
Consolidates the Central Bank of Sri Lanka (CBSL) and monetary authority functions of the central government through December 1985. The contra-entries to Treasury IMF accounts are included in *line 12a.* † Beginning in 1975, data are based on improved classification and sectorization. † Beginning in 1986 through 1995, data are based on partial coverage of IMF accounts. † Beginning in 1989, data are compiled from a new report form. † Beginning in January 1995, positions of the central bank with the commercial banks' offshore banking units are classified as positions with residents.

Deposit Money Banks:
Broad Money comprises narrow money and time and savings deposits held by the public with the commercial banks.

Comprises the commercial banks (domestic banking units and, beginning in January 1995, the offshore banking units). † Beginning in January 1995, commercial banks' offshore banking units have been reclassified from nonresident entities to resident entities and have been included in the consolidation. In addition, fifty percent of the deposits of nonresidents previously classified in foreign liabilities *(line 26c)* have been reclassified as domestic deposits.

Monetary Survey:
† See note on monetary authorities.

Money (National Definitions):

Reserve Money comprises currency issued by CBSL and deposits of commercial banks and public non-financial enterprises (government agencies and institutions) with the CBSL.

Narrow Money comprises currency in circulation and demand deposits held by the public (non-bank non-government resident sectors) with the commercial banks. Currency in circulation refers to currency issued by CBSL less the amount held by the commercial banks.

Interest Rates:

Discount Rate (End of Period):
Rate charged by the central bank on advances to commercial banks for their temporary liquidity needs.

Money Market Rate:
Maximum advance rate charged by commercial banks on inter-bank call loans.

Treasury Bill Rate:
Discount rate in the secondary market. † Beginning in August 1996, discount rate in the primary market.

Deposit Rate:
Weighted average rate on all commercial bank deposits excluding demand deposits; weights are the deposit amounts.

Lending Rate:
Weighted average prime lending rate of commercial banks; weights are the loan amounts.

Prices and Labor:

Share Prices (End of Month):
The All Share Price Index is an index of all equities traded on the Stock Exchange, base 1985. The index is weighted by the market capitalization of each equity.

Wholesale Prices:
Wholesale price index, all items, weights reference period: 1974.

Consumer Prices:
Source: Department of Census and Statistics. Weights Reference Period: 2006/07; Geographical Coverage: New index has been widened in the urban areas of the Colombo District i.e., Sri Jayawardenapura Municipal Council, Dehiwala – Mt. Layinia Municipal Council and Moratuwa Municipal Council; Kolonnawa Urban Council, Seethawakapura Urban Council, Maharagama Urban Council, Kesbawa Urban Council and Boralasgamuwa Urban Council; Number of Items in Basket: 373; Basis for Calculation: weights are derived from the Household Income and Expenditure Survey 2006–07.

International Transactions:

Trade data are from Central Bank of Sri Lanka. *Export* and *Import* data are adjusted for timing and coverage differences.

Volume of Exports:
Source: Central Bank of Sri Lanka. Weights Reference Period: 1997

Volume of Imports:
Source: Central Bank of Sri Lanka. Weights Reference Period: 1997

Unit Value of Exports:
Source: Central Bank of Sri Lanka. Weights Reference Period: 1997

Unit Value of Imports:
Source: Central Bank of Sri Lanka. Weights Reference Period: 1990.

Government Finance:

Annual data are as reported for the *Government Finance Statistics Yearbook (GFSY)* and cover budgetary central government. The fiscal year ends December 31.

National Accounts:

Source: Central Bank of Sri Lanka and Department of Census and Statistics. The National Accounts estimates are compiled based on the SNA 1993.

Sudan   732

Date of Fund Membership:
September 5, 1957

Standard Sources:
Central Bank of Sudan
Ministry of Finance and National Economy

Exchange Rates:
The pound was in circulation between the country's independence in 1956 and end-July 1999. On July 31, 1991 the dinar, equal to 10 pounds, was introduced. In January 2007 a new currency, the Sudanese pound (SDG), was introduced, replacing the old Sudanese dinar (SDD). The pound is equal to 100 old dinars (1 SDG = 100 SDD). The dinar remained in circulation alongside the pound until July 2007. In July 2011, the new pound was introduced to replace the old pound. The new pound is at par with the old pound.

Market Rate (End of Period and Period Average):
Effective 1992, a unified exchange rate system was introduced. Under the new system, the exchange rate is determined by a committee of local bankers, without official intervention, and is quoted uniformly by all commercial banks. Since 1992, all restrictions on foreign currency have been lifted.

International Liquidity:
† Beginning in March 2000, data reflect an improved classification of accounts.

Central Bank:
Consists of the Central Bank of Sudan (CBS) only. Beginning in July 2011, data exclude the Bank of South Sudan.
† Beginning in April 2006, data are based on a standardized report form (SRF) for central banks, which accords with the concepts and definitions of the IMF's *Monetary and Financial Statistics Manual (MFSM)*, 2000. Departures from the *MFSM* methodology are explained below.
Financial assets and liabilities for which financial instrument breakdown is unavailable are allocated to the financial instrument having the largest volume of transactions in the category.
Financial assets and liabilities for which economic sectorization is unavailable are allocated to the economic sector having the largest volume of transactions in the category.

Claims on Central Government include accumulated interest arrears representing the counterpart to interest payable by the CBS to foreign creditors on overdue government debt obligations.

Securities other than shares and shares and other equity are valued at acquisition cost rather than at market price or fair value.

Accrued interest is included in *Other Items (Net)* rather than in the outstanding amounts of the financial assets and liabilities.

For December 2001 through March 2006, data in the SRF format are compiled from pre-SRF data, which have less conformity with the *MFSM* methodology and therefore are not strictly comparable to data for later periods.

Departures from the *MFSM* methodology are explained below. Financial assets and liabilities for which financial instrument breakdown is unavailable are allocated to the financial instrument having the largest volume of transactions in the category. Financial assets and liabilities for which economic sectorization is unavailable are allocated to the economic sector having the largest volume of transactions in the category.

Securities other than shares and shares and other equity are valued at acquisition cost rather than at market price or fair value.

Accrued interest is included in *Other Items (Net)* rather than in the outstanding amounts of the financial assets and liabilities.

Other Depository Corporations:

Comprises commercial banks and the consolidation of postal savings deposits. Beginning in July 2011, data exclude commercial banks operating in South Sudan.

† Beginning in April 2006, data are based on a standardized report form (SRF) for other depository corporations, which accords with the concepts and definitions of the IMF's *Monetary and Financial Statistics Manual (MFSM)*.

For other depository corporations in Sudan, departures from the *MFSM* methodology are explained below.

Some positions with households are included in assets and liabilities with other sectors.

Accrued interest is included in *Other Items (Net)* rather than in the outstanding amounts of the financial assets and liabilities.

For December 2001 through March 2006, data have less conformity with the *MFSM* methodology and therefore are not strictly comparable to data for later periods. Departures from the *MFSM* methodology are explained below.

Financial assets and liabilities for which financial instrument breakdown is unavailable are allocated to the financial instrument having the largest volume of transactions in the category. Financial assets and liabilities for which economic sectorization is unavailable are allocated to the economic sector having the largest volume of transactions in the category.

Some positions with households are included in assets and liabilities with other sectors.

Accrued interest is included in *Other Items (Net)* rather than in the outstanding amounts of the financial assets and liabilities.

Depository Corporations:

† See notes on central bank and other depository corporations.

Monetary Aggregates:

Broad Money:

Broad Money calculated from the liability data in the sections for the central bank and other depository corporations accords with the concepts and definitions of the *MFSM* and is consistent with M2 described below.

Money (National Definitions):

M1 comprises currency outside depository corporations and transferable deposits. Currency outside depository corporations refers to notes and coins issued by the CBS less the amount held by the CBS and other depository corporations. Transferable deposits refer to current account deposits of other financial corporations, public nonfinancial corporations, and private sector with the depository corporations in national currency.

M2 comprises M1, other deposits in national currency, and foreign currency deposits of other financial corporations, public nonfinancial corporations, and private sector with the depository corporations.

Prices and Labor:

Consumer Prices:

Source: Bank of Sudan. Weights Reference Period: 2008; Geographical coverage: Urban and rural areas of Sudan; Number of items in basket: 173; Basis for calculation: The weights used to compile the CPI are based on data from the household income and expenditure survey of 2008.

International Transactions:

All trade value data are from Bank of Sudan. Prior to 1995, annual trade value data refer to the fiscal year ending June 30, and from 1995 onward, trade value data are on a calendar year basis (year ending December 31). For the 1994–95 fiscal year, exports are 421.7 million U.S. dollars and imports are 1,023.4 million U.S. dollars.

Balance of Payments:

† Balance of payments data from 2002 incorporate changes introduced following an IMF balance of payments statistics technical assistance mission in June 2003. The main changes relate to the reclassification of capital account flows to direct investment in the reporting economy and improved data sources on loan repayments of general government.

Government Finance:

Annual data are as reported in the *Government Finance Staitstics Yearbook* and cover budgetary central government. The fiscal year ends December 31.

National Accounts:

GDP data are from the Ministry of Finance and Economy. Prior to 1995, annual GDP refer to the fiscal year ending June 30, and from 1995 onward, annual GDP data are on a calendar-year basis (year ending December 31).

Suriname   366

Date of Fund Membership:

April 27, 1978

Standard Sources:

Central Bank of Suriname
General Bureau of Statistics

Exchange Rates:

On January 1, 2004, the Surinamese dollar, equal to 1,000 Surinamese guilders, replaced the guilder as the currency unit.

Official Rate (End of Period):

Central bank midpoint rate. Beginning July 1994, the Central Bank midpoint exchange rate was unified and became market determined. Beginning in March 2002, data reported correspond to the official rate.

International Liquidity:

Gold (National Valuation) (line 1and) is obtained by converting for current periods the value in national currency terms, as reported in the country's standard sources, using the prevailing exchange rate, as given in *line* **ae**. Beginning January 2006, gold holdings are valued at market prices.

Central Bank:

Consists of the Central Bank of Suriname (CBS) only.

† Beginning in May 2002, data are based on a standardized report form (SRF) for central banks, which accords with the concepts and definitions of the IMF's *Monetary and Financial Statistics Manual (MFSM)*, 2000.

For December 2001 through April 2002, data in the SRF format are compiled from pre-SRF data.

Other Depository Corporations:

Comprises commercial banks, a finance company, and two trust companies. Finance and trust companies are wholly owned by the commercial banks, on whom they almost exclusively rely to finance their operations. Data exclude credit unions, which accept deposits. Beginning in June 2006, includes credit unions.

† Beginning in May 2002, data are based on a standardized report form (SRF) for other depository corporations, which accords with the concepts and definitions of the *Monetary and Financial Statistics Manual (MFSM)*.

For December 2001 through April 2002, data in the SRF format are compiled from pre-SRF data not based in the *MFSM* methodology. Departures from the *MFSM* methodology are explained below.

Loans and deposits are disaggregated into only three sectors: central government, banks, and others.

Claims on Private Sector includes loans to public nonfinancial corporations.

Claims on Nonresidents and *Liabilities to Nonresidents* include all domestic credit and deposits in foreign currency.

Deposits of other depository corporations at the CBS, except correspondent accounts and reserve requirements, are included in *Other Items (Net)*.

Depository Corporations:

See notes on central bank and other depository corporations.

Monetary Aggregates:

Broad Money:

Broad Money calculated from the liability data in the sections for the central bank and other depository corporations accords with the concepts and definitions of the *MFSM*. Broad money includes currency issued by the central government. Broad money differs from M3 described below as M3 excludes for-

eign currency deposits. † Beginning in December 2010, broad money is consistent with M2 described below.

Money (National Definitions):

M1 comprises banknotes and coins in circulation; treasury notes; and demand deposits, other than central government deposits, with depository corporations in national currency. † Beginning in December 2010, comprises currency in circulation and transferable deposits in national and foreign currency with depository corporations, excluding central government deposits.

M2 comprises M1; time deposits, other than central government deposits, with a maturity of less than one year and ten percent of savings deposits, other than central government deposits, with depository corporations in national currency; and gold certificates held by the public. † Beginning in December 2010, comprises M1 and time and savings deposits in national and foreign currency with depository corporations, excluding central government deposits, and gold certificates held by the public.

M3 comprises M2 and time deposits with a maturity of more than one year and 90 percent of savings deposits, other than central government deposits, in national currency with depository corporations.

Interest Rates:

Central Bank Policy Rate (End of Period):

Short-term rate of less than six months at which the CBS extends credit to the commercial banks and the government.

Money Market Rate:

Simple average of rates at which commercial banks borrow funds in national currency in the interbank market.

Deposit Rate:

Weighted average rate offered by commercial banks on all savings and time deposits in national currency.

Deposit Rate in USD:

Weighted average rate offered by commercial banks on all savings and time deposits in U.S. dollars.

Deposit Rate in Euros:

Weighted average rate offered by commercial banks on all savings and time deposits in Euros.

Lending Rate:

Weighted average rate charged by commercial banks on all loans in national currency.

Lending Rate in USD:

Weighted average rate charged by commercial banks on all loans in U.S. dollars.

Lending Rate in Euros:

Weighted average rate charged by commercial banks on all loans in Euros.

Prices:

Consumer Prices:

Source: General Bureau of Statistics. Weights Reference Period 2007–2008; Geographical Coverage: Paramaribo, Wanica, Nickerie including Wageningen, Coronie, Saramacca, and Commewijne; Number of Items in Basket: 297; Basis for Calculation: Weights are based on the Household Budget Survey of 2007–2008.

International Transactions:

Trade data, which are compiled by the Central Bureau of Statistics have been updated with the Bank of Suriname balance of payments data on a cash basis for current periods.

National Accounts:

Source: Bank of Suriname. According to the country, the national accounts of Suriname are based, as far as possible, on the *1993 SNA*.

Swaziland 734

Date of Fund Membership:

September 22, 1969

Standard Sources:

Central Bank
Central Statistical Office

Exchange Rates:

Official Rate: (End of Period and Period Average):

The lilangeni is at par with the South African rand (see note on the page for South Africa for a description of the exchange rates).

Central Bank:

Consists of the Central Bank of Swaziland only.

† Beginning in August 2004, the data are based on a standardized report form (SRF) for central banks, which accords with the concepts and definitions of the IMF's *Monetary and Financial Statistics Manual (MFSM), 2000*. Departures from the *MFSM* methodology are explained below.

Some accrued interest is included in *Other Items (Net)* rather than in the outstanding amounts of the financial assets and liabilities. For December 2001 through July 2004, data in the SRF format are compiled from pre-SRF data not based on the *MFSM* methodology. Departures from the *MFSM* methodology are explained below.

Financial assets and liabilities not disaggregated by economic sector are allocated to the economic sector having the largest volume of transactions in the category.

Some accrued interest is included in *Other Items (Net)* rather than in the outstanding amounts of the financial assets and liabilities.

Other Depository Corporations:

Comprises commercial banks. Beginning in January 2006, includes the Swaziland Building Society.

† Beginning in August 2004, data are based on a standardized report form (SRF) for other depository corporations, which accords with the concepts and definitions of the *Monetary and Financial Statistics Manual (MFSM)*. For other depository corporations in Swaziland, departures from the *MFSM* methodology are explained below.

Some accrued interest is included in *Other Items (Net)* rather than in the outstanding amounts of the financial assets or liabilities.

For December 2001 through July 2004, data in the SRF format are compiled from pre-SRF data not based on the *MFSM*

methodology. Departures from the *MFSM* methodology are explained below.

Financial assets for which economic sectorization is unavailable are allocated to the economic sector having the largest volume of transactions in the category.

Monthly data on the sectorization of deposit liabilities are estimated based on data available on a quarterly basis.

Some accrued interest is included in *Other Items (Net)* rather than in the outstanding amounts of the financial assets and liabilities.

Depository Corporations:

Consolidation of central bank and other depository corporations.

Monetary Aggregates:

Broad Money:

Broad Money calculated from the liability data in the sections for the central bank and other depository corporations accords with the concepts and definitions of the *MFSM* and is consistent with M2 described below.

Money (National Definitions):

M1 comprises notes and coins in circulation outside the depository corporations, other financial corporations' deposits with the CBS in national currency, and demand deposits in national and foreign currency of the private sector, local authorities and town councils, nonfinancial public corporations, and other financial corporations with depository corporations.

M2 comprises M1 plus time and savings deposits in national and foreign currency of the private sector, local authorities and town councils, nonfinancial public corporations, and other financial corporations with depository corporations.

Interest Rates:

Discount Rate (End of Period):

Lowest rate at which the CBS discounts treasury bills to commercial banks.

Money Market Rate:

Interbank call deposit rate.

Treasury Bill Rate:

Yield on treasury bills with 91-days maturity auctioned by the CBS.

Savings Rate:

Midpoint rate offered by banks on savings deposits.

Deposit Rate:

Mid-point rate offered by commercial banks on three-month fixed term deposits.

Lending Rate:

Rate charged by banks to most creditworthy customers on short-term loans.

Prices and Labor:

Consumer Prices:

Source: Central Statistical Office. Weights Reference Period: 2001; Geographical Coverage: Nine urban centers; Number of Items in Basket: 390; Basis for Calculation: The weights are derived from the Swaziland Household Income and Expenditure Survey (SHIES) conducted in 2001.

International Transactions:

All trade value data are from the Central Bank. *Imports, c.i.f.* include customs duties, excises, and sales taxes paid and are therefore not comparable to corresponding balance of payments data.

Government Finance:

Data are derived from the Central Bank and cover the budgetary central government. External debt data cover both budgetary central government and public guaranteed debt. The fiscal year ends March 31.

National Accounts:

Source: Central Statistical Office. Data are prepared in accordance with the *SNA68*.

Sweden   144

Date of Fund Membership:

August 31, 1951

Standard Sources:

Sveriges Riksbank
National Institute of Economic Research
Central Bureau of Statistics

Exchange Rates:

Official Rate: (End of Period and Period Average):
Since November 19, 1992, midpoint rate in the Stockholm foreign exchange market at the time of the fixing of exchange quotations each business day. During the period May 17, 1991–November 18, 1992, the official rate was pegged to the European currency unit (ECU). Prior to May 17, 1991, the official rate was pegged to an index of a basket comprising 15 currencies.

International Liquidity:

Gold (National Valuation) (line 1and) is valued according to market prices. † Prior to January 2004, *(line 1and)* is equal to *Gold (Million Fine Troy Ounces) (line 1ad),* valued at SDR 35 per fine troy ounce and converted into U.S. dollars at the dollar/SDR rate **sa** on the country page for the United States. Source: OECD
Lines 7a.d and *7b.d* are obtained from detailed information with geographic breakdown and differ from *lines 21* and *26c.*
Lines 7a.d, 7b.d, 7e.d, and *7f.d:* † The banks' positions with their branches abroad are included.

Central Bank:

Consists of the Sveriges Riksbank only.
Data are compiled in accordance with the European Central Bank's framework for monetary statistics using the national residency approach.

Other Depository Corporations:

Comprises all resident units classified as other monetary financial institutions (other MFIs) in accordance with *1995 ESA* standards. Data are compiled in accordance with the European Central Bank's framework for monetary statistics using the national residence approach.

Depository Corporations:

See notes on central bank and other depository corporations.

Monetary Aggregates:

Broad Money:
Broad Money calculated from the liability data in the sections for the central bank and other depository corporations.

Money (National Definitions):
M0 comprises currency outside monetary financial institutions (MFIs), which is equal to currency in circulation minus currency held by MFIs.
M1 comprises M0 and Swedish crown and foreign currency demand deposits in MFIs from Swedish non-MFI, noncentral government sectors.
M2 comprises M1 and other Swedish crown and foreign currency deposits in MFIs from Swedish non-MFI, noncentral government sectors. Other deposits include time, savings, and other deposits with restrictions.
M3 comprises M2, repurchase agreements, money market fund shares, and debt securities with maturity less than 2 years issued by MFIs held by Swedish nonbank public.

Interest Rates:

Central Bank Policy Rate (End of Period):
Data refer to the reference rate set by the Riksbank at six-monthly intervals, and is based on the repurchase agreement rate applying at the end of the previous six-month period, rounded up to the nearest whole or half percentage point.

Discount Rate (End of Period):
Rate charged by the Riksbank to commercial banks on short-term loans. † Beginning in March 1992, official discount rate which was based on the average rate on six-month and five-year securities fixings during the previous quarter minus 2.5 percent.

Repurchase Rate:
Marginal rate charged by the Riksbank on the loans to banks. † Beginning in June 1994, the marginal rate has been replaced by the repurchase rate.

Money Market Rate:
Relates to the monthly average of daily rates for day-to-day interbank loans.

Treasury Bill Rate:
Rate on three-month treasury discount notes.

Deposit Rate:
From March 2000 onward, end-quarter average deposit rate of 11 largest commercial banks. † From December 1992 through February 2000, end-quarter average deposit rate at six largest banks. † Prior to December 1992, end-quarter average rate on savings deposits at deposit money banks.

Lending Rate:
From March 2000 onward, end-quarter average lending rate of 11 largest commercial banks. † From December 1992 through February 2000, rate on six largest banks' total lending, at end quarter. † Prior to December 1992, average rate on lending to households, at end-quarter.

Government Bond Yield:

Data refer to yields on government bonds maturing in 15 years. † Beginning January 1987, data refer to secondary market yields on bonds maturing in 10 years. This rate is used to measure long-term interest rates for assessing convergence among the European Union member states.

Prices, Production, Labor:

Share Prices (End of Month):

The general index refers to prices of all shares on the Stockholm Exchange, base December 28, 1979. † Beginning December 1995, refers to the OMX Stockholm Index, base December 31, 1995. The index is a capitalization-weighted index comprised of all shares listed on the A-List and O-List of the Stockholmsborsen. The other series are components of the general index. Forest industries share price index, base December 28, 1979, covers forest industries. Industrial share price index, base December 31, 2000, covers industrial conglomerates, vehicles and machinery, wholesalers, printing and office supplies, transportation, technical consultants, and miscellaneous industry subsectors. † Prior to December 1995, data refer to machinery/engineering industries share price index, base December 29, 1979, whose coverage differs from that of the industrials share price index.

Prices: Domestic Supply:

Source: Central Bureau of Statistics. Weights Reference Period: weights are updated annually; Sectoral Coverage: agriculture, forestry and fishing, mining and quarrying, manufacturing, electricity, gas, heating and water supply; Number of Items in Basket: approximately 5100 prices; Basis for Calculation: the weights are based on total sale values from the annual manufacturing statistics.

Consumer Prices:

Source: Central Bureau of Statistics. Weights Reference Period: calendar year 2003; Geographical Coverage: the whole country; Number of Items in Basket: 25,000 prices; Basis for Calculation: The weights are derived from national accounts estimates of private consumption expenditures and revised every year.

Wages: Hourly Earnings:

Central Bureau of Statistics data, weights reference period 1994. The index refers to basic wages and supplements for overtime and shiftwork and covers workers in mining, quarrying, and manufacturing.

Industrial Production:

Source: Central Bureau of Statistics. Weights Reference Period: 2005; Sectoral Coverage: Mining, manufacturing and electricity; Basis for Calculation: the weights used for aggregation are based on an annual survey of industrial production in manufacturing and the National Accounts.

Industrial Employment:

Central Bureau of Statistics series on employed labor force from January 1976, 16–64 years of age. Prior to 1976, the series related to ages 16–71. The monthly survey covers 22,000 persons selected from all over the country.

International Transactions:

Beginning January 1977, data refer to actual imports and exports of the period. Prior to January 1977, data refer to exports and imports for which customs documents were processed by the Customs Office during the period. *Exports* and *Imports c.i.f.:* Central Bureau of Statistics data. *Export* and *Import Prices:* Reference year = 2005; annual chain-linked Laspeyres index with data comprising 1800 items for the Swedish market, about 850 for the export market, and about 1500 for the import market.

Government Finance:

Data on general government are derived from source V. † From 1970 through 1993, cash data are as reported in the *Government Finance Statistics Yearbook* and refer to a fiscal year ending June 30. † Beginning in 1994, cash data cover the operations of the budgetary central government and are derived from the Central Bureau of Statistics. Domestic financing data include operations of the National Debt Office for liquidity purposes. Debt data are derived from Sveriges Riksbank and cover the budgetary central government only. The fiscal year ends December 31.

National Accounts:

Source: Central Bureau of Statistics. As indicated by the country, data are compiled in accordance with the methodology of the *1995 ESA*. *Line 93i* includes a statistical discrepancy. Beginning in 1999, data are sourced from the Eurostat database. Eurostat introduced chain-linked GDP volume measures to both annual and quarterly data with the release of the third quarter 2005 on November 30, 2005. Chain linked GDP volume measures are expressed in the prices of the previous year and re-referenced to 2012.

Switzerland 146

Date of Fund Membership:
May 29, 1992

Standard Sources:
Swiss National Bank
Message of the Federal Council to the Federal Assembly
Swiss Federal Statistical Office (Office federal de la statistique)

Exchange Rates:

Market Rate (End of Period and Period Average):
Midpoint rate.

International Liquidity:

Data for *line 1c.d* refer to Switzerland's lendings to the Fund. *Gold (National Valuation) (line 1and)* is obtained by converting the value in national currency terms, as reported in the country's standard sources, using the prevailing exchange rate, as given in *line* **de**, *line* **ae**, or *line* **we**.

Banks' foreign assets and foreign liabilities are equal to data reported in the text portion of the Swiss National Bank, converted at the prevailing spot rate (*line* **ae**). The institutional coverage provided is broader than deposit money bank coverage mainly because the foreign accounts of most private banks and foreign banks operating in Switzerland are included. *Lines 7a.d and 7b.d* cover their own foreign assets and liabilities of resident banks (including those of branches of foreign banks in Switzerland) that are subject to minimum reserve requirements on nonresident accounts. Nonresident branches of Swiss banks are treated as nonresident banks. Claims on and liabilities to Swiss citizens residing abroad, embassies, and international organizations residing in Switzerland are not included.

Lines 7k.d and 7m.d cover the trustee accounts of resident banks that are subject to minimum reserve requirements on nonresident accounts. A bank/nonbank distinction of these accounts is not available; however, it is known that *line 7k.d* consists mainly of claims on nonresident banks, whereas in *line 7m.d* the nonbank component is more dominant.

Monetary Authorities:

Consolidates the Swiss National Bank and monetary authority functions undertaken by the central government. The contraentry to treasury coin issues is included in *line 12a.* † Beginning in March 1997, *Central Government Deposits* includes Deposits of the Confederation. † Beginning in April 2005, data are based on an improved classification and sectorization of the accounts.

Deposit Money Banks:

† Before 1974, data cover all banks in Switzerland, with data on nonresident branches of Swiss banks being consolidated into the accounts of the parent bank. Beginning in December 1974, data cover resident banks which are subject to minimum reserves on external liabilities. † Beginning in August 1982, data cover all banks except for small Raiffeisen banks. † Beginning in December 1984, data reflect improved classification of accounts. † Beginning in December 1996, data reflect a new reporting format. Beginning in September 2006, data include all Raiffeisen banks. *Demand Deposits (line 24)* includes post office checking deposits with the counterpart adjustments made in *Claims on Central Government (line 22a)*.

Monetary Survey:

† See notes on monetary authorities and deposit money banks.

Other Banking Institutions:

Comprises trustee assets and liabilities of fiduciary operations by the deposit money banks. † Beginning in 1996, data reflect a new reporting format.

Money (National Definitions):

Base Money comprises currency in circulation and demand deposits of domestic banking institutions with the Swiss National Bank (SNB). Currency in circulation refers to notes and coins issued by the SNB. Beginning in 1995, the demand deposits of domestic banking institutions are adjusted for holdings of non-banks.

M1 comprises currency in circulation and demand and transferable savings deposits in national currency of other financial corporations, public nonfinancial corporations, and private sector with the SNB, banking institutions, and postal system savings accounts. Currency in circulation refers to notes and coins issued by the SNB less the amount held by banking institutions and postal savings system.

M2 comprises M1 and non-transferable savings deposits in national currency of other financial corporations, public nonfinancial corporations, and private sector with banking institutions less funds in mandatory occupational pension schemes and voluntary individual savings.

M3 comprises M2 and term deposits in national currency of

other financial corporations, public nonfinancial corporations, and private sector with banking institutions.

Interest Rates:

Central Bank Policy Rate (End of Period):
Data refer to official discount rates. Beginning in January 2000, data refer to the upper limit of the target range for three-month Swiss franc interbank market for unsecured loans set by the SNB.

Money Market Rate:
End-of-period rate of interest on overnight Swiss franc deposits in international markets.

Treasury Bill Rate:
Monthly average rate of interest on Federal Debt Register Claims.

Deposit Rate:
End-of-period rate of interest on three-month deposits with large banks. Beginning in January 2000, data are beginning-of-period rates. Beginning in January 2008 end-of-period interest on three-month deposits with approximately 50 banks.

Lending Rate:
Beginning-of-period rate of interest of Cantonal banks on first mortgages with variable interest rates. Beginning in January 2008 end-of-period rate of interest of approximately 50 banks on first mortgages with variable interest rates.

Government Bond Yield:
† Beginning in January 1998, data refer to spot interest rate on government bonds with 10-year maturity. Prior to that date, data cover government bonds with maturity of up to 20 years. Monthly data are based on prices of the last market day of the month. Quarterly and annual yields are end-of-period data.

Prices and Production:

Share Prices (End of Month):
Refers to the SBV–100 index, base April 1, 1987. Reflects data on closing quotations for a composition of the 100 most regularly traded shares. The composition of the index is updated semiannually.

Producer Prices:
Source: Swiss Federal Statistical Office. Weights Reference Period: weights are revised every five years; Sectoral Coverage: agriculture, forestry, quarrying, manufacturing, electricity, gas, and waste management; Number of Items in Basket: approximately 500 items; Basis for Calculation: subsequently the weights are revised and the index re-based every 5 years.

Prices: Home and Imported Goods:
Source: Swiss Federal Statistical Office. Weights reference period: December 2010; Basis for Calculation: the weights are based on the turnover value of domestic producers and importers.

Consumer Prices:
Source: Swiss Federal Statistical Office. Weights Reference Period: annually in December; Geographical Coverage: the entire country; Number of Items in Basket: 12 main groups; Basis for Calculation: the Household Budget Survey (HBS) conducted by the Swiss Federal Statistical Office (FSO) during January-December T–2 among 3000 private households of all socio-economic groups.

Industrial Production:
Source: Swiss Federal Statistical Office. Weights reference period: calendar year 1993; Sectoral Coverage: mining and quarrying,

manufacturing, and production and distribution of energy and water; Basis for Calculation: the weighting system is based on value added at factor costs taken from annual inquiry and on turnover obtained through a basic survey.

International Transactions:

Exports and Imports, c.i.f.:
Swiss Federal Statistical Office data. † Beginning in 1979, trade value data for the volume and unit value of imports included trade of gems, semi-precious stones, and antiques. Beginning in January 1, 1992, value data exclude diamonds, nonmonetary gold, works of art, collectors' pieces, antiques, and precious metals.

Volume and Unit Value Indices:
Swiss Federal Statistical Office data, weights reference period: 1997. † From 1997 onward, new methodology is used to calculate the indices.

Import Prices:
Source: Swiss Federal Statistical Office. For *line 76.x,* weights reference period: 2003, and the index is a component of the *Home & Imported Goods* index *(line 63s).*

Government Finance:

Quarterly and annual data are derived from the Swiss National Bank. Data cover the operations of the budgetary central government. The fiscal year ends December 31.

National Accounts:

Source: Swiss Federal Statistical Office. As indicated by the country, data are compiled in accordance with the methodology of the *1995 ESA.* Chain linked GDP volume measures are expressed according to 2005 prices.

Syrian Arab Republic   463

Date of Fund Membership:
April 10, 1947

Standard Sources:
Central Bank of Syria
Central Bureau of Statistics

Exchange Rates:

Principal Rate (End of Period and Period Average):
The principal rate is an officially determined exchange rate and it is used for the valuation of the Central Bank of Syria's foreign currency assets and liabilities.
Prior to January 2004, a number of different exchange rates were in use by other depository corporations to value their foreign currency positions depending on the sector of the transactor and the purpose of the transaction. Beginning in January 2004, the multiple exchange rates for public and private sector transactions have been replaced by two rates: *the state and public sector rate* which was used to value banks' foreign currency positions with the financial and nonfinancial public sector units, and *the free market rate* which was used by the banks to value foreign currency positions with the private sector. Beginning in January

2007, *the state and public sector rate* and *the free market rate* were unified into a single *foreign currency exchange rate.*

Secondary Rate (End of Period):
Beginning in January 2007, data refer to *the foreign currency exchange rate* which is used by the banks to value all foreign currency assets and liabilities. During January 2004 - December 2006, data refer to *the free market rate* which was used by the banks to value foreign currency positions with the private sector.

Tertiary Rate (End of Period):
During January 2004 - December 2006, data refer to *the state and public sector rate* which was used by the banks to value foreign currency positions with the financial and nonfinancial public sector units.

International Liquidity:

Gold (National Valuation) (line 1and) is obtained by converting the value in national currency terms, as reported in the country's standard sources, using the prevailing exchange rate, as given in *line* **wa** or **we.**

Central Bank:

Consists of the Central Bank of Syria (CBS) only.
† Beginning in January 2008, data are based on a standardized report form (SRF) for central banks, which accords with the concepts and definitions of the IMF's *Monetary and Financial Statistics Manual (MFSM),* 2000. Departures from the *MFSM* methodology are explained below.
Official rather than market exchange rate is used to convert foreign currency denominated accounts into national currency.
Monetary gold is valued at the official price (approximately 35 US dollars per troy ounce) rather than at market price.
Securities other than shares and shares and other equity are valued at acquisition cost rather than at market price or fair value.
For December 2001 through December 2007, data have less conformity with the *MFSM* methodology and therefore are not strictly comparable to data for later periods.

Other Depository Corporations:

Comprises public commercial banks. Beginning in January 2005, includes private commercial and Islamic banks and banks/branches operating in the Free Zone.
† Beginning in January 2008, data are based on a standardized report form (SRF) for other depository corporations, which accords with the concepts and definitions of the *MFSM.* For other depository corporations in Syria, departures from the *MFSM* methodology are explained below.
Securities other than shares and shares and other equity are valued at acquisition cost rather than at market price or fair value.
Commodity gold is valued at acquisition cost rather than at market price.
For December 2001 through December 2007, data have less conformity with the *MFSM* methodology and therefore are not strictly comparable to data for later periods. For valuation of foreign currency denominated positions prior to January 2007 refer to notes on *Exchange Rates.*

Depository Corporations:

† See notes on central bank and other depository corporations.

Monetary Aggregates:

Broad Money:

Broad Money (line 59m) calculated from the liability data in the sections for the central bank and other depository corporations accords with the concepts and definitions of the *MFSM* and is consistent with *Broad Money* (line 59mea) described below. Prior to January 2008, line 59m differs from line 59mea described below as line 59mea includes certain import deposits.

Money (National Definitions):

Reserve Money (M0) comprises currency issued and transferable and other deposits in national and foreign currency of banks and non-bank non-government resident sectors with the CBS.

M1 comprises currency outside banks, demand deposits in national currency of non-bank non-government resident sectors with depository corporations.

Quasi-Money comprises time, savings, foreign currency, and import deposits of non-bank non-government resident sectors with depository corporations.

Broad Money comprises *M1* and *Quasi-Money*.

Interest Rates:

Discount Rate (End of Period):

Rate at which the CBS discounts eligible commercial paper for banks not exceeding 120 days. The CBS also quotes several other rates for loans and advances on commercial paper, and for seasonal financing of agricultural and industrial operations. Advances against government securities bear a rate of one percent per annum. The CBS does not grant direct credit to businesses. The Credit and Monetary Council, together with the CBS, determine a ceiling for financing and rediscount operations of the Commercial Bank of Syria and other publicly-owned banks. Banks are permitted to exceed this ceiling with the consent of the Credit and Monetary Council and the Prime Minister. Borrowing from the CBS within the quantitative limits may be considered a right of the banks, but the CBS can finance banks more or less than the quantitative limits. The CBS started regular operations on August 1, 1956, with a discount rate of 3.50 percent per annum. On July 11, 1962, the rate was changed to the present level of five percent.

Deposit Rate:

Simple annual average rate offered by banks on one-year time deposits of the private and public sectors.

Lending Rate:

Rate at which the Commercial Bank of Syria discounts promissory notes held by the private sector. Beginning in January 2004, rate at which banks discount promissory notes held by the private and public sectors.

Prices and Production:

Share Prices (Period Average and End of Month):

Share price index of Damascus Securities Exchange (DSE), base January 1, 2010 refers to DSE weighted index (DWX). DWX covers shares of all companies listed in DSE weighted by market capitalization.

Wholesale Prices:

Source: Central Bank of Syria. Weights Reference Period: 2000; Coverage: all goods sold at wholesale markets in Damascus, ex-cept construction materials and highly fabricated goods; Number of items in basket: 163.

Consumer Prices:

Source: Central Bank of Syria. Weights Reference Period: 2005; Geographical Coverage: the whole country; Number of Items in Basket: 780; Basis for Calculation: the weights are derived from a household and expenditure survey conducted in 2003–2004.

Industrial Production:

Central Bank of Syria index, weights reference period 2000. Covers mining, manufacturing, electricity, and gas. The basic indicators used are quantities produced in 78 main industries in Syria.

International Transactions:

Exports and Imports, c.i.f.:

All data are from Central Bank of Syria. † Beginning in 2000, data have been calculated by authorities using a flexible exchange rate determined by the Ministry of Economy and Foreign Trade.

Trade indices:

Data are compiled on base 1990.

Government Finance:

Annual data are as reported for the *Government Finance Statistics Yearbook (GFSY)* and cover budgetary central government. The fiscal year ends December 31.

National Accounts:

Source: Central Bank of Syria. *Line 99b* includes a statistical discrepancy.

Tajikistan   923

Date of Fund Membership:

April 27, 1993

Standard Sources:

National Bank of Tajikistan
State Statistical Agency

Exchange Rates:

The Tajik ruble (TR) was introduced in May 1995. Beginning in November 2000, a new currency, the somoni (SM) replaced the Tajik ruble at the rate of SM 1 = TR 1000.

Official Rate: (End of Period and Period Average):

Prior to July 1, 2000, the official rate was established at the twice-weekly foreign exchange auctions in the Tajikistan Interbank Foreign Currency Exchange, which was eliminated in July 2000. Beginning in July 2000, the official rate is a weighted average of the established daily rates at the interbank foreign exchange market.

International Liquidity:

Gold (National Valuation) (line 1and) is equal to *Gold (Thousands of Fine Troy Ounces) (line 1ad)* valued at prevailing London market rates.

The foreign exchange data are in the process of being revised.

Central Bank:

Consists of the National Bank of Tajikistan (NBT) only.

† Beginning in January 2008, data are based on a standardized report form (SRF) for central banks, which accords with the concepts and definitions of the IMF's *Monetary and Financial Statistics Manual (MFSM)*, 2000. Departures from the *MFSM* methodology are explained below.

Accrued interest on holdings of securities and deposits offered is included in *Other Items (Net)* rather than as claims on and liabilities to the different economic sectors, respectively.

Securities are valued at acquisition cost rather than at current market price or fair value.

For January 2001 through December 2007, data in the SRF format are compiled from pre-SRF data which are not fully based on the *MFSM* methodology. Departures from the *MFSM* methodology are explained below.

Financial assets and liabilities for which financial instrument breakdown is unavailable are allocated to the financial instrument having the largest volume of transactions in the category.

Financial assets and liabilities not disaggregated by economic sector are allocated to the economic sector having the largest volume of transactions in the category.

Accrued interest is allocated to the sector having the largest volume of transactions in the category.

Securities are valued at acquisition cost rather than at current market price or fair value.

Other Depository Corporations:

Comprises domestic commercial banks and branches of foreign banks, nonbank credit institutions, and microcredit deposit organizations.

† Beginning in January 2008, data are based on a standardized report form (SRF) for other depository corporations, which accords with the concepts and definitions of the *Monetary and Financial Statistics Manual (MFSM)*. For other depository corporations in Tajikistan, departures from the *MFSM* methodology are explained below.

Accrued interest on liabilities is included in *Other Items (Net)* rather than as liabilities to the different economic sectors.

Securities and shares are valued at acquisition cost rather than at current market price or fair value.

For January 2001 through December 2007, data in the SRF format are compiled from pre-SRF data which are not fully based on the *MFSM* methodology. Departures from the *MFSM* methodology are explained below.

Financial assets and liabilities for which financial instrument breakdown is unavailable are allocated to the financial instrument having the largest volume of transactions in the category.

Financial assets and liabilities not disaggregated by economic sector are allocated to the economic sector having the largest volume of transactions in the category.

Accrued interest is allocated to the sector having the largest volume of transactions in the category.

Securities are valued at acquisition cost rather than at current market price or fair value.

Depository Corporations:

† See notes on central bank and other depository corporations.

Monetary Aggregates:

Broad Money:

Broad Money calculated from the liability data in the sections for the central bank and other depository corporations accords with the concepts and definitions of the *MFSM* and is consistent with M4 described below.

Broad Money (National Definitions):

M0 comprises currency in circulation.

M1 comprises M0; transferable deposits of other financial corporations and other resident sectors with the NBT in national currency; and transferable deposits of other financial corporations, state and local government, public nonfinancial corporations, and private sector (other nonfinancial corporations and other resident sectors) with other depository corporations in national currency.

M2 comprises M1; term deposits with maturity of less than one year of other nonfinancial corporations with the NBT in national currency; and term deposits with maturity of less than one year of other financial corporations, state and local government, public nonfinancial corporations, and private sector (other nonfinancial corporations and other resident sectors) with other depository corporations in national currency.

M3 comprises M2; deposits of other nonfinancial corporations with the NBT in foreign currency; and deposits of other financial corporations, state and local government, public nonfinancial corporations, and private sector (other nonfinancial corporations and other resident sectors) with other depository corporations in foreign currency.

Interest Rates:

Central Bank Policy Rate (End of Period):

Weighted average rate charged by commercial banks and non-bank credit institutions on loans to customers in national currency plus 200 basis points. Beginning on May 20, 2011, the rate is determined at the meetings of the Monetary Committee.

Central Bank Policy Rate (Foreign Currency) (End of Period):

Weighted average rate charged by commercial banks and non-bank credit institutions on loans to customers in foreign currency plus 200 basis points. Beginning on May 20, 2011, the rate is determined at the meetings of the Monetary Committee.

Refinancing Rate (End of Period):

National Bank of Tajikistan's (NBT) last credit auction rate plus a margin. † Beginning in January 2002, lowest rate charged by the NBT on loans to commercial banks, nonbank credit institutions, and microfinance institutions. Beginning on August 18, 2003, the rate is determined at the meetings of the Monetary Committee.

Central Bank Bill Rate:

Weighted average rate on accepted bids of NBT bills.

Money Market Rate:

Weighted average rate on loans between commercial banks and nonbank credit institutions in national currency. The rate is weighted by loan amounts.

Money Market Rate (Foreign Currency):

Weighted average rate on loans between commercial banks and nonbank credit institutions in foreign currency. The rate is weighted by loan amounts.

Treasury Bill Rate:
Weighted average rate on 91-day treasury bills in national currency.

Deposit Rate:
Weighted average rate offered by commercial banks on demand deposits and time deposits of all maturities in national currency. The rate is weighted by the outstanding amount of deposits. † Beginning in January 2002, weighted average rate offered by commercial banks and nonbank credit institutions on deposits (excluding demand deposits, trust accounts, and deposits of commercial banks and nonbank credit institutions) in national currency. The rate is weighted by deposit amounts.

Deposit Rate (Foreign Currency):
Weighted average rate offered by commercial banks and non-bank credit institutions on deposits (excluding demand deposits, trust accounts, and deposits of commercial banks and nonbank credit institutions) in foreign currency. The rate is weighted by deposit amounts.

Lending Rate:
Weighted average rate charged by commercial banks on loans of all types and maturities in national currency to nonbank sectors. The rate is weighted by the outstanding amount of loans. † Beginning in January 2002, weighted average rate charged by commercial banks and nonbank credit institutions on loans (excluding loans to commercial banks and nonbank credit institutions on loans (excluding loans to commercial banks and nonbank credit institutions and loans with zero interest rate) in national currency. The rate is weighted by loan amounts.

Lending Rate (Foreign Currency):
Weighted average rate charged by commercial banks and nonbank credit institutions on loans (excluding loans to commercial banks and nonbank credit institutions and loans with zero interest rate) in foreign currency. The rate is weighted by loan amounts.

Prices and Labor:

Producer Prices:
State Statistical Agency index. Coverage: manufacturing, electricity, and gas, which account for about 20–25 percent of total output of the economy; Number of items: 100; Basis for calculation: weights are derived from the annual production values of the industrial activities of the last but one year. In recent years, the weights have been updated annually to account for changes in product and activity.

Consumer Prices:
Source: State Statistical Agency. Geographical Coverage: Major cities and rural areas; Number of Items in Basket: 351; Basis for Calculation: Weights are derived from the annual Household Expenditure Survey, the last census was conducted in 2000.

International Transactions:

Source: State Statistical Agency.

National Accounts:

Source: State Statistical Agency. As indicated by the country, data are broadly in accordance with the *1993 SNA*.

Tanzania   738

Data refer to Tanzania, i.e., Tanzania Mainland, formerly Tanganyika, and Zanzibar, unless noted otherwise.

Date of Fund Membership:
September 10, 1962

Standard Sources:
Bank of Tanzania
National Bureau of Statistics

Exchange Rates:

Official Rate: (End of Period and Period Average):
Central bank midpoint rate.

Central Bank:
Consists of the Bank of Tanzania (BOT) only.
Data are based on a standardized report form (SRF) for central banks, which accords with the concepts and definitions of the IMF's *Monetary and Financial Statistics Manual (MFSM)*, 2000.

Other Depository Corporations:
Comprises commercial banks, Tanzania Investment Bank, Tanzania Postal Bank, Twiga Bancorp, Mwanga Rural Community Bank, and Mufindi Community Bank. † Beginning in June 2008, data are based on a standardized report form (SRF) for other depository corporations, which accords with the concepts and definitions of the IMF's *Monetary and Financial Statistics Manual (MFSM)*.
For December 2001 through May 2008 data are based on an SRF for other depository corporations, which accords with the concepts and definitions of the *MFSM*, except for the departures from the *MFSM* methodology explained below.
Claims on Private Sector includes holdings of import bills, domestic bills, banker's acceptances discounted, and shares and other equity issued by all resident sectors except those issued by other depository corporations and central and local governments.
Transferable and *Other Deposits Included in Broad Money* include accrued interest on deposits of nonresidents, central government, and other depository corporations.
Other Items (Net) includes accrued interest on loans from nonresidents and private sector.

Depository Corporations:
† See notes on central bank and other depository corporations.

Monetary Aggregates:

Broad Money:
Broad Money calculated from the liability data in the sections for the central bank and other depository corporations accords with the concepts and definitions of the *MFSM* and is consistent with M3 described below.

Money (National Definitions):
M0 comprises currency in circulation and commercial banks' legal reserve requirements and clearing/settlement accounts with the BOT in national currency.
M1 comprises currency in circulation outside depository corporations and demand deposits in national currency of other financial

corporations, local governments, public nonfinancial corporations, and private sector with depository corporations.

M2 comprises M1 and time and savings deposits in the national currency of other financial corporations, local governments, public nonfinancial corporations, and private sector with depository corporations.

M3 comprises M2 and foreign currency deposits of other financial corporations, local governments, public nonfinancial corporations, and private sector with depository corporations.

Interest Rates:

Discount Rate (End of Period):
Rate charged by the BOT on loans to commercial banks and overdrafts to government deposit accounts. It is derived from the weighted average yield of treasury bills of all maturities plus five percentage points. † Beginning in May 2007, weighted average repurchase agreement rate at which the BOT purchases/sells government securities from/to commercial banks. The maturity of the repurchase agreements range from overnight to 14 days. The rate is weighted by the volume of securities traded during the month.

Money Market Rate:
Weighted average rate charged by commercial banks on overnight interbank loans. The rate is weighted by the volume of overnight transactions during the month.

Treasury Bill Rate:
Rate on three-month treasury bills.

Savings Rate:
Weighted average rate offered by commercial banks on savings deposits. The rate is weighted by deposit amounts.

Deposit Rate:
Weighted average rate offered by commercial banks on three-month term deposits. The rate is weighted by deposit amounts.

Lending Rate:
Weighted average rate charged by commercial banks on loans. The rate is weighted by loan amounts.

Government Bond Yield:
Weighted average yield on successful bids of two-year treasury bonds.

Prices and Production:

Consumer Prices:
Source: National Bureau of Statistics. Weight Reference Period: 2007; Geographical Coverage: whole national territory; Number of Items in the Basket: 224 items; Basis of Calculation: 2007 Household Budget Survey (HBS).

Manufacturing Production:
Source: National Bureau of Statistics. Weight Reference Period: 2000; Coverage: manufacturing establishments that on average have a labor force of 50 persons or more. The index covers more than 300 establishments that are surveyed, contributing more than 85% to total manufacturing gross output; Basis of Calculation: weights have been taken from the output of the 2000 annual survey of industry production.

International Transactions:

Source: Bank of Tanzania.

Government Finance:

Data are compiled by the Ministry of Finance and disseminated in the Bank of Tanzania's web page and in sources A and B. Revenue, grants, and expenditure data cover operations of the budgetary central government. The fiscal year ends June 30.

National Accounts:

Source: National Bureau of Statistics. As indicated by the country, the data are compiled in the framework of the *1968 SNA* but also includes certain elements of the *1993 SNA*.

Thailand   578

Date of Fund Membership:

May 3, 1949

Standard Sources:

Bank of Thailand
Fiscal Policy Office, Ministry of Finance (dw.mof.go.th/foc/gfs)
National Economic and Social Development Board

Exchange Rates:

Official Rate: (End of Period and Period Average):
Average midpoint rate of all commercial banks. The official rate is determined on the basis of a weighted basket of currencies. † Effective July 2, 1997 the Bank of Thailand started operating a managed float for the baht exchange rate.

International Liquidity:

Gold (National Valuation) (line 1and) is the U.S. dollar value of official holdings of gold as reported in the country's standard sources. Gold is revalued annually at the end of the year.

Central Bank:

Consolidates the Bank of Thailand (BOT), Exchange Equalization Fund (EEF), and Financial Institutions Development Fund (FIDF). The EEF manages the foreign currency transactions of the BOT, and the FIDF is a fund managed by the BOT. The contra-entry to EEF foreign assets is included in *line 16d*. † Beginning in January 2003, the data are for the BOT only, inclusive of the EEF. † Beginning in January 2003, data are based on a standardized report form (SRF) for central banks, which accords with the concepts and definitions of the IMF's *Monetary and Financial Statistics Manual (MFSM)*, 2000. Departures from the *MFSM* methodology are explained below.
Financial derivatives are excluded from the data.
For December 2001 through December 2002, data in the SRF format are compiled from pre-SRF data not based on the *MFSM* methodology. Departures from the *MFSM* methodology are explained below.
Financial assets and liabilities not disaggregated by economic sector are allocated to the economic sector having the largest volume of transactions in the category.
Small amounts of foreign currency holdings are included along with BOT holdings of national currency. These holdings are deducted in the calculation of *Currency in Circulation*.
Though other depository corporations' claims on the BOT were

not directly distinguished from other financial corporations' claims on the BOT, separate data in some cases could be obtained on the basis of type of financial asset underlying a claim.

All bonds issued by the BOT are included in *Other Liabilities to Other Depository Corporations* in the absence of data on an individual economic sector's holdings, recognizing that other depository corporations are the principal holders of BOT bonds.

Gold holdings are revalued annually rather than on a monthly basis.

Accrued interest is included in *Other Items (Net)* rather than in the outstanding amounts of the financial assets and liabilities.

The liability account for *Shares and Other Equity* includes provisions for loan losses.

FIDF assets, mostly claims on financial and nonfinancial corporations, are included in *Other Items (Net)*.

Other Depository Corporations:

Comprises commercial banks, Government Savings Bank, Bank for Agriculture and Agricultural Cooperatives, Industrial Finance Corporation of Thailand, Government Housing Bank, finance companies, and Export-Import Bank of Thailand. † Beginning in January 2003, the data include the Small and Medium Enterprises Bank of Thailand, Islamic Bank of Thailand, savings cooperatives, and money-market mutual funds. Beginning in September 2004, the Industrial Finance Corporation of Thailand merged with the Thai Military Bank Public Company Ltd, a commercial bank. Data exclude thecredit unions and credit foncier companies, which have small amounts of deposits.

† Beginning in January 2003, data are based on a standardized report form (SRF) for other depository corporations, which accords with the concepts and definitions of the *Monetary and Financial Statistics Manual* (*MFSM*). For other depository corporations in Thailand, departures from the *MFSM* methodology are explained below.

Financial derivatives are excluded from the data.

Held-to-maturity securities are valued at acquisition cost rather than at current market price or fair value. Holdings of equity shares not traded in active markets are valued at acquisition cost rather than at current market price or fair value.

For December 2001 through December 2002, data in the SRF format are compiled from pre-SRF data not based on the *MFSM* methodology. Departures from the *MFSM* methodology are explained below.

Financial assets and liabilities for which economic sectorization is unavailable are allocated to the economic sector having the largest volume of transactions in the category.

Though data for other depository corporations were not directly distinguished from data for other financial corporations, separation of the data was based on the characteristics of the financial asset or liability. *Claims on Other Financial Corporations* includes some claims on other depository corporations.

Securities Other than Shares Included in Broad Money are not distinguished from *Securities Other than Shares Excluded from Broad Money*.

Accrued interest is included in *Other Items (Net)* rather than in the outstanding amounts of the financial assets or liabilities.

Depository Corporations:

† See notes on central bank and other depository corporations.

Other Financial Corporations:

Comprises insurance companies, pension and provident funds, non money-market mutual funds, asset management companies, Thai Asset Management Corporation, Financial Institutions Development Fund, Small Industry Credit Guarantee Corporation, and Secondary Mortgage Corporation. Beginning in December 2010, includes securities companies, leasing companies, credit card companies, and pawn shops. Data exclude financial auxiliaries.

Data are based on a standardized report form (SRF) for other financial corporations, which accords with the concepts and definitions of the *Monetary and Financial Statistics Manual* (*MFSM*). For other financial corporations in Thailand, departures from the *MFSM* methodology are explained below.

Some financial derivatives are excluded from the data.

Held-to-maturity securities are valued at acquisition cost rather than at current market price or fair value. Holdings of equity shares not traded in active markets are valued at acquisition cost rather than at current market price or fair value.

Financial Corporations:

See notes on central bank, other depository corporations, and other financial corporations.

Monetary Aggregates:

Broad Money:

Broad Money calculated from the liability data in the sections for the central bank and other depository corporations accords with the concepts and definitions of the *MFSM*. Broad money includes currency issued by the central government. Broad money (line 59m) differs from broad money (line 59mea) as line 59m includes small holdings of currency by the central government.

Money (National Definitions):

Narrow Money comprises currency outside depository corporations and transferable deposits in national currency of other financial corporations, local governments, public nonfinancial corporations, and private sector with other depository corporations.

Broad Money comprises currency outside depository corporations, including the currency issued by the government; transferable and other deposits of other financial corporations, local governments, public nonfinancial corporations, and private sector with other depository corporations; and securities issued by other depository corporations held by other financial corporations, local governments, public nonfinancial corporations, and private sector.

Interest Rates:

Central Bank Policy Rate (End of Period):

Policy rate is the rate announced by the Monetary Policy Committee in conducting monetary policy under the inflation-targeting framework. The monetary policy stance is signaled through the policy interest rate. Beginning on May 23, 2000, the 14-day repurchase rate was used as the policy interest rate. Beginning on January 16, 2007, the one-day repurchase rate was used. Beginning on February 12, 2008, with the closure of the BOT-run repurchase market, the one-day bilateral repurchase rate is used.

Discount Rate (End of Period):

Rate offered by the BOT on loans of last resort to commercial banks and finance companies.

Money Market Rate:
Rate on loans between commercial banks. † Beginning in January 1989, daily average of commercial banks' overnight rates for interbank lending.

Treasury Bill Rate:
Average rate on the total of accepted treasury bills sold at tender. † Beginning in February 2001, average of daily bidding yields on 91-day treasury bills.

Savings Rate:
End-of-period maximum rate offered by commercial banks on savings deposits.

Deposit Rate:
End-of-period maximum rate offered by commercial banks on six-month time deposits.

Lending Rate:
Minimum rate charged by commercial banks on loans to prime customers.

Government Bond Yield:
Maximum coupon rate on bonds allotted to other depository corporations and other financial corporations. † Beginning in September 1999, average bidding yield to maturity of government bonds with an interpolated remaining maturity of 10 years.

Prices:

Share Prices:
Composite stock price index of the Stock Exchange of Thailand, base April 30, 1975. The index covers common stocks and is weighted by market capitalization. The monthly index is calculated from the average of the daily closing quotations.

Producer Prices:
Source: Bank of Thailand. Weights Reference Period: 2005; Coverage: measures changes in the selling price received by domestic producers for their output; Number of Items in the Basket: 506 items; Basis for Calculation: the weights for major product groups are obtained from the 2005 input-output table. Disaggregated weights are based on turnover data obtained from surveys of major producers. The index is re-based and re-weighted each time the input-output table is revised.

Consumer Prices:
Source: Bank of Thailand. Weights Reference Period: 2011; Geographical Coverage: nationwide; Number of Items in the Basket: 373 items; Basis for Calculation: the weights are based on a Household Expenditure Survey conducted by the NSO in 2007 and normally re-based every four years.

International Transactions:

All trade data are from Bank of Thailand, based on customs records. *Exports* include re-exports. *Imports* include gold and exclude military aid.

Unit Value of Exports and Imports:
Bank of Thailand index numbers, national currency, base 1995. From January 1996 onward, unit value indices are calculated by using Fisher chained method. Volume indices are obtained by dividing value indices by Fisher chained unit value indices. *Export Volume* indices for individual commodities are based on Bank of Thailand data in metric tons. *Export Unit Value* indices for individual commodities are calculated for *IFS* from reported value and volume data. The rice

wholesale price index is the Thailand (Bangkok) index shown in the world table for commodity prices, and the rubber wholesale price index is the Malaysia (Singapore) index shown in the world table for commodity prices, both converted into baht at the period average exchange rate.

Government Finance:

Through September 2001, data are derived from Bank of Thailand and cover the operations of the consolidated central government. Expenditure exclude outlays financed through foreign loans and grants, and include the net deficits/surpluses of extra-budgetary accounts. Starting October 2001, data are derived from the Fiscal Policy Office, Ministry of Finance and cover the operations of the consolidated central government, including outlays financed through foreign loans and grants. However, data do not cover the complete operations of seven autonomous government agencies (which are extrabudgetary)-only transfers from the budgetary central government to these agencies are included in the data. The fiscal year ends September 30.

National Accounts:

Data are from the National Economic and Social Development Board. *Line 99b* is derived from the production accounts; therefore, it differs from the sum of the expenditure components presented here.

Timor-Leste 537

Date of Fund Membership:
July 23, 2002

Standard Sources:
Banking and Payments Authority
National Statistics Department (NSD)

Exchange Rates:

Market Rate (End of Period):
Timor-Leste uses the U.S. dollar as the official currency. The Banking and Payments Authority issues coins of small value to facilitate small transactions. These coins are fully backed by U.S. dollars.

International Liquidity:

Foreign Exchange (line 1d.d) comprises the Banking and Payments Authority's foreign currency holdings, liquid correspondent accounts with nonresident banks, and holdings of foreign securities.

Central Bank:

Consists of the Banking and Payments Authority (BPA) only.
Data are based on a standardized report form (SRF) for central banks, which accords with the concepts and definitions of the IMF's *Monetary and Financial Statistics Manual (MFSM)*, 2000. Departures from the *MFSM* methodology are explained below.
Prior to January 2008, *Claims on Nonresidents* and *Currency in Circulation* include coins in the vault of the BPA.
Accrued interest on liabilities not disaggregated by economic sector is allocated to the economic sector having the largest volume of transactions in the category.

Other Depository Corporations:

Comprises commercial banks and a microfinance institution. Beginning in October 2008, includes the rest of the microfinance institutions. Data exclude credit unions which have small amounts of short-term liabilities.

Data are based on a standardized report form (SRF) for other depository corporations, which accords with the concepts and definitions of the *Monetary and Financial Statistics Manual (MFSM)*. For other depository corporations in Timor-Leste, departures from the *MFSM* methodology are explained below.

Financial assets and liabilities for which economic sectorization is unavailable are allocated to the economic sector having the largest volume of transactions in the category.

Liabilities to Nonresidents includes small positions with other depository corporations.

Liabilities to Central Government includes deposits of public nonfinancial corporations.

Transferable Deposits Included in Broad Money includes deposits of some microfinance institutions.

Other Items (Net) includes small positions with nonresidents.

Accrued interest not disaggregated by economic sector is allocated to the economic sector having the largest volume of transactions in the category.

Depository Corporations:

See notes on central bank and other depository corporations.

Monetary Aggregates:

Broad Money:

Broad Money (line 59m) calculated from the liability data in the sections for the central bank and other depository corporations accords with the concepts and definitions of the *MFSM* and is consistent with broad money *(line 59mea)* described below.

Money (National Definitions):

Narrow Money comprises coins in circulation and transferable deposits in national and foreign currency of the private sector (other nonfinancial corporations and other resident sectors) with other depository corporations.

Quasi Money comprises other deposits of the private sector (other nonfinancial corporations and other resident sectors) with other depository corporations.

Broad Money comprises narrow money and quasi-money.

Interest Rates:

Savings Rate:

Weighted average rate offered by other depository corporations on savings deposits in U.S. dollars. The rate is weighted by deposit amounts.

Deposit Rate:

Weighted average rate offered by other depository corporations on one-month time deposits in U.S. dollars. The rate is weighted by deposit amounts.

Lending Rate:

Weighted average rate charged by other depository corporations on loans in U.S. dollars. The rate corresponds to the fixed rate charged by other depository corporations plus six-month Libor rate. The rate is weighted by loan amounts. † Beginning in April 2008, corresponds to the fixed rate charged by other depository corporations plus three-month Libor rate. The rate

is weighted by loan amounts. † Beginning in January 2011, corresponds to the fixed rate charged by other depository corporations plus six-month Libor rate. The rate is weighted by loan amounts.

Prices:

Consumer Prices:

Source: National Statistics Department. Geographical Coverage: prices are collected at regular monthly intervals for all items in the Dili region. Prices are also collected at regular quarterly intervals for all items from a representative selection of other regions throughout Timor-Leste. The measure for each item outside the Dili region is then estimated using the corresponding Dili region item price movement; Number of Items in Basket: 30 sub-groups or categories of like items; Basis for Calculation: Weights are based on the Household Income and Expenditure Survey (HIES) of 2010. The base year is 2001.

National Accounts:

Source: National Statistics Department. Data are prepared in accordance with the 2008 United Nations *System of National Accounts*.

Togo   742

Date of Fund Membership:
August 1, 1962

Standard Source:

Banque Centrale des Etats de l'Afrique de l'Ouest (Central Bank of West African States)

Togo is a member of the West African Economic and Monetary Union, together with Benin, Burkina Faso, Côte d'Ivoire, Guinea-Bissau, Mali, Niger, and Senegal. The Union, which was established in 1962, has a common central bank, the Central Bank of West African States (BCEAO), with headquarters in Dakar, and national branches in the member states. Mali and Guinea-Bissau joined the Union on June 1, 1984 and May 2, 1997, respectively.

Direction Générale de la Statistique et de la Comptabilité Nationale (DGSCN)

Exchange Rates:

Official Rate: (End of Period and Period Average):

Prior to January 1999, the official rate was pegged to the French franc. On January 12, 1994, the CFA franc was devalued to CFAF 100 per French franc from CFAF 50 at which it had been fixed since 1948. From January 1, 1999, the CFAF is pegged to the euro at a rate of CFA franc 655.957 per euro.

International Liquidity:

Gold is revalued on a quarterly basis at the rate communicated by the BCEAO, which corresponds to the lowest average fixing in the London market.

Monetary Authorities:

Comprises the national branch of the BCEAO only. The amount of currency outside banks is estimated by subtracting from the amount of CFA franc notes issued by Togo the estimated amounts of Togo's currency in the cash held by the banks of all member countries of the Union.

Deposit Money Banks:

Comprises commercial banks and development banks, and includes certain banking operations of the Treasury and the Post Office. The Treasury accepts customs duty bills (reported separately in *line 22d.i*). Through its many branches, the Postal Checking System acts as the main depository for the private sector in the interior of Togo. *Claims on the Private Sector (line 22d)* include doubtful and litigious debts. † Beginning in 1979, *Central Government Deposits (line 26d)* include the deposits of the public establishments of an administrative or social nature (EPAS) and exclude those of the savings bank; *Demand and Time Deposits (lines 24 and 25)* include deposits of the savings bank and exclude deposits of EPAS; and *Claims on Private Sector (line 22d)* exclude claims on other financial institutions.

Monetary Survey:

The data reported agree with Central Bank of West African States aggregates, as given in the table on the position of the monetary institutions. Valuation differences exist as a result of the *IFS* calculations of reserve position in the Fund and the SDR holdings, both components of *line 11,* based on Fund record. † Beginning in 1979, *Claims on Other Financial Institutions (line 32f)* includes claims of deposit money banks on other financial institutions; see deposit money bank notes for explanation of other break symbols.

Interest Rates:

Discount Rate (End of Period):
Basic discount rate offered by the BCEAO.

Repurchase Agreement Rate (End of Period):
Rate on repurchase agreements between the BCEAO and the banks.

Money Market Rate:
Rate paid on overnight interbank advances.

Deposit Rate:
Rate offered by banks on time deposits of CFAF 500,000–2,000,000 for under six months.

Prices and Labor:

Consumer Prices:
Source: Direction Générale de la Statistique et de la Comptabilité Nationale. Weights Reference Period: 2008; Geographical Coverage: Lomé metro area; Number of Items in Basket: 648; Basis for Calculation: The weights are derived from a household survey conducted from March 2008 to February 2009. The consumer price index follows the harmonized methodology proposed by the WAEMU.

International Transactions:

All trade data are from the Central Bank of West African States.

Government Finance:

The data are provided by the Central Bank of West African States and cover the consolidated central government. The fiscal year ends December 31.

National Accounts:

Source: Direction Générale de la Statistique et de la Comptabilité Nationale. Data are prepared in accordance with the 1968 United Nations System of National Accounts.

Tonga   866

Date of Fund Membership:
September 13, 1985

Standard Sources:
National Reserve Bank of Tonga
Statistics Department, Ministry of Finance

Exchange Rates:

Official Rate: (End of Period and Period Average):
The pa'anga was pegged at par to the Australian dollar from November 1976 through February 8, 1991. Beginning February 11, 1991, the value of the pa'anga was determined daily by reference to a weighted basket of currencies of Tonga's most important partners in trade and payments transactions. Beginning in November 1999, the official rate is the central bank midpoint rate.

International Liquidity:

Data for *Foreign Exchange (line 1d.d)* include small foreign exchange holdings by central government.

Central Bank:

Consists of the National Reserve Bank of Tonga (NRBT) only.
Data are based on a standardized report form (SRF) for central banks, which accords with the concepts and definitions of the IMF's *Monetary and Financial Statistics Manual (MFSM)*, 2000. Departures from the *MFSM* methodology are explained below.
Accrued interest not disaggregated by economic sector is allocated to the economic sector having the largest volume of transactions in the category.
Securities other than shares are valued at acquisition cost rather than at current market price or fair value.

Other Depository Corporations:

Comprises commercial banks and Tonga Development Bank.
Data are based on a standardized report form (SRF) for other depository corporations, which accords with the concepts and definitions of the *Monetary and Financial Statistics Manual (MFSM)*. For other depository corporations in Tonga, departures from the *MFSM* methodology are explained below.
Financial assets and liabilities for which economic sectorization is unavailable are allocated to the economic sector having the largest volume of transactions in the category.
Accrued interest is included in *Other Items (Net)* rather than in the outstanding amounts of the financial assets and liabilities.
Securities other than shares and shares and other equity are valued at acquisition cost rather than at current market price or fair value.

Depository Corporations:

See notes on central bank and other depository corporations.

Monetary Aggregates:

Broad Money:

Broad Money calculated from the liability data in the sections for the central bank and other depository corporations accords with the concepts and definitions of the *MFSM* and is consistent with M2 described below.

Money (National Definitions):

Reserve Money comprises currency in circulation and deposits of other depository corporations with the NRBT.

M1 comprises currency outside depository corporations and demand deposits of the private sector in national currency with other depository corporations.

Quasi-Money comprises time, savings, and foreign currency deposits of the private sector with other depository corporations.

M2 comprises M1 and quasi-money.

Interest Rates:

Deposit Rate:

Rate offered by commercial banks on six-month time deposits.

Lending Rate:

Maximum rate charged by the Bank of Tonga on loans. † Beginning in September 1993, average rate, which is the total interest received and accrued on all performing loans and overdrafts, charged by the Bank of Tonga as of the last business day of the quarter, divided by the average size of the portfolio during the quarter. † Beginning in July 1994, weighted average rate charged by commercial banks on loans. The rate is weighted by loan amounts.

Prices and Labor:

Consumer Prices:

Source: National Statistics Office. Weights Reference Period: October 2010; Geographical Coverage: Tongapatu division (main island of Tonga); Number of Items in Basket: 222; Basis for Calculation: the weights are derived from the Household Income and Expenditure Survey (HIES) 2009.

International Transactions:

All trade data are from the Statistics Department, Ministry of Finance.

National Accounts:

Data are as reported by the national authorities and are compiled on a fiscal year basis. The concepts and definitions used are broadly consistent with SNA93.

Trinidad and Tobago   369

Date of Fund Membership:

September 16, 1963

Standard Sources:

Central Bank of Trinidad and Tobago
Central Statistical Office

Exchange Rates:

Market Rate (End of Period and Period Average):

Effective April 13, 1993, the exchange rate of the TT dollar is market-determined. Prior to that date, the rates were based on a fixed relationship to the U.S. dollar.

International Liquidity:

Line 1d.d includes a share in small holdings of foreign exchange by the British Caribbean Currency Board.

Gold (National Valuation) (line 1and) is obtained by converting the value in national currency terms, as reported in the country's standard sources, using the prevailing exchange rate, as given in *line* **ae** or **we.**

External accounts of other financial institutions exclude nonbank financial institutions, namely, life insurance companies.

Monetary Authorities:

Consolidates the Central Bank of Trinidad and Tobago (CBTT) and monetary authority functions undertaken by the central government. † Beginning in December 1996, data are based on an improved sectorization of the accounts.

Deposit Money Banks:

Comprises commercial banks. † See note on monetary authorities.

Monetary Survey:

† See note on monetary authorities.

Other Banking Institutions:

Comprises post office savings deposits. † Beginning in December 1970, comprised other banklike institutions and development banks. Other banklike institutions comprise finance houses, merchant banks, trust and mortgage finance companies, and thrift institutions. † See note on monetary authorities.

Banking Survey:

† See note on monetary authorities.

Money (National Definitions):

Base Money comprises currency in circulation and commercial banks' deposits with the CBTT. Currency in circulation refers to notes and coins issued by the CBTT less the amount held by commercial banks and in the vaults of the CBTT.

M1A comprises currency in circulation, cashiers' cheques, and demand deposits in national currency of other financial corporations, state and local governments, public nonfinancial corporations, and private sector with commercial banks less cash items in the process of collection from other banks and net interbranch clearings. Currency in circulation refers to notes and coins issued by the CBTT less the amount held by commercial banks and in the vaults of the CBTT.

M1C comprises M1A and savings deposits in national currency of other financial corporations, state and local governments, public nonfinancial corporations, and private sector with commercial banks.

M2 comprises M1C and time deposits in national currency of other financial corporations, state and local governments, public nonfinancial corporations, and private sector with commercial banks.

M2* comprises M2 and foreign currency deposits of other financial corporations, state and local governments, public nonfinancial corporations, and private sector with commercial banks.
M3 comprises M2 and time and savings deposits in national currency of other financial corporations, state and local governments, public nonfinancial corporations, and private sector with other banking institutions.
M3* comprises M2*, time and savings deposits in national currency and foreign currency deposits of other financial corporations, state and local governments, public nonfinancial corporations, and private sector with other banking institutions.

Nonbank Financial Institutions:
Comprises insurance companies.

Interest Rates:

Discount Rate (End of Period):
Rate at which the Central Bank of Trinidad and Tobago lends to commercial banks.

Treasury Bill Rate:
Average tender rate for three-month bills. The Central Bank also sells treasury bills of the latest issue to commercial banks and to the public, normally at a slightly lower rate.

Savings Rate:
Median of ordinary savings deposits rates offered by commercial banks.

Deposit Rate:
Weighted average rate offered by commercial banks on 6-month time deposits in national currency. The rate is weighted by deposit amounts.

Deposit Rate (Foreign Currency):
Weighted average rate offered by commercial banks on 6-month time deposits and 6-month certificates of deposit in foreign currency. The rate is weighted by deposit amounts.

Lending Rate:
Median of basic prime rates charged by commercial banks on loans.

Prices and Production:

Share Prices (End of Month):
Composite price index covering commercial banking, conglomerates, manufacturing, property, trading, and nonbank finance shares quoted on the Trinidad and Tobago Stock Exchange, base January 1993. The index is computed every trading day by the Trinidad and Tobago Stock Exchange Limited based on share closing prices and outstanding listed share capital.

Producer Prices:
Source: Central Bank. Weights Reference Period: October 1978.

Consumer Prices:
Source: Central Bank. Weights Reference Period: January 2003; Basis for Calculation: Weights are based on the Household Budget Survey of 1997/1998.

Industrial Production:
Source: Central Bank. Weights Reference Period: 1995.

International Transactions:

Exports and Imports:
All trade value data are from the Central Bank as compiled by the Central Statistical Office, and include merchandise under Processing Agreement.

Government Finance:
Beginning 2003 annual and quarterly data are derived from preliminary fiscal statistics disseminated by the Central Bank (*Economic Bulletin*). The fiscal year ends September 30.

National Accounts:
Source: Central Bank.

Tunisia   744

Date of Fund Membership:
April 14, 1958

Standard Sources:
Central Bank
National Institute of Statistics

Exchange Rates:

Market Rate (End of Period and Period Average):
Central bank midpoint rate.

International Liquidity:
Gold (National Valuation) (line 1and) is obtained by converting the value in national currency terms, as reported in the country's standard sources, using the prevailing exchange rate, as given in *line* **de**, *line* **ae**, or *line* **we**.
Lines 7a.d and *7b.d* are derived from the accounts of commercial banks and exclude the foreign accounts of offshore banks operating in Tunisia.

Monetary Authorities:
Beginning in January 1998, items previously classified as *Claims on Deposit Money Banks (line 12e)* have been reclassified as *Claims on Private Sector (line 12d)*.

Deposit Money Banks:
Comprises commercial banks.

Monetary Survey:
Line 37r and *line 32d*: See note to section 10.

Other Banking Institutions:
Comprises the Economic Development Bank of Tunisia (BDET), previously known as the National Investment Corporation, the General Investment Bank (BGI), the Financial and Tourism Company (COFIT), the Tunisian National Savings Bank (CENT), the National Housing Savings Bank (CNEL), and the portfolio management companies (GEP, SIMPARI, SOFIGES, UF, and UTP). Data agree with those from the Central Bank.

Banking Survey:
Line 52d and *line 57r*: See note to section 10.

Interest Rates:

Discount Rate (End of Period):
Central Bank. The rate mainly applies to the rediscount of short-term commercial paper. Another rate exists that applies to the rediscount of financial paper and advances to banks in the form of guaranteed overdrafts. In November 1996 the Central Bank abolished its rediscount facility for preferential credit to certain sectors.

Money Market Rate:
Upper margin of interest on overnight interbank deposits.

Prices, Production, Labor:

Producer Prices:
Source: Central Bank. Weights Reference Period: 1990; Coverage: all industrial goods manufactured and sold on the local market; Number of Items in Basket: 347 products in ten industries; Basis for Calculation: weights are based on the value of the 1990 sales.

Consumer Prices:
Source: Central Bank. Weights Reference Period: 2000; Geographical Coverage: 18 communes representing the capital cities of governorates and communes having more than 50,000 inhabitants in 1994; Number of Items in Basket: 952; Basis for Calculation: weights are obtained from the 2000 Survey of Household Budgets and Consumption.

Industrial Production:
Source: National Institute of Statistics. Weights Reference Period: 1990; Sectoral Coverage: manufacturing, mining, and energy sectors, excluding construction and public works; Basis for Calculation: the weights for the index are derived on the basis of the value added to factor costs, by sector.

Mining Production:
Source: Central Bank. Weights Reference Period: 1990; no data were reported for 1984–1986.

Crude Petroleum Production:
The index is calculated from the Central Bank data in metric tons.

International Transactions:

All trade data are from the Central Bank.

Trade indices:
Data are compiled on weights reference period: 1990.

Government Finance:

Annual data are as reported for the *Government Finance Statistics Yearbook (GFSY)* and cover budgetary central government. The fiscal year ends December 31.

National Accounts:

Source: Central Bank.

Turkey   186

Date of Fund Membership:
March 11, 1947

Standard Sources:
Central Bank of the Republic of Turkey
State Institute of Statistics

Exchange Rates:
On January 1, 2005, the New Turkish Lira (TRY), equal to 1,000,000 Turkish lira, was introduced. On January 1, 2009, the New Turkish Lira (TRY) was redefined as Turkish Lira (TRY), equal to 1 New Turkish Lira.

Market Rate (End of Period and Period Average):
Official midpoint rate.

International Liquidity:
Gold (National Valuation) is equal to *Gold in Million Fine Troy Ounces* valued at US$369.1 per ounce between 1988–97 and US$300 per ounce in 1998. Beginning in 1999, *Gold (National Valuation)* item is valued according to national practice, in U.S. dollars. Beginning in August 2010, it is valued according to current market prices.

Central Bank:
Comprises the Central Bank of the Republic of Turkey (CBRT), inclusive of transactions with the IMF undertaken by the Government of the Republic of Turkey. Contra-entries to the Government's transactions with the IMF are made to *Other Items Net,* in line with the IMF's *Monetary and Financial Statistics Manual (MFSM), 2000.*
† Beginning in December 2002, data are based on a standardized report form (SRF) for central banks, which accords with the concepts and definitions of the *MFSM.*
For December 2001 through November 2002, data have less conformity with the *MFSM* methodology and therefore are not strictly comparable to data for later periods. Departures from the *MFSM* methodology are explained below.
Prior to November 2005, accrued interest was included in *Other Items (Net)* rather than in the outstanding amounts of the financial assets and liabilities and provisions for losses were included in *Shares and Other Equity* rather than in *Other Items (Net).*
Prior to November 2005, held-to-maturity securities were valued at acquisition cost rather than at market price or fair value.

Other Depository Corporations:
Comprises commercial banks and investment and development banks. Beginning in December 2005, includes money market funds (B-Type Liquid Funds).† Beginning in December 2002, data are based on an improved sectoral and instrument classification of accounts. † Beginning in December 2005, includes participation banks (formerly special finance houses) and B type money market funds. † Beginning in December 2002, data are based on a standardized report form (SRF) for other depository corporations, which accords with the concepts and definitions of the IMF's *Monetary and Financial Statistics Manual (MFSM).*

Depository Corporations:
See notes on central bank and other depository corporations.

Monetary Aggregates:
Broad Money:
Broad Money calculated from the liability data in the sections of the central bank and other depository corporations accords with the concepts and definitions of the *MFSM.* Broad money includes currency issued by the central government. Broad money differs from M3 described below as broad money includes small holdings of coins by the central bank and M3 excludes accrued interest on deposits and securities. Prior to December 2005, *Broad Money* differs from the national definition of M3YR which excluded accrued interest on deposits and securities and was discontinued.

Money (National Definitions):
Reserve money comprises currency in circulation, required and free reserves in national currency of commercial banks with the CBRT, and demand deposits of other financial corporations, state and local governments, public nonfinancial corporations, private sector, and social security institutions in national currency with

the CBRT. Currency in circulation refers to notes and coins issued by the CBRT and the Treasury. Beginning in August 2004, data are adjusted for inflation. Beginning in December 2005, includes required and free reserves of all other depository corporations.

M1 comprises currency in circulation and transferable deposits in national currency of other financial corporations, state and local governments, public nonfinancial corporations, and private sector in national currency with the CBRT and commercial banks. Currency in circulation refers to notes and coins issued by the CBRT and Treasury and cash in transit in national and foreign currency less the amount of notes and coins held by commercial banks. Beginning October 1999, excludes cash in transit. † Beginning December 2005, comprises currency in circulation and transferable deposits in national and foreign currency of other financial corporations, state and local governments, public nonfinancial corporations, private sector, and social security institutions in national currency with the CBRT and other depository corporations.

M2 comprises M1 and other deposits in national currency of other financial corporations, state and local governments, public nonfinancial corporations, and private sector with commercial banks. † Beginning December 2005, comprises M1 and other deposits in national and foreign currency with other depository corporations.

M3 comprises M2, deposits of government agencies and social security institutions in national currency with commercial banks, and time and savings deposits in national currency of nonbank financial institutions, central government, state and local governments, nonfinancial public enterprises, and private sector with the CBRT. † Beginning in December 2005, comprises M2, funds received from repurchase transactions by banking institutions and the CBRT with nonbank financial institutions, state and local governments, nonfinancial public enterprises, and private sector in national and foreign currency and deposits with money market funds (B-Type Liquid Funds). † Beginning in December 2010, includes securities other than shares issued by other depository corporations held by the private sector.

Interest Rates:

Central Bank Policy Rate (End of Period):
Interbank rate at which funds can be lent and borrowed for one day (overnight). The CBRT uses this base rate for monetary policy purposes. The level of the overnight rate has a direct effect on the level of interest rates for products such as savings, loans, and mortgages.

Discount Rate (End of Period):
Rate at which the central bank lends to eligible banks and state economic enterprises.

Treasury Bill Rate:
Weighted average auction rate on three-month Treasury bills.

Deposit Rate:
Rate on three-month time deposits denominated in national currency.

Prices and Production:

Share Prices:
Capitalization weighted index composed of National Market companies except investment trusts traded on the Instanbul Stock Exchange, base January 1986.

Wholesale Prices:
Source: State Institute of Statistics. Weights Reference Period: Weights are updated every year; Sectoral Coverage: agricultural, manufacturing, mining, and energy sectors nationwide; Number of Items in Basket: 770; Geographc Coverage: entire country; Basis for Calculation: weights used for the index are based on the industrial production data and agricultural and mining and energy censuses of 2005.

Consumer Prices:
Source: State Institute of Statistics. Weights Reference Period: Weights are updated every year; Geographical Coverage: the whole country; Number of Items in Basket: 446; Basis for Calculation: weights are derived from the continuous Household Budget Survey.

Industrial Production:
Source: State Institute of Statistics. Weights Reference Period: 2005; Sectoral Coverage: mining, manufacturing, electricity, gas, steam and air conditioning supply; Number of Items in Basket: 1383; Basis for Calculation: Weights are derived from Annual Business Survey for the production industries.

International Transactions:

Trade value and indices data in U.S. dollars are from the State Institute of Statistics.

The volume indices are of the Laspeyres type with 2003 weights, and the unit value indices use the Fisher formula.

Government Finance:

Data are as reported by the Ministry of Finance and cover the operations of the central government. The fiscal year ends December 31.

National Accounts:

Source: State Institute of Statistics. As indicated by the country, beginning in 1998, data are compiled in accordance with the methodology of the *1995 ESA*. Beginning in 1990, data are sourced from the Eurostat database. Chain linked GDP volume measures are expressed according to 1998 prices.

Uganda   746

Date of Fund Membership:
September 27, 1963

Standard Sources:
Bank of Uganda
Uganda Bureau of Statistics

Exchange Rates:

Principal Rate (End of Period and Period Average):
Central bank midpoint rate determined on the basis of a trade-weighted basket of currencies.

International Liquidity:

Foreign Exchange (line 1d.d) reflects the U.S. dollar value of foreign currency holdings, as reported by the Foreign Exchange Operations Department of the Bank of Uganda. † Prior to October 1984, data for *line 1d.d* are obtained by converting the shilling value of the Bank of Uganda's foreign exchange holdings, as maintained by the Accounts Department of the Bank of Uganda, using the prevailing exchange rate given in *line* **ae**.

Central Bank:

Consists of the Bank of Uganda (BoU) only.

Data are based on a standardized report form (SRF) for central banks, which accords with the concepts and definitions of the IMF's *Monetary and Financial Statistics Manual (MFSM)*, 2000.

Other Depository Corporations:

Comprises commercial banks. Data exclude savings and credit cooperative societies, credit institutions, and microfinance deposit institutions, which accept deposits.

Data are based on a standardized report form (SRF) for other depository corporations, which accords with the concepts and definitions of the *Monetary and Financial Statistics Manual (MFSM)*. Data in the SRF format are compiled from pre-SRF data which are not fully based on the *MFSM* methodology. For other depository corporations in Uganda, departures from the *MFSM* methodology are explained below.

Financial assets and liabilities for which economic sectorization is unavailable are allocated to the economic sector having the largest volume of transactions in the category. *Claims on Public Nonfinancial Corporations, Transferable Deposits Included in Broad Money*, and *Other Deposits Included in Broad Money* include some positions with the central government and local governments.

Financial assets and liabilities for which financial instrument breakdown is unavailable are allocated to the financial instrument having the largest volume of transactions in the category.

Accrued interest is included in *Other Items (Net)* rather than the outstanding amounts of the financial assets and liabilities.

Securities other than shares and shares and other equity are valued at acquisition cost rather than at current market price or fair value.

Depository Corporations:

See notes on central bank and other depository corporations.

Monetary Aggregates:

Broad Money:

Broad Money calculated from the liability data in the sectors of the central bank and commercial banks accords with the concepts and definitions of the *MFSM* and is consistent with M3 described below.

Money (National Definitions):

Base Money comprises of currency in circulation and commercial banks' deposits with the BoU.

M1 comprises currency in circulation outside the central bank and commercial banks and demand deposits in national currency of other financial corporations, local governments, public nonfinancial corporations, and private sector with depository corporations.

M2 comprises M1 and time and savings deposits in national currency of other financial corporations, local governments, public nonfinancial corporations, and private sector with depository corporations.

M2A comprises M2 and certificates of deposit in national currency of other financial corporations, local governments, public nonfinancial corporations, and private sector with depository corporations.

M3 comprises M2 and foreign currency deposits of other financial corporations, local governments, public nonfinancial corporations, and private sector with depository corporations.

Interest Rates:

Discount Rate (End of Period):

Rate charged by the BoU on loans to commercial banks, determined as a rate of interest not being less than one percent above the BoU's standard rediscount rate.

Treasury Bill Rate:

Rate on the 91-day treasury bills.

Savings Rate:

Weighted average rate offered by commercial banks on savings deposits. The rate is weighted by deposit amounts.

Deposit Rate:

Weighted average rate offered by commercial banks on three-month term deposits. The rate is weighted by deposit amounts.

Lending Rate:

Weighted average rate charged by commercial banks on loans. The rate is weighted by loan amounts.

Prices:

Producer Prices:

Source: Uganda Bureau of Statistics. Weights Reference Period: 2001; Sectoral Coverage: manufacturing sector, excluding utilities, mining, agriculture, etc.; Basis of Calculation: based on Gross Output derived from the 2000/01 Uganda Business Inquiry.

Consumer Prices:

Source: Uganda Bureau of Statistics. Weight Reference Period: July 2005-June 2006; Geographical Coverage: Kampala, Jinja, Mbale, Masaka, Mbarara, Gulu, and Arua; Number of Items in the Basket: 276 items; Basis of Calculation: based on the 2005/2006 Uganda National Household Survey (UNHS).

International Transactions:

Data are based on customs records from the Customs department of the Uganda Revenue Authority (URA), and are compiled by the Uganda Bureau of Statistics (UBOS), and the Bank of Uganda (BOU).

Imports, c.i.f.:

Data are for cash imports, imports without foreign exchange required, barter, and project imports valued at the official exchange rate.

Government Finance:

Data are reported by the Bank of Uganda and cover budgetary central government. † Prior to 2002, to the extent possible, existing subannual *IFS* data were converted to the main aggregates that are presented in the *GFSM 2001* Statement of Sources and Uses of Cash (see the Introduction of the monthly *IFS* publication for details). The fiscal year ends June 30.

National Accounts:

Source: Uganda Bureau of Statistics. Data are prepared in accordance with the 1968 United Nations System of National Accounts.

Ukraine 926

Date of Fund Membership:
September 3, 1992

Standard Sources:
National Bank of Ukraine
Ministry of Statistics of Ukraine

Exchange Rates:
On September 2, 1996, the Ukrainian hryvnia, equal to 100,000 karbovanets, was introduced.

Official Rate: (End of Period and Period Average):
The official rate is determined by the National Bank of Ukraine (NBU) and is set equal to the rate established at the Ukrainian interbank exchange market one day before the last business day of the period. Effective January 1, 2002, the exchange arrangement of Ukraine has been reclassified to the category conventional pegged arrangement.

International Liquidity:
Data for *Foreign Exchange (line 1d.d)* comprise NBU's convertible currency and other liquid claims on nonresidents denominated in convertible currencies.

Central Bank:
Consists of the National Bank of Ukraine (NBU) only.
† Beginning in December 2002, data are based on a standardized report form (SRF) for central banks, which accords with the concepts and definitions of the IMF's *Monetary and Financial Statistics Manual (MFSM)*, 2000.
For December 2001 through November 2002, data in the SRF format are compiled from pre-SRF data not fully based on the *MFSM* methodology. Departures from the *MFSM* methodology are explained below.
Shares and Other Equity includes provisions for loan losses.
Financial derivatives are not separately identified.
Holdings of government securities are valued at acquisition cost rather than at market price or fair value.

Other Depository Corporations:
Comprises state, joint-stock, and private commercial banks and the Savings Bank. Data exclude credit unions.
† Beginning in December 2002, data are based on a standardized report form (SRF) for other depository corporations, which accords with the concepts and definitions of the *Monetary and Financial Statistics Manual (MFSM)*.
For December 2001 through November 2002, data in the SRF format are compiled from pre-SRF data not fully based on the *MFSM* methodology. Departures from the *MFSM* methodology are explained below.
Accounts of depository corporations in liquidation are not included.
Shares and Other Equity includes provisions for loan losses.
Financial derivatives are not separately identified.
Holdings of government securities are valued at acquisition cost rather than at current market price or fair value.

Depository Corporations:
† See notes on central bank and other depository corporations.

Other Financial Corporations:
Comprises insurance corporations and pension funds. Beginning in December 2011, includes investment funds. Data exclude credit unions, other credit organizations, financial companies, pawnshops, and financial auxiliaries.
Data are based on a standardized report form (SRF) for other financial corporations, which accords with the concepts and definitions of the *Monetary and Financial Statistics Manual (MFSM)*. For other financial corporations in Ukraine, departures from the *MFSM* methodology are explained below.
Data for other financial corporations are available only on a quarterly basis.
Financial assets and liabilities for which financial instrument breakdown is unavailable are allocated to the financial instrument having the largest volume of transactions in the category.
Financial assets and liabilities for which economic sectorization is unavailable are allocated to the economic sector having the largest volume of transactions in the category.
Liability positions in financial derivatives of investment funds are included in *Other Items (Net)* rather than as liabilities to the corresponding economic sectors.
Other accounts receivable and payable of investment funds are included in *Other Items (Net)* rather than as claims on and liabilities to the corresponding economic sectors.
For December 2008 through December 2011, holdings of foreign currency are included in *Claims on Depository Corporations* rather than as *Claims on Nonresidents*.

Financial Corporations:
See notes on central bank, other depository corporations, and other financial corporations.

Monetary Aggregates:

Broad Money:
Broad Money calculated from the liability data in the sections for the central bank and other depository corporations accords with the concepts and definitions of the *MFSM* and is consistent with M3 described below.

Money (National Definitions):
Reserve Money comprises notes and coins issued by the NBU and demand deposits of other depository corporations and the private sector at the NBU in national currency.
M0 comprises notes and coins issued by the NBU, excluding holdings of the NBU and other depository corporations.
M1 comprises M0 and transferable deposits in national currency. Transferable deposits comprise liabilities of depository corporations on demand deposits (current account deposits and settlement accounts) in national currency of other financial corporations, nonfinancial corporations, households and nonprofit institutions serving households.
M2 comprises M1, transferable deposits in foreign currency, and other deposits in both national and foreign currency with the NBU and other depository corporations. Other deposits comprise liabilities of depository corporations on other demand deposits (target deposits, deposits on clearing accounts, deposits on accounts of VAT taxpayers), time deposits and deposits on registered saving certificates which belong to other financial corporations, nonfinancial corporations, households and nonprofit institutions serving households.
M3 comprises M2 and securities other than shares in both na-

tional and foreign currency. Securities other than shares included in M3 comprise liabilities of deposit corporations on time debt securities and bearer saving (deposit) certificates, obtained by other financial corporations, nonfinancial corporations, households and nonprofit institutions serving households.

Interest Rates:

Refinancing Rate (End of Period):
Basic rate at which the NBU extends refinancing loans to banks for a specified period.

Money Market Rate:
Weighted average rate on loans in national currency at the interbank market. The rate is weighted by daily loan amounts.

Money Market Rate (Foreign Currency):
Weighted average rate on loans in foreign currency at the interbank market. The rate is weighted by daily loan amounts.

Deposit Rate:
Weighted average rate offered by commercial banks on deposits in national currency. The rate is weighted by deposit amounts.

Deposit Rate (Foreign currency):
Weighted average rate offered by commercial banks on deposits in foreign currency. The rate is weighted by deposit amounts.

Lending Rate:
Weighted average rate charged by commercial banks on loans in national currency. The rate is weighted by loan amounts.

Lending Rate (Foreign Currency):
Weighted average rate charged by commercial banks on loans in foreign currency. The rate is weighted by loan amounts.

Prices, Production, Labor:

Share Prices (End of Month):
Capital weighted share price index covering shares quoted on the First Securities Trading System (PFTS), base October 1, 1997. The list of share of companies included in the index calculation includes the most liquid shares and is revised monthly.

Producer Prices:
Source: Ministry of Statistics of Ukraine. Weights Reference Period: weights are updated annually; Sectoral Coverage: all industrial activities that are classified by sections B, C, D, of the KVED (NACE); Numbers of Items in Basket: over 3,000 enterprises; Basis for Calculation: sources of weights are data of the production (output) value in base year at different aggregation levels and are updated yearly.

Consumer Prices:
Source: Ministry of Statistics of Ukraine. Weights Reference Period: Weights are updated annually; Geographical Coverage: all regions of the country; Number of Items in Basket: 335; Basis for Calculation: Weights are derived from annual household living condition survey (HLCS) and are updated yearly.

Wages:
Source: Ministry of Statistics of Ukraine. Geographic Coverage: entire country; Data show the average level of nominal monthly wages and salaries for employees in state and non-state sectors (including cooperatives, small enterprises, and industrial workshops/sections of collective farms and other nonindustrial organizations) per employee; Data do not cover businesses with less than 10 employees.

Industrial Production:
Source: Ministry of Statistics of Ukraine. Weights Reference Period: 2007; Sectoral Coverage: mining, manufacturing, production and distribution of electricity; Basis for Calculation: weight structure are data on distribution of gross value added by the industrial type of activity from the relevant individual indices for each product.

Industrial Employment:
Source: Ministry of Statistics of Ukraine. The coverage is the same as for wages.

International Transactions:

Source: Ministry of Statistics of Ukraine. *Exports (line 70..d)* and *Imports (line 71..d),* Data are based on cargo customs declarations and statistical reports of enterprise on goods not subject to declaration and State Statistics Committee estimates that use information from the Ministry of Fuel and Energy (imports of oil) and the National Joint Stock Company Naftogaz of Ukraine (exports/imports of the natural gas).

Government Finance:

Annual data are as reported for the *Government Finance Statistics Yearbook (GFSY)* and cover budgetary central government. The fiscal year ends December 31.

National Accounts:

Source: Ministry of Statistics of Ukraine. As indicated by the country, data are compiled in accordance with the methodology of the *1995 ESA* and the *1993 SNA*. The GDP components by production method and by income are produced during 2001–2006. At present, the GDP expenditure approach components are compiled. Chain linked GDP volume measures are expressed according to 2007 prices.

United Arab Emirates   466

Date of Fund Membership:
September 22, 1972

Standard Sources:
Central Bank
Department of Planning, Abu Dhabi

Exchange Rates:

Official Rate: (End of Period and Period Average):
Central bank midpoint rate.

International Liquidity:

Gold (National Valuation) (line 1and) is obtained by converting the value in national currency terms, as reported in the country's standard sources, using the prevailing exchange rate, as given in *line* **ae** or **we.**

Lines 7a.d and *7b.d* are the U.S. dollar equivalents of *lines 21* and *26c,* respectively. They exclude the foreign accounts of the restricted license banks (RLBs), first authorized in 1976. RLBs are not permitted to accept local currency deposits from nonbank residents but otherwise operate as commercial banks. RLB foreign assets and foreign liabilities, as reported by the Central Bank, are given in *lines 7k.d* and *7m.d,* respectively. The difference between these two lines essentially reflects the domestic credit extended by RLBs.

Monetary Authorities:

Consolidates the United Arab Emirates Central Bank (UAECB) and monetary authority functions undertaken by the central government. The contra-entry to Treasury IMF accounts, which are paid by the Government of Abu Dhabi, is included in *line 16d*.

The gold component of *line 11* is valued at the market-related cost of acquisition.

Beginning January 1990, data are provisional. Data for October and November 2011 are pending the completion of software upgrades to the UAECB's computer system.

Deposit Money Banks:

Consolidates the accounts of the commercial banks operating in the seven United Arab Emirates. Data for October and November 2011 are pending the completion of software upgrades to the UAECB's computer system.

Production:

Crude Petroleum Production:
Central Bank data covering production of the Abu Dhabi, Dubai, and Sharjah Fields. Data for current periods are based on production quantities as reported in the *Oil Market Intelligence.*

International Transactions:

Imports, c.i.f.:
Central Bank data covering imports into Dubai, Abu Dhabi, and Sharjah. Inter-emirate trade and transit trade are excluded, as are imports of gold and silver.

Government Finance:

Annual data are as reported for the *Government Finance Statistics Yearbook (GFSY)* and cover budgetary central government. The fiscal year ends December 31.

National Accounts:

Source: Central Bank.

United Kingdom 112

Date of Fund Membership:
December 27, 1945

Standard Sources:
Bank of England
Office for National Statistics

Exchange Rates:

Market Rate (End of Period and Period Average):
Midpoint rate at noon in the London market.

International Liquidity:

International Reserves (minus Gold) (line 1l.d) excludes the foreign assets of the central bank (Bank of England). This institutional separation reflects the fact that the ownership and purpose of the central government and Bank of England pools of foreign assets are different. The Exchange Equalization Account (EEA) holds the central government's foreign currency assets, owned by Her Majesty's Treasury but managed by the Bank of England

acting as its agent. The EEA was established in 1932 to provide a fund that could be used for "checking undue fluctuations in the exchange value of sterling" (Section 24 of the Finance Act 1932). Any U.K. government intervention in the foreign exchange market would therefore be conducted through the EEA. The Bank of England manages its own holdings of foreign assets and gold which mainly arise from the Bank's routine banking business with its customers, from its operations in the U.K. money markets, and from U.K. participation in the euro payment system, TARGET. In accordance with the Chancellor of the Exchequer's letter of May 6, 1997 to the Governor of the Bank of England, the Bank may intervene in the foreign exchange market in support of its monetary policy objective. The Bank of England's holdings of foreign assets are, therefore, not considered by the U.K. authorities to be part of the U.K.'s international reserves. Data on the Bank of England's holdings of liquid foreign assets (including Gold) are shown for completeness under *Other Liquid Foreign Assets (line 1e.d).* Net TARGET related balances are included in *Other Liquid Foreign Assets (line 1e.d).*

From April 1979 to June 1999, international reserves were valued using parity exchange rates; non-dollar holdings were revalued each year at the average of their exchange rates against the U.S. dollar in the three months up to the end of March. This system was amended in April 1980 in that the U.S. dollar valuation on the last working day of March was used if that was lower than the three-month average. The only exception to this was Gold for which a discount was also applied. Hence, beginning in April 1980, gold was valued at the lower of either the average of the London fixing price for the three months up to the end of March, less 25 percent, or at 75 percent of its final fixing price on the last working day in March.

Banking Institutions: Foreign Assets (line 7a.d) includes banking institutions' claims on foreign central monetary institutions (CMIs) and other nonresidents in the form of loans and advances, overdrafts, commercial bills, sterling denominated acceptances, and from end–1985, bonds issued by nonresidents. *Foreign Liabilities (line 7b.d)* includes banking institutions' liabilities to foreign CMIs, and other nonresidents.

The data on external liabilities and claims are as reported by the Bank of England.

Monetary Authorities:

† Beginning in July 1999, consolidates the accounts of the Bank of England's Issue and Banking Departments, and central government functions relating to the issue of coin. Prior to July 1999, consolidates the accounts of the Bank of England's Issue Department, central government functions relating to the issue of coin, and the EEA.

Foreign Assets (line 11) comprises monetary authorities' claims on nonresidents and includes gross TARGET related claims on the European Central Bank (ECB) and other member countries of the TARGET payment system. Beginning with the data for end-November 2000, *Foreign Assets* are affected by a change from gross to net presentation of positions relating to the TARGET (Trans-European Automated Real-Time Gross Settlement Express Transfer) euro clearing system. (See *Recording of TARGET system positions* under *European Economic and Monetary Union (EMU)* in the introduction to *IFS.) Reserve Money (line 14)* comprises the monetary liabilities of the monetary authorities: Issue Department notes and Treasury coin in circulation, plus bankers' restricted and unrestricted deposits at the Bank of England. *Foreign Liabilities (line 16c)* comprises monetary authority liabilities to nonresidents, including gross TARGET related liabilities to the ECB and other members of the TARGET payment system. Beginning with the data for end-November 2000, *Foreign Liabilities* are affected by a change from gross to net presentation of positions relating to the TARGET euro clearing system. (See *Recording of TARGET system positions* under *European Economic and Monetary Union (EMU)* in the introduction to *IFS*.) *Other Items (Net) (line 17r)* includes Bank of England claims on U.K. banking institutions.

Banking Institutions:

† A new system of bank returns was introduced in 1975. As a result of this change, (1) money at call and money placed overnight are now reported in *line 24* rather than in *line 25* – a shift of approximately 700 million pounds sterling – and (2) line 21 is estimated to have increased by about 1,3000 million pounds sterling. † Beginning in 1981, they comprise the U.K. monetary sector as described in the December 1981 issue of the Bank of England's Monetary and Financial Statistics, subject to the same exclusions as the banking sector. † Prior to 1987, building societies are treated as part of the private sector. Beginning in 1987, Comprises U.K. banks authorized under the Banking Act of 1987 and, beginning in January 1987, building societies as defined by the Building Societies Act of 1986. † In September 1992, a new balance sheet report form was introduced for the building society sector in the U.K., resulting in a discontinuity for most of the building society data. † Prior to September 1997, the accounts of certain institutions in the Channel Islands and the Isle of Man were included as part of the U.K. banking institutions sector.

Banking Survey:

A break in series occurs in July 1999 as a result of the change in the definition of the monetary authorities' sector. A break in series occurs in January 1987 as a result of a change in the coverage of banking institutions. A break in series occurs in September 1992 as a result of new balance sheet report forms for the building society sector.

Money (National Definitions):

M0 comprises notes and coin in circulation outside the Bank of England, plus bankers' operational balances with the Bank of England. M4 comprises notes and coin in circulation outside the Bank of England and banking institutions in the U.K., plus nonbank private sector sterling deposits held with U.K. banking institutions. † Beginning July 2009, refers to M4 excluding intermediate OFCs (M4^{ex}). Additional detail is available on the Bank of England website (www.bankofengland.co.uk/mfsd/iadb/notesiadb/m4adjusted.htm). M4 differs from *Money plus Quasi-Money (line 35l)* because it excludes private sector foreign currency deposits, and sterling and foreign currency deposits of official entities (local authorities and public enterprises).

Interest Rates:

Central Bank Policy Rate (End of Period):
Refers to the official bank rate, also called the Bank of England base rate or BOEBR, which is the rate that the Bank of England charges banks on secured overnight loans. It is the British government's key interest rate for enacting monetary policy.

Money Market Rate:
Data refer to the interbank offer rate for overnight deposits.

Treasury Bill Rate:
Bank of England. This is the tender rate at which 91-day bills are allotted, calculated from Bank of England data given in terms of the amount of the discount. Monthly data are averages of Friday data.

Treasury Bill Rate (Bond Equivalent):
Monthly data refer to the simple arithmetic average of the daily market yields on a bond equivalent basis for 91-day bills; this rate is used in calculating the SDR interest rate.
The *Eurodollar Rate in London* relates to three-month deposits. It is the average of daily quotations of broker bid rates at noon in London. Beginning December 1979, the data relate to the average of bid and offer rates at or near the end of the month.

Deposit Rate:
Office for National Statistics (*Financial Statistics*). With effect from January 1984, monthly data are end-period observations of average rates, for the four main London clearing banks, on instant access savings accounts with a median balance currently of £10,000. Prior to that date, data refer to the rate on seven-day notice accounts of the London clearing banks.

Lending Rate:
Data refer to the minimum base rate of the London clearing banks as reported by Bank of England.

Government Bond Yield:
Bank of England. These are theoretical gross redemption bond yields. Beginning June 1976, the calculations are based on a method described by Bank of England, June 1976. *Short-Term:* Issue at par with five years to maturity. † Beginning January 1984, refers to the average daily secondary market yield on 10-year fixed-rate government bonds. This rate is used to measure long-term interest rates for assessing convergence among the European Union member states. *Long-Term:* Issue at par with 20 years to maturity.

Prices, Production, Labor:

Share Prices (Period Average and End of Month):
The FTSE All-Share Index, base April 10, 1962, is a market capitalization weighted index representing the performance of all eligible companies listed on the London Stock Exchange's main market. FTSE All-Share Index constituents are traded on the London Stock Exchange's SETS and SETSmm trading systems.

FTSE 100:
The FTSE 100 Index, base January 3, 1984, is a market capitalization weighted index representing the performance of the 100 largest UK-domiciled blue chip companies. The FTSE 100 Index constituents are traded on the London Stock Exchange's SETS trading system.

Producer Prices:
Source: Office for National Statistics. Weights Reference Period: every five years; Sectoral Coverage: manufacturing industry; Number of Items in Basket: Approximately 7,000 price quotes are obtained covering 980 products; Basis for Calculation: the

weights are derived from data on sales in the base year as provided by the PRODCOM inquiry, the manufacturing products inquiry required by Eurostat. The index is re-based and the weights are revised every five years.

Consumer Prices:
Source: Office for National Statistics. Weights Reference Period: December of previous year; Geographical Coverage: all of the UK (i.e. England, Scotland, Wales and Northern Ireland); Number of Items in Basket: containing over 650 consumer goods and services from around 150 areas throughout the country; Basis for Calculation: Weights are derived from the National Accounts' estimates of household final monetary consumption expenditure (HFMCE). All weights are updated each year, with the basket of goods and services also revised each year. The CPI officially starts in January 1996. Estimates, which are broadly consistent with the data from 1996, are also available back to 1988.

Wages:
Source: Office for National Statistics. Reference Period: 2000. Sectoral Coverage: all industries except armed forces; Geographic Coverage: entire country including Great Britain but excluding Northern Ireland; Data refer to average monthly earnings.

Industrial Production:
Data are sourced from the OECD database. Weights Reference Period: 2008; Sectoral Coverage: mining and quarrying, manufacturing and electricity, gas and water supply sectors; Basis for Calculation: the monthly survey known as the Monthly Production Inquiry (MPI) is the main source of information for calculating the indices.

Employment, Seasonally Adjusted:
Source: Office for National Statistics. Data are taken from the *Employment Gazette* and refer to, for the entire U.K. economy, employees in employment, which covers salaried employees in all industries and services. Domestic servants, the self-employed, and military personnel are excluded.

International Transactions:

Value data on total *Exports* and *Imports* are from the Department of Trade and Industry. *Imports f.o.b.* are from the Office for National Statistics. The figures are on a balance of payments basis and include various coverage adjustments to the customs returns, such as the value of ships purchased abroad.

Trade indices are from the Office for National Statistics. Prior to 1970, trade indices refer to total unadjusted series. From January 1970. Volumes Indices refer to seasonally adjusted series.

Government Finance:

Data on general government are derived from source V. Monthly and quarterly cash data, which are not on a consolidated basis, are derived from sources B and S. Above-the-line transactions are compiled by the Office of National Statistics (ONS), while financing data are compiled by the Bank of England using different sources. Annual cash data, from 1999, are as reported in the *Government Finance Statistics Yearbook (GFSY)*. For the United Kingdom, *GFSY* data cover consolidated central government. The fiscal year ends December 31.

National Accounts:

Source: Office for National Statistics. *Line 99b.c* is "GDP-Average." By construction, the sum of the expenditure-based components is not equal to the "GDP-Average," leading to an official statistical discrepancy. As indicated by the country, data have been revised following the implementation of improved compilation methods and the *1993 SNA*. Beginning in 1999, euro data are sourced from the Eurostat database. Eurostat introduced chain-linked GDP volume measures to both annual and quarterly data with the release of the third quarter 2005 on November 30, 2005. Chain linked GDP volume measures are expressed in the prices of 2009.

United States   111

Date of Fund Membership:
December 27, 1945

Standard Sources:
Board of Governors of the Federal Reserve System
U.S. Department of Commerce
U.S. Treasury Department

Exchange Rates:
Data relate to the par value through June 1974 and to the rate determined through a method known as the standard "basket" valuation thereafter.

International Liquidity:
Foreign Exchange (line 1d.d) includes holdings of Treasury and the Federal Reserve System. Beginning November 1978, these holdings are valued at current market exchange rates or, where appropriate, at such other rates as may be agreed upon by the parties to the transactions. Consistent with reporting guidelines, it excludes outstanding reciprocal currency swaps with the European Central Bank, the Swiss National Bank, the Bank of England, the Bank of Japan, the Reserve Bank of Australia, and the National Bank of Denmark.
Lines 7a.d and *.7b.d* are derived from the U.S. Treasury International Capital (TIC) reports. They differ from the commercial banks' *Foreign Assets (line 21)* and *Foreign Liabilities (line 26c)*, reported in section 20, mainly because they include the accounts of international banking facilities (IBFs). See notes on commercial banks in the section on other depository corporations. † Beginning in 1978, *Other Depository Corporations: Assets (line .7a.d)* and *Other Depository Corporations: Liabilities (line .7b.d)* reflect a broader coverage of international banking facilities (IBFs). Beginning in December 2001, data are based on a new reporting system for other depository corporations.

Central Bank:
Consists of the Federal Reserve Banks (FED) only.
Data are based on a standardized report form (SRF) for central banks, which accords with the concepts and definitions of the IMF's *Monetary and Financial Statistics Manual (MFSM)*, 2000. Data in the SRF format are compiled from pre-SRF data derived from the *Bulletin* which are not fully based on the *MFSM* methodology. Departures from the *MFSM* methodology are explained below.
Beginning in October 2008, data refer to the last Wednesday of the month.
Financial derivatives are excluded from the data. Beginning in De-

cember 2007, central bank liquidity swaps are included.

Shares and other equity includes funds contributed by owners and retained earnings.

For December 2001 through July 2003, *Currency in circulation* was estimated.

Liabilities to Other Sectors includes some accounts with nonresidents. Accounts receivable and payable are included in *Other Items (Net)* rather than in the FED's claims on or liabilities to the corresponding economic sectors.

Accrued interest is included in *Other items (Net)* rather than in the outstanding amounts of the financial assets and liabilities.

Securities other than shares issued by the US Government and Federal agencies are valued at acquisition cost rather than at current market price or fair value.

Exchange rate revaluation account, which reflects the daily revaluation at mid-day market exchange rates of foreign currency denominated position, is included in *Other items (Net)* rather than in *Shares and Other Equity*.

Other Depository Corporations:

Comprises commercial banks, savings institutions, credit unions, and money market mutual funds. Commercial banks include U.S.-chartered commercial banks, foreign banking offices in the U.S., bank holding companies, and banks on U.S.-affiliated areas and exclude international banking facilities. Savings institutions include savings and loan associations, mutual savings banks, federal savings banks, and Massachusetts cooperative banks. Beginning in March 2009, excludes bank holding companies, which were reclassified as other financial corporations.

Data are based on a standardized report form (SRF) for other depository corporations, which accords with the concepts and definitions of the *Monetary and Financial Statistics Manual* (*MFSM*). Data in the SRF format are compiled from the data contained in the *Flow of Funds* (*FOF*) which are not fully based on the *MFSM* methodology. For other depository corporations in the United States, departures from the *MFSM* methodology are explained below.

Data are available only on a quarterly basis.

Financial derivatives and accounts payable/receivable are excluded from the data.

Financial assets and liabilities for which economic sectorization is unavailable are allocated to the economic sector based on an estimate. The estimate is calculated using *FOF* data as follows: the volume of a financial instrument recorded in the balance sheet of the other depository corporations multiplied by the percentage share of economic sectors recorded in balance sheet of the financial instruments.

Claim on Central Government includes a small portion of claims on public nonfinancial corporations.

Claims on State and Local Government includes a significant portion of claims on public nonfinancial corporations.

Shares and other equity comprises funds contributed by owners only.

The reported discrepancy between the total volume of assets and liabilities is included in *Other items (Net)*.

Securities other than shares are valued at acquisition cost rather than at current market price or fair value.

Depository Corporations:

See notes on central bank and other depository corporations.

Other Financial Corporations:

Comprises property-casualty insurance companies, life insurance companies, private pension funds, state and local government employee retirement funds, federal government retirement funds, mutual funds, closed-end and exchange-traded funds, government-sponsored enterprises (GSE), agency-and GSE-backed mortgage pools, issuers of asset-backed securities, finance companies, mortgage companies, real estate investment trust, security brokers and dealers, and funding corporations. Beginning in March 2009, includes holding companies.

Data are based on a standardized report form (SRF) for other financial corporations, which accords with the concepts and definitions of the *Monetary and Financial Statistics Manual* (*MFSM*). Data in the SRF format are compiled from data contained in the *FOF* which are not fully based on the *MFSM* methodology. For other financial corporations in United States, departures from the *MFSM* methodology are explained below.

Data are available only on a quarterly basis.

Financial derivatives are excluded from the data.

Financial assets and liabilities for which economic sectorization is unavailable are allocated to the economic sector based on an estimate. The estimate is calculated using the *FOF* data as follows: the volume of a financial instrument recorded in the balance sheet of the other financial corporations multiplied by the percentage share of economic sectors recorded in balance sheet of the financial instruments.

Claim on Central Government includes a small portion of claims on public nonfinancial corporations.

Claims on State and Local Government includes a significant portion of claims on public nonfinancial corporations.

Shares and other equity comprises funds contributed by owners only.

The reported discrepancy between the total volume of assets and liabilities is included in *Other items (Net)*.

Securities other than shares are recorded at acquisition cost rather than at current market price or fair value.

Financial Corporations:

See notes on central bank, other depository corporations, and other financial corporations.

Monetary Aggregates:

Broad Money:

Broad Money includes estimates of currency issued by the central government. Broad money calculated from the liability data in the sections for the central bank and other depository corporations differs from M2 described below as broad money excludes traveler's checks of nonbank issuers and does not exclude cash items in the process of collection, Federal Reserve float, and individual retirement account (IRA) and Keogh balances at other depository corporations. In addition, deposits included in broad money may be overstated due to the estimates to allocate these deposits to money holding sectors described in the note on the other depository corporations.

Money (National Definitions):

Monetary Base comprises (1) total reserves, (2) required clearing balances and adjustments to compensate for float at Federal Reserve Banks, (3) the currency component of the money stock, and (4) for all quarterly reporters on the "Report of Transaction

Accounts, Other Deposits and Vault Cash" and for all those weekly reporters whose vault cash exceeds their required reserves, the difference between current vault cash and the amount applied to satisfy current reserve requirements. Currency and vault cash figures are measured over computation periods ending on Mondays. *Seasonally adjusted monetary base*, break-adjusted monetary base consists of (1) seasonally adjusted, break-adjusted total reserves, (2) the seasonally adjusted currency component of the money stock, and (3), for all quarterly reporters on the "Report of Transaction Accounts, Other Deposits and Vault Cash" and for all those weekly reporters whose vault cash exceeds their required reserves, the seasonally adjusted, break-adjusted difference between current vault cash and the amount applied to satisfy current reserve requirements.

M1 comprises (1) currency outside the U.S. Treasury, Federal Reserve Banks, and the vaults of other depository corporations; (2) traveler's checks of nonbank issuers; (3) demand deposits at commercial banks (excluding those amounts held by other depository corporations, the U.S. government, and foreign banks and official institutions) less cash items in the process of collection and Federal Reserve float; and (4) other checkable deposits (OCDs), consisting of negotiable order of withdrawal (NOW) and automatic transfer service (ATS) accounts at depository institutions, credit union share draft accounts, and demand deposits at thrift institutions. *Seasonally adjusted M1* is constructed by summing currency, traveler's checks, demand deposits, and OCDs, each seasonally adjusted separately.

M2 comprises M1 plus (1) savings deposits (including money market deposit accounts); (2) small-denomination time deposits (time deposits in amounts of less than $100,000), less IRA and Keogh balances at other depository corporations; and (3) balances in retail money market mutual funds, less IRA and Keogh balances at money market mutual funds. *Seasonally adjusted M2* is constructed by summing savings deposits, small-denomination time deposits, and retail money funds, each seasonally adjusted separately, and adding this result to seasonally adjusted M1.

Interest Rates:

Central Bank Policy Rate (End of Period):
Refers to the federal funds rate, which is the rate at which private depository institutions (mostly banks) lend balances (federal funds) at the Federal Reserve to other depository institutions, usually overnight. It is the rate banks charge each other for loans.

Discount Rate (End of Period):
Rate at which the Federal Reserve Bank of New York discounts eligible paper and makes advances to member banks. Establishment of the discount rate is at the discretion of each Federal Reserve bank but is subject to review and determination by the Board of Governors in Washington every fourteen days; these rates are publicly announced. Borrowing from a Federal Reserve bank is a privilege of being a member of the Federal Reserve system. Borrowing may take the form either of discounts of short-term commercial, industrial, and other financial paper or of advances against government securities and other eligible collateral; most transactions are in the form of advances. Federal Reserve advances to or discounts for member banks are usually of short maturity up to fifteen days. Federal Reserve banks do not discount eligible paper or make advanced to members banks automati-

cally. Ordinarily, the continuous use of Federal reserve credit by a member bank over a considerable period of time is not regarded as appropriate. The volume of discount is consequently very small. † Effective January 9, 2003, the rate charged for primary credit replaces that for adjustment credit. Primary credit, which is broadly similar to credit programs offered by many, which is broadly similar to credit programs offered by many other central banks, is made available by the Federal Reserve Bank for short terms as a backup source of liquidity to other depository corporations that are in sound financial condition.

Federal Funds Rate:
Weighted average rate at which banks borrow funds through New York brokers. Monthly rate is the average of rates of all calendar days, and the daily rate is the average of the rate on a given day weighted by the volume of transaction.

Commercial Paper Rate:
Rate on three-month commercial paper of nonfinancial firms. Rates are quoted on a discount basis and interpolated from data on certain commercial paper trades settled by the Depository Trust Company. The trades represent sales of commercial paper by dealers or direct issuers to investors.

Treasury Bill Rate:
Weighted average yield on multiple-price auctions of 13-week treasury bills. Monthly averages are computed on an issue-date basis. Beginning on October 28, 1998, data are stop yields from uniform-price auctions.

Certificate of Deposit Rate:
Average of dealer offering rates on nationally traded certificates of deposits.

Lending Rate:
Base rate charged by banks on short-term business loans. Monthly rate is the average of rates of all calendar days and is posted by a majority of the top 25 insured U.S. chartered commercial banks.

Mortgage Rate:
Contract rate on 30-year fixed-rate first mortgages.

Government Bond Yield: Long-Term (line 61):
Yield on actively traded treasury issues adjusted to constant maturities. Yield on treasury securities at constant maturity are interpolated by the U.S. Treasury from the daily yield curve. This curve, which relates the yield on a security to its time to maturity, is based on the closing market bid yields on actively traded treasury securities in the over-the-counter market. These market yields are calculated from composites of quotations obtained by the Federal Reserve Bank of New York. Medium-Term rate refers to three-year constant maturities. Long-term rate refers to ten-year constant maturities.

Prices, Production, Labor:

Share Prices:
Price-weighted monthly average covering 30 blue chip stocks quoted in the Dow Jones Industrial Average (DJIA).

NASDAQ Composite:
Market capitalization-weighted index covering domestic and international-based common stocks, ordinary shares, American Depository Receipts (ADRs), shares of beneficial interest, REITs,

base February 5, 1971, Tracking Stocks and Limited Partnerships and excluding exchange traded funds, structured products, convertible debentures, rights, units, warrants and preferred issues.

S&P Industrials:
Laspeyres-type index based on daily closing quotations for companies in the Industrials on the New York Exchange, base 41–43.

Amex Average:
Total-market-value-weighted index that covers all common shares, warrants, and (ADRs) listed, base August 31, 1973.

Producer Prices:
Source: compiled by the Bureau of Labor Statistics (U.S. Department of Labor) and published by the U.S. Department of Commerce; Weights Reference Period: 1982; Coverage: the entire output of domestic goods-producing sectors; Number of Items in Basket: approximately 30,000 establishments providing close to 100,000 price quotations per month; Basis for Calculation: the weights are taken from the Economic Census conducted by the Census Bureau and are revised every five years.

Consumer Prices:
Source: compiled by the Bureau of Labor Statistics (U.S. Department of Labor) and published by the U.S. Department of Commerce. Weights reference period: 1982–1984; Geographical Coverage: covers all residents in urban areas; Number of Items in Basket: 305 entry level items representing all goods and services; Basis for Calculation: is computed using a modified Laspeyres methodology, the weights are derived from the Consumer Expenditure Surveys for 2003–2004, and the average for those two years. Historically weights have been revised once every 10 years; however, starting in 2002, weights will be revised every other year.

Wages: Hourly Earnings (Mfg):
Source: compiled by the Bureau of Labor Statistics (U.S. Department of Labor). In June 2003, the Current Employment Statistics survey converted to the 2002 North American Industry Classification System (NAICS) from 1987 Standard Industrial Classification System (SIC). NAICS emphasis on new, emerging, service-providing, and high-tech industries. Both current and historical data are now based on NAICS.

Industrial Production:
Source: Board of Governors of the Federal Reserve System. Weights Reference Period: 2007; Sectoral Coverage: manufacturing, mining, and electric and gas utilities; Basis for Calculation: the weights are based on annual estimates of value added.

Crude Petroleum Production:
Data are from Energy Information Administration, U.S. Department of Energy.

Nonagricultural Employment, Seasonally Adjusted:
Data are from the Board of Governors of the Federal Reserve System. and represent an establishment survey that covers all full- and part-time employees who worked during or received pay for the pay period that includes the 12th of the month. The survey excludes proprietors, self-employed persons, domestic servants, unpaid family workers, and members of the Armed Forces.

Labor:
Data are compiled by the Bureau of Labor Statistics (U.S. Department of Labor). Beginning in January 2000, Employment data presents statistics from two major surveys, the Current Population Survey (household survey) which provides the information on the labor force, employment, and unemployment that marked Household Data and the Current Employment Statistics Survey (establishment survey) which provides the information on the employment, hours, and earnings of workers on non-farm payrolls that marked Establishment Data.

International Transactions:
All trade value data are from the U.S. Bureau of Census web site. Total trade data include trade of the U.S. Virgin Islands. Beginning January 1975, data include exports and imports, respectively, of nonmonetary gold, which prior to January 1975 are excluded. † Beginning in 1987, all trade data are reported on the revised statistical month based on import entry and export declaration transaction dates, whereas previous data reflect import entries and export declarations transmitted to the U.S. Bureau of the Census during a fixed monthly processing period. Export and import price data are Laspeyres-type indices with 1995 trade weights and are compiled by the Bureau of Labor Statistics, U.S. Department of Labor. Volume indices are Paasche-type indices derived for *IFS* from import and export value data divided by the respective Laspeyres price indices. The f.a.s. (free alongside ship) value is the value of exports at the U.S. seaport, airport, or border port of export, based on the transaction price, including inland freight, insurance, and other charged incurred in placing the merchandise alongside the carrier at the U.S. port of exportation. The value, as defined, excludes the cost of loading the merchandise aboard the exporting carrier and also excludes freight, insurance, and any charges or transportation costs beyond the port of exportation.

Balance of Payments:
Data for *Business Travel* (credits and debits) include only *Expenditures by seasonal and border workers*. Other business travel services are included indistinguishably under *Personal Travel - Other* since source data do not distinguish between personal and other business travel.

Government Finance:
The monthly cash flow and balance sheet information are derived *from The Monthly Treasury Statement of Receipts and Outlays of the United States Government (MTS)* as prepared by the Financial Management Service, Department of the Treasury. This statement summarizes the financial activities of the Federal Government and off-budget Federal entities conducted in accordance with the Budget of the U.S. Government, i.e., receipts and outlays of funds, the surplus or deficit, and the means of financing the deficit or disposing of the surplus. Information is presented on a modified cash basis; receipts are accounted for on the basis of collections; refunds of receipts are treated as deductions from gross receipts; revolving and management fund receipts, reimbursements and refunds of monies previously expended are treated as deductions from gross outlays; and interest on the public debt (public issues) is recognized on the accrual basis. For the cash data the fiscal year ends September 30. Beginning in 2005, quarterly and annual accrual data on Central and General Government Operations are as reported by the Bureau of Economic Analysis (BEA). These data are derived from the National Income and Product Accounts (NIPAs) compiled by the BEA. For accrual data the fiscal year ends December 31.

National Accounts:

Source: Bureau of Economic Analysis (BEA), U.S. Department of Commerce. The National Income and Product Accounts (NIPAs) are, in general, consistent with the *1993 SNA*. Volume and price data are calculated using the chained Fisher formula. Quarterly data are seasonally adjusted at annual rates.

Uruguay 298

Date of Fund Membership:
March 11, 1946

Standard Sources:
Central Bank of Uruguay

Exchange Rates:
On March 1, 1993 the Uruguayan peso, equal to 1,000 new Uruguayan pesos, was introduced.

Market Rate (End of Period and Period Average):
Until June 19, 2002, the exchange rate was operated as a managed float. Effective June 20, 2002, the exchange rate regime was changed to a floating system.

International Liquidity:
Data for *Total Reserves minus Gold (line 1l.d)*, *Foreign Exchange (line 1d.d)*, and *Gold (lines 1ad and 1and)* include foreign exchange and gold holdings of the Central Bank of Uruguay (BCU) only. † Prior to March 1979, data include the holdings of the BCU and the Bank of the Republic of Uruguay. *Gold (National Valuation) (line 1and)* is the U.S. dollar value of official holdings of gold as reported in the country's standard sources.

Central Bank:
Consists of the Central Bank of Uruguay (CBU) only.
Data are based on a standardized report form (SRF) for central banks, which accords with the concepts and definitions of the IMF's *Monetary and Financial Statistics Manual (MFSM)*, 2000.

Other Depository Corporations:
Comprises private banks, the government-owned Banco de la República Oriental del Uruguay (BROU) and Banco Hipotecario del Uruguay (BHU), finance houses, and financial intermediation cooperatives.
Data are based on a standardized report form (SRF) for other depository corporations, which accords with the concepts and definitions of the *Monetary and Financial Statistics Manual (MFSM)*. Departures from the *MFSM* methodology are explained below. *Claims on Private Sector* includes claims on other financial corporations.

Depository Corporations:
See notes on central bank and other depository corporations.

Other Financial Corporations:
Comprises off-shore financial institutions only.
Data are based on a standardized report form (SRF) for other financial corporations, which accords with the concepts and defi-
nitions of the *Monetary and Financial Statistics Manual (MFSM)*. Departures from the *MFSM* methodology are explained below. *Claims on Private Sector* includes claims on other financial corporations.

Monetary Aggregates:

Broad Money:
Broad Money calculated from the liability data in the sections for the central bank and other depository corporations accords with the concepts and definitions of the *MFSM*. Broad money differs from M2 described below as M2 excludes foreign currency deposits of other financial corporations, local governments, public nonfinancial corporations, and private sector with depository corporations.

Money (National Definitions):
Base money comprises notes and coins in circulation, reserve requirement, demand and time deposits in national currency of other depository corporations, other financial corporations, local governments, public nonfinancial corporations, and private sector with the CBU, less reserve requirements constituted by the BROU on central government deposits in national currency. † Beginning in July 2007, includes certificates of deposits of less than 30 days issued by the CBU held by other financial corporations, local governments, public nonfinancial corporations, and private sector. † Beginning in September 2007, includes reserve requirements constituted by the BROU on central government deposits in national currency.
M1 comprises notes and coins in circulation outside the banking system and demand deposits in national currency of other financial corporations, local governments, public nonfinancial corporations, and private sector with depository corporations.
M2 comprises M1 and time and savings deposits in national currency of other financial corporations, local governments, public nonfinancial corporations, and private sector with depository corporations.

Interest Rates:

Central Bank Policy Rate (End of Period):
Monetary policy rate determined quarterly by the CBU's Monetary Policy Committee.

Discount Rate (End of Period):
Effective rate established by the CBU for financial assistance in national currency to the private banks.

Discount Rate (Foreign Currency) (End of Period):
Effective rate established by the BCU for financial assistance in foreign currency to the private banks.

Money Market Rate:
Effective overnight rate on loans between private banks. The rate is an average of the last three days of the month.

Treasury Bill Rate (Foreign Currency):
Weighted average rate on 182-day treasury bills denominated in foreign currency auctioned by the BCU. Rate is weighted by the number of bills auctioned.

Savings Rate:
Average of the rates most frequently offered on savings deposits in national currency in the last three days of each month by the

five most representative (determined as of July 1978) private banks. † Beginning in January 2002, average rate offered on savings deposits in national currency by private banks.

Savings Rate (Foreign Currency):
Average of the rates most frequently offered on savings deposits in foreign currency in the last three days of each month by the five most representative (determined as of July 1978) private banks. † Beginning in January 2002, average rate offered on savings deposits in foreign currency by private banks.

Deposit Rate:
Average of the rates most frequently offered on one- to six-month time deposits in national currency in the last three days of each month by the five most representative (determined as of July 1978) private banks. † Beginning in January 2002, average rate offered on one- to six-month time deposits in national currency by private banks.

Deposit Rate (Foreign Currency):
Average of the rates most frequently offered on one- to six-month time deposits in foreign currency in the last three days of each month by the five most representative (determined as of July 1978) private banks. † Beginning in January 2002, average rate offered on one- to six-month time deposits in foreign currency by private banks.

Lending Rate:
Average rates most frequently charged on ordinary loans in national currency not exceeding six months on the last day of each month by the five most representative (determined as of July 1978) private banks. † Beginning in January 2002, average rate charged on loans not exceeding six months in national currency by private banks.

Lending Rate (Foreign Currency):
Average rates most frequently charged on short-term commercial loans in foreign currency on the last day of each month by the five most representative (determined as of July 1978) private banks. † Beginning in January 2002, average rate charged on loans not exceeding six months in foreign currency by private banks.

Prices and Production:

Wholesale Prices:
Source: Central Bank. Index of wholesale prices, covering home and export goods in agriculture and manufacturing, base August 2001.

Consumer Prices:
Source: Central Bank. Weights Reference Period: December 2010; Geographical Coverage: Montevideo; Basis for Calculation: Household Expenditure and Income Survey.

Manufacturing Production:
Source: Central Bank.

International Transactions:

All trade data are from the Central Bank.

Government Finance:

Monthly and quarterly data are derived from the Central Bank and cover budgetary central government. The fiscal year ends December 31.

National Accounts:

Source: Central Bank. As reported by the country, quarterly data at constant prices are adjusted to the variable annual level by Denton's proportional method and may not add to yearly data.

Vanuatu   846

Date of Fund Membership:
September 28, 1981

Standard Sources:
Reserve Bank of Vanuatu
National Statistics Office

Exchange Rates:

Official Rate: (End of Period and Period Average):
The official exchange rate is determined on the basis of an undisclosed transactions-weighted basket of currencies.

Central Bank:
Consists of the Reserve Bank of Vanuatu (RBV) only.
Data are based on a standardized report form (SRF) for central banks, which accords with the concepts and definitions of the IMF's *Monetary and Financial Statistics Manual (MFSM)*, 2000. Departures from the *MFSM* methodology are explained below:
Holdings of central government securities and issuance of RBV bills are registered at face value rather than at current market price or fair value.

Other Depository Corporations:
Comprises branches of foreign banks and National Bank of Vanuatu.
Data are based on a standardized report form (SRF) for other depository corporations, which accords with the concepts and definitions of the *Monetary and Financial Statistics Manual (MFSM)*. For other depository corporations in Vanuatu, departures from the *MFSM* methodology are explained below:
Though accrued interest is included in the outstanding amounts of the financial assets and liabilities on a quarterly basis, it is included in *Other Items (Net)* for the intervening months.
Holdings of central government securities and RBV bills are registered at face value rather than at current market price or fair value.

Depository Corporations:
See notes on central bank and other depository corporations.

Other Financial Corporations:
Comprises the Credit Corporation, Vanuatu Agriculture Development Bank, and Vanuatu National Provident Fund (VNPF).
Data are based on a standardized report form (SRF) for other financial corporations, which accords with the concepts and definitions of the *Monetary and Financial Statistics Manual (MFSM)*. For other financial corporations in Vanuatu, departures from the *MFSM* methodology are explained below.
Data for the VNPF are only available on a quarterly basis.
Financial assets and liabilities for which financial instrument

breakdown is unavailable are allocated to the financial instrument having the largest volume of transactions in the category. Financial assets and liabilities for which economic sectorization is unavailable are allocated to the economic sector having the largest volume of transactions in the category.

In the absence of accrued interest for some financial instruments and sectors, accrued interest is estimated using the ratio of the volume of transactions with the corresponding financial instrument and sectors.

Securities and shares are valued at acquisition cost rather than at current market price or fair value.

Financial Corporations:

See notes on central bank, other depository corporations, and other financial corporations.

Monetary Aggregates:

Broad Money:

Broad Money calculated from the liability data in the sections for the central bank and other depository corporations accords with the concepts and definitions of the *MFSM* and differs from M2 described below as M2 includes central bank float.

Money (National Definitions):

Reserve Money comprises currency in circulation, banker's statutory reserve deposits (SRDs) and excess reserves, and transferable deposits in national currency of public entities excluding the central government with the RBV. Currency in circulation refers to notes and coins issued by the RBV. The RBV uses SRDs as monetary policy instruments calculated as ten percent of all deposits in national currency and transferable deposits in foreign currency. † Beginning in December 2001, comprises currency in circulation and bankers' SRDs and excess reserve deposits only.

M1 comprises currency in circulation, transferable deposits in national currency of state and local governments, public nonfinancial corporations, private sector, and other financial corporations with other depository corporations, and central bank float. Currency in circulation refers to notes and coins issued by the RBV less the amount held by other depository corporations. † Beginning in December 2001, comprises currency in circulation, transferable deposits in national currency of state and local governments, public nonfinancial corporations, private sector, and other financial corporations with depository corporations, and central bank float.

M2 comprises M1 and transferable deposits in foreign currency of state and local governments, public nonfinancial corporations, private sector, and other financial corporations with other depository corporations. † Beginning in December 2001, comprises M1, transferable deposits in foreign currency and time, fixed, and savings deposits in national and foreign currency of state and local governments, public nonfinancial corporations, private sector, and other financial corporations with depository corporations.

Interest Rates:

Discount Rate (End of Period):

Rate offered by the RBV on loans to commercial banks and overdrafts to the central government.

Money Market Rate:

Overnight interbank lending rate.

Deposit Rate:

Maximum representative rate offered by commercial banks on one to three-month time deposits.

Lending Rate:

Maximum representative rate charged by commercial banks on advances for commercial purposes.

Government Bond Yield:

Yield on three-year bonds. † Beginning in January 1989, yield on ten-year bonds.

Prices:

Consumer Prices:

Source: National Planning and Statistics Office. Weights Reference Period: first quarter 2000; Geographical Coverage: two urban centers of Vanuatu: Port Vila and Luganville; Number of Items in the Basket: 760 goods/services items for Vila, and 680 for Luganville; Basis for Calculation: the weights are derived from urban dwellers expenditure patterns through the 1998 household surveys.

International Transactions:

All trade data are from the National Planning and Statistics Office.

Venezuela, Rep. Bol.   299

Date of Fund Membership:

December 30, 1946

Standard Sources:

Central Bank of Venezuela

Exchange Rates:

On January 1, 2008, the new Venezuelan bolivar (VEF), equivalent to 1,000 old bolivares (VEB), was introduced.

Official Rate: (End of Period and Period Average):

Effective 1989, the multiple exchange rate system was replaced by a system of unified managed float that was maintained until June 1994. After a temporary closure, the exchange rate market was reopened on July 11, 1994 under a system of exchange controls at a fixed rate of 170 bolivares per U.S. dollar. On December 11, 1995, the official rate of the bolivar was devalued from 170 bolivares per U.S. dollar to 290 bolivares per U.S. dollar. Effective April 22, 1996 the exchange rate regime was changed to a managed float with full convertibility. On July 8, 1996 an exchange rate band system was introduced with a width of 7.5 percent each way around the central parity which moves according to the annual inflation target. Effective January 1, 2001, the exchange rate band was moved by 7.5 percent to set the central parity rate of the band to the actual level of the exchange rate. Effective February 13, 2002, the exchange rate regime was changed to a floating system. On February 4, 2003, the bolivar was fixed at Bs 1,598 per US$1 and, therefore, the exchange regime was reclassified to the category of conventional pegged arrangement.

Effective February 9, 2004, the bolivar was devalued and fixed at Bs 1,918 per US$1. Effective March 3, 2005, the bolivar was fixed at Bs 2,147 per US$1. On January 8, 2010, the bolivar was devalued and fixed at Bs 2.5935 per US$1. On January 1, 2011, the bolivar was devalued and fixed at Bs 4.2893 per US$1.

For the purpose of calculating effective exchange rates (lines **nec** and **rec**), a weighted average exchange rate index for U.S. dollars per bolivar is calculated as follows: Through November 1986, exchange rates were weighted by transactions in a basket of imports effected at various exchange rates; beginning December 1986, the rate is a weighted average of the market rate.

International Liquidity:

Gold (National Valuation) (line 1and) is the U.S. dollar value of official holdings of gold as reported in the country's standard sources.

Monetary Authorities:

Comprises the Central Bank of Venezuela (CBV) only. † Beginning in December 1987, data are based on an improved reporting system. † Beginning in July 1996, data reflect the introduction of a new plan of accounts, which provides an improved sectorization and classification of the accounts.

Deposit Money Banks:

Comprises commercial and universal banks. Universal banks began operations on November 26, 1996. Beginning in July 2006, includes development banks. Beginning in October 2011, includes investment banks, previously classified as other banking institutions, as they were acquired by universal banks † See note on monetary authorities.

Monetary Survey:

† See notes on monetary authorities and deposit money banks.

Other Banking Institutions:

Comprises mortgage banks, National Savings and Loan System, and investment banks. † Beginning in July 1996, includes financial leasing companies and investment funds. In July 2011 the National Savings and Loan System and financial leasing companies ceased operations. In October 2011, investment banks were reclassified as deposit money banks, ending the institutional coverage of the other banking institutions sector. † See note on monetary authorities.

Banking Survey:

† See notes on monetary authorities, deposit money banks, and other banking institutions.

Money (National Definitions):

Base Money comprises notes and coins in circulation, deposits of commercial and universal banks and the rest of the banking system in national currency and special deposits of the public in national currency.

M1 (Narrow Money) comprises currency in circulation and demand deposits of nonbank financial institutions, state and municipal governments, nonfinancial public enterprises, and private sector with deposit money banks. Currency in circulation refers to notes and coins issued by the BCV less the amount held by deposit money banks.. † Beginning in July 2006, comprises currency in circulation and demand and transferable savings deposits of nonbank financial institutions, state and municipal governments, nonfinancial public enterprises, and private sector with banking institutions. Currency in circulation refers to notes and coins issued by the Central Bank of Venezuela less the amount held by banking institutions.

M2 (Broad Money) comprises M1 and quasi-money. Quasi-money consists of savings and time deposits of nonbank financial institutions, state and municipal governments, nonfinancial public enterprises, and private sector with deposit money banks and unsecured bonds issued by deposit money banks held by the private sector. † Beginning in July 2006, comprises M1; nontransferable savings and time deposits of nonbank financial institutions, state and municipal governments, nonfinancial public enterprises, and private sector with banking institutions; and money market fund shares/units issued by banking institutions held by nonbank financial institutions, state and municipal governments, nonfinancial public enterprises, and private sector.

M3 (Extended Broad Money) comprises M2 and mortgage bonds issued by deposit money banks held by nonbank financial institutions, state and municipal governments, and private sector. † Beginning in July 2006, M3 comprises M2 and mortgage bonds issued by banking institutions.

Interest Rates:

Discount Rate (End of Period):
Rate charged by the Central Bank of Venezuela on credit to financial institutions through discounts, rediscounts, advances, and repurchase agreements.

Injection Rate (End of Period):
Rate used by the CBV to inject liquidity to the financial system.

Absorption Rate (End of Period):
Rate used by the CBV to absorb liquidity from the financial system.

Money Market Rate:
Weighted average rate on loans between financial institutions. The rate is weighted by loan amounts.

Savings Rate:
Weighted average rate offered by commercial and universal banks on savings deposits in national currency. The rate is weighted by deposit amounts.

Deposit Rate:
Weighted average rate offered by commercial and universal banks on 90-day time deposits in national currency. The rate is weighted by deposit amounts.

Lending Rate:
Average rate charged by commercial banks on loans. † Beginning in January 1990, weighted average rate charged by commercial and universal banks on industrial, agricultural, commercial, and car loans in national currency. The rate is weighted by loan amounts.

Government Bond Yield:
Effective weighted average yield on national public debt bonds traded in the Caracas Stock Exchange. † Beginning in January 1999, weighted average yield on national public debt bonds traded on the operations desk of the Central Bank of Venezuela. The yield is weighted by issuance amounts.

Prices, Production, Labor:

Share Prices (End of Month):
The index refers to the average of daily quotations of all shares on the Caracas Stock Exchange, base January 1, 1971. † Beginning in December 1993, the index refers to quotations on the last day of the month of all shares on the Caracas Stock Exchange, base December 1993.

Industrial Share Prices (End of Month):
Industrial share price index, base 1956/57. † Beginning in January 1958, the index refers to the average of daily quotations and covers ordinary and preference industrial shares quoted on the Caracas and Miranda exchanges, base 1968. † Beginning in January 1990, the index refers to the average of daily quotations of industrial shares on the Caracas Stock Exchange, base January 1, 1971. † Beginning in December 1993, the index refers to quotations on the last day of the month of industrial shares on the Caracas Stock Exchange, base December 1993.

Wholesale Prices:
Source: Central Bank of Venezuela. Weights Reference Period 1997, covering home-produced and imported goods for domestic consumption.

Consumer Prices (National):
Source: Central Bank of Venezuela. Weights Reference Period: 2007; Geographical Coverage: National; Number of Items in Basket: 362; Basis for Calculation: Weights are determined based on Households Expenditure Survey of 2004–2005.

Consumer Prices (Caracas and Maracaibo):
Source: Central Bank of Venezuela. Weights Reference Period: 2007; Geographical Coverage: Caracas and Maracaibo Metropolitan Area; Number of Items in Basket: 362; Basis for Calculation: Weights are determined based on Household Expenditure Survey of 2004–2005.

Crude Petroleum Production:
Central Bank of Venezuela data.

International Transactions:

Exports:
All data are from the Central Bank of Venezuela, except volume of petroleum exports, which is the average of crude and refined petroleum with 1995 values of exports as weights, computed for *IFS*. Data for exports from 2003 exclude petroleum exports.

Imports, c.i.f.:
Source: Central Bank of Venezuela. Data for current periods are based on incomplete enumeration of customs documents and are subject to subsequent upward revision. † Value data for exports and imports in bolivares are U.S. dollar equivalents at the secondary rate until June 1987 and at the principal rate from July 1987 through June 1988. Thereafter, the relation between values expressed in bolivares and in U.S. dollars is no longer determined by a uniform rate.

Government Finance:

Monthly and quarterly data are derived from Central Bank of Venezuela and cover budgetary central government only. † Prior to 2004, to the extent possible, existing subannual IFS data were converted to the main aggregates that are presented in the *GFSM 2001* Statement of Sources and Uses of Cash (see the Introduction of the monthly *IFS* publication for details). Beginning in 2004, annual data are as reported in the *Government Finance Statistics Yearbook (GFSY)* and cover the consolidated central government. The fiscal year ends December 31.

National Accounts:

Data are from the Central Bank of Venezuela. As indicated by the country, data are compiled according to the recommendations of the *1968 SNA*.

Vietnam   582

Date of Fund Membership:
September 21, 1956

Standard Source:
State Bank of Vietnam
General Statistics Office

Exchange Rates:

Market Rate (End of Period and Period Average):
Data refer to the midpoint of the average buying and selling rates quoted by the commercial banks authorized to deal in the organized foreign exchange market.

International Liquidity:

Data for *Foreign Exchange (line 1d.d)* are the U.S. dollar equivalents of the sum of foreign currency, investments in foreign securities, and deposits with foreign banks, as reported by the State Bank of Vietnam. The reported value in national currency terms is converted to the U.S. dollar value using the prevailing end-of-period exchange rate, as given in *line* **ae**.
Gold (Market Valuation) (line 1and) is obtained by converting the value of official holdings of gold in national currency terms, as reported by the State Bank of Vietnam, using the prevailing end-of-period exchange rate, as given in *line* **ae**.

Monetary Authorities:
Comprises the accounts of the State Bank of Vietnam.

Banking Institutions:

The SBV has expanded the coverage of the commercial banks used in compiling monetary statistics from 28 banks (before December 1999) to the credit institutions system as a whole in Vietnam (as of October 2011, there are 84 credit institutions and 46 foreign bank branches, more than previously as several credit institutions and foreign bank branches were established and came into operation.
Finance companies are credit institutions that are permitted to engage in some banking activities but not permitted to accept demand deposits and to provide payment services (according to the Law on Credit Institutions). The System of People's Credit Funds is permitted to accept demand deposits.
Bonds and Money Market Instruments (line 26a) include bills and bonds that are issued by credit institutions.

Interest Rates:

Central Bank Policy Rate (End of Period):
Rate charged by the State Bank of Vietnam on its lending facilities to all credit institutions. On December 12, 1997, the State Bank

Law required the State Bank of Vietnam to use the refinancing rate instrument to implement the national monetary policy.

Treasury Bill Rate:
Average monthly yield on 360-day treasury bills sold at auction.

Deposit Rate:
Average of rates at the end of period on 3-month deposits of four large state-owned commercial banks.

Lending Rate:
Average of rates at the end of period on short-term (less than 12 months) working capital loans of four large state-owned commercial banks.

Prices:

Share Prices (End of Month):
Data refer to the Vietnam Stock Exchange, base July 28, 2000. The Vietnam Stock Exchange is a capitalization-weighted index of all companies listed on the Ho Chi Minh Stock Exchange. Prior to March 1, 2002, the market only traded on alternate days.

Consumer Prices:
Source: General Statistics Office. Weight Reference Period: 2009; Geographical Coverage: 63 largest provinces representing the 8 economic regions; Number of Items in the Basket: 572 items; Basis of Calculation: the weights is derived from the 2008 Vietnam Household Living Standard Survey and relate to the expenditure pattern for households in each of the provinces.

International Transactions:
Source: General Statistics Office.

National Accounts:

Source: General Statistics Office. As indicated by the country, since 1996, concepts and definitions are in accordance with the *1993 SNA*.

WAEMU   759

The West African Economic Monetary Union (WAEMU) is a regional entity established by a treaty signed on January 10, 1994 and entered into force on August 1, 1994 after its ratification by all member countries. The aim of the treaty—built on the achievements of the West African Monetary Union (WAMU), established in 1962—was to create a new framework for fostering the achievement of the member countries' growth and development objectives. It was also to provide the credibility required to sustain the fixed exchange rate for the common currency.

The Union has a common central bank, the Central Bank of West African States (Banque centrale des États de l'Afrique de l'Ouest (BCEAO)), with headquarters in Dakar and national branches in the member states. WAEMU comprises eight francophone countries: Benin, Burkina Faso, Côte d'Ivoire, Guinea-Bissau, Mali, Niger, Senegal, and Togo. Mali and Guinea-Bissau joined the Union on June 1, 1984 and May 2, 1997, respectively. The BCEAO issues the common currency of the WAEMU member countries, the CFA franc (CFA stands for "Communauté financière africaine" since 1958; from 1945 through 1958, CFA stood for "Colonies françaises d'Afrique").

On December 17, 1993, the Council of Ministers of WAEMU decided to formally establish a regional financial market and mandated the BCEAO to carry out the project. The regional securities exchange (Bourse régionale des valeurs mobilières (BRVM)) was established as a private company in Abidjan and began operations in September 1998.

Compared to data published in the individual *IFS* pages for the WAEMU member countries, consolidated data published for the WAEMU as a whole embody two major methodological differences: (1) where relevant, a WAEMU-wide residency criterion is applied instead of a national residency criterion; (2) BCEAO headquarters' transactions are included in data presented in the sections "International liquidity" and "Monetary Authorities." BCEAO headquarters' transactions are not allocated to the member countries' national data.

Date of Fund Membership:
Benin (July 10, 1963), Burkina Faso (May 2, 1963), Côte d'Ivoire (March 11, 1963), Guinea-Bissau (March 24, 1977), Mali (September 27, 1963), Niger (April 24, 1963), Senegal (August 31, 1962), and Togo (August 1, 1962).

Standard Source:
Banque centrale des États de l'Afrique de l'Ouest (Central Bank of West African States)

Exchange Rates:

Official Rate: (End of Period and Period Average):
Prior to January 1999, the official rate was pegged to the French Franc. On January 12, 1994, the CFA franc (CFAF) was devalued to CFAF 100 per French franc from CFAF 50, which was the fixed rate adopted since 1948. From January 1, 1999 onward, the CFAF is pegged to the euro at the rate of CFAF 655.957 per euro.

Fund Position:
Data are the aggregation of positions of WAEMU countries.

International Liquidity:
Data include holdings by the BCEAO headquarters and the BCEAO agencies in member countries. *Gold (National Valuation) (line 1and)* is obtained by converting the value in national currency, as reported by the BCEAO source, using the prevailing exchange rate, as given in *line ae*. Gold in national currency is revalued by the BCEAO on a quarterly basis at the rate corresponding to the lowest average fixing in the London market.

Monetary Authorities:
Data, compiled from the BCEAO balance sheet, cover its headquarters and national agencies.

Deposit Money Banks:
This section consolidates national data by application of a WAEMU-wide residency criterion. For more details on national data, see country notes.

Interest Rates:

Repurchase Agreement Rate (End of Period):
Data refer to the rate on repurchase agreements between the BCEAO and banks. The repurchase agreements rate was formally established on October 1, 1993.

Money Market Rate:
Rate paid on overnight interbank advances.

Deposit Rate:
Rate offered by banks on time deposits of CFAF 500,000–2,000,000 with a maturity of less than six months.

Prices and Production:

Share Prices (Period Average and End of Month):
Regional Stock Exchange Composite Index, base 2005=100 covering all common shares listed on the BRVM.

BRVM 10 (Period Average and End of Month):
Regional Stock Exchange 10 Index, base 2005=100 covering the 10 most traded common shares on the BRVM.

Consumer Prices:
BCEAO harmonized index, weights reference period 2008. From January 2005, Guinea Bissau's CPI is taken into account in the calculation of the index.

National Accounts:

Source: Central Bank of West African States.

West Bank and Gaza   487

Standard Source:

Palestinian Monetary Authority

Exchange Rates *(End of Period)*:

The Israeli shekel, Jordanian dinar, and U.S. dollar co-circulate in the territory of West Bank and Gaza. The Palestinian Monetary Authority does not issue currency. The U.S. dollar is used for statistical reporting purposes. (See note on Exchange Rate for the United States).

Central Bank:

Consists of the Palestinian Monetary Authority (PMA) only.
† Beginning in December 2006, data are based on a standardized report form (SRF) for central banks, which accords with the concepts and definitions of the IMF's *Monetary and Financial Statistics Manual* (*MFSM*), 2000.
Departures from the *MFSM* methodology are explained below.
Securities held to maturity are valued at acquisition cost plus accrued interest rather than at market price or fair value.
Accrued interest is included in *Other Items* (*Net*) rather than in the outstanding amounts of the financial assets or liabilities.
For December 2001 through November 2006, data have less conformity with the *MFSM* methodology and therefore are not strictly comparable to data for later periods.

Other Depository Corporations:

Comprises commercial banks under the PMA's supervisory authority.
† Beginning in December 2006, data are based on a standardized report form (SRF) for other depository corporations, which accords with the concepts and definitions of the *MFSM*. For other depository corporations in West Bank and Gaza, departures from the *MFSM* methodology are explained below.
Transferable and *Other deposits included in Broad Money* include some deposits of extra-budgetary central government units.
Claims on *private sector* includes some claims on other financial corporations.

Securities held to maturity are valued at acquisition cost minus impairment loss (loss of value for two consecutive years or more) rather than at market price or fair value.
Accrued interest is included in *Other Items* (*Net*) rather than in the outstanding amounts of the financial assets or liabilities.

Depository Corporations:

† See notes on central bank and other depository corporations.

Monetary Aggregates:

Broad Money:
Broad Money (line 59m) calculated from the liability data in the sections for the central bank and other depository corporations accords with the concepts and definitions of *MFSM* and is consistent with *Broad Money* (line 59mea).

Money (National Definitions):
Monetary Base comprises required reserves; current, time, and saving accounts and certificates of deposit issued to resident commercial banks and to non-central government non-bank resident sectors.
Broad Money comprises current, time, and saving accounts, and certificates of deposit issued to non-central government non-bank resident sectors.

Interest Rates:

Deposit Rate:
Weighted average rate offered by commercial banks on deposits of all clients in U.S. dollars. The rate is weighted by deposit amounts.

Lending Rate:
Weighted average rate charged by commercial banks on loans to all clients in U.S. dollars. The rate is weighted by loan amounts.

Yemen, Republic of   474

Date of Fund Membership:

Central Statistical OrganizationMay 22, 1970
The Republic of Yemen succeeded to the membership of the Yemen Arab Republic and of the People's Democratic Republic of Yemen on May 22, 1990.

Standard Sources:

Central Bank of Yemen
Central Statistical Organization

Exchange Rates:

Market Rate (End of Period and Period Average):
† Starting on July 1, 1996, data refer to the market rate. Prior to July 1, 1996, data refer to the official rate, which was pegged to the U.S. dollar. The official rate applied to most government transactions and was also referred to as the principal rate within the multiple exchange rate regime in effect prior to July 1, 1996. Effective January 1996, the official rate was changed from Yrls 50.04 to Yrls 100.08 per U.S. dollar. Effective March 29, 1995, the official rate was changed from Yrls 12.01 to Yrls 50.04 per U.S. dollar.

Monetary Authorities:

Comprises the Central Bank of Yemen. † Starting in December 1999, data are based on improved classification due to more detailed reporting.

Deposit Money Banks:

Comprises commercial and Islamic banks. † Starting in December 1999, data are based on improved classification due to more detailed reporting.

Monetary Survey:

See notes on monetary authorities and deposit money banks.

Interest Rates:

Central Bank of Yemen.

Discount Rate (End of Period):
The rate at which the Central Bank of Yemen rediscounts government securities.

Treasury Bill Rate:
Simple annualized rate on three-month treasury bills.

Deposit Rate:
Rate on savings deposits, which is a minimum rate on deposits at commercial banks set by the Central Bank of Yemen.

Lending Rate:
Simple arithmetic average of the maximum and minimum rates on short-term loans extended to the private sector by commercial banks.

Prices:

Consumer Prices:
Source: Central Statistical Organization. Weights reference period: 2008; Geographical coverage: 20 urban areas selected among the most important regions, representing all private households residing permanently in urban areas of Yemen and about 18% of the population. Number of items in basket: 449; Basis for calculation: Laspeyres index, prices are collected at varying frequencies from outlets in Sana's and Aden. Weights are derived from the household budget survey conducted by the Central Statistical Organization. The last survey was conducted during January-December, 2008 among 13461 private households of all socio-economic groups.

International Transactions:

Source: Central Statistical Organization. Exports include re-exports.

Government Finance:

Annual data are as reported for the *Government Finance Statistics Yearbook (GFSY)* and cover budgetary central government. The fiscal year ends December 31.

National Accounts:

Source: Central Statistical Organization.

Zambia   754

Date of Fund Membership:

September 23, 1965

Standard Sources:

Bank of Zambia
Central Statistical Office

Exchange Rates:

Official Rate: (End of Period and Period Average):
Bank of Zambia base rate. Prior to July 2003, the rate was determined in the auction market, with a 1.6 percent spread between buying and selling rates. Afterwards, it is calculated as the midpoint between the simple average of the primary dealers bid and offer rates. Beginning 1st January 2013, the Zambian Kwacha (ZMK) was redenominated. The New Kwacha (ZMW) is equal to 1000 Zambian Kwacha (ZMK).

International Liquidity:

Data for *line 1d.d* include small foreign exchange holdings by the government.
Gold (National Valuation) (line 1and) is obtained by converting the value in national currency terms, as reported in the country's standard sources, using the prevailing exchange rate, as given in *line* **dg** or *line* **ag**.

Central Bank:

Consists of the Bank of Zambia (BOZ) only.
† Beginning in January 2003, data are based on a standardized report form (SRF) for central banks, which accords with the concepts and definitions of the IMF's *Monetary and Financial Statistics Manual (MFSM)*, 2000. Departures from the *MFSM* methodology are explained below.
Overdrafts are netted against the deposits, rather than presented as loans to/from the corresponding economic sector.
For December 2001 through December 2002, data in the SRF format are compiled from pre-SRF data not based in the *MFSM* methodology. Departures from the *MFSM* methodology are the same as the ones detailed for January 2003 onwards.

Other Depository Corporations:

Comprises commercial banks (including three banks in liquidation), building societies, and the National Savings and Credit Bank.
† Beginning in January 2003, data are based on a standardized report form (SRF) for other depository corporations, which accords with the concepts and definitions of the *Monetary and Financial Statistics Manual (MFSM)*. Departures from the *MFSM* methodology are explained below.
Claims on Private Sector includes a large amount of loans to other financial corporations.
Transferable Deposits Included in Broad Money and *Other Deposits Included in Broad Money* include deposits of the central government in foreign currency.
Some other depository corporations record repurchase agreements as the outright buying or selling of the securities, rather than as collateralized loans.
For December 2001 through December 2002, data in the SRF format are compiled from pre-SRF data not based in the *MFSM* methodology. Departures from the *MFSM* methodology, other than those detailed for January 2003 onwards, are explained below.
Transferable Deposits Included in Broad Money and *Other Deposits Included in Broad Money* include some deposits of the central government in national currency.
Accrued interest on treasury bills is included in *Other Items (Net)* rather than in the outstanding amounts of the securities.

Depository Corporations:

† See notes on central bank and other depository corporations.

Monetary Aggregates:

Broad Money:
Broad Money calculated from the liability data in the sections of the central bank and other depository corporations accords with the concepts and definitions of the *MFSM*. Broad money differs slightly from M3 described below as M3 also includes bills payable.

Money (National Definitions):
Monetary base comprises currency in circulation, depository corporations' positive current account balances with the central bank, statutory reserves of depository corporations (on the public's local and foreign currency deposits) and any other deposits other than those of the depository corporations but excluding government deposits.

M1 comprises currency in circulation outside depository corporations plus demand deposits in national currency, other than those of the central government, with the BOZ and other depository corporations, and bills payable.

M2 comprises M1 plus savings and time deposits in national currency and demand deposits in foreign currency, other than those of the central government, with other depository corporations.

M3 comprises M2 plus savings and time deposits in foreign currency, other than those of the central government, with commercial banks.

Interest Rates:

Discount Rate (End of Period):
Rate charged by the BOZ on loans to commercial banks.

Treasury Bill Rate:
Average rate on treasury bills.

Savings Rate:
Rate offered by commercial banks on savings deposits.

Deposit Rate:
Rate offered by commercial banks on three- to six-month deposits.

Lending Rate:
Rate charged by commercial banks on overdrafts.

Prices and Production:

Share Prices:
General index covering shares quoted in the Lusaka Stock Exchange, base January 1997.

Wholesale Prices:
Bank of Zambia index, weights reference period: 1966.

Consumer Prices:
Source: Central Statistical Office. Weights Reference Period: 1993–1994; Geographical Coverage: whole national territory; Number of Items in Basket: 357; Basis for Calculation: 1993/94 Household Budget Survey, Laspeyres index.

Industrial Production and Mining Production:
Bank of Zambia indices, † weights reference period: 1980.

International Transactions:

All trade value data are from the Central Statistical Office.

Government Finance:

Annual data are as reported for the *Government Finance Statistics Yearbook (GFSY)* and cover budgetary central government. The fiscal year ends December 31.

National Accounts:

Source: Central Statistical Office. The data are compiled in the framework of the *1968 SNA*.

Zimbabwe   698

Date of Fund Membership:
September 29, 1980

Standard Sources:
Reserve Bank of Zimbabwe
Central Statistical Office

Exchange Rates:

On August 1, 2006, the new dollar (ZWN), equivalent to 1,000 of the old dollar (ZWD) was introduced. Due to adoptability issues by the Reserve Bank of Zimbabwe, the ZWN code was expired and ZWD remained as the valid currency code. In September 2007 the Zimbabwe dollar (ZWD) was devalued against the US dollar. The official rate was adjusted from the previous rate of 250 ZWD per US dollar to the new rate of 30,000 ZWD per US dollar. On August 1, 2008, the third Zimbabwe dollar (ZWR), equivalent to 10,000,000,000 of the second Zimbabwe dollar (ZWN), was introduced. On February 2, 2009, the fourth Zimbabwe dollar (ZWI), equivalent to 1,000,000,000,000 of the third Zimbabwe dollar (ZWR), was introduced. The third dollar (ZWR) circulated alongside the fourth dollar (ZWI) and remained legal tender until June 30, 2009.

Official Rate: (End of Period and Period Average):
Central bank midpoint rate. The official rate was pegged to a trade-weighted basket of currencies. As of June 30, 2001, the official rate is pegged to the U.S. dollar.

International Liquidity:

Gold holdings are valued on the first of each month at 50 percent of the daily average price of the Zurich closing quotation for the three-month period ended on the last day of the preceding month.

Monetary Authorities:

Comprises the Reserve Bank of Zimbabwe only.

Deposit Money Banks:

Consolidates the commercial banks, the discount houses, and the accepting houses. † Prior to December 1984, *line 22d* includes claims on state and local governments and claims on public financial enterprises. Subsequently, these claims have been identified and omitted from the series.

Monetary Survey:

Data for *Money (line 34)* agree with data for M1 as published by the Reserve Bank of Zimbabwe; however, data for *Quasi-Money* (line 35) differ from data for "near-money" as published by the Reserve Bank of Zimbabwe. "Near-money" is defined as fixed deposits (including savings deposits) with commercial banks with a maturity of less than 30 days, while quasi-money is equal to the sum of savings and fixed deposits at the deposit money banks and the quasi-monetary liabilities of the Reserve Bank. Therefore, M2 (total money and near-money), as published by the Reserve Bank of Zimbabwe, differs from the sum of *lines 34* and *35*. † See note on deposit money banks.

Other Banking Institutions:
Comprises the finance houses, the Post Office Savings Bank, and the building societies.

Banking Survey:
† See note on deposit money banks.

Interest Rates:

Discount Rate (End of Period):
Rate charged by the Reserve Bank of Zimbabwe on loans to banks. † Beginning in December 1998, rate charged on rediscounted loans and repurchase agreements.

Money Market Rate:
Rate charged by discount houses to buy three-month bankers' acceptances.

Treasury Bill Rate:
Yield on 91-day treasury bills.

Deposit Rate:
Rate offered by commercial banks on three-month deposits.

Lending Rate:
Rate charged by commercial banks on loans.

Prices, Production, Labor:

Industrial Share Prices:
Capital weighted share price index covering industrial shares quoted on the Zimbabwe Stock Exchange (ZSE), base 1967.

Consumer Prices:
Source: Central Statistical Office. Weights Reference Period: 1995; Geographical Coverage: Whole national territory; Number of Items in Basket: 337; Basis for Calculation: The weights are derived from the Income, Consumption and Expenditure Survey conducted in 1995/96.

Manufacturing Production:
Central Statistical Office index of volume of production of the manufacturing sector (all groups), 1980 = 100.

International Transactions:

All trade data are from the Central Statistical Office. *Exports* include re-exports and are valued "Free On Rail" (F.O.R.) at point of dispatch.

Government Finance:

Annual data are as reported for the *Government Finance Statistics Yearbook (GFSY)* and cover consolidated central government. The fiscal year ends June 30.

National Accounts:

Lines 99a and *99b* include a statistical discrepancy.